KU-094-645

GOOD GUIDE TO
DOG
FRIENDLY
PUBS, HOTELS
AND B&Bs 2005

This edition first published in Great Britain in 2005

1 3 5 7 9 10 8 6 4 2

© Random House Group Ltd 2005

First published by
Ebury Press
Random House, 20 Vauxhall Bridge Road, London SW1V 2SA

Random House Australia (Pty) Limited
20 Alfred Street, Milsons Point, Sydney,
New South Wales 2061, Australia

Random House New Zealand Limited
18 Poland Road, Glenfield, Auckland 10, New Zealand

Random House South Africa (Pty) Limited
Endulini, 5A Jubilee Road, Parktown 2193, South Africa

The Random House Group Limited Reg. No. 954009

www.randomhouse.co.uk

A CIP catalogue record for this book is available from the British Library.

ISBN 0091904846

Papers used by Ebury Press are natural, recyclable products made from wood grown in sustainable forests.

Text design and typesetting by Textype, Cambridge.

Jacket design by Main Artery

Cover image © Zefa

Printed and bound by Cox & Wyman Ltd, Reading, Berkshire

GOOD GUIDE TO
DOG
FRIENDLY
PUBS, HOTELS
AND B&Bs 2005

EDITED BY ALISDAIR AIRD AND FIONA STAPLEY
MANAGING EDITOR KAREN FICK
WALKS CONSULTANT TIM LOCKE
ADDITIONAL RESEARCH FIONA WRIGHT

EBURY PRESS

Contents

Introduction

All of us on the staff of this guide own dogs and like going away with them. So we're rather well placed to know what places suit dog owners best – but we could never have put this book together without the help of the many thousands of reports we have had over the years from readers of our companion guides.

We have chosen just under 1,000 places with a real welcome for dogs and their owners. These are all places which we would have no hesitation in including in a 'non-dog' guide book – indeed, many of them are distinguished entries in one of our sister publications. They span a tremendous range of styles, from simple B&Bs or farmhouses through cheerful pubs and venerable inns to luxurious hotels. We have put particular effort into tracking down places with plenty of good walks nearby.

Although the emphasis in the book is more on places to stay in, several hundred are equally welcoming if you just want to drop in for a meal. In particular, most of the pubs we have included are happy to serve meals in a bar where dogs are allowed (we have actually included some pubs which are great for a meal with your dog but may not allow them in the bedrooms – so check the entry).

This new expanded edition of our popular guide to dog friendly establishments draws heavily on some 47,000 reports from readers of our other guides. We are very grateful to them for their help. Special thanks to Dennis Jenkin, J and C Whelan, Lynda and Trevor Smith, Kevin Thorpe, Dr D J and Mrs S C Walker, Mike and Lynn Robinson, John and Hiro Charles, George Atkinson, Ian Phillips, Tony and Maggie Harwood, Peter Craske, John and Joan Nash, Michael Rowse, Martin and Karen Wake, Ian and Ruth Laurence, Michael and Ann Cole, Brian Dawes, Ian Arthur, Edward Pearce, Steve Whalley, Ian Clare, and Ian and Celia Abbott.

Do please help us with your own reports. Simply send an e-mail to *dogs@goodguides.com*, or write to Dogs, FREEPOST TN1569, WADHURST, TN5 7BR – no stamp needed if you post in the UK.

Ten tips for top dog holidays

Making sure your dog enjoys a break as much as you do boils down mainly to common sense and a little forethought. And do think of other people – a little consideration for staff and other visitors goes a long way.

1. Always phone the establishment to discuss with the owners or manager what their rules are regarding dogs BEFORE you book a room. If you turn up with two large rottweilers without pre-booking, you might not get the warm reception you were hoping for. Many places set aside bedrooms that are particularly suitable for dogs, such as ground-floor rooms or rooms with access to the outside. And often, there is a small charge for dogs – confirm this when booking.

2. Check your pet insurance to see that it covers personal liability – knocking over furniture, tripping people up, and so forth.

3. Check which areas your dog is allowed into, as many places will not allow them in dining areas.

4. Most establishments will not allow dogs to be left alone in bedrooms as they could become unhappy, anxious or bored and then might howl endlessly or even end up chewing the room to pieces.

5. Make sure to take your dog's own bedding, a towel for drying muddy paws, and any favourite toys. Some places do provide bowls and food but often it's best to stick to regular mealtimes and the food they are used to.

6. Hairy dogs need a really thorough brushing beforehand, to minimise errant hairs.

7. Obviously, you wouldn't want to take a really unsociable dog away. Many proprietors have dogs and other animals of their own (and children of course), and therefore will not want a visiting pet that is difficult with them – or with other guests.

8. Do remember to keep your dog under control all the time – we find that it's more relaxing to keep even the best-behaved dogs on leads.

9. Make sure when you leave that there is no evidence that your dog has been there – either inside or out.

10. If you are hoping to explore the area, most proprietors will be able to point you in the direction of good nearby walks, and some attractions have facilities where you can leave your dog in special kennels; it is worth checking this beforehand.

Top Dog Awards

From our thousand places which are really great for breaks with your dog, we have picked out three which in their very different ways really stand out:

To pamper your dog:
Holne Chase (Ashburton, Devon) even has a dog spa, besides lots of treats and lovely walks
To pamper yourself:
Magnificent **Cliveden** (Taplow, Buckinghamshire) cossets you with Thames-side luxury, while your dog is treated royally too
For muddy-paw adventurers:
Other dogs at the splendidly informal **Druidstone Hotel** (Broad Haven, Wales), with its virtually private beach on a magnificent remote coast, quickly welcome your dog into the pack.

In the countryside with your dog

Many dogs appreciate the countryside as much as their owners do. Whether your dog likes the hills, open heaths or coastal landscapes, there is plenty of choice across Britain. However, there's by no means unlimited access, and the law requires you to keep your dog under control and put it on a lead when crossing fields with livestock in (a farmer actually has the right to shoot dogs that are worrying his farm animals).

Places you can generally walk your dog in England and Wales are:
- **Public roads**, though they're obviously not always ideal.
- Most **beaches**. Some popular beaches ban dogs in the summer, and – even more than anywhere else – it is always considerate to clean up after your dog on beaches.
- Paths and tracks on **National Trust land** (apart from National Trust gardens and house estates, where you need a ticket to get in, though some of these welcome dogs on leads) that are dedicated as public land and have free access: these include areas of coast, woodland and open land.
- **Canal towpaths** unless there's a sign to the contrary.
- Paths and tracks in areas of forest owned by the **Forestry Commission**, though these may be temporarily closed during felling operations.
- Anywhere along a **public footpath**, **public bridleway** or **public byway** (the three together are also known generically as **public rights of way**). Bridleways are also open to horse-riders and cyclists, and

byways are open to all traffic, so unless these have a paved surface they can be a lot more muddy in wet weather. Public rights of way are normally signposted from roads, and once you're on them there may be **waymark arrows** (red for byways, blue for bridleways and yellow for footpaths). There are also paths where the landowner allows access as '**permissive paths**' or '**licensed paths**' but which aren't formally public rights of way; here the landowner has the right to close the path at any time.

• **Access land** in uncultivated countryside, where you have a '**right to roam**' under new legislation (the Countryside and Rights of Way Act) that is now coming into effect, area by area (see below).

• **Scotland** has a quite different law about access to the countryside. There are some legal rights of way, but not many, and they aren't shown as such on OS maps. Generally things get by on an informal basis: there's a general tolerance towards walkers, who can effectively go anywhere on moorland and mountains outside the grouse-shooting and deer-stalking seasons. Dogs may not be welcome on moorland because of nesting game birds; look out for notices, or check locally at tourist information centres.

What the right to roam means

The new law on right to roam in four million acres of uncultivated land is the most radical change to countryside access for more than half a century. The new law that has created these access areas is being phased in region by region, beginning with South East and Lower North West England in September 2004, Central Southern England in December 2004, Upper North West and North East England in May 2005, Wales in (probably) spring 2005, South West England in July 2005, and West and East England in November 2005.

The new law allows access on foot only to many areas of moors, mountains, downland, heaths and registered commons that have been designated as access land. Here you'll have the right to walk freely and don't have to stick to paths, although in places vegetation and the lie of the land won't make it universally possible to go absolutely everywhere. This law doesn't cover all uncultivated land – just the bits that have been designated and mapped (some of it may have been open informally for years). And it doesn't cover farmland, woods, coast or parkland; even in areas of open-looking hills such as the South Downs, the access areas are quite confined.

How you get on to the access land won't always be that easy to work out. At first, there's likely to be some confusion, as not all access points (gates, stiles and so on) will be mapped, and there will be some access land which will not be possible to get into as it's surrounded by private land and with no rights of way leading to it. So there's likely to be a phase where things are left to settle down while walkers' desire lines are identified and further access arrangements are sorted out.

It's safest to assume that you don't have access unless you've got the relevant OS map or can find a sign showing its status. OS Explorer 1:25,000 scale maps (see below) will show where these access areas are, and the OS hopes to publish these soon after the phasing-in dates for each region (see above).

In spite of these minor uncertainties, though, generally it's good news for dog owners and walkers as it really opens up some spectacular landscapes that have been out of bounds for generations. However, do note the restrictions: you must keep dogs on a lead if near livestock, and at all times during March to July; dogs may also, at any time, be banned temporarily or permanently from some areas of land such as places where birds tend to nest. You also aren't allowed to ride a horse, cycle, light fires, camp or feed livestock; if you do, you lose your right to roam for 72 hours. There may also be local restrictions on night-time access.

Getting information

- **Websites showing access areas with right to roam**: the Countryside Agency, www.ca-mapping.co.uk, covers all of England (select region, then map type – conclusive is the final version – then type in a grid reference or place name); the Countryside Commission for Wales, www.ccw.gov.uk/mapping.
- **OS maps** Wherever you are in England and Wales, the first point of reference is the local Ordnance Survey (OS) map: both the purple-covered Landranger series (at a scale of 1:50,000, or about one and a quarter inches to the mile) and the orange-covered Explorer series (at a scale of 1:25,000, or about two and a half inches to the mile) show rights of way (green crosses for byways, long green dashes for bridleways and short green dashes for footpaths; sometimes these are partly overprinted with green diamonds denoting long-distance routes like the Cotswold Way); on Landranger maps it's the same set of symbols, but with red instead of green. Access land designated under the 2004 legislation is to be shown with a yellow wash and a dark orange border, on Explorer maps only; they'll also show with an *i* in an orange circle the points of 'primary access', where there's an information board and a way in to the access land; but other gates and stiles giving you access on to the land won't be shown. Areas of other land that are always open as access land (National Trust, National Trust for Scotland and Forestry Commission) are shown on Explorer and Landranger maps with purple boundaries.
- **Dog stiles and gates** Bridleways and byways use gates rather than stiles, which makes things much easier for dog walking, as some stiles are baffling for dogs. But you usually need local knowledge to find out whether a particular public footpath is going to be suitable for your dog

in its provision of stiles and gates. Some councils and landowners are increasingly installing easily climbed stiles, or gates rather than stiles, or excellent stiles with dog gates built into them – and there's now a legal requirement for councils to take into account the needs of the less mobile when stiles or gates are installed. In the meantime, finding out if a certain path has dog-friendly stiles or gates isn't straightforward. Some local tourist information centres stock leaflets showing stile-free walks suitable for dogs.

Factual Details

We list opening hours for pubs, whether they have a restaurant, and if they offer bar food. Standard food times in pubs is from 12-2, 7-9 Monday to Saturday (food service often stops a bit earlier on Sundays). If food times are significantly different to this, we list the times. We note days when we know pubs do not do food or are closed altogether, but suggest you should play safe on Sundays and check first before planning an expedition that depends on getting a meal there. Pubs that are out of the way may cut down on cooking times if they're quiet, which they tend to be except at holiday times. The bedroom price we show is for a double room, normally including full english breakfast. A price before the / is for single occupancy, and a B or S against the price indicates a private bathroom or shower.

For hotel and B&B accommodation, the price we show is the total for two people sharing a double or twin-bedded room with its own bathroom for one night in high season. It includes a full english breakfast, VAT and any automatic service charge that we know about. We say if dinner is included in this total price, which it may be for some of the more remote places. If a price appears at the end of an entry, it indicates the additional cost of accommodating a dog.

Many hotels have very good value short break prices, especially out of season, so it's always worth asking.

If we know that the back rooms are the quietest or the front ones have the best views or the ones in the new extension are more spacious, then we say so.

We always mention a restaurant if we know there is one and we commend food if we have information supporting a positive recommendation. Many B&Bs will recommend nearby pubs for evening meals if they do not offer dinner.

Dog Quiz

1. How many dogs are there in the UK?
2. What was the name of the Edinburgh dog who sat by his master's grave for 14 years until his death?
3. How many teeth does an adult dog have?
4. What was the name of Bill Sykes's dog in the musical *Oliver*?
5. What is the largest domestic dog breed?
6. In the film *A Dog's Life*, what was the name of Charlie Chaplin's doggy co-star?
7. What is the top speed of the average dog?
8. Blue Peter's first puppy was called what?
9. What was the name of the dog that cocks his ear at the gramophone for His Master's Voice?
10. In greek mythology who was Orion's pet, the namesake for the Dog Star?
11. What was the name of the bearded collie in *Peter Pan*?
12. Can you be fined for dog mess?
13. In 1923, Lord Carnarvon's dog suddenly howled, keeled over and died at the exact moment King Tutankhamen's tomb was opened. What was her name?
14. In egyptian mythology what was the name of the ancient egyptian version of Satan who was depicted as a greyhound or pharaoh hound?
15. In the Famous Five books, what was the dog called?
16. In 1957, the Soviet Union launched the first living creature into space aboard Sputnik 2. What was the little dog's name?
17. Mr Punch, of Punch and Judy, had a frequent doggy companion. What was his name?
18. A lot is said about human obesity. Which dog breeds are most likely to be overweight?
19. What was the dog in the film *The Wizard of Oz* called?
20. In the cross-country film *The Incredible Journey*, what was the name of the golden retriever that accompanied the cat and bulldog?
21. What was the name of the dog that sailed up the Thames with Three Men in a Boat?
22. Who was Dick Dastardly's sidekick?
23. What was Pickles famous for?
24. Spike chased Tom and Jerry, but what was Spike's puppy called?

25. Who did Gnasher belong to?
26. What was Lassie's real name?
27. Which breed of dog doesn't bark?
28. What was the name of Pongo's wife?
29. Who wrote 'Love Me, Love My Dog'?
30. What did Shaggy feed his dog?
31. Who was K9's time-travelling owner?
32. Where did Snoopy sleep?
33. What is the correct name of the 'animals' VC'?
34. How many times more powerful than a human's nose is a dog's?
35. Which of these is poisonous to dogs: chocolate, daffodil bulbs, apple seeds, lily pollen?
36. What is the name of David Blunkett's current guide dog?

See page 368 for answers

Calendar of Dog Events

All the events listed here include something of interest to the dog owner, and organisers have told us that well behaved dogs are welcome on a lead. Dates were provisional at the time of going to press so please ring to confirm before you set out, and it's probably worth checking that 'dog welcome' guidelines haven't changed since we checked this information.

BEDFORDSHIRE
July
9 Old Warden

Bedfordshire County Show at the English School of Falconry with dog shows and working dog displays – till 10 Jul (01767) 627527

September
17 Old Warden

Bedfordshire Steam and Country Fair at the Shuttleworth Collection: working dog demonstrations, steam tractors, heavy horses, working crafts, motor show – till 18 Sep (01767) 627288

CHESHIRE
June
21 Tabley

Cheshire County Show: livestock, dog show (over 100 classes), horses, flowers, food hall with live demonstrations, crafts, country pursuits, hundreds of trade stands and main ring events – till 22 Jun (01829) 760020

August
14 Knutsford

Fun Dog Show at Tatton Park: ten novelty classes including saddest eyes, waggiest tail and scruffiest dog, and fun agility course (01625) 534400

CUMBRIA
August
17 Threlkeld

Sheepdog Trials (017687) 79032
27 Patterdale

Sheepdog Trials (01768) 864671

DERBYSHIRE
August
16 Dove Dale
Sheepdog Trials – till 17 Aug (07989) 150889
29 Hope
Show and Sheepdog Trials at The Showground (01433) 620905
September
17 Hayfield
Sheepdog Trials and Country Show at Spray House Farm – till 18 Sep (01663) 746653/733644
3 Chatsworth
Country Fair: dog agility, terrier racing and dog and fun dog show, lurcher racing, sheepdog and gundog trials, grand ring, hot air balloons, trade and craft stands – till 4 Sep (01328) 701133

DEVON
July
6 Mortehoe
Sheepdog and Falconry Display: Weds evening from 6pm at Borough Farm. Some dogs may not like the falcons – till 31 Aug (01271) 870056
28 Totnes
Totnes and District Show: terrier racing, possibly sheepdog display, livestock, donkeys, rabbits, craft tent, over 100 trade stands, show jumping and main ring entertainment (01548) 821070

DORSET
May
30 Sherborne
Country Fair at Sherborne Castle: dog scurries (test your dog's speed against the clock, dog show, dog agility displays and gundogs inc an international retriever event. Also falconry, craft stalls and demonstrations of country crafts and skills, main ring attractions, rural and leisure pursuits demonstrations and heavy horses (01935) 813182

HAMPSHIRE
May
29 Romsey
Hampshire Country Show at Broadlands, inc dog agility and scurries – till 30 May (01794) 505010
30 Highclere
Southern Counties Game and Country Fair at Highclere Castle: world–class acts, falconry, sheepdogs, gun dogs, terriers and lurchers, shooting, pet dog show and trade shows – till 31 May (01635) 253210
July
9 Buriton
Country Park Show inc dog agility at Queen Elizabeth Country Park – till 10 Jul (023) 9259 5040

26 Brockenhurst

New Forest and County Show: large agricultural and equestrian event with international showjumping, terrier racing, working hounds, horses, cattle, sheep, goats, flower show, crafts, forestry, ring displays and around 450 display stands – till 28 Jul (01590) 622400

ISLE OF WIGHT
April
23 Binstead

Canine Show at Brickfields Horse Country (01983) 566801

NORFOLK
June
25 Sandringham

Country Show and Horse Driving Trials at Sandringham House inc dog events – till 26 Jun (01553) 772675

29 Norwich

Royal Norfolk Show: livestock, dog shows, trade stands, arena displays, flower show, arts and crafts – till 30 Jun (01603) 748931

July
2 Snetterton

Summer Show and Horse Show: arena displays, trade stands, also dog show, agility and flyball (0870) 366 6924

16 Holkham

Country Fair at Holkham Hall: dog agility, terrier racing and show, fun dog show, lurcher racing, sheepdog and gundog trials, grand ring, hot air balloons, trade and craft stands – till 17 Jul (01328) 710227

WARWICKSHIRE
August
27 Stoneleigh

Town and Country Festival at Stoneleigh Park: top dog ring events, fun dog shows, canine makeovers, discover breeds, dog scurry (test your dog's speed against the clock) and international flyball – till 29 Aug (024) 7669 6969

SCOTLAND
January
22 Aviemore

Sled Dog Rally: take the ski road from Aviemore, at Coylum Bridge continue on the ski road. After approx 3 miles, Loch Morlich will be on your right. Heronsfield car park is past the loch on the right – till 23 Jan (01908) 609796

WALES
April
16 Builth Wells

Working and Pastoral Breeds of Wales Championship Dog Show at the Royal Welsh Showground (01639) 823078

August
18 Tregaron
National Welsh Sheepdog Trials – till 20 Aug (01974) 298414
25 Monmouth
Monmouthshire Show at Vauxhall Fields: biggest one-day agricultural show in Wales with a variety of main and countryside ring attractions, horses, livestock, big dog show, craft marquee, shopping mall, food hall and trade stands (01291) 691160

Bedfordshire

Dog Friendly Pubs

BIDDENHAM
Three Tuns *Village signposted from A428 just W of Bedford*
Handy if you're in the area, this thatched village pub is popular for its very good value enjoyable bar food. It can draw a crowd (particularly at lunchtime) so it's worth booking. The low-beamed lounge is fairly straightforward with wheelback chairs round dark wood tables, window seats and pews on a red turkey carpet, and country paintings. Even more down-to-earth, the green-carpeted public bar (readers have found it a bit smokey in here, but the dining area is no smoking) has photographs of local sports teams, darts, table skittles and dominoes. Standard but tasty food is served in good sized helpings and includes dishes such as soup, sandwiches, steak and kidney pie, steak braised in tarragon and red wine and meat or vegetable lasagne; Sunday roast and puddings. On handpump, Greene King Abbot is well kept alongside a guest such as Everards Tiger. There are seats in the attractively sheltered spacious garden, and a big decked terrace has lots of picnic-sets. The very good children's play area has swings for all ages.
Greene King ~ Tenant Kevin Bolwell ~ Real ale ~ Bar food (12-2, 6-9; not Sun evening) ~ (01234) 354847 ~ Children in eating area of bar ~ Dogs welcome ~ Open 11.30-2.30, 6-11; 12-3, 7-10.30 Sun

BROOM
Cock *High Street; from A1 opposite northernmost Biggleswade turn-off, follow Old Warden 3, Aerodrome 2 signpost, and take first left signposted Broom*
You'll appreciate this 300-year-old place if you like your pubs simple and unspoilt – its four quietly cosy rooms have survived almost untouched over the years. Original latch doors lead from one little room to another, where you'll find warming winter log fires, low ochre ceilings, stripped panelling, and farmhouse tables and chairs on antique tiles. There's no bar counter, and the very well kept Greene King IPA, Abbot and Ruddles County are tapped straight from casks by the cellar steps off a central corridor. Straightforward bar food. The restaurant is no smoking; piped (perhaps classical) music, darts, table skittles, cribbage and dominoes. There are

picnic-sets and flower tubs on the terrace by the back lawn; caravanning and camping facilities are available.

Greene King ~ Tenants Gerry and Jean Lant ~ Real ale ~ Bar food (12-2.30, 7-9; not Sun evening) ~ Restaurant ~ (01767) 314411 ~ Children in restaurant and family room ~ Dogs allowed in bar ~ Open 12-3(4 Sat), 6-11; 12-4, 7-10.30 Sun

HOUGHTON CONQUEST
Knife & Cleaver *Between B530 (old A418) and A6, S of Bedford*
Dishes at this attractive 17th-c dining pub are stylishly presented, contemporary and fully flavoured, with the same care taken over ingredients and cooking in the bar as with the separate more elaborate (and pricier) restaurant menu. While some readers find it a bit too restauranty for their tastes, others are grateful to find such well prepared and fairly priced food in an area where pubs serving really good meals are a little thin on the ground. Beware that it does get very busy, and on Saturday evening and Sunday lunchtime if the restaurant is fully booked they may not serve bar meals. The comfortably civilised bar has dark panelling which is reputed to have come from nearby ruined Houghton House, as well as maps, drawings and old documents on the walls, and a blazing fire in winter. The airy white-walled no smoking conservatory restaurant has rugs on the tiled floor and lots of hanging plants. There's also a no smoking family room. Service is really welcoming and efficient. Well kept Batemans XB and Fullers London Pride on handpump, Stowford Press farm cider, around 30 good wines by the glass, and over 20 well aged malt whiskies; unobtrusive piped music. There are tables on the terrace alongside a neatly kept appealing garden, and the church opposite is worth a look.

Free house ~ Licensees David and Pauline Loom ~ Real ale ~ Bar food (12-2.30(2 Sat), 7-9.30; not Sun or bank hol evenings; but see text about wknds) ~ Restaurant ~ (01234) 740387 ~ Children in eating area of bar, restaurant and family room ~ Dogs allowed in bedrooms ~ Open 12-2.30(2 Sat, 3 Sun), 7-11; closed Sun evening, 27-30 Dec ~ Bedrooms: £53B/£68B

NORTHILL
Crown *Ickwell Road; village signposted from B658 W of Biggleswade*
Prettily cottagey, this black and white thatched pub stands just across from the church in a green and peaceful village, with picnic-sets under cocktail parasols out in front looking over the village pond. The smallish bar has a big open fire, flagstones and low heavy beams, comfortable bow window seats, and well kept Greene King IPA and Abbot Batemans XXB on handpump from the copper-topped counter; good coffee comes with a jug of cream, and refills if you want. On the left is a carpeted side room with Leech hunting prints (from Mr Sponge's Sporting Tour) and reproduction brewery mirrors. On the right, the airy main dining room has elegantly laid tables on bare boards, witty contemporary fashion-hat cartoons and some appealing nude drawings and paintings, with steps up to a smaller more intimate side room. Throughout, the atmosphere is warm and relaxed, thanks particularly to the concerned and friendly service; daily papers; fairly

unobtrusive piped music. Enjoyable food includes lunchtime sandwiches, daily roast or sausage and mash, ricotta and spinach cannelloni topped with provençal sauce and pie or curry of the day; daily puddings; no smoking restaurant. Outside, a sheltered side terrace has more picnic-sets, and opens into a very large garden with a few widely spaced canopied tables, plenty of trees and shrubs, a good play area, and masses of room for children to run around.

Greene King ~ Tenant Marian Hawkes-Blodau ~ Real ale ~ Bar food (12-2.30, 6.30-9.30; not Sun evening) ~ Restaurant ~ (01767) 627337 ~ Children in eating area of bar and restaurant ~ Dogs allowed in bar ~ Open 11.30-3, 6-11; 12-4 (maybe later in summer) Sun; closed 25 Dec evening

OLD WARDEN
Hare & Hounds *Village signposted off A600 S of Bedford and B658 W of Biggleswade*

Still fresh from its refurbishment over a year ago, this welcoming pub is popular for its thoughtfully prepared food. Breads and ice cream are home-made, and where possible they use local ingredients – such as pork from the surrounding Shuttleworth estate. Rambling around a central servery, and painted warmly cosy red and cream, the four beamed rooms have dark standing timbers, comfortable upholstered armchairs and sofas on stripped flooring, light wood tables and coffee tables, a woodburning stove in an inglenook fireplace and fresh flowers on the bar. Prints and photographs depict the historic aircraft in the Shuttleworth Collection just up the road. Charles Wells Eagle and Bombardier and a guest such as Greene King Old Speckled Hen are well kept on handpump, and the half a dozen or so wines by the glass include some from the local Southill estate. Service from well turned out staff is attentive and friendly, and two rooms are no smoking. The village itself is part of the Shuttleworth estate and was built about 200 years ago in a swiss style. The glorious sloping garden, which stretches up to pine woods behind the pub, dates back to the same period and style (more tables at the side on a small terrace, and a couple in front), and there are some substantial walks nearby. Though there's an ample car park, they sometimes need to commandeer the grounds of the village hall as an overflow.

Charles Wells ~ Lease Jane Hasler ~ Real ale ~ Bar food (12-2, 6.30-9.30; 12-4 Sun; not Sun evening) ~ Restaurant ~ (01767) 627225 ~ Children in family room ~ Dogs allowed in bar ~ Open 12-3, 6-11; 12-10.30 Sun; closed Mon exc lunchtime bank hols

PEGSDON
Live & Let Live *B655 W of Hitchin*

This rambling old place has been much extended from its snugly traditional tiled and panelled core, with a big beamed dining room behind the cosier salmon-painted rooms at the front, separated by a double-sided fireplace. There are fresh flowers on the sewing machine tables, stripped brick floors, rustic pictures and gun displays on the walls, and a nice, chatty feel. In summer the big back garden has a startling array of hanging baskets and flowers, as well as tables and chairs on a terrace, and picnic-sets on the long lawn, with views of the Chiltern Hills (a track leads straight up almost opposite). There's just as much colour in the winter, when the bars are transformed by particularly good decorations at Christmas. Tasty bar food but there may be a wait for meals at the busiest periods. Well kept Brakspears, Fullers London Pride, Marstons Pedigree, and a guest such as Youngs on handpump, and a comprehensive wine list with plenty by the glass. Most parts are no smoking; piped music. Though the pub's postal address is Hertfordshire, it's actually in Bedfordshire, which bulges down here almost as if it's determined just to capture this nice pub.

Free house ~ Licensees Ray and Maureen Scarbrow ~ Real ale ~ Bar food (12-2.30, 6.45-9.30) ~ Restaurant ~ (01582) 881739 ~ Children in eating area of bar and restaurant ~ Dogs allowed in bar ~ Open 12-11(10.30 Sun) ~ Bedrooms: £57.50S/£57.50S

RISELEY

Fox & Hounds *High Street; village signposted off A6 and B660 N of Bedford*
You can choose your own piece of steak from the cold counter (you're charged by the weight) and watch it cooked on an open grill at this very welcoming pub. Other, fairly robust dishes are listed on blackboards. Even if you don't see anything you fancy, it's worth asking: they're very obliging here, and will try to cope with particular food requests. It's a happy bustling place that has been cheerily run by the same jovial landlord and his wife for over a decade. Service is normally very attentive, but it does get busy, and as they don't take bookings on Saturday night you may have to wait for your table and food. A relaxing lounge area, with comfortable leather chesterfields, lower tables and wing chairs, contrasts with the more traditional pub furniture spread among timber uprights under the heavy low beams; unobtrusive piped classical or big band piped music. Charles Wells Eagle and Bombardier with perhaps a changing guest such as Shepherd Neame Spitfire are kept well on handpump, alongside a decent collection of other drinks including bin-end wines and a range of malts and cognacs. An attractively decked terrace with wooden tables and chairs has outside heating, and the pleasant garden has shrubs and a pergola.

Charles Wells ~ Managers Jan and Lynne Zielinski ~ Real ale ~ Bar food (12-1.45, 6.30-9.30 (12-2, 7-9 Sun)) ~ Restaurant ~ (01234) 708240 ~ Children welcome ~ Dogs allowed in bar ~ Open 11.30-2.30, 6.30-11; 12-3, 7-10.30 Sun

Dog Friendly Hotels, B&Bs and Farms

ASPLEY GUISE

Moore Place *The Square, Aspley Guise, Milton Keynes, Buckinghamshire MK17 8DW (01908) 282000 £75*, plus special breaks; 64 well equipped, pretty rms. Elegant, restored Georgian house in lovely gardens, with cocktail bar and lounge, enjoyable food and nice breakfasts in no smoking restaurant, and friendly, helpful staff; cl 27 Dec-31 Jan; disabled access; dogs in bedrooms, reception and lounge; plenty of nearby walks

FLITWICK

Flitwick Manor *Church Rd, Flitwick, Bedford, Bedfordshire MK45 1AE (01525) 712242* £208, plus special breaks; 17 thoughtfully decorated rms. 17th-c country house surrounded by interesting gardens, with log fire in entrance hall, comfortable lounge and library, and smart restaurant with fine french wines and imaginative food using home-grown and local produce; tennis, putting, croquet; dogs in downstairs bedrooms

MARSTON MORETEYNE

White Cottage *Marston Hill, Marston Moreteyne, Cranfield, Bedfordshire MK43 0QJ (01234) 751766* £48; 6 comfortable rms. Neatly kept, white painted no smoking cottage with fine views across the gardens and countryside, residents' lounge, super breakfasts in attractive dining room (good evening meals weekdays only), and a friendly, relaxed atmosphere; dogs in bedrooms weekends only; fenced-off garden and nearby country walks

SANDY

Highfield Farm *Tempsford Rd, Sandy, Bedfordshire SG19 2AQ (01767) 682332* £65 (Directly off A1 S-bound carriageway just S of Tempsford flyover); 10 rms (some in charmingly converted barn). Neatly kept whitewashed house (no smoking) set well away from A1 and surrounded by attractive arable farmland; warmly friendly, helpful owner, open fire in comfortable sitting room, and breakfasts in pleasant dining room; disabled access; dogs welcome in bedrooms; £15

Berkshire

Dog Friendly Pubs

ALDWORTH

Bell *A329 Reading—Wallingford; left on to B4009 at Streatley*

'If ever I lived out of the country, the thought of a Sunday lunchtime summer or winter at the Bell would have me racing to the nearest airport' writes one reader, who has been coming to this 14th-c country pub for 20 years. Bewitchingly unspoilt, it's simply furnished with benches around the panelled walls, an ancient one-handed clock, beams in the shiny ochre ceiling, and a woodburning stove; rather than a bar counter for service, there's a glass-panelled hatch. What sets it apart is the genuine friendliness of the welcome: the same family have run it for over 200 years, and you are made to feel at home immediately. A convivial atmosphere is helped along by a ban on games machines, mobile phones and piped music; darts, shove-ha'penny, dominoes, and cribbage. Well priced Arkells BBB and Kingsdown are superbly kept alongside Old Tyler, Dark Mild and a monthly guest on handpump from the local West Berkshire Brewery; no draught lager. They also serve good house wines and winter mulled wine. Excellent value bar food is limited to filled hot crusty rolls such as honey-roast ham, pâté, cheddar, stilton or brie, smoked salmon, crab, tongue or salt beef; in winter they also do home-made soup. The quiet, old-fashioned pub garden is by the village cricket ground, and behind the pub there's a paddock with farm animals. In summer morris dancers visit sometimes, while at Christmas local mummers perform in the road by the ancient well-head (the shaft is sunk 400 feet through the chalk). It tends to get busy at weekends; dogs must be kept on leads.

Free house ~ Licensee H E Macaulay ~ Real ale ~ Bar food (11-2.30, 6-10; 12-2.45, 7-10 Sun; not Mon) ~ No credit cards ~ (01635) 578272 ~ Children must be well behaved ~ Dogs welcome ~ Open 11-3, 6-11; 12-3, 7-10.30 Sun; closed Mon exc bank hols, 25 Dec

BOXFORD

Bell *Back road Newbury—Lambourn; village also signposted off B4000 between Speen and M4 junction 14*

You can choose from a whopping 60 different wines by the glass and 12 champagnes by the flute at this civilised mock Tudor inn. If wine is not your thing, they also stock a range of whiskies, and they've four changing beers such as Badger Best, Bass, Wadworths 6X and Shepherd Neame Spitfire well kept (under light blanket pressure) on handpump. The long-standing landlord cleverly manages to maintain a relaxed, country local atmosphere, and service is friendly and cheerful. Quite long but cosy, the bar has a nice mix of racing pictures, old Mercier advertisements, red plush cushions for the mate's chairs, some interesting bric-a-brac, and a log-effect fire at one end. Pool, cribbage, shove-ha'penny, dominoes, TV, and piped music. From an extensive menu, good portions of well cooked bar food, with puddings such as chocolate brownie with home-made vanilla ice-cream or bread and butter pudding. Most people eat in the rather smart, no smoking restaurant area on the left, but you can also dine on the attractive covered and heated terrace (prettily lit at night). The side courtyard has white cast-iron garden furniture. More reports please.

Free house ~ Licensee Paul Lavis ~ Real ale ~ Bar food (12-2(3 Sun), 7-9.45) ~ Restaurant ~ (01488) 608721 ~ Children welcome ~ Dogs allowed in bar and bedrooms ~ Open 11-11; 12-4, 7-11 Sun ~ Bedrooms: £50S/£60S

BRAY

Crown *1¼ miles from M4 junction 9; A308 towards Windsor, then left at Bray signpost on to B3028; High Street*

A friendly place with a good mix of customers, the emphasis at this 14th-c pub is on the enjoyable (though not cheap) food. Dishes are cooked to order. Best to arrive early as it does get busy, and they recommend you book if you want to eat in the restaurant. Throughout, there are lots of beams (some so low you have to mind your head), and plenty of old timbers handily left at elbow height where walls have been knocked through. The partly panelled main bar has oak tables, leather backed armchairs, and a roaring fire. One dining area has photographs of WWII aeroplanes. It's especially cosy in winter when you really feel the benefit of the three log fires; good service. Well kept Brakspears Special, Courage Best and Directors on handpump along with a decent choice of wines. There are tables and benches out in a sheltered flagstoned front courtyard (which has a flourishing grapevine), and in the large back garden.

Scottish Courage ~ Tenants John and Carole Noble ~ Real ale ~ Bar food (not Sun or Mon evenings) ~ Restaurant ~ (01628) 621936 ~ Children in restaurant ~ Dogs allowed in bar ~ Open 11-3, 6-11; 12-3, 7-10.30 Sun; closed 25, 26 Dec

CRAZIES HILL

Horns *From A4, take Warren Row Road at Cockpole Green signpost just E of Knowl Hill, then past Warren Row, follow Crazies Hill signposts*

The comfortable bars of this tiled and whitewashed cottage have rugby mementos on the walls, exposed beams, open fires and stripped wooden

tables and chairs, while the no smoking barn room is opened up to the roof like a medieval hall. The food here is popular, and it's essential to book a table at weekends if you want to eat from the bar menu (it gets particularly busy on Sunday lunchtimes). Dishes could include seafood pancake or aubergine topped with roasted mediterranean vegetables and toasted mozzarella, and coq au vin, along with fish specials from Billingsgate; good puddings, and they also do lunchtime baguettes. Well kept Brakspears Bitter, Special, and seasonal ales on handpump, a thoughtful wine list, and several malt whiskies; they make a good bloody mary. A gentrified country atmosphere is helped along by the absence of a jukebox, fruit machine and piped music. There's access to the large landscaped garden (which has a play area) from the garden bar with its open fire. No dogs in the evening.
Brakspears ~ Tenant A J Hearn ~ Real ale ~ Bar food (not Sun evening) ~ Restaurant ~ (0118) 940 1416 ~ Children allowed in barn room ~ Dogs allowed in bar ~ Open 11.30-3(3.30 Sat), 6-11; 12-5.30, 7-10.30 Sun; cl Sun evening in winter; closed 25 Dec

INKPEN

Crown & Garter *Inkpen signposted with Kintbury off A4; in Kintbury turn left into Inkpen Road, then keep on into Inkpen Common*
Tucked away up a narrow country lane, this 16th-c brick-built pub is handy for good downland walks, and you can pick up local walks leaflets here free. Surprisingly substantial for somewhere so remote-feeling, it has an appealing low-ceilinged bar, a few black beams, and an attractive variety of mainly old prints and engravings on walls painted cream or shades of pink. The relaxed central bar serves well kept Arkells Moonlight and West Berkshire Mr Chubbs and Good Old Boy on handpump. Three areas radiate from here; our pick is the parquet-floored part by the raised log fire, which has a couple of substantial old tables, a huge old-fashioned slightly curved settle, and a neat little porter's chair decorated in commemoration of the Battle of Corunna (the cats' favourite seat – they've three). Other parts are carpeted, with a good mix of well spaced tables and chairs, and nice lighting; they've recently re-decorated the no smoking restaurant. The long side garden is lovely in summer, with picnic-sets and a play area, by shrubs and a big oak tree. From an imaginative menu, dishes might be wild mushroom risotto with parmesan shavings, cod and pancetta fishcakes, or chickpea burgers, various thai curries or half a roast duck with orange and Grand Marnier sauce (highly recommended by readers), and puddings such as pear crumble with cinnamon custard. They do a popular OAP bargain lunch (Wednesday to Friday). In a separate single-storey building, the well equipped bedrooms form an L around a pretty garden; good breakfasts.
Free house ~ Licensee Gill Hern ~ Bar food (not Mon-Tues lunchtime) ~ Restaurant ~ (01488) 668325 ~ Children welcome ~ Dogs allowed in bar ~ Open 12-3, 5.30-11; 12-11 Sat; 12-3, 7-10.30 Sun; closed Mon and Tues lunchtime ~ Bedrooms: £50B/£70B

RUSCOMBE

Royal Oak *Ruscombe Lane (B3024 just E of Twyford)*

One of our regular reporters who lives a few minutes' walk away tipped us off about the interesting changes here just in time for us to inspect anonymously shortly before going to press with this new edition – and confirm that this is indeed a nice find. We were struck by the immediate sense of welcome, the feeling that they really want to look after you well here, whether you want just a drink, a light snack, or a full meal. It's open plan, carpeted more or less throughout (not the cheerful side garden room), and well laid out so that each bit is fairly snug, yet keeps the overall feel of a lot of people enjoying themselves. A good variety of furniture runs from dark oak tables to big chunky pine ones, with mixed seating to match (the deeply squashy sofa we had our own eye on was bagged by another couple – inviting, though it would have meant eating off a very low table). Contrasting with the exposed ceiling joists, mostly unframed modern paintings and prints decorate the walls, mainly dark terracotta over a panelled dado; one back area has a big bright fruity cocktail mural. There is an eclectic blackboard food choice; they have plans to introduce an italian food night on Mondays. Well kept Fullers London Pride and Youngs on handpump, and half a dozen nicely chosen wines in two glass sizes; the restaurant and conservatory are no smoking. Service is quick and friendly; on our visit they had 1950s/60s piped music. Picnic-sets are ranged around a venerable central hawthorn in the garden behind, which has a barbecue area. We look forward to hearing from readers who have stayed overnight. *Enterprise ~ Tenants Jenny and Stefano Buratta ~ Real ale ~ Bar food (not Sun/Mon evenings) ~ Restaurant ~ (0118) 934 5190 ~ Children in eating area of bar, restaurant and family room ~ Dogs welcome ~ Open 12-3, 5.30-11; 12-10.30 Sun ~ Bedrooms: £35/£50*

SHINFIELD

Magpie & Parrot *2.6 miles from M4 junction 11, via B3270; A327 just SE of Shinfield – heading out on Arborfield Road, keep eyes skinned for small hand-painted green 'Nursery' sign on left, and Fullers 'bar open' blackboard*

A real charmer, this unexpected combination of pub and plant nursery. They raise good value alpines, perennials and bedding plants in the glasshouses and shade house here, and unless you already knew you'd never guess that the little brick roadside cottage includes a genuine pub (as indeed it did in the early 19th c). Go in through the lobby (with its antiquated telephone equipment) and you find a cosy and inviting high-raftered room with a handful of small polished tables – each with a bowl of peanuts – and a comfortable mix of individualistic seats from Victorian oak thrones to a red velveteen sofa, not to mention the armchair with the paw-printed cushion reserved for Spencer the labrador. Everything is spick and span, from the brightly patterned carpet to the plethora of interesting bric-a-brac covering the walls: miniature and historic bottles, dozens of model cars and vans, veteran AA badges and automotive instruments, mementoes of a pranged Spitfire (ask about its story – they love to chat here). Well kept Fullers London Pride on handpump from the small corner counter, a good range of malt whiskies and of soft drinks; very hospitable landlady; a warm log or coal fire. What a nice relaxed place to while away an hour or so in the afternoon! There are teak tables on the back terrace, and an immaculate lawn beyond; the outside lavatories surely qualify for some sort of award. In the summer they have hog roasts. Note the unusual opening hours; no children inside.

Free house ~ Licensee Mrs Carole Headland ~ Real ale ~ No credit cards ~ (0118) 988 4130 ~ Dogs allowed in bar ~ Open 12-7; 12-3 Sun

STANFORD DINGLEY

Bull *From M4 junction 12, W on A4, then right at roundabout on to A340 towards Pangbourne; first left to Bradfield, and at crossroads on far edge of Bradfield (not in centre) turn left signposted Stanford Dingley; turn left in Stanford Dingley*
Reasonably priced for the area, the six well kept real ales on handpump at this attractive 15th-c brick pub could include Bass, Brakspears Bitter, Loddon Hoppit and West Berkshire Good Old Boy, Dr Hexters Healer, and Skiff. The beamed tap room is firmly divided into two by standing timbers hung with horsebrasses. The main part has an old brick fireplace, cushioned seats carved out of barrels, a window settle, wheelback chairs on the red quarry tiles, and an old station clock; a carpeted section has an exposed wattle and daub wall. The half-panelled lounge bar reflects the motorsport and classic car interests of the licensees; on some summer Saturdays owners of classic cars and motorcycles gather in the grounds. Besides tasty lunchtime (and Sunday evening) snacks, you can choose from tempting daily specials. There is a different evening menu with home-made puddings; they also do children's dishes and Sunday roasts. The dining room (and saloon bar at weekends) is no smoking; dominoes, ring-the-bull and piped music. In front of the building are some big rustic tables and benches, and to the side the big garden has plenty of seats. Morris men visit in August, and on St George's Day and New Year's Day.

Free house ~ Licensees Robert and Kate Archard, Robin and Carol Walker ~ Real ale ~ Bar food (12-2.30, 6.30-9.30; not Sun evening Oct-Mar) ~ Restaurant ~ (0118) 974 4409 ~ Children in eating area of bar and restaurant ~ Dogs allowed in bar ~ Open 12-3, 6-11; 12-3, 7-10.30 Sun ~ Bedrooms: £60S/£75S

Old Boot *Off A340 via Bradfield, coming from A4 just W of M4 junction 12*
The beamed bar of this stylish 18th-c pub has two welcoming fires (one in an inglenook) and bunches of fresh flowers. Everything is neatly kept, with fine old pews, settles, old country chairs, and well polished tables, attractive fabrics for the old-fashioned wooden-ring curtains, and some striking pictures and hunting prints. The tranquil sloping back garden and terrace have pleasant rural views, and there are more tables out in front of the pub. Enjoyable bar food from an interesting menu. The dining conservatory is no smoking. Three well kept beers such as Archers Best, local Loddon Hoppit and West Berkshire Good Old Boy on handpump, and good, generously poured wine; the landlord is friendly.

Free house ~ Licensees John and Jeannie Haley ~ Real ale ~ Bar food ~ Restaurant ~ (0118) 974 4292 ~ Children in eating area of bar and restaurant ~ Dogs allowed in bar ~ Open 11-3, 6-11

WINDSOR

Two Brewers *Park Street, off High Street next to Mews*

There's lots to keep your eyes occupied at this charmingly old-fashioned pub, and around the bar are a plethora of tickets, for everything from Royal Ascot to the final of *Pop Idol*. Rambling around a central servery, each of the three quaint but cosily civilised bare-board rooms has a different feel. The red room on the left is our favourite, with a big armchair and wooden floors, sizeable piles of magazines, and a rarely used, discreetly tucked-away TV. Chalkboards record events of the day in history, and there are distinctive old pews and tables. The back bar leading off has a champagne theme, with hundreds of corks lining the walls, particularly around a big mirror above the fireplace. The bar on the right has stripped tables, and a stack of daily papers. Their wide-ranging, fairly priced wine list has several by the glass (including champagne), and Courage Best and Fullers London Pride are well kept on handpump along with a guest such as Wadworths 6X; you can buy cigars here too. Although all the tables are given over to diners (and the friendly staff will try their best to squeeze you in), it's best to book if you want to enjoy the good bar food. They also do a choice of Sunday roasts. Most dishes have a £1 surcharge in the evening. Bustling but pleasantly relaxed atmosphere; piped jazz throughout. There are a few tables out in front, under an array of hanging baskets; dogs are treated to a bowl of water. The pub is handily set next to the entrance to Windsor Great Park's Long Walk, and there are plenty of big car parks nearby. Please note that they don't allow children.

Free house ~ Licensee Robert Gillespie ~ Real ale ~ Bar food (12-2.30, 6.30-10 Mon-Thurs; 12-2.30 Fri; 12-4 wknds) ~ Restaurant ~ (01753) 855426 ~ Dogs welcome ~ Open 11.30-11; 12-10.30 Sun; closed 25 Dec evening

WINTERBOURNE

Winterbourne Arms *3.7 miles from M4 junction 13; A34 S, then cutting across to B4494 Newbury—Wantage from first major slip-road, and follow Winterbourne signs*

We went to press shortly before this lovely countryside pub changed hands, and although we don't expect any big changes, it would be a good idea to check the opening times if you're coming from any distance. The bars are interestingly decorated with a collection of old irons around the fireplace, early prints and old photographs of the village, and a log fire; piped music. The peaceful view over the rolling fields from the big bar windows cleverly avoids the quiet road, which is sunk between the pub's two lawns. There's a decent wine list with 13 wines by the glass (served in elegant glasses), and three real ales such as Adnams Broadside, Fullers London Pride and West Berkshire Good Old Boy are well kept on handpump. Besides lunchtime sandwiches, they offer an interesting range of main dishes; puddings too. The little no smoking restaurant area was once a bakery, and you can still see the original bakers' ovens. The pub is in a charming spot, and there are nearby walks to Snelsmore and Donnington. In summer, flowering tubs and hanging baskets, brighten up the picnic-sets, and there's a big weeping willow in the garden. Reports on the new regime please.

Free house ~ Licensee Frank Adams ~ Real ale ~ Bar food (not Sun evening, or Mon) ~ Restaurant ~ (01635) 248200 ~ Children in eating area of bar and restaurant ~ Dogs allowed in bar ~ Open 12-3, 6-11; 12-3 Sun; closed Sun pm, all day Mon

Dog Friendly Hotels, B&Bs and Farms

HUNGERFORD
Bear Hotel *41 Charnham St, Hungerford, Berkshire RG17 0EL (01488) 682512* **£87**, plus special breaks; 41 comfortable, attractive rms with antiques and beams in older ones, and some with views over the river. Civilised and carefully restored hotel with open fires, plentiful bar food and well kept real ales in Courtyard Bar (open all day), and a relaxing brasserie restaurant; dogs welcome in bedrooms

HUNGERFORD
Marshgate Cottage *Marsh Lane, Hungerford, Berkshire RG17 0QN (01488) 682307* **£62**; 10 individually decorated rms. Family-run little hotel backing on to Kennet & Avon Canal, with residents' lounge and bar, super breakfasts, a friendly atmosphere, and seats overlooking water and marsh, and in sheltered courtyard; plenty to see nearby; disabled access; dogs by arrangement

MAIDENHEAD
Sheephouse Manor *Sheephouse Rd, Maidenhead, Berkshire SL6 8HJ (01628) 776902* **£69**; 9 individually decorated no smoking rms. 16th-c former farmhouse with original beams, timber floors and antique pine doors, open fireplaces, English breakfasts, and two acres of gardens, children's playground, and two donkeys; plenty of pubs and restaurants nearby for evening meals; self-catering also; disabled access; dogs welcome in cottages

PANGBOURNE
Copper *Church Rd, Pangbourne, Berkshire RG8 7AR (0118) 984 2244* **£90**, plus winter breaks; 22 attractive, modern rms, some overlooking the quiet gardens. Carefully restored Victorian hotel a short walk from the Thames and the setting for Kenneth Grahame's novel *Wind in the Willows* which he wrote while living in the cottage next door; open fires, a bustling bistro bar, a quiet lounge, and good food using home-grown and local produce in pretty dining room with terrace; dogs welcome in annexe bedrooms only

STREATLEY
Swan at Streatley *High St, Streatley, Reading, Berkshire RG8 9HR (01491) 878800* **£148**, plus special breaks; 46 attractive rms, many overlooking the

water. Well run, friendly riverside hotel with comfortable, relaxed lounges, consistently good food in attractive newly refurbished restaurant, popular leisure club with indoor fitness pool, restored Magdalen College Barge, and flower-filled gardens; disabled access; dogs welcome in bedrooms; £15

Buckinghamshire

Dog Friendly Pubs

BOVINGDON GREEN
Royal Oak *¼ mile N of Marlow, on back road to Frieth signposted off West Street (A4155) in centre*

The emphasis at this stylish rambling country pub is on the high quality food. There's a good selection of skilfully prepared dishes from a seasonally changing blackboard menu; a good few tables may have reserved signs (it's worth booking ahead, especially on Sundays). Several attractively decorated areas open off the central bar, the half-panelled walls variously painted in pale blue, green or cream: the cosiest part is the low-beamed room closest to the car park, with three small tables, a woodburner in an exposed brick fireplace, and a big pile of logs. Throughout there's a mix of church chairs, stripped wooden tables and chunky wall seats, with rugs on the partly wooden, partly flagstoned floors, co-ordinated cushions and curtains, and a very bright, airy feel. It's a well organised and civilised place, and thoughtful extra touches set the tone, with a big, square bowl of olives on the bar, smart soaps and toiletries in the lavatories, and carefully laid out newspapers; most tables have fresh flowers or candles. A terrace with good solid tables leads to an appealing garden with plenty more, and there's a smaller garden at the side as well (all the staff get a shift looking after the garden). They serve 13 wines by the glass, and well kept Brakspears, Fullers London Pride and Marlow Rebellion on handpump; hard-working and helpful staff, piped music. The pub is part of a little group which comprises the Alford Arms in Frithsden (see Hertfordshire) and the Swan at Denham (see Buckinghamshire).

Enterprise ~ Lease Trasna Rice Giff and David Salisbury ~ Real ale ~ Bar food (12-2.30(3 Sun), 7-10) ~ (01628) 488611 ~ Children in eating area of bar and restaurant ~ Dogs allowed in bar ~ Open 11-11; 12-10.30 Sun; closed 25-26 Dec

CHALFONT ST GILES
White Hart *Three Households (main street, W)*

This former community local has recently been well reworked as a good dining pub. It does still have a proper civilised front bar where drinkers are welcome, with broadsheet daily papers, bar stools, one or two pub tables and a couple of liberally cushioned dark green settees, and well kept Greene King IPA, Triumph, Morlands Original and Old Speckled Hen on handpump. However, the main emphasis is on the food side, with a spreading extended dining area, mainly bare boards (the bright acoustics make for a lively medley of chatter – sometimes rather on the noisy side when it's busy), and white walls decorated with lots of foody cartoons. The food is good, carefully cooked modern british cooking. There are two menus, with sandwiches, duck salad, and mussels or fishcakes on the short bar one, and an interesting main menu. They do small helpings for children, and there is a good choice of wines by the glass. Service from the neatly dressed young staff is friendly, helpful and efficient. A sheltered back terrace has squarish picnic-sets under cocktails parasols, with more beyond in the garden, which has a neat play area; the comfortable newly done 11-room bedroom block is on the other side (breakfasts are good).

Greene King ~ Lease Scott MacRae ~ Real ale ~ Bar food (12-2, 6.30(7 Sun)-9.30) ~ Restaurant ~ (01494) 872441 ~ Children in eating area of bar and restaurant ~ Dogs allowed in bar ~ Open 11.30-2.30, 6(5.30 Fri/Sat)-11; 12-10.30 Sun; 12-3, 7-10.30 Sun in winter ~ Bedrooms: £77.50S/£97.50S

CHENIES

Red Lion *2 miles from M25 junction 18; A404 towards Amersham, then village signposted on right; Chesham Road*
Handy for the M25, this well run pub is a good all-rounder with well kept beers, a welcoming atmosphere and tasty home-made food. The bustling unpretentious L-shaped bar has comfortable built-in wall benches by the front windows, other traditional seats and tables, and original photographs of the village and traction engines; there's also a small no smoking back snug and a dining room. Benskins Best, Marlow Rebellion Lion Pride (brewed for the pub and highly recommended by readers), Wadworths 6X, and a guest beer are kept in top condition on handpump. There's a terrific choice on the inventive menu, and handily lots of the dishes come in two sizes. The hanging baskets and window boxes are pretty in summer, and there are picnic-sets on a small side terrace. No children, games machines or piped music.

Free house ~ Licensee Mike Norris ~ Real ale ~ Bar food (12-2, 7-10(9.30 Sun)) ~ (01923) 282722 ~ Dogs allowed in bar ~ Open 11-2.30, 5.30-11; 12-3, 6.30-10.30 Sun; closed 25 Dec

DENHAM

Swan *¼ mile from M40 junction 1 or M25 junction 16; follow Denham Village signs*
In a charming village street, among old tiled, wisteria-clad buildings, this civilised pub is a popular place for a well cooked meal. Along with lunchtime sandwiches (not weekends), you'll find high quality, beautifully presented dishes. A good wine list includes over a dozen by the glass, and they keep Courage Best and Directors and Morrells Oxford Blue on handpump; excellent courteous staff, and a friendly bustling atmosphere.

It's stylishly furnished, with a nice mix of antique and old-fashioned chairs, and solid tables, with individually chosen pictures on the cream and warm green walls, rich heavily draped curtains, inviting open fires (usually lit) and fresh flowers; piped music. The extensive garden is floodlit at night, and leads from a sheltered terrace with tables to a more spacious lawn. It can get busy at weekends, and parking may be difficult.

Scottish Courage ~ Lease Mark Littlewood ~ Real ale ~ Bar food (12-2.30(3 Sun), 7-10) ~ (01895) 832085 ~ Children welcome ~ Dogs allowed in bar ~ Open 11-11; 12-10.30 Sun; closed 26 Dec

EASINGTON

Mole & Chicken *From B4011 in Long Crendon follow Chearsley, Waddesdon signpost into Carters Lane opposite the Chandos Arms, then turn left into Chilton Road*

An excellent choice for a special meal, this enjoyable dining pub is set in lovely countryside. The open–plan layout is cleverly done, so that all the different parts seem quite snug and self-contained without being cut off from what's going on, and the atmosphere is relaxed and sociable. The beamed bar curves around the serving counter in a sort of S–shape, and there are pink walls with lots of big antique prints, flagstones, and (even at lunchtime) lit candles on the medley of tables to go with the nice mix of old chairs; good winter log fires. Although customers do drop in for just a drink, you'll probably feel you're missing out if you're not eating; you must book to be sure of a seat. Delicious, generously served food, with daily specials. They serve a good choice of wines (with decent french house wines), over 40 malt whiskies, and well kept Fullers London Pride, Greene King IPA and Hook Norton Best on handpump. The garden, where they sometimes hold summer barbecues and pig and lamb roasts, has quite a few tables and chairs.

Free house ~ Licensees A Heather and S Ellis ~ Real ale ~ Bar food ~ Restaurant ~ (01844) 208387 ~ Children welcome ~ Dogs allowed in bar ~ Open 12-3, 6-11; 12-10.30 Sun; closed 25 Dec ~ Bedrooms: £50S/£65B

FORD

Dinton Hermit *SW of Aylesbury*

Tucked away in pretty countryside, this welcoming 16th-c stone cottage has a very old print of John Bigg, the supposed executioner of King Charles I and the man later known as the Dinton Hermit. With a huge inglenook fireplace (good log fire in winter), the bar has scrubbed tables and comfortable cushioned and wicker-backed mahogany-look chairs on a nice old black and red tiled floor, with white-painted plaster on very thick uneven stone walls; the extended back dining area is very much in character, with similar furniture on quarry tiles. A nice touch are the church candles lit throughout the bar and restaurant, and there are hundreds of bottles of wine decorating the walls and thick oak bar counter. Although locals do still drop in for just a drink, there's quite an emphasis on the enjoyable food. Generously served dishes and home-made puddings; they also do lunchtime sandwiches. Alongside well kept Fullers London

Pride and Vale Wychert on handpump, they serve a changing guest such as Adnams, and there's a decent choice of wines; friendly and attentive service, and a congenial atmosphere. As we went to press, the huge garden was being landscaped; barbecues in summer and live jazz events. The comfortable, well decorated bedrooms are in a sympathetically converted barn.

Free house ~ Licensees John and Debbie Colinswood ~ Real ale ~ Bar food (not Sun evening) ~ Restaurant ~ (01296) 747473 ~ Children in eating area of bar and restaurant, must be over 12 in evening ~ Dogs allowed in bar ~ Open 11-11; 12-4 Sun; closed Sun evening ~ Bedrooms: /£80B

GREAT HAMPDEN

Hampden Arms *Village signposted off A4010 N and S of Princes Risborough*
This quietly set pub is on the edge of Hampden Common (and right opposite the village cricket pitch), so there are good walks nearby. Although the emphasis is on the well prepared food, the friendly staff do make drinkers feel welcome; they also do lunchtime sandwiches. The beige-walled front room has broad dark tables with a few aeroplane pictures and country prints, and the back room has a slightly more rustic feel, with its cushioned wall benches and big woodburning stove. Well kept Adnams and Hook Norton on handpump, and Addlestone's cider from the small corner bar. There are tables out in the tree-sheltered garden.

Free house ~ Licensees Louise and Constantine Lucas ~ Real ale ~ Bar food ~ Restaurant ~ (01494) 488255 ~ Children welcome ~ Dogs welcome ~ Open 12-3, 6-11

HAMBLEDEN

Stag & Huntsman *Turn off A4155 (Henley—Marlow road) at Mill End, signposted to Hambleden; in a mile turn right into village centre*
This handsome brick and flint pub is set opposite a church on the far edge of one of the prettiest Chilterns villages; it's just a field's walk from the river. In fine weather you'll have to be quick if you want to bag one of the seats in the spacious and neatly kept country garden. The half-panelled, L-shaped lounge bar has low ceilings, a large fireplace, and upholstered seating with wooden chairs on the carpet. Attractively simple, the public bar serves well kept Rebellion IPA, Wadworths 6X, and a guest beer such as Loddon Hoppit on handpump, and they've farm cider, and good wines; darts, dominoes, cribbage, shove-ha'penny, and piped music. There's a dining room, and a cosy snug at the front; friendly and efficient service, and a buoyant atmosphere. Well liked and reasonably priced bar food.

Free house ~ Licensees Hon. Henry Smith and Andrew Stokes ~ Real ale ~ Bar food (not Sun evenings) ~ (01491) 571227 ~ Children in eating area of bar and restaurant ~ Dogs allowed in bar ~ Open 11-2.30(3 Sat), 6-11; 12-3, 7-10.30 Sun; closed 25 Dec, evenings 26 Dec and 1 Jan ~ Bedrooms: £58B/£68B

HAWRIDGE COMMON

Full Moon *Hawridge Common; left fork off A416 N of Chesham, then follow for 3.5 miles towards Cholesbury*
This prettily set little country local is bustling with a friendly mix of locals,

walkers and visitors. The low-beamed rambling bar is the heart of the building, with oak built-in floor-to-ceiling settles, ancient flagstones and flooring tiles, hunting prints, and an inglenook fireplace. In summer, you can sit at seats on the terrace (which has an awning and outside heaters for cooler evenings) and gaze over the windmill nestling behind; plenty of walks over the common from here. The enjoyable menu includes meat, poultry and game from an organic butcher. Both the restaurants are no smoking. They keep six real ales on handpump, with regulars such as Adnams, Bass, Brakspears Special, and Fullers London Pride, and weekly changing guests such as Courage Best and Wadworths 6X; piped music, and good service.

Enterprise ~ Lease Peter and Annie Alberto ~ Real ale ~ Bar food (not Sun evening) ~ Restaurant ~ (01494) 758959 ~ Children welcome ~ Dogs allowed in bar ~ Open 12-3, 5.30-11; 12-11 Sat; 12-10.30 Sun; closed 25 Dec

HEDGERLEY

White Horse *2.4 miles from M40 junction 2: at exit roundabout take Slough turnoff, then take Hedgerley Lane (immediate left) following alongside M40. After 1.5 miles turn right at T-junction into Village Lane*

The fine range of seven or eight real ales at this proper country local are all tapped from the cask in a room behind the tiny hatch counter. Greene King IPA and Marlow Rebellion are well kept alongside five daily changing guests from anywhere in the country, with good farm cider and belgian beers too; their regular ale festivals are very popular. The cottagey main bar has plenty of character, with lots of beams, brasses and exposed brickwork, low wooden tables, some standing timbers, jugs, ball-cocks and other bric-a-brac, a log fire, and a good few leaflets and notices about future village events. There is a little flagstoned public bar on the left. On the way out to the garden, which has tables and occasional barbecues, they have a canopy extension to help during busy periods. The atmosphere is jolly with warmly friendly service from the long-standing licensees and cheerful staff. At lunchtimes they do bar food such as sandwiches and changing straightforward hot dishes. In front are lots of hanging baskets, with a couple more tables overlooking the quiet road. There are good walks nearby, and the pub is handy for the Church Wood RSPB reserve. It can get crowded at weekends.

Free house ~ Licensees Doris Hobbs and Kevin Brooker ~ Real ale ~ Bar food (lunchtime only) ~ (01753) 643225 ~ Children in canopy extension area ~ Dogs allowed in bar ~ Open 11-2.30, 5-11; 11-11 Sat; 12-10.30 Sun

MENTMORE

Stag *Village signposted off B488 S of Leighton Buzzard; The Green*

They've around 50 different kinds of wine at this pretty village pub, and they're all available by the glass. With a relaxed atmosphere, the small civilised lounge bar has low oak tables, attractive fresh flower arrangements, and an open fire; the more simple public bar leading off has shove-ha'penny, cribbage and dominoes. Well kept Wells Bombardier, Eagle and IPA and maybe a guest from Greene King on handpump, and champagne cocktails. There are seats too out on the pleasant flower-filled front terrace looking across towards Mentmore House, and a charming, well tended, sloping garden. Good, reasonably priced lunchtime bar food includes interesting sandwiches, salads and hot dishes; changing evening menu. Part of the more formal restaurant is no smoking.

Charles Wells ~ Lease Jenny and Mike Tuckwood ~ Real ale ~ Bar food (not Mon evenings) ~ Restaurant ~ (01296) 668423 ~ Children in restaurant and eating area of bar but must be over 12 in evening ~ Dogs allowed in bar ~ Open 12-11(10.30 Sun); may be shorter opening hours in winter

NEWTON LONGVILLE
Crooked Billet *Off A421 S of Milton Keynes; Westbrook End*

Wine-lovers will find it hard to tear themselves away from this thatched dining pub (in a slightly unusual position by a modern housing estate), as there are over 400 wines by the glass to choose from, with plans to add a further 100. Although it manages to feel like a proper pub, the focus is very much on the adventurous (though not cheap) food. At lunchtime as well as sandwiches and wraps, there's a choice of thoughtfully prepared dishes, made with lots of local ingredients, and unusual puddings; they also do a good cheeseboard. Reserve your table well in advance if you want to eat in the evening in the no smoking restaurant. The brightly modernised and extended bar has beam and plank ceilings, some partly green-painted walls, sporting trophies on the shelves, and usually a few chatting locals. Well kept Greene King IPA and Abbot, and a couple of guests such as Everards Tiger and Wadworths 6X on handpump, 30 malt whiskies, and 30 cognacs and armagnacs. There are tables out on the lawn.

Greene King ~ Lease John and Emma Gilchrist ~ Real ale ~ Bar food (lunchtime only, not Mon) ~ Restaurant ~ (01908) 373936 ~ Children in restaurant ~ Dogs allowed in bar ~ Open 12-2.30, 5.30-11; 12-11 Sat; 12-4, 7-11 Sun; closed Mon lunchtime, 25-26 Dec, 1 Jan

PRESTWOOD
Polecat *170 Wycombe Road (A4128 N of High Wycombe)*

Lovely in summer, the attractive garden of this cheerfully run pub has lots of bulbs in spring, and colourful hanging baskets, tubs, and herbaceous plants; there are quite a few picnic-sets under parasols on neat grass out in front beneath a big fairy-lit pear tree, with more on a big well kept back lawn. Opening off the low-ceilinged bar are several smallish rooms with an assortment of tables and chairs, various stuffed birds as well as the stuffed white polecats in one big cabinet, small country pictures, rugs on bare boards or red tiles, and a couple of antique housekeeper's chairs by a good open fire; the Gallery room is no smoking. The pub attracts a loyal following, and at lunchtime there tend to be chatty crowds of middle-aged diners, with a broader mix of ages in the evening; readers like the friendly, relaxed atmosphere. Enjoyable, home-made dishes from a popular menu, with blackboard specials; and they also do lunchtime snacks and puddings. You can choose from 16 wines by the glass, and Flowers IPA, Greene King Old Speckled Hen, Marstons Pedigree and a guest are well kept on

handpump at the flint bar counter; a good few malt whiskies too; piped music. Readers recommend the nearby farm shop.
Free house ~ Licensee John Gamble ~ Real ale ~ Bar food (12-2, 6.30-9; not Sun evening) ~ Restaurant ~ No credit cards ~ (01494) 862253 ~ Children in family room ~ Dogs allowed in bar ~ Open 11.30-2.30, 6-11; 12-3 Sun; closed Sun evening, evenings 24 and 31 Dec, all day 25-26 Dec

SKIRMETT
Frog *From A4155 NE of Henley take Hambleden turn and keep on; or from B482 Stokenchurch—Marlow, take Turville turn and keep on*
You'll find a good mix of customers and a warm welcome at this bustling country inn, set right in the heart of the Chiltern Hills. A side gate leads to a lovely garden with a large tree in the middle, and the unusual five-sided tables are well placed for attractive valley views. Inside, although brightly modernised, it still has something of a local feel with leaflets and posters near the door advertising raffles and so forth. Neatly kept, the beamed bar area has a mix of comfortable furnishings, a striking hooded fireplace with a bench around the edge (and a pile of logs sitting beside it), big rugs on the wooden floors, and sporting and local prints around the salmon painted walls. The function room leading off is sometimes used as a dining overflow. You must book in advance if you want to eat the good, freshly cooked food which is served by very friendly staff; irresistible home-made puddings. The restaurant and family room are no smoking; piped music. Three well kept real ales such as Fullers London Pride, Rebellion IPA and Young's Bitter on handpump, a good range of wines, quite a few whiskies, and various coffees. The appealing bedrooms make a nice base for the area. Henley is close by, and just down the road is the delightful Ibstone windmill; there are many surrounding hiking routes.
Free house ~ Licensees Jim Crowe and Noelle Greene ~ Real ale ~ Bar food (12-2.30, 6.30-9.30; not winter Sun evening) ~ Restaurant ~ (01491) 638996 ~ Children in restaurant and family room ~ Dogs allowed in bar ~ Open 11-3, 6.30(6 Fri/Sat)-11; 12-4, 6-10 Sun; closed Sun evening Oct-May ~ Bedrooms: £55B/£65B

TURVILLE
Bull & Butcher *Off A4155 Henley—Marlow via Hambleden and Skirmett*
Handily open all day, this black and white timbered pub is in a lovely Chilterns valley among ancient cottages. There are seats on the lawn by fruit trees in the attractive garden which has a children's play area, and they hold barbecues in the summer. Big helpings of well presented bar food, with specials and home-made puddings; they do children's helpings, and readers are keen on their Sunday lunch. As well as some three dozen wines by the glass, they serve well kept Brakspears Bitter, Special, and a seasonal guest on handpump alongside Hook Norton Mild; Addlestone's cider, and a good choice of juices too; piped jazz. There are two low-ceilinged, oak-beamed rooms (the Windmill lounge is no smoking), and the bar has a deep well incorporated into a glass-topped table, with tiled floor, cushioned wall settles and an inglenook fireplace. The village is popular with television and

film companies; *The Vicar of Dibley*, *Midsomer Murders* and *Chitty Chitty Bang Bang* were all filmed here. A fine place to end up after a walk (though no muddy boots), the pub does get crowded at weekends.
Brakspears ~ Tenants Hugo and Lydia Botha ~ Real ale ~ Bar food (12-2.30(3 Sat), 7-9.45; 12-4 Sun and bank hol Mon) ~ Restaurant ~ (01491) 638283 ~ Children in eating area of bar and restaurant ~ Dogs allowed in bar ~ Open 11-11; 12-10.30 Sun; closed 25 Dec evening

Dog Friendly Hotels, B&Bs and Farms

AYLESBURY
Hartwell House *Oxford Rd, Aylesbury, Buckinghamshire HP17 8NL (01296) 747444 £260*, plus special breaks; 46 rms, some large and well equipped, others with four-posters and fine panelling, inc 10 secluded suites in restored 18th-c stables with private garden and statues. Elegant Grade I listed building with Jacobean and Georgian façades, wonderful decorative plasterwork and panelling, fine paintings and antiques, a marvellous Gothic central staircase, splendid morning room, and library, exceptional service, fine wines, and excellent food; 90 acres of parkland with ruined church, lake and statues, and spa with indoor swimming pool, saunas, gym and beauty rooms, and informal buttery and bar; tennis, croquet and fishing; children over 8; good disabled access; dogs in Hartwell Court

MARLOW
Compleat Angler *Bisham Rd, Marlow, Buckinghamshire SL7 1RG (01628) 484444 £218*, plus special breaks; 64 pretty, individually furnished rms overlooking garden or river. Famous Thames-side hotel with comfortable panelled lounge, balconied bar, spacious beamed restaurant, imaginative food, and prompt service; tennis, croquet, coarse fishing and boating; disabled access; dogs welcome in bedrooms; £10

TAPLOW
Cliveden *Taplow, Maidenhead, Berkshire SL6 0JF (01628) 668561 £225* (plus £7 each paid to National Trust), plus special breaks; 39 luxurious, individual rms with maid unpacking service and a butler's tray. Superb Grade I listed stately home with gracious, comfortable public rooms, fine paintings, tapestries and armour, and a surprisingly unstuffy atmosphere; lovely views over the magnificent NT Thames-side parkland and formal gardens (open to the public); imaginative food in the two no smoking restaurants with lighter meals in the conservatory, friendly breakfasts around a huge table, and impeccable staff; pavilion with swimming pool, gym, etc.; tennis, squash, croquet, and boats for river trips; they are kind to children; dogs in bedrooms, with beds, blankets and menu available

WESTBURY
Mill Farmhouse *Westbury, Brackley, Northamptonshire NN13 5JS* (01280) 704843 £50; 3 pretty rms. Carefully restored miller's house on large farm, and a colourful big garden with swimming pool; plenty of original features and open fire in comfortable sitting/dining room, oak furniture and plenty of hunting prints; charming owners and good light suppers if ordered; two self-contained flats, too; disabled access; dogs welcome in bedrooms by arrangement

WINSLOW
Bell *Market Sq, Winslow, Buckingham, Buckinghamshire MK18 3AB* (01296) 714091 £64; 43 rms. Carefully furnished and elegant black and white timbered inn with beams and open fires, plush hotel bar, all-day coffee lounge, enjoyable bar food, and good lunchtime and evening carvery in restaurant; disabled access; dogs welcome in bedrooms

Cambridgeshire

Dog Friendly Pubs

CAMBRIDGE
Cambridge Blue *85 Gwydir Street*
The rather charming collection of rowing memorabilia at this quiet back street pub includes the bow section of the Cambridge boat that famously rammed a barge and sank before the start of the 1984 boat race. Chris Lloyd the landlord rowed for Cambridge, and there's such a nice selection of rowing photographs you feel you're browsing through someone's family snaps. Two uncluttered rooms are simply decorated with old-fashioned bare-boards style furnishings, candles on the tables and a big collection of oars, and are completely no smoking; cribbage, dominoes, chess and draughts. An interesting range of seven regularly changing well kept real ales on handpump are (with the odd exception such as Fullers) picked from East Anglian breweries such as Adnams, City of Cambridge, Hobsons, Iceni, Nethergate, Potton Brewery or Woodfordes; they also have a decent choice of wines and malt whiskies and fresh orange juice. Reasonably priced straightforward bar food is served in an attractive little conservatory dining area, and includes a cold table with game or picnic pies, nut roast and various quiches; also daily specials and Sunday roast. Children like the surprisingly rural feeling and large back garden and its wendy house.
Free house ~ Licensees Chris and Debbie Lloyd ~ Real ale ~ Bar food (12-2.30, 6-9.30; not 25 Dec) ~ (01223) 505110 ~ Children welcome in conservatory ~ Dogs welcome ~ Open 12-2.30(3 Sat), 5.30-11; 12-3, 6-10.30 Sun

Free Press *Prospect Row*
Pubby and cheerful, this unspoilt old place is completely no smoking. In winter you can read a newspaper by the log fire which warms its simple but characterfully sociable bare-board rooms, and in summer the sheltered paved garden at the back is quite a sun-trap. Over the years loyal customers have donated little items that are displayed in old printing trays, which are hung up among old newspapers, printing memorabilia and a collection of oars. Real ale lovers enjoy the well kept Greene King IPA, Abbot and Mild and a guest such as Batemans on handpump; cribbage, dominoes and shove-ha'penny. Good value tasty bar food is served in generous helpings.

Greene King ~ Tenant Donna Thornton ~ Real ale ~ Bar food (12-2, 6-8.30; not Sun evening) ~ (01223) 368337 ~ Children welcome ~ Dogs welcome ~ Open 12-2.30(3 Sat), 6-11; 12-3, 7-10.30 Sun; closed 25-26 Dec, 1 Jan

Live & Let Live *40 Mawson Road; off Mill Road SE of centre*
For entertainment value, the drink to order at this friendly old local is their speciality, a 'Brownie-Boy Shandy'. It's a mix of two farm ciders and when one is ordered the welcoming landlord rings the bell and announces 'and another'. And it's worth sticking around until last orders, for his closing speech to thank everybody for coming. He stocks a good range of real ales with regulars such as Everards Tiger and Nethergate Umbel, and guests from brewers such as Crouch Vale, Featherstone, Milton and Tring on handpump too, as well as over a dozen malts, belgian beers on tap, lots of belgian bottled beers and farm cider. Down to earth but popular, the heavily timbered brickwork rooms have sturdy varnished pine tables with pale wood chairs on bare boards, real gas lighting, lots of interesting old country bric-a-brac, some steam railway and brewery memorabilia and posters about local forthcoming events; cribbage, dominoes. The eating area of the bar is no smoking until 9pm. Simple but good value home-made food, Sunday roast and all-day breakfast (weekends only).
Burlison Inns ~ Lease Peter Wiffin ~ Real ale ~ Bar food (12-2(3 Sun), 6(7 Sun)-9) ~ (01223) 460261 ~ Children in eating area of bar ~ Dogs allowed in bar ~ Folk most Sat evenings ~ Open 11.30-2.30(3 Sat), 5.30(6 Sat)-11; 12-3, 7-10.30 Sun

ELTON
Black Horse *B671 off A605 W of Peterborough and A1(M); Overend*
This rather nice-looking honey brick dining pub happily combines a cosy traditional interior with a good choice of tasty food. There's all you'd expect in a country inn from the welcoming atmosphere to roaring fires, hop-strung beams, a homely and comfortable mix of furniture (no two tables and chairs seem the same), antique prints, and lots of ornaments and bric-a-brac including an intriguing ancient radio set. Dining areas at each end of the bar have parquet flooring and tiles, and the stripped stone back lounge towards the partly no smoking restaurant has an interesting fireplace. Bass, Everards Tiger, Nethergate Suffolk County and a guest from a brewer such as Caledonian are well kept on handpump, alongside an extensive wine list with over a dozen wines by the glass. The enjoyable food is very popular so you may need to book. The big garden is prettily divided into separate areas with super views across Elton Hall park, some tables shaded by horse chestnut trees and a couple of acres of grass for children to play.
Free house ~ Licensee John Clennell ~ Real ale ~ Bar food (12-2, 6-9; not Sun evening; maybe tapas summer afternoons) ~ Restaurant ~ (01832) 280240 ~ Children welcome ~ Dogs allowed in bar ~ Open 12-11; 12-5 Sun; 12-3, 6-11 winter; closed Sun evening

ELY
Fountain *Corner of Barton Square and Silver Street*
Very simple and traditional with no music, fruit machines or even food,

this genteel, if basic, town corner pub is the type of place that's nice to come to for a chat. You'll find a real mix of age groups, and the atmosphere is pleasant and inclusive. They serve well kept Adnams Bitter and Broadside, Fullers London Pride and a changing guest such as Timothy Taylors Landlord on handpump. Old cartoons, local photographs, regional maps and mementoes of the neighbouring King's School punctuate the elegant dark pink walls, and neatly tied-back curtains hang from golden rails above the big windows. Above one fireplace is a stuffed pike in a case, and there are a few antlers dotted about – not to mention a duck at one end of the bar; everything is very clean and tidy. A couple of tables are squeezed on to a tiny back terrace. Note the limited opening times.

Free house ~ Licensees John and Judith Borland ~ Real ale ~ No credit cards ~ (01353) 663122 ~ Children welcome away from bar until 8pm ~ Dogs welcome ~ Open 5-11; 12-2, 6-11 Sat; 12-2, 7-10.30 Sun

FEN DITTON
Ancient Shepherds *Off B1047 at Green End, The River signpost, just NE of Cambridge*

Readers enjoy the tasty food and well kept beer at this pleasantly welcoming pub. Perhaps the nicest room is the softly lit central lounge, where you can't fail to be comfortable on one of the big fat dark red button-back leather settees or armchairs at low solid indonesian tables, by the warm coal fire, and all tucked in by heavy drapes around the window seat with its big scatter cushions. Above a black dado the walls (and ceiling) are dark pink, and decorated with little steeplechasing and riding prints, and comic fox and policeman ones. On the right the smallish convivial more pubby bar with its coal fire serves Adnams and Greene King IPA on handpump, while on the left is a pleasant no smoking restaurant (piped music in here). A decent choice of good bar food. The licensees' new west highland terrier Billie might be around outside food service times.

Pubmaster ~ Tenant J M Harrington ~ Real ale ~ Bar food (lunchtimes only) ~ Restaurant ~ (01223) 293280 ~ Children in eating area of bar and restaurant ~ Dogs allowed in bar ~ Open 12-2.30, 6-11; 12-5.30 Sun; closed Sun evening

HELPSTON
Blue Bell *Woodgate; off B1443*

The very good value OAP weekday lunchtime menu and smaller helpings of quite a few dishes draw an older set to this friendly place. Other good honest food too. There is plenty of red plush here, including cushions for the three oak settles, pictures on the bar's dark brown panelling-effect walls, a nice collection of antique and country prints, big china ornaments, lots of tankards, mugs and horsebrasses overhead, and an enormous brass platter above the small fireplace. The corner bar counter has well kept Adnams, Everards Tiger and Old Original and a guest such as Moles Holy Moley on handpump, and the good coffee comes with fresh cream; piped music, cribbage and dominoes. The comfortable flagstoned no smoking dining room on the right, with stripped joists and some stripped stone, gives the greatest impression of the building's age; John Clare the early

19th-c peasant poet was born next door and originally worked here. Wheelchair access; there may be faint piped pop music. A sheltered terrace has plastic garden tables under outdoor heaters.
Free house ~ Licensee Aubrey Sinclair Ball ~ Real ale ~ Bar food (not Sun, Mon evenings) ~ Restaurant ~ (01733) 252394 ~ Children welcome ~ Dogs allowed in bar ~ Open 11.30-2.30, 5-11; 11.30-11 Sat; 12-10.30 Sun

HEYDON
King William IV *Off A505 W of M11 junction 10*
The lovingly put together interior of this rambling dining pub is filled with a charming jumble of rustic implements from ploughshares, yokes and iron tools, cowbells, beer steins, samovars, brass or black wrought-iron lamps, copper-bound casks and milk ewers, harness, horsebrasses and smith's bellows, to decorative plates, cut-glass and china ornaments. In winter its beamed nooks and crannies are warmed by a hearty log fire, and in summer the wooden deck has teak furniture and outdoor heaters; there are more seats in the pretty garden. It all rather reflects the landlady's enjoyable character. Bar food includes around ten vegetarian dishes. Part of the restaurant is no smoking. Well kept real ales such as Adnams Best, Greene King IPA, Ruddles and a guest such as City of Cambridge Darwins Downfall on handpump; they also do cocktails. Fruit machine.
Free house ~ Licensee Elizabeth Nicholls ~ Real ale ~ Bar food (12-2, 6.30-10; 12-3, 7-10 Sun) ~ Restaurant ~ (01763) 838773 ~ Children in eating area of bar ~ Dogs allowed in bar ~ Open 11-3, 6-11; 12-3, 7-10.30 Sun

HINXTON
Red Lion *Between junctions 9 and 10, M11; just off A1301 S of Great Shefford*
There's plenty of age to this very attractive pink-washed and twin-gabled inn. The dusky mainly open-plan bustling bar (no smoking on Sundays) has leather chesterfields on wooden floors; cribbage, dominoes. Off here there are high-backed upholstered settles in an informal dining area, and the smart no smoking restaurant is filled with mirrors, pictures and assorted clocks. Food is attractively presented and tasty, and includes a Sunday roast. Adnams, Greene King IPA, Woodfordes Wherry and perhaps a guest such as Adnams Regatta are well kept on handpump alongside just over half a dozen changing wines by the glass. In the tidy, attractive garden there's a pleasant terrace with picnic-sets, a dovecote and views of the village church. The pub is not far from the Imperial War Museum, Duxford.
Free house ~ Licensee Alex Clarke ~ Real ale ~ Bar food ~ Restaurant ~ (01799) 530601 ~ Children welcome ~ Dogs allowed in bar ~ Open 11-3, 6-11; 12-4, 7-10.30 Sun

KEYSTON
Pheasant *Village loop road; from A604 SE of Thrapston, right on to B663*
Immaculately kept throughout, this long low thatched white inn is known for its imaginative food and comfortably civilised atmosphere. The oak-beamed spreading bar has open fires, simple wooden tables and chairs on

deep coloured carpets, guns on the pink walls, and country paintings. The excellent wine list includes an interesting choice of reasonably priced bottles and around 15 wines by the glass (plus three champagnes); fine port and sherry too. There's also well kept Adnams Bitter with changing guests such as Nethergate Suffolk County and Potton Village Bike on handpump, and freshly squeezed juices. The pub is no smoking throughout, except in the bar. Under a new chef, well prepared food is served, using carefully sourced ingredients; and there's a set price two-course lunch menu (Monday-Saturday). Seats out in front of the building.

Huntsbridge ~ Licensees Johnny Dargue and John Hoskins ~ Real ale ~ Bar food (12-2, 6.30-9.30) ~ Restaurant ~ (01832) 710241 ~ Children welcome ~ Dogs allowed in bar ~ Open 12-3, 6-11; 12-2.30, 6.30-10.30 Sun

PETERBOROUGH
Brewery Tap *Opposite Queensgate car park*

A two-storey high glass wall running down one side of this enormous pub gives a fascinating view of the massive copper-banded stainless brewing vessels that turn out the very good Oakham beers that are produced at what is said to be one of the largest microbreweries in Europe. Bishops Farewell, Helterskelter, JHB and White Dwarf are their own Oakham beers, and they are served alongside up to eight guests from breweries scattered all over the country. There's an easy-going relaxed feel to the design of the place which is a striking conversion of an old labour exchange, with blue-painted iron pillars holding up a steel-corded mezzanine level, light wood and stone floors, and hugely enlarged and framed newspaper cuttings on its light orange or burnt red walls. It's stylishly lit by a giant suspended steel ring with bulbs running around the rim, and steel-meshed wall lights. A band of chequered floor tiles traces the path of the long sculpted light wood bar counter, which is boldly backed by an impressive display of bottles in a ceiling-high wall of wooden cubes. A sofa seating area downstairs provides a comfortable corner for a surprisingly mixed bunch of customers from young to old. It gets very busy in the evening. The extensive choice of very good thai bar food is prepared by thai chefs. Prices in 2005 are expected to be up a little, though it should still be very good value. The pub is sadly under threat of being turned into a parking complex.

Own brew ~ Licensees Stuart Wright, Jamie Howley, Jessica Loock ~ Real ale ~ Bar food (12-2.30, 6-9.30; 12-9.30 Fri/Sat) ~ Restaurant ~ (01733) 358500 ~ Children welcome ~ Dogs welcome ~ Occasional live music ~ Open 12-11(till 1.30am Fri/Sat); 12-10.30 Sun; closed 25-26 Dec, 1 Jan

REACH
Dyke's End *From B1102 E of A14/A1103 junction, follow signpost to Swaffham Prior and Upware – keep on through Swaffham Prior (Reach signposted from there); Fair Green*

With its weather-worn inn-sign, big front yew tree, adjacent church and charming village-green setting, this looks every inch the classic village pub. Its village character runs deep: a few years ago a consortium of locals bought it, to save it from being turned into a private house – more recently, it was sold to the current landlord, who has managed to keep and even build on its warm-hearted villagey feel. A high-backed winged settle screens off the door, and the simply decorated ochre-walled bar has stripped heavy pine tables and pale kitchen chairs on dark boards with one or two rugs, a few rather smarter dining tables on parquet flooring in a panelled section on the left, and on the right a step down to a red-carpeted bit with the small red-walled servery, and sensibly placed darts at the back. All the tables have lit candles in earthenware bottles, and on our visit a big bowl of lilies brightened up the serving counter almost as much as the well kept Adnams and Woodfordes and three guests from brewers such as Adnams, Greene King and Elgoods on handpump, also country cider. A wide range of enjoyable food, using local and seasonal produce. The evening restaurant is upstairs. Service is pleasant and efficient, the atmosphere chatty and relaxed, piped music (such as Bach cello suites) unobtrusive, and we gather the piano sometimes gets a hearing. The front grass has picnic-sets under big green canvas parasols.

Free house ~ Licensee Simon Owers ~ Real ale ~ Bar food (not Sun evening, Mon) ~ Restaurant ~ (01638) 743816 ~ Children in eating area of bar ~ Dogs allowed in bar ~ Open 12-2.30, 6-10.30; 12-2, 7-10.30 Sun; closed Mon lunchtime

Dog Friendly Hotels, B&Bs and Farms

DUXFORD

Duxford Lodge *Ickleton Rd, Duxford, Cambridgeshire CB2 4RU (01223)* *836444* £**105**; 15 good-sized, warm rms, 2 with four-posters. Carefully run late Victorian hotel in an acre of neatly kept landscaped gardens, with a welcoming, relaxed atmosphere, individually chosen modern paintings and prints, a restful little lounge, decent wines, enjoyable modern cooking in the airy no smoking restaurant, and good breakfasts; partial disabled access; dogs welcome in some bedrooms

ELY

Lamb *2 Lynn Rd, Ely, Cambridgeshire CB7 4EJ (01353) 663574* £**95**; 31 comfortable rms. Pleasant, neatly kept old coaching inn (newly refurbished) near cathedral, with two smart bars, enjoyable food in an attractive restaurant, very friendly staff, and good car parking; dogs welcome in bedrooms; £10

HUNTINGDON

Old Bridge *1 High St, Huntingdon, Cambridgeshire PE18 6TQ (01480)* *451591* £**150**, plus wknd breaks; 24 excellent rms with CD stereos and power showers. Creeper-covered Georgian hotel with pretty lounge, log fire in panelled bar, imaginative british cooking and extensive wine list in the no smoking restaurant and less formal lunchtime room (nice murals), and quick courteous service; riverside gardens; partial disabled access; dogs welcome in bedrooms, bar and lounge

SIX MILE BOTTOM
Swynford Paddocks *Six Mile Bottom, Newmarket, Cambridgeshire CB8 0UE (01638) 570234* £**135**; 15 individually furnished rms with good bthrms. Gabled country house in neat grounds overlooking stud paddocks; carefully furnished rooms with fresh flowers and log fires, bar decorated with Brigadier memorabilia (a tribute to the great racehorse who is buried in the hotel grounds), conservatory Garden Room, a relaxed atmosphere, good food, and friendly service; tennis, putting and croquet; disabled access; dogs welcome in bedrooms

WANSFORD
Haycock *London Rd, Wansford, Peterborough, Cambridgeshire PE8 6JA (01780) 782223* £**115**, plus special breaks; 50 individually decorated rms. 16th-c golden stone inn with relaxed, comfortable and carefully furnished lounges and pubby bar; pretty lunchtime café, smart restaurant with good food, excellent wines and efficient friendly service; garden with boules, fishing and cricket; disabled access. The little village it dominates is attractive, with a fine bridge over the Nene, and a good antiques shop; dogs welcome in some bedrooms

Cheshire

Dog Friendly Pubs

ALDFORD
Grosvenor Arms *B5130 Chester—Wrexham*
Hugely popular, this very well run pub is an excellent all-rounder, with enjoyable food, a great choice of drinks, swift friendly service and if that wasn't enough, it's handily open all day too. Lovely on summer evenings, the airy terracotta-floored conservatory has lots of huge low hanging flowering baskets and chunky pale wood garden furniture, and opens on to a large elegant suntrap terrace and neat lawn with picnic-sets, young trees and a tractor. Inside, it's spacious and open plan, with a traditional feel, and a buoyantly chatty atmosphere prevails in the huge panelled library. Tall bookshelves line one wall, and lots of substantial tables are well spaced on the handsome board floor. Several quieter areas are well furnished with good individual pieces. There are plenty of interesting pictures, and the lighting is welcoming; cribbage, dominoes, Trivial Pursuit and Scrabble. A tempting choice of whiskies includes 100 malts, 30 bourbons, and 30 from Ireland, and all 20 wines (largely new world) are served by the glass. Flowers IPA, Caledonian Deuchars IPA and Robinsons Best are well kept on handpump with a couple of guests from brewers such as Freeminer and Derwent. A good choice of well presented bar food, with mouth-watering puddings; best to book on weekend evenings. The pub is a favourite with families and can get very busy.
Brunning & Price ~ Managers Gary Kidd and Jeremy Brunning ~ Real ale ~ Bar food (12-10(9 Sun and bank hols); not 25 Dec, or 26 and 31 Dec evenings) ~ (01244) 620228 ~ No children inside after 6pm ~ Dogs allowed in bar ~ Open 11.30-11; 12-10.30 Sun

ASTON
Bhurtpore *Off A530 SW of Nantwich; in village follow Wrenbury signpost*
'Every beer-drinker's dream' according to one reader, this marvellous roadside pub serves a truly awesome range of drinks. The pub takes its unusual name from the town in India, where local landowner Lord Combermere won a battle, and the carpeted lounge bar bears some indian influences, with a growing collection of exotic artefacts (one turbaned

statue behind the bar proudly sports a pair of Ray-Bans), as well as good local period photographs, and some attractive furniture. At lunchtime or earlyish on a weekday evening the atmosphere is cosy and civilised, but even on weekends, when it gets packed, the cheery staff cope superbly. Tables in the comfortable public bar are reserved for people not eating, and the snug area and dining room are no smoking; darts, dominoes, cribbage, pool, TV and fruit machine. More than 1,000 different superbly kept real ales pass through the 11 handpumps every year, including some really unusual ones. Alongside Hanbys Drawwell, you might find Abbeydale Absolution and Belfry, Copper Dragon Dark, Dark Star Over the Moon, Gales Frolic, Moorhouses Bursting Bitter, Salopian Golden Thread, and Titanic Longitude, and they also serve continental beers such as Bitburger Pils, Pilsner Urquell and Timmermans Peach Beer, with dozens of unusual bottled beers and fruit beers. If you're not a beer fan, there's still a great deal to choose from, with a tempting selection of farm ciders and perries, 100 different whiskies, and a good wine list (with fine wines and fruit wines). The enjoyable menu has snacks (not Friday or Saturday night), as well as other reasonably priced dishes and a choice of about six delicious home-made indian curries; puddings too.

Free house ~ Licensee Simon George ~ Real ale ~ Bar food (12-2, 7-9; 12-9 Sun) ~ Restaurant ~ (01270) 780917 ~ Well behaved children lunchtime and early evenings ~ Dogs allowed in bar ~ Open 12-2.30(3 Sat), 6.30-11; 12-10.30 Sun; closed 25-26 Dec, 1 Jan ~ Bedrooms: £30S/£40S

BARTHOMLEY

White Lion *A mile from M6 junction 16; from exit roundabout take B5078 N towards Alsager, then Barthomley signposted on left*

The main bar of this lovely 17th-c black and white thatched pub feels timeless, with its blazing open fire, heavy oak beams dating back to Stuart times (mind your head), attractively moulded black panelling, Cheshire watercolours and prints on the walls, latticed windows, and thick wobbly old tables. Up some steps, a second room has another welcoming open fire, more oak panelling, a high-backed winged settle, a paraffin lamp hinged to the wall, and shove-ha'penny, cribbage and dominoes; local societies make good use of a third room. Outside, seats and picnic-sets on the cobbles have a charming view of the attractive village, and the early 15th-c red sandstone church of St Bertiline across the road is well worth a visit. At lunchtime, friendly and efficient staff serve good value sandwiches, as well as daily roasts or stilton and local roast ham ploughman's; they have plans to refurbish the kitchen. It's best to arrive early on weekends to be sure of a table. Well kept real ales on handpump include Burtonwood Bitter and Top Hat, with a couple of guests such as Belhaven 70/- and Wadworths 6X; no noisy games machines or music. The cottage behind the pub is available to rent.

Burtonwood ~ Tenant Terence Cartwright ~ Real ale ~ Bar food (lunchtime only, not Thurs) ~ (01270) 882242 ~ Children welcome away from public bar ~ Dogs welcome ~ Open 11.30-11(5-11 only Thurs); 12-10.30 Sun; closed Thurs afternoon

BUNBURY

Dysart Arms *Bowes Gate Road; village signposted off A51 NW of Nantwich; and from A49 S of Tarporley – coming this way, coming in on northernmost village access road, bear left in village centre*

Tables on the terrace and in the neatly kept slightly elevated garden of this popular dining pub are lovely in summer, with views of the splendid church at the end of the pretty village, and the distant Peckforton Hills beyond. Nicely laid out spaces ramble around the pleasantly lit central bar. Under deep venetian red ceilings, the knocked-through cream-walled rooms have red and black tiles, some stripped boards and some carpet, a comfortable variety of well spaced big sturdy wooden tables and chairs, a couple of tall bookcases, some carefully chosen bric-a-brac, properly lit pictures, and good winter fires. One area is no smoking. They've lowered the ceiling in the more restauranty end room (with its book-lined back wall), and there are lots of plants on the window sills. You'll find an interesting selection of 16 wines by the glass, and Thwaites Bitter and Timothy Taylors Landlord are well kept on handpump, along with a couple of guests such as Hanby Drovers and Weetwood Eastgate. Interesting, well presented dishes from a changing menu and a tasty cheeseboard.

Brunning & Price ~ Managers Darren and Elizabeth Snell ~ Real ale ~ Bar food (12-2.15, 6-9.30; 12-(9 Sun)9.30 Sat) ~ (01829) 260183 ~ No children under 10 after 6pm ~ Dogs allowed in bar ~ Open 11.30-11; 12-10.30 Sun; closed 25 Dec, evenings 26 Dec and 1 Jan

CHESTER

Albion *Park Street*

Run by the same landlord for over 30 years, this old-fashioned corner pub is tucked away in a quiet part of town just below the Roman Wall. The atmosphere is peacefully relaxed and chatty, and the lack of piped music, noisy machines and children make the pub especially popular with a loyal following of older visitors. Throughout the rooms you'll find an absorbing collection of World War I memorabilia: big engravings of men leaving for war, and similarly moving prints of wounded veterans, are among the other more expected aspects – flags, advertisements, and so on. The post-Edwardian décor is appealingly muted, with floral wallpaper, appropriate lamps, leatherette and hoop-backed chairs, a period piano, a large mangle, and cast-iron-framed tables; there's an attractive side dining room too. Service is friendly, though race-goers are discouraged, and they don't like people rushing in just before closing time; it can get smoky. Well kept real ales such as Cains Bitter, Jennings Cumberland, and Timothy Taylors Landlord on handpump and maybe a guest, with over 25 malt whiskies, new world wines, and fresh orange juice; the pub cat is called Kitchener. Big portions of hearty bar food (made with lots of local ingredients); it can get very busy at lunchtime. New bedrooms are due to open in 2005.

Punch ~ Lease Michael Edward Mercer ~ Real ale ~ Bar food (12-2, 5(6 Sat)-8, not Sun evening) ~ Restaurant ~ No credit cards ~ (01244) 340345 ~ Dogs allowed in bar ~ Open 12-3, 5(6 Sat)-11; 12-11 Fri; 12-3, 7-10.30 Sun

EATON
Plough *A536 Congleton—Macclesfield*

There's a nicely civilised feel to this handsome 17th-c village pub, a well run place where the various extensions and extra facilities have been conceived with some aplomb. The appealingly designed bedrooms are in a converted stable block, and the old raftered barn at the back – used as the restaurant – was moved here piece by piece from its original home in Wales. Smart but welcoming, the neat bar has plenty of beams and exposed brickwork, comfortable armchairs and cushioned wooden wall seats, long red curtains leading off to a cosy no smoking room, mullioned windows, and a big stone fireplace; there are a couple of snug little alcoves. The big tree-filled garden is attractive, with good views of the nearby hills, and there are picnic-sets on the lawn and a smaller terrace. Very good home-made bar food; they also do a three-course Sunday lunch. Hydes Bitter and Jekylls Gold and Wadworths 6X on handpump, and a decent expanding wine list; happy hour between 4 and 7 (not Sun). Service is friendly and attentive. Regular quiz and curry nights; piped music.

Free house ~ Licensee Mujdat Karatas ~ Real ale ~ Bar food ~ Restaurant ~ (01260) 280207 ~ Dogs allowed in bar ~ Open 11-11; 12-10.30 Sun ~ Bedrooms: £50B/£70B

HIGHER BURWARDSLEY
Pheasant *Burwardsley signposted from Tattenhall (which itself is signposted off A41 S of Chester) and from Harthill (reached by turning off A534 Nantwich—Holt at the Copper Mine); follow pub's signpost on up hill from Post Office; OS Sheet 117 map reference 523566*

Popular with walkers and motorists, this half-timbered and sandstone 17th-c pub is well placed for the Sandstone Trail along the Peckforton Hills. It's a great place if you like views: on a clear day the telescope on the terrace lets you make out the pier head and cathedrals in Liverpool, while from the well spaced tables inside you can see right across the Cheshire plain. The bar has a bright modern feel, with wooden floors and light-coloured furniture. The see-through fireplace is said to house the largest log fire in the county, and there's a pleasant no smoking conservatory. Besides lunchtime sandwiches and ploughman's made with freshly baked bread, they provide superbly cooked dishes. Good service from the friendly young staff. Four very well kept ales on handpump from the local Weetwood brewery, and over 30 malts; piped music, daily newspapers. A big side lawn has picnic-sets, and on summer weekends they sometimes have barbecues. Be warned that there's a flight of stairs to the entrance.

Free house ~ Licensee Simon McLoughlin ~ Real ale ~ Bar food (12-2.30, 6.30-9.30; Sun 12-4, 6.30-8.30) ~ Restaurant ~ (01829) 770434 ~ Children welcome ~ Dogs welcome ~ Open 12-11; 12-10.30 Sun ~ Bedrooms: £65B/£80B

PEOVER HEATH
Dog *Off A50 N of Holmes Chapel at the Whipping Stocks, keep on past Parkgate into Wellbank Lane; OS Sheet 118 map reference 794735; note that this*

village is called Peover Heath on the OS map and shown under that name on many road maps, but the pub is often listed under Over Peover instead
The pretty garden of this friendly, civilised pub is nicely lit on summer evenings, and underneath colourful hanging baskets there are picnic-sets on the peaceful lane. The main bar is very comfortable, with easy chairs and wall seats (including one built into a snug alcove around an oak table), and two wood-backed seats built in either side of a coal fire, opposite which logs burn in an old-fashioned black grate. Well kept Hydes, Moorhouses Black Cat, Weetwood Best and a guest from a brewer such as Copper Dragon on handpump, Addlestone's cider, 35 different malt whiskies, and eight wines by the glass; darts, pool, dominoes, TV and piped music. Service is very friendly and helpful. Enjoyable, reasonably priced bar food. The dining room is no smoking; it's a good idea to book at weekends. There are picnic-sets too out on the rear lawn. It's a pleasant walk from here to the Jodrell Bank Centre and Arboretum.
Free house ~ Licensee Steven Wrigley ~ Real ale ~ Bar food (12-2.30, 6-9; 12-8.30 Sun; not evenings 25, 26 Dec) ~ Restaurant ~ (01625) 861421 ~ Children in eating area of bar and restaurant ~ Dogs allowed in bar ~ Live music one Friday in month ~ Open 11.30-3, 4.30-11; 11.30-11 Sat; 12-10.30 Sun ~ Bedrooms: £55B/£75B

WINCLE
Ship *Village signposted off A54 Congleton—Buxton*
Tucked away in scenic countryside, this is said to be one of the oldest pubs in Cheshire. Great for relaxing in after a walk (there are plenty nearby to choose from), the two old-fashioned and simple little tap rooms have thick stone walls, and a coal fire; no piped music or games machines. Four well kept ales include Moorhouses Premier and Timothy Taylors Landlord with a couple of guests on handpump such as Copper Dragon Best and Storm Windgather, and they also have belgian beers, Westons cider and fruit wines; dominoes. Tasty bar food with specials; puddings might include home-made banoffee pie. On Saturday evenings and Sunday lunchtimes (when it's best to book) it can get busy, and you might have to park on the steep, narrow road outside. A small garden has wooden tables. They sell their own book of local walks (£3).
Free house ~ Licensee Giles Henry Meadows ~ Real ale ~ Bar food (not Mon) ~ Restaurant ~ (01260) 227217 ~ Children in family room ~ Dogs allowed in bar ~ Open 12-3, 7(5.30 Fri)-11; 12-11 Sat; 12-10.30 Sun; closed Mon (exc bank hols)

WRENBURY
Dusty Miller *Village signposted from A530 Nantwich—Whitchurch*
Charming even on a chilly, foggy winter's day, this attractively converted 19th-c mill enjoys a lovely peaceful setting by the Shropshire Union Canal. In fine weather picnic-sets on the gravel terrace, among rose bushes by the water, are a great place to sit – you get to them either by the towpath or by a high wooden catwalk over the River Weaver. Inside you get a good view of the striking counter-weighted drawbridge going up and down, from a

series of tall glazed arches. The modern main bar area is comfortable, with long low-hung hunting prints on green walls, and the mixture of seats flanking the rustic tables includes tapestried banquettes, an ornate church pew and wheelback chairs; further in, a quarry-tiled part by the bar counter has an oak settle and refectory table. There's quite an emphasis on the food, and good, well presented dishes (made with mostly local ingredients); they also do sandwiches. The restaurant and five tables in the bar are no smoking; fresh flowers on tables. Friendly, eager-to-please staff serve well kept real ales such as Cwmbran Double Hop, Robinsons Hatters Mild, Unicorn Old Tom on handpump; eclectic piped music, dominoes. The pub can get very crowded in fine weather.

Robinsons ~ Tenant Mark Sumner ~ Real ale ~ Bar food (12-2, 6.30-9.30, all day Sun in summer; not Mon in winter) ~ Restaurant ~ (01270) 780537 ~ Children in eating area of bar and restaurant ~ Dogs allowed in bar ~ Open 12-3, 6-11; 11-11 Sat; 12-10.30 Sun; 12-3, 6-11 Sat/Sun in winter; closed Mon afternoon in winter

Dog Friendly Hotels, B&Bs and Farms

BEESTON
Wild Boar Hotel *Whitchurch Rd, Beeston, Tarporley, Cheshire CW6 9NW* (01829) 260309 £105.75, plus special breaks; 37 rms with appealing touches such as fresh fruit. Striking timbered 17th-c former hunting lodge, much extended over the years, with relaxed and comfortable bars and lounges, enjoyable bar meals and formal beamed restaurant, and friendly, professional service; disabled access; dogs in ground-floor bedrooms only; £5

BICKLEY MOSS
Cholmondeley Arms *Cholmondeley, Malpas, Cheshire SY14 8HN (01829) 720300* £65, plus special breaks; 6 rms. Airy converted Victorian schoolhouse close to castle and gardens (famously, Cholmondeley is pronounced 'Chumley'), with lots of atmosphere, very friendly staff, interesting furnishings, open fire, excellent imaginative bar food, and very good choice of wines; disabled access; dogs in bedrooms and in pub too if well behaved

CHESTER
Castle House *23 Castle St, Chester, Cheshire CH1 2DS (01244) 350354* £50, plus special breaks; 5 comfortable rms, 3 with own bthrm. Small carefully preserved 16th-c guest house in the middle of the city, with helpful friendly owners, and fine breakfasts in room with original fireplace, timbers and ceiling; dogs welcome in bedrooms

FULLERS MOOR

Frogg Manor *Nantwich Rd, Broxton, Chester, Cheshire CH3 9JH (01829)*
782629 £**100**, plus special breaks; 7 lavishly decorated rms with thoughtful
extras. Enjoyably eccentric Georgian manor house full of ornamental frogs
and antique furniture, open fires and ornate dried-flower arrangements, a
restful upstairs sitting room, cosy little bar, a large collection of 30s/40s
records, and good English cooking in elegant dining room which leads to
conservatory overlooking the gardens; disabled access; dogs welcome in
bedrooms

HOOLE

Hoole Hall *Warrington Rd, Hoole, Chester, Cheshire CH2 3PD (01244)*
408800 £**94.90**, plus special breaks; 97 well equipped rms, some no
smoking. Extended and attractively refurbished 18th-c hall with five acres of
gardens, good food in two restaurants, and friendly service; good disabled
access; dogs welcome in downstairs bedrooms with doors to terrace

KNUTSFORD

Longview *51-55 Manchester Rd, Knutsford, Cheshire WA16 0LX (01565)*
632119 £**72.50**, plus special breaks; 26 rms. Friendly Victorian hotel with
attractive period and reproduction furnishings, open fires in original
fireplaces, pleasant cellar bar, ornate restaurant, and good well presented
food; cl Christmas; dogs welcome in bedrooms

MACCLESFIELD

Sutton Hall Hotel *Bullocks Lane, Sutton, Macclesfield, Cheshire SK11 0HE*
(01260) 253211 £**94.95**; 9 marvellous rms. Welcoming and secluded
historic baronial hall, full of character, with stylish rooms, high black
beams, stone fireplaces, suits of armour and so forth, friendly service, and
good food; can arrange clay shooting/golf/fishing; partial disabled access;
dogs welcome in bedrooms

MOBBERLEY

Laburnum Cottage *Knutsford Rd, Mobberley, Knutsford, Cheshire WA16*
7PU (01565) 872464 £**57**; 5 pretty rms. Neatly kept and friendly no
smoking country guest house in an acre of landscaped garden; relaxed
atmosphere in comfortable lounge with books, a sunny conservatory, and
very good food; dogs by arrangement in annexe

POTT SHRIGLEY

Shrigley Hall *Shrigley Park, Pott Shrigley, Macclesfield, Cheshire SK10 5SB*
(01625) 575757 £**130**, plus special breaks; 150 smart well equipped rms,
some with country views. In over 260 acres of parkland, this impressive
country house has a splendid entrance hall with several elegant rooms
leading off, enjoyable food in the orangery and restaurant, and good service
from friendly staff; championship golf course, fishing, tennis, and leisure
centre in former church building; plenty to do nearby; disabled access; dogs
welcome in bedrooms

SANDBACH

Old Hall *High St, Sandbach, Cheshire CW11 1AL (01270) 761221* £**70**, plus special breaks; 11 comfortable rms. Fine Jacobean timbered hotel with lots of original panelling and fireplaces, relaxing lounge, friendly welcome, and popular, attractive restaurant; disabled access; dogs in bedrooms

TARPORLEY

Swan *50 High St, Tarporley, Cheshire CW6 0AG (01829) 733838* £**77**, plus special breaks; 16 rms. Well managed Georgian inn with a good mix of individual tables and chairs in attractive bar, well kept real ales, decent wines, and quite a few malt whiskies, good food from extensive menu, nice breakfasts, and friendly staff; limited disabled access; dogs welcome in coach house annexe bedrooms

WORLESTON

Rookery Hall *Main Rd, Worleston, Nantwich, Cheshire CW5 6DQ (01270) 610016* £**110**, plus special breaks; 46 individually decorated rms. Fine early 19th-c hotel in 38 acres of lovely parkland, with elegant lounges, log fires, intimate panelled restaurant with enjoyable food, and friendly service; disabled access; dogs in coach house bedrooms; £25

Cornwall

Dog Friendly Pubs

ALTARNUN
Rising Sun *Village signposted off A39 just W of A395 junction; pub itself NW of village, so if coming instead from A30, keep on towards Camelford*
In an attractive spot on the NE edge of Bodmin Moor, this cheerful 16th-c pub is likely to be full of chatty locals and their dogs on even the wettest and windiest weekday lunchtimes, with the barmaids absolutely in the thick of things. On the Land's End Trail, it's handy too for longer-distance walkers. The low-beamed L-shaped main bar has bare boards and polished Delabole slate flagstones, some stripped stone, a couple of coal fires, guns on the wall, and plain traditional furnishings. The central bar has well kept Bass, Cotleigh Tawny, Greene King IPA and Marstons Pedigree on handpump, and decent house wines. The food is hearty home cooking, and the regular menu includes three sausages made specially for the pub. A small back area has darts, fruit machine and a pool table, with a second pool table in the carpeted room beyond (no dogs allowed in that one). The main bar can get a bit smoky sometimes. There are tables outside; they have bedrooms, but we have had no news of these from readers yet. Screened off by high evergreens, the field opposite has space for caravans. The village itself (with its altarless church – hence the name) is well worth a look.
Free house ~ Licensee Jim Manson ~ Real ale ~ Bar food ~ Restaurant ~ No credit cards ~ (01566) 86636 ~ Dogs allowed in bar ~ Open 11-3, 5.30-11; 11-11 Sat; 12-10.30 Sun ~ Bedrooms: £20/£40

BLISLAND
Blisland Inn *Village signposted off A30 and B3266 NE of Bodmin*
Run by a knowledgeable landlord, this welcoming local stocks a fine range of eight or more perfectly kept real ales. Every inch of the beams and ceiling is covered with beer mats (or their particularly wide-ranging collection of mugs), and the walls are similarly filled with beer-related posters and memorabilia. A blackboard lists the day's range, which has a firm emphasis on brews from Cornwall. They also have a changing farm cider, fruit wines and real apple juice. Above the fireplace another blackboard has the choice of enjoyable, hearty home-made food, including

a number of good pies (the gravy for the steak and ale is made purely from beer, without any water), fresh fish, and a popular Sunday lunch (booking advisable); service is cheerful and friendly. The partly flagstoned and carpeted no smoking lounge has a number of clocks and barometers on one wall, a rack of daily newspapers for sale, a few standing timbers, and a good chatty atmosphere. Note children are allowed only in the separate, plainer family room (with darts, euchre, and pool), though there are plenty of picnic-sets outside; dominoes and cribbage. The Camel Trail cycle path is close by. As with many pubs in this area, it's hard to approach without negotiating several single-track roads.

Free house ~ Licensees Gary and Margaret Marshall ~ Real ale ~ Bar food (12-2.30(2 Sun), 6.30-9.30(9 Sun) ~ (01208) 850739 ~ Children in family room ~ Dogs welcome ~ Live music Sat evening ~ Open 11.30-11; 12-10.30 Sun

CADGWITH

Cadgwith Cove Inn *Down very narrow lane off A3083 S of Helston; no nearby parking*

Set in a working fishing cove at the bottom of a steep village (it's best to park at the top and walk down), this remains an old-fashioned and bustling thatched local. Its two snugly dark front rooms have plain pub furnishings on their mainly parquet flooring, a log fire in one stripped stone end wall, lots of local photographs including gig races, cases of naval hat ribands and of fancy knot-work, and a couple of compass binnacles. Some of the dark beams have ships' shields and others have spliced blue rope hand-holds. Well kept Flowers IPA, Greene King Abbot, Sharps Doom Bar, and Wadworths 6X on handpump. A plusher pink back room has a huge and colourful fish mural. The daily specials tend to be the things to go for in the food line, with an emphasis on fresh local fish; also home-made hot dishes and puddings. Best to check food times in winter. The left-hand room has darts, dominoes and cribbage, and there may be 1960s piped music. A good-sized front terrace has green-painted picnic-sets, some under a fairy-lit awning, looking down to the fish sheds by the bay. Coast Path walks are superb in both directions.

Pubmaster ~ Lease David and Lynda Trivett ~ Real ale ~ Bar food ~ Restaurant ~ (01326) 290513 ~ Children in restaurant ~ Dogs welcome ~ Folk club Tues, Cornish singing Fri ~ Open 12-3, 7-11; 12-11 Fri and Sat; 12-10.30 Sun; closed evening 25 Dec ~ Bedrooms: £25/£50(£70S)

CONSTANTINE

Trengilly Wartha *Simplest approach is from A3083 S of Helston, signposted Gweek near RNAS Culdrose, then fork right after Gweek; coming instead from Penryn (roads narrower), turn right in Constantine just before Minimarket (towards Gweek), then pub signposted left in nearly a mile; at Nancenoy, OS Sheet 204 map reference 731282*

It's quite a surprise to find such an extremely popular inn tucked away on a peaceful hillside not far from the Helford River. There's a pretty landscaped garden with some tables under large parasols, an international sized piste for boules, and a lake; lots of surrounding walks. Inside, the long low-beamed main bar has a woodburning stove and attractive built-in high-backed settles boxing in polished heavy wooden tables, and at one end, shelves of interesting wines with drink-in and take-out price labels (they run their own retail and wholesale wine business). The bright no smoking conservatory is good for families; darts, shove-ha'penny, dominoes and cribbage. Popular bar food includes lunchtime ploughman's with home-made breads and pickles, their own sausages and plenty of daily specials. You can eat the restaurant food in the bar but not vice versa; they offer many dishes in helpings for smaller people. Well kept Sharps Cornish Coaster and Skinner's Betty Stogs tapped from the cask. Over 50 malt whiskies (including several extinct ones), up to 20 wines by the glass (from a fine list of over 250), and around 10 armagnacs. The pub does get very busy at peak times and there may be a wait for a table then.

Free house ~ Licensees Nigel Logan and Michael Maguire ~ Real ale ~ Bar food (12-2.15(2 Sun), 6.30(7 Sun)-9.30; not 25 or 31 Dec) ~ Restaurant ~ (01326) 340332 ~ Children welcome ~ Dogs allowed in bar and bedrooms ~ Open 11-3, 6.30-11; 12-3, 7-10.30 Sun ~ Bedrooms: £49B/£78B

DULOE
Olde Plough House *B3254 N of Looe*
The two communicating rooms in this neatly kept and popular pub have lovely dark polished Delabole slate floors, some turkey rugs, a mix of pews, modern high-backed settles and smaller chairs, foreign banknotes on the beams, and three woodburning stoves. The décor is restrained – prints of waterfowl and country scenes, and a few copper jugs and a fat wooden pig perched on window sills. Well liked and reasonably priced food at lunchtime includes a roast of the day; different choices in the evening. One room is no smoking; piped music. Well kept Bass and Sharps Doom Bar on handpump, and sensibly priced wines. There is a small more modern carpeted dining room, and a few picnic-sets out by the road. The two friendly jack russells are called Jack and Spot, and the cat, Willow.

Free house ~ Licensees Gary and Alison Toms ~ Real ale ~ Bar food (not 25 Dec) ~ Restaurant ~ (01503) 262050 ~ Children in eating area of bar ~ Dogs allowed in bar ~ Open 12-2.30, 6.30-11; 12-2.30, 7-10.30 Sun; closed evenings 25-26 Dec

HELFORD
Shipwrights Arms *Off B3293 SE of Helston, via Mawgan*
Now a free house, this thatched pub looks down over the pretty wooded creek (at its best at high tide) and can be reached by foot ferry (open April to the end of October) from Helford Passage (01326) 250770 or by car, though it is quite a walk from the nearest car park. There are seats on the terrace making the most of the water views, and plenty of surrounding walks, including a long-distance coastal path that goes right past the door. Inside, there's quite a nautical theme, with navigation lamps, models of ships, sea pictures, drawings of lifeboat coxswains, and shark fishing photographs. A dining area has oak settles and tables; winter open fire. Well kept Castle Eden and Sharps Doom Bar on handpump, a good wine list,

and bar food; also summer evening barbecue dishes and home-made puddings; piped music. Dogs must be kept on a lead.

Free house ~ Licensee Charles Herbert ~ Real ale ~ Bar food (not Sun or Mon evenings in winter) ~ (01326) 231235 ~ Children welcome ~ Dogs welcome ~ Open 11-2.30, 6-11; 12-2.30, 7-10.30 Sun; closed Sun and Mon evenings

KINGSAND

Halfway House *Fore Street, towards Cawsand*

For a weekend break, this well run and attractive inn is just the place to be. There are plenty of chatty locals, a friendly welcome, enjoyable beer and food (including nice breakfasts), and comfortable bedrooms. There are marvellous surrounding walks, too, especially in the cliff area at Rame Head, and the picturesque village is well placed for visiting Mount Edgcumbe House and Country Park, and the new diving venue at Whitsand Bay. The simply furnished but quite smart bar is mildly Victorian in style, and rambles around a huge central fireplace, with low ceilings, and soft lighting. Popular bar food using local produce includes daily specials and constantly changing home-made puddings. They open for morning coffee and serve summer afternoon teas. The restaurant is no smoking. Well kept Courage Best, Marstons Pedigree, Sharps Doom Bar, and a beer made for the pub by Sharps, called Cawking, on handpump kept under light blanket pressure, and decent wines. To reach the inn, you can either park in the council car park and walk through the narrow hilly streets down towards the sea, or park in the private car park next to the inn.

Free house ~ Licensees Hudi and Shauna Honig ~ Real ale ~ Bar food ~ Restaurant ~ (01752) 822279 ~ Children welcome ~ Dogs allowed in bar and bedrooms ~ Open 11-11; 12-10.30 Sun; 12-3, 7-11 in winter ~ Bedrooms: £30S/£60B

LANLIVERY

Crown *Signposted off A390 Lostwithiel—St Austell (tricky to find from other directions)*

The same company that owns the popular Springer Spaniel at Treburley (see entry) have taken over this inn, and indeed, have installed the licensee from over there, too. There will be quite a few changes over the next few months including a kitchen extension and various refurbishments. But the small, dimly lit public bar still has its heavy beams, slate floor and built-in wall settles, and attractive alcove of seats in the dark former chimney. A much lighter room leads off, with beams in the white boarded ceiling, some settees in one corner, cushioned black settles, a small cabinet with wood turnings for sale, and a little fireplace with an old-fashioned fire; there's also another similar small room. No noisy games machines or music. Well liked bar food at lunchtime and different evening dishes include changing local fish; also daily specials and puddings such as sticky toffee pudding and summer fruit crumble. Well kept Sharps Coaster, Doom Bar, and a couple of beers named for the pub, Crown and Glory, on handpump; local cider. Darts, dominoes and cribbage. The slate-floored porch room has lots of succulents and a few cacti, and wood-and-stone seats, and at the far end of the restaurant is a no smoking sun room, full of more plants, with tables and benches. There's a sheltered garden with granite-faced seats, white cast-iron furniture, and several solid wooden tables. The Eden Project is only ten minutes away. We'd be grateful for reports on the changes.

Wagtail Inns ~ Licensee Andrew Brotheridge ~ Real ale ~ Bar food (12-2, 6-9.15) ~ Restaurant ~ (01208) 872707 ~ Children in eating area of bar and restaurant ~ Dogs allowed in bar ~ Trad jazz every 2nd Sun of month; music nights during week in winter ~ Open 12-11; 12-10.30 Sun; 12-3, 6-11 in winter; closed 25 Dec ~ Bedrooms: £50S/£70S

MITHIAN
Miners Arms *Just off B3285 E of St Agnes*
New licensees have taken over this 16th-c pub but seem to have settled in quickly. Several cosy little rooms and passages are warmed by winter open fires, and the small back bar has an irregular beam and plank ceiling, a wood block floor, and bulging squint walls (one with a fine old wall painting of Elizabeth I); another small room has a decorative low ceiling, lots of books and quite a few interesting ornaments. The Croust Room is no smoking; piped music. Bar food includes home-made soup, a vegetarian dish, crab salad, rack of lamb, and puddings. Well kept Morlands Old Speckled Hen and Sharps Doom Bar on handpump, and several wines by the glass. There are seats on the back terrace, with more on the sheltered front cobbled forecourt.

Inn Partnership (Pubmaster) ~ Lease Mr and Mrs K Hodge ~ Real ale ~ Bar food ~ (01872) 552375 ~ Children in restaurant ~ Dogs allowed in bar ~ Open 12-2.30, 6-11; 12-11 Sat; 12-10.30 Sun

MYLOR BRIDGE
Pandora *Restronguet Passage: from A39 in Penryn, take turning signposted Mylor Church, Mylor Bridge, Flushing and go straight through Mylor Bridge following Restronguet Passage signs; or from A39 further N, at or near Perranarworthal, take turning signposted Mylor, Restronguet, then follow Restronguet Weir signs, but turn left down hill at Restronguet Passage sign*
On a peaceful sunny day, it would be hard to find a pub in such an idyllic position. Thatched and medieval, it faces a sheltered waterfront, and you can sit on the long floating pontoon with a drink and while away an hour or so watching children crabbing and customers arriving by boat. Inside, the several rambling, interconnecting rooms have low wooden ceilings (mind your head on some of the beams), beautifully polished big flagstones, cosy alcoves with leatherette benches built into the walls, old race posters, two large log fires in high hearths (to protect them against tidal floods); half the bar area is no smoking – as is the restaurant. Bar food includes good local crab sandwiches, cornish crab cakes with citrus and orange flesh dressing and daily specials. They also serve afternoon teas in summer. Well kept Bass, and St Austell HSD, Tinners, and Tribute on handpump, several wines by the glass, and local cider. It does get very crowded in summer, and parking is difficult at peak times. Good surrounding walks.

St Austell ~ Tenant John Milan ~ Real ale ~ Bar food (12-3, 6.30-9) ~ Restaurant ~ (01326) 372678 ~ Children in eating area of bar and restaurant ~ Dogs allowed in bar ~ Open 11-11; 12-10.30 Sun

PERRANWELL
Royal Oak *Village signposted off A393 Redruth—Falmouth and A39 Falmouth—Truro*
This pretty and quietly set stone-built village pub is welcoming and relaxed, with a buoyant gently upmarket atmosphere. Its roomy carpeted bar has horsebrasses and pewter and china mugs on its black beams and joists, plates and country pictures on its cream-painted stone walls, and cosy wall and other seats around its tables. It rambles around beyond a big stone fireplace (with a good log fire in winter) into a snug little nook of a room behind, with just a couple more tables. Good, interesting food includes super tapas (available at all times the bar is open), lunchtime specials and evening choices like roast rack of lamb. In summer, booking for their great value Thursday night lobster specials is essential, and they make good proper sandwiches (ask, if you don't see them on the menu). The restaurant area is no smoking. Well kept Bass, Flowers IPA, and Sharps Special on handpump from the small serving counter, wines by the glass (the wine list is well balanced and not over long), a particularly good landlord, and prompt friendly service; piped music and shove-ha'penny. There are some picnic-sets out by the quiet village lane.
Free house ~ Licensee Richard Rudland ~ Real ale ~ Bar food (12-2.30, 7-9.30) ~ Restaurant ~ (01872) 863175 ~ Children in restaurant ~ Dogs allowed in bar ~ Open 11-3, 6-11; 12-3, 6-10.30 Sun

PHILLEIGH
Roseland *Between A3078 and B3289, just E of King Harry Ferry*
Despite the many holiday visitors, this busy little pub still manages to be a genuine local with plenty of cheerful banter in the small lower back bar, maybe a game of cards, and a relaxed, friendly atmosphere. The helpful and efficient staff offer a welcome to all – dogs and children included – and do their utmost at peak times to serve you as quickly as possible. The two bar rooms (one with flagstones and the other carpeted) have wheelback chairs and built-in red-cushioned seats, open fires, old photographs and some giant beetles and butterflies in glasses, and maybe the large pub cat. Good, interesting, if not cheap, bar food, and daily specials such as well liked, if hot, thai green chicken curry. You must book to be sure of a table; the restaurant is no smoking. Well kept Bass, Greene King Old Speckled Hen, Ringwood Best, and Sharps Doom Bar on handpump, a good wine list with quite a few by the glass, and several malt whiskies. Dominoes and cribbage. The pretty paved front courtyard is a lovely place to sit in the lunchtime sunshine beneath the cherry blossom, and the pub is handy for Trelissick Gardens and the King Harry ferry.
Authentic Inns ~ Lease Colin Phillips ~ Real ale ~ Bar food (12-2.30, 6-9.30) ~ Restaurant ~ (01872) 580254 ~ Children in eating area of bar and restaurant ~ Dogs welcome ~ Live jazz Sun ~ Open 11-11; 12-10.30 Sun; 11-3, 6-11 winter ~ Bedrooms: /£80B

PORT ISAAC

Slipway *Middle Street; limited foreshore parking, or use top car park and walk down*

Low dark beams, Delabole slate flagstones and some stripped stone walling give something of a cellar feel to this small and friendly family-run bar. It's entirely unpretentious, not at all 'hotelish' though pleasantly civilised, with one or two nice touches like the appealing local watercolours (for sale). Service is quick and particularly helpful; they have Sharps Doom Bar on handpump, and decent wines by the glass. The lunchtime bar menu gives an attractive choice without being overlong. Visitors have found them happy to modify dishes to suit children. You can also choose from the menu for the comfortable two-level beamed restaurant, which concentrates on beautifully cooked fresh local fish, particularly the abundance of lobster and crab for which the village is famous in season – around May to October. There may be piped music. The position could hardly be bettered, at the foot of this delightful steep conservation village, and just across from the slipway down to the beach where crabbing boats are pulled up for the night, and the fish and seafood sales point is located. Overlooking the cove, the crazy-paved terrace has solid teak tables and chairs under an awning. This hotel dates from the 16th c; we have not yet heard from any readers who have stayed here, but would expect it to be a good place to stay, if you don't mind steep stairs.

Free house ~ Licensees Mark and Kep Forbes ~ Real ale ~ Bar food (12-6, 7-9.30) ~ Restaurant ~ (01208) 880264 ~ Children welcome ~ Dogs allowed in bedrooms ~ Open 11-11; 12-10.30 Sun; may close Mon and Tues in Jan ~ Bedrooms: £67.50B/£90B

PORTHLEVEN

Ship *Village on B3304 SW of Helston; pub perched on edge of harbour*

One reader was delighted to find that after a gap of 40 years, this old fisherman's pub really hadn't changed much. What certainly can't change is the marvellous view over the pretty working harbour and out to sea – if you are lucky, you might be able to bag a window seat inside or one of the tables out in the terraced garden; at night, the harbour is interestingly floodlit. The knocked-through bar has log fires in big stone fireplaces and some genuine character. The no smoking family room is a conversion of an old smithy and has logs burning in a huge open fireplace. Popular, if not cheap, bar food with daily specials; the candlelit dining room also enjoys the good view. Well kept Courage Best, Greene King Old Speckled Hen, and Sharps Doom Bar on handpump; friendly service. Dominoes, cribbage, fruit machine and piped music.

Free house ~ Licensee Colin Oakden ~ Real ale ~ Bar food (12-9 in summer) ~ (01326) 564204 ~ Children in family room ~ Dogs welcome ~ Open 11.30-11; 12-10.30 Sun

SENNEN COVE
Old Success *Off A30 Land's End road*

From the terraced garden of this well placed, old-fashioned seaside hotel, there are marvellous views of the surf of Whitesands Bay. The beamed and timbered bar has plenty of lifeboat memorabilia, including an RNLI flag hanging on the ceiling; elsewhere are ships' lanterns, black and white photographs, dark wood tables and chairs, and a big ship's wheel that doubles as a coat stand. Bar food includes locally baked cornish pasty and daily specials such as 12oz T-bone steak. Well kept Sharps Doom Bar and Special and Skinners Cornish Knocker and Heligan Honey on handpump. Service is friendly and efficient, even in the height of summer; it's less hectic out of season. The upper bar and restaurant are no smoking. Piped music, TV; quiz night most Fridays. Bedrooms are basic but comfortable, enjoying the sound of the sea; they also do self-catering suites. Land's End is a pleasant walk away, and the clean beach is very attractive — as well as a big draw for surfers.

Free house ~ Licensee Martin Brooks ~ Real ale ~ Bar food (12-2.30, 6-9.30) ~ Restaurant ~ (01736) 871232 ~ Children in eating area of bar and restaurant ~ Dogs allowed in bar ~ Open 11-11; 12-10.30 Sun ~ Bedrooms: £31(£44B)/£88B

ST ANNS CHAPEL
Rifle Volunteer *A390*

Main road pubs, especially on holiday routes, are not exactly racing certainties if you are hoping to find good food. Here's one you can bank on, though. What's more, it's kept a pleasantly pubby feel in its two front bars. The main one on the left has a log fire in its big stone fireplace, cushioned pews and country kitchen chairs, a turkey rug on its parquet floor, and a relaxed ochre and green décor; on the right, the Chapel Bar has similar furnishings on its dark boards, another open fire, and motorcycle prints on its cream walls. They have well kept Sharps Doom Bar, Coaster and Special on handpump, over 70 whiskies, and decent wines by the glass; piped music, darts, pool, dominoes, TV and skittle alley. The food changes daily, with a concentration on fresh produce, and imaginative touches perking up standard menu items. Service is friendly; it can be slow on busy nights. The modern back dining room has picture windows to take advantage of a very wide view that stretches down to the Tamar estuary and Plymouth. An elevated astroturf deck beside it has some tables, with more in the garden which slopes away below. A skittle alley doubles as a function room. We have not yet heard from readers who have used the bedrooms here.

Free house ~ Licensees Frank and Lynda Hilldrup ~ Real ale ~ Bar food ~ Restaurant ~ (01822) 832508 ~ Children in restaurant and family room ~ Dogs allowed in bar ~ Blues last Fri of month ~ Open 12-2.30, 6-11; 12-3, 6.30-10.30 Sun ~ Bedrooms: £30B/£50B

ST BREWARD

Old Inn *Old Town; village signposted off B3266 S of Camelford, also signed off A30 Bolventor–Bodmin*

To get here, just head for the church which is a landmark for miles around – the pub originally housed the monks who built it. There's a friendly welcome for both regulars and visitors (quite a few of our readers are on foot, cycling or with dogs), and the spacious middle bar has plenty of seating on the fine broad slate flagstones, banknotes and horsebrasses hanging from the low oak joists that support the ochre upstairs floorboards, and plates on the stripped stonework; two massive granite fireplaces date back to the 11th c. Good, straightforward bar food includes a lunchtime breakfast, and daily specials like a home-made pie; home-made puddings too. The restaurant and family room are no smoking. Well kept Bass, and Sharps Doom Bar, Eden and Special on handpump, all their wines available by the glass, and quite a few malt whiskies; sensibly placed darts, piped music, and fruit machine. Picnic-sets outside are protected by low stone walls. There's plenty of open moorland behind, and cattle and sheep wander freely into the village. In front of the building is a very worn carved stone; no one knows exactly what it is but it may be part of a Saxon cross.

Free house ~ Licensee Darren Wills ~ Real ale ~ Bar food (11-2(3 Sun), 6-9) ~ Restaurant ~ (01208) 850711 ~ Children in eating area of bar and family room ~ Dogs allowed in bar ~ Open 11-11; 12-10.30 Sun; 11-3, 6-11 Mon-Thurs in winter

TREBURLEY

Springer Spaniel *A388 Callington—Launceston*

Owned by the same company that now runs the Crown at Lanlivery (see earlier entry), this bustling roadside pub has a new licensee, again, but readers are quick to voice their enthusiasm. There's been a little refurbishment, but the relaxed, friendly bar still has a lovely, very high-backed settle by the woodburning stove in the big fireplace, high-backed farmhouse chairs and other seats, and pictures of olde-worlde stagecoach arrivals at inns; this leads into a cosy room with big solid teak tables. Up some steps from the main bar is the beamed, attractively furnished, no smoking restaurant. Good, enjoyable food from lunchtime sandwiches to daily specials like local venison and mushroom casserole, and assorted puddings. Well kept Sharps Doom Bar, Coaster, and a beer named for the pub on handpump, a good wine list, local cider, and a few malt whiskies; cribbage and dominoes.

Wagtail Inns ~ Licensee Craig Woolley ~ Real ale ~ Bar food (12-2, 6-9) ~ Restaurant ~ (01579) 370424 ~ Children in eating area of bar and restaurant ~ Dogs allowed in bar ~ Open 12-3, 6-11; 12-3, 7-10.30 Sun; closed 25 Dec

TREMATON

Crooked Inn *Off A38 just W of Saltash*

A long well-lit drive leads you down to this surprisingly isolated but relaxed and friendly inn. The bar is more or less open plan, with high bar stools by the curved stone counter, mates' chairs and brocaded stools around a mix of tables in front of the big open fireplace, and a piano for impromptu entertainment. Down a step is the lower lounge with heavier stripped beams, upholstered settle seating, and another fireplace with a woodburning stove. A new conservatory leads off this, with ceiling fans, a growing vine, and doors opening out onto the new decking area which looks over the garden and valley below. For children there are swings, a slide built into the hillside, a tree house, and trampoline. Sheep, ducks, a pig, pigmy goat, and two dogs roam the grounds, and a rather fine horse may be nibbling the lawn. Well kept Sharps Own and Doom Bar, Skinners Cornish Knocker, and St Austell HSD on handpump, and a decent wine list; piped music. Generous helpings of bar food includes home-made curry of the day, fresh local cod in crispy batter, and daily specials. The bedrooms (which we would be grateful for reports on) overlook the courtyard where there are seats, and maybe some feathered friends.

Free house ~ Licensees Sandra and Tony Arnold ~ Real ale ~ Bar food (12-3, 6-9.30) ~ (01752) 848177 ~ Children welcome ~ Dogs welcome ~ Open 11-11; 12-10.30 Sun ~ Bedrooms: £45B/£70B

Dog Friendly Hotels, B&Bs and Farms

BODINNICK

Old Ferry *Bodinnick, Fowey, Cornwall PL23 1LX (01726) 870237* £**70**; 12 comfortable and spacious rms, most with own bthrm and river views. 400-year-old inn in lovely situation overlooking Fowey estuary; back flagstoned bar partly cut into the rock, real ales, comfortable residents' lounge with french windows opening onto a terrace, and decent food in both bar and little evening restaurant; quiet out of season; cl 25 Dec; dogs everywhere except restaurant; £3

CARNE BEACH

Nare Hotel *Carne Beach, Veryan, Truro, Cornwall TR2 5PF (01872) 501279* £**300**, plus special breaks; 36 lovely rms to suit all tastes – some stylish ones overlook garden and out to sea. Attractively decorated and furnished hotel in magnificent clifftop position with secluded gardens, outdoor and indoor swimming pools, tennis, sailboarding and fishing; antiques, fresh flowers and log fires in the airy, spacious day rooms, very good food in two restaurants (one with a more relaxed atmosphere), wonderful breakfasts, and run by staff who really care; ideal for quiet family hols, with safe sandy beach below; disabled access; dogs welcome; from £10 inc daily meal

CONSTANTINE BAY

Treglos Hotel *Constantine Bay, Padstow, Cornwall PL28 8JH (01841) 520727* £**141**, plus special breaks; 42 light rms, some with balcony. Quiet and relaxed hotel close to good sandy beach, and in the same family for 30

years; comfortable traditional furnishings, log fires, good food, friendly helpful staff, sheltered garden plus playground and adventure equipment, indoor swimming pool, table tennis, table football and pool table, and children's playroom with electronic games; self-catering apartments; cl Dec–Feb; children over 7 in evening restaurant; disabled access; dogs welcome in bedrooms by arrangement (if small); £5; lovely nearby walks

CRANTOCK

Crantock Bay Hotel *West Pentire, Crantock, Newquay, Cornwall TR8 5SE* *(01637) 830229* £80, plus special breaks; 32 comfortable rms, most with coastal views. In a lovely setting on the West Pentire headland, facing the Atlantic and a huge sheltered sandy beach, this relaxed and informal hotel has been run by the same friendly family for 50 years; four acres of grounds, an indoor swimming pool, toddlers' pool, sauna and exercise room, all-weather tennis court, a putting course and children's play area; two lounges, bar lounge and restaurant, enjoyable food using local produce, and nice afternoon teas; cl Dec–Feb; families most welcome; lots to do nearby; disabled access and facilities; dogs welcome in bedrooms; £3

FALMOUTH

Penmere Manor *Mongleath Rd, Falmouth, Cornwall TR11 4PN (01326) 211411* £98, plus special breaks; 37 spacious rms. Run by the same owners for 34 years, this quietly set Georgian manor has five acres of subtropical gardens and woodland, heated outdoor swimming pool, giant chess, croquet, and leisure centre with indoor swimming pool, gym, and sauna; particularly helpful friendly staff, an evening pianist, and enjoyable food in restaurant and informal bar; disabled access; dogs welcome in some bedrooms; £3.50

FALMOUTH

Prospect House *1 Church Rd, Falmouth, Cornwall TR10 8DA (01326) 373198* £60; 3 lovely rms named after sailing ships, and little kitchenette for teas, coffee and biscuits. Built for a local packet-ship captain, this Georgian house is set on the Penryn River in a walled garden; original features such as panelled mahogany doors and painted cornices, a comfortable elegant guest lounge with an open fireplace, good traditional english breakfasts taken around large antique table in the dining room (no evening meals), and a restful atmosphere; dogs welcome if well behaved; £2.50; nearby river walks

FOWEY

Fowey Hall *Fowey, Cornwall PL23 1ET (01726) 833866* £150 inc dinner; 24 rms inc 11 suites and 4 pairs of interconnecting rms. Fine Gothic-style mansion in five acres of grounds overlooking the harbour and run along the same lines as their other hotels – eg Woolley Grange, Bradford-on-Avon (see Wiltshire chapter); marble fireplaces, baroque plasterwork, panelling, antiques, big potted plants, two enjoyable restaurants, marvellous facilities for children inc supervised nursery, and covered swimming pool, croquet and badminton; dogs welcome away from dining areas if on lead; £7

FOWEY
Marina Hotel *17 Esplanade, Fowey, Cornwall PL23 1HY (01726) 833315*
£135, plus special breaks; 18 rms, several with lovely views (some with balcony). Friendly Georgian hotel in fine position overlooking Fowey River and open sea (private access from secluded walled garden); refurbished, comfortable lounge/reading room, cheerfully decorated bar, attractive dining room overlooking the water, very good food (super fresh fish and shellfish), and helpful service; disabled access; dogs welcome in bedrooms and some other areas

GILLAN
Tregildry *Gillan, Manaccan, Helston, Cornwall TR12 6HG (01326) 231378* **£190** inc dinner, plus special breaks; 10 attractive rms with fine views over Falmouth Bay. Elegantly furnished hotel in four acres of grounds with private access to the cove below; spacious comfortable lounges, fresh flowers, books and magazines, a restful atmosphere, very good food in attractive restaurant, enjoyable breakfasts, and kind, courteous service; cl Nov–Feb; children over 8; dogs welcome in bedrooms only

LISKEARD
Well House *St Keyne, Liskeard, Cornwall PL14 4RN (01579) 342001* **£115**, plus special breaks; 9 individually designed rms with fine views. Light and airy Victorian country house, recently redecorated, with warm, friendly owners, courteous staff, comfortable drawing room, cosy little bar, and particularly good food and fine wines in dining room overlooking terrace and lawns; three acres of gardens with hard tennis court, swimming pool and croquet lawn; children over 8 in evening restaurant; dogs welcome away from reception areas and restaurant

LOOE
Talland Bay Hotel *Porthallow, Looe, Cornwall PL13 2JB (01503) 272667* **£130**, plus special breaks; 23 charming rms with sea or country views. Down a little lane between Looe and Polperro, this restful partly 16th-c country house has lovely subtropical gardens just above the sea; comfortable drawing room with log fire, smaller lounge with library, fresh flowers, courteous service, good food in pretty oak-panelled dining room, and pleasant afternoon teas; heated outdoor swimming pool, putting, croquet; children over 5 in evening restaurant (high tea for younger ones); dogs welcome in bedrooms by arrangement; £7.50

MAWNAN SMITH
Meudon Hotel *Mawnan Smith, Falmouth, Cornwall TR11 5HT (01326) 250541* **£190** inc dinner, plus special breaks; 29 well equipped comfortable rms in separate wing. Run by the same caring family for over 36 years, this is an old stone mansion with a newer wing, in beautiful subtropical gardens laid out 200 years ago by R. W. Fox; fine views from the dining room, comfortable lounge with log fire and fresh flowers, good english cooking, and old-fashioned standards of service; cl Jan; disabled access; dogs welcome in bedrooms; £10

MITHIAN

Rose-in-Vale Country House Hotel *Mithian, St Agnes, Cornwall TR5 0QD (01872) 552202* £**132**, plus special breaks; 18 pretty rms inc 2 suites. Secluded and quietly set Georgian house in four acres of neatly kept gardens, with comfortable spacious day rooms, a friendly atmosphere, helpful, long-standing local staff, and good food in enlarged dining room; ducks on ponds, a trout stream, outdoor swimming pool, badminton and croquet, plus a sauna and solarium; children over 7 in evening in public rooms and restaurant (high tea for smaller ones); cl Jan-Feb; disabled access; dogs welcome in bedrooms; £4.95

MULLION

Caunce Head *Predannack, Mullion, Cornwall TR12 7HA (01326) 240128* £**55**; 2 restful rms with farmland views. Handsome 17th-c stone house set back from Mullion Cliffs in lovely countryside with a peaceful atmosphere, comfortable sitting room with antiques, log fire, and plants, fine Aga-cooked breakfasts, and wonderful walks from the door; children over 12; dogs welcome in bedrooms

MULLION

Polurrian Hotel *Mullion, Helston, Cornwall TR12 7EN (01326) 240421* £**220** inc dinner, plus special breaks; 39 rms, some with memorable sea view. White clifftop hotel in lovely gardens with path down to sheltered private cove below, a restful atmosphere in the comfortable lounges and bright cocktail bar, fresh flowers, good food using fresh local ingredients (pianist and sea views in the dining room), enjoyable breakfasts, leisure club with heated swimming pool, and outdoor pool, badminton, tennis, mini-golf, squash and croquet; particularly good for families; limited disabled access; dogs welcome in bedrooms; £8; must be on lead in grounds

PADSTOW

St Petroc's Hotel & Bistro *4 New St, Padstow, Cornwall PL28 8EA (01841) 532700* £**110**; 10 comfortable rms. Attractive little hotel (under the same ownership as the Seafood Restaurant) with lounges, a reading room, an airy dining room overlooking the terraced garden, good quickly served food from a short bistro-type menu (plenty of fish), a sensible wine list, and friendly atmosphere; dogs welcome away from bistro

PENZANCE

Abbey Hotel *Abbey St, Penzance, Cornwall TR18 4AR (01736) 366906* £**120**; 9 charming rms. Stylish little 17th-c house close to harbour with marvellous views, a relaxed atmosphere in comfortable drawing room full of flowers, fine paintings and antiques, a good set menu in small Abbey Restaurant next door and pretty garden; cl Jan; children over 7 in dining room; dogs welcome in bedrooms

PENZANCE

Georgian House Hotel *20 Chapel St, Penzance, Cornwall TR18 4AW (01736) 365664* £50; 10 comfortable rms, most with own bthrm. Warmly friendly little hotel, once the home of the Mayor of Penzance and close to the harbour and shopping centre, with helpful owner and staff, very good breakfasts in attractive dining room, reading lounge and private parking; dogs very welcome and given a bonio for breakfast

PORT ISAAC

Port Gaverne Hotel *Port Gaverne, Port Isaac, Cornwall PL29 3SQ (01208) 880244* £75, plus special breaks; 14 comfortable rms. Lovely place to stay and an excellent base for area (dramatic coves, good clifftop walks and lots of birds); big log fires in well kept bars, relaxed lounges, decent bar food, good restaurant food and fine wines; also, restored 18th-c self-catering cottages; cl 1st 2 wks Feb; children over 7 in restaurant; dogs welcome away from dining room; £3.50

PORTSCATHO

Rosevine *Porthcurnick Beach, Portscatho, Cornwall TR2 5EW (01872) 580206* £172, plus special breaks; 17 rms, 6 in courtyard annexe. Imposing house set above a fine beach with an attractive, semi-tropical garden, traditionally decorated lounges (one has views of the garden and sea) and bar, enjoyable food including lots of fish and local produce in pretty, no smoking restaurant, and genuinely friendly staff; indoor swimming pool, games room and children's playroom; cl Oct-beginning Feb; dogs welcome in bedrooms

SALTASH

Erth Barton *Elmgate, Saltash, Cornwall PL12 4QY (01752) 842127* £80; 3 rms. Lovely old manor house with its own chapel, peaceful rooms with lots of books, pictures and big fireplaces, good enjoyable food, bird-watching in the surrounding estuaries, and riding (you can bring your own horse); children over 12; dogs welcome in bedrooms

SENNEN

Land's End Hotel *Sennen, Penzance, Cornwall TR19 7AA (01736) 871844* £140, plus special breaks; 33 elegant airy rms, many with splendid sea views. Comfortable hotel right on the clifftop with fine sea views, good food in attractive conservatory-style restaurant, elegant seating areas, informal bar with lots of malt whiskies, and helpful staff; lots to do nearby; dogs welcome away from bar and restaurant; £10

ST MAWES

Rising Sun *The Square, St Mawes, Truro, Cornwall TR2 5DJ (01326) 270233* £130; 8 rms. Small, attractive old hotel in popular picturesque waterside village, with harbour views, large comfortable and airy lounge with bustling bar area, elegant no smoking conservatory restaurant, very good food majoring on local fish, super breakfasts, and charming terrace; dogs welcome in bedrooms and bar

TREVAUNANCE COVE
Driftwood Spars *Trevaunance Cove, St Agnes, Cornwall TR5 0RT (01872) 552428* £**78**; 15 attractive, comfortable bdrms, some with sea view, 8 in separate building. Friendly family-owned hotel dating from the 17th c and just up the road from the beach and dramatic cove; woodburner in comfortable lounge, main bar with large open fire, upstairs gallery, beamed ceilings, helpful staff and enjoyable food; live music wknds; cl 25 Dec; dogs in bedrooms and bars; £3

Isles of Scilly

BRYHER
Hell Bay *Bryher, Isles of Scilly TR23 0PR (01720) 422947* £**200** inc dinner; 24 bdrms and suites, many with stunning sea views. Relaxed and peaceful hotel on the western tip of the island's rugged coastline and in extensive private grounds with outdoor heated swimming pool, golf, boules and croquet; light, airy contemporary décor and original sculptures and paintings from the owners' private collections, residents' lounge, and sea-view restaurant with plenty of local fish and shellfish; boat trips, fishing, diving and water sports; cl Jan/Feb; disabled access; dogs welcome in bedrooms

ST AGNES
Coastguards *St Agnes, Isles of Scilly TR22 0PL (01720) 422373* £**75** inc dinner; 2 rms with views of the sea. Peacefully set former coastguard cottages with open fire, interesting artefacts, and sea views in the sitting room, enjoyable homely dinners and breakfasts, friendly, helpful owners, and big garden; no smoking; cl Nov–Mar; children over 12; dogs welcome in bedrooms only

ST MARTIN'S
St Martin's on the Isle *Lower Town, St Martin's, Isles of Scilly TR25 0QW (01720) 422092* £**160**, plus special breaks; 30 attractively decorated rms, most with fine sea views. Welcomed by the manager as you step off the boat, you find this stone-built hotel set idyllically on a white sand beach, with stunning sunsets; comfortable, light and airy split-level bar-lounge with doors opening onto the terrace, lovely flower arrangements, genuinely friendly professional staff, sophisticated food in main restaurant (lighter lunches in the bar), and a fine wine list; they are particularly kind to children, with buckets and spades to borrow, videos and high tea (they must be over 9 in evening restaurant); fine walks (the island is car free), launch trips to other islands, and good bird-watching; small swimming pool; cl Nov–end Feb; disabled access; dogs welcome in bedrooms; £15

Cumbria

Dog Friendly Pubs

AMBLESIDE
Golden Rule *Smithy Brow; follow Kirkstone Pass signpost from A591 on N side of town*

It's the atmosphere and genuine welcome from both the landlord and chatty, friendly regulars that makes this straightforward town local appealing to visitors. The bar has lots of local country pictures decorating the butter-coloured walls, horsebrasses on the black beams, built-in leatherette wall seats, and cast-iron-framed tables; dominoes and cribbage. There is a no smoking back room with TV (not much used), a left-hand room with darts and a fruit machine, and a further room down a few steps on the right, with lots of seats and an internet cubicle. Well kept Robinsons Hatters Mild, Hartleys XB, Cumbrian Way, and Best Bitter, and Cwmbran Double Hop on handpump; pork pies, jumbo scotch eggs, and filled rolls. There's a back yard with benches, and especially colourful window boxes. The golden rule referred to in its name is a brass measuring yard mounted over the bar counter.

Robinsons ~ Tenant John Lockley ~ Real ale ~ No credit cards ~ (015394) 32257 ~ Children welcome until 9pm ~ Dogs welcome ~ Open 11-11; 12-10.30 Sun

APPLEBY
Royal Oak *B6542/Bongate is E of the main bridge over the River Eden*

Despite new owners and a new licensee, this old-fashioned coaching inn remains popular with both locals and visitors. The oak-panelled public bar has a relaxed atmosphere and a good open fire, and the beamed lounge has old pictures on the timbered walls, some armchairs and a carved settle, and a panelling-and-glass snug enclosing the bar counter. Bar food at lunch-time; evening dishes such as home-made salmon and crab fishcakes with a sweet chilli dip, steak in ale pie, lamb cutlets with honey, mint and rosemary sauce. The restaurant is no smoking. Well kept Black Sheep and John Smiths, and a couple of guests on handpump. There are seats on the front terrace, and attractive flowering tubs, troughs and hanging baskets. You can get here on the scenic Leeds/Settle/Carlisle railway (best to check times and any possible delays to avoid missing lunch).

Landmark Inns ~ Manager Nigel Duffin ~ Real ale ~ Bar food (12-2.30, 6-9; all day Sun) ~ Restaurant ~ (01768) 351463 ~ Children in eating area of bar and restaurant ~ Dogs allowed in bar ~ Open 11-11; 12-10.30 Sun ~ Bedrooms: £35B/£69B

ARMATHWAITE
Dukes Head *Off A6 S of Carlisle*
Readers have very much enjoyed their visits to this warmly welcoming village pub over the last year. The civilised lounge bar has oak settles and little armchairs among more upright seats, oak and mahogany tables, antique hunting and other prints, and some brass and copper powder-flasks above the open fire. Using as much local produce as possible, the good, popular food includes freshly made soup with croûtons, hot potted Solway shrimps, well liked roast duckling, and daily specials. The restaurant is no smoking. Well kept Jennings Cumberland and Tetleys Mild on handpump, and home-made lemonade; dominoes, and a separate public bar with darts and table skittles. There are tables out on the lawn behind; boules. You can hire bicycles.
Pubmaster ~ Tenant Henry Lynch ~ Real ale ~ Bar food ~ Restaurant ~ (016974) 72226 ~ Children in eating area of bar and restaurant ~ Dogs allowed in bar and bedrooms ~ Open 12-11; 12-10.30 Sun ~ Bedrooms: £32.50(£35.50S)/£52.50(£55.50S)

BOUTH
White Hart *Village signposted off A590 near Haverthwaite*
The bar in this traditional Lakeland inn has recently been extended and now has a no smoking area. Many customers come to enjoy the fine range of well kept real ales on handpump: Black Sheep, Jennings Cumberland, and Tetleys, and changing guests such as Brysons Shifting Sands, Foxfield Hoad Mild, and Timothy Taylors Landlord. They also have 40 malt whiskies. The sloping ceilings and floors show the building's age, and there are lots of old local photographs and bric-a-brac – farm tools, stuffed animals, a collection of long-stemmed clay pipes – and two woodburning stoves. The games room has darts, pool, dominoes, fruit machine, TV, table football and juke box; piped music. Bar food (using local meat) includes pizzas, vegetarian chilli and daily specials like pork medallions and black pudding or Herdwick lamb. The restaurant is no smoking. Seats outside, and plenty of surrounding walks.
Free house ~ Licensees Nigel and Peter Barton ~ Real ale ~ Bar food (12-2, 6-8.45; not Mon or Tues lunchtime) ~ Restaurant ~ (01229) 861229 ~ Children in eating areas until 9pm ~ Dogs allowed in bedrooms ~ Live music maybe Thurs or Sun ~ Open 12-2, 6-11; 12-11 Sat; 12-10.30 Sun; closed Mon and Tues lunchtimes(exc bank hols) ~ Bedrooms: £20(£35S)(£25B)/£40(£70S)(£50B)

BROUGHTON MILLS
Blacksmiths Arms *Off A593 N of Broughton-in-Furness*
Friendly new licensees have taken over this charming little pub, and readers have been quick to voice their enthusiasm. Three of the four simply but

attractively decorated small rooms have open fires, as well as ancient slate floors, and well kept Dent Aviator, Hawkshead Bitter, and Jennings Cumberland on handpump, and summer farm cider. Bar food is very good and they use meat from local farms, and local game and fish; home-made puddings such as sticky toffee pudding or raspberry crème brûlée. There are three smallish dining rooms (the back one is no smoking). Darts, dominoes, cribbage, and children's books and games. Pretty summer hanging baskets and tubs of flowers in front of the building.

Free house ~ Licensees Mike and Sophie Lane ~ Real ale ~ Bar food (12-2, 6-9; not Mon lunchtime) ~ Restaurant ~ (01229) 716824 ~ Children welcome ~ Dogs welcome ~ Open 12-11; 12-10.30 Sun; 5-11 Mon (closed winter Mon), 12-2.30, 5-11 Tues-Fri in winter; closed 25 Dec

CROSTHWAITE
Punch Bowl *Village signposted off A5074 SE of Windermere*

The excellent, imaginative food in this bustling 16th-c inn continues to draw warm praise from our readers, and quite a few were particularly pleased to also find plenty of locals enjoying the well kept Black Sheep, and Coniston Bluebird and XB on handpump, and a chat. There are several separate areas carefully reworked to give a lot of space, and a high-raftered central part by the serving counter with an upper minstrel's gallery on either side; much of the pub is no smoking. Steps lead down into a couple of small rooms on the right, and there's a doorway through into two more airy rooms on the left. It's all spick and span, with lots of tables and chairs, beams, pictures by local artist Derek Farman, and an open fire. As well as a popular set-price lunch Tuesdays-Saturdays, the menu might include sandwiches, cream of mushroom and smoked bacon soup, crab and prawn gateau, chargrilled fell-bred rib-eye steak with creamy pepper sauce, and various puddings. They also have a three-course Sunday lunch; a carefully chosen wine list with 20 by the glass, and several malt whiskies. There are some tables on a terrace stepped into the hillside. This is a nice place to stay.

Free house ~ Licensee Steven Doherty ~ Real ale ~ Bar food (12-2, 6-9; not Sun evening or Mon) ~ Restaurant ~ (015395) 68237 ~ Children welcome ~ Dogs allowed in bar ~ Open 11-11; 12-3 Sun; closed Sun evening, all day Mon, 2 wks Jan ~ Bedrooms: £37.50B/£65B

DALTON-IN-FURNESS
Black Dog *Holmes Green, Broughton Road; 1 mile N of town, beyond A590*

A former farmhouse, this is a simple, comfortable local that's lifted out of the ordinary by the cheery licensee who runs it; access is from the terrace in the car park. The unpretentious bar has beer mats and brasses around the beams, two log fires, partly tiled and flagstoned floor, and plain wooden tables and chairs; the eating area is no smoking. Good value hearty bar food – all home-made – includes daily specials and puddings. The six real ales change constantly but might include Abbeydale Absolution, Barngates Tag Lag, Copper Dragon Golden Pippin, Hart Mild, Roosters Yankee, and Charles Wells Eagle on handpump; they also have several farm ciders and perries, home-made elderflower cordial and lemonade, and children's milkshakes. Table skittles, darts, shove-ha'penny, cribbage, and dominoes. A side terrace has a few plastic tables and chairs. The pub is handy for the South Lakes Wild Animal Park.

Free house ~ Licensee Jack Taylor ~ Real ale ~ Bar food (12-8 summer weekdays, 12-9 all weekends; best to phone for winter weekday lunchtime serving) ~ (01229) 462561 ~ Children welcome ~ Dogs allowed in bar ~ Open 12-11; 12-10.30 Sun; 4.30-11 weekdays in winter; may be closed winter weekday lunchtimes ~ Bedrooms: £17.50(£26S)/£42S

HAWKSHEAD

Drunken Duck *Barngates; the hamlet is signposted from B5286 Hawkshead— Ambleside, opposite the Outgate Inn; or it may be quicker to take the first right from B5286, after the wooded caravan site; OS Sheet 90 map reference 350013*

Even at the start of this civilised place's journey from country pub to something much more restauranty, there was a school of thought that regretted those changes, feeling it didn't fit the bill for this walking area. The fact that two more rooms have now been turned into another dining area, leaving just a last tiny toehold for drinkers, means that this can hardly be considered as a pub any more – a shame for us, as we've always had a real soft spot for it. There's a good winter fire in one traditional beamed room with cushioned old settles and a mix of chairs, a newly refurbished snug, and as we've said those two rooms off the bar which have now been knocked into one, making another dining area with an oak floor and dark leather seating. Everywhere is no smoking except the little bar area. Imaginative, if pricy, food. Their own Barngates Chesters Strong & Ugly, Cracker Ale, Tag Lag, and Catnap are kept on handpump with Yates Bitter as a guest, and a fine wine list has over 20 by the glass. Seats on the front verandah have stunning views and there are quite a few rustic wooden chairs and tables at the side, sheltered by a stone wall with alpine plants along its top; the residents' garden has been recently reworked.

Own brew ~ Licensee Steph Barton ~ Real ale ~ Bar food (12-2.30, 6-9) ~ Restaurant ~ (015394) 36347 ~ Children in eating area of bar and restaurant ~ Dogs allowed in bar ~ Open 11.30-11; 12-10.30 Sun; closed evening 25 Dec ~ Bedrooms: £86.75B/£115B

Kings Arms *The Square*

Bustling and pleasant, this inn is set on a glorious square. There are traditional pubby furnishings, some fine original Elizabethan beams (including the figure of a medieval king holding up the ceiling, carved recently), and Black Sheep, Coniston Bluebird, Hawkshead Bitter, and Tetleys on handpump; 30 malt whiskies, summer cider, locally made damson gin, and a decent wine list. Piped music, fruit machine, shove-ha'penny, dominoes and cribbage. Enjoyable bar food at lunchtime; in the evening, there might be chargrilled local trout on rocket and roast pepper salad, and trio of fell-bred minted lamb chops; also daily specials and puddings like home-made sticky toffee pudding or banoffi pie. The restaurant is no smoking. As well as bedrooms, they offer self-catering cottages.

Free house ~ Licensees Rosalie and Edward Johnson ~ Real ale ~ Bar food (12-2.30,

6-9.30) ~ Restaurant ~ (015394) 36372 ~ Children welcome ~ Dogs allowed in bar and bedrooms ~ Open 11-11; 12-10.30 Sun ~ Bedrooms: £38(£43S)/£66(£76S)

INGS
Watermill *Just off A591 E of Windermere*
It is quite remarkable that the cheerful, hard-working licensee in this very popular pub manages to keep his 16 regularly changing real ales in such tip-top condition. On handpump, there might be Black Sheep Best and Special, Coniston Bluebird, Hawkshead Bitter, Lees Moonraker, Moorhouses Black Cat, Theakstons Best and Old Peculier, with changing guests like Hart Retrievers Legend, Marlow Rebellion Blonde, Oakham JHB, Orkney Dark Island, Tirril Bewshers, Timothy Taylors Landlord, and York Final Whistle; also, over 60 bottled beers, farm cider, and up to 50 malt whiskies. Cleverly converted from a wood mill and joiner's shop, the bars have a friendly, bustling atmosphere, a happy mix of chairs, padded benches and solid oak tables, bar counters made from old church wood, open fires, and interesting photographs and amusing cartoons by a local artist. The spacious lounge bar, in much the same traditional style as the other rooms, has rocking chairs and a big open fire; two areas are no smoking. Generous helpings of tasty bar food include home-made pâté, cumberland sausage or home-made chicken pie, and daily specials such as vegetable bake and local venison casserole. Darts, cribbage and dominoes. There are seats in the front garden. Lots to do nearby. Note that even residents cannot book a table for supper.
Free house ~ Licensee Brian Coulthwaite ~ Real ale ~ Bar food (12-4.30, 5-9) ~ (01539) 821309 ~ Children in family room ~ Dogs allowed in bar and bedrooms ~ First Tues of month storytelling club, 3rd Tues of month folk ~ Open 12-11(10.30 Sun); closed 25 Dec ~ Bedrooms: £32S/£70B

KESWICK
Swinside Inn *Only pub in Newlands Valley, just SW; OS Sheet 90 map reference 242217*
Looking over a quiet valley to the high crags and fells around Grisedale Pike, this friendly country inn has been recently refurbished but has kept many of its original 17th-c features. The long bright public bar has traditional wheelbacks and red and cream wall banquettes, and well kept Jennings Cumberland, Theakstons Best, and a guest on handpump; a central chimney with an open fire divides off the games area, which has pool, fruit machine, TV, cribbage and dominoes. There are two no smoking dining rooms and two further open fires. Tasty bar food includes cod in their own beer batter or home-made lasagne, and puddings like sticky toffee pudding. Seats in the garden and on the upper and lower terraces make the most of the view.
Jennings ~ Lease Joyce and Jim Henderson ~ Bar food (12-2, 6-8.45) ~ (017687) 78253 ~ Children welcome ~ Dogs allowed in bar ~ Open 11-11; 12-10.30 Sun ~ Bedrooms: £45S/£60S

LITTLE LANGDALE

Three Shires *From A593 3 miles W of Ambleside take small road signposted The Langdales, Wrynose Pass; then bear left at first fork*

From seats on the terrace here, there are lovely views over the valley to the partly wooded hills below Tilberthwaite Fells, with more seats on a well kept lawn behind the car park, backed by a small oak wood. Inside, the comfortably extended back bar has stripped timbers and a beam-and-joist stripped ceiling, antique oak carved settles, country kitchen chairs and stools on its big dark slate flagstones, Lakeland photographs lining the walls, and a warm winter fire in the modern stone fireplace with a couple of recesses for ornaments; an arch leads through to a small, additional area. Bar food at lunchtime may include home-made fishcake with lime and cucumber crème fraîche or home-made terrine, and cumberland sausage or a home-made pie of the day; more elaborate evening dishes. Most of the inn is no smoking (apart from the main bar). Well kept Jennings Bitter and Cumberland, and a guest such as Coniston Old Man or Hawkshead Bitter on handpump, 40 malt whiskies, and a decent wine list; darts, cribbage and dominoes. The three shires are Cumberland, Westmorland and Lancashire, which used to meet at the top of the nearby Wrynose Pass.

Free house ~ Licensee Ian Stephenson ~ Real ale ~ Bar food (12-2, 6-8.45; no evening meals midweek in Dec or Jan) ~ Restaurant ~ (015394) 37215 ~ Children welcome ~ Dogs allowed in bar ~ Open 11-10.30(11 Sat); 12-10.30 Sun; 11-3, 8-10.30 midweek in winter; closed 25 Dec ~ Bedrooms: /£72B

LOWESWATER

Kirkstile Inn *From B5289 follow signs to Loweswater Lake; OS Sheet 89 map reference 140210*

The Loweswater Brewery in this 16th-c inn is now well established and produces Grassmoor and Melbreak ales on site. They also keep Coniston Bluebird, Hawkshead Bitter and Yates Bitter on handpump. The bar is low-beamed and carpeted, with a roaring log fire, comfortably cushioned small settles and pews, and partly stripped stone walls; slate shove-ha'penny board. Well liked bar food includes pâté en croûte with home-made cumberland sauce, lunchtime filled baked potatoes, and mushroom and lentil bake; also daily specials and puddings like crème brûlée, sherry trifle or fruit crumble; friendly staff. The restaurant, lounge and bedrooms are no smoking. You can enjoy the view from picnic-sets on the lawn, from the very attractive covered verandah in front of the building, and from the bow windows in one of the rooms off the bar.

Own brew ~ Licensees Roger and Helen Humphreys ~ Real ale ~ Bar food (12-2, 6-9) ~ Restaurant ~ (01900) 85219 ~ Children welcome ~ Dogs allowed in bar and bedrooms ~ Jazz once a month ~ Open 11-11; 11-10.30 Sun; closed 25 Dec ~ Bedrooms: £40B/£60(£70B)

NEAR SAWREY

Tower Bank Arms *B5285 towards the Windermere ferry*

As Beatrix Potter's Hill Top Farm (owned by the National Trust) backs onto this little country inn, and it features in *The Tale of Jemima Puddleduck,* there are lots of customers at peak times. The low-beamed main bar has a fine log fire in the big cooking range, high-backed settles on the rough slate floor, local hunting photographs, postcards of Beatrix Potter, and signed photographs of celebrities on the walls, a grandfather clock, and good traditional atmosphere. Well kept Theakstons Old Peculier and Best and Charles Wells Bombardier and a couple of guests like Adnams Broadside or Barngates Tag Lag on handpump, as well as lots of malt whiskies, and belgian fruit beers and other foreign beers. Appreciated food includes home-made soup, Morecambe Bay potted shrimps, home-made cheese flan, a vegetarian dish or cumberland sausage, and steaks; friendly staff. Darts, dominoes, cribbage and piped music. Seats outside have pleasant views of the wooded Claife Heights. This is a good area for golf, sailing, bird-watching, fishing (they have a licence for two rods a day on selected waters in the area), and walking, but if you want to stay at the pub, you'll have to book well in advance.

Free house ~ Licensee Philip Broadley ~ Real ale ~ Bar food (not 25 Dec) ~ Restaurant ~ (015394) 36334 ~ Children in eating area of bar lunchtime, but in restaurant only, in evenings ~ Dogs welcome ~ Open 11-3, 5.30-11; 12-3, 5.30(6 in winter)-10.30 Sun ~ Bedrooms: £40B/£57B

SANDFORD

Sandford Arms *Village and pub signposted just off A66 W of Brough*

Tucked away in a very small village by the River Eden, this neat and welcoming little inn was once an 18th-c farmhouse. The compact and comfortable no smoking dining area is on a slightly raised balustraded platform at one end of the L-shaped carpeted main bar, which has stripped beams and stonework, well kept Black Sheep and a guest like Hesket Newmarket Skiddaw Special Bitter on handpump, a good range of malt whiskies, and nice new world house wines (including ones from the Sandford Estate – no connection); dominoes, and Sunday quiz evening. The two sons do the cooking, and the food might include grilled black pudding with mustard sauce, salads or home-made pie of the day, salmon fillet with parsley sauce; and puddings like highland trifle. There's also a more formal separate dining room (open if pre-booked), and a second bar area with broad flagstones, charming heavy-horse prints, an end log fire, and darts and piped music. Some picnic-sets outside.

Free house ~ Licensee Susan Stokes ~ Real ale ~ Bar food (12-1.45, 6.30(7 Sun, Mon)-8.30; not Mon, Weds, Thurs lunchtimes, not Tues) ~ Restaurant ~ (017683) 51121 ~ Children welcome ~ Dogs allowed in bar ~ Open 12-1.45, 6.30(7 Weds, Thurs, Sun)-11(10.30 Sun; closed Mon lunchtime, all day Tues) ~ Bedrooms: £50B/£60B

SANTON BRIDGE

Bridge Inn *Off A595 at Holmrook or Gosforth*

Run by a cheerful and helpful licensee, this traditional little black and white Lakeland inn has fell views and seats out in front by the quiet road. The turkey-carpeted bar has stripped beams, joists and standing timbers, a coal and log fire, and three rather unusual timbered booths around big stripped tables along its outer wall, with small painted school chairs and tables elsewhere. Bar stools line the long concave bar counter, which has well kept Jennings Bitter, Cumberland, Cocker Hoop and Sneck Lifter, and a guest such as Marstons Pedigree on handpump; good big pots of tea, speciality coffees, and maybe well reproduced piped nostalgic pop music, darts and dominoes. Bar food includes home-made soup, salads, cumberland sausage, steak and kidney pie and vegetarian stir-fry; also daily specials and Sunday carvery. The back bistro is no smoking (no children under 10 in here), the small reception hall has a rack of daily papers, and there's a comfortable more hotelish lounge (with an internet café) on the left. *Jennings ~ Tenants John Morrow and Lesley Rhodes ~ Real ale ~ Bar food (12-2.30, 6-9.30) ~ Restaurant ~ (01946) 726221 ~ Children in eating area of bar and restaurant ~ Dogs allowed in bar and bedrooms ~ Live music 1st Thurs of month ~ Open 11-11; 12-10.30 Sun ~ Bedrooms: £40(£45S)/£55(£60B)*

SEATHWAITE
Newfield Inn *Duddon Valley, near Ulpha (ie not Seathwaite in Borrowdale)*
In a quieter corner of the Lakes, this is an enjoyable pub to visit. It is well run and neatly kept with a friendly welcome for both visitors and regulars. The slate-floored bar has a genuinely local and informal atmosphere, with wooden tables and chairs, and some interesting pictures, and well kept Caledonian Deuchars IPA, Hawkshead Bitter, Jennings Bitter and York Stonewall on handpump. There's a comfortable side room and a games room with darts, bar billiards, shove-ha'penny, cribbage and dominoes. Good value bar food includes filled baked potatoes, home-made lasagne, salmon fillet with lime butter; daily specials like home-made meat and potato pie, and puddings such as pear and chocolate crumble. The grill room is no smoking; piped music. There are good walks from the doorstep so it's not surprising that walkers and climbers crowd in at weekends, and there are tables out in the nice garden with good hill views. The pub owns and lets the next-door self-catering flats.
Free house ~ Licensee Paul Batten ~ Real ale ~ Bar food (12-9) ~ Restaurant ~ (01229) 716208 ~ Children in eating area of bar and restaurant ~ Dogs allowed in bar ~ Open 11-11; 12-10.30 Sun

TROUTBECK
Queens Head *A592 N of Windermere*
Readers have enjoyed staying at this civilised inn, and as well as good traditional breakfasts, you might be offered something different such as field mushrooms on an oatmeal pancake with feta cheese. The big rambling original U-shaped bar has a little no smoking room at each end, beams and flagstones, a very nice mix of old cushioned settles and mates' chairs around some sizeable tables (especially the one to the left of the door), and a log fire in the raised stone fireplace with horse harness and so forth on either side of it in the main part, with a log fire in the other; some trumpets, cornets and saxophones on one wall, country pictures on others, stuffed pheasants in a big glass case, and a stag's head with a tie around his neck, and a stuffed fox with a ribbon around his neck. A massive Elizabethan

four-poster bed is the basis of the finely carved counter where they serve Boddingtons, Coniston Bluebird and Jennings Bitter, with guests such as Hawkshead Bitter or Tirrell Old Faithful on handpump. The newer dining rooms (where you can also drop in for just a drink) are similarly decorated to the main bar, with oak beams and stone walls, settles along big tables, and an open fire. Popular bar food includes home-made soup with home-made bread, steak, ale and mushroom cobbler, mixed bean and lentil strudel, fillet of salmon with coriander risotto and haunch of local venison on braised red cabbage; proper food for children and a three-course, set-price menu. Piped music. Seats outside have a fine view over the Trout valley to Applethwaite moors.

Free house ~ Licensees Mark Stewardson and Joanne Sherratt ~ Real ale ~ Bar food ~ Restaurant ~ (015394) 32174 ~ Children welcome ~ Dogs allowed in bar ~ Open 11-11; 12-10.30 Sun; closed 25 Dec ~ Bedrooms: /£95S(£105B)

ULVERSTON
Bay Horse *Canal Foot signposted off A590 and then you wend your way past the huge Glaxo factory*

Once a staging post for coaches that crossed the sands of Morecambe Bay to Lancaster in the 18th century, this civilised hotel is at its most informal at lunchtime. The bar, notable for its huge stone horse's head, has a relaxed atmosphere despite its smart furnishings: attractive wooden armchairs, some pale green plush built-in wall banquettes, glossy hardwood traditional tables, blue plates on a delft shelf, and black beams and props with lots of horsebrasses. Magazines are dotted about, there's a handsomely marbled green granite fireplace, and decently reproduced piped music; darts, shove-ha'penny, cribbage and dominoes. Good, imaginative bar food might include home-made cream of potato, leek and watercress soup, home-made cheese and herb pâté, fresh crab and salmon fishcakes on a white wine and fresh herb cream sauce, and home-made puddings. Well kept Jennings Best and Cumberland, and a guest like Bass on handpump, a decent choice of spirits, and a carefully chosen and interesting wine list with quite a few from South Africa. The no smoking conservatory restaurant has fine views over Morecambe Bay (as do the bedrooms) and there are some seats out on the terrace. Please note, the bedroom price includes dinner as well.

Free house ~ Licensee Robert Lyons ~ Real ale ~ Bar food (lunchtime only; not Mon) ~ Restaurant ~ (01229) 583972 ~ Children in eating area of bar and in restaurant if over 12 ~ Dogs allowed in bar and bedrooms ~ Open 11-11; 12-10.30 Sun ~ Bedrooms: /£160B

Dog Friendly Hotels, B&Bs and Farms

ALSTON
Lovelady Shield Country House *Nenthead Rd, Alston, Cumbria CA9 3LF (01434) 381203* £180 inc dinner, plus special breaks; 12 rms. In a

lovely setting with River Nent running along bottom of garden (tennis and croquet), this handsome country house has a tranquil atmosphere, courteous staff, log fires in comfortable rooms (no smoking in sitting room or restaurant), and very good food inc fine breakfasts; children over 7 in evening restaurant; dogs welcome in bedrooms; £5

AMBLESIDE
Wateredge Inn *Borrans Rd, Ambleside, Cumbria LA22 0EP (015394) 32332* £**90**, plus special breaks; 21 good comfortable rms. Beautifully placed, warmly welcoming inn with neat gardens running down to Lake Windermere (embarkation point for cruising the lake); light airy bar (with fine views) and lounge, good meals in no smoking dining area (more lovely views), and excellent service; cl 4 days over Christmas; disabled access; dogs welcome in bedrooms and part of bar

APPLEBY
Appleby Manor *Roman Rd, Appleby, Cumbria CA16 6JB (01768) 351571* £**128**, plus special breaks; 31 well equipped rms in original house (the nicest), coach house annexe or modern wing. Very friendly family-run hotel with fine views over Appleby Castle and Eden valley, log fires in two of the three comfortable lounges, relaxed bar with wide range of whiskies, excellent service, good interesting food in panelled restaurant, and leisure centre; enjoyed by families; cl 24–26 Dec; disabled access; dogs in coach house bedrooms only; £10

BARBON
Barbon Inn *Barbon, Carnforth, Cumbria LA6 2LJ (015242) 76233* £**65**; 10 simple but comfortable rms, some with own bthrm. Small friendly 17th-c village inn in quiet spot below fells, with relaxing bar, traditional lounge, good meals in candlelit dining room, and helpful service; lots of good tracks and paths all around; dogs in bedrooms

BASSENTHWAITE LAKE
Armathwaite Hall Hotel *Bassenthwaite Lake, Keswick, Cumbria CA12 4RE (017687) 76551* £**196**, plus special offers; 42 rms. Turreted 17th-c mansion in 400 acres of deerpark and woodland; handsome public rooms with lovely fireplaces, fine panelling, antiques, paintings and fresh flowers, good french and english cooking, a super wine list, and helpful staff; snooker room, croquet, pitch–and–putt, tennis court, indoor swimming pool, gym and beauty salon, fishing, archery and clay pigeon shooting, jogging and mountain-bike tracks, and free children's club; disabled access; dogs welcome in bedrooms; £10

BASSENTHWAITE LAKE
Pheasant *Bassenthwaite Lake, Cockermouth, Cumbria CA13 9YE (017687) 76234* £**140**, plus special breaks; 16 comfortable rms. Civilised hotel with delightfully old-fashioned pubby bar, restful lounges with open fire, antiques, fresh flowers and comfortable armchairs, and interesting gardens

merging into surrounding fellside woodlands; cl 25 Dec; children over 8; disabled access; dogs in bar and in Garden Lodge bedrooms

BRAMPTON
Farlam Hall *Hallbankgate, Brampton, Cumbria CA8 2NG (016977) 46234* £265 inc dinner, plus special breaks; 12 comfortable rms. Charmingly Victorian (though parts are much older) and very civilised country house with log fires in spacious lounges, excellent attentive service, good 4-course dinner using fine china and silver, marvellous breakfasts, and peaceful, spacious grounds with croquet lawn and small pretty lake; cl 25-30 Dec; children over 5; disabled access; dogs welcome but not to be left alone at any time

BUTTERMERE
Bridge *Buttermere, Cockermouth, Cumbria CA13 9UZ (017687) 70252* £112.50, plus special breaks; 21 comfortable rms. Comfortable hotel surrounded by some of the best steep countryside in the county, with beamed bar, open fire and deep armchairs in sitting room, good food in bar and no smoking restaurant, real ales, quite a few malt whiskies, and a friendly atmosphere; self-catering also; cl 2 wks Jan; children over 7 in dining room; dogs welcome in bedrooms and hall; £5

CARTMEL
Uplands *Haggs Lane, Cartmel, Grange-Over-Sands, Cumbria LA11 6HD (01539) 536248* £168 inc dinner, plus special breaks; 5 pretty rms. Comfortable Edwardian house in two acres of grounds (plenty of wildlife) with views over to Morecambe Bay; large, attractively decorated lounge, welcoming owners, an informal atmosphere, very good modern food in the no smoking restaurant cooked by the owner, and super breakfasts; cl Mon, Jan-Feb; children over 8; walks from the front door; dogs welcome away from public rooms

CROOK
Wild Boar *Crook, Windermere, Cumbria LA23 3NF (015394) 45225* £119, plus special offers; 36 rms. Comfortable well run, extended hotel with period furnishings and log fires in its ancient core, attentive service, and good food in no smoking dining room; free access to nearby leisure club and discounts on watersports; children's club at sister hotel, The Lowwood; dogs welcome in bedrooms

CROSBY ON EDEN
Crosby Lodge *High Crosby, Crosby on Eden, Carlisle, Cumbria CA6 4QZ (01228) 573618* £130, plus special breaks; 11 spacious rms (2 in stable conversion). Imposing and carefully converted country house in attractive mature grounds, with comfortable and appealing individual furnishings, enjoyable home-made food using local produce in no smoking restaurant, friendly long-established owners, and nice surrounding countryside; cl Christmas/New Year; limited disabled access; dogs in courtyard bedrooms; £5

DENT

Sportsmans *Cowgill, Dent, Sedbergh, Cumbria LA10 5RG (01539) 625282*
£47, plus winter breaks; 5 rms with shared bthrm. Unassuming
comfortable pub notable for its wonderful position in Dentdale by the
River Dee overlooking the Settle—Carlisle railway, and walks in all
directions; guests' sitting room (no TV reception but plenty of videos,
dvds, books and magazines), open log fires, real ales, and good value home-
made food; dogs welcome in bedrooms by arrangement; £5

DERWENT WATER

Lodore Falls *Borrowdale, Keswick, Cumbria CA12 5UX (017687) 77285*
£138, plus special breaks; 71 well equipped rms. Long-standing but well
updated big holiday hotel with lots of facilities in 40 acres of lakeside
gardens and woodlands, comfortable day rooms, elegant restaurant, leisure
club, tennis and squash, outdoor swimming pool, and games room;
particularly well organised for families with NNEB nannies and so forth;
self-catering house too; children over 6 in evening restaurant (high tea is
offered); dogs welcome in bedrooms; £5

ELTERWATER

Britannia Inn *Elterwater, Ambleside, Cumbria LA22 9HP (015394) 37210*
£100, plus special breaks; 9 rms, several recently refurbished. Simple
charmingly traditional pub in fine surroundings opposite village green, with
a happy friendly atmosphere (it does get very busy at peak times), hearty
home cooking inc superb breakfast, comfortable, upgraded no smoking
lounge and bustling bar, real ales, and Sun evening quiz; fine walks all
around; cl 25 Dec; dogs welcome away from residents' lounge and dining
room

ENNERDALE BRIDGE

Shepherds Arms *Ennerdale, Cleator, Cumbria CA23 3AR (01946) 861249*
£63; 8 rms. Set on the popular Coast-to-Coast path and with wonderful
surrounding walks, this welcoming inn has a convivial bar, a woodburning
stove, carpeted main bar with coal fire and a homely variety of comfortable
seats, and a new no smoking conservatory; cheerful and obliging service,
substantial bar food using local meat and fish and only fresh vegetables, well
kept real ales, and a good choice of wines by the glass; a couple of daily
papers; cl 2 wks Feb; dogs in bedrooms and bar

FAR SAWREY

Sawrey *Far Sawrey, Ambleside, Cumbria LA22 0LQ (015394) 43425* £63,
plus special breaks; 18 rms. Friendly hotel well placed at the foot of Claife
Heights, with simple pubby and smarter bars, friendly staff, good straightforward food, and seats on pleasant lawn; cl Christmas; kind to children;
partial disabled access; dogs welcome in bedrooms as long as not left alone;
£2.50

GARRIGILL
Ivy House *Garrigill, Alston, Cumbria CA9 3DU (01434) 382501* £49, plus special breaks; 3 rms. 17th-c farmhouse in fine scenery on Alston Moor, with a comfortable guest lounge, open fire and plenty of books, games and newspapers, helpful welcoming owners, and good breakfasts (packed lunches, too); dogs welcome anywhere

GRASMERE
Swan *Keswick Rd, Grasmere, Ambleside, Cumbria LA22 9RF (015394) 35551* £116, plus special breaks; 38 rms, most with fine views. Smart and friendly 17th-c hotel in beautiful fell-foot surroundings, with beams and inglenooks, elegant no smoking dining room, enjoyable food, and attractive garden; lovely walks; partial disabled access; dogs in some bedrooms

IREBY
Overwater Hall *Ireby, Carlisle, Cumbria CA5 1HH (017687) 76566* £110, plus special breaks; 11 rms. Relaxed and friendly family-run hotel, partly castellated, in 18 acres of gardens and woodland; log fire in traditionally furnished, comfortable drawing room, good imaginative food in cosy dining room, hearty breakfasts, and lots of walks; cl Jan; children over 5 in restaurant (high tea 5pm); partial disabled access; dogs in bedrooms, bar and hall

KENDAL
Low Jock Scar *Selside, Kendal, Cumbria LA8 9LE (01539) 823259* £64; 5 rms, most with own bthrm. Relaxed and friendly small country guesthouse in six acres of garden and woodland, with residents' lounge, and good home cooking (picnic lunches on request); no smoking; cl Nov-mid-Mar; children over 12; dogs welcome in bedrooms

LANGDALE
Old Dungeon Ghyll *Great Langdale, Ambleside, Cumbria LA22 9JY (015394) 37272* £90, plus special breaks; 13 rms, some with shared bthrm. Friendly, simple and cosy walkers' and climbers' inn dramatically surrounded by fells, wonderful views and terrific walks; cosy residents' lounge and popular food – best to book for dinner if not a resident; cl Christmas; dogs in bedrooms

LORTON
New House Farm *Lorton, Cockermouth, Cumbria CA13 9UU (01900) 85404* £98, plus special breaks; 6 rms with wonderful hillside views. Friendly no smoking 17th-c house (not a working farm) in 15 acres, with beams and rafters, flagstones, open fires, and three residents' lounges, very good food inc game and fish caught by owner, home-made scones and preserves, a thoughtful wine list – and lots of walks; children over 6; dogs welcome in bedrooms

MUNGRISDALE

Mill Hotel *Mungrisdale, Penrith, Cumbria CA11 0XR (017687) 79659*
£90, plus special breaks; 9 rms, most with own bthrm. Very friendly small
streamside hotel, beautifully placed in lovely valley hamlet hidden away
below Blencathra, with open fire in cosy and comfortable sitting room,
good imaginative 5-course evening meals, and a small carefully chosen
wine list; cl Nov-beginning Mar; they are kind to children; disabled access;
dogs welcome in bedrooms

RYDAL WATER

White Moss House *White Moss, Ambleside, Cumbria LA22 9SE (015394)
35295* £154 inc dinner, plus special breaks; 6 thoughtfully furnished and
comfortable little rms in main house plus separate cottage let as one unit
with 2 rms. Bought by Wordsworth for his son, this attractive stripped-
stone country house – set in charming mature grounds overlooking the
lake – is a marvellously relaxing place to stay, with owners who have been
there for over 20 years, a comfortable lounge, excellent fixed-price 5-
course meals in pretty no smoking dining room, a fine wine list, and
exemplary service; free fishing and free use of local leisure club; cl Dec-Jan;
no toddlers; dogs in cottage

SCALES

Scales Farm *Scales, Threlkeld, Cumbria CA12 4SY (01768) 779660* £58;
6 comfortable, well equipped rms, 3 with ground-floor access. Converted
17th-c no smoking farmhouse with wide stretching views, a friendly
welcome, woodburning stove and wide screen TV in homely beamed
lounge, traditional english breakfasts in large dining room (good pub next
door for evening meals), and packed lunches on request; fine walks; dogs
welcome in bedrooms; £3

SEATOLLER

Seatoller House *Borrowdale, Keswick, Cumbria CA12 5XN (017687)
77218* £95; 10 spotless, comfortable rms. Friendly house-party atmosphere
in 17th-c house that has been a guesthouse for over 100 years, with self-
service drinks and board games in comfortable lounges (no TV), and good
no-choice fixed-time hearty dinner (not Tues) served at two big oak tables;
packed lunches; two acres of grounds and many walks from doorstep
(house is at the foot of Honister Pass); cl Dec-Mar; children over 5 in
dining room; disabled access; dogs welcome in bedrooms

TIRRIL

Queens Head *Tirril, Penrith, Cumbria CA10 2JF (01768) 863219* £70,
plus special breaks; 7 lovely rms. Bustling very welcoming inn with
flagstones and bare boards in the bar, spacious back restaurant (mostly no
smoking), low beams, black panelling, inglenook fireplace and old-
fashioned settles in older part, good interesting food inc snacks and OAP
specials, and well kept real ales (inc their own brews); babies welcome but
older children must be over 13; dogs in bedrooms and bars; £5

WASDALE HEAD

Wasdale Head Hotel *Wasdale Head, Seascale, Cumbria CA20 1EX* *(019467) 26229* £**98**, plus special breaks; 9 simple but warmly comfortable pine-clad rms, with 3 more luxurious ones in farmhouse annexe. Old flagstoned and gabled walkers' and climbers' inn in magnificent setting surrounded by steep fells, with micro-brewery (tours welcome), civilised day rooms, popular home cooking, good wine list, huge breakfasts, and cheerfully busy public bar; steam room; self-catering cottages; partial disabled access; dogs welcome in bedrooms; £3

WATERMILLOCK

Leeming House *Watermillock, Ullswater, Penrith, Cumbria CA11 0JJ* *(017684) 86622* £**130**, plus special breaks; 40 cosseting rms, many with beautiful views. Well run extended hotel in 20 acres of quiet lakeside grounds, with log fires in comfortable lounges, cosy panelled bar, fine food in lovely no smoking dining room, and good courteous service; boating and fishing; high teas for young children; good provision for disabled; dogs welcome in bedrooms only; £10

WATERMILLOCK

Rampsbeck Country House *Watermillock, Penrith, Cumbria CA11 0LP* *(017684) 86442* £**110**, plus special breaks; 19 attractive rms, some with balconies. 18th-c hotel in 18 acres by Lake Ullswater with extensive lake frontage and seats on sunny terrace; open fire in the cosy sitting room, french windows into the garden from the plush, comfortable lounge, friendly attentive staff, and carefully prepared food in the attractive dining room; croquet; lots to do nearby; cl Jan-mid-Feb; no children in evening dining room; dogs welcome in bedrooms

WINDERMERE

Langdale Chase Hotel *Windermere, Cumbria LA23 1LW (015394) 32201* £**130**, plus special breaks; 27 rms, many with marvellous lake view. Welcoming family-run hotel in lovely position on the edge of Lake Windermere with bathing from the hotel jetty; croquet, putting and rowing, afternoon tea on the terraces, gracious oak-panelled rooms with antiques, paintings, fresh flowers, open fires, very good food (huge breakfasts, too), and friendly service; disabled access; dogs in bedrooms, and in bar and lounges at management discretion

Derbyshire

Dog Friendly Pubs

ALDERWASLEY

Bear *Village signposted with Breanfield off B5035 E of Wirksworth at Malt Shovel; inn ½ mile SW of village, on Ambergate—Wirksworth high back road*

The several small dark rooms at this enchantingly unspoilt village pub have low beams, bare boards and ochre walls, a great variety of old tables, and seats running from brocaded dining chairs and old country-kitchen chairs to high-backed settles and antique oak chairs carved with traditional Derbyshire motifs. One little room is filled right to its built-in wall seats by a single vast table. There are log fires in huge stone fireplaces, candles galore, antique paintings and engravings, plenty of Staffordshire china ornaments and no fewer than three grandfather clocks. Despite the treasures, this is a proper easy-going country local, with dominoes players clattering about beside canaries trilling in a huge Edwardian-style white cage (elsewhere look out for the talkative cockatoos, an african grey parrot, and budgerigars). The sensibly imaginative food is popular so you may need to book. Made mostly with ingredients from local farms and growers, and listed on a daily changing blackboard, dishes might include beer battered haggis balls in whisky sauce, root vegetable stew with cheddar mash, or lamb shank in mint jus, and puddings such as rhubarb crumble. Service is friendly and helpful. They have a fine range of interesting wines, and three changing real ales such as Bass, Marstons Pedigree, and Timothy Taylors Landlord on handpump. There are peaceful country views from well spaced picnic-sets out on the side grass, and it's popular with walkers. There's no obvious front door – you get in through the plain back entrance by the car park.

Free house ~ Licensee Nicky Fletcher-Musgrave ~ Real ale ~ Bar food (12-9.30) ~ Restaurant ~ (01629) 822585 ~ Children welcome away from bar ~ Dogs welcome ~ Open 12-11 ~ Bedrooms: £35S/£70S

BRASSINGTON

Olde Gate *Village signposted off B5056 and B5035 NE of Ashbourne*

The charming interior of this lovely old ivy-clad inn is an absolute treat.

The timelessly relaxing public bar is traditionally furnished, with a fine ancient wall clock, rush-seated old chairs, antique settles, including one ancient black solid oak one, and roaring log fires. Gleaming copper pots sit on a 17th-c kitchen range, pewter mugs hang from a beam, and a side shelf boasts a collection of embossed Doulton stoneware flagons. To the left of a small hatch-served lobby, another cosy beamed room has stripped panelled settles, scrubbed-top tables, and a blazing fire under a huge mantelbeam. Stone-mullioned windows look out across lots of tables in the pleasant garden (boules in summer) to small silvery-walled pastures, and in fine weather the small front yard with a few benches is a nice place to sit (listen out for the village bell-ringers practising on Friday evenings). Although the date etched on the building reads 1874, it was originally built in 1616, from magnesian limestone and timbers salvaged from Armada wrecks, bought in exchange for locally mined lead. Bar food, from a regularly changing menu, is mostly home-made; also puddings such as lemon pie (highly recommended by readers). The dining room is no smoking; the back bar is prettily candlelit at night. Well kept Marstons Pedigree and a guest such as Adnams Broadside on handpump, and a good selection of malt whiskies; cribbage and dominoes. Carsington reservoir is only a five-minute drive away.

Marstons (W & D) ~ Tenant Paul Burlinson ~ Real ale ~ Bar food (not Sun evening or Mon) ~ (01629) 540448 ~ Children over 10 ~ Dogs welcome ~ Open 12-2.30 (possibly earlier if quiet; 3 Sat), 6-11; 12-3, 7-10.30 Sun; closed Mon exc bank hols

BUXTON

Bull i' th' Thorn *Ashbourne Road (A515) 6 miles S of Buxton, near Hurdlow*
Themed food nights are a feature at this rather intriguing cross between a medieval hall and a straightforward roadside dining pub, with sizzle and griddle on Monday, seafood on Tuesday, steak on Wednesday, vegetarian on Thursday (when they add ten extra dishes to a bar menu that already lists about that number) and curries on Friday night. There's lots to look at inside, and among the lively old carvings that greet you on your way in is one of the eponymous bull caught in a thornbush (the pub's name comes from a hybrid of its 15th-c and 17th-c titles, the Bull and Hurdlow House of Hurdlow Thorn), and there are also images of an eagle with a freshly caught hare, and some spaniels chasing a rabbit. In the hall, which dates from 1471, a massive central beam runs parallel with a forest of smaller ones, there are panelled window seats in the embrasures of the thick stone walls, handsome panelling, and old flagstones stepping gently down to a big open fire. It's furnished with fine long settles, an ornately carved hunting chair, a longcase clock, a powder-horn, and armour that includes 17th-c german helmets, swords, and blunderbusses and so forth. Stuffed animals' heads line the corridor that leads to a candlelit hall, used for medieval themed evening banquets. An adjoining room has pool and dominoes. A simple no smoking family room opens on to a terrace and big lawn, and there are more tables in a sheltered angle in front. They serve Robinsons Best on handpump.

Robinsons ~ Tenant Annette Maltby-Baker ~ Real ale ~ Bar food (9.30-9) ~ Restaurant ~ (01298) 83348 ~ Children in restaurant and family room ~ Dogs welcome ~ Open 9.30-11(10.30 Sun) ~ Bedrooms: /£60B

DERBY

Brunswick *Railway Terrace; close to Derby Midland railway station*
The plain brick exterior of this railwaymen's hostelry, at the apex of a row of preserved railway cottages, gives no clue to the treasure trove of beers inside. Up to 17 real ales, on handpump or tapped from the cask, include seven which are produced in the purpose-built brewery tower which is tucked away behind the pub (Father Mikes Dark Rich Ruby, Old Accidental, Second Brew Usual, Railway Porter, Triple Hop and Triple Gold) as well as around 10 regularly changing widely sourced guests such as Batemans, Everards Tiger, Holdens Golden Glow, Marstons Pedigree, and Timothy Taylors Landlord; farm cider is tapped from the cask. You can tour the brewery (£7.50 including a meal and a pint). The welcoming high-ceilinged bar has heavy well padded leather seats, whisky-water jugs above the dado, and a dark blue ceiling and upper wall, with squared dark panelling below. The no smoking room is decorated with little old-fashioned prints and swan's neck lamps, and has a high-backed wall settle and a coal fire; behind a curved glazed partition wall is a chatty family parlour narrowing to the apex of the triangular building. Interesting wall displays tell you about the history and restoration of the building, and there are interesting old train photographs; darts, dominoes, cribbage, fruit machine and TV. Tasty, good value bar food from a limited menu; on Sunday they do rolls only. There are two outdoor seating areas, including a terrace behind. They'll gladly give dogs a bowl of water.
Everards ~ Licensee Graham Yates ~ Real ale ~ Bar food (12-5 Mon-Sat) ~ No credit cards ~ (01332) 290677 ~ Children in family room ~ Dogs welcome ~ Jazz Thurs evenings ~ Open 11-11; 12-10.30 Sun

EYAM

Miners Arms *Signposted off A632 Chesterfield—Chapel-en-le-Frith*
In the couple of years that the cheery licensees have been at this welcoming pub they've really brought it up to scratch. It's very well run, and the friendly owners and helpful chatty staff contribute strongly to the pleasantly relaxed and civilised atmosphere. Very cosy in winter, the three little neatly kept plush beamed rooms each have their own stone fireplace. It gets nicely lively in the evening, when locals drop in for a well kept pint. Good home-made bar food includes sausage of the day and mash or roast of the day, pie of the day, and puddings such as delicious trifle and bread and butter pudding. They have Bass, Stones and a guest such as Greene King Old Speckled Hen on handpump; cribbage, dominoes and piped music. Bedrooms are nicely decorated, and breakfasts are good. This is an excellent base for exploring the Peak District, and there are decent walks nearby, especially below Froggatt Edge. Eyam is famous for the altruism of its villagers, who isolated themselves during the plague to save the lives of others in the area.

*New Century Inns ~ Tenants John and Michele Hunt ~ Real ale ~ Bar food
(12-2(3 Sat, Sun), 6-9; not Sun evening) ~ Restaurant ~ (01433) 630853 ~
Children in eating area of bar and restaurant ~ Dogs allowed in bar and bedrooms ~
Monthly jazz suppers ~ Open 12-11(10.30 Sun); closed 25 Dec ~ Bedrooms:
/£60B*

FENNY BENTLEY
Bentley Brook *A515 N of Ashbourne*

Very much a family-run operation, this substantial timbered inn has been in
the same capably friendly hands for just under 30 years and has a range of
attractions on offer. The main bar area is traditional but with quite an airy
feel, thanks to big windows, fairly high ceilings and quite a few mirrors,
with well lit pictures, some brassware and decorative plates on the neat
white walls, wheelback and other chairs around plenty of dark polished
tables on the bare boards, and a log fire in the stone fireplace between the
two linked areas. Food here is good. They use herbs, fruit and some
vegetables from their own garden, and you can buy their own preserves,
sausages and so forth from their little kitchen shop. A separate smarter no
smoking restaurant has its own menu. Well worth trying is the attractively
priced Leatherbritches ales they brew here, and which are increasingly
available in other pubs we list. The range includes Goldings, Ashbourne,
Belter, Hairy Helmet and Bespoke, and at their May bank holiday beer
festival you get a chance to taste the full range (and dozens of other beers),
but usually they have just a selection on handpump, alongside a guest such
as Marstons Pedigree, and local Saxon farm cider; well reproduced piped
music, dominoes, chess, cards, Jenga and board games. Picnic-sets under
cocktail parasols on a broad flower-festooned terrace look down over a
pleasant lawn and proper barbecue area, and they have summer barbecues,
boules, croquet, skittles and a good play area. The streamside grounds
include a wildflower meadow, and room for campers, and the location is
handy for Dovedale.

*Own brew ~ Licensees David and Jeanne Allingham ~ Real ale ~ Bar food (12-9)
~ Restaurant ~ (01335) 350278 ~ Dogs allowed in bar and bedrooms ~ Open
11-11; 12-10.30 Sun ~ Bedrooms: £50B/£72.50B*

FOOLOW
Bulls Head *Village signposted off A623 Baslow—Tideswell*

There's a buoyantly friendly atmosphere in the simply furnished flagstoned
bar at this neatly kept welcoming pub, with a couple of quieter areas set out
for a relaxing meal. A step or two takes you down into what may once
have been a stables, with its high ceiling joists, some stripped stone, and a
woodburning stove. On the other side, a smart no smoking dining room
has more polished tables set in cosy stalls. Interesting photographs include a
good collection of Edwardian naughties. The wide range of enjoyable food
is popular, so you may need to book at the weekend; three succulent roasts
on Sunday. Tetleys is well kept alongside three changing guests such as
Adnams, Black Sheep and Shepherd Neame Spitfire; piped music and darts.
You can buy basic provisions here (milk, eggs, bread, and so forth), which

is handy, as there's no shop in this upland village. It's an appealing village, surrounded by rolling stone-walled pastures – good walks nearby mean it's popular with ramblers. Picnic-table sets at the back have nice views, and the small pretty green has a medieval cross and a pond.

Free house ~ Licensees William and Leslie Bond ~ Real ale ~ Bar food (12-2, 7-9(5-8 Sun)) ~ Restaurant ~ (01433) 630873 ~ Children in eating area of bar, restaurant and family room ~ Dogs allowed in bar ~ Live folk Fri evening ~ Open 12-3(2 Sat), 6.30-11; 12-2, 5-8 Sun; closed Mon ~ Bedrooms: £40S/£65S

HATHERSAGE

Scotsmans Pack *School Lane, off A625*

Well placed for walkers and close to the church where Little John is said to be buried, this welcoming local is a comfortable place for a good, quietly civilised meal. There's been a pub on the spot for centuries, though the current building dates from around 1900. The most comfortable area is on the left as you enter, with a fireplace, and patterned wallpaper somewhat obscured by a splendid mass of brasses, stuffed animal heads and the like. Elsewhere there's plenty of dark panelling, lots of mugs and plates arranged around the bar, and a good few tables, many with reserved signs (it's worth booking ahead, particularly at weekends). The wide range of food might include a good choice of sandwiches, a well regarded steak pie and several vegetarian dishes. Burtonwood Bitter and Top Hat on handpump, along with a monthly changing guest like Wadworths 6X; service remains prompt and cheery even when busy. They have regular quiz and bingo nights. One area is no smoking. Outside is a small but very pleasant patio, next to a trout-filled stream.

Free house ~ Licensee Nick Beagrie ~ Real ale ~ Bar food (12-2, 6-9) ~ (01433) 650253 ~ Children welcome till 9 ~ Dogs welcome ~ Open 11-3, 5.30-11; 11-11 Sat; 12-10.30 Sun ~ Bedrooms: £32B/£61B

HOGNASTON

Red Lion *Village signposted off B5035 Ashbourne—Wirksworth*

The open-plan oak-beamed bar at this well run welcoming pub has a relaxing almost bistro feel. An attractive mix of old tables (candlelit at night) and old-fashioned settles and other seats are arranged on ancient flagstones. There are three open fires, and a growing collection of teddy bears among other bric-a-brac and copies of *Country Life*; the conservatory restaurant is no smoking. The generously served, nicely presented food here is popular, and from a frequently changing, fairly priced menu, dishes could include home-made soup, mushroom stroganoff or roast beef, pork or lamb, and sticky toffee pudding. They've well kept Bass, Greene King Old Speckled Hen and Marstons Pedigree, and perhaps a guest such as Whim Hartington on handpump, and you can get country wines; piped music, dominoes and cribbage. It's in a lovely peaceful spot, handy for Carsington Reservoir, and bedrooms are big and comfortable.

Free house ~ Licensee Pip Price ~ Real ale ~ Bar food (12-2, 6.30-9; not Sun evening, not Mon) ~ Restaurant ~ (01335) 370396 ~ Children in restaurant ~

Dogs allowed in bar ~ Open 12-3, 6-11.30(7-10.30 Sun); closed Mon lunchtime ~ Bedrooms: £50S/£80S

HOLBROOK

Dead Poets *Village signposted off A6 S of Belper; Chapel Street*

Tucked into a quiet street, this low white-painted pub continues to serve a great selection of eight real ales. Alongside well kept Everards Original, Greene King Abbot, Marstons Pedigree, Timothy Taylors Landlord and Burton Bridge Golden Delicious, a couple of guests could be from brewers such as Church End, Clarks or Holdens, on handpump or served by the jug from the cellar; also farm cider and several country wines. The regular beer festivals here are very popular. It's very dark inside, with low black beams in its ochre ceiling, stripped stone walls with some smoked plaster, and broad flagstones. Candles burn on scrubbed tables, there's a big log fire in the end stone fireplace, high-backed winged settles form snug cubicles along one wall, and there are pews and a variety of chairs in other intimate corners and hide-aways. The décor makes a few nods to the pub's present name (it used to be the Cross Keys), and includes some old prints of Derby. Alongside cobs (nothing else on Sundays), bar food is limited to a few good value hearty dishes. There's a good atmosphere, and a nice mix of customers, male and female; well reproduced piped music. Behind is a sort of verandah room, with lanterns, fairy lights and a few plants, and more seats out in the yard, with outdoor heaters.

Everards ~ Licensee William Holmes ~ Real ale ~ Bar food (lunchtimes Mon-Sat) ~ No credit cards ~ (01332) 780301 ~ Children in family room ~ Dogs welcome ~ Poetry night 1st Tues in month ~ Open 12-3, 5-11; 12-11 Fri-Sat; 12-10.30 Sun

KIRK IRETON

Barley Mow *Village signposted off B5023 S of Wirksworth*

The landlady at this unspoilt rural gem recently celebrated her 70th birthday, so it's good to know that she's well looked after by her huge newfoundland, Hector. Other than that, little changes here from year to year – the dimly lit passageways and narrow stairwells of this tall gabled Jacobean brown sandstone inn have a timeless atmosphere, helped along by traditional furnishings and civilised old-fashioned service. It's a place to sit and chat, and though the only games you'll find here are dominoes and cards it still pulls in a good crowd of youngsters and local old folk at weekends, and walkers at other times. The small main bar has a relaxed pubby feel, with antique settles on the tiled floor or built into the panelling, a roaring coal fire, four slate-topped tables, and shuttered mullioned windows. Another room has built-in cushioned pews on oak parquet and a small woodburning stove, and a third room has more pews, a tiled floor, beams and joists, and big landscape prints. One room is no smoking. In casks behind a modest wooden counter are well kept (and reasonably priced) Archers, Hook Norton Best and Old Hooky, Whim Hartington and possibly a guest from another small brewery such as Cottage or Storm; farm ciders too. Lunchtime filled rolls are the only food; the good home-made evening meals are reserved for residents staying in the comfortable rooms. There's a decent-sized garden, and they've opened a post office in what used to be the pub stables. Handy for Carsington Water, the pretty hilltop village is in good walking country.

Free house ~ Licensee Mary Short ~ Real ale ~ No credit cards ~ (01335) 370306 ~ Children in a side room lunchtime only ~ Dogs allowed in bedrooms ~ Open 12-2, 7-11(10.30 Sun); closed 25 Dec and 1 Jan ~ Bedrooms: £30S/£50B

LADYBOWER RESERVOIR
Yorkshire Bridge *A6013 N of Bamford*

This big roadside hotel is a very popular stop near the Ladybower, Derwent and Howden reservoirs (immortalised by the World War II Dambusters). Service is friendly and obliging, and there's a cheerful bustling atmosphere. One area has a country cottage feel, with floral wallpaper, sturdy cushioned wall settles, Staffordshire dogs and toby jugs on a big stone fireplace with a warm coal-effect gas fire, china on delft shelves, a panelled dado and so forth. Another extensive area, with another fire, is lighter and more airy with pale wooden furniture, good big black and white photographs and lots of plates on the walls. The Bridge Room has yet another coal-effect fire and oak tables and chairs, and the small no smoking conservatory gives pleasant views across a valley to steep larch woods. The bar and Bridge Room have no smoking areas too. In summer it's a good idea to arrive early, to be sure of a table. The enjoyable menu, which has lots of generously served traditional dishes, includes lunchtime sandwiches, home-made steak and kidney pie, specials and puddings such as lemon meringue pie; they also do children's meals. All three dining rooms are no smoking; the restaurant is for residents only. Well kept on handpump are Black Sheep, Stones, Theakstons Old Peculier and Timothy Taylors Landlord; darts, dominoes, fruit machine and piped music; disabled lavatories.

Free house ~ Licensees Trevelyan and John Illingworth ~ Real ale ~ Bar food (12-2, 6-9(9.30 Fri, Sat); 12-8.30 Sun) ~ Restaurant ~ (01433) 651361 ~ Children in eating area of bar, restaurant and family room ~ Dogs welcome ~ Open 11-11; 12-10.30 Sun ~ Bedrooms: £47B/£64B

LITTON
Red Lion *Village signposted off A623, between B6465 and B6049 junctions; also signposted off B6049*

The enjoyable local atmosphere and good value tasty food are what readers like about this welcoming 17th-c village pub, where the cheerily friendly landlord makes everyone feel like a regular. The two inviting homely linked front rooms have low beams and some panelling, and blazing log fires. There's a bigger back room (no smoking during food service) with good-sized tables, and large antique prints on its stripped stone walls. The small bar counter has well kept Barnsley Bitter, Black Sheep, Theakstons Old Peculier and Timothy Taylors Landlord on handpump, with decent wines and 30 malt whiskies; shove-ha'penny, cribbage, dominoes and table skittles. Fresh tasting bar food such as rabbit casserole and chicken and mushroom pancakes. The peaceful tree-studded village green in front of this is pretty, and there are good walks nearby. A good time to visit is during the annual village well-dressing carnival (usually the last weekend in June), when villagers create a picture from flower petals, moss and other natural materials, and at Christmas a brass band plays carols. No children under 6.

Free house ~ Licensees Terry and Michele Vernon ~ Real ale ~ Bar food (12-2, 6-8.30 (not Sun evening)) ~ (01298) 871458 ~ No children under 6 ~ Dogs welcome ~ Open 12-3, 6-11; 12-11 Fri, Sat; 12-10.30 Sun ~ Bedrooms: /£48(£55S)

OVER HADDON

Lathkil *Village and inn signposted from B5055 just SW of Bakewell*

The views from this pleasantly unpretentious hotel are spectacular – the walled garden is a good place to sit and soak them in. Steeply down below the pub lies one of the quieter of the dales, Lathkil Dale – a harmonious landscape of pastures and copses. Not surprisingly the pub is very popular with walkers (who can leave their muddy boots in the pub's lobby, and they're not fussy about dress here) so it's best to arrive early in fine weather. Five reasonably priced real ales include Charles Wells Bombardier and Whim Hartington, which are well kept alongside a couple of guests from brewers such as Black Sheep, Cottage and Theakstons. They have a few unusual malt whiskies and a good range of new world wines (not cheap). The airy room on the right as you go in has a nice fire in the attractively carved fireplace, old-fashioned settles with upholstered cushions and chairs, black beams, a delft shelf of blue and white plates, original prints and photographs, and big windows. On the left, the spacious and sunny no smoking dining area doubles as a restaurant in the evenings. The changing blackboard menu could include tasty home-made soup, fish pie or a vegetarian dish and venison in red wine; puddings too. There are darts, bar billiards, shove-ha'penny, backgammon, dominoes, cribbage, and piped music.

Free house ~ Licensee Robert Grigor-Taylor ~ Real ale ~ Bar food (lunchtime) ~ Restaurant ~ (01629) 812501 ~ Children in restaurant and family room ~ Dogs allowed in bar and bedrooms ~ Open 11.30-3, 6.30(7 winter)-11; 11.30-11 Sat; 12-10.30 Sun ~ Bedrooms: £37.50S/£70B

SHARDLOW

Old Crown *3 miles from M1 junction 24, via A50: at first B6540 exit from A50 (just under 2 miles) turn off towards Shardlow – pub E of Shardlow itself, at Cavendish Bridge, actually just over Leics boundary*

Early feedback since Burtonwood's recent takeover of this 17th-c coaching inn suggests very little has changed, and readers have found the new landlady pleasantly helpful. Some of the former landlord's memorabilia left with him, but the bustling bar is still packed with hundreds of jugs and mugs hanging from the beams, and brewery and railway memorabilia and advertisements and other bric-a-brac still cover the walls (even in the lavatories). Half a dozen well kept real ales on handpump include Bass, Burtonwood Top Hat and Marstons Pedigree, with a couple of guests such as Marston Moor Cromwell and Moorhouses Black Cat, and they have a nice choice of malt whiskies; fruit machine and piped music. Bar food with good specials, and puddings such as chocolate sponge and spotted dick; best to book for Sunday lunch. Handy for the A6 as well as the M1, the pub was once a deportation point for convicts bound for the colonies.

Burtonwood ~ Tenant Monique Johns ~ Real ale ~ Bar food (lunchtime) ~ Restaurant ~ (01332) 792392 ~ Children welcome ~ Dogs allowed in bar ~ Open 11-11; 12-10.30 Sun; 11-3, 5-11 winter; 12-3, 7-10.30 Sun winter ~ Bedrooms: £35S/£45S

SHELDON
Cock & Pullet *Village signposted off A6 just W of Ashford*

The flagstoned bar of this popular place feels as if it's been here for centuries, so it's quite a surprise to discover that the building was converted into a pub only ten years ago. The friendly family that run it have created a proper traditional village local, taking great pains to include the sort of mismatched furnishings and features that other pubs have taken decades to amass. As well as low beams, exposed stonework, and scrubbed oak tables and pews, the small, cosy rooms have 24 fully working clocks (one for every hour of the day), whose decorous chimes further add to the relaxed, peaceful atmosphere. Well kept Bass, Black Sheep, and Timothy Taylors Landlord on handpump. As well as good sandwiches and a choice of popular Sunday roasts, dishes on the shortish menu are highly praised by readers. A fireplace is filled with flowers in summer, and around it are various representations of poultry, including some stuffed. A plainer room has pool and a TV; there's also a no smoking snug. At the back is a pleasant little terrace with tables and a water feature. The pub is a year-round favourite with walkers (it can be busy at weekends); the pretty village is just off the Limestone Way.

Free house ~ Licensees David and Kath Melland ~ Real ale ~ Bar food (12-2.30, 6-9) ~ (01629) 814292 ~ Children welcome ~ Dogs allowed in bar ~ Open 11-11; 12-10.30 Sun; closed 25 Dec ~ Bedrooms: £30S/£55S

WARDLOW
Three Stags Heads *Wardlow Mires; A623 by junction with B6465*

One reader was delighted to find five customers, eight dogs and two blazing fires on his Sunday lunchtime visit to this simple but friendly white-painted cottage. Genuinely traditional, this is a real find if you like your pubs basic and full of character, and enjoy a chat with friendly locals at the bar. It's situated in a natural sink, so don't be surprised to find the floors muddied by boots in wet weather (and the dogs even muddier). Warmed right through by a cast-iron kitchen range, the tiny flagstoned parlour bar has old leathercloth seats, a couple of antique settles with flowery cushions, two high-backed windsor armchairs and simple oak tables (look out for the petrified cat in a glass case). Four well kept real ales on handpump are Abbeydale Absolution, Black Lurcher (brewed for the pub at a hefty 8% ABV) and Matins, and Broadstone Charter Ale; they've lots of bottled continental and english beers (the stronger ones aren't cheap), and in winter they do a roaring trade in mugs of steaming tea – there might be free hot chestnuts on the bar; cribbage and dominoes, nine men's morris and backgammon. Food is hearty and home-made, and the seasonal menu notably countrified; the hardy plates are home-made (the barn is a pottery workshop). You can book the tables in the small no smoking dining parlour. The front terrace looks across the main road to the distant hills. Please note the opening times.

Free house ~ Licensees Geoff and Pat Fuller ~ Real ale ~ Bar food ~ No credit cards ~ (01298) 872268 ~ Dogs welcome ~ Folk music most Sat evenings and alternate Fri ~ Open 7-11 Fri; 12-11 Sat, Sun and bank hols; closed Mon-Thu

WOOLLEY MOOR
White Horse *Badger Lane, off B6014 Matlock—Clay Cross*
A very good play area with a wooden train, boat, climbing frame and swings, and a puzzle sheet and crayons with their meal means children are well catered for at this attractive old pub. It's in a delightful spot and picnic-sets in the well maintained garden (with its own boules pitch) have lovely views across the Amber Valley. A sign outside shows how horses and carts carried measures of salt along the toll road in front – the toll bar cottage still stands at the entrance of Badger Lane (a badger was the haulier who transported the salt). Still very much in its original state, the bustling tap room has a pleasant chatty atmosphere, well kept Adnams Broadside and Black Sheep and a changing guest such as Fullers London Pride; decent wines too, and efficient friendly service. There is piped music in the lounge and no smoking conservatory (great views of the Ogston reservoir from here). Bar food is enjoyable, good value and generously served; home-made puddings include a changing cheesecake and chocolate and Baileys mousse. It's best to book for the linen-laid restaurant.

Musketeers ~ Managers Keith Hurst and Forest Kimble ~ Real ale ~ Bar food (12-2, 6-9; 12-7 Sun; not Sun evening) ~ Restaurant ~ (01246) 590319 ~ Children welcome away from tap room ~ Dogs allowed in bar ~ Live music last Fri in month ~ Open 12-3, 6-11; 12-10.30 Sun

Dog Friendly Hotels, B&Bs and Farms

ASHBOURNE
Callow Hall *Mappleton Rd, Ashbourne, Derbyshire DE6 2AA* (01335) 300900 £130, plus special breaks; 16 lovely well furnished rms, excellent bthrms. Quietly smart and friendly Victorian mansion up a long drive through grounds with fine trees and surrounded by marvellous countryside; comfortable drawing room with open fire, fresh flowers and plants, and period furniture, very good traditional food using home-grown produce in warmly decorated dining room, excellent breakfasts, and kind hosts; good private fishing; cl 25-26 Dec; disabled access; dogs welcome in bedrooms

BAKEWELL

Hassop Hall *Hassop, Bakewell, Derbyshire DE45 1NS (01629) 640488*
£94, plus winter breaks; 13 gracious rms. Mentioned in the Domesday
Book, in lovely parkland surrounded by fine scenery, this handsome hotel
has antiques and oil paintings, an elegant drawing room, oak-panelled bar,
good food and friendly service; tennis; no accommodation 3 nights over
Christmas; partial disabled access; dogs welcome in bedrooms by prior
arrangement

BIGGIN-BY-HARTINGTON

Biggin Hall *Biggin-by-Hartington, Buxton, Derbyshire SK17 0DH (01298)
84451* £76, plus special breaks; 20 spacious rms with antiques, some in
converted 18th-c stone building and in bothy. Cheerfully run 17th-c house
in quiet grounds with a very relaxed atmosphere, two comfortable sitting
rooms, log fires; freshly cooked straightforward food with an emphasis on
free-range wholefoods served at 7pm in the attractive dining room, and
packed lunches if wanted; children 12 and over; limited disabled access;
dogs welcome in annexe only, by arrangement

BIRCH VALE

Waltzing Weasel *New Mills Rd, Birch Vale, High Peak, Derbyshire SK22
1BT (01663) 743402* £78; 8 lovely rms. Attractive traditional inn with
open fire, some handsome furnishings, daily papers and plants in quiet
civilised bar, very good food using the best seasonal produce in charming
back restaurant (fine views), excellent puddings and cheeses, obliging
service; children over 7 in restaurant; disabled access; dogs in bedrooms and
bar

DOVE DALE

Peveril of the Peak *Thorpe, Ashbourne, Derbyshire DE6 2AW (08704)
008109* £110, plus special breaks; 46 rms. Relaxing hotel in pretty village
amidst some of the finest scenery in the Peak District and with 11 acres of
grounds; comfortable sofas and log fire in spacious lounge, modern bar and
attractive restaurant overlooking the garden, friendly staff, and good english
cooking; tennis; wonderful walking nearby; disabled access; dogs welcome
away from restaurant

GRINDLEFORD

Maynard Arms *Main Rd, Nether Padley, Grindleford, Hope Valley,
Derbyshire S32 2HE (01433) 630321* £85, plus special breaks; 10 rms.
Comfortable hotel with log fire and good Peak District views from the
first-floor lounge, smart welcoming bar, good choice of food, popular
evening restaurant, and particularly attentive service; good walks nearby;
disabled access; dogs welcome in bedrooms

HOPE

Underleigh House *Edale Rd, Hope, Castleton, Derbyshire S33 6RF
(01433) 621372* £69, plus special breaks; 6 thoughtfully decorated rms. In

unspoilt countryside, this spotlessly kept converted barn has fine views from the comfortable sitting room, hearty breakfasts with good home-made preserves enjoyed around communal table in flagstoned dining room, friendly cheerful owners, attractive gardens; terrific walks on the doorstep, packed lunches can be arranged; cl Christmas and New Year; children over 12; dogs by prior arrangement

KIRK IRETON

Barley Mow *Kirk Ireton, Ashbourne, Derbyshire DE6 3JP (01335) 370306* £50; 5 rms. Tall, Jacobean, walkers' inn with lots of woodwork in series of interconnecting bar rooms, a solid-fuel stove in beamed residents' sitting room, and well kept real ales; close to Carsington Reservoir; cl Christmas and New Year; dogs in one ground-floor room

MATLOCK

Riber Hall *Matlock, Derbyshire DE4 5JU (01629) 582795* £136, plus special breaks; 14 lovely beamed rms. Elizabethan manor house in pretty grounds surrounded by peaceful countryside, with antique-filled heavily beamed rooms, fresh flowers, two elegant dining rooms with enjoyable food and fine wines, and tennis and croquet; dogs welcome in bedrooms; £5

MONSAL HEAD

Monsal Head Hotel *Monsal Head, Buxton, Derbyshire DE45 1NL (01629) 640250* £50, plus special breaks; 7 very good rms, some with lovely views. Comfortable and enjoyable small hotel in marvellous setting high above the River Wye, with horsey theme in bar (converted from old stables), freshly prepared decent food using seasonal produce, and good service; cl 25 Dec; dogs welcome in bedrooms and part of pub; £5

ROWSLEY

Peacock *Rowsley, Matlock, Derbyshire DE4 2EB (01629) 733518* £125, plus special breaks; 16 comfortable rms. Smart 17th-c country house hotel by River Derwent (private fishing in season), with well kept gardens, friendly staff, interesting and pleasant old-fashioned inner bar, spacious and comfortable lounge, and very popular restaurant; dogs welcome in bedrooms; £5

Devon

Dog Friendly Pubs

ASHPRINGTON

Durant Arms *Village signposted off A381 S of Totnes; OS Sheet 202 map reference 819571*

Run by charming and helpful licensees who really care. Readers have very much enjoyed their visits – as somewhere to spend a few nights, for a particularly good meal out, and as a place for a drink and a chat in the spotless bar. The beamed open-plan bar has several open fires, lamps and horsebrasses, fresh flowers, and a mix of seats and tables on the red patterned carpet; there's a lower carpeted lounge too, with another open fire. With quite an emphasis on dining and all the food cooked to order, there might be good liver and onions or spinach and mushroom lasagne, and home-made puddings such as blackberry and apple pie; best to book if you want to be sure of a table. The no smoking dining room has lots of oils and watercolours by local artists on the walls. Good, attentive service. St Austell Dartmoor Best and Tribute on handpump, and Luscombe cider; no games machines but they do have piped music. The back terrace has wooden garden furniture and there's a water feature.

Free house ~ Licensees Graham and Eileen Ellis ~ Real ale ~ Bar food ~ Restaurant ~ (01803) 732240 ~ Children in family room ~ Dogs allowed in bar ~ Open 11.30-2.30, 6.30-11; 12-2.30, 7-10.30 Sun ~ Bedrooms: £40B/£70B

BRANSCOMBE

Masons Arms *Main Street; signposted off A3052 Sidmouth—Seaton, then bear left into village*

This thatched 14th-c longhouse is set in a village surrounded by little wooded hills in National Trust territory, and close to the sea. At its heart is the rambling low-beamed main bar with a massive central hearth in front of the roaring log fire (spit roasts on Tuesday and Sunday lunch and Friday evenings), windsor chairs and settles, slate floors, ancient ships' beams, and a bustling atmosphere created by a good mix of customers. The no smoking Old Worthies bar also has a slate floor, a fireplace with a two-sided woodburning stove, and woodwork that has been stripped back to the original pine. There's also the original no smoking restaurant (warmed by one side of the woodburning stove), and the newer Waterfall Restaurant, set slightly away from the pub, and with an open kitchen so you can watch the chefs at work (closed on Sunday and Monday evenings). Using as much local and organic produce as possible, the very good bar food includes lunchtime sandwiches, panini with fillings, bisque of local crab, confit of duck leg with spiced pickled red cabbage, pot-roasted local pheasant, daily specials, and puddings like dark chocolate crème brûlée; children's meals available too. Well kept Bass, Otter Ale and Bitter, and a couple of guests from maybe Branscombe Vale or Cotleigh on handpump; they hold a popular beer festival in July, and keep 33 malt whiskies, 15 wines by the glass, and local farm cider. Occasional darts. Outside, the quiet flower-filled front terrace has tables with little thatched roofs, extending into a side garden. Writing so enthusiastically about this favourite pub naturally focuses a great deal of attention on it. This last year, merciless scrutiny has shown up occasional shortcomings in service, but we should stress that the overall picture is still very positive.

Free house ~ Licensees Murray Inglis, Mark Thompson, and Tim Manktelow-Gray ~ Real ale ~ Bar food ~ Restaurant ~ (01297) 680300 ~ Children in eating area of bar ~ Dogs allowed in bar ~ Occasional live duo ~ Open 11-11; 12-10.30 Sun; 11-3, 6-11 in winter ~ Bedrooms: £30(£60B)/£50(£100B)

BROADHEMBURY

Drewe Arms *Signposted off A373 Cullompton—Honiton*

In the 16 years Mr and Mrs Burge have run this fine old pub, we've never had a poor report, and with their son Andrew now in charge of the kitchen, we hope this can continue. It's a civilised but friendly place and a favourite with a great many readers, and despite the emphasis on the marvellous fish dishes, the small bar area has kept its lovely local chatty atmosphere so that anyone walking in for just a drink would not feel at all out of place. The bar has neatly carved beams in its high ceiling, and handsome stone-mullioned windows (one with a small carved roundabout horse), and on the left, a high-backed stripped settle separates off a little room with flowers on the three sturdy country tables, plank-panelled walls painted brown below and yellow above with attractive engravings and prints, and a big black-painted fireplace with bric-a-brac on a high mantelpiece; some wood carvings, walking sticks, and framed watercolours for sale. The flagstoned entry has a narrow corridor of a room by the servery with a couple of tables, and the cellar bar has simple pews on the stone floor; the dining room is no smoking. The food is unfailingly good with daily specials such as spicy crab soup, warm salmon salad, whole langoustines, wing of skate with black butter, and sea bream; some meaty choices too and excellent seasonal partridge; puddings like bread pudding with whisky butter sauce. Best to book to be sure of a table. Well kept Otter Bitter, Ale, and Bright tapped from the cask, and a very good wine list laid out extremely helpfully – including quite a few by the glass. There are picnic-sets in the lovely garden which has a lawn stretching back under the shadow of chestnut trees towards a church with its singularly melodious hour-bell. Thatched and very pretty, the 15th-c pub is in a charming village of similar cream-coloured cottages.

Free house ~ Licensees Kerstin and Nigel Burge ~ Real ale ~ Bar food (not Sun evening) ~ Restaurant ~ (01404) 841267 ~ Well behaved children in eating area of bar ~ Dogs allowed in bar ~ Open 11-3, 6-11; 12-3 Sun; closed Sun evening, 25 and 31 Dec

BUCKLAND BREWER

Coach & Horses *Village signposted off A388 S of Monkleigh; OS Sheet 190 map reference 423206*

The heavily beamed bar in this 13th-c thatched house has a bustling pubby atmosphere, comfortable seats (including a handsome antique settle), a woodburning stove in the inglenook, and maybe Harding the friendly cat – who is now 18; a good log fire also burns in the big stone inglenook of the cosy lounge. A small back room has darts and pool. Bar food includes home-made curries, daily specials such as stilton, spinach and mushroom pasta bake, and locally caught skate, and puddings like lemon and lime mousse. The restaurant is no smoking. Well kept Bass, Fullers London Pride, and a guest beer on handpump; dominoes, fruit machine, skittle alley, and piped music. There are tables on a terrace in front, and in the side garden. Please note, they no longer offer bed and breakfast.

Free house ~ Licensees Oliver Wolfe and Nicola Barrass ~ Real ale ~ Bar food (not 25 Dec or evening 26 Dec) ~ Restaurant ~ (01237) 451395 ~ Children welcome ~ Dogs allowed in bar ~ Open 12-3, 6-11; 12-3, 7-10.30 Sun

BUCKLAND MONACHORUM

Drake Manor *Off A386 via Crapstone, just S of Yelverton roundabout*

Near Buckland Abbey and the lovely Garden House, this charming little pub is popular with locals and visitors. The heavily beamed public bar on the left has brocade-cushioned wall seats, prints of the village from 1905 onwards, some horse tack and a few ship badges on the wall, and a really big stone fireplace with a woodburning stove; a small door leads to a low-beamed cubby hole where children are allowed. The snug Drake's Bar has beams hung with tiny cups and big brass keys, a woodburning stove in an old stone fireplace hung with horsebrasses and stirrups, a fine stripped pine high-backed settle with a partly covered hood, and a mix of other seats around just four tables (the oval one is rather nice). On the right is a small, beamed no smoking dining room with settles and tables on the flagstoned floor. Shove-ha'penny, darts, euchre, dominoes and fruit machine. Enjoyable bar food includes lunchtime baguettes as well as soup, crab cakes, home-made steak and kidney pie or roasted vegetable and feta filo tart; daily specials too. Well kept Courage Best, Greene King Abbot and Sharps Doom Bar on handpump, around 70 malt whiskies, and a decent wine list with nine by the glass. The floral displays at the front of the building are very attractive all year round, and the sheltered back garden – where there are picnic-sets – is prettily planted.

Innspired Inns ~ Lease Mandy Robinson ~ Real ale ~ Bar food (12-2, 7-10(9.30 Sun)) ~ Restaurant ~ (01822) 853892 ~ Children in restaurant and in small area off main bar ~ Dogs allowed in bar ~ Open 11.30-2.30(3 Sat), 6.30-11; 12-3, 7-10.30 Sun

CHERITON BISHOP
Old Thatch Inn *Village signposted from A30*

Friendly, professional new licensees have taken over this 16th-c pub and are very keen to keep a strong emphasis on both drinks and food, and not to be thought of as a restaurant with a bar. The lounge and the rambling beamed bar (the only place where you can smoke) are separated by a large open stone fireplace (lit in the cooler months), and have Adnams Broadside, Otter Ale, Sharps Doom Bar, and a guest like Princetown Jail Ale on handpump; several wines by the glass. The daily specials are interesting and popular: home-made carrot and coriander soup, gateau of fresh local crab and cucumber with lemon mayonnaise, and pheasant breast wrapped in bacon and cranberry sauce. Also, lunchtime sandwiches or baguettes, and home-made puddings like hot chocolate brownie or rhubarb crumble. The family room leads onto the terrace with a thatched water well; piped music.

Free house ~ Licensees David and Serena London ~ Real ale ~ Bar food ~ Restaurant ~ (01647) 24204 ~ Children in eating area of bar, restaurant and family room ~ Dogs allowed in bar ~ Open 11.30-3, 6-11; 12-3, 7-10.30 Sun; closed winter Sun evenings ~ Bedrooms: £39B/£60B

CLAYHIDON
Merry Harriers *3 miles from M5 junction 26: head towards Wellington; turn left at 1st roundabout signposted Ford Street and Hemyock, then after a mile turn left signposted Ford Street; at hilltop T-junction, turn left towards Chard – pub is 1½ miles on right*

Customers do drop into this charmingly laid out dining pub for just a drink and feel quite comfortable doing so, although there is no doubt that there is quite a strong emphasis on the good restauranty food. As well as lunchtime sandwiches, the enjoyable dishes might include Brixham scallops in thyme and garlic butter, hand-carved ham with free-range eggs, local squash and vegetable curry, local steaks, confit of Quantock duck on onion marmalade, and home-made puddings. Several small linked green-carpeted areas have comfortably cushioned pews and farmhouse chairs, lit candles in bottles, a woodburning stove with a sofa beside it, and plenty of horsey and hunting prints and local wildlife pictures. Two dining areas have a brighter feel with quarry tiles and lightly timbered white walls. You can only smoke in the bar area; dominoes and chess. Well kept Juwards (Moor) Bishops Somerset Ale, Cotleigh Barn Owl, and Otter Head on handpump, 10 wines by the glass, several bottled belgian beers, 18 malt whiskies, and local Bollhayes farm cider and apple juice. There are two dogs, Annie who likes real ale, and Nipper who only has three legs. Picnic-sets on a small terrace, with more in a sizeable garden sheltered by shrubs and the old skittle alley; this is a good walking area. No children except on Sunday lunchtimes and must be over 6. More reports please.

Free house ~ Licensees Barry and Chris Kift ~ Real ale ~ Bar food (not Sun evening or Mon) ~ Restaurant ~ (01823) 421270 ~ Dogs allowed in bar ~ Open 12-3, 7-11; 12-3 Sun; closed Sun evening, Mon

COCKWOOD

Anchor *Off, but visible from, A379 Exeter—Torbay*

Even on a chilly midweek day in winter, you have to arrive early at this extremely popular fishy place to get a table – and there's usually a queue to get in. They do two sittings in the restaurant on winter weekends and every evening in summer to cope with the crowds. There are 30 different ways of serving mussels, 14 ways of serving scallops, 10 ways of serving oysters, and four 'cakes' such as crab cakes or mussel cakes. Non-fishy dishes feature as well, including home-made steak and kidney pudding, and children's dishes. But despite the emphasis on food, there's still a pubby atmosphere, and they keep six real ales on handpump or tapped from the cask: Bass, Fullers London Pride, Greene King Abbot and Old Speckled Hen, Otter Ale and Wadworths 6X. Also, a rather good wine list (12 by the glass – they do monthly wine tasting evenings September-June), 30 brandies, 90 malt whiskies, and west country cider. The small, low-ceilinged, rambling rooms have black panelling, good-sized tables in various alcoves, and a cheerful winter coal fire in the snug; the cosy restaurant is no smoking. Darts, dominoes, cribbage, fruit machine and piped music. From the tables on the sheltered verandah you can look across the road to the bobbing yachts and crabbing boats in the harbour.

Heavitree ~ Tenants Mr Morgan and Miss Sanders ~ Real ale ~ Bar food (12-3, 6.30-10(9.30 Sun)) ~ Restaurant ~ (01626) 890203 ~ Children in restaurant ~ Dogs allowed in bar ~ Open 11-11; 12-10.30 Sun; closed evening 25 Dec

COLEFORD

New Inn *Just off A377 Crediton—Barnstaple*

It is not easy to get the balance right between a proper pub, a good restaurant, and a comfortable, well equipped inn, but this 13th-c place seems to have mastered it. It's an L-shaped building with the servery in the 'angle', and interestingly furnished areas leading off it: ancient and modern settles, spindleback chairs, plush-cushioned stone wall seats, some character tables – a pheasant worked into the grain of one – and carved dressers and chests; also, paraffin lamps, antique prints and old guns on the white walls, and landscape plates on one of the beams, with pewter tankards on another. The resident parrot Captain is chatty and entertaining. Good, interesting food using local produce, daily specials, and puddings. The restaurant is no smoking. Well kept Badger Best, Ring O' Bells Bodmin Boar, and a guest beer on handpump, and quite a range of malt whiskies, ports and cognacs. Fruit machine (out of the way up by the door),and piped music. There are chairs, tables and umbrellas on decking under the willow tree along the stream, and more on the terrace.

Free house ~ Licensees Paul and Irene Butt ~ Real ale ~ Bar food (till 10(9.30 Sun)) ~ Restaurant ~ (01363) 84242 ~ Children in eating area of bar and in restaurant ~ Dogs allowed in bar ~ Open 12-2.30, 6-11; 12-3, 7-10.30 Sun; closed 25 and 26 Dec ~ Bedrooms: £60B/£75B

CULMSTOCK
Culm Valley *B3391, off A38 E of M5 junction 27*

Interesting and even a little quirky (the landlord's own words), this village inn at first glance looks a bit scruffy. Inside, it's actually rather civilised and run by accommodating and friendly people. The licensee and his brother import wines from smaller french vineyards, so you can count on a few of those (they offer 50 wines by the glass), as well as some unusual french fruit liqueurs, Somerset cider brandies, good sherries and madeira, local ciders, and an excellent range of real ales tapped from the cask. You'll usually find between five and nine mostly local brews, such as Archers Spirit of St George, Cotleigh Cuckoo or Peregrine, Glastonbury Excalibur, O'Hanlons Yellowhammer, Otter Bright, and Teignworthy Old Moggie, but the choice can swell to 17 during their occasional beer festivals. The very good bar food usually comes with a choice of helping size; their tapas are very popular. There's a good thriving mix of locals and visitors in the salmon-coloured bar, which has well worn upholstered chairs and stools, a big fireplace with some china above it, newspapers, and a long stripped wooden bar counter; further along is a dining room with chalkboard menu, and a small room at the front. Cribbage and dominoes. Old photographs show how the railway line used to run through what's now the car park. Outside, tables are very attractively set overlooking the bridge and the River Culm. The gents' are in an outside yard.

Free house ~ Licensee Richard Hartley ~ Real ale ~ Bar food (may not do food Sun evenings) ~ Restaurant ~ No credit cards ~ (01884) 840354 ~ Children welcome away from bar ~ Dogs welcome ~ Open 12-3, 6-11(10.30 Sun); poss all day in good weather ~ Bedrooms: £30B/£55B

DOLTON
Union *B3217*

New licensees took over this pleasant village inn just before we went to press, so we are keeping our fingers crossed that things won't change too much. The little lounge bar has a cushioned window seat, two cushioned benches, and some dark pine country chairs with brocaded cushions, as well as dagging shears, tack, country prints and brass shell cases. On the right, and served by the same stone bar counter, is another bar with a chatty atmosphere and liked by locals: heavy black beams hung with brasses, antique housekeepers' chairs, a small settle snugged into the wall, and various dining chairs on the squared patterned carpet; the big stone fireplace has some brass around it, and on the walls are two land-felling saws, antlers, some engravings and a whip. Bar food includes sandwiches and various home-made hot dishes; the restaurant is no smoking. Well kept St Austell Tribute and Teignworthy Reel Ale on handpump, and decent wines; piped music. Outside on a small patch of grass in front of the building are some rustic tables and chairs. More reports on the new regime, please.

Free house ~ Licensees Mr P Thomas, Miss A Thomas, and Mrs D Thomas ~ Real ale ~ Bar food (not Weds) ~ Restaurant ~ (01805) 804633 ~ Children in eating area of bar and restaurant ~ Dogs allowed in bar and bedrooms ~ Open 11-3, 6-11; 12-10.30 Sun; closed Wednesdays ~ Bedrooms: £35S/£55S(£65B)

EAST BUDLEIGH
Sir Walter Raleigh *High St*
In a pretty thatch-and-cob village, this charming pub is run by a warmly welcoming licensee. There's a low-beamed bar with lots of books on shelves, a cosily chatty atmosphere, and well kept Adnams Broadside, Otter Bitter and Charles Wells Bombardier on handpump; reasonably priced wines. The attractive restaurant down a step from the bar is no smoking. Lunchtime bar food is very good and using fresh local produce might include home-made sausages, extremely popular steak and kidney pie, plenty of local fish such as sole, plaice, bass, lobster and crab, and home-made puddings like bakewell tart. There's a fine church with a unique collection of carved oak bench ends, and the pub is handy for Bicton Park gardens. Raleigh himself was born at nearby Hayes Barton, and educated in a farmhouse 300 yards away. Parking is about 100 yards away. No children.
Enterprise ~ Lease Lindsay Mason ~ Real ale ~ Bar food (lunchtime) ~ Restaurant ~ (01395) 442510 ~ Dogs allowed in bar ~ Open 12-3, 6-11; 12-3, 7-10.30 Sun

EXMINSTER
Turf Hotel *Follow the signs to the Swan's Nest, signposted from A739 S of village, then continue to end of track, by gates; park, and walk right along canal towpath – nearly a mile; there's a fine sea view out to the mudflats at low tide*
The cheerful, caring licensees of this isolated pub work really hard to make this the friendly place it is. On a lovely sunny day, a trip here makes a really memorable day out. You cannot reach it by car. You must either walk (which takes about 20 minutes along the ship canal) or cycle, and there's a 60-seater boat which brings people down the Exe estuary from Topsham quay (15-minute trip, adults £3, child £2); there's also a canal boat from Countess Wear Swing Bridge every lunchtime. Best to phone the pub for all sailing times. For those arriving in their own boat there is a large pontoon as well as several moorings. The decking area with outdoor rotisserie for chicken and pig roasts and outside bar is very popular. Inside, the pleasantly airy bar has church pews, wooden chairs and alcove seats on the polished bare floorboards, and pictures and old photographs of the pub and its characters over the years on the walls; woodburning stove and antique gas fire. From the bay windows there are views out to the mudflats (full of gulls and waders at low tide). Good bar food (using as much local produce as possible) includes a big choice of sandwiches, toasties and filled baked potatoes; puddings too. The dining room is no smoking. Well kept Otter Bitter, Bright, and Ale, and a guest beer on handpump, Green Valley and Dragon Tears farm ciders, locally pressed apple juice, and cappuccino and espresso coffee; cribbage, dominoes and piped music. The garden has a children's play area built using a lifeboat from a liner that sank off the Scilly Isles around 100 years ago. Please note, they no longer do bedrooms, though you could hire their Red Indian teepee.
Free house ~ Licensees Clive and Ginny Redfern ~ Real ale ~ Bar food (12-2.30(3 summer), 7-9.30; not Sun evening) ~ (01392) 833128 ~ Children welcome ~ Dogs welcome ~ Open 11.30-11; 11.30-10.30 Sun; closed Nov-Feb

HARBERTON
Church House *Village signposted from A381 just S of Totnes*
Parts of this ancient village pub may in fact be Norman and some of the
oldest sections have benefited from being hidden for centuries. The open-
plan bar has some magnificent medieval oak panelling, and the latticed glass
on the back wall is almost 700 years old and one of the earliest examples of
non-ecclesiastical glass in the country. Furnishings include attractive 17th-
and 18th-c pews and settles, candles, and a large inglenook fireplace with a
woodburning stove; one half of the room is set out for eating. The family
room is no smoking. Under the new licensee, bar food includes home-
made soup, garlic and cheese mushrooms, local sausages, salads, fresh fillet
of plaice, and local rump steak. Well kept Butcombe Bitter, Courage Best,
Marstons Pedigree and St Austell Tribute on handpump, farm cider, 14
wines by the glass, and several malt whiskies; piped music, darts, cribbage
and dominoes. More reports please.
*Coast & Country Inns ~ Licensee Martin Ward ~ Real ale ~ Bar food ~ (01803)
863707 ~ Children in family room ~ Dogs welcome ~ Open 12-2.30(3 Sat), 6-
11; 12-3, 7-11 Sun ~ Bedrooms: £30B/£60B*

HOLNE
Church House *signposted off B3357 W of Ashburton*
There are fine moorland views from the pillared porch here (where
regulars tend to gather), and plenty of surrounding walks – the short
quarter-hour one from the Newbridge National Trust car park to the pub
is rather fine. Inside, the lower bar has stripped pine panelling and an 18th-c
curved elm settle, and is separated from the lounge bar by a 16th-c
heavy oak partition; open log fires in both rooms. Bar food includes
lunchtime filled baked potatoes, sandwiches and baguettes, home-made
pâté, and favourites like steak in ale pie or rabbit casserole; more elaborate
choices in the evening. The restaurant and eating area of the bar are no
smoking. Well kept Butcombe Bitter, Summerskills Best Bitter, and
Teignworthy Reel Ale on handpump, a dozen wines by the glass, and
organic cider, apple juice and ginger beer; darts. Morris men and clog
dancers in the summer. Charles Kingsley (of *The Water Babies* fame) was
born in the village.
*Free house ~ Licensee J Silk ~ Real ale ~ Bar food ~ Restaurant ~ (01364)
631208 ~ Children in eating area of bar and restaurant ~ Dogs welcome ~ Open
12-2.30(3 Sat), 7-11(10.30 in winter); 12-3, 7-10.30 Sun; closed Mon in
winter ~ Bedrooms: £33S/£55(£66B)*

HORNDON
Elephants Nest *If coming from Okehampton on A386 turn left at Mary Tavy
Inn, then left after about ½ mile; pub signposted beside Mary Tavy Inn, then
Horndon signposted; on the Ordnance Survey Outdoor Leisure Map it's named as
the New Inn*
This is an isolated old pub on the lower slopes of Dartmoor, with benches
on the spacious lawn in front that look over dry-stone walls to the pastures
and the rougher moorland above; they have their own cricket pitch. Inside,

the bar has a good log fire, flagstones, and a beams-and-board ceiling; there are two other rooms plus a no smoking dining room and garden room. Well kept Palmers IPA and Copper and St Austell HSD, and a guest such as Exmoor Gold, Otter Bright or Teignworthy Beachcomber on handpump, 10 wines by the glass, farm cider, and proper tea and coffee; friendly service. Enjoyable bar food includes home-made soup, local cheese and biscuits, home-made sausage with onion gravy, pink bream in wine and cream, home-made puddings, and a choice of Sunday roasts; children's dishes too.

Free house ~ Licensee Peter Wolfes ~ Real ale ~ Bar food (12-2.15, 6.30-9) ~ (01822) 810273 ~ Children in dining room only ~ Dogs allowed in bar ~ Folk music 1st and 3rd Weds of month ~ Open 12-3, 6.30-11; closed Sun evening, all day Mon

IDDESLEIGH
Duke of York B3217 Exbourne—Dolton

This is a smashing pub and very much enjoyed by a good mix of customers. The bar is full of friendly locals (plenty of chat and no noisy games machines or piped music), the food is first rate, and it's a nice place to stay with excellent breakfasts. The bar has a lot of character, with rocking chairs by the roaring log fire, cushioned wall benches built into the wall's black-painted wooden dado, stripped tables, and other homely country furnishings, and well kept Adnams Broadside, Cotleigh Tawny, and a guest such as Sharps Doom Bar tapped from the cask; freshly squeezed orange and pink grapefruit juice, and 10 wines by the glass. Generous helpings of good bar food includes sandwiches, grilled or battered fish and chips, delicious scallops wrapped in smoked bacon or crab mayonnaise, vegetable korma, and double lamb chop with rosemary and garlic gravy; it can get a bit cramped at peak times. Cribbage, dominoes, shove-ha'penny and darts. Through a small coach arch is a little back garden with some picnic-sets. Fishing nearby.

Free house ~ Licensees Jamie Stuart and Pippa Hutchinson ~ Real ale ~ Bar food (all day) ~ Restaurant ~ (01837) 810253 ~ Children welcome ~ Dogs welcome ~ Open 11-11; 12-10.30 Sun ~ Bedrooms: £30B/£60B

LOWER ASHTON
Manor Inn Ashton signposted off B3193 N of Chudleigh

Particularly at weekends, it's best to book ahead to be sure of a table in this popular creeper-covered pub. There's a good mix of customers, although the left-hand room with its beer mats and brewery advertisements on the walls is more for locals enjoying the well kept Princetown Jail Ale, RCH Pitchfork, Teignworthy Reel Ale, and a constantly changing guest on handpump; 10 wines by the glass and local cider. On the right, two rather more discreet rooms have a wider appeal, bolstered by the good, popular home-made food which might include lots of filled baked potatoes, home-made burgers with various toppings, home-cooked ham and egg or beef and mushroom in ale, plus a good choice of changing specials such as vegetable and nut curry; puddings available as well. Shove-ha'penny. The

garden has lots of picnic-sets under cocktail parasols (and a fine tall Scots pine), and pretty hanging baskets. No children inside.
Free house ~ Licensees Geoff and Clare Mann ~ Real ale ~ Bar food (12-1.30, 7-9.30; not Mon exc bank hols) ~ (01647) 252304 ~ Dogs welcome ~ Open 12-2(2.30 Sat), 6.30-11; 12-2.30, 7-10.30 Sun; closed Mon (exc bank hols)

LUSTLEIGH
Cleave *Village signposted off A382 Bovey Tracey—Moretonhampstead*
As this delightful thatched 15th-c pub is deservedly popular with walkers, it's best to arrive around midday to avoid a bit of a wait at the bar. The low-ceilinged no smoking lounge bar has attractive antique high-backed settles, cushioned wall seats, and wheelback chairs around the tables on its patterned carpet, granite walls, and a roaring log fire. A second bar has similar furnishings, a large dresser, harmonium, an HMV gramophone, and prints, and the no smoking family room has crayons, books and toys for children. Good bar food listed on daily changing boards might includehome-made smoked mackerel pâté, local sausages, popular home-made steak and kidney in stout pie, and half a honey-roast duckling; the dining room is no smoking. Well kept Greene King Abbot, Otter Ale and Wadworths 6X on handpump kept under light blanket pressure, quite a few malt whiskies, and a dozen wines by the glass. The sheltered garden is neat and very pretty, and the summer hanging baskets and flowerbeds are lovely. Until the car parking field in the village is opened during the summer, parking can be very difficult.
Heavitree ~ Tenant A Perring ~ Real ale ~ Bar food ~ Restaurant ~ (01647) 277223 ~ Children in family room ~ Dogs welcome ~ Open 11-3, 6.30-11; 11.30-3, 6.30-10.30 Sun; closed Mon Oct-Mar

LYDFORD
Castle Inn *Off A386 Okehampton—Tavistock*
After a walk in the beautiful nearby river gorge (owned by the National Trust; closed November-Easter), this pink-washed Tudor inn is a relaxing place for a refreshing drink. It has a lot of character and charm, and the twin-roomed bar has country kitchen chairs, high-backed winged settles and old captains' chairs around mahogany tripod tables on big slate flagstones. One of the rooms has low lamp-lit beams, a sizeable open fire, masses of brightly decorated plates, some Hogarth prints, and, near the serving counter, seven Lydford pennies hammered out in the old Saxon mint in the reign of Ethelred the Unready, in the 11th century. The bar area has a bowed ceiling with low beams, a polished slate flagstone floor, and a stained-glass door with the famous Three Hares; there's a snug with high-backed settles which is used by families. Good, enjoyable bar food includes stuffed mushrooms, ploughman's or greek salad, home-made lasagne, home-cooked ham with an apricot and mango sauce, a pie of the day, and breast of local duckling. Well kept Fullers London Pride, Otter Ale and Wadworths 6X on handpump, and 11 wines by the glass; piped music, darts, cribbage and dominoes.
Heavitree ~ Tenant Richard Davies ~ Real ale ~ Bar food ~ Restaurant ~

*(01822) 820241 ~ Children in restaurant ~ Dogs allowed in bar and bedrooms ~
Open 11.30-11; 12-10.30 Sun ~ Bedrooms: £45B/£65B*

Dartmoor Inn *Downton, on A386*

There's no doubt that most customers in this well run and very popular
place are here to enjoy the exceptionally good food, but locals and
weekend walkers do drop into the small bar for a pint of well kept Fullers
London Pride, Otter Ale or St Austell Dartmoor Best on handpump.
Taken in one of the other four interestingly decorated rooms, the
lunchtime bar menu might offer a bowl of tomato soup with a nutmeg
cream, cod and chips with a green mayonnaise or omelette with smoked
salmon and asparagus; also puddings such as jasmine-scented crème brûlée
with vanilla tuiles or bakewell pudding with clotted cream. A two-course
set lunch or dinner is also available. An interesting and helpfully short wine
list offers six good wines by the glass. The overall feel is of civilised but
relaxed elegance: matt pastel paintwork in soft greens and blues, naive farm
and country pictures, little side lamps supplemented by candles in black
wrought-iron holders, basketwork, dried flowers, fruits and gourds, maybe
an elaborate bouquet of fresh flowers. The whole pub is no smoking.
There are tables out on the terrace, with a track straight up on to the
moors.

*Free house ~ Licensee Philip Burgess ~ Real ale ~ Bar food (lunchtime only; not Mon)
~ Restaurant ~ (01822) 820221 ~ Children welcome ~ Dogs allowed in bar ~
Occasional live jazz ~ Open 11.30-3, 6-11; 12-2.30 Sun; closed Sun evening, Mon*

MARLDON

Church House *Just W of Paignton*

There's a genuinely warm welcome for all from the helpful and friendly
staff in this attractive, charming inn. The spreading bar (half of which is no
smoking) has a relaxed atmosphere and several different areas that radiate
off the big semi-circular bar counter. The main bar has interesting
windows, some beams, dark pine chairs around solid tables on the turkey
carpet, and yellow leather bar chairs; leading off here is a cosy little candlelit
room with just four tables on the bare-board floor, a dark wood dado and
stone fireplace, and next to this is the attractive, no smoking restaurant with
a large stone fireplace. At the other end of the building, a characterful room
is split into two parts with a stone floor in one bit and a wooden floor in
another (which has a big woodburning stove). Extremely good, interesting
bar food includes tasty smoked haddock, mussel and potato chowder with a
poached egg, home-made chicken liver and mushroom pâté, broccoli and
three cheese pasta, loin of pork with sweet and sour sauce, local sirloin
steak, and king prawns in paprika and sour cream; efficient service even
when busy. Well kept Bass, Fullers London Pride, Greene King IPA, and
St Austell Dartmoor Best on handpump, and 12 wines by the glass; skittle
alley. There are three grassy terraces with picnic-sets behind.

*Whitbreads ~ Lease Julian Cook ~ Real ale ~ Bar food (12-2, 7-9.30) ~
Restaurant ~ (01803) 558279 ~ Children welcome ~ Dogs allowed in bar ~
Open 11.30-2.30, 5-11; 11.30-11 Sat; 12-10.30 Sun ~ Bedrooms: /£60B*

MEAVY
Royal Oak *Off B3212 E of Yelverton*
On the edge of Dartmoor in a peaceful rustic village, this partly 15th-c pub
has seats on the green in front and by the building itself. Inside, the heavy-
beamed L-shaped bar has pews from the church, red plush banquettes and
old agricultural prints and church pictures on the walls; a smaller bar –
where the locals like to gather – has flagstones, a big open hearth fireplace
and side bread oven. Promptly served by friendly staff, the well liked bar
food at lunchtime includes filled baked potatoes and baguettes, home-made
vegetable lasagne and home-made steak and kidney pie; in the evening
there might be garlic mushrooms, pork escalope with apple and cider sauce,
salmon and steaks. The lounge bar is no smoking during food times. Well
kept Princetown IPA and Jail Ale, and maybe Bass and Sharps Doom Bar
on handpump. The ancient oak from which the pub gets its name is just
close by. No children inside. More reports please.
*Free house ~ Licensee Ann Davis ~ Real ale ~ Bar food ~ (01822) 852944 ~
Dogs welcome ~ Open 11-3, 6.30-11; 12-3, 6.30-10.30 Sun*

MOLLAND
London *Village signposted off B3227 E of South Molton, down narrow lanes*
Although it is a little off the beaten track, this proper Exmoor inn is worth
the diversion for its chatty and informal atmosphere undisturbed by piped
music or noisy games machines. The two small linked rooms by the old-
fashioned central servery have lots of local stag-hunting pictures, tough
carpeting or rugs on flagstones, cushioned benches and plain chairs around
rough stripped trestle tables, a table of shooting and other country
magazines, ancient stag and otter trophies, and darts, table skittles and
dominoes; maybe working dogs from local shoots (there is a bowl of water
left for them by the good log fire). On the left an attractive beamed room
has accounts of the rescued stag which lived a long life at the pub some 50
years ago, and on the right, a panelled dining room with a great curved
settle by its fireplace has particularly good hunting and gamebird prints.
Honest bar food includes filled baked potatoes, savoury pancakes and a dish
of the day; evening choices like chicken and stilton wrapped in bacon with
a white wine sauce. The dining room is no smoking. A small hall with
stuffed birds and animals and lots of overhead baskets has a box of toys, and
there are good country views from a few picnic-sets out in front. The low-
ceilinged lavatories are worth a look, with their Victorian mahogany and
tiling (and in the gents' a testament to the prodigious thirst of the village
cricket team). And don't miss the next-door church, with its untouched
early 18th-c box pews – and a spring carpet of Tenby daffodils in the
graveyard.
*Free house ~ Licensees M J and L J Short ~ Real ale ~ Bar food ~ Restaurant ~
No credit cards ~ (01769) 550269 ~ Children in family room, in eating area of bar
and in restaurant ~ Dogs allowed in bar and bedrooms ~ Open 11.30-2.30, 6-11;
12-2.30, 7-10.30 Sun ~ Bedrooms: /£50B*

NEWTON FERRERS

Dolphin *Riverside Road East – follow Harbour dead end signs*

In summer the two terraces across the lane are the place to be: by day they have a grandstand view of the boating action on the busy tidal River Yealm below the cottages on these steep hillsides, and at night the floodlit church over in Noss Mayo makes a lovely focal point. Service out here is quick and friendly, as it is in the 18th-c pub itself. The L-shaped bar has a few low black beams, slate floors, some white-painted plank panelling, and simple pub furnishings including cushioned wall benches and small winged settles; chatty and relaxed out of season, it can get packed in summer. Enjoyable food includes sandwiches, fresh cod and home-made vegetable lasagne; daily specials such as scallops in garlic butter; puddings. Bass, Sharps Doom Bar, and a Skinners brew for the pub are kept well on handpump, Heron Valley cider, organic apple juice, and 9 wines by the glass; they have darts, a popular quiz night on Wednesdays in winter, and the pub is decorated with lots of coastal watercolours (for sale). The carpeted family area is up a few steps at the back, and there is a no smoking restaurant upstairs. Parking by the pub is very limited, with more chance of a space either below or above.

Free house ~ Licensee Sandra Dunbar Rees ~ Bar food ~ Restaurant ~ (01752) 872007 ~ Children in eating area of bar ~ Dogs welcome ~ Open 12-2.30(3 Sat), 6-11; 12-3, 7-10.30 Sun; opens 12.30 in winter

NOMANSLAND

Mount Pleasant *B3131 Tiverton—South Molton*

This is the sort of friendly and relaxed place where you often have to step over dogs and farmers' wellies to get in. There's a new bay window extension to fit an extra four tables, and the long bar is divided into three, with huge fireplaces each end, one with a woodburning stove under a low dark ochre black-beamed ceiling, the other with a big log fire. A nice informal mix of furniture on the patterned carpet includes an old sofa with a colourful throw, old-fashioned leather dining chairs, pale country kitchen chairs and wall pews, and tables all with candles in attractive metal holders; there are country prints and local photographs including shooting parties. The bar, with plenty of bar stools, has well kept Cotleigh Tawny and Barn Owl, and Marstons Pedigree on handpump, and decent wines. Generous helpings of well liked bar food, using local produce, includes an all-day breakfast, beef stroganoff or steak and kidney pie, fillets of bass, and puddings. On the left a high-beamed stripped stone no smoking dining room with a stag's head over the sideboard was once a smithy, and still has the raised forge fireplace. Piped music, fruit machine, TV and darts; picnicsets under smart parasols in the neat back garden. Samuel the spaniel comes in to say hello at closing time. More reports please.

Free house ~ Licensees Anne Butler, Karen Southcott and Sarah Roberts ~ Real ale ~ Bar food (all day) ~ Restaurant ~ (01884) 860271 ~ Children welcome ~ Dogs allowed in bar ~ Open 11.30-11; 12-10.30 Sun; closed evening 25 Dec, 1 Jan

NOSS MAYO
Ship *Off A379 via B3186, E of Plymouth*
The terrace in front of this rather smart pub has recently been refurbished. It's an idyllic spot in summer, and you can sit at the octagonal wooden tables and look over the inlet; visiting boats can tie up alongside – with prior permission. Parking is restricted at high tide. Inside, the two thick-walled bars have a happy mix of dining chairs and tables on the wooden floors, log fires (so hot you might not want to sit too close!), bookcases, dozens of local pictures, newspapers and magazines to read, and a friendly, chatty atmosphere. All of the first floor is no smoking; board games and dominoes. Good food (which can be eaten anywhere in the pub and features much local produce) might include curried vegetable soup, smoked duck salad, a vegetable stir-fry, sausages with mustard mash, black pudding, onions and gravy, a tapas plate for two to share, and grilled lemon sole; cheerful, helpful staff. Well kept Princetown Dartmoor IPA, Summerskills Tamar, and guests like Keltek Magik or Blackawton 44 Special on handpump, lots of malt whiskies, and eight wines by the glass. It does get very busy, particularly in fine weather.
Free house ~ Licensees Lesley and Bruce Brunning ~ Real ale ~ Bar food (12-9.30) ~ Restaurant ~ (01752) 872387 ~ Children allowed before 7pm ~ Dogs allowed in bar ~ Open 11.30-11; 12-10.30 Sun

PETER TAVY
Peter Tavy Inn *Off A386 near Mary Tavy, N of Tavistock*
It's best to get to this attractive old stone inn early to be sure of, not only a table, but a parking space. The low-beamed bar has a good bustling atmosphere, high-backed settles on the black flagstones by the big stone fireplace (a fine log fire on cold days), smaller settles in stone-mullioned windows, a snug, no smoking side dining area, and efficient service. Popular food at lunchtime might include red lentil and sun-blush tomato pâté, chicken and bacon tartlet, ploughman's with a choice of six local cheeses, and chicken supreme; in the evening there might be crab and avocado tian, venison steak Diane, salmon with risotto, and duck breast with plum sauce. Home-made puddings such as rich chocolate and nut tart. Well kept Princetown Jail Ale and Summerskills Tamar and Sharps Doom Bar, with a couple of guests from breweries like Blackawton or Sutton on handpump, kept under light blanket pressure; local farm cider, 30 malt whiskies and nine wines by the glass; piped music and darts. From the picnic-sets in the pretty garden, there are peaceful views of the moor rising above nearby pastures.
Free house ~ Licensees Graeme and Karen Sim ~ Real ale ~ Bar food ~ Restaurant ~ (01822) 810348 ~ Children in restaurant and family room ~ Dogs welcome ~ Open 12-3, 6-11(10.30 Sun); closed 25 Dec and evenings 24, 25 and 31 Dec

POSTBRIDGE
Warren House *B3212 ¼ mile NE of Postbridge*
This is just the place to head for after a walk on Dartmoor. The cosy bar has a fireplace at either end (one is said to have been kept almost continuously

alight since 1845), and is simply furnished with easy chairs and settles under a beamed ochre ceiling, wild animal pictures on the partly panelled stone walls, and dim lighting (fuelled by the pub's own generator); there's a no smoking family room. Good no-nonsense home cooking includes locally made meaty or vegetable pasties, home-made rabbit pie or home-made vegetable curry, daily specials, and home-made puddings such as chocolate truffle torte. Well kept Badger Tanglefoot, Ringwood Old Thumper, Sharps Doom Bar, and a guest like Shepherd Neame Spitfire on handpump, local farm cider, and malt whiskies. Darts, pool, cribbage and dominoes; maybe piped music. There are picnic-sets on both sides of the road that enjoy the moorland views.

Free house ~ Licensee Peter Parsons ~ Real ale ~ Bar food (all day summer and winter weekends; more restricted in winter) ~ (01822) 880208 ~ Children in family room ~ Dogs welcome ~ Open 11-11; 12-10.30 Sun; may shut weekday afternoons in winter

POUNDSGATE
Tavistock Inn *B3357 continuation*
Sir Arthur Conan Doyle wrote *The Hound of the Baskervilles* while staying in this picturesque, family-run 15th-c local. It's in a Dartmoor-edge village and moorland walks start and finish at the pub or pass it en route; boots and even waders are welcome, as are dogs on a lead – there's a bowl of water outside for them, and maybe if they are lucky, a dog biscuit behind the bar. Some original features include a narrow-stepped granite spiral staircase, original flagstones, ancient log fireplaces, and beams, and there's a friendly atmosphere and a good mix of locals and visitors. Well kept Courage Best, Wadworths 6X and a guest such as Wychwood Hobgoblin Best on handpump, decent wines, and a few malt whiskies. Tasty traditional bar food includes filled baguettes, filled baked potatoes, yorkshire pudding filled with sausages, baked beans and onions or home-made lasagne, and steaks. Tables on the front terrace and pretty flowers in stone troughs, hanging baskets, and window boxes, and more seats in the quiet back garden with a gazebo overlooking the children's play area; lovely scenery.

InnSpired ~ Lease Peter and Jean Hamill ~ Real ale ~ Bar food (12-2, 6-9; not Mon evening Oct-Easter) ~ (01364) 631251 ~ Children allowed if over 4 ~ Dogs allowed in bar ~ Open 11-3, 6-11; 12-3, 7-10.30 Sun

RATTERY
Church House *Village signposted from A385 W of Totnes, and A38 S of Buckfastleigh*
This is one of Britain's oldest pubs, and the spiral stone steps behind a little stone doorway on your left as you come in date from about 1030. There are massive oak beams and standing timbers in the homely open-plan bar, large fireplaces (one with a little cosy nook partitioned off around it), windsor armchairs, comfortable seats and window seats, and prints on the plain white walls; the no smoking dining room is separated from this room by heavy curtains, and there's also a separate no smoking lounge area. Bar food includes devilled whitebait, ploughman's, battered cod or sausages,

creamy coconut chicken curry, vegetable lasagne, and puddings. Well kept Greene King Abbot, Hook Norton Old Hooky, Otter Ale and St Austell Dartmoor Best on handpump, several malt whiskies, and a decent wine list. The garden has picnic benches on the large hedged-in lawn, and peaceful views of the partly wooded surrounding hills.

Free house ~ Licensee Ray Hardy ~ Real ale ~ Bar food ~ Restaurant ~ (01364) 642220 ~ Children welcome ~ Dogs allowed in bar ~ Open 11-2.30, 6-11; 12-2.30, 6-10.30 Sun

SIDBURY

Hare & Hounds *3 miles N of Sidbury, at Putts Corner; A375 towards Honiton, crossroads with B3174*

At mealtimes particularly, this very well run roadside pub is extremely full of cheerful customers, but as it is open all day, the crowds can be avoided. It is so much bigger inside than you could have guessed from outside, rambling all over the place, but despite this, the very friendly and efficient staff will make you welcome and serve you promptly. There are two good log fires (and rather unusual wood-framed leather sofas complete with pouffes), heavy beams and fresh flowers throughout, some oak panelling, plenty of tables with red leatherette or red plush-cushioned dining chairs, window seats and well used bar stools too; it's mostly carpeted, with bare boards and stripped stone walls at one softly lit no smoking end. At the opposite end of the pub, on the left, another big dining area has huge windows looking out over the garden. As you come in, the first thing you see is the good popular daily carvery counter, with a choice of joints, and enough turnover to keep up a continuous supply of fresh vegetables. Other food includes sandwiches or baguettes, home-made pie of the day, local steaks, and daily specials such as cauliflower cheese topped with crispy bacon. Well kept Branscombe Summa Vale and Otter Ale and Bitter tapped from the cask; side room with a big-screen sports TV. Alley skittles and piped music. The big garden, giving good valley views, has picnic-sets, a play area enlivened by a pensioned-off fire engine, and a small strolling flock of peafowl.

Free house ~ Licensee Peter Cairns ~ Real ale ~ Bar food (all day) ~ Restaurant ~ (01404) 41760 ~ Children welcome ~ Dogs allowed in bar ~ Live music Sun lunchtimes in marquee ~ Open 10-11.30; 12-10.30 Sun

SLAPTON

Tower *Signposted off A379 Dartmouth—Kingsbridge*

The new licensees seem to have settled easily into this fine old place, and as the same chef stayed on, the food is as good as ever. The low-ceilinged beamed bar has armchairs, low-backed settles and scrubbed oak tables on the flagstones or bare boards, open log fires, and well kept Adnams Best, Badger Tanglefoot, and St Austell Dartmoor Best on handpump; several wines by the glass. At lunchtime, the popular food includes home-made ham, asparagus and baby leek terrine, italian antipasto, trio of local sausages with onion gravy, roasted vegetables with tagliatelle, and beef and mushroom in ale pie; in the evening, there might be crab and prawn tower with light basil oil, mushroom stroganoff, slow-cooked lamb shank, pheasant supreme, and roast bass. Puddings such as double chocolate and orange truffle torte, vanilla crème brûlée or sticky toffee pudding with toffee sauce; piped music. The lane up to the pub is very narrow and parking can be pretty tricky.

Free house ~ Licensees Annette and Andrew Hammett ~ Real ale ~ Bar food ~ Restaurant ~ (01548) 580216 ~ Children in eating area of bar ~ Dogs welcome ~ Open 12-3, 6-11; 12-3, 7-10.30 Sun ~ Bedrooms: £35S/£55S

TORBRYAN

Old Church House *Most easily reached from A381 Newton Abbot—Totnes via Ipplepen*

Built in 1400 on the site of a very ancient cottage, this pub once housed the workmen restoring the part-Saxon church with its battlemented Norman tower. Bustling and neatly kept, the bar on the right of the door is particularly attractive, and has benches built into the fine old panelling as well as the cushioned high-backed settle and leather-backed small seats around its big log fire. On the left there are a series of comfortable and discreetly lit lounges, one with a splendid deep Tudor inglenook fireplace with a side bread oven. Enjoyable bar food at lunchtime includes home-made soup, cauliflower cheese, chicken curry, and roast lamb or beef; evening choices such as pâté or grilled sardines, pork in apple and mustard sauce or cod in a prawn and white wine sauce. Puddings like chocolate pecan torte and black cheery cheesecake. Well kept Palmers Dorset Gold, Skinners Betty Stogs, seasonal ale from Teignworthy, and a beer named for the pub on handpump, and around 25 malt whiskies; piped music, dominoes and cribbage. Plenty of nearby walks.

Free house ~ Licensees Richard and Carolyn McFadyen ~ Real ale ~ Bar food ~ Restaurant ~ (01803) 812372 ~ Children in restaurant and family room ~ Dogs welcome ~ Open 12-3, 6-11; 12-3, 7-10.30 Sun ~ Bedrooms: £50S/£85B

TORCROSS

Start Bay *A379 S of Dartmouth*

There are often queues outside this extremely popular dining pub before it opens, so to be sure of a table, you must get there early. Local fishermen work off the beach right in front of the pub and deliver all kinds of fish, a local crabber drops the crabs at the back door, and the landlord enjoys catching plaice, scallops and bass. Apart from the wonderful choice of fish (available in different sizes), other food includes sandwiches, vegetable lasagne, steaks and children's meals. They do warn of delays at peak times. Well kept Bass and Flowers Original or Otter Ale on handpump, and maybe Heron Valley cider and fresh apple juice, and local wine from the Sharpham Estate. The unassuming main bar is very much set out for eating with wheelback chairs around plenty of dark tables or (round a corner) back-to-back settles forming booths; there are some photographs of storms buffeting the pub and country pictures on its cream walls, and a winter coal fire; a small chatty drinking area by the counter has a brass ship's clock and barometer. The winter games room has darts and shove-ha'penny; there's more booth seating in a no smoking family room with sailing boat pictures. There are seats (highly prized) out on the terrace overlooking the three-mile pebble beach, and the freshwater wildlife lagoon of Slapton Ley is just behind the pub.

Whitbreads ~ Tenant Paul Stubbs ~ Real ale ~ Bar food (11.30-2, 6-10) ~ (01548) 580553 ~ Children in family room ~ Dogs welcome ~ Open 11.30-11; 12-10.30 Sun; 11.30(12 Sun)-2.30, 6-11(10.30 Sun) in winter

WINKLEIGH
Kings Arms *Village signposted off B3220 Crediton—Torrington; Fore Street*
Lively and friendly, this popular, well run thatched village pub welcomes visitors and locals alike. There's an attractive main bar with beams, some old-fashioned built-in wall settles, scrubbed pine tables and benches on the flagstones, and a woodburning stove in a cavernous fireplace; another woodburning stove separates the bar from the dining rooms (one is no smoking). Well liked bar food includes home-made soup, chicken liver and brandy pâté, filled baked potatoes or omelettes, vegetable roulade, chicken stir-fry or curry of the day, and puddings like rhubarb crumble or marmalade steam pudding. Well kept Butcombe Bitter, Flowers IPA and Skinners Cornish Knocker on handpump, local cider, and decent wines; darts, cribbage, dominoes, and shove-ha'penny. There are seats out in the garden.

Enterprise ~ Lease Chris Guy and Julia Franklin ~ Real ale ~ Bar food (all day) ~ Restaurant ~ (01837) 83384 ~ Children welcome ~ Dogs welcome ~ Open 11-11; 12-10.30 Sun

WONSON
Northmore Arms *A30 at Merrymeet roundabout, take 1st left on old A30, through Whiddon Down; new roundabout and take left onto A382; then right down lane signposted Throwleigh/Gidleigh. Continue down lane over hump-back bridge; turn left to Wonson; OS Sheet 191 map reference 674903*
Down narrow high-hedged lanes on the north-east edge of Dartmoor, this secluded cottage is all the more remarkable in this area for being open all day. It's almost as if time has stood still here. The two small connected beamed rooms – modest and informal but civilised – have wall settles, a few elderly chairs, five tables in one room and just two in the other. There are two open fires (only one may be lit), and some attractive photographs on the stripped stone walls; darts, dominoes, and cribbage. Besides well kept ales such as Adnams Broadside, Cotleigh Tawny and Exe Valley Dobs, they have good house wines, and simple but reasonably priced food such as filled baked potatoes, feta, spinach and mushroom flan, roast lamb with garlic potatoes and Tuesday curries. The ladies' lavatory is up steep steps and some feel the gents' could do with some refurbishment. The steep garden has been made larger and new tables and chairs were arriving as we went to press – it's all very peaceful and rustic; excellent walking from the pub (or to it, perhaps from Chagford or Gidleigh Park). The car park is larger this year. Castle Drogo is close by.

Free house ~ Licensee Mrs Mo Miles ~ Real ale ~ Bar food (all day Mon-Sat;

12-2.30, 7-9 Sun) ~ (01647) 231428 ~ Well behaved children in family room ~ Dogs allowed in bar ~ Open 11-11; 12-10.30 Sun ~ Bedrooms: /£35

WOODLAND
Rising Sun *Village signposted off A38 just NE of Ashburton – then keep eyes peeled for Rising Sun signposts (which may be hidden in the hedges); pub N of village itself, near Combe Cross*

Although people do drop into this friendly pub for just a drink, there's quite an emphasis on the popular, frequently changing food: fried local pigeon breast with orange salad, home-cooked ham with free range egg and home-made chips or ploughman's with four local cheeses, spiced chick peacakes with home-made tomato sauce, fillet of lemon sole and roast rack of local lamb; home-made puddings such as white chocolate marquise or rhubarb crumble; Sunday roast as well. The dining area is no smoking. There's an expanse of softly lit red plush button-back banquettes and matching studded chairs, partly divided by wooded banister rails, masonry pillars and the odd high-backed settle. A forest of beams is hung with thousands of old doorkeys, and a nice part by the log fire has shelves of plates and books, and old pictures above the fireplace. Well kept Princetown Jail Ale, Sharps Doom Bar, and maybe a guest like Moor Avalon on handpump, 12 wines by the glass, and local Luscombe cider; cheerful service. The family area has various toys (and a collection of cookery books). There are some picnic-sets in the spacious garden, which has a play area including a redundant tractor.

Free house ~ Licensee Heather Humphreys ~ Real ale ~ Bar food (12-2.15(3 Sun), 6(7 Sun)-9.15) ~ Restaurant ~ (01364) 652544 ~ Children in restaurant and family room ~ Dogs welcome ~ Open 11.45-3, 6-11; 12-3, 7-10.30 Sun; closed Mon (exc bank hols) ~ Bedrooms: £38B/£60B

Dog Friendly Hotels, B&Bs and Farms

ALLERFORD
West Lynch Farm *West Lynch, Allerford, Somerset TA24 8HJ* (01643) 862816 £55; 3 rms. Listed 15th-c National Trust farmhouse in six acres of landscaped gardens and paddocks on the edge of Exmoor; lots of original features, antiques and persian rugs, homely lounge with woodburning stove, super breakfasts with their own honey and home-made marmalade, and lots of animals; falconry tuition and hawking all year, a collection of owls and birds of prey, clay pigeon shooting, and riding; children over 5; dogs welcome by arrangement; £5

ASHBURTON
Holne Chase *Ashburton, Newton Abbot, Devon TQ13 7NS* (01364) 631471 £145, plus winter breaks; 17 comfortable and individually furnished rms, many with views over the Dart Valley, and some split-level

suites in converted stables. Marvellously peaceful ex-hunting lodge of Buckfast Abbey, in 70 acres with sweeping lawns and plenty of woodland walks, a mile of Dart fishing, shooting and riding on Dartmoor; cheerful welcoming owners, comfortable public rooms with log fires, very good modern english cooking using home-grown vegetables, and enjoyable breakfasts and afternoon teas (home-made breads and so forth); children over 12 in evening restaurant; dogs welcome away from restaurant; £7.50; treats, menu and dog spa

BIGBURY-ON-SEA
Henley *Folly Hill, Bigbury-on-Sea, Kingsbridge, Devon TQ7 4AR (01548) 810240* £**86**; 6 compact rms. Renovated Edwardian cottage with fine views of the Avon estuary, Burgh Island, and beyond; lounge and conservatory dining room with magnificent sea views, deep wicker chairs and polished furniture, binoculars and books, good, enjoyable food from a small menu, super breakfasts, and steep, private path down the cliff to a sandy bay; cl Nov–Mar; dogs welcome in bedrooms; £2

BOLBERRY
Port Light *Bolberry, Salcombe, Devon TQ7 3DY (01548) 561384* £**112** inc dinner; 6 pleasant rms with lovely views.   Clifftop former RAF radar station (an easy walk from Hope Cove) with a warmly friendly welcome, good home-made food (super fresh fish) in attractive bar and restaurant, woodburner, and good outdoor children's play area; dogs welcome

BAMPTON
Bark House *Oakford Bridge, Bampton, Devon EX16 9HZ (01398) 351236* £**79**; 5 cottagey rms with teddies, 4 with own bthrm. Charming hotel with lovely rural views, garden with croquet and plenty of surrounding walks; caring, hospitable owners, open fires and low beams in comfortable homely sitting and dining rooms, delicious food using local produce, a thoughtful little changing wine list, and super breakfasts; dogs welcome in bedrooms

BISHOP'S TAWTON
Halmpstone Manor *Bishop's Tawton, Barnstaple, Devon EX32 0EA (01271) 830321* £**100**; 5 pretty rms. Quietly relaxing small country house with log fire in comfortable sitting room, enjoyable food in panelled dining room, good breakfasts, caring service, an attractive garden, and nice views; plenty to do nearby; cl Christmas, New Year; dogs welcome away from restaurant

BOVEY TRACEY
Edgemoor Hotel *Haytor Rd, Bovey Tracey, Newton Abbot, Devon TQ13 9LE (01626) 832466* £**120**, plus special breaks; 17 charming rms. Ivy-covered country house in neatly kept gardens on the edge of Dartmoor, with newly refurbished comfortable lounge and bar, log fires, good modern english cooking in elegant restaurant; cl 1 wk after Christmas; no children; limited disabled access; dogs in Woodland Wing bedrooms with back door leading to private patio

BRATTON FLEMING

Bracken House Hotel *Bratton Fleming, Barnstaple, Devon EX31 4TG* (01598) 710320 £**130** inc dinner; 8 rms. Peacefully set little hotel, once a rectory, on the edge of Exmoor in eight acres of gardens and woodland with plenty of wildlife – they also care for injured owls; a genuine welcome from the friendly owners, comfortable drawing room with a small bar, library with books on the area, plenty of owl ornaments and house plants, open fires, hearty breakfasts, and enjoyable aga-cooked evening meals using local produce; children over 12; dogs welcome if well behaved; £2

CHAGFORD

Easton Court *Sandy Park, Chagford, Newton Abbot, Devon TQ13 8JN* (01647) 433469 £**72**; 5 comfortable rms. Extended Tudor thatched longhouse in four acres of gardens and paddocks, with a relaxed and informal atmosphere, hearty breakfasts in guest lounge/breakfast room, helpful, friendly owners, and lots to do nearby; plenty of surrounding pubs and restaurants; children over 10; disabled access; dogs welcome in bedrooms; £2.50

CHAGFORD

Gidleigh Park *Chagford, Newton Abbot, Devon TQ13 8HH* (01647) 432367 £**440** inc dinner, plus winter breaks; 15 opulent and individual rms with fruit and flowers. Exceptional luxurious Dartmoor-edge mock Tudor hotel with deeply comfortable panelled drawing room, wonderful flowers, conservatory overlooking the fine grounds (40 acres, with walks straight up on to the moor), log fires, particularly fine cooking and a fine wine list, and caring staff; children over 7 in restaurant; cl 2 wks Jan; dogs welcome in bedrooms

CLAWTON

Court Barn Hotel *Clawton, Holsworthy, Devon EX22 6PS* (01409) 271219 £**80**, plus special breaks; 8 individually furnished rms. Charming country house in five pretty acres with croquet, 9-hole putting green, small chip-and-putt course, and tennis and badminton courts; comfortable lounges, log fires, library/TV room, good service, imaginative food and award-winning wines (and teas), and a quiet relaxed atmosphere; they are kind to families; dogs welcome in bedrooms; £4

DARTMOUTH

Royal Castle *11 The Quay, Dartmouth, Devon TQ6 9PS* (01803) 833033 £**105.90**, plus special breaks; 25 individually furnished rms. Well restored mainly Georgian hotel (part 16th c) overlooking the inner harbour – great views from most rooms; lively and interesting public bar with open fires and beams, quiet library/lounge with antiques, drawing room overlooking the quayside, winter spit-roasts in lounge bar, elegant upstairs seafood restaurant, decent bar food, and friendly staff; dogs welcome in bedrooms and bar

EXETER
Edwardian Hotel *30-32 Heavitree Rd, Exeter, Devon EX1 2LQ (01392) 276102* £**60**, plus special breaks; 12 individually furnished rms, 3 with four-posters. Popular guesthouse, recently renovated, close to cathedral and city centre, with pretty lounge, enjoyable breakfasts in attractive dining rooms, and warmly friendly and knowledgeable resident owners; plenty of places nearby for evening meals; cl 25–26 Dec; partial disabled access; dogs welcome in bedrooms

Hotel Barcelona *Magdalen St, Exeter, Devon EX2 4HY (01392) 281000* £**108.90**, plus special breaks; 46 beautifully furnished rms with CD-player and video, and lovely bthrms. Stylishly modern, converted Victorian eye hospital filled with bright posters and paintings, a bar with 1950s-style furniture and fashionable cocktails, a smart but informal no smoking restaurant overlooking the big walled garden, with a woodburning oven for pizza cooking plus other good value contemporary choices, a nightclub featuring 1950s films noir and live entertainment, and very helpful staff; disabled access; dogs welcome in bedrooms; £15

Royal Clarence *Cathedral Yard, Exeter, Devon EX1 1HB (01392) 319955* £**130**, plus special breaks; 55 newly refurbished rms and suites, many with fine views across to Exeter Cathedral. Georgian-style hotel on the lovely Cathedral Yard with comfortably modern public rooms, exceptional modern cooking using the best of local produce and an excellent wine list in the Michael Caines restaurant, a more informal, bustling café bar, and the popular Well House pub; dogs welcome in bedrooms; £7

EXFORD
Crown *Exford, Minehead, Devon TA24 7PP (01643) 831554* £**99**; 17 rms. Comfortably upmarket coaching inn on the village green in Exmoor National Park with a delightful back water garden – a lovely summer spot with trout stream, gently sloping lawns, tall trees and plenty of tables; brightly refurbished lounge with very relaxed feel, hunting prints on cream walls, old photographs of the area, and smart cushioned benches; real ales, a good wine list, and enjoyable modern cooking in no smoking candlelit dining room with simpler meals in the bar; a good base for walking; children over 7; dogs in bedrooms

GALMPTON
Burton Farm *Galmpton, Kingsbridge, Devon TQ7 3EY (01548) 561210* £**70**; 14 pretty rms. Welcoming working farm in lovely countryside with dairy herd and pedigree sheep (guests can enjoy farm activities) and traditional farmhouse cooking using home-produced ingredients; own tea time and play area for children; no smoking; dogs welcome in cottage

GITTISHAM
Combe House *Gittisham, Honiton, Devon EX14 0AD (01404) 540400* £**138**, plus winter breaks; 15 individually decorated pretty rms with lovely

views. Peaceful, Grade I listed, Elizabethan country hotel in gardens with 400-year-old cedar of Lebanon, and walks around the 3,500-acre estate; elegant sitting rooms with fine panelling, antiques, portraits and fresh flowers, a happy relaxed atmosphere, very good food in restaurant and faithfully restored Georgian kitchen, and fine wines; can hire the house for special occasions and meetings; dogs welcome away from restaurant

HAWKCHURCH

Fairwater Head Country House *Hawkchurch, Axminster, Devon EX13 5TX (01297) 678349* £**140**; 20 rms, most with country views. Edwardian hotel in quiet, flower-filled gardens with genuinely friendly, attentive owners and staff, open fire in comfortable lounge hall, a well stocked bar and wine cellar, and enjoyable food in no smoking restaurant; croquet; dogs in bedrooms; £5

HAYTOR VALE

Rock Inn *Haytor Vale, Newton Abbot, Devon TQ13 9XP (01364) 661305* £**85**, plus special breaks; 9 individual rms. Civilised old coaching inn on the edge of Dartmoor National Park, with good food (inc fresh fish), a nice mix of visitors and locals in the two rooms of the panelled bar, open fires, no smoking restaurant, courteous service, and big garden; walking, fishing, riding and golf nearby; cl 25 Dec; dogs welcome in some bedrooms; £5.50

HEXWORTHY

Forest Inn *Hexworthy, Princetown, Yelverton, Devon PL20 6SD (01364) 631211* £**65**; 10 cosy, comfortable rms, most with own bthrm. Country inn in fine Dartmoor setting, popular with walkers and anglers; varied menu in both bar and restaurant, local ales, good choice of wines, and welcoming staff; cl 25 Dec; dogs welcome

HOLNE

Wellpritton Farm *Holne, Ashburton, Devon TQ13 7RX (01364) 631273* £**50**, plus special breaks; 5 pretty rms. Small friendly Dartmoor farm set in 15 acres with horses, goats and chickens and lovely views from terrace and garden; comfortable sitting room, good, completely home-made evening meals using local produce, and enjoyable breakfasts; cl Christmas week; children under 5 by arrangement; disabled access; dogs welcome in bedrooms; £2.50

LEWDOWN

Lewtrenchard Manor *Lewdown, Okehampton, Devon EX20 4PN (01566) 783256* £**200**, plus special breaks; 9 well equipped rms with fresh flowers and period furniture. Lovely Elizabethan manor house in garden with fine dovecot and surrounded by peaceful estate with shooting, fishing and croquet; dark panelling, ornate ceilings, antiques, fresh flowers, and log fires, a friendly welcome, relaxed atmosphere, and candlelit restaurant with very good imaginative food; children over 8; partial disabled access; dogs welcome in bedrooms; £10

LIFTON
Arundell Arms *Fore St, Lifton, Devon PL16 0AA (01566)* 784666 £**136**, plus special breaks; 27 well equipped rms, 5 in annexe over the road. Carefully renovated old coaching inn with 20 miles of its own waters – salmon and trout fishing and a long-established fly-fishing school; comfortable sitting room, log fires, super food in both bar and elegant restaurant, carefully chosen wines, and kind service from local staff; new eating area in attractive terraced garden; cl 3 nights over Christmas; disabled access; dogs allowed away from restaurant; £4

MALBOROUGH
Soar Mill Cove Hotel *Malborough, Salcombe, Devon TQ7 3DS (01548)* 561566 £**220** inc dinner, plus special breaks; 17 comfortable rms that open on to garden. Neatly kept single-storey building in idyllic spot by peaceful and very beautiful cove on NT coast (excellent walks), with lovely views, extensive private grounds, tennis/putting, and warm indoor pool; outstanding service, log fires, very good food (marvellous fish) in restaurant and coffee shop, and they are particularly kind to children of all ages: microwave, fridge and so forth, for little ones, own high tea or smaller helpings of most meals, fully equipped laundry, a play room, table tennis and snooker, swings, and donkey and pony; cl Nov-Jan; disabled access; dogs welcome in bedrooms

MEMBURY
Lea Hill *Membury, Axminster, Devon EX13 7AQ (01404)* 881881 £**70**, plus winter breaks; 4 individually furnished rms. Thatched, no smoking 14th-c longhouse in 8 acres of secluded grounds inc their own par 3, 9-hole golf course, and lovely views; comfortable beamed rooms, flagstones and beams, relaxed and friendly owners, and nice breakfasts, morning coffee, and afternoon tea with home-made cakes and cream teas; self-catering, too; children over 5; dogs in bedrooms and guest lounge (if other guests are agreeable)

MORETONHAMPSTEAD
Great Sloncombe Farm *Moretonhampstead, Newton Abbot, Devon TQ13 8QF (01647)* 440595 £**52**; 3 rms – the big double is the favourite. Lovely 13th-c farmhouse on a working dairy and stock farm, with friendly owners, carefully polished old-fashioned furniture in oak-beamed lounge, decent food, hearty breakfasts, log fires, a relaxed atmosphere, and good nearby walking and bird-watching; no smoking; children over 8; dogs welcome in bedrooms

NORTHAM
Yeoldon House *Durrant Lane, Northam, Bideford, Devon EX39 2RL (01237)* 474400 £**105**, plus special breaks; 10 individually decorated rms. Quietly set hotel in two acres by the River Torridge, with a warmly friendly and relaxed atmosphere, a comfortable lounge, good food using local produce in the attractive dining room, and helpful service; lots to do nearby; cl Christmas; dogs welcome in bedrooms and lounge

NORTH BOVEY
Gate House *North Bovey, Newton Abbot, Devon TQ13 8RB (01647) 440479* £64, plus special breaks; 3 charming rms. 15th-c thatched cottage in picturesque village, with huge granite fireplace in attractive beamed sitting room, breakfasts and candlelit evening meals in beamed dining room, tea with home-made cakes, friendly owners, and outdoor swimming pool in peaceful garden; plenty to do nearby; no children; dogs welcome in bedrooms

PARKHAM
Penhaven *Rectory Lane, Parkham, Bideford, Devon EX39 5PL (01237) 451711* £140; 12 spacious rms inc suites in cottages. Former rectory in lovely grounds with plenty of wildlife – the local badgers come onto the lawn at night; friendly, peaceful atmosphere, big fire in the lounge, lounge bar, and good dinner party-style food (smashing vegetarian choices) in no smoking dining room that overlooks the wood and garden; cl Jan; children over 10; dogs welcome in bedrooms only; £3

PORLOCK
Andrews on the Weir *Porlock Weir, Minehead, Somerset TA24 8PB (01643) 863300* £80; 5 rms, some with sea view. Victorian villa housing a restaurant-with-rooms overlooking the harbour; country house-style décor, imaginative modern british cooking using first-class local produce (Exmoor hill lamb, fish freshly landed on the nearby quay, and west country cheeses are excellent), lovely puddings, and a well chosen wine list; cl Jan; children over 12; dogs welcome in bedrooms

Seapoint *Redway, Porlock, Minehead, Somerset TA24 8QE (01643) 862289* £53, plus winter breaks; 3 rms. Surrounded by the Exmoor hills and with views of Porlock Bay, this no smoking Edwardian guesthouse has a comfortable sitting room with winter log fire, a friendly and relaxing atmosphere, enjoyable home-made food in candlelit dining room, and fine breakfasts; cl Dec/Jan; they are kind to children; dogs welcome in bedrooms

POSTBRIDGE
Lydgate House *Postbridge, Yelverton, Devon PL20 6TJ (01822) 880209* £120; 7 rms. Friendly and relaxed Victorian country house in a secluded wild Dartmoor valley spot (lots of wildlife), with a log fire in the comfortable sitting room, good, simple modern cooking in candlelit conservatory dining room, and fine breakfasts (light lunches and picnics are available); good walks from the door; children over 12; dogs if well behaved are welcome

SALCOMBE
Tides Reach *Cliff Rd, South Sands, Salcombe, Devon TQ8 8LJ (01548) 843466* £202 inc dinner, plus special breaks; 35 rms, many with estuary views. Unusually individual resort hotel run by long-serving owners in

pretty wooded cove by the sea, with airy luxury day rooms, big sea aquarium in cocktail bar, good restaurant food using fresh local produce, friendly efficient service, and squash, snooker, leisure complex, health area, and big heated pool; windsurfing etc, beach over lane, and lots of coast walks; cl Dec-Jan; children over 8; dogs welcome in bedrooms; £5

SANDY PARK

Mill End *Sandy Park, Chagford, Newton Abbot, Devon TQ13 8JN (01647) 432282* **£140**, plus special breaks; 15 attractive rms with fine bthrms and views. Quietly set former flour mill with waterwheel in neatly kept grounds below Dartmoor with 600 yards of private salmon and trout fishing, access to miles of game fishing and still-water fishing on local lakes; comfortable lounges, carefully prepared interesting food, fine breakfasts, and cream teas on the lawn, and good service; cl 2 wks Jan; partial disabled access; dogs welcome with towels and so forth; £10

SELWORTHY

Hindon Farm *Selworthy, Minehead, Somerset TA24 8SH (01643) 705244* **£50**; 3 rms. Organic Exmoor hill farm of 500 acres with sheep, pigs, cattle, donkeys and ducks; lovely walks from the door to the heather moors; fine breakfasts using their own organic bacon, sausages, eggs and fresh baked bread; self-catering cottage with free organic produce hamper on arrival; own organic farm shop; cl Christmas and New Year; dogs in bedrooms; £3

SHEEPWASH

Half Moon *Sheepwash, Beaworthy, Devon EX21 5NE (01409) 231376* **£78**, plus special breaks; 14 rms inc some in converted stables. Civilised heart-of-Devon hideaway in colourful village square with 10 miles of private salmon, sea trout and brown trout fishing on the Torridge, a neatly kept friendly bar, solid old furnishings and big log fire, good wines, lovely evening restaurant, lunchtime bar snacks; cl 20-27 Dec; limited disabled access; dogs welcome away from dining room

SIDFORD

Salty Monk *Church St, Sidford, Exeter, Devon EX10 9QP (01395) 513174* **£95**; 5 cottagey rms, some with spa baths. 16th-c former salt house (where monks trading in salt stayed on their way to Exeter) with leather armchairs in comfortable lounge, good food using local produce cooked by the owners and taken in the newly extended, no smoking restaurant, and quiet garden; cl 2 wks Jan; walks nearby; dogs welcome in bedrooms with outside door and in lounge if on lead; £3

SOUTH ZEAL

Oxenham Arms *South Zeal, Okehampton, Devon EX20 2JT (01837) 840244* **£70**, plus special breaks; 8 rms. Grandly atmospheric old inn dating back to 12th c and first licensed in 1477 (a neolithic standing stone still forms part of the wall in the TV room); elegant beamed and panelled bar with chatty relaxed atmosphere and open fire, a wide choice of enjoyable food and wines, and charming ex-monastery small garden; dogs welcome away from dining room

STAVERTON
Sea Trout *Staverton, Totnes, Devon TQ9 6PA (01803) 762274* £74; 10 cottagey rms. Comfortable pub in quiet hamlet near River Dart with two relaxed beamed bars, log fires, popular food in bar and airy dining conservatory, and terraced garden with fountains and waterfalls; cl Christmas; disabled access; dogs in bedrooms

STOCKLAND
Kings Arms *Stockland, Honiton, Devon EX14 9BS (01404) 881361* £65; 3 rms. Cream-faced thatched pub with elegant rooms, open fires, first-class food in bar and evening restaurant (esp fish), and interesting wine list; skittle alley, live music Sat, Sun pm; cl 25 Dec; dogs in bedrooms

STOKE GABRIEL
Gabriel Court *Stoke Gabriel, Totnes, Devon TQ9 6SF (01803) 782206* £98, plus special breaks; 19 rms, some in former hay lofts. In a walled Elizabethan garden, this attractive family-run manor has quiet relaxing lounges (winter log fire), enjoyable traditional english food, and courteous helpful staff; outdoor heated swimming pool and croquet lawn; dogs welcome away from dining room; £2.50

THURLESTONE
Thurlestone Hotel *Thurlestone, Kingsbridge, Devon TQ7 3NN (01548) 560382* £98; 67 comfortable rms, many with sea or country views. Owned by the same family since 1896, this well run hotel is in lovely grounds with marvellous views over the coast, and tennis and squash courts, badminton court, swimming pool, golf course, and super play area for children; stylish and spacious public rooms, relaxing cocktail bar, imaginative food in attractive no smoking restaurant, and courteous helpful staff; lots for families; marvellous nearby beaches and walks, and fishing, riding and sailing on request; dogs welcome in bedrooms; £6

TWO BRIDGES
Prince Hall *Two Bridges, Yelverton, Devon PL20 6SA (01822) 890403* £140, plus special breaks; 8 attractive spacious rms. Surrounded by Dartmoor National Park, this tranquil, recently refurbished 18th-c country house is run by caring friendly owners and their helpful staff; lovely views from convivial bar, comfortable sitting room, and cosy dining room, open fires, very good evening meals, enjoyable breakfasts, and lots of fine walks; cl mid-Dec to mid-Feb; children over 10; dogs welcome away from restaurant

WOOLACOMBE
Woolacombe Bay Hotel *Woolacombe, Devon EX34 7BN (01271) 870388* £130, plus special breaks; 64 rms. Carefully extended Victorian

hotel in six acres of gardens running down to a splendid three-mile Blue Flag beach; quiet comfortable lounges, elegant high-ceilinged restaurant with chandeliers, bustling bistro for light lunches, two bars, and splendid facilities for children: indoor and outdoor pools and paddling pools, a children's club plus teenage activities, a crèche, discos and bands, board games and books, and billiard room, pool tables and table tennis; 9-hole approach golf, tennis, squash, and gym, sunbed, jacuzzi, and steam room; golf, riding and surfing nearby, and lovely unspoilt surrounding countryside; cl Jan to mid-Feb; dogs in mews apartments; £10

Dorset

Dog Friendly Pubs

CERNE ABBAS
Royal Oak *Long Street*

With delicious bar food, welcoming service and a good choice of drinks, this picturesque creeper-covered Tudor dining pub is well worth a detour. Made using good quality, mostly local ingredients (with herbs grown in the garden), well presented dishes include lunchtime sandwiches, wild mushroom stroganoff, and local venison sausage and mash; also puddings such as wild berry crumble, and an interesting cheese platter; smaller portions are available for children. The three flagstoned communicating rooms have sturdy oak beams, lots of shiny black panelling, an inglenook with an oven, and warm winter log fires. The stone walls and the ceilings are packed with all sorts of small ornaments from local photographs to antique china, brasses and farm tools; candles on tables, and fresh flowers, occasional piped music. It's smoothly run by the enthusiastic licensees, and the staff are pleasant and efficient. Butcombe, Greene King Old Speckled Hen, Quay Weymouth, and St Austell Dartmoor are served from handpumps on the uncommonly long bar counter. They also do around a dozen wines by the glass, and 15 malt whiskies; fruit teas and good coffee too. The enclosed back garden is very pleasant, with Purbeck stone terracing and cedarwood decking, comfortable chairs, and tables under cocktail parasols, and outdoor heaters. On sunny summer afternoons they sometimes serve drinks and snacks out here. Readers tell us parking can be a problem at busy times.

Free house ~ Licensees David and Janice Birch ~ Real ale ~ Bar food ~ Restaurant ~ (01300) 341797 ~ Children in eating area of bar ~ Dogs allowed in bar ~ Open 11.30-3, 6.30(6 Sat)-11; 12-3, 7-10.30 Sun; closed 25 Dec

CHIDEOCK
Anchor *Seatown signposted off A35 from Chideock*

This strikingly set pub nestles dramatically beneath the 188-metre (617-ft) Golden Cap pinnacle, just a few steps from the cove beach and very near the Dorset Coast Path. Ideally placed for the lovely sea and cliff views, there are seats and tables on the spacious front terrace; get here really early in summer if you want to bag a seat. Even out of season it's a pleasure, after a walk by the stormy sea, when the sometimes overwhelming crowds have gone. The little bars feel especially snug then, with roaring winter fires, some sea pictures and lots of interesting local photographs, a few fossils and shells, simple but comfortable seats around neat tables, and low white-planked ceilings; the family room is no smoking. Friendly, efficient staff serve well kept Palmers 200, IPA and Copper on handpump (under light blanket pressure in winter only), and there's a decent little wine list; piped, mainly classical, music. Tasty bar food, and specials such as spinach and feta pie and whole grilled plaice; puddings like apple cake and clotted cream; children's menu too. There are plans to upgrade the lavatories.

Palmers ~ Tenants Paul Wiscombe and Ben Ambridge ~ Real ale ~ Bar food (all day in summer) ~ (01297) 489215 ~ Children welcome ~ Dogs welcome ~ Open 11-11; 12-10.30 Sun; 11-3, 6-11 winter

COLEHILL

Barley Mow *From roundabout junction of A31 Ferndown bypass and B3073 Wimborne road, follow Colehill signpost up Middlehill Road, pass Post Office, and at church turn right into Colehill Lane; OS Sheet 195 map reference 032024*

The cosy low-beamed main bar of this attractive part-thatched and part-tiled former drovers' cottage has a good winter fire in the huge brick inglenook, attractively moulded oak panelling, some Hogarth prints, and a relaxed dining atmosphere. The friendly staff serve very well kept Badger Best, Tanglefoot and a seasonal ale on handpump, and they've a dozen fruit wines. The cat is called Misty, unobtrusive piped music and a fruit machine. Big helpings of home-made bar food could include salmon fishcakes, steak and kidney pie or mediterranean vegetable lasagne, and puddings such as tiramisu; they also do a Sunday roast; an extension to the main bar is set for diners. Sheltered by oak trees, there's a big, pleasant, enclosed lawn at the back with a boules pitch. The pub is specially striking in summer, when colourful flowers in tubs and hanging baskets are set off vividly against the whitewash; there are some nice country walks nearby.

Badger ~ Manager Bruce Cichocki ~ Real ale ~ Bar food ~ (01202) 882140 ~ Children in family room ~ Dogs allowed in bar ~ Open 11-3, 5.30-11; 12-3, 7-10.30 Sun

CORFE CASTLE

Fox *West Street*

Full of character, this very traditional pub is beautifully set with the evocative ruins of Corfe Castle rising up behind the pleasant suntrap garden (reached through a pretty flower-hung side entrance). Much of the pub is built from the same stone as the castle – it's particularly evident in an ancient fossil-dotted alcove and in the pre-1300 stone fireplace. Tiny and atmospheric, the front bar has closely set tables and chairs, a romantic painting of the castle depicting it in its prime, and other pictures above panelling, old-fashioned iron lamps, and hatch service. An ancient well in the lounge bar has been glassed over and lit from within; no piped music or games machines. Tapped from the cask, three to six well kept real ales might include Greene King Abbot and Old Speckled Hen, Fullers London Pride, Timothy Taylors Landlord, Wadworths 6X and Worthington 1744. Big portions of tasty bar food includes home-made soup, ploughman's, and daily specials such as chicken balti and 15oz rib-eye steak. Children are only allowed in the garden. The countryside surrounding this National Trust village is well worth exploring, and there's a local museum opposite. *Free house ~ Licensees Graham White and Miss Annette Brown ~ Real ale ~ Bar food ~ (01929) 480449 ~ Dogs welcome ~ Open 11-3, 6.30-11; 12-3, 7-11 Sun; closed 25 Dec*

EAST CHALDON

Sailors Return *Village signposted from A352 Wareham—Dorchester; from village green, follow Dorchester, Weymouth signpost; note that the village is also known as Chaldon Herring; OS Sheet 194 map reference 790834*

Usefully for walkers, this well extended thatched pub is open all day, and they serve six real ales on handpump: alongside Hampshire Strongs Best and Ringwood Best, you might find four well kept guests such as Archers City Boy, Badger Tanglefoot, Hop Back Summer Lightning and Young's Special; they also have country wines and several malt whiskies. The pub is set in lovely countryside, close to Lulworth Cove, and from nearby West Chaldon, a bridleway leads across to join the Dorset Coast Path by the National Trust cliffs above Ringstead Bay. Picnic-sets, benches and log seats on the grass in front look down over cow pastures to the village, and you can wander to the interesting little nearby church or enjoy a downland walk from the pub. The flagstoned bar still keeps much of its original country-tavern character, while the newer part has unfussy furnishings, old notices for decoration, and open beams showing the roof above. A wide choice of straightforward bar food such as baguettes, chilli con carne, and lamb shoulder. The no smoking dining area has solid old tables in nooks and corners; darts, cribbage, dominoes, TV and piped music. Although fairly isolated it gets very busy at weekends, especially in fine weather. *Free house ~ Licensees Mike Pollard, Claire Kelly and David Slater ~ Real ale ~ Bar food (12-2, 6-9(9.30 Fri/Sat); 12-9(9.30 Fri/Sat)Thurs-Sun in summer) ~ Restaurant ~ (01305) 853847 ~ Children in restaurant ~ Dogs allowed in bar ~ Open 11-11; 12-10.30 Sun*

EAST MORDEN

Cock & Bottle *B3075 between A35 and A31 W of Poole*

The interesting, well cooked bar food is so popular that it's a good idea to book if you want to eat at this particularly welcoming pub. From a changing bar menu dishes might include fresh prawn bisque, home-cured salmon gravlax, stuffed vine leaves with spiced vegetable risotto, and marinated duck breast; also puddings such as apple and cinnamon suet pudding with fresh vanilla sauce, and lunchtime sandwiches. There's a children's menu, and they do half helpings of some main courses. The interior is divided into several communicating areas (mostly laid out for dining), with heavy rough beams, some stripped ceiling boards, squared panelling, a mix of old furnishings in various sizes and degrees of antiquity, small Victorian prints and some engaging bric-a-brac. There's a roaring log fire, and comfortably intimate corners each with just a couple of tables. Although the emphasis is on dining there's still a pubby wood-floored public bar with piped music, a fruit machine, and a sensibly placed darts alcove. This in turn leads on to yet another individually furnished dining room. Most of the restaurant is no smoking, and they have some disabled facilities. As well as a good choice of decent house wines (including half a dozen by the glass), they have well kept Badger Best, K&B and Tanglefoot on handpump; helpful service from the pleasant staff. There are a few picnic-sets outside, a garden area, and an adjoining field with a nice pastoral outlook.

Badger ~ Tenant Peter Meadley ~ Real ale ~ Bar food (12-2, 6(7 Sun)-9) ~ Restaurant ~ (01929) 459238 ~ Children in restaurant ~ Dogs allowed in bar ~ Open 11-2.30(3 Sat), 6-11; 12-3, 7-10.30 Sun

MIDDLEMARSH
Hunters Moon *A352 Sherborne—Dorchester*
Opened in 2002 after a thorough-going refurbishment (and renaming – it used to be the White Horse), this is now a comfortable, neatly kept and welcoming country inn with good food and drink. It rambles around through several largely no smoking linked areas, with a great variety of tables and chairs, plenty of bric-a-brac from decorative teacups, china ornaments and glasses through horse tack and brassware to quite a collection of spirits miniatures. Beams, some panelling, soft lighting from converted oil lamps, three log fires (one in a capacious inglenook), and the way that some attractively cushioned settles form booths all combine to give a cosy relaxed feel. The food (made with lots of local produce) includes lunchtime sandwiches, home-made game pie, chargrilled vegetables and pasta or fishcakes, and puddings such as treacle tart. Well kept Caledonian Six Nations, Palmers Dorset Gold and St Austell Tribute on handpump, with decent wines by the glass, proper coffee, and a good range of spirits and soft drinks; service is good, and the piped pop music is faint. The neat lawn has circular picnic-sets as well as the more usual ones; the new bedrooms are in what was formerly a skittle alley and stable block.

Free house ~ Licensees Liz and Brendan Malone ~ Real ale ~ Bar food ~ (01963) 210966 ~ Children in eating area of bar ~ Dogs allowed in bar ~ Open 11-3, 6-11; 12-3, 6-10.30 Sun ~ Bedrooms: £45S/£60S

MUDEFORD
Ship in Distress *Stanpit; off B3059 at roundabout*
The décor in the bar's two cottagey rooms is good fun: well worth a close look round at quiet times, when you've room to move freely. All sorts of more or less nautical bric-a-brac spans the gamut from rope fancywork and brassware through lanterns, oars and ceiling nets and ensigns to a somewhat murky aquarium, boat models, and the odd piratical figure. Besides a good few boat pictures, the room on the right has masses of snapshots of locals caught up in various waterside japes, under its glass tabletops. Service is friendly, and they have well kept Adnams Broadside, Bass, Brakspears

Three Sheets and Ringwood Best on handpump, and good wines by the glass; darts, fruit machine, a couple of TV sets, and the sort of dated piped pop music that fits in rather well. All this cheery clutter, and the homely old leather sofas alongside more orthodox pub furnishings, might give you the idea that this is just an entertaining local. Don't be fooled. The carefully cooked fresh local fish and seafood is good and imaginative. The menu includes bar snacks (not Friday and Saturday night), with other dishes such as Brixham scallops, lobster salad and grilled dover sole; puddings such as strawberry mousse with vodka-minted strawberries; they also do steak and a vegetarian dish, and you can get cream teas in summer. A spreading and appealing two-room restaurant area, as cheerful in its way as the bar, has a light-hearted mural sketching out the impression of a window open on a sunny boating scene, and another covering its dividing wall with vines. There are tables out on the back terrace; look out for the two springer spaniels.

Punch ~ Tenants S Canning and Dennis Smith ~ Real ale ~ Bar food (all day in summer) ~ Restaurant ~ (01202) 485123 ~ Children in restaurant ~ Dogs allowed in bar ~ Open 10-11(10.30 Sun)

PAMPHILL

Vine *Off B3082 on NW edge of Wimborne: turn onto Cowgrove Hill at Cowgrove signpost, then turn right up Vine Hill*

Two tiny bars make up this charmingly simple and unspoilt country pub, on the National Trust's Kingston Lacy estate. In 1991 the Trust bought the pub from Whitbreads, though it's run independently by the family who have been tenants now for three or four generations. They certainly look after it extremely well – it has that well cared-for feel that matters so much in places like this. One room with a warm coal-effect gas fire has three tables, the other just half a dozen or so seats on its lino floor, some of them huddling under the stairs that lead up to an overflow room. Local photographs (like the regular with his giant pumpkin) and notices decorate the painted panelling, with a few animal prints and decorative plates. At weekends and in summer it can get very busy – there are walks all around on National Trust land. In winter they have good mulled wine as well as well kept ales such as Stonehenge Danish Dynamite and Youngs on handpump, and simple food including fresh sandwiches; service is friendly. There are picnic-sets and benches out on a sheltered gravel terrace, and more share a heated and fairy-lit verandah with a grapevine. Round the back a patch of grass has a climbing frame. No children inside.

Free house ~ Licensee Mrs Sweatland ~ Real ale ~ Bar food (lunchtime only) ~ (01202) 882259 ~ Dogs welcome ~ Open 11-2.30, 7-11; 12-3, 7-10.30 Sun

SHERBORNE

Digby Tap *Cooks Lane; park in Digby Road and walk round corner*

Handy for the glorious golden stone abbey, this down-to-earth old-fashioned ale house serves around four or five superbly kept beers on handpump. Mostly from West Country brewers such as Exmoor, Otter, Sharps and St Austell, the beers change regularly, with around 20 different types a week. Not a pub for those seeking sophistication, the interior is simple but full of character, and the flagstoned main bar is relaxed and friendly with a good mix of customers. Several small games rooms have pool, cribbage, fruit machine, TV and piped music. Large portions of reasonably priced, straightforward bar food includes tasty soup, filled baked potatoes, and daily specials such as gammon and pineapple. There are some seats outside.

Free house ~ Licensees Peter Lefevre and Nick Whigham ~ Real ale ~ Bar food (12-1.45, not evenings, or Sun) ~ No credit cards ~ (01935) 813148 ~ Children welcome in eating area of bar at lunchtime ~ Dogs welcome ~ Open 11-2.30, 5.30-11; 11-3, 6-11 Sat; 12-3, 7-10.30 Sun; closed 1 Jan

STOURTON CAUNDLE

Trooper *Village signposted off A30 E of Milborne Port*

Opposite Enid Blyton's former farm (better known as Finniston Farm in one of her Famous Five books), this appealing little stone-built pub now has friendly new licensees. The tiny low-ceilinged bar on the left has cushioned pews and wheelback chairs, a cabinet of sports trophies, charity bookshelves, over 80 horse bits, and lots of good horsebrasses on their leathers decorating the big stripped stone fireplace, which now has an oak pew built into it. There's another big fireplace in the stripped stone dining room on the right; cribbage, dominoes, shove-ha'penny, TV, darts, piped music, and a skittle alley. Simple lunchtime snacks (made with local produce) and a handful of hot meals such as cod and chips, and steak and kidney pie; children's meals too. Two or three well kept real ales on handpump might include Archers Best and Hop Back Crop Circle. There are a few picnic-sets out in front and in its side garden, by a stream which is cut into a deep stone channel along the village lane.

Free house ~ Licensees Roger and Rachel Paull ~ Real ale ~ Bar food (lunchtime Tues-Sat only) ~ (01963) 362405 ~ Children welcome ~ Dogs welcome ~ Open 12-2.30, 7-11; 12-11(10.30 Sun) wknds; 12-2.30, 7-11(10.30 Sun) in winter; closed Mon lunchtime

TARRANT MONKTON

Langton Arms *Village signposted from A354, then head for church*

As we went to press, the friendly licensees were in the process of re-building part of this pretty 17th-c pub, after a fire which destroyed the thatched roof and first floor, but they hope to have fully re-opened by the time this Guide comes out. Whether you're a family looking for a leisurely lunch or a dog-walker after a well kept pint, you can expect a cheerful welcome here. Alongside Hop Back Best and a beer from Ringwood, they serve three constantly changing guests from brewers such as Cottage, Hampshire and Scattor Rock on handpump; there's an annual beer festival. The fairly simple beamed bar has a huge inglenook fireplace, settles, stools at the counter and other mixed dark furniture, and the public bar has a jukebox, darts, pool, a fruit machine, TV, cribbage and dominoes; piped music. The no smoking bistro restaurant is in an attractively reworked barn, and the skittle alley doubles as a no smoking family room during the day. With some really interesting choices, the enjoyable menu includes bar snacks such as filled baguettes, and pork and leek sausages and chips, with other dishes like crispy haddock goujons, game pie and local steaks; puddings such as home-made steamed coffee and walnut pudding or local ice-creams; children's meals as well. There's a very good wood-chip children's play area in the garden, and your dog may be lucky enough to be offered a free sausage. Tarrant Monkton is a charming village (with a ford that can flow quite fast in wet weather), and is well located for local walks and exploring the area. The comfortable en-suite bedrooms are in a modern block at the back; good breakfasts.

Free house ~ Licensees Barbara and James Cossins ~ Real ale ~ Bar food (11.30-2.30(3 Sun), 6-9; 11.30-9.30 Sat) ~ Restaurant ~ (01258) 830225 ~ Children in restaurant and family room ~ Dogs allowed in bedrooms ~ Open 11-11; 12-10.30 Sun ~ Bedrooms: £50B/£70B

WEST BAY
West Bay *Station Road*
'Excellent' is a word that crops up frequently when readers are describing this superbly run seaside pub. If you've come to eat you're in for a treat (though it's so popular, booking is virtually essential even on a winter weekday), especially if you like fish. There's always at least ten fresh fish dishes to choose from. Other imaginative dishes (they use local suppliers wherever possible) might be steak and kidney casserole with mustard dumplings and duck breast with stir-fried vegetables; lunchtime bar snacks such as sandwiches or prawn and smoked salmon salad. They also do children's meals. The friendly hands-on licensees and cheerful staff help generate an enjoyably relaxed atmosphere. An island servery separates the fairly simple bare-boards front part with its coal-effect gas fire and mix of sea and nostalgic prints from a cosier carpeted no smoking dining area with more of a country kitchen feel. Well kept Palmers IPA, Copper and 200 on handpump, good house wines (with ten by the glass), and whiskies; decent piped music, and a skittle alley (the local team meets here). A dining terrace has tables outside; there's plenty of parking. Readers very much like staying in the quiet and homely bedrooms; delicious breakfasts.

Palmers ~ Tenants John Ford and Karen Trimby ~ Real ale ~ Bar food (not Sun evening exc bank hols) ~ Restaurant ~ (01308) 422157 ~ Children in restaurant ~ Dogs allowed in bar ~ Open 11-2.30, 6-11; 12-3 Sun; closed Sun evening exc bank hols ~ Bedrooms: £50B/£65B

WEST BEXINGTON
Manor Hotel *Village signposted off B3157 SE of Bridport; Beach Road*
Mentioned in the Domesday Book, this well liked stone-built hotel is a relaxing place to spend the night. You can see the sea from the smart no smoking Victorian-style conservatory (which has airy furnishings and lots of plants), the comfortable lounge with its log fire, the bedrooms, and also the garden, where there are picnic-sets on a small lawn with flowerbeds lining the low sheltering walls; a much bigger side lawn has a children's play area. The bustling downstairs cellar bar has horsebrasses on the walls,

stools and low-backed chairs (with one fat seat carved from a beer cask) under the black beams and joists, as well as heavy harness over the log fire; piped music. Enjoyable bar food might include delicious fish soup, crab and asparagus pancakes, mushroom stroganoff or duck leg casserole; puddings such as chocolate roulade; the good restaurant is no smoking. It's well run, and the helpful staff go out of their way to make visitors feel welcome, and are kind to families with young children. Well kept Butcombe Gold and Quay Harbour Master on handpump, quite a few malt whiskies, and several wines by the glass. The pub is just a stroll from lovely if tiring walks on Chesil Beach and the cliffs above; there are stunning views from the approach road.

Free house ~ Licensees Peter King and Sheree Lynch ~ Real ale ~ Bar food ~ Restaurant ~ (01308) 897616 ~ Children welcome ~ Dogs allowed in bar ~ Open 11-11; 12-10.30 Sun ~ Bedrooms: £75B/£120S(£120B)

Dog Friendly Hotels, B&Bs and Farms

BEAMINSTER
Bridge House *3 Prout Bridge, Beaminster, Dorset DT8 3AY (01308) 862200* £**110**; 14 rms, more spacious in main house. 13th-c priest's house, family owned, with open fire in sitting room, cosy bar, breakfast room overlooking the attractive walled garden, good food using local produce in Georgian dining room, friendly service, and an informal, relaxed atmosphere; cl 30-31 Dec; dogs welcome in coach house bedrooms; walks in surrounding countryside

BOURNEMOUTH
Langtry Manor *26 Derby Rd, Eastcliff, Bournemouth, Dorset BH1 3QB (01202) 553887* £**149.50**, plus special breaks; 25 pretty rms, some in the manor, some in the lodge. Built by Edward VII for Lillie Langtry, with lots of memorabilia, relaxed public rooms, helpful friendly staff, and good food inc Edwardian banquet every Sat evening; no children; disabled access; dogs welcome in bedrooms; £10

BRIDPORT
Britmead House *West Bay Rd, Bridport, Dorset DT6 4EG (01308) 422941* £**66**, plus special breaks; 8 rms. Extended Victorian hotel with lots to do nearby, comfortable lounge overlooking garden, attractive dining room, good breakfasts, and kind helpful service; disabled access; dogs welcome in bedrooms

DORCHESTER
Maiden Castle Farm *Dorchester, Dorset DT2 9PR (01305) 262356* £**60**; 4 rms. Victorian farmhouse in 2 acres of gardens in the heart of Hardy country and set beneath the prehistoric earthworks from which the farm

takes its name; views of the hill fort and countryside, nice breakfasts, afternoon tea with home-made cakes, and comfortable traditionally furnished sitting room which overlooks the garden; dogs welcome in bedrooms

EAST KNIGHTON

Countryman *East Knighton, Dorchester, Dorset DT2 8LL (01305) 852666* £72; 6 rms. Attractively converted and much liked pair of old cottages with open fires and plenty of character in the main bar which opens into several smaller areas, no smoking family room, half a dozen real ales, imaginative, generously served food inc nice breakfasts and a hot carvery in large restaurant, and courteous staff; cl 25 Dec; dogs welcome

EVERSHOT

Summer Lodge *Evershot, Dorchester, Dorset DT2 0JR (01935) 83424* £260, plus special breaks; 24 big, individually decorated rms. Beautifully kept, peacefully set former dower house with lovely flowers in the comfortable and elegantly furnished day rooms, excellent food using the best local produce in most attractive restaurant overlooking pretty garden, delicious breakfasts and afternoon tea, and personal caring service; indoor swimming pool, tennis and croquet; children over 7 in evening restaurant; partial disabled access; dogs welcome in bedrooms; £7.50

FARNHAM

Museum Inn *Farnham, Blandford Forum, Dorset DT11 8DE (01725) 516261* £75; 8 rms. Odd-looking thatched building with various effortlessly civilised areas – flagstoned bar with big inglenook fireplace, light beams and good comfortably cushioned furnishings, dining room with a cosy hunt theme, and what feels rather like a contemporary version of a baronial hall, soaring up to a high glass ceiling, with dozens of antlers and a stag's head looking down on to a long wooden table and church-style pews; excellent food, three real ales, a fine choice of wines, and very good attentive service; dogs in bar and bedrooms

KINGSTON

Kingston Country Courtyard *West St, Kingston, Corfe Castle, Wareham, Dorset BH20 5LH (01929) 481066* £60; 10 rms in most attractive farm building conversion. A collection of stylish suites and apartments in beautifully decorated houses keeping much original character and charm, and with wonderful views over Corfe Castle, Arne peninsula, and the Isle of Wight; enjoyable full english or continental breakfasts in Old Cart Shed dining room; self-catering too; lots to do nearby; cl Dec/Jan; good disabled access; dogs welcome in bedrooms; £5

LOWER BOCKHAMPTON

Yalbury Cottage *Lower Bockhampton, Dorchester, Dorset DT2 8PZ (01305) 262382* £94, plus special breaks; 8 rms overlooking garden or fields. Very attractive family-run 16th-c thatched house with a relaxed friendly atmosphere, and low beams and inglenook fireplaces in comfortable lounge and dining room; carefully cooked often imaginative food, good wines, and attractive mature garden; dogs welcome in bedrooms; £5

LYME REGIS
White House *Silver St, Lyme Regis, Dorset DT7 3HR (01297) 443420* **£54**; 7 rms. A short walk from the beach, this small Georgian house has nice back views of the coastline, a friendly atmosphere, books, maps and local information in big comfortable lounge, full english breakfast in attractive dining room, and packed lunches and flasks on request; cl Christmas and New Year; dogs welcome in bedrooms; £1; plenty of surrounding walks

SHIPTON GORGE
Innsacre Farmhouse *Shipton Lane, Shipton Gorge, Bridport, Dorset DT6 4LJ (01308) 456137* **£80**; 4 rms. 17th-c no smoking farmhouse in 10 acres of lawns, woodland and nature trails and tucked away in a little valley; french country-style furnishings, a simple and comfortable lounge with a woodburning stove in big inglenook fireplace, good, interesting no-choice evening meals (by arrangement) in a dinner party atmosphere in the beamed dining room, nice breakfasts that include brioche, pastries and pancakes as well as a traditional english choice, packed lunches for walkers, and an informal, friendly atmosphere; fishing nearby; dogs welcome away from dining room; £10

STUDLAND
Knoll House *Studland, Swanage, Dorset BH19 3AH (01929) 450450* **£276** inc lunch and dinner; 80 comfortable rms. Spacious, very well run hotel owned by the same family for over 45 years, in 100 acres with marvellous views of Studland Bay and direct access to the fine 3-mile beach; relaxed friendly atmosphere, particularly helpful staff, super food in dining room overlooking the gardens, cocktail bar, TV lounge, and excellent facilities for families: attractive children's dining room (with proper food and baby food, microwave, own fridge, etc.), well equipped play room, table tennis, pool and table football, heated outdoor pool and health spa, tennis courts, small private golf course, marvellous adventure playground, and nearby sea fishing, riding, walking, sailing and windsurfing; cl end Oct-Easter; children over 8 in evening dining room; disabled access; dogs welcome away from dining rooms, pool and spa; £4

STURMINSTER NEWTON
Plumber Manor *Hazelbury Bryan Rd, Plumber, Sturminster Newton, Dorset DT10 2AF (01258) 472507* **£170**, plus special breaks; 16 very comfortable rms, some in nearby period buildings; many in the house itself overlook the peaceful, pretty garden and down the stream with herons and even maybe egrets. Handsome 17th-c, family-run house in quiet countrys- ide, with warm fires, a convivial well stocked bar, attractive writing room/lounge, resident black labradors, good interesting food inc tempting

puddings in three dining rooms, nice breakfasts, a relaxed atmosphere, and exceptionally friendly helpful service; tennis; cl Feb; children welcome by prior arrangement; disabled access; dogs welcome in bedrooms

WIMBORNE MINSTER

Beechleas *17 Poole Rd, Wimborne, Dorset BH21 1QA (01202) 841684* £99, plus special breaks; 9 attractive, comfortable rms. Carefully restored Georgian house with open fires in cosy sitting room and charming dining room, airy conservatory overlooking walled garden, enjoyable Aga-cooked food using organic produce, nice breakfasts, and friendly helpful owners; lots to do and see nearby; cl 24 Dec–mid-Jan; partial disabled access; dogs welcome in bedrooms by arrangement

YELLOWHAM WOOD

Yellowham Farmhouse *Yellowham Wood, Dorchester, Dorset DT2 8RW (01305) 262892* £56, plus special breaks; 2 comfortable no smoking rms. Peaceful place close to the town but surrounded by 120 acres of farmland and 130 acres of woodland; newly built sitting/garden room for residents, good breakfasts, evening meal by arrangement, tennis court and croquet; children over 4; dogs welcome in bedrooms

Essex

Dog Friendly Pubs

CHAPPEL
Swan *Wakes Colne; pub visible just off A1124 Colchester—Halstead*
Even a 74-mile round trip isn't enough to deter one couple from coming to this deservedly popular old timbered pub. A treat for fish-lovers, there's an excellent range of superbly cooked fresh fish. Other bar food includes lunchtime filled baguettes, as well as chicken curry or calves liver and bacon; home-made puddings such as plum crumble. They also do a simple children's menu. The pub is splendidly set, with the River Colne running through the garden on its way downstream to an impressive Victorian viaduct. Big overflowing flower tubs and french street signs lend the sheltered suntrap cobbled courtyard a continental feel, and gas heaters mean that even on cooler evenings you can still sit outside. The spacious and low-beamed rambling bar has standing oak timbers dividing off side areas, plenty of dark wood chairs around lots of dark tables for diners, a couple of swan pictures and plates on the white and partly panelled walls, and a few attractive tiles above the very big fireplace. The central bar area keeps a pubbier atmosphere, with regulars dropping in for a drink; fruit machine, cribbage, dominoes and piped music. One of the lounge bars is no smoking. Well kept Greene King IPA and Abbot and a guest such as Morland Tanners Jack on handpump are swiftly served by the friendly staff; they've wines by the glass, and just under two dozen malt whiskies. The Railway Centre (a must for train buffs) is only a few minutes' walk away.
Free house ~ Licensee Terence Martin ~ Real ale ~ Bar food (12-2.30, 6.30-10(10.30 Sat); 12-3, 6.30-9.30 Sun) ~ Restaurant ~ (01787) 222353 ~ Children in eating area of bar and restaurant ~ Dogs allowed in bar ~ Open 11-3, 6-11; 11-11 Sat; 12-10.30 Sun

FINGRINGHOE
Whalebone *Follow Rowhedge, Fingringhoe signpost off A134, the part that's just S of Colchester centre; or Fingringhoe signposted off B1025 S of Colchester*
A good way to start the day, you can get a tasty breakfast (from 10-11.30am) at this civilised and relaxing pub. The pale yellow-washed interior has been very nicely done out, its three room areas airily opened

together, leaving some timber studs; stripped tables on the unsealed bare boards have a pleasant mix of chairs and cushioned settles. Roman blinds with swagged pelmets, neat wall lamps, a hanging chandelier and local watercolours (for sale) are good finishing touches. Although you'll feel welcome if you're just after a drink (the staff are friendly and courteous), the main focus is the imaginative, freshly cooked food. An enticing choice of dishes is listed on a blackboard over the small but warming coal fire; they also do weekday lunchtime sandwiches and baguettes (they let you choose your own fillings), and children's meals. Greene King IPA and Old Speckled Hen are well kept alongside a couple of guests such as Ridleys Prospect and Mighty Oak Burntwood on handpump, and there are decent house wines; piped music. Pleasant on a fine day, the back garden, with gravel paths winding through the grass around a sizeable old larch tree, has picnic-sets with a peaceful valley view; they sometimes have plays out here in summer. Readers recommend stopping off at the Fingringhoe Wick Nature Reserve.

Free house ~ Licensees Sam and Victoria Burroughes ~ Real ale ~ Bar food (10-2.30, 7-9.30) ~ (01206) 729307 ~ Children in family room ~ Dogs welcome ~ Open 10-3, 5.30-11; 10-11(10.30 Sun) wknds

FULLER STREET

Square & Compasses *From A12 Chelmsford—Witham take Hatfield Peverel exit, and from B1137 there, follow Terling signpost, keeping straight on past Terling towards Great Leighs; from A131 Chelmsford—Braintree, turn off in Great Leighs towards Fairstead and Terling*

Tuesday night is sausage and mash night at this civilised little country pub, and you can choose from around 20 different varieties of sausage. Along with the stuffed birds, traps and brasses which adorn the L-shaped beamed bar, there are otter tails, birds' eggs and old photographs of local characters, many of whom still use the pub. This comfortable and well lit carpeted bar has a woodburning stove as well as a big log fire; shove-ha'penny, table skittles, cribbage and dominoes; disabled lavatories. Very well kept Nethergate Suffolk County and Ridleys IPA are tapped from the cask, and they've also decent french regional wines. Besides lunchtime sandwiches, good home-made dishes include changing specials such as beer-battered cod and chips, properly cooked rib-eye steak, and sticky toffee pudding; on Sunday evenings they have a limited menu. There are gentle country views from tables outside.

Free house ~ Licensees Howard Potts and Ginny Austin ~ Real ale ~ Bar food (12-2.30, 7-9.30(10 Sat); 12-2.30, 7-8.30 Sun; not Mon) ~ Restaurant ~ (01245) 361477 ~ Children welcome away from bar ~ Dogs welcome ~ Open 11.30-3, 6.30(7 in winter)-11; 12-3, 7-10.30 Sun; closed Mon exc bank hol Mon lunchtime

GOSFIELD

Green Man *3 miles N of Braintree*

It's worth trying to catch the help-yourself cold table at this smart dining pub: you can choose from home-cooked ham and pork, turkey, tongue, beef and poached or smoked salmon, as well as game pie, salads and home-made pickles. If you want something hot, big portions of bar food (served with fresh vegetables and home-made chips) from a mostly traditional english menu; or you can choose from snacks such as soup, sandwiches and filled baked potatoes; puddings might be fruit pie or treacle tart. Even midweek it's a good idea to book. The two little bars have a happy relaxed atmosphere (or you can sit outside in the garden), and the staff are exceptionally friendly. Many of the decent nicely priced wines are available by the glass, and they've very well kept Greene King IPA and Abbot on handpump; pool and a jukebox.

Greene King ~ Lease Debbie With and Tony Bowen ~ Real ale ~ Bar food (not Sun evening) ~ Restaurant ~ (01787) 472746 ~ Children in restaurant ~ Dogs allowed in bar ~ Open 11-3, 6-11; 12-4, 7-10.30 Sun

HORNDON-ON-THE-HILL

Bell *M25 junction 30 into A13, then left into B1007 after 7 miles, village signposted from here*

Seven real ales, an outstanding choice of wines, and imaginative food make this bustling 15th-c village inn a popular choice with readers. The heavily beamed bar has some antique high-backed settles and benches, rugs on the flagstones or highly polished oak floorboards, and a curious collection of ossified hot cross buns hanging from a beam. They stock over a hundred well chosen wines from all over the world, including 16 by the glass, and you can buy very fairly priced bottles off-sales. They're keen on supporting local brewers: three swiftly rotating guests such as Mauldons Suffolk Pride, Mighty Oak Burntwood and Charles Wells Bombardier are well kept on handpump alongside Bass, Crouch Vale Brewers Gold and Greene King IPA. They hold occasional beer festivals. The ambitious menu changes frequently, and is available in the bar and no smoking restaurant; you may need to book. Beautifully presented dishes might include roast salmon with smoked salmon crust and wild garlic or roast rib of beef with caramelised onions and fennel and balsamic crème fraîche, with puddings such as white chocolate, rhubarb and mascarpone trifle. There is a separate bar menu and they also do a popular olives, bread and butter platter. Centuries ago, many important medieval dignitaries would have stayed here, as it was the last inn before travellers heading south could ford the Thames at Highams Causeway.

Free house ~ Licensee John Vereker ~ Real ale ~ Bar food (12-2, 6.30(7 Sun)-9.45; not bank hol Mon or 25/26 Dec) ~ Restaurant ~ (01375) 642463 ~ Children in eating area of bar and restaurant ~ Dogs allowed in bar and bedrooms ~ Open 11-2.30(3 Sat), 5.30(6 Sat)-11; 12-4, 7-10.30 Sun; closed bank hol Mon, and 25/26 Dec ~ Bedrooms: /£65B

LITTLE BRAXTED

Green Man *Kelvedon Road; village signposted off B1389 by NE end of A12 Witham bypass — keep on patiently*

On a fine afternoon, picnic-sets in the pleasant sheltered garden behind this pretty brick pub are a good place to while away an hour or two. Inside the welcoming little lounge has an interesting collection of bric-a-brac, including 200 horsebrasses, some harness, mugs hanging from a beam, and a lovely copper urn; it's especially cosy in winter when you'll really feel the benefit of the open fire. The tiled public bar has books, darts, shove-ha'penny, cribbage, dominoes and a video machine. Welcoming staff serve Ridleys IPA, Rumpus and Old Bob on handpump, along with several malt whiskies. Reasonably priced, hearty bar food such as filled baguettes or baked potatoes, sausages and creamed potatoes, and a couple of daily specials such as steak and ale pie and minted lamb shank, while puddings might be treacle tart. The pub is tucked away down an isolated country lane.

Ridleys ~ Tenant Neil Pharaoh ~ Real ale ~ Bar food ~ (01621) 891659 ~ Dogs allowed in bar ~ Open 11.30-3, 6-11; 12-3.30, 7-10.30 Sun

LITTLE WALDEN
Crown *B1052 N of Saffron Walden*
The cosy low-beamed bar of this friendly 18th-c low white cottage has a good log fire in the brick fireplace, bookroom-red walls, flowery curtains and a mix of bare boards and navy carpeting. Seats, ranging from high-backed pews to little cushioned armchairs, are spaced around a good variety of closely arranged tables, mostly big, some stripped. The small red-tiled room on the right has two little tables; piped local radio. The big draw are the four or five well kept real ales tapped straight from the cask, which might include Adnams, Greene King IPA and Abbot, and a couple of changing guests such as City of Cambridge Boathouse and Mauldons Bitter. Hearty bar food includes home-made lasagne and steak and ale pie, with daily specials on blackboards such as vegetable curry, smoked haddock mornay, cold seafood platter and beef stroganoff; puddings might be tasty apple crumble or bread and butter pudding. There are tables out on a side patio.

Free house ~ Licensee Colin Hayling ~ Real ale ~ Bar food (not Mon evening) ~ (01799) 522475 ~ Children in eating area of bar and restaurant ~ Dogs welcome ~ Trad jazz Weds evening ~ Open 11.30-3, 6-11; 12-10.30 Sun ~ Bedrooms: £45S/£60S

STAPLEFORD TAWNEY
Mole Trap *Tawney Common, which is a couple of miles away from Stapleford Tawney and is signposted off A113 just N of M25 overpass – keep on; OS Sheet 167 map reference 500013*
Although it's tucked away in what seems like the back of beyond, this country pub is usually humming with customers. The smallish carpeted bar (mind your head as you go in) has black dado, beams and joists, brocaded wall seats, library chairs and bentwood elbow chairs around plain pub tables, and steps down through a partly knocked-out timber stud wall to a similar area. There are a few small pictures, 3-D decorative plates, some dried-flower arrangements and (on the sloping ceiling formed by a staircase beyond) some regulars' snapshots, with a few dozen beermats stuck up around the serving bar. It's especially cosy in winter, when you can fully

appreciate the three blazing coal fires. As well as Fullers London Pride, they have three constantly changing guests such as Crouch Vale Brewers Gold, Hop Back Summer Lightning and Timothy Taylors Landlord on handpump; the piped radio tends to be almost inaudible over the contented chatter. Bar food includes lasagne, lamb curry and steak, or fresh daily fish; they do a roast on Sunday. Outside are some plastic tables and chairs and a picnic-set, and there's a growing tribe of resident animals, many rescued, including friendly cats, rabbits, a couple of dogs, goats and horses. The pub is run with considerable individuality by forthright licensees. Do make sure children behave well here if you bring them.

Free house ~ Licensees Mr and Mrs Kirtley ~ Real ale ~ Bar food (not Sun evening) ~ No credit cards ~ (01992) 522394 ~ Well behaved children in family room ~ Dogs welcome ~ Open 11.30-3, 6-11; 12-4, 6.30-10.30 Sun

STOW MARIES

Prince of Wales *B1012 between S Woodham Ferrers and Cold Norton Posters*
As well as five interesting, frequently changing real ales on handpump from brewers such as Everards, Mauldons, Phoenix, Ridleys and Stonehenge, you'll also find four draught belgian beers at this appealingly laid-back pub; several bottled beers, farm cider, and vintage ports too. Although the cosy and chatty low-ceilinged rooms appear unchanged since the turn of the last century, they've in fact been renovated in a traditional style. Few have space for more than one or two tables or wall benches on the tiled or bare-boards floors, though the room in the middle squeezes in quite a jumble of chairs and stools. Besides sandwiches or ciabattas, generously served dishes (with good fish specials) could include ham, egg and chips, deep-fried calamari, lamb shank with raspberry beer and mash, and puddings such as sticky toffee pudding; one of the dining areas is now no smoking. On Thursday evenings in winter they fire up the old bread oven to make pizzas in the room that used to be the village bakery, while in summer on some Sundays they barbecue unusual fish (also steaks for the less adventurous). There are seats and tables in the back garden, and between the picket fence and the pub's white weather boarded frontage is a terrace with herbs in Victorian chimney pots. On most bank holidays and some Sundays, there are live bands, and they've a marquee for summer weekends.

Free house ~ Licensee Rob Walster ~ Real ale ~ Bar food (12-2.30, 7-9.30; 12-9 Sun) ~ (01621) 828971 ~ Children in family room ~ Dogs welcome ~ Open 11-11; 12-10.30 Sun

WENDENS AMBO

Bell *B1039 just W of village*
The small cottagey low-ceilinged rooms of this village pub have brasses on ancient timbers, wheelback chairs around neat tables, comfortably cushioned seats worked into snug alcoves, quite a few pictures on the cream walls, and an inviting open fire. A real bonus in summer, the extensive back garden has plenty to keep children entertained, with a wooden wendy house, crazy golf (£1), a sort of mini nature-trail wandering off through the shrubs, and a big tree-sheltered lawn; they're

currently landscaping the meadow at the bottom. Nicely lit up in the evenings, you can eat out on the suntrap patio; look out for Reggie and Ronnie the goats (who have a habit of escaping). Adnams Broadside and Ansells Mild are well kept on handpump, along with a couple of changing guests such as Fullers London Pride and Shepherd Neame Spitfire. Friendly service from the new landlord and his staff; cribbage, dominoes and piped music. Tasty bar food includes sandwiches, sausages and mash, steak, mushroom and ale pie and puddings; the dining room is no smoking. The pub is handy for Audley End.

Free house ~ Licensees Martin Housen and Elizabeth Silk ~ Real ale ~ Bar food (12-2, 6-9, not Sun evenings) ~ Restaurant ~ (01799) 540382 ~ Children welcome away from bar ~ Dogs welcome ~ Open 11.30-2.30, 5-11; 11.30-11 Fri/Sat; 12-10.30 Sun

Dog Friendly Hotels, B&Bs and Farms

BURNHAM-ON-CROUCH

White Harte *The Quay, Burnham-on-Crouch, Essex CM0 8AS (01621) 782106* £78; 19 rms, 11 with own bthrm. Old-fashioned 17th-c yachting inn on quay overlooking the River Crouch with its own jetty; high ceilings, oak tables, polished parquet flooring, sea pictures, panelling, residents' lounge, and decent food in bar and restaurant; dogs welcome; £3

GREAT DUNMOW

Starr Restaurant *Market Place, Great Dunmow, Essex CM6 1AX (01371) 874321* £115, plus special breaks; 8 individually decorated rms in old stable block. Family run, rather smart restaurant-with-rooms in former 15th-c pub with open fire in rustic bar, first rate food in airy beamed no smoking dining room, an excellent wine list, and helpful, professional service; dogs welcome in bedrooms only

PLESHEY

Yew Tree Farm *Pleshey, Chelmsford, Essex CM3 1HX (01245) 231229* £50; 2 attractive rms. Peacefully set farmhouse with a warm welcome from the charming owners, good english breakfasts, croquet lawn and exercise paddock; no smoking; cl Christmas; dogs in bedrooms by prior arrangement

Gloucestershire

Dog Friendly Pubs

ALMONDSBURY

Bowl *1¼ miles from M5 junction 16 (and therefore quite handy for M4 junction 20; from A38 towards Thornbury, turn first left signposted Lower Almondsbury, then first right down Sundays Hill, then at bottom right again into Church Road*

A popular break from the M5, this bustling pub is prettily set with a church next door and lovely flowering tubs, hanging baskets, and window boxes. Well kept on handpump, they serve around half a dozen real ales such as Bass, Bath Barnstormer and Gem, Courage Best, Moles Best, and Smiles May Fly; piped music and fruit machine. The long beamed bar is neatly kept, with terracotta plush-patterned modern settles, dark green cushioned stools and mates' chairs around elm tables, horsebrasses on stripped bare stone walls, and big winter log fire at one end, with a woodburning stove at the other. Besides filled baguettes, enjoyable bar food includes interesting salads, steak and kidney pie or crispy duck noodles, and specials such as thai chicken curry, and puddings like apple and blackberry crumble; half helpings of some main courses are available for children under 12. They ask to keep your credit card behind the bar. In good weather, the seats outside get snapped up quickly.

Free house ~ Licensee Miss E Alley ~ Real ale ~ Bar food (12-2.30, 6-10; 12-8 Sun, not 25 Dec) ~ Restaurant ~ (01454) 612757 ~ Children in eating area of bar and restaurant ~ Dogs allowed in bar and bedrooms ~ Open 11.30-3, 5(6 Sat)-11; 12-10.30 Sun; closed 25 Dec ~ Bedrooms: £44.50S/£71S

BARNSLEY

Village Pub *B4425 Cirencester—Burford*

They make their own bread at this smart and rather civilised dining pub – a great place to come if you're in need of a treat. The menu changes twice a day, and good (but not cheap) lunchtime dishes might include country terrine with home-made chutney, cold beef salad, and smoked haddock with fresh laver bread; evening dishes such as steamed mussels or roast quail with grilled courgettes and aubergine; puddings might feature coconut tart with strawberry sorbet. Calm and relaxing, the low-ceilinged communicating rooms (one is no smoking) have oil paintings, plush chairs, stools, and window settles around polished candlelit tables, and country magazines and newspapers to read. Well kept Hook Norton Bitter and Wadworths 6X, with maybe a guest such as Archers Best on handpump, local cider and apple juice, and around 14 wines by the glass; service is swift and courteous. The sheltered back courtyard has plenty of good solid wooden furniture under umbrellas, outdoor heaters and its own outside servery.

Free house ~ Licensees Tim Haigh and Rupert Pendered ~ Real ale ~ Bar food (12-3, 7-10) ~ Restaurant ~ (01285) 740421 ~ Children in eating area of bar and restaurant ~ Dogs welcome ~ Open 11-3, 6-11; 11-11 Sat; 12-10.30 Sun ~ Bedrooms: £65S/£80S(£105B)

BLAISDON
Red Hart *Village signposted off A4136 just SW of junction with A40 W of Gloucester; OS Sheet 162 map reference 703169*

The flagstoned main bar of this welcoming pub, tucked away in the Forest of Dean, has cushioned wall and window seats, traditional pub tables, a big sailing-ship painting above the log fire, and a thoroughly relaxing atmosphere – helped along by well reproduced piped bluesy music, and maybe Spotty the perky jack russell. On the right, there's an attractive beamed two-room no smoking dining area with some interesting prints and bric-a-brac, and on the left you'll find additional dining space for families. They serve five well kept real ales such as Hook Norton Best, Otter Head, Timothy Taylors Landlord, RCH Pitchfork and Uley Bitter on handpump, and there's a decent wine list; cribbage, dominoes, shove-ha'penny and table skittles. Enjoyable bar food includes home-made soup, breaded plaice, and sirloin steak with bubble and squeak; specials such as crab tartlets, moussaka, and lamb fillet; children's meals too. There are some picnic-sets in the garden and a children's play area, and at the back of the building is a large space for barbecues.

Free house ~ Licensee Guy Wilkins ~ Real ale ~ Bar food ~ Restaurant ~ (01452) 830477 ~ Children in eating area of bar, restaurant and family room ~ Dogs allowed in bar ~ Open 11.30-3, 6ish-11; 12-3.30, 7-10.30 Sun

BLEDINGTON
Kings Head *B4450*

The main bar of this classic-looking Cotswold pub is full of ancient beams and other atmospheric furnishings (high-backed wooden settles, gateleg or pedestal tables), and there's a warming log fire in the stone inglenook with a big black kettle hanging in it. To the left of the bar a drinking space for locals (popular with a younger crowd in the evening) has benches on the wooden floor, a woodburning stove, and darts, cribbage, TV and piped music; on Sunday lunchtimes it's used by families. The lounge looks on to the garden. Besides an excellent wine list, with eight by the glass (champagnes too), you'll find well kept Hook Norton Best, and a couple of guests from brewers such as Burton Bridge and Goff's on handpump, and they've also over 20 malt whiskies, organic cider and perry, and local apple juice; readers warn it can get smoky. Interesting and often of award standard (though not cheap), bar food might include toasted panini, home-made duck spring rolls with sweet chilli sauce or haddock, salmon and prawn pie with mash; evening dishes such as seared king scallops, tagliatelle with wild mushrooms and crispy leeks, and home-made puddings like treacle tart; they also do a selection of interesting cheeses. The dining room is no smoking. Set in a peaceful village, the pub overlooks the green where there might be ducks pottering about; there are seats in the back garden; aunt sally.

Free house ~ Licensees Nicola and Archie Orr-Ewing ~ Real ale ~ Bar food ~ Restaurant ~ (01608) 658365 ~ Children in restaurant and family room ~ Dogs allowed in bar ~ Open 11(12 Sat)-3, 6-11; 12-3, 6.30-10.30 Sun; closed 25/26 Dec ~ Bedrooms: £50B/£95S(£70B)

BRIMPSFIELD
Golden Heart *Nettleton Bottom (not shown on road maps, so we list the pub instead under the name of the nearby village); on A417 N of the Brimpsfield turning*

This bustling pub is 'a good place for a break after a long drive'. The main low-ceilinged bar is divided into three cosily distinct areas, with a roaring log fire in the huge stone inglenook fireplace in one, traditional built-in settles and other old-fashioned furnishings throughout, and quite a few brass items, typewriters, exposed stone, and wood panelling. A comfortable parlour on the right has another decorative fireplace, and leads into a further room that opens onto the terrace; two rooms are no smoking. A good selection of bar food includes popular vegetarian specials, with other choices such as malaysian beef curry and wild boar with orange and nutmeg; also sandwiches, omelettes, steaks and puddings; they have a children's menu. As well as decent wines, friendly staff serve well kept Archers Golden Best and Timothy Taylors Landlord, with a couple of guests such as Bass and Wickwar Cotswold Way on handpump; there's an August bank holiday beer festival. From the rustic cask-supported tables on the suntrap terrace, there are pleasant views down over a valley; nearby walks. If you are thinking of staying here, bear in mind that the nearby road is a busy all-night link between the M4 and M5.

Free house ~ Licensee Catherine Stevens ~ Real ale ~ Bar food (12-3, 6-10; 12-10 Sun) ~ (01242) 870261 ~ Children in family room ~ Dogs welcome ~ Open 11-3, 5.30-11; 11-11 Fri and Sat; 12-10.30 Sun ~ Bedrooms: £35S/£55S

CHEDWORTH
Seven Tuns *Village signposted off A429 NE of Cirencester; then take second signposted right turn and bear left towards church*

This cosy little 17th-c pub is a pleasant place to drop into for a drink after a visit to the famous Roman villa nearby. A good winter log fire in the big stone fireplace warms the snug little lounge on the right, which has comfortable seats and decent tables, sizeable antique prints, tankards hanging from the beam over the serving bar, and a partly boarded ceiling. Down a couple of steps, the public bar on the left has an open fire, and this opens into a no smoking dining room with another open fire; as we went to press the upstairs skittle alley was about to be renovated and gain its own bar. Well kept Youngs Bitter and Waggle Dance, and a guest on handpump, and lots of malt whiskies; darts, cribbage, shove-ha'penny, dominoes, and piped music. There's a short choice of tasty bar food such as lunchtime sandwiches or baguettes, ham and eggs, and seafood stir-fry with prawns and monkfish; puddings such as bread and butter pudding. Service can be slow at times. Across the road is a little walled raised terrace with a waterwheel and a stream, and there are plenty of tables both here and under cocktail parasols on a side terrace. There are nice walks through the valley. *Youngs ~ Tenant Mr Davenport-Jones ~ Real ale ~ Bar food ~ (01285) 720242 ~ Children in eating area of bar and restaurant ~ Dogs welcome ~ Open 11-11; 12-10.30 Sun; 11-3, 6-11 in winter*

CHIPPING CAMPDEN
Eight Bells *Church Street (which is one way – entrance off B4035)*
Doing very well at the moment, this fine old pub has a large terraced garden with plenty of seats, and striking views of the almshouses and church. Inside are heavy oak beams with massive timber supports, stripped stone walls, cushioned pews and solid dark wood furniture on the broad flagstones, daily papers to read, and log fires in up to three restored stone fireplaces. Part of the floor in the no smoking dining room has a glass inlet showing part of the passage from the church by which Roman Catholic priests could escape from the Roundheads. Very good food might include home-made soup, crispy duck pancake with apple, honey and ginger chutney, vegetable moussaka, pork medallions, and fried bass with mediterranean vegetables; home-made puddings such as maple syrup sponge with custard; they also do lunchtime (not Sunday) ciabatta. Alongside a guest such as Marstons Pedigree, they serve Hook Norton Best and Old Hooky on handpump from the fine oak bar counter; country wines, and decent coffee. Piped music, darts, cribbage, and dominoes. Handy for the Cotswold Way walk to Bath, the pub is popular with walkers. They've recently refurbished the bedrooms. *Free house ~ Licensee Neil Hargreaves ~ Real ale ~ Bar food (12-2(2.30 Fri/Sat), 6.30-9.30; 12.30-3, 7-9 Sun) ~ Restaurant ~ (01386) 840371 ~ Children in restaurant and family room ~ Dogs allowed in bar ~ Open 12-3, 5.30-11; 11-11 Sat; 12-10.30 Sun; closed 25 Dec ~ Bedrooms: £50B/£85.95B*

COLN ST ALDWYNS
New Inn *On good back road between Bibury and Fairford*
A meal at this smart inn, set in a peaceful Cotswold village, is a fine reward after a pleasant riverside walk to Bibury. Spotlessly kept, the two main rooms are attractively furnished and decorated, and divided by a central log fire in a neat stone fireplace with wooden mantelbeam and willow-pattern plates on the chimney breast; there are also low beams, some stripped stonework around the bar servery with hops above it, oriental rugs on the red tiles, and a mix of seating from library chairs to stripped pews. Down a slight slope, a further room has a coal fire in an old kitchen range at one end, and a white pheasant on the wall. Skilfully cooked (though not cheap), well presented dishes might include vine tomato and buffalo

mozzarella salad with basil pesto, tomato and mushroom risotto, thai chicken, and steak with green peppercorn sauce; puddings such as steamed chocolate and orange pudding with chocolate sauce; lunchtime sandwiches also. The restaurant is no smoking. Well kept real ales such as Archers Village, Hook Norton Best, and Wadworths 6X on handpump, and they've eight good wines by the glass, and several malt whiskies. The split-level terrace has plenty of seats, and you can get popular day tickets for fly fishing on the river in the water meadows.

Free house ~ Licensee Angela Kimmett ~ Real ale ~ Bar food ~ Restaurant ~ (01285) 750651 ~ Children in eating area of bar; must be over 10 in restaurant ~ Dogs allowed in bar and bedrooms ~ Open 11-11; 12-10.30 Sun ~ Bedrooms: £90S/£120B

COWLEY

Green Dragon *Off A435 S of Cheltenham at Elkstone, Cockleford signpost; OS Sheet 163 map reference 970142*

Gathering much support from readers, this attractive stone-fronted dining pub was a cider house when it first opened in 1643. Cosy and genuinely old-fashioned, the two bars have big flagstones and wooden boards, beams, two stone fireplaces (welcoming fires in winter), candle lit tables, and a woodburning stove. The furniture and the bar itself in the upper Mouse Bar were made by Robert Thompson, and little mice run over the hand-carved chairs, tables and mantelpiece; the larger Lower Bar is no smoking. The food here is good, and well presented dishes (which you can eat anywhere) could include lunchtime sandwiches (not Sunday), wilted spinach with onion welsh rarebit, breaded lemon sole goujons with hollandaise sauce, or fried black pudding with pork loin chop and sage butter, and 10oz rib-eye steak; puddings such as lemon and almond pudding with raspberries; they also do children's meals. The upstairs restaurant is no smoking. Good service from the friendly and helpful young staff, and a buoyant bustling atmosphere. Well kept real ales include Butcombe Bitter, Courage Directors, Hook Norton Best and a guest on handpump; piped music. Terraces outside overlooking Cowley Lake and the River Churn, and the pub is a good centre for the local walks.

Buccaneer Holdings ~ Manager Mhari Ashworth ~ Real ale ~ Bar food (12-2.30, 6-10; 12-9.30 Sat/Sun) ~ Restaurant ~ (01242) 870271 ~ Children welcome ~ Dogs welcome ~ Open 11(12 Sun)-11 ~ Bedrooms: /£65S(£65B)

DUNTISBOURNE ABBOTS

Five Mile House *Off A417 at Duntisbourne Abbots exit sign; then, coming from Gloucester, pass filling station and keep on parallel to main road; coming from Cirencester, pass under main road then turn right at T-junction*

An enjoyable all-rounder, this welcoming 300-year-old coaching inn is a great place to bring visitors. The front room has a companionable bare-boards drinking bar on the right, with wall seats around the big table in its bow window and just one other table. On the left is a flagstoned hallway tap room snug formed from two ancient high-backed settles by a woodburning stove in a tall carefully exposed old fireplace; newspapers to read. There's a small cellar bar, a back restaurant down steps, and a family room on the far side; cribbage, dominoes and darts. The lounge and cellar bar are no smoking. The food here is proper pubby stuff, but the way the landlord cooks it wins great acclaim from readers. The menu includes lunchtime open sandwiches, gammon steak with egg and pineapple or local trout with prawn and lemon butter; evening dishes such as home-made soup and shoulder of lamb stuffed with redcurrant and mint; also daily specials such as home-made faggots with herby mash and onion gravy, and puddings such as treacle tart. It's a good idea to book on weekends and in the evenings. Friendly staff serve well kept Donningtons BB, Timothy Taylors Landlord and Youngs Bitter, with a local guest such as Wye Valley Butty Bach on handpump (the cellar is temperature-controlled), and they've got interesting wines (strong on new world ones). The gardens have nice country views; the country lane was once Ermine Street, the main Roman road from Wales to London.

Free house ~ Licensees Jo and Jon Carrier ~ Real ale ~ Bar food (12-2.30, 6-9.30; 12-2.30, 7-9 Sun) ~ Restaurant ~ (01285) 821432 ~ Children welcome if well behaved ~ Dogs allowed in bar ~ Open 12-3, 6-11; 12-3, 7-10.30 Sun

EWEN
Wild Duck *Village signposted from A429 S of Cirencester*
They serve more than 25 wines by the glass at this civilised 16th-c inn, which is quietly placed on the edge of a peaceful village. The high-beamed main bar has a nice mix of comfortable armchairs and other seats, paintings on the red walls, crimson drapes, a winter open fire, candles on tables, and magazines to read; overlooking the garden, the residents' lounge has a handsome Elizabethan fireplace and antique furnishings. Besides Duckpond Bitter (brewed especially for the pub), you'll find well kept real ales such as Charles Wells Bombardier, Greene King Old Speckled Hen, Sharps Doom Bar, and Theakstons Best and Old Peculier, and several malt whiskies; piped music (which can be obtrusive). Good, though not cheap, dishes from a changing menu might include home-smoked duck breast with rocket salad, roast rack of pork on leek, bacon and cheese mash, seared tuna steak on sweet potato mash, and a tempting choice of puddings such as warm apple and sultana cake with vanilla sauce and chocolate ice-cream. The service, though normally good, could perhaps sometimes do with more supervision. Pleasant in summer, the neatly kept and sheltered garden has wooden tables and seats. Beware, unless you pay in advance for your bar food, or have booked, you will be asked to leave your credit card with them.

Free house ~ Licensees Tina and Dino Mussell ~ Real ale ~ Bar food (12-2, 6.45-10; 12-2.30, 7-9.30 Sun) ~ Restaurant ~ (01285) 770310 ~ Children in eating area of bar and restaurant ~ Dogs allowed in bar and bedrooms ~ Open 11-11; 12-10.30 Sun ~ Bedrooms: £60B/£80B

GUITING POWER
Hollow Bottom *Village signposted off B4068 SW of Stow-on-the-Wold (still called A436 on many maps)*
The comfortable beamed bar of this friendly and relaxed 17th-c inn has lots

of racing memorabilia including racing silks, tunics and photographs (it's owned by a small syndicate that includes Peter Scudamore and Nigel Twiston-Davies). There's a winter log fire in an unusual pillar-supported stone fireplace, and the public bar has flagstones and stripped stone masonry and racing on TV; newspapers to read, darts, cribbage, dominoes, Spoof, and piped music. Fullers London Pride, Hook Norton, and a guest such as Timothy Taylors Landlord are well kept on handpump, they've 15 malt whiskies, and half a dozen wines by the glass; the staff are friendly and obliging. Besides adventurous specials such as grilled red snapper with pesto and pine kernels, a wide choice of enjoyable bar food could include filled baked potatoes, home-made cottage pie or lasagne; they also do a Sunday carvery. From the pleasant garden behind are views towards the peaceful sloping fields. The bedrooms are good value, and there are decent walks nearby.

Free house ~ Licensees Hugh Kelly and Charles Pettigrew ~ Real ale ~ Bar food (12-9 (snacks during the afternoon rather than meals)) ~ Restaurant ~ (01451) 850392 ~ Children in eating area of bar and restaurant ~ Dogs allowed in bar and bedrooms ~ Open 11-11; 12-10.30 Sun ~ Bedrooms: £45B/£65B

KINGSCOTE

Hunters Hall *A4135 Dursley—Tetbury*
Well run and civilised with a warmly welcoming atmosphere, this creeper-covered inn has held a continuous licence for over 500 years. There's quite a series of bar rooms and lounges with fine high Tudor beams and stone walls, a lovely old box settle, sofas and miscellaneous easy chairs, and sturdy settles and oak tables on the flagstones in the lower-ceilinged, cosy public bar. You can eat the enjoyable, freshly prepared food in the airy end room or there are more tables in the Gallery upstairs. Served by helpful and friendly staff, the well thought out menu might include lunchtime sandwiches (not Sunday), seafood chowder, pork and leek sausages with mustard mashed potatoes or grilled trout, and 8oz fillet steak. The Retreat Bar and restaurant (where there is piped music) are no smoking. A back room – relatively untouched – is popular with local lads playing pool; darts, cribbage, shove-ha'penny, fruit machine, TV and jukebox. On handpump, they've well kept Greene King Abbot and Ruddles Best, and Uley Hogs Head. The garden has seats, and a wooden fortress, play house and swings for children. The bedrooms are good value and well maintained.

Old English Inns ~ Tenant Stephanie Ward ~ Real ale ~ Bar food ~ Restaurant ~ (01453) 860393 ~ Children welcome ~ Dogs allowed in bar and bedrooms ~ Open 11-11; 12-10.30 Sun ~ Bedrooms: £55B/£90B

LITTLE BARRINGTON

Inn For All Seasons *On A40 3 miles W of Burford*
Not only does this civilised old inn have a good wine list with a dozen by the glass (and 100 bin ends), but the food here is very good too. Deliciously cooked fresh fish is their speciality, and a typical choice might include grilled sardines, poached skate wing with baby caper and shallot butter sauce, and grilled dover sole. If you prefer meat, you can choose from well presented dishes such as home-made pork faggots with creamed potatoes

and red wine and onion jus, chargrilled scotch rump steak with chunky chips; lunchtime snacks too, and puddings might be chocolate brownie with chocolate sauce and double cream. The attractively decorated, mellow lounge bar has low beams, stripped stone and flagstones, old prints, leather-upholstered wing armchairs and other comfortable seats, country magazines to read, and a big log fire (with a big piece of World War II shrapnel above it); readers tell us there can be traffic noise. Well kept Bass, Sharps Doom Bar and Wadworths 6X on handpump, and they've over 60 malt whiskies; cribbage, dominoes, TV and piped music. The pleasant garden has tables and a play area; there are walks straight from the inn. It gets very busy during Cheltenham Gold Cup Week – when the adjoining field is pressed into service as a helicopter pad.

Free house ~ Licensees Matthew and Heather Sharp ~ Real ale ~ Bar food (11-2.30, 6-9.30) ~ Restaurant ~ (01451) 844324 ~ Children welcome ~ Dogs allowed in bar and bedrooms ~ Open 10.30-2.30, 6-11; 12-2.30, 7-10.30 Sun ~ Bedrooms: £56.50B/£97B

MISERDEN

Carpenters Arms *Village signposted off B4070 NE of Stroud; also a pleasant drive off A417 via the Duntisbournes, or off A419 via Sapperton and Edgeworth; OS Sheet 163 map reference 936089*

Set in an idyllic Cotswold estate village, this properly run pub is as warmly welcoming to drinkers as it is to diners. The two open-plan bar areas have low beams, nice old wooden tables, seats with the original little brass name plates on the backs, and some cushioned settles and spindlebacks on the bare boards; also, stripped stone walls with some interesting bric-a-brac, and two big log fires; the small no smoking dining room has dark traditional furniture. A sizeable collage (done with Laurie Lee) has lots of illustrations and book covers signed by him. As well as lunchtime filled baguettes, enjoyable dishes (made with lots of local produce) might include home-made cheese and pepper quiche, fishcakes or chicken breast with honey and mustard sauce, pie of the day, and specials such as grilled shark steak with tomato and pesto sauce, and beef wellington; pleasant and efficient service. Well kept Greene King IPA and Wadworths 6X, and a guest such as Smiles Bitter on handpump, country wines, and darts. There are seats out in the garden; the nearby gardens of Misarden Park are well worth visiting.

Free house ~ Licensee Johnny Johnston ~ Real ale ~ Bar food ~ Restaurant ~ (01285) 821283 ~ Children in eating area of bar and in restaurant until 9pm ~ Dogs allowed in bar ~ Occasional country music and summer morris dancing ~ Open 11.30-2.30, 6-11; 11-3, 6-11 Sat; 12-3, 7-10.30 Sun

NAILSWORTH

Weighbridge *B4014 towards Tetbury*

The speciality at this deservedly popular and very welcoming pub (now with a new landlord) is the delicious 2 in 1 pies, which they have been serving for more than 20 years. They come in a large bowl, and half the bowl contains the filling of your choice while the other is full of home-made cauliflower cheese (or broccoli mornay or root vegetables), and topped with pastry: turkey and trimmings, salmon in a creamy sauce, steak and mushroom, or chicken, ham and leek in a cream and tarragon sauce (you can also have mini versions or straightforward pies). Enjoyable bar food also includes chilli con carne or moussaka, and puddings such as banana crumble. The relaxed bar has three cosily old-fashioned rooms (one is no smoking) with stripped stone walls, antique settles and country chairs, and window seats. The black beamed ceiling of the lounge bar is thickly festooned with black ironware – sheepshears, gin-traps, lamps, and a large collection of keys, many from the old Longfords Mill opposite the pub; good disabled access and facilities. Upstairs is a raftered hayloft with an engaging mix of rustic tables; no noisy games machines or piped music. Uley Old Spot and Wadworths 6X are well kept alongside a guest such as Uley Laurie Lee on handpump, they've 14 wines (and champagne) by the glass, and Westons cider. Behind is a sheltered landscaped garden with picnic-sets under umbrellas.

Free house ~ Licensee Howard Parker ~ Real ale ~ Bar food (12-9.30) ~ (01453) 832520 ~ Children in family room till 9pm ~ Dogs welcome ~ Open 12-11; 12-10.30 Sun; closed 25, 31 Dec

NORTH NIBLEY

New Inn *Waterley Bottom, which is quite well signposted from surrounding lanes; inn signposted from the Bottom itself; one route is from A4135 S of Dursley, via lane with red sign saying Steep Hill, 1 in 5 (just SE of Stinchcombe Golf Course turn-off), turning right when you get to the bottom; OS Sheet 162 map reference 758963*

Peacefully set in lovely South Cotswold countryside, this is a splendid place to relax in before embarking on one of the many nearby walks. Well kept Bath Gem Bitter and SPA, Cotleigh Tawny, Greene King Abbot and a guest such as Burton Bridge Bitter are dispensed from Barmaid's Delight (the name of one of the antique beer engines). The friendly licensees also serve Thatchers cider, around 50 malt whiskies, and they import their own french wines; there's a beer festival on the last weekend in June. The lounge bar has cushioned windsor chairs and varnished high-backed settles against the partly stripped stone walls, and dominoes, cribbage, TV, and sensibly placed darts in the simple public bar. Outside, there are lots of seats on the lawn, and there's also a neat terrace; three boules pitches. A short choice of home-made bar food includes sandwiches or toasties, beef and mushroom casserole, poached plaice, and rib-eye steak with garlic potatoes; they've redecorated the dining areas.

Free house ~ Licensees Jackie and Jacky Cartigny ~ Real ale ~ Bar food (12-2, 6-9, not Mon/Tues) ~ (01453) 543659 ~ Children welcome ~ Dogs allowed in bar ~ Open 12-2.30, 6(7 Mon)-11; 12-11 Sat; 12-10.30 Sun; closed Mon lunchtime

OLDBURY-ON-SEVERN

Anchor *Village signposted from B4061*

Thankfully the new licensees at this welcoming pub have managed to retain the good combination of proper village local with plenty of chatty regulars, and dining pub with enjoyable food. Well priced for the area, they've Bass, Butcombe Bitter, Theakstons Old Peculier and Wickwar BOB well kept on handpump or tapped from the cask, and you'll find over 75 malts, and a decent choice of good quality wines, with a dozen by the glass. The neatly kept lounge has modern beams and stone, a mix of tables including an attractive oval oak gateleg, cushioned window seats, winged seats against the wall, oil paintings by a local artist, and a big winter log fire. Diners can eat in the lounge or bar area or in the no smoking dining room at the back of the building and the menu is the same in all rooms. Using local produce, home-made dishes might be soup, creamy risotto with marinated artichokes, shepherd's pie, and 8oz sirloin steak; puddings such as sticky toffee pudding; instead of chips they offer a choice of roast, new, sautéed, baked or dauphinois potatoes. In summer (when the hanging baskets and window boxes are lovely) you can eat in the pretty garden. They have wheelchair access and a disabled lavatory; darts and cribbage, and boules too. Plenty of walks to the River Severn and along the many footpaths and bridleways, and St Arilda's church nearby is interesting, on its odd little knoll with wild flowers among the gravestones (the primroses and daffodils in spring are lovely).

Free house ~ Licensees Michael Dowdeswell and Mark Sorrell ~ Real ale ~ Bar food (12-2,7(7.30 Sun)-9.30) ~ Restaurant ~ (01454) 413331 ~ Children in restaurant ~ Dogs allowed in bar ~ Open 11.30-3, 6.30-11; 11.30-11 Sat; 12-10.30 Sun

SAPPERTON

Bell *Village signposted from A419 Stroud—Cirencester; OS Sheet 163 map reference 948033*

This particularly well run pub continues to be a real favourite with our readers, and no wonder: whether you're a walker or a local, a day-tripping family or a couple out for a special meal, you'll be made to feel genuinely welcome. Freshly cooked with high quality ingredients, imaginative dishes change regularly but might include pigeon faggot on potato cake, home-made butternut and red pepper ravioli, braised local beef blade with sweet potato mash or steamed halibut supreme with cheesy leek mash; puddings such as maple and mascarpone cheesecake with poached pear and nutmeg ice; they also do an excellent lunchtime ploughman's. There are three separate, cosy rooms with stripped beams, a nice mix of wooden tables and chairs, country prints and modern art on stripped stone walls, one or two attractive rugs on the flagstones, roaring log fires and woodburning stoves, fresh flowers, and newspapers and guidebooks to browse. As well as more than a dozen wines by two sizes of glass, and champagne by the flute, they serve well kept Uley Old Spot, Wickwar Cotswold Way and Goff's Jouster, and a guest such as Hook Norton Best on handpump; Weston's cider too. A hit with children, Harry the springer spaniel is very sociable. There are tables out on a small front lawn and in a partly covered and very pretty courtyard, for eating outside. Good surrounding walks, and horses have their own tethering rail (and bucket of water).

Free house ~ Licensees Paul Davidson and Pat Le Jeune ~ Real ale ~ Bar food (not 25 Dec) ~ Restaurant ~ (01285) 760298 ~ Children welcome till 6.30pm ~ Dogs welcome ~ Open 11-2.30, 6.30-11; 12-3, 7-10.30 Sun; closed 25 Dec and evenings 26 and 31 Dec

ST BRIAVELS
George *High Street*
Seats on the flagstoned terrace behind this attractive white-painted pub overlook a grassy former moat to the silvery 12th-c castle built as a fortification against the Welsh; an ancient escape tunnel connects the castle to the pub. With a welcoming, bustling atmosphere, the three rambling rooms have old-fashioned built-in wall seats, some booth seating, cushioned small settles, toby jugs and antique bottles on black beams over the servery, and a large stone open fireplace; a Celtic coffin lid dating from 1070, discovered when a fireplace was removed, is now mounted next to the bar counter. Popular enjoyable home-made dishes could include rabbit casserole, moroccan lamb, or fresh bass, and home-made puddings such as lemon meringue and crumble. The dining room and restaurant are no smoking; piped music. Friendly and courteous staff serve well kept Freeminer Bitter, Fullers London Pride, and RCH Pitchfork, with a couple of guests from brewers such as Archers and Freeminer on handpump; also 15 malt whiskies, farm cider, and country wines. Lots of walks start nearby but muddy boots must be left outside; outdoor chess.
Free house ~ Licensee Bruce Bennett ~ Real ale ~ Bar food ~ Restaurant ~ (01594) 530228 ~ Children in eating area of bar and restaurant ~ Dogs allowed in bar ~ Open 11-2.30, 6.30-11; 12-2.30, 7-10.30 Sun ~ Bedrooms: £35S/£50S

TETBURY
Trouble House *A433 towards Cirencester, near Cherington turn*
Although the main focus at this pub is on the freshly prepared food, you can still drop in for just a drink, and there are 14 wines by the glass to choose from. Furnishings are mainly close-set stripped pine or oak tables with chapel chairs, some wheelback chairs and the odd library chair, and there are attractive mainly modern country prints on the cream or butter-coloured walls. The rush-matting room on the right is no smoking, and on the left there's a parquet-floored room with a chesterfield by the big stone fireplace, a hop-girt mantelpiece, and more hops hung from one of its two big black beams. In the small saggy-beamed middle room, you can commandeer one of the bar stools, where they have well kept Wadworths IPA and Henrys Original on handpump; piped music and cribbage. The ambitious menu might include fried smoked haddock and parsley dumplings, roasted guinea fowl with pea and bacon broth or calves sweetbreads with pea and broad bean puree, with puddings such as strawberry and raspberry gratin, and an interesting selection of cheeses; friendly service. They sell quite a few of their own preserves such as tapenade or preserved tomatoes with onions. You can also sit out at picnic-sets on the gravel courtyard behind.
Wadworths ~ Tenants Michael and Sarah Bedford ~ Real ale ~ Bar food (not Sun or Mon) ~ Restaurant ~ (01666) 502206 ~ Children in restaurant ~ Dogs welcome ~ Open 11-3, 6.30(7 winter)-11; closed Sun and Mon; around 2 wks over Christmas and New Year

WINCHCOMBE
White Hart *High Street (B4632)*

Like the landlady, the friendly staff at this interesting place (more café-bar than pub) are virtually all swedish, and this is reflected in the delicious swedish specials. On Friday and Sunday lunchtimes and Wednesday evenings, they do a popular smorgasbord buffet. Otherwise, big plates of well prepared food might include a delicious scandinavian seafood platter, meatballs in creamy sauce, and smorgasbord platter, alongside more traditional lunchtime bar snacks; puddings such as apple and cinnamon cheesecake. There's also a pizzeria (not open Monday). The main area has mates' chairs, dining chairs and small modern settles around dark oak tables (candlelit at night) on black-painted boards, cream walls, and what amounts to a wall of big windows giving on to the village street – passers-by knock on the glass when they see their friends inside. A smaller no smoking back area has its kitchen tables and chairs painted pale blue-grey, and floor matting. A downstairs bar, with black beams, stripped stone above the panelled dado, and pews and pine tables on the good tiles, may be open too at busy times. Well kept Greene King IPA and Old Speckled Hen, Wadworths 6X, and a changing guest such as Goff's White Knight on handpump, and a good choice of wines by the glass – brought to your table unless you're sitting at the big copper-topped counter. There's a good mix of all ages, and an enjoyably relaxed atmosphere; daily papers, laid-back piped music. The back car park is rather small.

Enterprise ~ Lease Nicole Burr ~ Real ale ~ Bar food (all day) ~ Restaurant ~ (01242) 602359 ~ Children in restaurant, and away from bar till 9pm ~ Dogs allowed in bar and bedrooms ~ Occasional jazz evenings ~ Open 11-11; 12-10.30 Sun ~ Bedrooms: £55B/£65B

Dog Friendly Hotels, B&Bs and Farms

BIBURY
Bibury Court *Bibury, Cirencester, Gloucestershire GL7 5NT (01285) 740337*
£135, plus special breaks; 18 individual rms, some overlooking garden. Lovely peaceful mansion dating from Tudor times, in beautiful gardens, with an informal friendly atmosphere, panelled rooms, antiques, huge log fires, conservatory, a fine choice of breakfasts, and good interesting food; partial disabled access; dogs welcome in bedrooms, bar and lounge; £5

BIBURY
Swan *Bibury, Cirencester, Gloucestershire GL7 5NW (01285) 740695* £160, plus special breaks; 18 very pretty individually decorated rms. Handsome creeper-covered hotel on the River Coln, with private fishing and attractive formal gardens; lovely flowers and log fires in carefully furnished comfortable lounges, a cosy no smoking parlour, good food in opulent

dining room, nice breakfasts, and attentive staff; disabled access; dogs in bedrooms; £10

BROAD CAMPDEN

Malt House *Broad Campden, Chipping Campden, Gloucestershire GL55 6UU (01386) 840295* £**118.50**; 7 rms with sloping floors and mullioned windows. 16th-c house in an unspoilt Cotswold village with ancient oak panelling, old beams, open fires, antiques and home-grown flowers, and a peaceful old-fashioned atmosphere; dinner party-type evening meals, super breakfasts, afternoon teas with home-made biscuits and cakes (served in the thatched summer house in warm weather), and friendly staff and owners; 3-acre garden with croquet; cl Christmas; dogs welcome in bedrooms; £10

CHELTENHAM

Alias Hotel Kandinsky *Bayshill Rd, Cheltenham, Gloucestershire GL50 3AS (01242) 527788* £**95**; 48 large, stylish and well equipped rms. White-painted Regency hotel with an interesting mix of old and new furnishings, antiques and modern paintings, big pot plants, lots of mirrors, unusual collections on walls, tiled or wooden floors, and a relaxed, informal atmosphere; enjoyable modern food in bustling Café Paradiso, friendly bar, willing young staff, downstairs cocktail bar, and seats out on decked terrace; they are kind to families; disabled access; dogs in bedrooms

CHIPPING CAMPDEN

Cotswold House *The Square, Chipping Campden, Gloucestershire GL55 6AN (01386) 840330* £**175**; 20 rms. Imposing Regency house in lovely town and run by warmly friendly 'hands-on' owners; beautiful central staircase, relaxing drawing room with log fire, good british cooking in modern brasserie or restaurant, a cosseting atmosphere, sunny terraces, and formal garden; plenty to see nearby; disabled access; dogs welcome in bedrooms

CLEARWELL

Tudor Farmhouse *Clearwell, Coleford, Gloucestershire GL16 8JS (01594) 833046* £**80**, plus special breaks; 21 cottagey rms. Carefully restored Tudor farmhouse and stone cottages with landscaped gardens and surrounding fields; lots of beams and panelling, oak doors and sloping floors, inglenook fireplaces, delicious food in no smoking candlelit restaurant, and friendly staff; cl Christmas; disabled access; dogs in bedrooms

CORSE LAWN

Corse Lawn House *Corse Lawn, Gloucestershire GL19 4LZ (01452) 780771* £**135**, plus special breaks; 19 pretty, individually furnished rms. Magnificent Queen Anne building with comfortable and attractive day rooms, a distinguished restaurant with imaginative food and excellent wines (there's a less pricey bistro-style operation too), warmly friendly staff, a relaxed atmosphere, and an indoor swimming pool, tennis court, croquet, and horses in 12 acres of surrounding gardens and fields; cl 24-26 Dec; disabled access; dogs welcome away from restaurant

GUITING POWER

Guiting Guest House *Post Office Lane, Guiting Power, Cheltenham, Gloucestershire GL54 5TZ (01451) 850470* £**80**; 7 pretty rms with thoughtful extras. 16th-c Cotswold stone guesthouse with inglenook fireplaces, beams, and rugs on flagstones, two sitting rooms, enjoyable evening meals by candlelight, attentive owners, and a very relaxed atmosphere; cl Christmas week; dogs in bedrooms

NORTH CERNEY

Bathurst Arms *North Cerney, Cirencester, Gloucestershire GL7 7BZ (01285) 831281* £**65**; 5 pleasant rms. Civilised and handsome old inn with lots of atmosphere, a nice mix of polished old furniture and a fireplace at each end of the beamed and panelled bar, small no smoking dining room, imaginative food, quite a few well chosen wines by the glass, well kept real ales, and an attractive garden running down to the River Churn; lots of surrounding walks; dogs welcome in bedrooms

PAINSWICK

Painswick Hotel *Kemps Lane, Painswick, Stroud, Gloucestershire GL6 6YB (01452) 812160* £**140**, plus special breaks; 19 individually furnished, comfortable rms with views of the village or countryside. 18th-c Palladian mansion – once a grand rectory – with fine views, antiques and paintings in the elegant rooms, open fires, good food using the best local produce, a thoughtful wine list, and a relaxed, friendly atmosphere; garden with croquet lawn; they are kind to families; dogs welcome in some bedrooms; £25

PARKEND

Edale House *Folly Rd, Parkend, Lydney, Gloucestershire GL15 4JF (01594) 562835* £**51**, plus special breaks; 5 rms, most with own bthrm. No smoking Georgian house opposite cricket green and backing on to Nagshead Nature Reserve; comfortable, homely sitting room, honesty bar, very good food in attractive dining room, and a relaxed atmosphere; children over 12; dogs in bedrooms and lounge; £3

STOW-ON-THE-WOLD

Grapevine *Sheep St, Stow-on-the-Wold, Cheltenham, Gloucestershire GL54 1AU (01451) 830344* £**130**, plus special breaks; 22 individually decorated, attractive, no smoking rms. Warm, friendly and very well run hotel with antiques, comfortable chairs and a relaxed atmosphere in the lounge, a beamed bar, and imaginative food in the attractive, sunny restaurant with its 70-year-old trailing vine; partial disabled access; dogs in bedrooms, bar and lounge if small and well behaved

Old Stocks *The Square, Stow-on-the-Wold, Cheltenham, Gloucestershire GL54 1AF (01451) 830666* £**90**, plus special breaks; 18 rms. Well run 16th/17th-c Cotswold stone hotel with cosy welcoming small bar, beams and open fire, comfortable residents' lounge, good food, friendly staff, and sheltered garden; cl 18-28 Dec; disabled access; dogs welcome away from restaurant, £5

THORNBURY

Thornbury Castle *Castle St, Thornbury, Bristol BS35 1HH (01454) 281182* £195; 25 opulent rms, some with big Tudor fireplaces or fine oriel windows. Impressive and luxuriously renovated early 16th-c castle with antiques, tapestries, huge fireplaces and mullioned windows in the baronial public rooms, three dining rooms (one in the base of a tower), fine cooking, extensive wine list (inc wine from their own vineyard), thoughtful friendly service, and vast grounds inc the oldest Tudor gardens in England; partial disabled access; dogs at manager's discretion; £10

Hampshire

Dog Friendly Pubs

AXFORD
Crown *B3046 S of Basingstoke*
On a warm day, the suntrap terrace in the sloping shrub-sheltered garden behind this tucked-away country pub is a popular place for a drink; there are also picnic-sets out in front. Inside, the three compact rooms ramble around the central servery and open together enough to build a chatty atmosphere – each keeping its own character: appealing late 19th-c local villager photographs, cream walls, patterned carpet and stripped boards on the left, for instance, abstract prints on pale terracotta walls and rush carpeting on the right. Furnishings are largely stripped tables and chapel chairs, and each room is candlelit at night, with a small winter log fire; daily papers, piped music and TV. Well kept Bass, Cheriton Pots Ale, and Triple fff Moondance and Altons Pride on handpump, and nine wines by the glass. Bar food includes filled baked potatoes, filled ciabattas, haddock and spring onion fishcakes, vegetarian pasta, home-made pie of the day, and specials like crocodile or kangaroo kebabs. There are lovely walks around Moundsmere, and in the woods of Preston Oak Hills (bluebells in May).
Free house ~ Licensee Steve Nicholls ~ Real ale ~ Bar food (all day summer weekends) ~ Restaurant ~ (01256) 389492 ~ Children in eating area of bar and restaurant ~ Dogs allowed in bar ~ Open 12-3, 6-11; 12-11(10.30 Sun) Sat; 12-3, 6-11 weekends in winter

BENTWORTH
Sun *Sun Hill; from A339 coming from Alton, the first turning takes you there direct; or in village follow Shalden 2¼, Alton 4¼ signpost*
This tucked-away friendly pub is a thoroughly good all-rounder. It's very popular with both locals and visitors, there's a fine choice of eight real ales, food is enjoyable and promptly served, and the staff are welcoming and efficient. The two little traditional communicating rooms have high-backed antique settles, pews and schoolroom chairs, olde-worlde prints and blacksmith's tools on the walls, and bare boards and scrubbed deal tables on the left; big fireplaces with roaring winter fires and candles make it especially snug in winter; an arch leads to a brick-floored room with

another open fire. Well kept Badger Fursty Ferret, Cheriton Pots Ale, Fullers London Pride, Gales HSB, Hogs Back TEA, Ringwood Best, Stonehenge Pigswill, and Timothy Taylors Landlord on handpump; several malt whiskies. Good home-made bar food includes creamy garlic mushrooms, yorkshire pudding with roast beef or pork and leek sausages, fresh tagliatelle, well liked cumberland sausage with onion gravy or venison in Guinness, and puddings. There are seats out in front and in the back garden, and pleasant nearby walks.

Free house ~ Licensee Mary Holmes ~ Real ale ~ Bar food ~ (01420) 562338 ~ Children in eating area of bar ~ Dogs welcome ~ Open 12-3, 6-11; 12-10.30 Sun

EAST TYTHERLEY

Star *Off B3084 N of Romsey; turn off by railway crossing opposite the Mill Arms at Dunbridge*

A new lounge area has been created in this consistently well run inn and furnished with leather sofas and tub chairs, and the bar and restaurant have been redecorated. Most customers come to enjoy the good food: home-made soup, smoked haddock terrine, warm tomato and basil tart, steak, kidney and Guinness pudding, and fillet of beef with roasted shallots and garlic topped with foie gras; vegetables are extra. They also offer a two-course or three-course menu. The bar has log fires in attractive fireplaces, horsebrasses and saddlery, and a mix of comfortable furnishings; there's a lower lounge bar, and a cosy and pretty no smoking restaurant. Ringwood Best and a guest such as Hydes Fine & Dandy are well kept on handpump, they've several malt whiskies, and a thoughtful wine list with around ten by the glass; shove-ha'penny, and a popular skittle alley for private dining. You can sit out on a smartly furnished terrace, and a children's play area has play equipment made using local reclaimed wood. The well liked bedrooms overlook the village cricket pitch (which is used every Tuesday and Saturday through the summer), and breakfasts are highly thought of. Good nearby walks.

Free house ~ Licensees Paul and Sarah Bingham ~ Real ale ~ Bar food (not Mon exc bank hols) ~ Restaurant ~ (01794) 340225 ~ Children in eating area of bar and restaurant ~ Dogs allowed in bar ~ Open 11-2.30, 6-11; 12-2.30, 7-10.30 Sun; closed Mon exc bank hols; closed evening 25 Dec, closed 26 Dec ~ Bedrooms: £50S/£70S

EASTON

Chestnut Horse *3.6 miles from M3 junction 9: A33 towards Kings Worthy, then B3047 towards Itchen Abbas; Easton then signposted on right – bear left in village*

In a quiet, pretty village with thatched cottages, this rather up-market 16th-c dining pub offers a friendly welcome from particularly kind and efficient staff. Although inside it's all opened together, the pub manages to retain the cosy feel of small separate rooms, with a really snug décor: candles and fresh flowers on the tables, log fires in cottagey fireplaces, comfortable furnishings, black beams and joists hung with all sorts of jugs, mugs and chamber-pots, and lots of attractive pictures of wildlife and the local area. The two restaurants are no smoking. Very good – though not cheap – food at lunchtime includes caesar salad, toasted ciabatta sandwiches, home-made mackerel pâté, home-made lasagne and popular beer-battered fish; evening main courses such as stuffed roasted red peppers, and chicken fillet stuffed with sun-dried tomato and mozzarella; also fish specials and two-course and three-course lunch and early evening options (not available on Sunday lunch or weekend evenings). Well kept Courage Best, Fullers London Pride, and Chestnut Horse (brewed specially for the pub by Itchen Valley) on handpump, 12 wines and a champagne by the glass, and more than 50 malt whiskies; fairly unobtrusive piped music. There are good tables out on a smallish sheltered decked area with colourful flower tubs and baskets; plenty of Itchen Valley walks.

Free house ~ Licensees John and Jocelyn Holland ~ Real ale ~ Bar food (12-2, 6.45-9.30) ~ Restaurant ~ (01962) 779257 ~ Children welcome ~ Dogs allowed in bar ~ Open 11-11; 12-10.30 Sun; closed Sun evenings in winter

FRITHAM

Royal Oak *Village signposted from exit roundabout M27 junction 1; quickest via B3078, then left and straight through village; head for Eyeworth Pond*

As well as ponies and pigs out on the green, there's plenty of livestock close to this charming brick-built thatched pub as it is part of a working farm; gentle views across forest and farmland, fine surrounding walks, and a neatly kept big garden where summer barbecues are held (they have a marquee for poor weather). Inside, the three neatly kept, simple bar rooms have a proper traditional atmosphere, antique wheelback, spindleback, and other old chairs and stools with colourful seats around solid tables on the new oak flooring, and prints and pictures involving local characters on the white walls; restored panelling, black beams, and two roaring log fires. Well kept Cheriton Pots Ale, Hop Back Summer Lightning and Ringwood Best and Fortyniner, along with guests such as Archers Village Bitter, Cheriton Village Elder, and Palmers Dorset Gold tapped from the cask; they hold a beer festival in September. Darts, dominoes, shove-ha'penny and cribbage, and the back bar has quite a few books. The pub attracts a good mix of customers, and the staff are friendly. Simple lunchtime food is limited to home-made soup, ploughman's with home-made pâté, home-cooked pork pie, and gammon or cumberland sausage ring.

Free house ~ Licensees Neil and Pauline McCulloch ~ Real ale ~ Bar food (lunchtime only) ~ No credit cards ~ (023) 8081 2606 ~ Children welcome but must be well behaved ~ Dogs welcome ~ Open 11-3, 6-11; 11-11 Sat; 12-10.30 Sun

HAWKLEY

Hawkley Inn *Take first right turn off B3006, heading towards Liss ¼ mile from its junction with A3; then after nearly 2 miles take first left turn into Hawkley village – Pococks Lane; OS Sheet 186 map reference 746292*

Cheerful and unpretentious, this country local is popular with real ale lovers as there are usually half a dozen constantly changing beers, well kept and often from small breweries: one from Downton (new to us), Itchen

Valley Fat Controller, King Red River and Horsham Best Bitter, and RCH East Street Cream; they have their own cider, too. The opened-up bar and back dining room have a simple décor – big pine tables, a moose head, dried flowers, and prints on the mellowing walls; parts of the bar can get a bit smoky when it's busy, but there is a no smoking area to the left of the bar. Besides good soups such as bacon and mushroom, stilton and celery or tomato and watercress, swiftly served tasty bar food includes cottage pie or spinach and ricotta tart, pork and cider sausages, and beef stew. Also puddings such as spotted dick; friendly service. The pub is on the Hangers Way Path, and at weekends there are plenty of walkers; tables and a climbing frame in the pleasant garden.

Free house ~ Licensee Al Stringer ~ Real ale ~ Bar food (not Sun evening) ~ (01730) 827205 ~ Children welcome until 8pm ~ Dogs welcome ~ Open 12-2.30(3 Sat), 6-11; 12-3, 7-10.30 Sun

LONGSTOCK
Peat Spade *Village signposted off A30 on W edge of Stockbridge, and off A3057 Stockbridge—Andover*

There's no doubt that while locals do drop in for a pint and a chat, the emphasis in this well run place is very much on the good, interesting food; to be sure of a table, it is best to book in advance. The roomy and attractive squarish main bar is airy and high-ceilinged, with pretty windows, well chosen furnishings and a nice show of toby jugs and beer mats around its fireplace. A rather elegant no smoking dining room leads off, and there are doors to a big terrace. Served by helpful, pleasant staff and using local (and often organic) produce, the sensibly short menu might typically include cabbage and bacon soup, smoked haddock mousse, borlotti bean and tarragon casserole, lamb curry, baked fillet of cod with cheese crust, and aberdeen angus rib-eye steak; puddings such as fresh lemon delight. Well kept Batemans Spring Blonde, Hop Back GFB, and Ringwood Fortyniner on handpump, and several wines by the glass from a carefully chosen list. There are teak seats on the terrace, with more in the pleasant little garden, and maybe free range chickens, two cats, Cleo the cocker spaniel and Mollie the diabetic dog (who is not allowed to be fed). There are plenty of surrounding walks – along the Test Way at the end of the road and in the water meadows in Stockbridge, and Longstock Water Gardens is at the end of the village, and open alternate summer Sundays.

Free house ~ Licensees Bernie Startup and Sarah Hinman ~ Real ale ~ Bar food ~ Restaurant ~ No credit cards ~ (01264) 810612 ~ Children welcome ~ Dogs welcome ~ Open 11.30-3, 6.30-11; 12-3 Sun; closed Sun evening, all Mon

LYMINGTON
Kings Head *Quay Hill; pedestrian alley at bottom of High Street, can park down on quay and walk up from Quay Street*

Rambling darkly up and down steps and through timber dividers, this 17th-c pub has tankards hanging from great rough beams, and is mainly bare boarded, though there's a rug or two here and there. Lighting is dim, and even in daytime they light the candles on the tables – a great mix from

an elegant gateleg to a huge chunk of elm, with a nice old-fashioned variety of seating too; the local pictures include good classic yacht photographs. One cosy upper corner past the serving counter has a good log fire in a big fireplace, its mantelpiece a shrine to all sorts of drinking from beer tankards to port and champagne cases: they have well kept Adnams Bitter, Fullers London Pride, Gales HSB, Greene King IPA, and a seasonal Ringwood ale on handpump. Enjoyable food includes crispy duck salad with soy sauce, ginger and lemongrass, pasta with smoked chicken and bacon in creamy parmesan sauce, home-made steak and mushroom in ale pie, and specials such as home-made chicken liver pâté and mixed fish grill with lemon and parsley butter. A wall rack holds daily papers; piped pop music.
Inn Partnership (Pubmaster) ~ Lease Paul Stratton ~ Bar food (12-2.10, 6-10) ~ Restaurant ~ (01590) 672709 ~ Children welcome ~ Dogs welcome ~ Open 11-3, 5-11; 11-11 Sat; 12-10.30 Sun

MICHELDEVER
Half Moon & Spread Eagle *Village signposted off A33 N of Winchester; then follow Winchester 7 signpost almost opposite hall*
Under the friendly new licensees, this country local has remained a popular village pub. The simply decorated and beamed bar has heavy tables and good solid seats, and a woodburning stove at each end; a no smoking area leads off. Well liked bar food includes fried foie gras with apples and calvados sauce or ploughman's, brochette of the day with salad, sausages of the week or mushroom, pepper and parmesan risotto, thai chicken curry and wok-fried tiger prawns with garlic butter; also puddings like orange crème brûlée. Well kept Greene King IPA and Abbot, and guests such as Caledonian 80/- or St Austell Tribute on handpump; darts, pool, fruit machine, cribbage, and piped music. There are seats on a sheltered back terrace, and picnic-sets and a play area on the recently upgraded garden. This is a good starting point for exploring the Dever Valley, and there are lots of pleasant walks nearby.
Greene King ~ Tenants Christina Nicholls, Richard Tolfree, and Alex Tolfree ~ Real ale ~ Bar food ~ Restaurant ~ (01962) 774339 ~ Children welcome ~ Dogs allowed in bar ~ Open 12-3, 6-11; 12-3, 7-10.30 Sun

MINSTEAD
Trusty Servant *2.2 miles from M27 junction 1; keep on A31 for just over a mile, then turn left into village; also signposted off A337 Cadnam—Lyndhurst*
Suiting this scattered and prettily wooded New Forest hamlet with its wandering ponies, this welcoming 19th-c pub has a pleasantly relaxed feel – and a bonus for walkers on warm summer days is that its big airy dining room, with plenty of open windows, is pleasantly cool then. This is a pretty room, with comfortable chairs. The two opened-together rooms of the bar area (they also open through into the dining room) have a rather more local feel, with assorted chairs, carpet and bare boards, some Victorian and sporting prints, and an old piano (some of the regulars have been known to have a strum when the mood takes them). A varied choice of very good generous food, nicely presented on big plates, might include home-made

steak and kidney pie, double egg, ham and chips or liver and bacon, sizzling thai vegetable stir-fry, local skate wing, and daily specials such as whole bass or medallions of beef with coriander mash and roasted baby vegetables. In season, they do good game dishes, particularly pheasant. Service is friendly and commendably quick even when all the tables inside and in the good-sized side and back garden are full. They have well kept changing ales such as Fullers London Pride, Ringwood Best and Wadworths 6X on handpump, and decent house wines and country wines. The bedrooms are simple and pleasant, and they do a good breakfast. The nearby church is interesting for its unspoilt Georgian interior, and Sir Arthur Conan Doyle is buried in its graveyard; there are plenty of easy walks all around.

Enterprise ~ Lease Tony and Jane Walton ~ Real ale ~ Bar food (12-9.30) ~ Restaurant ~ (023) 8081 2137 ~ Children in restaurant ~ Dogs allowed in bar ~ Pianist alternate Fri evening ~ Open 11-11; 12-10.30 Sun ~ Bedrooms: £30S/£60S

NORTH GORLEY
Royal Oak *Ringwood Road; village signposted off A338 S of Fordingbridge*

As this 17th-c thatched pub (originally a hunting lodge) is on the edge of the New Forest, there are usually ponies and cattle roaming around; ducks on the big pond across the road, and a neatly kept sheltered back garden with plenty of seating and a play area for children. Inside, there's a quiet, comfortable and neatly refurbished no smoking lounge on the left, though we prefer the busier main bar on the right: carpeted too, with a corner gas stove, old copper and heavy horse decorations, and steps down to an attractive L-shaped eating area. This has a mix of dark pine tables and pleasant old-fashioned chairs on bare boards, and a further no smoking part with pine booth seating. Friendly and efficient staff serve the well liked popular food which at lunchtime includes sandwiches, home-made lasagne and sausages, or seafood linguine; evening dishes such as moules marinière, wild mushroom risotto or whole rack of ribs glazed with hickory sauce. Well kept Fullers London Pride, Ringwood Best, and a guest such as Adnams Broadside on handpump, decent wines, and several malt whiskies; fruit machine, TV, piped music and boules.

Enterprise ~ Lease Sharon Crush and Tom Woods ~ Real ale ~ Bar food (12-2.30, 6-9, but all day during school summer holidays) ~ Restaurant ~ (01425) 652244 ~ Children welcome ~ Dogs welcome ~ Pianist alternate Fri evening; monthly band Sun ~ Open 11-11; 12-10.30 Sun

OVINGTON
Bush *Village signposted from A31 on Winchester side of Alresford*

As this is such a lovely spot, and the back garden of this picturesquely set little cottage runs down to the River Itchen, it's not surprising to find quite a few customers on a warm sunny day; but it's well worth visiting in spring, too, when the nearby banks are covered in snowdrops and daffodils. Inside, the rooms have a nice old-fashioned décor, and the low-ceilinged bar has cushioned high-backed settles, elm tables with pews and kitchen chairs, masses of old pictures in heavy gilt frames on the walls, and a roaring fire on one side with an antique solid fuel stove opposite. Well kept Wadworths 6X, IPA, JCB, and seasonal guests on handpump, and several country wines and malt whiskies; cribbage, dominoes and board games. The sociable scottish springer spaniel is called Paddy. Bar food – not cheap – includes home-made chicken liver pâté, leek and mushroom cottage pie with smoked garlic mash or local trout fillets with hazelnut and coriander butter; puddings such as chocolate and black cherry bread and butter pudding; efficient, friendly service. Two rooms are no smoking. Please note that if you want to bring children it's best to book, as there are only a few tables set aside for families.

Wadworths ~ Managers Nick and Cathy Young ~ Real ale ~ Bar food (not Sun evening) ~ (01962) 732764 ~ Well behaved children in small family area ~ Dogs welcome ~ Open 11-3, 6-11; 12-2.30, 7-10.30 Sun

PETERSFIELD

Trooper *From B2070 in Petersfield follow Steep signposts past station, but keep on up past Steep, on old coach road; OS Sheet 186 map reference 726273*

'A good all-rounder' is how many of our readers describe this particularly well run pub. The landlord really goes out of his way to make customers feel welcome, the beers are well kept and from local breweries, the food is extremely good, and it's a comfortable place to stay. There's an island bar, tall stools by a broad ledge facing big windows that look across to rolling downland fields, blond wheelback and kitchen chairs and a mix of tripod tables on the bare boarded or red tiled floor, little persian knick-knacks here and there, quite a few ogival mirrors, big baskets of dried flowers, lit candles all around, fresh flowers, logs burning in the stone fireplace, and good piped music; newspapers and magazines to read. The raftered restaurant is most attractive; the pub is no smoking except for around the bar counter. Very good food (best to book to be sure of a table) might include chicken and wild mushroom puff, locally cured hand-carved ham with free range egg or chilli con carne, thai glazed vegetable skewers with chilli and pepper noodles, slow-roasted half shoulder of lamb and wild boar steak; well liked breakfasts. The four well kept real ales change frequently but might include Cheriton Pots Ale, Ringwood Best and Fortyniner, and Triple fff Moondance on handpump, and they have decent house wines. There are lots of picnic-sets on an upper lawn and more on the partly covered sunken terrace which has french windows to the dining area. The horse rail in the car park ('horses only before 8pm') does get used.

Free house ~ Licensee Hassan Matini ~ Real ale ~ Bar food ~ Restaurant ~ (01730) 827293 ~ Children welcome ~ Dogs allowed in bar ~ Open 12-2, 6-11; 12-2, 7-10.30 Sun; closed 25 and 26 Dec, 1 Jan ~ Bedrooms: £69S(£62B)/ £89S(£79B)

ROWLAND'S CASTLE

Castle Inn *Village signposted off B2148/B2149 N of Havant; Finchdean Road, by junction with Redhill Road and Woodberry Lane*

In a pleasant village with good surrounding walks, this is a cheerful and chatty pub with helpful, smart staff. There are two appealing smallish eating rooms on the left. The front one (no smoking) has rather nice simple mahogany chairs around sturdy scrubbed pine tables, one quite long, rugs on flagstones, a big fireplace, and quite a lot of old local photographs on its ochre walls; the back one is similar, but with bare boards, local water colour landscapes by Bob Payne for sale, and cases of colourful decorative glassware from nearby Stansted Park. Popular bar food at lunchtime includes sandwiches and filled baguettes, a vegetarian dish of the day, a pie or curry of the day, and daily specials; evening choices such as smoked mackerel pâté and leg of lamb steak with rosemary and garlic. Well kept Gales Butser, GB and HSB and a seasonal guest on handpump, and country wines. There is a small separate public bar on the right; disabled access and facilities are good, and the garden behind has picnic-sets.

Gales ~ Licensees Jan and Roger Burrell ~ Bar food (12-9; not after 3pm on winter Sun and Mon) ~ Restaurant ~ (023) 9241 2494 ~ Children in eating area of bar only ~ Dogs allowed in bar ~ Open 11-11; 12-10.30 Sun ~ Bedrooms: /£30

SPARSHOLT
Plough *Village signposted off B3049 (Winchester—Stockbridge), a little W of Winchester*

With helpful, friendly staff, excellent food, good beer, and a bustling atmosphere, it's not surprising that this well run place is so popular. Everything is neatly kept, and the main bar has an interesting mix of wooden tables and chairs, and farm tools, scythes and pitchforks attached to the ceiling; two no smoking areas. On daily changing blackboards, the interesting bar food might include chilli and chickpea cakes with an avocado salsa, loin of pork on garlic sweet potatoes, salmon and crab fishcakes, braised faggots with bubble and squeak, beef fillet stuffed with goats cheese and pinenuts; also puddings like poached pear and caramel ice-cream; to be sure of a table or a long wait, you must book a table in advance. Well kept Wadworths IPA, JCB, 6X, a seasonal ale, and maybe a guest on handpump, and an extensive wine list. There's a children's play fort, and plenty of seats on the terrace and lawn.

Wadworths ~ Tenants R C and K J Crawford ~ Real ale ~ Bar food ~ (01962) 776353 ~ Children welcome ~ Dogs welcome ~ Open 11-3, 6-11; 12-3, 6-10.30 Sun; closed 25 Dec

STOCKBRIDGE
Grosvenor *High Street*

This handsome Georgian country-town coaching inn has been attractively restored and refurbished by its new owners. The high-ceilinged main bar's pleasantly restrained decoration is now entirely in keeping with the distinction of the building itself, with a good log fire, some sporting pictures and *Vanity Fair* caricatures of former jockeys. Well divided into separate room areas, it is comfortable and relaxing. Service is cheerful and efficient; they have well kept Greene King IPA, Abbot and Ruddles County on handpump, a dozen enjoyable wines by the glass, and decent coffee. Bar food includes soup such as sweet roasted pepper and tomato, crab cakes with sweet chilli sauce, home-made lasagne, home-made steak in ale pie and beer-battered cod. The impressive partly oak-panelled dining room has some attractive late 19th-c pictures of horse race winners from the stables of the hotel's then owner, who was Master of the Danebury Harriers. A back conservatory has more tables. A couple of pavement tables stand out beside the imposing front portico, with more tables in the good-sized back garden, prettily laid out with attractive plantings and a small lily pond. We have not heard yet from any readers who have stayed since the management changes, but would expect good value. This is an appealing small town, with good antiques shops, the National Trust Common Marsh along the River Test, and downland walks all around.

Greene King ~ Managers Colin and Valerie Holman ~ Real ale ~ Bar food ~ Restaurant ~ (01264) 810606 ~ Children welcome ~ Dogs allowed in bar ~ Open 11-11; 12-10.30 Sun ~ Bedrooms: £80B/£95B

TICHBORNE

Tichborne Arms *Village signposted off B3047*

This is a proper country pub – charmingly old-fashioned and friendly. The comfortable square-panelled room on the right has wheelback chairs and settles (one very long), a log fire in the stone fireplace, and latticed windows. On the left is a larger, livelier, partly panelled room used for eating. The pictures and documents on the walls inside recall the bizarre Tichborne Case (a mystery man from Australia claimed fraudulently to be the heir to this estate); friendly golden labrador. Home-made bar food includes sandwiches, stilton mushrooms, coronation chicken salad, spinach and ricotta cannelloni, pies such as chicken, tarragon and mushroom, steak, ale and stilton or fish, and lamb shank; puddings might include hot plum tart or rhubarb and ginger crumble. Well kept Ringwood Best and Wadworths 6X, and a couple of guests tapped from the cask, a decent choice of wines by the glass, country wines and farm cider; sensibly placed darts, bar billiards, shove-ha'penny, dominoes, cribbage and piped music. Picnic-sets outside in the big well kept garden, and a petanque pitch. You can expect to find quite a few walkers here during the day, as the Wayfarers Walk and Itchen Way pass close by, and many fine walks lead off in all directions. No children inside.

Free house ~ Licensees Keith and Janie Day ~ Real ale ~ Bar food (12-1.45, 6.30-9.45) ~ Restaurant ~ (01962) 733760 ~ Dogs welcome ~ Open 11.30-2.30, 6-11; 12-3, 7-10.30 Sun; closed evenings 25 and 26 Dec and evening 1 Jan

UPHAM

Brushmakers Arms *Shoe Lane; village signposted from Winchester—Bishops Waltham downs road, and from B2177 (former A333)*

Bustling and attractive old village local with a comfortable L-shaped bar divided in two by a central brick chimney – there's a woodburning stove in the raised two-way fireplace. It has comfortably cushioned wall settles and chairs, a variety of tables including some in country-style stripped wood, a few beams in the low ceiling, and quite a collection of ethnic-looking brushes; there's also a little snug. Dominoes, cribbage, fruit machine, shove-ha'penny and sensibly placed darts. Reasonably priced and well kept Ballards Best, Ringwood Best, and Charles Wells Bombardier on handpump. Bar food includes lunchtime snacks such as filled baked potatoes, ploughman's, and ham and egg, as well as sardines in garlic, mushroom stroganoff, local partridge with stilton and bacon sauce, steaks, and home-made puddings. The big garden is well stocked with mature shrubs and trees, and there are picnic-sets on a sheltered back terrace among lots of tubs of flowers, with more on the tidy tree-sheltered lawn. Good walks nearby.

Free house ~ Licensee Tony Mottram ~ Real ale ~ Bar food ~ (01489) 860231 ~ Children in eating area of bar ~ Dogs allowed in bar ~ Open 11-3, 5.45-11; 11-3.30, 6-11 Sat; 12-3.30, 7-10.30 Sun

WELL
Chequers *Off A287 via Crondall, or A31 via Froyle and Lower Froyle*
This is a friendly place with a good welcome for all – best to get there soon after it opens as it fills up quickly. The low-beamed rooms have lots of alcoves, wooden pews, brocaded stools and a few GWR carriage lamps, and the panelled walls are hung with 18th-c country-life prints and old sepia photographs of locals enjoying a drink; roaring winter log fire, fruit machine, dominoes, chess and Jenga. Generous helpings of very tasty bar food includes duck and orange pâté with tangy fruit and cider chutney, warm chicken and bacon salad, home-made burger topped with bacon and brie or honey-roast ham and egg with bubble and squeak, feta, sun-blush tomato and olive salad, steak in ale pie, or pork and herb sausages on mustard mash with onion gravy; the restaurant is no smoking. Well kept Badger Best, Tanglefoot, and Fursty Ferret on handpump, and decent wines. The vine-covered terrace is a very pleasant place to sit in summer and the spacious back garden has picnic-sets too. They provide bowls of water and biscuits for dogs.

Badger ~ Managers Sonia Henderson and Tim Llewellyn ~ Real ale ~ Bar food (12-3(4 Sat and Sun), 6-9.30(8.30 Sun)) ~ Restaurant ~ (01256) 862605 ~ Children in restaurant ~ Dogs allowed in bar ~ Open 12-3, 6-11; 12-11 Sat; 12-10.30 Sun

Dog Friendly Hotels, B&Bs and Farms

BEAULIEU
Montagu Arms *Palace Lane, Beaulieu, Brockenhurst, Hampshire SO42 7ZL (01590) 612324 £160*, plus special breaks; 23 individually decorated pretty rms. Attractive creeper-clad hotel with lovely terraced garden, comfortable sitting room, conservatory lounge, very good food in beamed restaurant and more informal brasserie, and attentive staff; their health club is in the nearby village of Brockenhurst; disabled access; dogs in bedrooms and lounge area

BROCKENHURST

Cloud Hotel *Meerut Rd, Brockenhurst, Hampshire SO42 7TD (01590)* *622165* £104; 18 pretty rms. Neatly kept and friendly hotel with New Forest views, several cosy lounges, log fires and fresh flowers, an intimate little bar, dancing memorabilia highlighting the career of the owner, and good food in attractive no smoking restaurant; cl 27 Dec-14 Jan; children over 8; partial disabled access; dogs welcome in bedrooms; £10

CHERITON

Flower Pots *Cheriton, Alresford, Hampshire SO24 0QQ (01962) 771318* £60; 4 rms. Unspoilt and quietly comfortable village local run by very friendly family, with two pleasant little bars, log fire, decent bar food, super own-brew beers, and old-fashioned seats on the pretty lawns; no credit cards; no accommodation Christmas and New Year; no children; dogs in bedrooms and bars if well behaved

HURSTBOURNE TARRANT

Esseborne Manor *Hurstbourne Tarrant, Andover, Hampshire SP11 0ER (01264) 736444* £130, plus special breaks; 15 individually decorated rms. Small stylish Victorian manor with a relaxed, friendly atmosphere, comfortable lounge and snug little bar, good modern cooking, log fires in elegant dining room, and courteous staff; neat gardens with tennis and croquet; special arrangement with local golf club and health and leisure centre; disabled access; dogs welcome in bedrooms

LYMINGTON

Efford Cottage *Milford Rd, Everton, Lymington, Hampshire SO41 0JD (01590) 642315* £55, plus winter breaks; 3 comfortable rms. Spacious Georgian cottage near New Forest with an acre of garden, marvellous breakfasts inc home-baked bread and home-made jams and preserves, and good parking; no children; dogs in bedrooms; £2

Stanwell House *High St, Lymington, Hampshire SO41 9AA (01590) 677123* £120, plus special breaks; 29 pretty rms. Handsome town house with comfortable attractively furnished lounge, cosy little bar, good imaginative food, and pretty walled back garden; dogs in bedrooms; £15

LYNDHURST

Poussin at Parkhill *Beaulieu Rd, Lyndhurst, Hampshire SO43 7FZ (023) 8028 2944* £110, plus special breaks; 19 carefully furnished, spacious and comfortable rms. 18th-c former hunting lodge reached by a long drive through wood-flanked New Forest pastures; a nice, informal, family-run atmosphere, big welcoming peaceful lounge/hall with sofas, easy chairs, a writing desk, a good log fire and daily papers, and an inner hall with a grand piano and longcase clock; the pink-carpeted lounge has another big log fire, lots of sofas and deep easy chairs and low tables, and big windows looking over a narrow flagstoned terrace and pond-side lawn; a little library with lots of books, smallish cosy bar, and pretty, formal restaurant with conservatory-style extension; quite excellent, beautifully presented food, a good wine list with an exceptionally good choice of wines by the glass, and enjoyable breakfasts with home-preserved fruits and home-made jams and marmalade; children over 8 in dining room; dogs in cottage bedroom with own walled garden; £10

MILFORD ON SEA
Westover Hall *Park Lane, Milford on Sea, Lymington, Hampshire SO41 0PT* *(01590) 643044* **£165**, plus winter breaks; 12 individually furnished rms, 6 with sea views. Victorian mansion in marvellous spot near peaceful beach, views of Christchurch Bay, Isle of Wight and the Needles rocks; impressive original features inc dramatic stained glass, magnificent oak panelling, and ornate ceilings, very good food using the best local produce in grand (but not stuffy) candlelit restaurant overlooking garden and sea, lighter lunches in lounge bar also with water views, sunny terrace, and helpful friendly staff; dogs welcome in bedrooms; £10

OWER
Ranvilles Farm House *Pauncefoot Hill, Romsey, Hampshire SO51 6AA* *(023) 8081 4481* **£55**; 4 attractively decorated rms with antique furniture. Dating from the 13th c when Richard de Ranville came from Normandy and settled with his family, this Grade II★ listed house is in five quiet acres of gardens and paddock, with warmly friendly owners and enjoyable breakfasts; no evening meals; cl 25 and 26 Dec; disabled access; dogs welcome in bedrooms

SPARSHOLT
Lainston House *Sparsholt, Winchester, Hampshire SO21 2LT (01962)* *863588* **£115**, plus wknd breaks; 50 spacious, individually decorated rms. Close to Winchester, this elegant William and Mary hotel stands in 63 acres of fine parkland, with tennis court, croquet, fishing, archery, and clay pigeon shooting; fresh flowers and paintings in relaxing, elegant lounge, panelled bar and restaurant, a fine wine list, and modern english cooking; gym; disabled access; dogs in bedrooms, lounge and reception area; £10

WINCHESTER
Wykeham Arms *75 Kingsgate St, Winchester, Hampshire SO23 9PE* *(01962) 853834* **£90**; 14 well equipped attractive rms. Very well run, smart old town inn, close to cathedral, with interestingly furnished bustling bars, two small dining rooms serving delicious daily changing food (very good breakfasts, too), fine wines (lots by the glass), and prompt friendly service; several no smoking areas; cl 25 Dec; dogs in some bedrooms and bar; £5

Herefordshire

Dog Friendly Pubs

AYMESTREY
Riverside Inn *A4110; N off A44 at Mortimer's Cross, W of Leominster*
At the back of this idyllically placed black and white timbered inn, there are picnic-sets by a flowing river, and rustic tables and benches up above in a steep tree-sheltered garden – a beautifully sheltered former bowling green, too. Residents are offered fly-fishing (they have fishing rights on a mile of the River Lugg), and a free taxi service to the start of the Mortimer Trail; pleasant circular walks start from here. The rambling beamed bar has several cosy areas and the décor is drawn from a pleasant mix of periods and styles, with fine antique oak tables and chairs, stripped pine country kitchen tables, fresh flowers, hops strung from a ceiling wagon-wheel, horse tack, and nice pictures; you can only smoke in one specified area. Warm log fires in winter, while in summer big overflowing flower pots frame the entrances; shove-ha'penny, cribbage, and piped music. Well kept Woods Shropshire Lad, Wye Valley Dorothy Goodbodys Golden Ale, and a guest such as Spinning Dog Pit Stop on handpump, local farm ciders and apple juice, 22 malt whiskies, and seven wines by the glass. The landlord likes to talk to his customers and service is good. Enjoyable bar food includes freshly made baguettes, local gammon steak with parsley sauce and locally smoked salmon and prawn salad; also starters such as fried local chicken livers and bacon on toasted brioche and main courses like seared fillet of brill on summer vegetables. It does get busy at weekends, so booking would be wise.
Free house ~ Licensees Richard and Liz Gresko ~ Real ale ~ Bar food ~ Restaurant ~ (01568) 708440 ~ Children in eating area of bar and restaurant ~ Dogs welcome ~ Open 11-4(3 in winter), 6-11; may open all day if busy; 11-11 Sat; 12-10.30 Sun; closed 25 Dec ~ Bedrooms: £40B/£65B

BRIMFIELD
Roebuck Inn *Village signposted just off A49 Shrewsbury—Leominster*
'First class' is how several of our readers describe this well run and smart country dining pub. The friendly, cheerful landlord and his efficient staff are sure to make you welcome, the beers are well kept, and the food

extremely good; it's also a comfortable place to stay. Each of the three rambling bars has a different but equally civilised atmosphere. The quiet old-fashioned snug is where you might find locals drinking and playing dominoes and cribbage by an impressive inglenook fireplace. Pale oak panelling in the 15th-c main bar makes for a quietly relaxed atmosphere, and the Brimfield Bar with a big bay window and open fire is light and airy. The brightly decorated cane-furnished airy dining room is no smoking. Absolutely everything, right down to the bread and relishes, is home-made, and, at lunchtime, snacks might include platters with assorted cheeses, home-cooked ham, roast sirloin of beef or grilled cumberland sausages, and specials such as faggots, venison casserole, cottage pie or pizza. More elaborate choices include a ragout of fresh mushrooms in puff pastry with port and tarragon scented jus, smoked chicken ravioli with a white bean cappuccino, and seared scallops; also puddings like apricot and almond steamed pudding or three chocolate terrine. They have an interesting reasonably priced wine list, a carefully chosen range of spirits and Stowford Press cider. Seats out on the enclosed terrace.

Free house ~ Licensees Mr and Mrs Jenkins ~ Real ale ~ Bar food ~ Restaurant ~ (01584) 711230 ~ Children in eating area of bar till 9pm ~ Dogs allowed in bar ~ Open 11.30-3, 6.30-11; 12-3, 7-10.30 Sun; closed 25 and 26 Dec ~ Bedrooms: /£70S(£70B)

SELLACK

Lough Pool *Back road Hoarwithy—Ross-on-Wye*

Particularly well run, this attractive black and white timbered cottage continues to serve very good food while firmly remaining a traditional pub. The beamed central room has kitchen chairs and cushioned window seats around wooden tables on the mainly flagstoned floor, sporting prints, bunches of dried flowers and fresh hop bines, and a log fire at one end with a woodburner at the other. Other rooms lead off, gently brightened up with attractive individual furnishings and nice touches like the dresser of patterned plates. The same interesting menu – which changes daily – is available in the chatty bar as well as the restaurant, and might include sandwiches, cream of celeriac soup, a plate of spanish charcuterie or blue cheese soufflé with walnut and watercress salad, chargrilled liver and bacon with crispy fried onions, spatchcocked poussin with yoghurt and cumin and sweet and sour sauce, and pink bream with curried leeks, mussels and saffron braised potatoes; puddings such as warm chocolate fondant or lemon and elderflower pannacotta with shortbread. The restaurant is no smoking. Well kept John Smiths, and Wye Valley Bitter or Butty Bach on handpump, a good range of malt whiskies, local farm ciders and a well chosen reasonably priced wine list. Service is good. There are plenty of picnic-sets on its neat front lawned area, and pretty hanging baskets; plenty of bridleways and surrounding walks.

Free house ~ Licensee Stephen Bull ~ Real ale ~ Bar food ~ Restaurant ~ (01989) 730236 ~ Children in eating area of bar and restaurant ~ Dogs allowed in bar ~ Open 11.30-2.30, 6.30-11; 12-2, 7-10.30 Sun; closed Sun evening, all day Mon in winter

ST OWEN'S CROSS

New Inn *Junction A4137 and B4521, W of Ross-on-Wye*

The hanging baskets all around this unspoilt black and white timbered coaching inn are quite a sight, and in summer the big enclosed garden here really comes into its own; fine views stretch over rolling countryside to the distant Black Mountains. Inside, both the lounge bar (with a buoyant local atmosphere) and the no smoking restaurant have huge inglenook fireplaces, intriguing nooks and crannies, settles, old pews, beams and timbers. Lunchtime bar food includes home-made chicken liver pâté, ploughman's, home-made lasagne, a curry of the day and home-made steak and kidney pie; in the evening there might be extras such as trout fillets wrapped in bacon (caught by the chef), local duckling in a chinese-style plum sauce, and steaks. Friendly and pleasant service. Well kept Tetleys and Wadworths 6X alongside Brains Reverend James and Marstons Pedigree on handpump, local cider and perry, and a fair choice of malt whiskies; darts, shove-ha'penny, cribbage, dominoes, and piped music. Be very careful if you do use the A4137 – this is England's second most dangerous road.

Free house ~ Licensee Graham Gumley ~ Real ale ~ Bar food (12-2, 6.15-9) ~ Restaurant ~ (01989) 730274 ~ Children welcome ~ Dogs welcome ~ Open 12-2.30(3 Sat), 6-11; 12-4, 7-10.30 Sun ~ Bedrooms: £40S/£70S(£80B)

TITLEY

Stagg *B4355 N of Kington*

There have been several changes to this well known dining pub over the last year or so. Their new barn conversion, as we went to press, was virtually finished which will give them a further dining room with doors onto the terrace. This increased space should mean that the bar is freed up from people all eating, thus giving those who just want a drink and a chat a bit more space. They have also bought a Georgian vicarage four minutes away and plan to open guest accommodation; the two-acre garden will also incorporate a vegetable and herb garden for the kitchen. The landlord/chef uses local suppliers wherever possible, so you can be sure of good, fresh often organic ingredients. The pubbier blackboard menu (not available Saturday evening or Sunday lunchtime) has up to 10 choices which could include three-cheese ploughman's, pasta with home-made pesto, crispy duck leg with cider sauce, and smoked haddock risotto. On the more elaborate restaurant menu (which can also be eaten in the bar) you might find venison carpaccio with truffled celeriac salad, fried foie gras with apple jelly, bass fillet and local beef with stuffed savoy cabbage. Puddings such as dark and white chocolate mousse cake or rum baba with local clotted cream. There's also a choice of around 14 british cheeses. The food can take quite a while to come and helpings can strike some people as small. The dining rooms are no smoking. A carefully chosen wine list with 10 wines and champagne by the glass, well kept Hobsons Best and Town Crier, and a guest like Black Sheep or Greene King Ruddles County on handpump, and a fine collection of malt whiskies, and local farm cider and perry and apple juice; cribbage and dominoes. The bar, though comfortable and hospitable, is not large, and the atmosphere is civilised rather than lively. The garden has chairs and tables on a terrace.

Free house ~ Licensees Steve and Nicola Reynolds ~ Real ale ~ Bar food (not Sun evening or Mon) ~ Restaurant ~ (01544) 230221 ~ Children welcome ~ Dogs allowed in bar ~ Open 12-3, 6.30-11; 12-3.30 Sun; closed Sun evening, Mon, 25 and 26 Dec, 1 Jan ~ Bedrooms: £50B/£70B

Dog Friendly Hotels, B&Bs and Farms

GLEWSTONE
Glewstone Court *Glewstone, Ross-on-Wye, Herefordshire HR9 6AW* (01989) 770367 **£104**; 8 well equipped rms. Elegant, partly Georgian and partly Victorian country house set in neat grounds with a fine cedar of Lebanon and views over Ross-on-Wye; long-standing, warmly welcoming owners and staff, comfortable and relaxing public rooms, and good food in antique-filled dining room; croquet; cl 24–26 Dec; dogs welcome in bedrooms, bar and lounge; £5

HEREFORD
Castle House *Castle St, Hereford, Herefordshire HR1 2NW (01432) 356321* **£175**; 15 rms. Stylish and elegant Georgian hotel near the cathedral with garden views overlooking the tranquil moat, a restful lounge and bar, beautifully presented ambitious food using first-class ingredients in smart restaurant, and impeccable service; dogs welcome in bedrooms

KINGTON
Penrhos Court *Lyonshall, Kington, Herefordshire HR5 3LH (01544)* 230720 **£100**, plus special breaks; 17 elegant rms. Beautifully restored 13th-c hall in six acres, with fine beams and flagstones, a magnificent hall for their organic dining, a huge wood fire, and very good carefully cooked food using seasonal organic home-grown herbs and vegetables; they run regular food and health courses; cl Jan; disabled access; dogs in self-catering unit; £2.50

LEDBURY
Feathers *25 High St, Ledbury, Herefordshire HR8 1DS (01531) 635266* **£99**, plus special breaks; 19 carefully decorated rms making the most of the old beams and timbers. Very striking, mainly 16th-c, black and white hotel with a relaxed atmosphere, log fires, comfortable lounge hall with country antiques, beams and timbers, particularly enjoyable food and friendly service in hop-decked Fuggles bar, a good wine list, and a fine mix of locals and visitors; health and leisure spa with indoor swimming pool; dogs welcome in bedrooms

PUDLESTON
Ford Abbey *Pudleston, Leominster, Herefordshire HR6 0RZ (01568)* 760700 **£115**; 6 luxury suites, one with own sitting room. Former

Benedictine Abbey dating in part back to the 12th c and surrounded by 320 acres of farmland; elegant and comfortable drawing room with inglenook fireplaces, cosy study, a restful atmosphere, friendly staff, and good food using the best local produce (and some from their own farm); indoor heated swimming pool, fitness centre and self-catering lodges; good disabled access; dogs welcome in bedrooms; £10; must be on lead in grounds

Hertfordshire

Dog Friendly Pubs

ASHWELL
Three Tuns *Off A505 NE of Baldock; High Street*
In a delightful village full of enjoyable corners and buildings, including St Mary's Church with its soaring tower, this pleasant flower-decked 18th-c hotel has a nicely old-fashioned atmosphere. It's popular with walkers at summer weekends, as the landscape around rolls enough to be interesting, and views on higher ground are far ranging. There's an air of Victorian opulence in the cosy lounge with its relaxing chairs, big family tables, lots of pictures, stuffed pheasants and fish, and antiques. The simpler more modern public bar has pool, darts, cribbage, dominoes, a fruit machine, SkyTV, and Greene King IPA, Abbot and a guest on handpump, and there's a good choice of wines; piped light classical music. Served by friendly attentive staff, changing home-made bar food might include soup, devilled whitebait, vegetarian pasta bake, chicken, ham and mushroom pie, and roast partridge with stuffing and leek and mushroom sauce; home-made puddings; no smoking dining room. The substantial shaded garden has boules, and picnic-sets under apple trees; lavatories are down a steep flight of steps. One of the six bedrooms has a four-poster bed, and another its own dressing room; we still have not heard from readers who have stayed here.
Greene King ~ Tenants Claire and Darrell Stanley ~ Real ale ~ Bar food (12-2.30, 6.30-9.30; all day Sat/Sun) ~ Restaurant ~ (01462) 742107 ~ Children in eating area of bar and restaurant ~ Dogs allowed in bar ~ Live entertainment Fri or Sat ~ Open 11-11; 12-10.30 Sun ~ Bedrooms: £39(£59B)/£59S(£69B)

BATFORD
Gibraltar Castle *Lower Luton Road; B653, S of B652 junction*
One area of this friendly, traditional low-beamed roadside pub on the north side of Harpenden gives way to soaring rafters and gives it something of the feel of a hunting lodge. Throughout are glass cases housing an interesting collection of militaria including rifles, swords, medals, uniforms and bullets. The rest of the long carpeted bar has a pleasant old fireplace, comfortably cushioned wall benches, and a couple of snugly intimate window alcoves, one with a fine old clock. Well kept Fullers Chiswick,

ESB, London Pride and a seasonal brew on handpump, a good range of malt whiskies, well made irish coffee, and a thoughtful choice of wines by the glass; board games and piped music. The tasty bar food varies according to season and might include spinach and ricotta pancake, smoked salmon stuffed with prawns and seafood sauce, steak and ale pie, exotic fish according to availability, and home-made puddings. Booking is recommended for their very popular good value Sunday roast. There are tables and chairs on a new, safely enclosed decked back terrace, a few tables in front by the road, and pretty hanging baskets and tubs dotted around.

Fullers ~ Tenant Hamish Miller ~ Real ale ~ Bar food (12-2.30, 7-9; 12-4 Sun) ~ Restaurant ~ (01582) 460005 ~ Children in eating area of bar ~ Dogs welcome ~ Jam session Tues evening ~ Open 11.30-3, 5-11; 11.30-11 Sat; 12-10.30 Sun

CHAPMORE END

Woodman *Off B158 Wadesmill—Bengeo; 300 yards W of A602 roundabout, keep eyes skinned for discreet green sign to pub pointing up otherwise unmarked narrow lane; OS Sheet 166 map reference 328164*

A haven of daytime tranquillity, this delightfully unspoilt early Victorian local is tucked away close to the duck pond of a small hamlet, and is popular with walkers and cyclists. The two little linked rooms have plain seats around stripped pub tables, flooring tiles or broad bare boards, log fires in period fireplaces, cheerful pictures for sale, lots of local notices, and darts on one side, with a piano (and a couple of squeeze boxes) on the other; shove-ha'penny, cribbage and dominoes. They have well kept Greene King IPA, Abbot, a house mix of the two, and a Greene King guest such as St Austell Triumph tapped from the cask, as well as five malt whiskies. A good choice of good value lunchtime sandwiches and a couple of daily dishes. From their very small kitchen they also manage to conjure up a simple Thursday evening meal giving one main dish such as home-made steak and kidney pudding and a pudding or home-made ice-cream – best to book ahead. Service is friendly and helpful, and in past seasons (when there's an R in the month) they've done monthly oyster nights. There are picnic-sets out in front under a couple of walnut trees; a bigger garden behind has boules and a good fenced play area; there are pet rabbits in the garden as well as a pub cat. The car park has little room.

Greene King ~ Tenants Drs D R Davis and A C Yates ~ Real ale ~ Bar food (lunchtime and Thurs evening) ~ No credit cards ~ (01920) 463143 ~ Dogs welcome ~ Open 12-3, 6-11 (5.30-11 Fri); 12-11 Sat; 12-10.30 Sun

FRITHSDEN

Alford Arms *From Berkhamsted take unmarked road towards Potten End, pass Potten End turn on right, then take next left towards Ashridge College*

This is the county's leading food pub, so booking at the weekend is essential. It's pleasantly secluded though by no means undiscovered, by a village green and surrounded by National Trust woodland (with plenty of possibilities for walkers). Fashionably refurbished by thoughtful licensees, it is an elegantly casual place for a very good meal out. The interior has

simple prints on pale cream walls, with areas picked out in blocks of
Victorian green or dark red, and an appealing mix of good furniture from
Georgian chairs to old commode stands on bare boards and patterned
quarry tiles. It's all pulled together by luxurious richly patterned curtains.
Very good and successfully innovative bar food is served by charming staff,
and might include rustic bread with roast garlic and balsamic olive oil, oak-
smoked bacon on bubble and squeak with hollandaise sauce and poached
egg, fettucine with asparagus and artichoke, and grilled scotch rib-eye steak
with chips and home-made ketchup; also puddings such as treacle and
hazelnut tart. Good sweet wines. Smoking is allowed throughout. Well
kept Brakspears, Flowers Original, Marstons Pedigree and Morrells Oxford
Blue on handpump; piped jazz, darts. They have plenty of tables out in
front.

*Enterprise ~ Lease Becky and David Salisbury ~ Real ale ~ Bar food (12-2.30(3
Sun), 7-10) ~ Restaurant ~ (01442) 864480 ~ Children in eating area of bar and
restaurant ~ Dogs allowed in bar ~ Open 11-11; 12-10.30 Sun*

Dog Friendly Hotels, B&Bs and Farms

CHIPPERFIELD
Two Brewers *Chipperfield, King's Langley, Hertfordshire WD4 9BS (01923)
265266* £**69.50**; 20 comfortable rms. Comfortable and very neatly kept
country hotel with relaxing views of pretty village green, dark beams, bow
windows, antique settles, log fires, and good bar and restaurant food;
pleasant nearby walks; partial disabled access; dogs in bedrooms; £5

KNEBWORTH
Homewood *Knebworth, Hertfordshire SG3 6PP (01438) 812105* £**70**; 2
rms. Lovely Lutyens-designed house in six beautiful acres; elegant rooms
with antiques and tapestries and interestingly decorated by the owner, good
breakfasts, evening meals by prior arrangement, and five cats and a friendly
dog; cl 20 Dec-5 Jan; dogs welcome in bedrooms

UGLEY
Harewood *Snakes Lane, Ugley, Bishop's Stortford, Hertfordshire CM22 6HW
(01279) 813907* £**70**; 2 rms, 1 with own sitting area. Victorian house in
four acres of landscaped gardens in a quiet village, welcoming, friendly
owners, good breakfasts using local produce served around a communal
table in elegant dining room, and TV lounge; no smoking; croquet; dogs
welcome in bedrooms

Isle of Wight

Dog Friendly Pubs

BEMBRIDGE
Crab & Lobster *Foreland Fields Road, off Howgate Road (which is off B3395 via Hillgate Road)*

The wonderful view from the coastal bluff over The Solent alone justifies the search for this obscurely located clifftop pub, and the terrace, bedrooms and window seats make the most of its position, within strolling distance of the beach. There's more room inside than you'd expect from the frontage, which is prettily bedecked with flower baskets in summer. The attractively decorated interior has a civilised, almost parlourish style, with lots of yachting memorabilia and old local photographs. They serve a very good choice of eight or nine changing fresh local seafood specials every day, from sardines in garlic butter and lemon, through moules marinière and tasty home-made crab cakes, to whole lobster. Other very well prepared food includes duck pâté, baked potatoes, home-made lasagne and fish pie, pork steaks with mozzarella and rosemary, and spicy baked local crab in the shell; also puddings such as spotted dick. Due to open at Easter after refurbishment, the restaurant is no smoking. Well kept Flowers Original, Greene King IPA, a guest such as Goddards Fuggle-Dee-Dum on handpump, decent house wines, country wines from the barrel, a large selection of malt whiskies, good coffee; piped music (even in the lavatories), darts, dominoes and cribbage. It does get very popular, so best to get there early or late at lunchtime.
Whitbreads ~ Lease Richard, Adrian and Pauline Allan ~ Real ale ~ Bar food (12-2.30, 6-9.30) ~ Restaurant ~ (01983) 872244 ~ Children in eating area of bar and restaurant ~ Dogs allowed in bar ~ Open 11-11; 12-10.30 Sun; 11-3, 6-11 weekdays in winter ~ Bedrooms: £40B/£80B

BONCHURCH
Bonchurch Inn *Bonchurch Shute; from A3055 E of Ventnor, turn down to Old Bonchurch opposite Leconfield Hotel*

Beneath a steep and rocky slope and cut into the side of the hill, this is not at all a conventional-looking pub, with its origins as stables for the nearby manor house, hence its unusual arrangement of separate bar, restaurant, rooms and kitchens spread round a cobbled courtyard. Since gaining its

licence in the 1840s, little has changed. Its various buildings form the sides of a small cobbled central courtyard. Tables, a fountain and pergola out here are nicely enclosed, giving it a slightly continental feel on warm summer days. The furniture-packed Victorian bar has a good chatty atmosphere, and conjures up images of salvaged shipwrecks, with its floor of narrow-planked ship's decking, and seats like the ones that old-fashioned steamers used to have. A separate entrance leads to the very simple no smoking family room (a bit cut off from the congenial atmosphere of the public bar). As well as Courage Directors and a guest ale tapped from the cask, there are italian wines by the glass, a few bottled french wines, darts, bar billiards, shove-ha'penny, dominoes and cribbage. The welcoming landlord is italian, and the menu reflects this with several good value dishes such as lasagne, spinach cannelloni and seafood risotto, as well as sandwiches, chilli chicken with rice and sirloin steak; for puddings they have ice-creams and sorbets; there is a £1 charge for credit cards. The no smoking restaurant is just across the courtyard (the lounge bar has also been made no smoking), and the pub owns a holiday flat for up to six people.
Free house ~ Licensees Ulisse and Gillian Besozzi ~ Real ale ~ Bar food ~ Restaurant ~ (01983) 852611 ~ Children in family room ~ Dogs welcome ~ Open 11-3, 6.30-11; 12-3, 7-10.30 Sun ~ Bedrooms: /£50B

FRESHWATER

Red Lion *Church Place; from A3055 at E end of village by Freshwater Garage mini-roundabout, follow Yarmouth signpost, then take first real right turn signposted to Parish Church*
In some choice walking country near the reedy Yar Estuary and tucked well away, this red-brick pub has kept a genuine local atmosphere that visitors without smaller children tend to appreciate. It's so popular that if you want to eat here it's a good idea to book ahead. Enjoyable bar food includes sandwiches and fish and chips; very well prepared imaginative daily specials are listed on a big blackboard behind the bar, and might include soup such as parsnip and apple, herring roes on toast, steak and kidney pie, and puddings such as rhubarb crumble or home-made ice-cream. There's a bustling atmosphere in the comfortably furnished open-plan bar, which has open fires, low grey sofas and sturdy country-kitchen style furnishings on mainly flagstoned floors, with bare boards at one end, and lots of local pictures and photographs and china platters on the walls. Well kept Flowers Original, Fullers London Pride and Wadworths 6X, plus a guest ale such as Goddards on handpump, and the good choice of wines includes 16 by the glass; service could be friendlier at times. Fines on mobile phone users go to charity (they also collect a lot for the RNLI); there's a fruit machine but no music, and smoking is permitted throughout. There are tables on a carefully tended grass and gravel area at the back (some under cover), behind which is the kitchen's herb garden, and a couple of picnic-sets in a quiet square at the front, by the church.
Enterprise ~ Lease Michael Mence ~ Real ale ~ Bar food ~ (01983) 754925 ~ Children over 10 ~ Dogs allowed in bar ~ Open 11.30-3, 5.30-11; 11.30-4, 6-11 Sat; 12-3, 7-10.30 Sun

SHALFLEET
New Inn *A3054 Newport—Yarmouth*
Just a stroll away from the quay at an inlet of the yacht-filled Newtown
estuary is this welcoming 18th-century fishermen's pub that aptly
specialises in fresh fish dishes. Well known for their crab or lobster salad and
seafood platter, they also have a great choice of up to 12 fresh fish dishes a
day. A little crab shack in the garden sells potted shrimps and crab
sandwiches, and there's a new decked garden area. Other dishes include
smoked venison with green fig chutney, chicken breast with honey and
cream, alongside a short menu with sandwiches, filled baguettes, home-
made lasagne, home-made pie and rump steak. You will need to book, and
there may be double sittings in summer. The partly panelled flagstoned
public bar has yachting photographs and pictures, a boarded ceiling,
scrubbed pine tables and a roaring log fire in the big stone hearth, and the
carpeted beamed lounge bar has boating pictures and a coal fire. The snug
and gallery (with slate floors, bric-a-brac and more scrubbed pine tables) are
no smoking. Well kept Badger Best, Bass, Flowers Original, Marstons
Pedigree and Ventnor Golden on handpump, and around 60 wines (six
sold by the glass); piped music.
*Whitbreads ~ Lease Mr Bullock and Mr McDonald ~ Real ale ~ Bar food (12-
2.30, 6-9.30) ~ Restaurant ~ (01983) 531314 ~ Children in eating area of bar
~ Dogs welcome ~ Open 12-3, 6-11(10.30 Sun)*

VENTNOR
Spyglass *Esplanade, SW end; road down very steep and twisty, and parking
nearby can be difficult – best to use the pay-and-display (free in winter) about 100
yards up the road*
The location right up beside the sea wall makes the pub terrace an idyllic
place to bask in the sunshine and take in the view, and there's a fascinating
array of mostly seafaring bits and pieces to look at inside too. Among the
memorabilia are wrecked rudders, ships' wheels, old local advertisements,
rope-makers' tools, stuffed seagulls, an Admiral Benbow barometer and an
old brass telescope. The bustling mainly quarry-tiled interior is snug and
pubby, and the atmosphere is buoyant; fruit machine, piped music and
nightly entertainment. Usefully served all day, generous helpings of good,
very fairly priced bar food include soup, home-made chilli, home-made
fisherman's pie and sirloin steak; daily specials such as seafood chowder,
cauliflower cheese and seafood casserole. They have well kept Badger Best,
Badger Tanglefoot, Ventnor Golden and possibly several guests such as
Gribble Fursty Ferret on handpump. There are strolls westwards along the
coast towards the Botanic Garden as well as heftier hikes up on to St
Boniface Down and towards the eerie shell of Appuldurcombe House, and
the pub owners don't mind muddy boots; no smoking area.
*Free house ~ Licensees Neil and Stephanie Gibbs ~ Real ale ~ Bar food (all day) ~
(01983) 855338 ~ Children in eating area of bar ~ Dogs allowed in bar ~ Live
entertainment every night ~ Open 10.30-11(10.30 Sun) ~ Bedrooms: /£55B*

Dog Friendly Hotels, B&Bs and Farms

BONCHURCH
Lake Hotel *Bonchurch, Ventnor, Isle of Wight PO38 1RF (01983) 852613*
£72, plus special breaks; 20 rms. Early 19th-c country house in two acres
of pretty gardens, 400 metres from beach; lots of flowers and plants in three
light and airy lounges (one is an attractive conservatory), a well stocked bar,
and good food in neat restaurant; cl Dec–Feb; children over 3; partial
disabled access; dogs welcome in bedrooms; small ones £3, large ones £5

SEAVIEW
Priory Bay Hotel *Priory Croft, Priory Rd, Seaview, Isle of Wight PO34 5BU
(01983) 613146* £150, plus special breaks; 18 individually furnished rms
with 10 more in cottages. Former Tudor farmhouse with Georgian and
more recent additions in grounds leading to a fine sandy private beach with
a beach bar (good for lunch); lovely day rooms with comfortable sofas,
books and magazines on coffee tables, pretty flower arrangements,
imaginative food in restaurant with charming Georgian murals and
elaborate plasterwork, and an informal, relaxed atmosphere; outdoor
swimming pool, tennis, croquet, and a nine-hole par three golf course;
disabled access; dogs in cottages in grounds; £10

SEAVIEW
Seaview Hotel *High St, Seaview, Isle of Wight PO34 5EX (01983) 612711*
£95, plus special breaks; 17 attractively decorated rms, some with sea views
and private drawing rooms. Small, friendly and spotlessly kept hotel with
fine ship photographs in the chatty and relaxed front dining bar, an
interesting old-fashioned back bar, good imaginative bar food, and a highly
regarded evening restaurant; cl 3 days over Christmas; proper high tea for
children (must be over 5 in evening restaurant); partial disabled access; dogs
welcome away from restaurant; bring own bedding

TOTLAND
Sentry Mead Hotel *Totland Bay, Isle of Wight PO39 0BJ (01983) 753212*
£100; 14 pretty rms. Victorian country house hotel in flower-filled
gardens overlooking The Solent and 100 yards from the beach; traditionally
furnished rooms, open fire in lounge, a bar area and airy conservatory,
caring, attentive staff, and good food in stylish restaurant; dogs welcome by
arrangement, if well behaved; £3

VENTNOR
Royal Hotel *Belgrave Rd, Ventnor, Isle of Wight PO38 1JJ (01983) 852186*
£115, plus special breaks; 55 well equipped rms. Friendly Victorian hotel
with fine sea views, neat gardens with heated outdoor pool, spacious and
comfortable day rooms, cosy candlelit bar with open fire, good food in
attractive restaurant, and helpful service; cl 1st 2 wks Jan; disabled access;
dogs welcome in bedrooms only; £15

YARMOUTH

George Hotel *Quay St, Yarmouth, Isle of Wight PO41 0PE (01983)
760331* £**175**; 17 comfortable rms. 17th-c house by the harbour, with
gardens leading to little private beach; a fine flagstoned hall, fresh flowers
and open fires, a convivial bar and attractive residents' sitting room with
marvellously relaxing atmosphere, imaginative enjoyable food in informal
brasserie and smart restaurant, hearty breakfasts, and prompt courteous
service; motor yacht for hire; dogs welcome in bedrooms; £7.50

Kent

Dog Friendly Pubs

BIDDENDEN
Three Chimneys *A262, 1 mile W of village*
It's worth arriving early at this pretty ochre-coloured country pub for the very good food, which can be eaten in the bar or restaurant. Superbly cooked, but not cheap, dishes might include baked field mushrooms with caramelised red onions, thai-style crab cakes, sautéed lambs liver and bacon with mash and port and roasted venison; puddings such as strawberry and vanilla crème brulée; they'll also serve ploughman's in the garden. The rambling, low-beamed series of small, very traditional rooms have plain wooden furniture and old settles on flagstones and coir matting, some harness and sporting prints on the stripped brick walls, and good log fires. The simple public bar has darts, dominoes and cribbage. French windows in the civilised candlelit bare-board restaurant open onto the garden, which has picnic-sets (some nice and shady on a hot day), and a smart terrace area has tables and outdoor heaters. They've a good wine list, local Biddenden cider, several malt whiskies, and Adnams Best, Bass, Harveys Best, and Shepherd Neame Bishops Spitfire are tapped straight from the cask; friendly service from the knowledgeable staff. Nearby, Sissinghurst Gardens are well worth a visit; no muddy boots.
Free house ~ Licensee Craig Smith ~ Real ale ~ Bar food (12-1.50, 7-9) ~ Restaurant ~ (01580) 291472 ~ Children in eating area of bar and restaurant ~ Dogs allowed in bar ~ Open 11.30-3, 6-11; 12-3, 7-10.30 Sun; closed 25 Dec

BOUGH BEECH
Wheatsheaf *B2027, S of reservoir*
Thoughtful touches at this enjoyably bustling pub include piles of smart magazines to read, tasty nibbles, chestnuts to roast, mulled wine in winter, and summer Pimms. Full of history, there are masses of interesting things to look at inside, and the older part of the building is thought to have been a hunting lodge belonging to Henry V. The neat central bar and the long front bar (with an attractive old settle carved with wheatsheaves) have unusually high ceilings with lofty oak timbers, a screen of standing timbers and a revealed king post; dominoes, and board games. Divided from the

central bar by two more rows of standing timbers – one formerly an outside wall to the building – is the snug, and another bar. Other similarly aged features include a piece of 1607 graffiti, 'Foxy Holamby', thought to have been a whimsical local squire. There are quite a few horns and heads, as well as a sword from Fiji, crocodiles, stuffed birds, swordfish spears, and the only matapee in the south of England on the walls and above the massive stone fireplaces. It's appealing outside too: there are plenty of seats, and flowerbeds and fruit trees in the sheltered side and back gardens, and shrubs help divide it into various areas, so it doesn't feel too crowded even when it's full. Greene King IPA and Old Speckled Hen, Harveys and Shepherd Neame Master Brew are well kept on handpump, and they've also farm cider, a decent wine list, several malt whiskies, and a range of local fruit juices. Besides lunchtime snacks, the extensive menu might include soup, poached smoked haddock with mash or thai green chicken curry, and beef wellington, with puddings such as apple and caramel pancakes; swift and friendly service.

Enterprise ~ Lease Liz and David Currie ~ Real ale ~ Bar food (12-10) ~ (01732) 700254 ~ Children in part of eating area of bar ~ Dogs welcome ~ Contemporary folk and country Weds 9pm ~ Open 11-11; 12-10.30 Sun

BOYDEN GATE

Gate Inn *Off A299 Herne Bay—Ramsgate – follow Chislet, Upstreet signpost opposite Roman Gallery; Chislet also signposted off A28 Canterbury—Margate at Upstreet – after turning right into Chislet main street keep right on to Boyden; the pub gives its address as Marshside, though Boyden Gate seems more usual on maps*

On fine summer evenings, you can sit at the picnic-sets on the sheltered side lawn of this refreshingly old-fashioned pub and listen to the contented quacking of a multitude of ducks and geese, coots and moorhens out on the marshes (they sell food for them – 10p a bag). Inside the winter inglenook log fire serves both the well worn quarry-tiled rooms, and there are flowery-cushioned pews around tables of considerable character, hop bines hanging from the beam and attractively etched windows; the atmosphere is properly pubby. Well kept Shepherd Neame Spitfire and Master Brew, and a seasonal ale are tapped from the cask by the long-standing landlord, and you can also get interesting bottled beers, a fine range of 14 wines by the glass, and country wines; shove-ha'penny, dominoes and cribbage. From the straightforward menu, reasonably priced bar meals include a fine choice of sandwiches, lots of filled baked potatoes, quite a few different ploughman's, and salads, pasta, omelettes or spicy hotpots; no chips. The eating area is no smoking at lunchtime.

Shepherd Neame ~ Tenant Christopher Smith ~ Real ale ~ Bar food (12-2, 6-8.45) ~ No credit cards ~ (01227) 860498 ~ Well behaved children welcome ~ Dogs welcome ~ Open 11-2.30, 6-11; 12-4, 7-10.30 Sun

BROOKLAND

Woolpack *On A259 from Rye, about 1 mile before Brookland, take the first right turn signposted Midley where the main road bends sharp left, just after the expanse of Walland Marsh; OS Sheet 189 map reference 977244*

The friendly landlord of this early 15th-c cottage plans to hold barbecues in the sheltered garden, which has recently been expanded, with plenty of picnic-sets, well developed shrubs, and pretty hanging baskets; it's all nicely lit up in the evenings. Inside, the ancient entrance lobby has an uneven brick floor and black-painted pine-panelled walls, and on the right, the simple but homely main bar has basic cushioned plank seats in the massive inglenook fireplace (a lovely log fire on chilly days), a painted wood-effect bar counter hung with lots of water jugs, and some ships' timbers that may date from the 12th c in the low-beamed ceiling. On the quarry-tiled floor is a long elm table with shove-ha'penny carved into one end, other old and newer wall benches, chairs at mixed tables with flowers and candles, and photographs of the locals on the walls. To the left of the lobby is a sparsely furnished little room, and an open-plan games room with central hearth, modern bar counter, and locals playing darts or pool; cribbage, fruit machine and piped music. Fairly priced and well kept Shepherd Neame Master Brew, Spitfire and a seasonal brew on handpump; look out for the two pub cats Liquorice and Charlie Girl. Hearty bar food from a reasonably priced menu includes good home-made soup, home-made steak pie, chilli, lasagne or stilton and vegetable bake, tasty cold pies, salmon fillet, and mixed grill or sirloin steak; changing specials, and puddings such as spotted dick; children's menu too.

Shepherd Neame ~ Tenant Barry Morgan ~ Real ale ~ Bar food (12-2, 6-9) ~ (01797) 344321 ~ Children in family room ~ Dogs welcome ~ Open 11-3, 6-11 (all day during school hols); 11-11 Sat; 12-10.30 Sun

CHIDDINGSTONE
Castle Inn *Village signposted from B2027 Tonbridge—Edenbridge*
You can choose from an impressive list of wines at this cosy rambling old pub, an inn since 1730. The handsome, carefully modernised beamed bar has well made settles forming booths around the tables, cushioned sturdy wall benches, an attractive mullioned window seat in one small alcove, and latticed windows (a couple of areas are no smoking); darts, shove-ha'penny, dominoes and cribbage. In summer, there are tables in front of the building facing the church, with more in the pretty secluded vine-hung garden. They serve well kept Larkins Traditional (brewed in the village, and in winter they have Porter too), along with Harveys Best and a guest on handpump, and there's a good range of malt whiskies. Popular (though not cheap) bar food includes lunchtime open sandwiches, chilli con carne or curry, with other dishes such as ham hock terrine, mixed seafood risotto and seared calves liver; puddings such as lavender pannacotta; no chips. They do a two-course lunch on Sunday, and there's a children's menu; afternoon tea too. It's best to avoid peak times as it gets very busy, there can be a wait and service can be variable. It's worth wandering around this National Trust village, to look at the picturesque cluster of unspoilt Tudor houses; the licensees publish three circular walks from the village.

Free house ~ Licensee Nigel Lucas ~ Real ale ~ Bar food (11-9.30, not 25 Dec) ~ Restaurant ~ (01892) 870247 ~ Children in eating area of bar and restaurant ~ Dogs welcome ~ Open 11-11; 12-10.30 Sun

DARGATE

Dove *Village signposted from A299*

Lovely in fine weather, the sheltered garden of this tucked-away dining
pub has roses, lilacs, peonies and many other flowers, picnic-table sets
under pear trees, a dovecote with white doves, a rockery and pool, and a
swing. You have to book some time in advance if you want to enjoy the
very good restaurant-style food, and at busy times (when they may finish
serving food early), you may not even be able to get a lunchtime baguette
unless you've booked. Well cooked, generously served dishes could
include bacon, avocado and rocket salad, prawns with garden herbs and
pickled ginger, and scotch beef fillet with shallots and garlic; puddings such
as passion fruit crème brûlée; friendly service. With a relaxed atmosphere,
the charmingly unspoilt rambling rooms have photographs of the pub and
its licensees throughout the past century on the walls, a good winter log
fire, and plenty of seats on the bare boards; piped music. Well kept
Shepherd Neame Master Brew on handpump. The pub is set down a
network of narrow lanes in a quiet hamlet; a bridlepath leads up from the
pub (along the quaintly named Plumpudding Lane) into Blean Wood.
*Shepherd Neame ~ Tenants Nigel and Bridget Morris ~ Real ale ~ Bar food (12-
2.30(1.30 Sun, Tues), 7-9; not Mon, or evenings Sun or Tues) ~ (01227)
751360 ~ Well behaved children in eating area of bar ~ Dogs allowed in bar ~
Open 12-3, 6-11; 12-3, 7-10.30 Sun; closed Mon exc bank hols, and Sun and
Tues evenings*

DEAL

Kings Head *Beach Street, just off A258 seafront roundabout*

A real sight in summer when it's festooned with brightly coloured hanging
baskets and window boxes, this handsome three-storey Georgian inn is just
across the road from the promenade and the sea; there are picnic-sets out
on a broad front paved terrace side area. Four comfortable bar rooms work
their way round a central servery, and the walls, partly stripped masonry,
are decorated with marine architectural drawings, maritime and local
pictures and charts, and other material underlining connections with the
Royal and Merchant Navies; another area has an interesting collection of
cricket memorabilia. There are a couple of warming flame-effect gas fires;
it can get smoky. Well kept real ales might include Bass, Fullers London
Pride, Greene King IPA and Shepherd Neame Master Brew on handpump;
piped music, fruit machines and TV. Generous helpings of straightforward
bar food such as filled baguettes and omelettes; two-course Sunday lunch.
In the evening, particularly Friday night, it can be crowded with young
people, who may be attracted by the games machines in the daytime too.
Beware that traffic wardens here are vigilant during the week; there's pay-
and-display (two-hour limit) parking opposite, and another (three-hour
limit) just a few minutes' walk away.
*Courage (S & N) ~ Lease Graham Stiles and Shirley Russell ~ Real ale ~ Bar
food (12-3, 6-9) ~ (01304) 368194 ~ Children in family room ~ Dogs welcome
~ Open 10-11; 12-10.30 Sun ~ Bedrooms: £45S/£59B*

GROOMBRIDGE
Crown *B2110*
Prettily set at the end of a row of picturesque cottages overlooking the steep village green, this tile-hung old smugglers' haunt is handily placed for a visit to Groombridge Place Gardens. The snug beamed rooms (get there early if you want a seat) have a jumble of bric-a-brac including old teapots, pewter tankards, and antique bottles, and there's a log fire in the big brick inglenook. The walls, mostly rough yellowing plaster with some squared panelling and timbering, are decorated with small topographical, game and sporting prints, and a circular large-scale map with the pub at its centre. The no smoking end room (normally for eaters) has fairly close-spaced tables with a variety of good solid chairs, and a log-effect gas fire in a big fireplace. Picnic-sets out in front on a brick terrace are very popular in summer. From the long copper-topped bar counter, they serve Greene King Abbot and IPA, Harveys and Larkins on handpump; shove-ha'penny, dominoes, cribbage and Scrabble. Tasty bar food includes lunchtime soup, devilled whitebait, and chicken and leek pie, while in the evening you might find half a roast barbary duck and lamb rump steak, with puddings such as lemon and shortbread cheesecake. A public footpath across the road beside the small chapel leads through a field to Groombridge Place Gardens.
Free house ~ Licensee Peter Kilshaw ~ Real ale ~ Bar food (12-3, 7-9; not Sun evening) ~ Restaurant ~ (01892) 864742 ~ Children in eating area of bar and restaurant ~ Dogs allowed in bar ~ Open 11-3, 6-11; 11-11 Sat; 12-10.30 Sun; 11-3, 6-11 Sat, 12-3, 7-10.30 Sun in winter ~ Bedrooms: £40/£45(£60S)

HUCKING
Hook & Hatchet *3½ miles from M2 junction 5; A249 towards Maidstone, then after a mile turn left at Hucking signpost into narrow lane; Church Road*
This recently reworked isolated country pub seems all set to become a big favourite. It stands alone on the edge of the Woodland Trust's Hucking Estate, nearly a square mile of woods, farmland and downland now open to the public (free), with plenty of interesting walks – the pub gives away a useful map. Inside, the pub is a haven of civilised comfort. Around a central chimneypiece with fireplaces each side, a variety of well spaced seats spreads over broad polished boards, from a leather armchair and low sofa covered with bright scatter-cushions to pews, cushioned stools and chairs around sturdy tables. There are one or two pictures on the smooth pink walls, varnished joists in the cream ceiling, and comfortable backed seats along the long rather smart bar counter, with its well kept Fullers London Pride and guest beers such as Adnams Broadside and Harveys Best on handpump (served in lined glasses); they have a good choice of wines by the glass. The food is enjoyable too, including soup, filled baked potatoes, pasta, a fry-up and good interesting pies such as smoked haddock with turmeric and spinach; children's dishes too, and evening restaurant dishes such as bass. The softly lit no smoking dining room has high-backed settles forming intimate booths around some of its tables, and another side area is also no smoking. There are tables out on a heated verandah, and lots of

picnic-sets in the carefully laid out garden, which has a good play area at one end, and a field with plenty of space for children to let off steam in. Two nice touches: the boot-washing tap, and what is certainly the best pub hitching rail for visiting horses that we've seen (they also encourage customers to debox here – with notice).

Free house ~ Licensee Adam Silverton ~ Real ale ~ Bar food (12-2.30(3 Sun), 6.30-9.30; not Sun evening) ~ Restaurant ~ (01622) 880830 ~ Children welcome ~ Dogs allowed in bar ~ Live music Thurs ~ Open 12-11(10.30 Sun)

IDEN GREEN

Woodcock *Iden Green is signposted off A268 E of Hawkhurst and B2086 at W edge of Benenden; in village at crossroads by bus shelter follow Standen Street signpost, then fork left just before the orchard down Woodcock Lane (maybe a signpost to pub here) – beware that there is an entirely different Iden Green just 10 miles away near Goudhurst*

Recently taken over by new licensees, this bustling and friendly little local country pub is tucked away on the edge of Standen Wood. Snugly comfortable, the small flagstoned bar has stripped brick walls and very low ceilings bearing down heavily on a couple of big standing timbers; you'll find a comfortable sofa and armchairs by a warming woodburning stove, and chunky big old pine tables tucked snugly into little nooks; darts, shove-ha'penny, and piped local radio. Enthusiastic young staff serve well kept Greene King IPA, Abbot and Old Speckled Hen, along with a changing guest such as Rother Valley Level Best on handpump. Generously served, enjoyable bar food such as baguettes, burgers, garlic chicken escalope, and puddings such as home-made crème brûlée; you may need to book at weekends when it can get very busy. The partly panelled dining area opens on to a verandah, and there are seats in the pretty side garden. The car park is across the road.

Greene King ~ Lease Mark and Tracy Coxhead ~ Real ale ~ Bar food (not Sun evening) ~ Restaurant ~ (01580) 240009 ~ Children in eating area of bar ~ Dogs allowed in bar ~ Open 11-11; 12-10.30 Sun

LANGTON GREEN

Hare *A264 W of Tunbridge Wells*

A great place for a civilised summer meal, the sheltered terrace (now with lighting and heaters) at this thriving Edwardian roadside pub has picnic-sets looking out on to a tree-ringed green. With a good sociable atmosphere, the knocked-through rooms have big windows and high ceilings giving a pleasant feeling of space: dark-painted dados below light walls, oak furniture and turkey carpets on stained wooden floors, old romantic pastels, and plenty of bric-a-brac (including a huge collection of chamber-pots). Interesting old books, pictures and two big mahogany mirror-backed display cabinets crowd the walls of a big chatty room at the back, which has lots of large tables (one big enough for at least a dozen) on a light brown carpet; from here french windows lead to the terrace. The front bar (piped music here) is well liked by drinkers; shove-ha'penny, cribbage and dominoes. Service is good, and the atmosphere is pubby and sociable. A wide choice of superbly cooked food changes every day, but might include potato, leek and cheddar cheese hash cakes, braised venison shank in mustard sauce, seared tuna with tomato and saffron risotto, and 10oz rib-eye steak; tempting puddings such as treacle tart with honeycomb ice-cream; they also do snacks such as fish finger sandwich and hot beef granary roll. To be sure of a table it's best to book. Greene King IPA and Abbot are well kept alongside a couple of guests such as Greene King Old Speckled Hen and Wadworths 6X on handpump, they have lots of wines by the glass, and over 50 malt whiskies. Parking is not easy at peak times unless you get here early.

Brunning & Price ~ Tenant Christopher Little ~ Real ale ~ Bar food (12-9.30) ~ Restaurant ~ (01892) 862419 ~ Children in eating area of bar till 7pm ~ Dogs allowed in bar ~ Open 11-11; 12-10.30 Sun

NEWNHAM

George *The Street; village signposted from A2 just W of Ospringe, outside Faversham*

The several atmospheric spreading rooms at this well run pub have lots for you to look at – dressers with teapots, prettily upholstered mahogany settles, dining chairs and leather carving chairs around candlelit tables, table lamps and gas-type chandeliers, and rugs on the waxed floorboards; open fires, fresh flowers, quite a few pictures, and hop bines hanging from the beams. They've a dozen wines by the glass, well kept Shepherd Neame Master Brew, Bishops Finger and Spitfire, and seasonal beers on handpump, and good coffee; piped music. Very good food, served by pleasant staff, includes lunchtime sandwiches or baguettes, home-made chinese fishcakes, chicken, smoked bacon and mushroom tagliatelle, vegetable curry or steak and kidney pudding; changing specials such as fresh fillets of bass with fresh asparagus and hollandaise, and home-made puddings; the restaurant is no smoking. The spacious sheltered garden has some picnic-sets, and there are pleasant nearby walks.

Shepherd Neame ~ Tenant Marc Perkins ~ Real ale ~ Bar food ~ Restaurant ~ (01795) 890237 ~ Children welcome ~ Dogs allowed in bar ~ Open 11-3, 6.30-11; 11-4, 6.30-10.30 Sun; closed evenings 26 Dec and 1 Jan

OARE

Shipwrights Arms *S shore of Oare Creek, E of village; coming from Faversham on the Oare road, turn right into Ham Road opposite Davington School; or off A2 on B2045, go into Oare village, then turn right towards Faversham, and then left into Ham Road opposite Davington School; OS Sheet 178 map reference 016635*

They only serve Kent-brewed beers at this charmingly unspoilt 17th-c tavern: tapped straight from the cask, a typical selection might be well kept Goachers Gold Star, Mild and Shipwrecked and Hopdaemon Golden Braid and Incubus. The three simple little bars are dark and cosy, and separated by standing timbers and wood part-partitions or narrow door arches. There's a medley of seats from tapestry cushioned stools and chairs to black wood-panelled built-in settles forming little booths, pewter tankards over the bar counter, boating jumble and pictures, flags or boating pennants on the ceilings, several brick fireplaces, and a good woodburning stove. There may be piped local radio; cribbage and dominoes. Reasonably priced bar food includes sausage and mash, home-baked ham and egg or cod in crispy batter, and puddings such as cherry pancakes; part of the eating area is no smoking. Three feet below sea level, the pub is situated in the middle of marshland, and there's plenty of surrounding birdlife. An interesting approach is a walk from the village through the tangle of boatyard; or you can moor a boat in the creek which runs just below the Saxon Shore Way (up a bank from the front and back gardens of the pub). Parking can be difficult at busy times.

Free house ~ Licensees Derek and Ruth Cole ~ Real ale ~ Bar food (not Sun or Mon evenings, not Mon in winter) ~ Restaurant ~ (01795) 590088 ~ Children in dining room ~ Dogs welcome ~ Open 11-3(4 Sat), 6-11; 12-4, 6-10.30 Sun; closed Mon in winter

PENSHURST
Bottle House *Coldharbour Lane, Smarts Hill; leaving Penshurst SW on B2188 turn right at Smarts Hill signpost, then bear right towards Chiddingstone and Cowden; keep straight on*
You may have trouble deciding what to eat at this very popular and welcoming pub – the range of well cooked dishes is awesome. Served all day by the friendly and obliging staff, the interesting menu could include smoked salmon mousse with lemon chutney, vietnamese spring rolls, chicken, king prawn and chorizo jambalaya, and skate wing with capers and lemon butter; around 10 enticing puddings and children's meals too. On weekdays if you eat between 5 and 6.30, you get a 25% discount. Neatly kept, the low-beamed front bar has a well worn brick floor that extends behind the polished copper-topped bar counter, and big windows look onto a terrace with climbing plants and hanging baskets around picnic-sets under cocktail parasols, and beyond to views of quiet fields and oak trees. The unpretentious main red-carpeted bar has massive hop-covered supporting beams, two large stone pillars with a small brick fireplace (with a stuffed turtle to one side), and old paintings and photographs on mainly plastered walls; quite a collection of china pot lids, with more in the no smoking low-ceilinged dining room. Several cosy little areas lead off the main bar – all can be booked for private parties; one room is covered in sporting pictures right up to the ceiling, and another has pictures of dogs. Harveys and Larkins are well kept on handpump, and they have local wine; unobtrusive piped music. Good surrounding walks.

Free house ~ Licensees Gordon and Val Meer ~ Real ale ~ Bar food (12-10(9.30 Sun)) ~ Restaurant ~ (01892) 870306 ~ Children welcome ~ Dogs allowed in bar ~ Open 11-11; 12-10.30 Sun; closed 25 Dec

PLUCKLEY
Dering Arms *Pluckley Station, which is signposted from B2077*
Fish-lovers are in for a treat at this striking old dutch-gabled pub, which was originally built as a hunting lodge on the Dering Estate. Skilfully cooked by the long-standing licensee, dishes might include provençal fish

soup or half a dozen irish oysters, whole crab salad and grilled dover sole. If you don't like fish, other choices might be pie of the day, leg of lamb with couscous, and confit of duck; they sell oysters to take away. The stylishly plain high-ceilinged main bar has a variety of good solid wooden furniture on stone floors, and a roaring log fire in the great fireplace; dominoes, cribbage and shove-ha'penny. The smaller half-panelled back bar has similar dark wood furnishings, and they've recently added a new bar with woodburning stove, comfortable armchairs, and a grand piano. The extensive wine list is very good; also well kept Dering Ale (made for the pub by Goachers), home-made lemonade, local cider and quite a few malt whiskies. The big simple bedrooms have old ad hoc furnishings. Classic car meetings are held here on the second Sunday of the month, and they have regular special events such as wine tasting evenings and summer garden parties.

Free house ~ Licensee James Buss ~ Real ale ~ Bar food ~ Restaurant ~ (01233) 840371 ~ Children welcome ~ Dogs allowed in bar ~ Open 11.30(11 Sat)-3.30, 6-11; 12-3.30, 7-10.30 Sun; closed 26/27 Dec ~ Bedrooms: £35/£45

Rose & Crown *Mundy Bois – spelled Monday Boys on some maps – off Smarden Road SW of village centre*

You can now enjoy the home-made bar food at this quietly set pub on the new terrace. Bar snacks might include baguettes, chargrilled burger, pizza, and steak and kidney pie, or you can choose from the restaurant menu dishes such as fried scallops with creamy hollandaise sauce, mushroom and pepper stroganoff, and aberdeen angus fillet steak; also children's menu. The bar menu is also available in the cosy candlelit restaurant (not Friday and Saturday evenings). The relaxed Village Bar, with its massive inglenook fireplace (favourite spot of Ted the pub labrador), leads on to a little pool room; TV and piped music. Shepherd Neame Master Brew and a couple of guests such as Greene King IPA and Wadworths 6X are well kept on handpump, and they've a sensibly priced wine list (country wines too), plenty of malt whiskies, and farm cider; disabled facilities. There are seats in the garden, which has a children's play area.

Free house ~ Licensees Peter and Helen Teare ~ Real ale ~ Bar food ~ Restaurant ~ (01233) 840393 ~ Children in eating area of bar and restaurant ~ Dogs welcome ~ Open 11.30-3, 6-11; 11.30-11 Sat; 12-10.30 Sun; 11.30-3, 6-11 Sat; 12-3, 6-10.30 Sun in winter

SELLING
Rose & Crown *Signposted from exit roundabout of M2 junction 7: keep right on through village and follow Perry Wood signposts; or from A252 just W of junction with A28 at Chilham, follow Shottenden signpost, then right turn signposted Selling, then right signposted Perry Wood*

The cottagey garden behind this welcoming 16th-c pub is something special. Charming in summer, it's attractively planted with climbers, ramblers and colourful plants, and there are plenty of picnic-sets, a neatly kept children's play area, bat and trap, and a small aviary; a new pergola (planted with vines and clematis) is fairy-lit at night, with cartwheel-back benches. The flowering tubs and hanging baskets in front are pretty too, and the terrace has outdoor heaters. Inside you'll find well kept Adnams Southwold, Goachers Mild and Harveys Best on handpump, along with a changing guest, local cider, a good range of malts and decent wines in good measures. Around the central servery there are pretty fresh flowers by each of the sturdy corner timbers, hop bines strung from the beams, and an interesting variety of corn-dolly work – more in a wall cabinet in one cosy side alcove, and much more again down steps in the comfortably cottagey no smoking restaurant. Apart from a couple of old-fashioned housekeepers' chairs by the huge fireplace (filled in summer with a colourful mass of silk flowers interlaced with more corn dollies and so forth), the seats are very comfortably cushioned, and there's a winter log fire; the walls have recently been re-painted in soft yellow and red. The licensees are friendly and attentive, and there's a pleasant atmosphere; cribbage, shove-ha'penny, dominoes and piped music. Besides tasty daily specials such as beef in mustard, caribbean chicken or stilton and asparagus pancake, bar food includes home-made soup, baked potatoes, chicken, ham and leek pie or spaghetti bolognese; lots of puddings on show in a cold cabinet down steps in a small family room. Readers recommend the Sunday roast beef, and they do children's meals. The pub is surrounded by natural woodland, with good walking.

Free house ~ Licensees Richard and Jocelyn Prebble ~ Real ale ~ Bar food (not Sun or Mon evenings) ~ Restaurant ~ (01227) 752214 ~ Children in restaurant and family room ~ Dogs allowed in bar ~ Open 11-3, 6.30-11; 12-3, 7-10.30 Sun; closed evenings 25/26 Dec and 1 Jan

SMARDEN

Chequers *Off A20 in Charing, via Pluckley; or off A274 at Standen just under 1 mile N of its junction with A262; The Street*

In an attractive village, this 14th-c inn is handily open all day. A walkway in the attractive landscaped garden leads to a pond with fish and waterfowl, and there's an arbour with climbing plants; the terrace has nice green metal tables and chairs on the York stone. With a pleasantly relaxed atmosphere and chatting locals, the cosy and comfortable bar has well kept Adnams, Bass, Harveys Best, and a guest such as Kelham Island Easy Rider on handpump. They've a decent wine list, with 10 wines by the glass, and several malt whiskies; piped music. Well presented bar food (not served on Saturday evening – only restaurant meals then), made with fresh local produce, could include ploughman's, gammon and eggs, fisherman's pie and home-made chicken curry; you can also choose dishes from the restaurant menu such as tempura prawns with sweet chilli sauce, pork tenderloin with mushroom and brandy sauce, or chargrilled rib-eye steak. There are elegant reproduction tables and chairs in the dining area, and they've added another no smoking restaurant. Readers enjoy staying here, and they do good breakfasts.

Free house ~ Licensee Lisa Bullock ~ Bar food (12-2.30, 6-9.30(not Sat evening)) ~ Restaurant ~ (01233) 770217 ~ Children in eating area of bar and restaurant ~ Dogs allowed in bar ~ Open 11-11; 12-10.30 Sun ~ Bedrooms: £40B/£70S(£70B)

STAPLEHURST
Lord Raglan *About 1½ miles from town centre towards Maidstone, turn right off A229 into Chart Hill Road opposite Cross at Hand Garage; OS Sheet 188 map reference 785472*

You'll find no piped music or games machines at this unpretentious and simple yet quite civilised country inn, just nice little conversational nooks. The interior is quite compact, with a narrow bar – you walk in almost on top of the counter and chatting locals – widening slightly at one end to a small area with a big log fire in winter. In the other direction it works its way round to an intimate area at the back, with lots of wine bottles lined up on a low shelf. Everywhere you look on the low beams are masses of hops, and the mixed collection of comfortably worn dark wood furniture on quite well used dark brown carpet tiles and nice old parquet flooring is mostly 1930s. They serve well kept Goachers Light and Harveys Best, along with a guest from a brewer such as Woods on handpump; a good wine list too, and summer farm cider. Enjoyable bar food, up on blackboard menus, includes a few pubby staples such as sandwiches, macaroni cheese or chilli con carne, as well as more elaborate dishes such as smoked venison and pickled walnut and chicken breast with white wine and mushroom sauce; home-made puddings too. Small french windows lead out to an enticing little high-hedged terraced area with white plastic tables and chairs, and there are wooden picnic-sets in the side orchard; reasonable wheelchair access.

Free house ~ Licensees Andrew and Annie Hutchison ~ Real ale ~ Bar food (12-2.30, 7-10; not Sun) ~ Restaurant ~ (01622) 843747 ~ Children welcome ~ Dogs welcome ~ Open 12-3, 6-11; closed Sun

Dog Friendly Hotels, B&Bs and Farms

ASH
Great Weddington *Weddington, Ash, Canterbury, Kent CT3 2AR (01304) 813407* £92; 3 pretty bdrms. Regency country house surrounded by farmland and extensive gardens, with log fire in drawing room, enjoyable breakfasts and evening meals, and a relaxing atmosphere; no smoking; cl Christmas and New Year; children over 8; dogs welcome in bedrooms by arrangement only

BIDDENDEN
Bishopsdale Oast *Biddenden, Ashford, Kent TN27 8DR (01580) 292321* £70.50; 5 large, homely rms with king-size beds and country views. Large double-kiln oast house in four acres of wild and cultivated gardens, beams and original features, good breakfasts and imaginative dinner (excellent cheeseboard and home-grown vegetables) eaten on terrace or in dining room, and friendly owners; cl Christmas; dogs welcome in downstairs bedrooms; £5

BOUGHTON LEES
Eastwell Manor *Eastwell Park, Boughton Lees, Ashford, Kent TN25 4HR*
(01233) 219955 £**220**, plus special breaks; 62 prettily decorated rms in
hotel and 19 courtyard cottages (some cottages have their own garden and
can also be booked on self-catering basis). Fine Jacobean-style manor
(actually rebuilt in the 1920s) in 62 acres with croquet lawn, tennis court,
two boules pitches and putting green; grand oak-panelled rooms, open
fires, comfortable leather seating, antiques and fresh flowers, courteous
helpful service, and extremely good food; health and fitness spa with 20–
metre indoor pool and 14 treatment rooms, and lots of walks; disabled
access; dogs welcome in mews cottages only; £15

CANTERBURY
Cathedral Gate *36 Burgate, Canterbury, Kent CT1 2HA (01227) 464381*
£**90**, plus special breaks; 27 rms, 12 with own bthrm and some
overlooking cathedral. 15th-c hotel that predates the adjoining sculpted
cathedral gateway; bow windows, massive oak beams, sloping floors,
antiques and fresh flowers, continental breakfast in little dining room or
your own room, and a restful atmosphere; municipal car parks a few
minutes away; dogs in bedrooms

PLUCKLEY
Elvey Farm *Pluckley, Ashford, Kent TN27 0SU (01233) 840442* £**69.50**;
10 rms, some in the oast house roundel, some in original barn and stable
block. 15th-c farmhouse in secluded spot on 75-acre working family farm,
with timbered rooms, inglenook fireplace, and french windows from
lounge onto sun terrace; ample play areas for children; partial disabled
access; dogs welcome in bedrooms

TUNBRIDGE WELLS
Spa Hotel *Langton Rd, Tunbridge Wells, Kent TN4 8XJ (01892) 520331*
£**138.50**, plus wknd breaks; 69 individually decorated rms. Run by the
same family for three generations, this Georgian hotel stands in 14 acres of
landscaped gardens; comfortable and quietly decorated, partly no smoking
lounge, a popular and attractive bar with equestrian paintings and
photographs, good enjoyable food in Regency-style restaurant, a carefully
chosen wine list, and friendly long-serving staff; leisure centre with indoor
heated swimming pool and well equipped gym; tennis court and pony
riding; disabled access; dogs welcome in bedrooms; £25

Lancashire
(with Greater Manchester and Merseyside)

Dog Friendly Pubs

BISPHAM GREEN
Eagle & Child *Maltkiln Lane (Parbold—Croston road, off B5246)*
Since the friendly former landlady came back out of retirement to run this striking red-brick pub, we've had a flood of happy reports from readers. Well divided by stubs of walls, the largely open-plan bar is appealingly simple and civilised. Attractively understated old furnishings include a mix of small oak chairs around tables in corners, an oak coffer, several handsomely carved antique oak settles (the finest apparently made partly from a 16th-c wedding bed-head), and old hunting prints and engravings. There's coir matting in the no smoking snug, and oriental rugs on flagstones in front of the fine old stone fireplaces; unobtrusive piped music. You'll find quite an emphasis on the well cooked food, and besides snacks (not Saturday evening), fish and chips or steak and ale pie, the friendly and helpful staff serve interesting daily changing specials such as spiced meatballs and chilli jam, chicken breast and chorizo, or baked strawberry grouper; puddings like gooseberry cobbler. A good range of well kept beers includes Moorhouses Black Cat and Thwaites, with four changing guest ales from brewers such as Hanby, Hart, Jennings and Phoenix. They also have changing farm cider, decent wines, some country wines and two dozen or more malt whiskies. The pub holds a popular beer festival in May; the dog's called Harry. You can watch players competing on the neat bowling green outside, and the pub can provide bowls for anyone who wants to try the crowns, which fool even the most experienced bowlers. A nice wild garden has crested newts and nesting moorhens.
Free house ~ Licensee Monica Evans ~ Real ale ~ Bar food (12-2, 6-8.30(9 Fri, Sat); 12-8.30 Sun) ~ Restaurant ~ (01257) 462297 ~ Children away from main bar ~ Dogs welcome ~ Open 12-3, 5.30-11; 12-10.30 Sun

BLACKSTONE EDGE
White House *A58 Ripponden—Littleborough, just W of B6138*
A haven for walkers (the Pennine Way crosses the road outside), this

imposing 17th-c pub is high up on the bleak and moody moors with panoramic views stretching for miles into the distance. Inside the atmosphere is cheery, and the cosily bustling main bar has a turkey carpet in front of a blazing coal fire, and a large-scale map of the area. The snug Pennine Room opens off here, with brightly coloured antimacassars on its small soft settees; there's also a dining extension. A spacious room on the left has comfortable seating, and a big horseshoe window has impressive moorland views; fruit machine. Theakstons Best is promptly served by the friendly staff along with a couple of guests from brewers such as Archers and Jennings; also farm cider and malt whiskies. The reasonably priced menu might include tasty bar food such as soup, cumberland sausage with egg or beef curry, salmon, and home-made apple pie. Muddy boots can be left in the porch.

Free house ~ Licensee Neville Marney ~ Real ale ~ Bar food (12-2, 6.30-9.30; 12-9 Sun) ~ (01706) 378456 ~ Children welcome ~ Dogs allowed in bar ~ Open 12-3, 6.30-11; 12-11 Sun

LITTLE ECCLESTON

Cartford *Cartford Lane, off A586 Garstang—Blackpool, by toll bridge*
Peacefully placed by a toll bridge over the River Wyre (tidal here), this handy pub serves up to seven very well kept real ales. Aside from a couple from Hart (their own good microbrewery behind the pub, with brewery tours by arrangement), you'll find Boddingtons, Fullers London Pride and up to four changing ales from interesting brewers such as Goose Eye, Moorhouses, Phoenix and Rooster; also decent house wines and several malt whiskies. The rambling interior has oak beams, dried flowers, a log fire and an unusual layout on four different levels, with uncoordinated seating areas; pool, darts, fruit machine, dominoes, TV and piped music. Two levels are largely set for dining (the upstairs part is no smoking). Straightforward bar food includes steak and mushroom pie, lemon sole, curries, and 10oz sirloin steak. There are tables out in a garden (not by the water), with a play area; the pub has fishing rights along 1½ miles of the river.

Own brew ~ Licensee Andrew Mellodew ~ Real ale ~ Bar food (12-2, 6.30-9.30; 12-9 Sun) ~ Restaurant ~ (01995) 670166 ~ Children in eating area of bar and restaurant ~ Dogs welcome ~ Open 12-3, 6.30-11; 12-10.30 Sun ~ Bedrooms: £36.95B/£48.95B

MELLOR

Oddfellows Arms *Heading out of Marple on A626 towards Glossop, Mellor is the next road after B6102, signposted off on the right at Marple Bridge; keep on for nearly 2 miles up Longhurst Lane and into Moor End Road*
No piped music or games machines spoil the relaxed and chatty atmosphere at this civilised old pub. What draws most customers here is the enjoyable food, and it's a good idea to get here early to be sure of a table. Served by friendly staff, a wide choice of dishes might include mussel chowder, lamb rogan josh, hot thai chicken with lychees, and steaks, and specials such as chicken satay skewers and cajun swordfish steak; puddings might be rhubarb and ginger mousse or spotted dick. The pleasant low-

ceilinged flagstoned bar has nice open fires; there's a small no smoking restaurant upstairs. Served with or without a sparkler, Adnams Southwold, Marstons Best, Phoenix Arizona and a weekly changing guest such as Cottage Golden Arrow are well kept on handpump; they've eight wines by the glass. There are a few tables out by the road. It can be tricky to secure a parking space when they're busy.

Free house ~ Licensee Robert Cloughley ~ Real ale ~ Bar food (not Sun evening, Mon, or a few days over Christmas) ~ Restaurant ~ (0161) 449 7826 ~ Children allowed till 8.30pm ~ Dogs welcome ~ Open 12-3, 5.30-11(7-10.30 Sun); closed Mon, and a few days over Christmas

UPPERMILL

Church Inn *From the main street (A607), look out for the sign for Saddleworth Church, and turn off up this steep narrow lane – keep on up!*

Seats on a small terrace outside this ancient and isolated local look up towards the moors, with more out in a garden – and anything from rabbits, ducks and geese to horses and a couple of peacocks. The fairly priced own-brewed Saddleworth beers are a big draw, and Saddleworth More, Ayrtons, Bert Corner, Hopsmacker, Rueben's Bitter, Shaftbender, and seasonal ales, are well kept alongside a couple of guests such as Boggart Hole Clough Boggart Bitter or Dark Star on handpump; several malt whiskies and farm cider too. The big unspoilt L-shaped main bar has high beams and some stripped stone; one window at the end of the bar counter looks down over the valley, and there's also a valley view from the quieter no smoking dining room. The comfortable furnishings include settles and pews as well as a good individual mix of chairs, and there are lots of attractive prints, staffordshire and other china on a high delft shelf, jugs, brasses and so forth; TV and occasional unobtrusive piped music. The horse-collar on the wall is worn by the winner of their annual gurning (or face-pulling) championship (part of the lively Rush Cart Festival, usually held over the August bank holiday), and handbells here are the church bellringers' practice set. Children and dogs are made to feel very welcome, and there's an increasing army of rescued cats. Reasonably priced bar food such as sandwiches, steak and ale pie, jumbo cod, roast beef, and puddings such as banoffi pie; children's meals too.

Own brew ~ Licensee Julian Taylor ~ Real ale ~ Bar food (12-2.30, 5.30-9; 12-9 Sat/Sun and bank hols) ~ Restaurant ~ (01457) 872415 ~ Children welcome ~ Dogs welcome ~ Open 12-11(10.30 Sun); closed from 3-7.30pm 25 Dec

WHEELTON

Dressers Arms *2.1 miles from M61 junction 8; A674 towards Blackburn, then in Wheelton fork right into Briers Brow; 3.6 miles from M65 junction 3, also via A674*

Handy from the motorway, this converted cottage row is well liked for its food and its very good range of beers, including at least one from their own microbrewery. It's much bigger than it looks from the outside, with a series of genuinely atmospheric, low-beamed little rooms that remain darkly cosy even on the sunniest of days, full of old oak and traditional features, including a handsome old woodburning stove in the flagstoned main bar.

Candles on tables add to the welcoming feel, and there are newspapers, magazines and a couple of stuffed animals in glass cases; two areas are no smoking. One particularly snug room has windows overlooking the brewing equipment. They usually keep eight real ales on at once, such as their own Big Franks and possibly Annastasia, as well as the more familiar Boddingtons, Fullers London Pride, Shepherd Neame Spitfire, Tetleys, Timothy Taylors Landlord and Worthington Best; also around 20 malt whiskies, and some well chosen wines. The good locally sourced bar food includes hot filled baguettes, several vegetarian dishes, liver and onions or sausage and mash, and blackboard specials such as green thai curry; also Sunday roasts and straightforward children's meals. The licensees are great pet-lovers, and have a couple of dogs and cats. On the first floor is a cantonese restaurant. Lots of picnic-sets on a terrace in front of the pub; they have a very big car park, across the road.

Own brew ~ Licensees Steve and Trudie Turner ~ Real ale ~ Bar food (12-2.30, 5-9; 12-9 weekends) ~ Restaurant ~ (01254) 830041 ~ Children in eating area of bar ~ Dogs welcome ~ Open 11-11; 12-10.30 Sun

YEALAND CONYERS
New Inn *3 miles from M6 junction 35; village signposted off A6*
A handy place to stop if you need a break from the nearby M6, this 17th-c ivy-covered village pub is open all day. The simply furnished little beamed bar on the left has a cosy village atmosphere, with its log fire in the big stone fireplace, and cribbage and dominoes. On the right, two communicating no smoking cottagey dining rooms have dark blue furniture, shiny beams and an attractive kitchen range. Well kept Hartleys XB and Hartleys Cumbria Way on handpump, around 30 malt whiskies, winter mulled wine and maybe summer home-made lemonade; piped music. There's a bustling atmosphere with plenty of locals and visitors. The same menu runs through the dining rooms and bar, and dishes might include soup, cajun potato skins, cumberland sausage or lentil and red pepper curry, with specials such as fried duck breast with orange sauce. A sheltered lawn at the side has picnic-sets among roses and flowering shrubs.

Robinsons ~ Tenants Bill Tully and Charlotte Pinder ~ Real ale ~ Bar food (11.30(12 Sun)-9.30) ~ Restaurant ~ (01524) 732938 ~ Children welcome ~ Dogs allowed in bar ~ Open 11.30-11; 12-10.30 Sun

Dog Friendly Hotels, B&Bs and Farms

ASHWORTH VALLEY
Leaches Farm *Ashworth Rd, Rochdale, Lancashire OL11 5UN (01706) 41117 £40*; 3 rms, shared bthrm. Creeper-clad 17th-c hill farm with really wonderful views, massive stone walls, beams and log fires; self-catering too; cl 22 Dec-2 Jan; children over 8; dogs in bedrooms by arrangement

BLACKPOOL
Imperial Hotel *North Promenade, Blackpool, Lancashire FY1 2HB (01253) 623971* £**118**, plus special breaks; 183 well equipped pretty rms, many with sea views. Fine Victorian hotel overlooking the sea, with spacious and comfortable day rooms, lots of period features, enjoyable food and fine wines, and a full health and fitness club with indoor swimming pool, gym, sauna and so forth; children's club during summer, Christmas and Easter; lots to do nearby; disabled access; dogs welcome in bedrooms; £15

BROMLEY CROSS
Last Drop Village Hotel *Hospital Rd, Bromley Cross, Bolton, Lancashire BL7 9PZ (01204) 591131* £**88**; 128 rms. Big well equipped hotel complex cleverly integrated into olde-worlde pastiche village complete with stone-and-cobbles street of gift and teashops, bakery, etc, even a spacious creeper-covered pub with lots of beamery and timbering, popular buffet, and heavy tables out on attractive flagstoned terrace; disabled access; dogs welcome in bedrooms; £10

CAPERNWRAY
New Capernwray Farmhouse *Capernwray, Carnforth, Lancashire LA6 1AD (01524) 734284* £**75**; 3 comfortable rms. Pretty 300-year-old ex-farmhouse (no smoking) in two acres of grounds, with helpful friendly owners, characterful drawing room, stone walls and beams, and candlelit dinner with an informal house-party atmosphere; cl Nov-Feb; children over 10; dogs welcome in bedrooms by arrangement; must be fed outside

CHIPPING
Gibbon Bridge Hotel *Green Lane, Chipping, Preston, Lancashire PR3 2TQ (01995) 61456* £**120**, plus special breaks; 29 spacious individual rms, inc 22 split-level suites, most with views of the Bowland Hills. Country hotel on the edge of the Forest of Bowland, with beautiful landscaped gardens, and old-fashioned values of quality and personal service; attractively presented food using home-grown produce in airy restaurant and adjoining conservatory, a quiet relaxing atmosphere, and fine wines; health and gym area; tennis court; a good base for walking and short driving trips; good disabled access; dogs in two restricted bedrooms

COWAN BRIDGE
Hipping Hall *Cowan Bridge, Kirkby Lonsdale, Carnforth, Lancashire LA6 2JJ (01524) 271187* £**96**, plus special breaks; 7 pretty rms, 5 in main hotel, 2 cottage suites across courtyard (with self-catering facilities). Relaxed country-house atmosphere and delicious food in handsome small hotel, an open fire, a lovely beamed Great Hall with minstrels' gallery, and four acres of walled gardens; fine walks from front door; cl Christmas and New Year; children over 12; dogs in cottage suites

HURST GREEN

Shireburn Arms *Whalley Rd, Hurst Green, Clitheroe, Lancashire BB7 9QJ* *(01254) 826518* £**75**, plus special breaks; 18 rms. Lovely 17th-c country hotel with a refined but friendly atmosphere, an airy modernised bar, comfortable lounge, open fires, well presented enjoyable food, good service, and fine view of the Ribble Valley from the conservatory; disabled access; dogs welcome in bedrooms if well behaved; £10

MANCHESTER

Malmaison *Piccadilly, Manchester M1 3AQ (0161) 278 1000* £**154.50**; 167 chic rms with CD player, in-house movies, smart bthrms, and really good beds. Stylishly modern hotel with comfortable contemporary furniture, exotic flower arrangements, bright paintings, very efficient service, french brasserie, generous breakfasts, and free gym; good disabled access; dogs welcome in bedrooms; £10

MANCHESTER

Rossetti *107 Piccadilly, Manchester M1 2DB (0161) 247 7744* £**105**; 61 well equipped modern rms with eclectic décor (14 are no smoking) and 5 suites – each floor offers 50s-style diners with help-yourself tea, coffee, croissants, fruit and cereals. Formerly the headquarters of the Horrocks cotton dynasty, this impressive hotel has stylish rooms with lots of mirrors, old tiling, parquet floors, huge gold-painted ironwork columns, and lots of artwork; good mediterranean cooking in no smoking café (brazilian jazz all day), enjoyable breakfasts, basement cocktail bar, and cheerful informal service; dogs welcome in bedrooms

WADDINGTON

Backfold Cottage *The Square, Waddington, Clitheroe, Lancashire BB7 3JA* *(01200) 422367* £**57**; 3 rms. Tiny 17th-c cottage in cobbled street, attractive millennium clock on the front, beautiful antique furnishings (inc a doll's house in the lounge); very good service, all-day snacks, and candlelit evening meals (bring your own wines); nearby walks; children at owner's discretion; cl Christmas; dogs welcome by special arrangement only; £5

WHITEWELL

Inn at Whitewell *Whitewell, Clitheroe, Lancashire BB7 3AT (01200)* *448222* £**94**; 17 rms, some with open peat fires. Civilised Forest of Bowland stone inn on the River Hodder, with seven miles of trout, salmon and sea trout fishing, and grounds with views down the valley; interesting period furnishings, plenty of room, highly praised food (as well as coffee and cream teas all day), fine wines (they house a wine merchant), and courteous service; dogs in bedrooms

Leicestershire and Rutland

Dog Friendly Pubs

CLIPSHAM

Olive Branch *Take B668/Stretton exit off A1 N of Stamford; Clipsham signposted E from exit roundabout*

Still doing very well, this civilised stone-built country dining pub produces delicious food and stocks a good range of drinks to go with your meal. The friendly obliging staff are happy to help you choose from the enticing selection of blackboard wines, which includes interesting bin ends, old clarets and unusual sherries. They've also well kept Grainstore Olive Oil with a guest such as Timothy Taylors Landlord on handpump, also freshly squeezed fruit juices, home-made lemonade, good coffee, and winter mulled wine. The emphasis though is on the food, and it's worth booking or arriving early for a table, especially at lunchtime when they do a good value two-course meal, but not Sunday when they do three courses. Carefully made, using lots of fresh local produce, imaginative dishes change daily, but might include excellent honey-roast confit of duck leg with sweet potato and spring onions, sausage cassoulet with crispy vegetables, and roast local partridge with game chips; irresistible puddings. A nice touch is the board of home-baked bread they bring for you to slice yourself, and we liked the cheeseboard too. There are dark joists and beams in the various smallish attractive rambling room areas, a cosy log fire in the stone inglenook fireplace (they use old menus to light it), and an interesting mix of pictures, some by local artists, country furniture and books (many bought at antique fairs by one of the partners – ask if you see something you like, as much is for sale). Two of the dining rooms are no smoking; shove-ha'penny, and there may be unobtrusive piped music. Lovely in summer, there are picnic-sets out on a heated terrace, with more on the neat lawn sheltered in the L of its two low buildings.

Free house ~ Licensees Sean Hope, Ben Jones and Marcus Welford ~ Real ale ~ Bar food ~ Restaurant ~ (01780) 410355 ~ Children welcome ~ Dogs allowed in bar ~ Open 12-3, 6-11; 12-11(10.30 Sun) Fri, Sat; closed Fri afternoon in winter

COTTESMORE

Sun *B668 NE of Oakham*

The tasty food is quite a draw at this 17th-c thatched and stone-built village pub, and as there aren't many tables in the rooms off the bar, it pays to get here early in winter, or even book; in fine weather, you can also eat out on the terrace. Meals are served by friendly efficient staff, and include baked camembert for two, baguettes, calves liver or lamb shank, and specials such as cajun chicken caesar salad and salmon, cod and prawn fishcakes; home-made puddings too. Along with stripped pine furnishings, there's a winter log fire in the stone inglenook, and pictures on the olive and terracotta walls; one dining area is no smoking; piped music, and boules outside. Besides decent wines, they serve Adnams and Everards Tiger along with a guest such as Highwood Tom Woods Bomber County on handpump; generous coffee as well.

Everards ~ Tenant David Johnson ~ Real ale ~ Bar food (not Sun evening, Mon) ~ Restaurant ~ (01572) 812321 ~ Children welcome ~ Dogs allowed in bar ~ Open 11.30-2.30, 6.30-11; 12-3, 7-10.30 Sun; closed Mon

EXTON

Fox & Hounds *Signposted off A606 Stamford—Oakham*

Italian licensees at this handsome old country coaching inn add a gentle mediterranean lean to the good well presented bar food, and wine list (with a good range by the glass). As well as fresh ciabattas or grilled paninis, you might find mediterranean seafood salad, tasty pasta dishes, rack of lamb with rosemary or home-made steak and kidney pie; excellent coffee; no smoking dining room. Quietly civilised, the comfortable high-ceilinged lounge bar has some dark red plush easy chairs as well as wheelback seats around lots of pine tables, maps and hunting prints on the walls, fresh flowers, and a winter log fire in a large stone fireplace. The separate public bar has a more pubby atmosphere, with pool, darts, dominoes and piped music. Friendly competent staff serve well kept real ales such as Grainstore Springtime, Timothy Taylors Landlord, with perhaps a guest such as Greene King IPA on handpump. Seats among large rose beds on the pleasant well kept back lawn look out over paddocks, and the tranquil village green with its tall trees out in front is most attractive. Only a couple of miles away from Rutland Water, the pub is a useful stop for walkers on the Viking Way.

Free house ~ Licensees Valter and Sandra Floris ~ Real ale ~ Bar food (not Sun evening) ~ Restaurant ~ (01572) 812403 ~ Children welcome ~ Dogs allowed in bar ~ Open 11-3, 6-11; 12-3, 7-10.30 Sun ~ Bedrooms: £28/£42

KEGWORTH

Cap & Stocking *A mile or so from M1 junction 24: follow A6 towards Loughborough; in village, turn left at chemist's down one-way Dragwall opposite High Street, then left and left again, into Borough Street*

The three rooms of this backstreet local are an intriguing throwback to another age. The brown paint and etched glass in the right-hand room make it seem as if little has changed since the 1940s, and they serve Bass from a stainless steel jug; you'll also find Greene King IPA on handpump. The two determinedly simple but cosy front rooms both have their own coal fire and an easy-going feel, and furnishings include big cases of stuffed birds and locally caught fish, fabric-covered wall benches and heavy cast-iron-framed tables, and a cast-iron range; cribbage, dominoes, trivia and piped music. The back room has french windows to the pretty, secluded garden, where there may be floodlit boules and barbecues in summer. Straightforward bar food and daily specials such as thai chicken.

Punch ~ Tenants Graham and Mary Walsh ~ Real ale ~ Bar food (11.30-1.45, 6.30-8.45) ~ No credit cards ~ (01509) 674814 ~ Children welcome ~ Dogs welcome ~ Open 11.30-2.30, 6.30-11; 12-2.30, 7-10.30 Sun

MARKET OVERTON
Black Bull *Village signposted off B668 in Cottesmore*
Fresh fish features quite strongly on the specials board at this friendly old thatched stone-built pub – there may be 16oz fish and chips, bass, halibut and tilapia. A good range of other tasty dishes (served in generous helpings) could include battered whitebait, sweet and sour sizzling vegetables, stilton lamb or pasta of the day. The main dining room has a no smoking area and service is friendly. With a cheerfully bustling atmosphere, the low black-beamed bar has raspberry walls, red plush stools and cushioned spindleback chairs at dark wood pub tables, and flowers on the sills of its little curtained windows. They serve well kept Greene King IPA, Morlands Original and a guest such as Greene King Triumph on handpump; piped music and fruit machine.

Free house ~ Licensees John and Val Owen ~ Real ale ~ Bar food ~ Restaurant ~ (01572) 767677 ~ Children welcome ~ Dogs allowed in bar ~ Open 11-2.30, 6-11; 12-3, 7-10.30 Sun ~ Bedrooms: £35S/£48S

MEDBOURNE
Nevill Arms *B664 Market Harborough—Uppingham*
This enjoyable old pub is cheerily unpretentious, with a friendly welcome from the well liked long-serving licensees. The inviting main bar has a buoyant atmosphere, two log fires in stone fireplaces at either end, chairs and small wall settles around its tables, and a lofty dark-joisted ceiling; piped music. Much needed at busy times, a spacious back room by the former coachyard has pews around more tables, and some toys to amuse children. In summer most people prefer to eat at the tables out on the grass by the dovecote. Hearty home-made food from a short but reasonably priced menu, with blackboard specials such as pork with peppers and chicken with stilton and leeks. They have well kept Adnams, Fullers London Pride, Greene King Abbot and two changing guests such as Bass and Wadworths 6X, on handpump, and about two dozen country wines. A wide choice of games includes darts, shove-ha'penny, cribbage, dominoes, table skittles, and on request other board games and even table football; look out for Truffles the cat, and the two inquisitive great danes, Cleo and her son Bertie. The building itself is attractive, with handsome stonework and imposing latticed mullioned windows, and you get to it by a footbridge

over the little duck-filled River Welland. The church over the bridge is worth a visit. The bedrooms are in two neighbouring cottages, and the first-class breakfasts are served in the pub's sunny conservatory.

Free house ~ Licensees Nicholas and Elaine Hall ~ Real ale ~ Bar food (12-2, 7-9.30) ~ (01858) 565288 ~ Children welcome ~ Dogs allowed in bar ~ Open 12-2.30(3 Sat, Sun), 6-11 ~ Bedrooms: £45B/£55B

NEWTON BURGOLAND

Belper Arms *Village signposted off B4116 S of Ashby or B586 W of Ibstock*

The friendly landlord is very hands-on, and there's a good pubby atmosphere at this popular roadside place. Although very opened up, many ancient interior features reflect the various stages in its development (heavy beams, changing floor levels and separate areas with varying floor and wall materials) and give it an enjoyably intimate feel. Parts are said to date back to the 13th c, and much of the exposed brickwork certainly looks at least three or four hundred years old. A big freestanding central chimney has a fire one side and a range on the other, with chatty groups of captains' chairs. There are lots of interesting bits and pieces dotted around, from a suit of old chain mail, to a collection of pewter teapots, some good antique furniture and the story of the pub ghost (Five to Four Fred) which is framed on the wall. They hold a beer festival during the August bank holiday, but usually have well kept Greene King IPA, Hook Norton Best, Marstons Pedigree and a couple of guests from brewers such as J W Lees and Smiles on handpump; nine wines by the glass. Pleasant piped music and dominoes. Tasty bar food includes smoked haddock rarebit with tomato salad, curry of the day, mediterranean vegetable lasagne, and sirloin steak; also specials and puddings, and a three-course Sunday lunch. The restaurant is very big, and service can slow down when they get busy. A rambling garden has boules, cricket nets and children's play area, and works its way round the pub to teak tables and chairs on a terrace, and a steam-engine-shaped barbecue; there's a good campsite here too.

Mercury Taverns ~ Manager Guy Wallis ~ Real ale ~ Bar food (12-2.30, 7-9.30) ~ Restaurant ~ (01530) 270530 ~ Children welcome ~ Dogs allowed in bar ~ Open 12-3, 6-11; all day Fri-Sun

OAKHAM

Grainstore *Station Road, off A606*

As soon as you arrive at this converted three-storey Victorian grain warehouse, you get the feel of a working brewery, from the bustle of deliveries leaving the building to the vats of beer which you can see through glass doors in the functional open-plan bar. The brewery is a traditional tower brewhouse, with raw materials starting on the upper floor and the finished beer coming out on the bottom floor. Laid back or lively, depending on the time of day, the interior is plain and functional, with wide well worn bare floorboards, bare ceiling boards above massive joists (and noises of the workings above) which are supported by red metal pillars, a long brick-built bar counter with cast-iron bar stools, tall cask tables and simple elm chairs. Their fine beers (Grainstore Cooking,

Rutland Panther, Steamin' Billy, Triple B and Ten Fifty) are served traditionally at the left end of the bar counter, and through swan necks with sparklers on the right; the friendly staff are happy to give you samples. At lunchtimes alongside soup they serve dutchman's breakfast (three eggs, ham, cheese and bread), as well as a few reasonably priced dishes, with perhaps a special such as mushroom and mustard puff. In summer they open huge glass doors onto a terrace stacked with barrels, and with picnic-sets; sporting events on TV, fruit machine, bar billiards, cribbage, dominoes, darts, giant Jenga and bottle-walking. Loading trucks used to pass right through the building; disabled access. You can tour the brewery by arrangement, and they do take-aways. It's very handy for the station.

Own brew ~ Licensee Tony Davis ~ Real ale ~ Bar food (11.30-2.15, not evenings or Sun) ~ (01572) 770065 ~ Children welcome ~ Dogs allowed in bar ~ Live music once a month on Sun afternoon, Sun evening and Thurs evening ~ Open 11-11; 12-10.30 Sun

OLD DALBY

Crown *By school in village centre turn into Longcliff Hill*

Three or four intimate little rooms at this tucked-away creeper-covered former farmhouse have black beams, one or two antique oak settles, a mix of carvers and wheelback chairs, hunting and other rustic prints, and open fires; the snug is no smoking. Outside, you'll find cast-iron furniture and rustic tables and chairs on the terrace, hanging baskets and urns of flowers; steps lead down through the sheltered sloping lawn with boules. Bar food includes ciabattas, sausage and mash, pasta dishes and goats cheese tart. The dining room has paintings by a local artist and a pleasantly relaxed bistro feel. Local Belvoir Brewery, Charles Wells Bombardier, Courage Directors and three guests such as Greene King Old Speckled Hen, Marstons Pedigree or Theakstons Old Peculier are well kept on handpump or tapped straight from the cask; darts and cribbage.

Free house ~ Licensees Mr and Mrs Hayle ~ Real ale ~ Bar food (12-2.30, 6.30-9.30; not Mon lunchtime or Sun evening) ~ Restaurant ~ (01664) 823134 ~ Children in eating area of bar and restaurant ~ Dogs allowed in bar ~ Open 12-3, 6-11(7-10.30 Sun); closed Mon lunchtime

SOMERBY

Stilton Cheese *High Street; off A606 Oakham—Melton Mowbray, via Cold Overton, or Leesthorpe and Pickwell; can also be reached direct from Oakham via Knossington*

Lots of local activity, and diners in for a meal keep the atmosphere at this welcoming 16th-c pub enjoyably bustling and cheerful. The hop-strung beamed bar/lounge has dark carpets, lots of country prints on its stripped stone walls, a collection of copper pots, a stuffed badger and plenty of restful seats; shove-ha'penny, cribbage, dominoes, board games and piped music. Five handpumps serve well kept local Grainstore Ten Fifty, Marstons Pedigree, and Tetleys along with two thoughtfully sourced guests from brewers such as John O'Gaunt or Tring, and they've a good choice of wines, and about two dozen malt whiskies. Well cooked (there are three chefs in the family) and reasonably priced bar meals might include local sausages and mash or lasagne, battered cod or chicken tikka masala, and tasty specials such as stilton-stuffed mushrooms or home-made venison and mushroom pie, and monkfish provençal; also children's meals. The restaurant is no smoking. The terrace has wooden seating and outdoor heaters.

Free house ~ Licensees Carol and Jeff Evans ~ Real ale ~ Bar food (12-2, 6(7 Sun)-9) ~ Restaurant ~ (01664) 454394 ~ Children in restaurant and family room ~ Dogs allowed in bedrooms ~ Open 12-3, 6-11(7-10.30 Sun) ~ Bedrooms: /£35

STATHERN
Red Lion *Off A52 W of Grantham via the brown-signposted Belvoir road (keep on towards Harby – Stathern signposted on left); or off A606 Nottingham—Melton Mowbray via Long Clawson and Harby*

The unassuming exterior of this gourmet pub is deceptive. It's run by the team behind the Olive Branch in Clipsham (see entry) and has the same enjoyable mix of good (though not cheap) food, well chosen wines, and civilised atmosphere. They have a kitchen shop where you can buy produce and fully prepared dishes. Bar food ingredients are sourced locally, they smoke their own meats and make their own preserves and pickles. The twice daily changing menu offers a good choice which might include smoked haddock and leek tart, fried calves liver with mustard mash and tarragon jus, roast gressingham duck breast, and puddings such as rhubarb crumble with ginger ice-cream. They also do a limited two-course set menu. The splendid range of drinks takes in well kept Brewsters Wicken Women from just down the road, Grainstore Olive Oil, a couple of changing guest beers such as Fullers London Pride and Caledonian Deuchars IPA, draught belgian beer, freshly squeezed orange and grapefruit, several ciders and fruit punches, and a varied wine list with just under a dozen by the glass. There's a relaxed country pub feel to the yellow room on the right, a relaxing lounge with sofas, a fireplace, and a big table with books, papers and magazines; it leads off the smaller, more traditional flagstoned bar, with terracotta walls, another fireplace with a pile of logs beside it, and lots of beams and hops. Dotted around are various oddities picked up by one of the licensees on visits to Newark Antiques Fair: some unusual lambing chairs for example, and a collection of wooden spoons. A little room with tables set for eating leads to the long, narrow main dining room in what was once the pub's skittle alley, and out to a nicely arranged suntrap garden, with good hardwood furnishings spread over its lawn and terrace, and an unusually big play area behind the car park, with swings, climbing frames and so on.

Free house ~ Licensees Sean Hope, Ben Jones and Marcus Welford ~ Real ale ~ Bar food ~ Restaurant ~ (01949) 860868 ~ Children welcome ~ Dogs allowed in bar ~ Open 12-3, 6-11; 12-11 Fri, Sat; 12-6 Sun

Dog Friendly Hotels, B&Bs and Farms

EMPINGHAM

White Horse *Main St, Empingham, Oakham, Rutland LE15 8PR (01780) 460221* £65, plus special breaks; 13 pretty rms, some in a delightfully converted stable block. Attractive, bustling old inn, handy for Rutland Water; a relaxed and comfortable atmosphere, a big log fire and fresh flowers in open-plan lounge, big helpings of very enjoyable food inc fine breakfasts, coffee and croissants from 8am, and cream teas all year; attractive no smoking restaurant, well kept real ales, and efficient friendly service; cots/high chairs; cl 25 Dec; good disabled access; dogs welcome in bedrooms; £5

MELTON MOWBRAY

Sysonby Knoll *Asfordby Rd, Melton Mowbray, Leicestershire LE13 0HP (01664) 563563* £73; 30 rms, most facing a central courtyard, and 6 in annexe. Family-run Edwardian brick house on the edge of a bustling market town; reception and lounge areas furnished in period style, winter open fire, friendly owners and excellent service, generous helpings of imaginative food including lots of puddings in newly refurbished airy restaurant, and five acres of gardens leading down to the River Eye where guests may fish; no smoking except in bar; cl 24 Dec–2 Jan; dogs welcome away from restaurant; plenty of nearby walks

STAPLEFORD

Stapleford Park *Stapleford, Melton Mowbray, Leicestershire LE14 2EF (01572) 787522* £232.65; 52 individually designed rms, plus cottage. Luxurious country house, extravagantly restored, in lovely large grounds with riding and stabling, tennis, croquet, putting green, 18-hole championship golf course, trout fishing, falconry, and clay pigeon shooting; lots of opulent furnishings, fine oil paintings and an impressive library, delicious restaurant food, enthusiastic owner, and warmly welcoming staff; health spa and indoor swimming pool; cots/babysitting; disabled access; dogs in bedrooms and most public areas; £15

STRETTON

Ram Jam Inn *Great North Rd, Stretton, Oakham, Rutland LE15 7QX (01780) 410776* £74.10; 7 comfortable and well equipped rms. Actually on the A1, this civilised place has a comfortable airily modern lounge bar, a café bar and bistro, good interesting food quickly served all day from open-plan kitchen, and useful small wine list; large garden and orchard; cl 25 Dec; dogs welcome in bedrooms

UPPINGHAM

Lake Isle *16 High St East, Uppingham, Oakham, Rutland LE15 9PZ (01572) 822951* £75, plus special breaks; 12 rms with home-made biscuits, sherry and fresh fruit, and three cottage suites. In a charming market town, this 18th-c restaurant-with-rooms has an open fire in the attractive lounge, a redecorated bar (once a barber's where the schoolboys had their hair cut), good, imaginative food in refurbished restaurant (enjoyable breakfasts, too), a carefully chosen wine list, and a small and pretty garden; dogs welcome in cottage suites

Lincolnshire

Dog Friendly Pubs

SOUTH WITHAM

Blue Cow *Village signposted just off A1 Stamford—Grantham (with brown sign for pub)*

The two real ales they serve at this old stone-walled country pub are brewed by the friendly landlord in the building next door. Thirlwells Best (named after the licensees) and Witham Wobbler are available on handpump, and if the landlord is around he'll happily give you a little tour, and sell you some to take home (perhaps even in a recycled Coke bottle). With a good relaxed atmosphere, the two appealing individual bars are separated by a big central open-plan counter. One dark-beamed room has bentwood chairs at big hardwood tables, wickerwork and panelling, and prettily curtained windows. The second room has big black standing timbers and beams, partly stripped stone walls, shiny flagstones and a dark blue flowery carpet; piped music, TV, cribbage and dominoes. Just inside the entrance lobby you pass an endearing little water feature on floodlit steps that go down to the cellar. Reasonably priced, enjoyable bar food includes tasty home-made soup, salmon balls, chicken curry or vegetable pancake, and duck breast with potato rösti. The garden has tables on a pleasant terrace.

Own brew ~ Licensees Dick and Julia Thirlwell ~ Real ale ~ Bar food (12-2.30, 6-9.30) ~ Restaurant ~ (01572) 768432 ~ Children in eating area of bar, restaurant and family room ~ Dogs allowed in bar and bedrooms ~ Open 12-11 ~ Bedrooms: £40S/£45S(£55B)

SURFLEET

Mermaid *Just off A16 N of Spalding, on B1356 at bridge*

In summer, they hold regular barbecues and hog roasts at this genuinely old-fashioned dining pub, and the pretty garden has lots of seats and a terrace with thatched parasols, and its own bar; a children's play area is safely walled from the River Glen which runs beside the pub. Inside, it looks largely unchanged since the 70s, but everything is well cared for and fresh-looking. A small central glass-backed bar counter (complete with original Babycham décor) serves two high-ceilinged rooms, which have huge netted sash windows, green patterned carpets, beige Anaglypta dado, brass platters, navigation lanterns and horse tack on cream textured walls, and a mixture of banquettes and stools; cribbage, dominoes, and piped music. Two steps down, the restaurant is decorated in a similar style. Besides enjoyable lunchtime snacks such as hamburgers and omelettes, generous helpings of home-made food (served on hot plates) might include fried mushrooms with garlic, cream and crispy bacon, cottage pie or aubergine and vegetable galette; also daily specials such as fisherman's pie. Adnams Broadside, John Smiths and possibly a guest such as Charles Wells Bombardier are well kept on handpump; obliging service from the welcoming staff.

Free house ~ Licensee Chris Bustance ~ Real ale ~ Bar food (12-2.30, 6.30-9.30(6-10 Fri/Sat); 12-2.30, 6.30-9 Sun) ~ Restaurant ~ (01775) 680275 ~ Children welcome ~ Dogs welcome ~ Open 11-11; 12-10.30 Sun

WOOLSTHORPE

Chequers *The one near Belvoir, signposted off A52 or A607 W of Grantham*
Up a short dead-end off the main street, this 17th-c coaching inn continues its journey into the 21st c with some subtle redecoration. Its core, the heavy-beamed main bar, is still dominated by the huge boar's head above a good log fire in the big brick fireplace, set off now by a gentle up-to-date colour scheme. Its two big tables, one a massive oak construction, have a comfortable mix of seating including some handsome leather chairs and leather banquettes. Among cartoons on the wall are some of the illustrated claret bottle labels from the series commissioned from famous artists, initiated by the late Baron Philippe de Rothschild. The lounge on the right has been smartened up with a deep red colour scheme, and new leather sofas. On the left, there are more leather seats in a dining area housed in what was once the village bakery. A corridor leads off to the light and airy main restaurant, with contemporary pictures and a newly uncovered 1920s sprung dance floor. As well as decent house wines (with 24 wines by the glass), and 50 single malts, they serve three or four well kept real ales on handpump such as Adnams Best, Fullers London Pride, Hardys & Hansons Best, and Marstons Pedigree; also organic drinks and fruit pressés. Bar food includes lunchtime soup, toasted brie and parma ham, ploughman's, and sausages and mash, with evening dishes such as chargrilled chicken breast and stuffed rabbit leg with chorizo, spinach and wild mushrooms; puddings might include chocolate bread and butter pudding with chocolate sauce. There are nice teak tables, chairs and benches outside, and beyond some picnic-sets on the edge of the pub's cricket field; boules too, and views of Belvoir Castle.

Free house ~ Licensee Justin Chad ~ Real ale ~ Bar food ~ Restaurant ~ (01476) 870701 ~ Children welcome ~ Dogs allowed in bar and bedrooms ~ Open 12-3, 5.30-11; 12-5.30 Sun; closed Sun evening ~ Bedrooms: £40S/£50S

Dog Friendly Hotels, B&Bs and Farms

LINCOLN
D'Isney Place *Eastgate, Lincoln LN2 4AA (01522) 538881* £**95**, plus special breaks; 17 charming rms. Friendly 18th-c hotel with lovely gardens (one wall of the cathedral close forms its southern boundary), a relaxed and homely atmosphere, good breakfasts using free-range eggs served on bone china in your room (there are no public rooms), and friendly owners; partial disabled access; dogs welcome in bedrooms

SPALDING
Cley Hall *22 High St, Spalding, Lincolnshire PE11 1TX (01775) 725157* £**75**; 12 smart rms, 8 in annexe. Handsome Georgian manor house overlooking the River Welland with attractive back gardens, comfortable seating areas, very good, popular food in the no smoking Garden Restaurant and more informal bistro, and friendly, helpful staff; dogs welcome in bedrooms

STAMFORD
George *71 St Martins, Stamford, Lincolnshire PE9 2LB (01780) 750700* £**110**, plus special breaks; 47 individually decorated rms. Ancient former coaching inn with a quietly civilised atmosphere, sturdy timbers, broad flagstones, heavy beams and massive stonework, and open log fires; good food in Garden Lounge, restaurant and courtyard (in summer), an excellent range of drinks inc very good value italian wines, and welcoming staff; well kept walled garden and sunken croquet lawn; disabled access; dogs welcome in bedrooms and some other areas (not the restaurant)

WINTERINGHAM
Winteringham Fields *1 Silver St, Winteringham, Scunthorpe, Lincolnshire DN15 9ND (01724) 733096* £**125**; 10 pretty rms (3 off courtyard). Thoughtfully run restaurant-with-rooms in 16th-c manor house with comfortable and very attractive Victorian furnishings, beams and open fires, really excellent, inventive and beautifully presented food (inc a marvellous cheeseboard) in no smoking dining room, fine breakfasts, exemplary service, and an admirable wine list; cl 2 wks Christmas, 1 wk Mar, 1 wk Aug, last wk Oct; disabled access; babes in arms and children over 8; dogs welcome in bedrooms (not to be left unattended)

Norfolk

Dog Friendly Pubs

BLAKENEY
Kings Arms *West Gate Street*
There's always a happy throng of chatty customers in this bustling, friendly pub that has been run by the same licensees for 30 years. The three simply furnished, knocked-through pubby rooms have low ceilings, some interesting photographs of the licensees' theatrical careers, other pictures including work by local artists, and what must be the smallest cartoon gallery in England – in a former telephone kiosk. Look out for the brass plaque on the wall that marks a flood level. Two small rooms are no smoking, as is the airy garden room; darts, fruit machine, shove-ha'penny, table skittles and dominoes. Well kept Greene King Old Speckled Hen and Marstons Pedigree, and a couple of changing guests often from Adnams and Woodfordes on handpump; good efficient service. Reasonably priced, well liked bar food includes filled baked potatoes, ploughman's, grilled prawns in garlic butter, vegetable lasagne, battered cod, haddock or plaice, and puddings like home-made fruit crumble. Lots of tables and chairs plus swings for children in the large garden. The pub is just a short stroll from the harbour, and there are good nearby walks.
Free house ~ Licensees John Howard and Marjorie Davies ~ Real ale ~ Bar food (12-9.30(9 Sun)) ~ (01263) 740341 ~ Children welcome ~ Dogs welcome ~ Open 11-11; 12-10.30 Sun ~ Bedrooms: /£60S

BRANCASTER STAITHE
White Horse *A149 E of Hunstanton*
Cleverly, this particularly well run inn manages to appeal to a wide mix of customers. Locals tend to congregate for a chat and a pint in the front bar, those wanting to enjoy the very good, imaginative food head for the big conservatory, and the delightful, airy bedrooms attract customers all year round. It's all more or less open-plan. In the front bar there are good local photographs on the left, with bar billiards and maybe piped music, and on the right is a quieter group of cushioned wicker armchairs and sofas by a table with daily papers, and local landscapes for sale. This runs into the no smoking back conservatory with well spaced furnishings in unvarnished

country-style wood, and some light-hearted seasidey decorations; through the big glass windows you can look over the sun deck to the wide views of the tidal marshes and Scolt Head Island beyond. Well kept Adnams Bitter, Fullers London Pride, and Woodfordes Nelsons Revenge and Wherry on handpump from the handsome counter, manned by exceptionally friendly young staff; they also have 15 malt whiskies and about a dozen wines by the glass from an extensive and thoughtful wine list. The good menu changes twice a day, and as well as lunchtime choices such as home-made roasted tomato, garlic and basil soup, poached salmon fishcake with spinach and sorrel sauce, and their own sausage with white onion sauce, there might be cured salmon and asparagus salad, fresh home-made pasta, roast loin of pork, and roast rib-eye steak with garlic creamed potatoes. The coast path runs along the bottom of the garden, and if you stay they do an excellent breakfast.

Free house ~ Licensees Cliff Nye and Kevin Nobes ~ Real ale ~ Bar food (lunchtime only) ~ Restaurant ~ (01485) 210262 ~ Children in eating area of bar and restaurant ~ Dogs allowed in bar ~ Open 11-11; 12-10.30 Sun ~ Bedrooms: /£104B

BURNHAM THORPE
Lord Nelson *Village signposted from B1155 and B1355, near Burnham Market*
As Nelson was born in this sleepy village it's no surprise to find lots of pictures and memorabilia of him lining the walls, and there are recipes for unusual rum concoctions called Nelson's Blood and Lady Hamilton's Nip. The little bar has well waxed antique settles on the worn red flooring tiles and smoke ovens in the original fireplace, and an eating room has flagstones, an open fire, and more pictures of Nelson; there are two no smoking rooms. Well kept Greene King IPA and Abbot, and Woodfordes Nelsons Revenge and Wherry tapped from the cask in a back stillroom, and 11 wines by the glass; friendly, obliging staff. Enjoyable daily changing bar food using lots of fresh local ingredients might include home-made salmon mousse or local cockles, a plate of filo prawns, scampi, whitebait and squid rings, home-made ratatouille or bangers and mash with onion gravy, lamb cutlets with rosemary, and puddings such as crème brûlée or home-made chocolate brownies; the eating areas are no smoking. Shove-ha'penny, cribbage and dominoes. There's a good-sized play area in the very big garden, and they are kind to children.

Greene King ~ Lease David Thorley ~ Real ale ~ Bar food (not Sun evening or Mon in winter) ~ Restaurant ~ (01328) 738241 ~ Children in eating area of bar and restaurant ~ Dogs allowed in bar ~ Live bands every 2nd Thurs Oct-June ~ Open 11(12 in winter)-2.30(3 Sat), 6-11; 12-3, 6.30-10.30 Sun; closed winter Mon

CLEY NEXT THE SEA
Three Swallows *Off A149 E of Blakeney; in village, turn into Holt Road and head for church at Newgate Green*
You will be warmly welcomed in this village local by the new licensee, the friendly locals, and tabby cats. The unpretentious carpeted bar on the right

has a mix of pubby furnishings including long green leatherette benches around high leathered tables, a good log fire in the small fireplace at one end, and team photographs and pictures of local old boys above its dark dado; cribbage and dominoes. Well kept Adnams Best, and Greene King IPA and Abbot on handpump served from a counter richly carved with fantastical figures and faces, with a handsome carved mirror backing; a couple of steps lead up to a small family eating area. There's a second log fire in the informal no smoking stripped pine restaurant on the left. Good bar food now includes home-made soup, fresh seasonal crab, filled baked potatoes, spicy thai-style king prawns, ham and free range eggs or spinach, tomato and mushroom lasagne, or a popular daily roast; also specials like venison in red wine, puddings such as fruit pie and a children's menu. Below the handsome flint church tower, the big garden has picnic-sets on two grass terraces, and is prettily planted with flowering shrubs; there's a prominent water feature with a surprisingly grandiose fountain, and a wooden climbing frame, budgerigar aviary and goat pen for children. Handy for the salt marshes, the pub is liked by bird-watchers. The bedrooms are simple and comfortable, and they do particularly good, generous breakfasts.

Pubmaster ~ Tenant Brian Pennington ~ Real ale ~ Bar food (12-2, 6-9; 12-9 Fri-Sun) ~ (01263) 740526 ~ Children in eating area of bar and restaurant ~ Dogs allowed in bar ~ Open 11-11; 12-10.30 Sun; 11-3, 5.30-11 Mon-Thurs in winter; closed 25 Dec ~ Bedrooms: £40S/£60B

ERPINGHAM

Saracens Head *At Wolterton – not shown on many maps; Erpingham signposted off A140 N of Aylsham, keep on through Calthorpe, then where road bends right take the straight-ahead turn-off signposted Wolterton*

The bedrooms in this gently civilised dining pub have recently been redecorated and two new ones added; they are still hoping to add a conservatory bar. The two-room bar is simple and stylish, with high ceilings, terracotta walls, and red and white striped curtains at its tall windows – all lending a feeling of space, though it's not actually large. There's a mix of seats from built-in leather wall settles to wicker fireside chairs as well as log fires and flowers, and the windows look out on to a charming old-fashioned gravel stableyard with picnic-sets. A pretty little five-table parlour on the right, in cheerful nursery colours, has another big log fire. Well kept Adnams Bitter and Woodfordes Wherry on handpump, an interesting wine list, local apple juice, and decent malt whiskies; the atmosphere is enjoyably relaxed, and the landlord and his daughter charming and friendly. The imaginative bar food is so popular, you must book to be sure of a table. The changing menu could have starters and snacks such as local mussels with cider and cream, crispy fried aubergine with garlic mayonnaise, or red onion and goats cheese tart; main courses like baked cromer crab with mushrooms and sherry, roast local pheasant with calvados and cream, plump scallops with bacon and white wine, and pot-roast leg of lamb; puddings such as chocolate pot with orange jus. The Shed next door (run by Mr Dawson-Smith's daughter Rachel) is a

workshop and showcase for furniture and interior pieces.
Free house ~ Licensee Robert Dawson-Smith ~ Real ale ~ Bar food ~ Restaurant
~ (01263) 768909 ~ Children welcome ~ Dogs allowed in bedrooms ~ Open
11.30-3.30, 6-11; 12-3.30, 7-10.30 Sun; closed 25 Dec and evening 26 Dec ~
Bedrooms: £45B/£75B

GREAT CRESSINGHAM
Windmill *Village signposted off A1065 S of Swaffham; Water End*
All sorts of rooms and side areas ramble cosily around the island servery in
this carefully extended black-beamed pub, and there's a variety of pubby
furniture from pews and wheelback chairs to red leatherette or plush settles,
and masses of mainly rustic bric-a-brac and pictures, particularly big
sentimental Victorian lithographs. The walls are mainly painted a warm
terracotta pink, though there is some stripped brick and flint, and big log
fireplaces are re-equipped with electric look-alikes in warmer weather. The
separate more formal dining room and garden room are no smoking. Bar
food includes home-made spicy steak and ale pudding, lemon and black
pepper chicken fillet, rump steak, and daily specials such as vegetable
lasagne and pork in cider pie; children's meals too. Well kept Adnams
Bitter and Broadside, Greene King IPA and Windy Miller Quixote
(brewed for the pub) on handpump, with a couple of guest beers such as
Batemans XXXB and O'Hanlons Royal Oak, decent sensibly priced wines,
25 malt whiskies, friendly attentive staff. Off a back corridor with a fruit
machine is a neat well lit pool room, and one side snug has a big sports TV;
also darts, shove-ha'penny, table skittles, cribbage, dominoes, and faint
piped music. A good-sized stretch of neatly kept grass behind has picnic-
sets and a well equipped play area, including a sandpit; a caravan site almost
opposite is well screened by trees. It's been run by the same family for 50
years.
Free house ~ Licensee M J Halls ~ Bar food (12-2, 6-10) ~ Restaurant ~ (01760)
756232 ~ Children in restaurant and family room ~ Dogs allowed in bar ~
Country and Western on Tues nights ~ Open 11-3, 6-11; 12-3.30, 6-10.30
Sun

HORSEY
Nelson Head *Signposted off B1159 (in series of S-bends) N of Great Yarmouth*
Run by a friendly landlord, this simple place has two homely unpretentious
little rooms furnished with straightforward but comfortable seats (including
four tractor-seat bar stools), bits of shiny bric-a-brac, and small local
pictures for sale; good fire, geraniums on the window sill, and quite a mix
of customers. The garden has picnic-sets and an outside marquee.
Woodfordes Wherry and (of course) Nelsons Revenge are well kept on
handpump; cribbage, dominoes, shove-ha'penny, and piped music. Bar
food includes filled baguettes, home-made soup, vegetable chilli, chicken
in lemon and tarragon, good home-made steak and kidney pie, and fresh
local cod; the restaurant is no smoking. The pub sign is often hidden by
trees in summer; Horsey Windmill and the beach (pleasant walks from here
to Winterton-on-Sea) are just down the road.

Free house ~ Licensee Reg C Parsons ~ Real ale ~ Bar food (12-2, 6.15-8.30) ~ Restaurant ~ No credit cards ~ (01493) 393378 ~ Children in family room ~ Dogs allowed in bar ~ Open 11-3, 6-11(10 on Mon-Weds evenings in winter); 12-3, 6-10.30 Sun

ITTERINGHAM
Walpole Arms *Village signposted off B1354 NW of Aylsham*
This red-brick dining pub has a biggish open-plan bar with exposed beams, stripped brick walls, little windows, and a mix of dining tables. As well as snacks such as summer sandwiches, gloucester old spot pork pie, pasta with creamed mushrooms, rocket and parmesan, and smoked mackerel and spring onion fishcakes, the menu might include terrine of smoked chicken, salad of octopus stewed in red wine, singapore-style rabbit, and gigot of lamb with ratatouille; puddings such as cheesecake with apricot purée; the attractive restaurant is no smoking. Well kept Adnams Bitter and Broadside, and a Woodfordes beer named for the pub plus Wherry on handpump; they've also a well chosen wine list with up to 15 by the glass. Behind the pub is a two-acre landscaped garden.
Free house ~ Licensee Richard Bryan ~ Real ale ~ Bar food (12-2.30, 7-9; not Sun evening) ~ Restaurant ~ (01263) 587258 ~ Children welcome ~ Dogs allowed in bar ~ Open 12-3, 6-11; 12-3, 7-10.30 Sun

LETHERINGSETT
Kings Head *A148 just W of Holt*
Children love this unpretentious pub (which is not surprisingly full of families) and the emphasis is on keeping them amused. There's a play castle, living willow tunnel, toys, bikes and games (the garden is large enough not to be overwhelmed by this), and a particularly good children's menu with plenty of choices – they even do home-made baby food. The pub is pleasantly set, in grounds well back from the road, opposite a church with an unusual round tower, and it's not far from an interesting working water mill. Inside, the bar has metal-legged tables, a couple of armchairs and log fires, with various interesting prints, pictures and other items, including a signed poem by John Betjeman. There's also a small plush lounge, and a separate games room with darts, pool, TV, shove-ha'penny, dominoes, cribbage, fruit machines, and piped music. Tasty bar food from the straightforward, reasonably priced menu includes home-made soup, a three-egg omelette, ploughman's and salads, vegetarian chilli pasta bake or lamb cutlets and steaks; also daily specials and puddings such as home-made chocolate profiteroles; there's a braille menu too. Friendly and efficient staff serve well kept ales from local breweries like Elgoods, Greene King Abbot, Woodfordes, and Wolf; milk shakes, slush puppies, children's (and adults') cocktails, and decent wines. The pub's popularity with families does mean that housekeeping can, at busy times, become something of a lost cause.
Free house ~ Licensees David and Pamela Watts ~ Real ale ~ Bar food (all day) ~ (01263) 712691 ~ Children welcome ~ Dogs welcome ~ Live bands Sat evening ~ Open 11-11; 12-10.30 Sun

SNETTISHAM

Rose & Crown *Village signposted from A149 King's Lynn—Hunstanton just N of Sandringham; coming in on B1440 from the roundabout just N of village, take first left turn into Old Church Road*

Extremely popular with a wide mix of customers, this pretty white cottage has a very thoughtfully put together interior, with a separate character for each of the different areas: an old-fashioned beamed front bar with black settles on its tiled floor, and a great log fire; another big log fire in a back bar with the landlord's sporting trophies and old sports equipment; a no smoking bar with a colourful but soothing décor (this room is favoured by people eating); and another warmly decorated room, lovely for families, with painted settles and big old tables, leads out to the garden. Some nice old pews and other interesting furniture sit on the wooden floor of the main dining room, and there are shelves with old bottles and books, and old prints and watercolours. All three restaurant areas are no smoking. At lunchtime, the good, interesting bar food might include chilli and mint marinated olives, roast chicken livers with braised chicory and beetroot vinaigrette, fried sardines and linguine with hot paprika meatballs; evening choices such as crispy italian bacon, egg and rocket salad, aromatic pork belly, red mullet and king prawn tom yam and noodle broth, and chargrilled marinated sirloin steak with potato and swiss cheese pie; puddings like chocolate parve with orange salad. Well kept Adnams Broadside, Bass, Fullers London Pride, and Greene King IPA on handpump, 20 wines by the glass, organic fruit juices, and farm cider. Smart new café-style aluminium and blue chairs with matching blue tables, cream parasols and an outdoor heater have been added to the colourful enclosed garden with its herbaceous borders, flowering shrubs, and two spectacular willow trees; there's also a wooden fort for children.

Free house ~ Licensee Anthony Goodrich ~ Real ale ~ Bar food (12-2(2.30 weekends and summer holidays), 6.30-9(9.30 Fri, Sat)) ~ Restaurant ~ (01485) 540099 ~ Children in restaurant and family room ~ Dogs welcome ~ Open 11-11; 12-10.30 Sun ~ Bedrooms: £50B/£80B

STIFFKEY

Red Lion *A149 Wells—Blakeney*

The new licensee doesn't seem to have made any dramatic changes to this bustling pub. The oldest parts of the simple bars have a few beams, aged flooring tiles or bare floorboards, and big open fires; also, a mix of pews, small settles and a couple of stripped high-backed settles, a nice old long deal table among quite a few others, and oil-type or lantern wall lamps. Well kept Greene King IPA and Abbot, and Woodfordes Wherry and a guest from Woodfordes on handpump, and 10 wines by the glass; dominoes and cribbage. Good home-made bar food now includes thai spring rolls, deep-fried local whitebait, vegetable lasagne, curries, cottage pie or fish pie, and rump steak or venison steak with plum compote; seasonal offerings such as cromer crab salad or crab and prawn cakes, and roast pheasant; winter Sunday roasts. The back restaurant and conservatory are both no smoking. A back gravel terrace has proper tables and seats, with more on grass further up beyond; there are some pleasant walks nearby.

Free house ~ Licensee Andrew Waddison ~ Real ale ~ Bar food ~ Restaurant ~ (01328) 830552 ~ Children welcome ~ Dogs welcome ~ Open 11-11; 12-10.30 Sun

TIVETSHALL ST MARY
Old Ram *A140 15 miles S of Norwich, outside village*

Friendly and well run, this popular place handily serves food all day. The spacious country-style main room has lots of stripped beams and standing timbers, antique craftsmen's tools on the ceiling, a huge log fire in the brick hearth, a turkey rug on rosy brick floors, and a longcase clock. It's ringed by smaller side areas, and one no smoking dining room has striking navy walls and ceiling, swagged curtains and an open woodburning stove; this leads to a second comfortable mainly no smoking dining room and gallery. A wide choice of well liked bar food includes an open sandwich of the day, duck breast salad, local sausages with onion gravy, spaghetti with king prawns, salmon, crayfish tails, garlic and chilli, calves liver and bacon; also specials like king scallops in garlic butter, and pork medallions with a mushroom and shallot cream sauce, and puddings such as lemon tart or crème brûlée with ginger shortbread. There's an OAP two-course lunch and a breakfast menu. Unobtrusive fruit machine, TV, cribbage, dominoes, and piped music. Well kept Adnams, Bass, Timothy Taylors, and Woodfordes Wherry on handpump, 28 wines by the glass, fresh orange, apple, pineapple and carrot juice, milkshakes, and 20 malt whiskies. The sheltered flower-filled terrace of this much extended pub is very civilised, with outdoor heaters and big green parasols.

Free house ~ Licensee John Trafford ~ Real ale ~ Bar food (all day) ~ Restaurant ~ (01379) 676794 ~ Children in eating area of bar and in restaurant, but under 7s must leave by 8pm ~ Dogs welcome ~ Open 11-11; 12-10.30 Sun; closed 25-26 Dec ~ Bedrooms: £60.50B/£83B

UPPER SHERINGHAM
Red Lion *B1157; village signposted off A148 Cromer—Holt, and A149 just W of Sheringham*

This is a smashing little pub run by a cheerful landlady. There's always a buoyant atmosphere and plenty of chatty regulars, and visitors are made very welcome. The two modest but charming little bars have stripped high-backed settles and country-kitchen chairs on the red tiles or bare boards, terracotta-painted walls, a big woodburning stove, and newspapers to read; the red-walled snug is no smoking. It's best to book a table if you want to enjoy the good bar food: home-made soup, stilton-stuffed mushrooms, sweet and sour chicken, vegetable curry, lambs liver in port and orange gravy, and around 10 fresh fish dishes with various sauces. The restaurant gets very busy especially at weekends during the holiday season. Well kept Greene King IPA, Woodfordes Wherry and a guest on handpump, with around 12 malt whiskies and decent wines; dominoes and card games. They are still hoping to add six new bedrooms and a

conservatory dining area to this traditional–looking flint cottage.
*Free house ~ Licensee Sue Prew ~ Real ale ~ Bar food (12-2, 6.30-9) ~
Restaurant ~ No credit cards ~ (01263) 825408 ~ Children in restaurant and
family room ~ Dogs welcome ~ Open 11.30-11; 12-10.30 Sun; 11-3, 6.30-11
winter weekdays; 12-4 Sun in winter; closed winter Sun evenings ~ Bedrooms:
/£45*

WELLS-NEXT-THE-SEA
Crown *The Buttlands*
Since Chris and Jo Coubrough have taken over this 16th-c coaching inn,
readers have been quick to voice their warm enthusiasm. The beamed bar
is a friendly place with an informal mix of furnishings on the stripped
wooden floor, local photographs on the red walls, a good selection of
newspapers to read in front of the open fire, and well kept Adnams Best
and Broadside and Woodfordes Wherry on handpump; 15 wines by the
glass. The sunny no smoking conservatory with wicker chairs on the tiled
floor, beams, and modern art is where families with well behaved children
can sit, and there's a pretty no smoking restaurant; piped music. Served by
friendly young staff, the very good modern bar food might include chicken
and bacon terrine with chargrilled vegetables, deep–fried fishcakes, sandwiches with home-made crisps, dressed crab salad or a well liked tapas slate
with interesting appetisers, and moroccan spiced lamb burger with butter
bean and new potato salad; puddings such as chocolate bread and butter
pudding with crème anglaise. You can sit outside on the sheltered sun-deck.
*Free house ~ Licensees Chris and Jo Coubrough ~ Real ale ~ Bar food (12-2.30,
6.30-9.30) ~ Restaurant ~ (01328) 710209 ~ Children welcome ~ Dogs allowed
in bar ~ Open 11-11; 12-10.30 Sun ~ Bedrooms: £60B/£95B*

Dog Friendly Hotels, B&Bs and Farms

BLAKENEY
Blakeney Hotel *Blakeney, Holt, Norfolk NR25 7NE (01263) 740797*
£166, plus special breaks; 63 very comfortable rms, many with views over
the salt marshes and some with own little terrace. Overlooking the harbour
with fine views, this friendly hotel has comfortable and appealing public
rooms, good food, very pleasant staff, indoor swimming pool, saunas, spa
bath, billiard room, and safe garden; very well organised for families, with
plenty to do for them nearby; good disabled access; dogs welcome in
bedrooms; £3

BURNHAM MARKET
Hoste Arms *Market Pl, Burnham Market, King's Lynn, Norfolk PE31 8HD
(01328) 738777* **£108**, plus special breaks; 36 comfortable rms. Handsome
inn on green of lovely Georgian village, with a smartly civilised atmosphere, attractive bars, some interesting period features, big log fires,

conservatory lounge, stylish food (plus morning coffee and afternoon tea), well kept real ales and good wines, and professional friendly staff; big new awning covering a sizeable eating area in the garden; partial disabled access; dogs in bedrooms and some other areas; £7.50

MELTON CONSTABLE
Burgh Parva Hall *Holt Rd, Melton Constable, Norfolk NR24 2PU (01263) 862569* £50; 2 rms. Lovely, partly 16th-c longhouse with lovely country views, friendly, helpful owners, a relaxed atmosphere in the big rooms, rugs, pictures and nice old furniture, home-grown produce for evening meals (if arranged in advance), and marvellous breakfasts using their own eggs; dogs in bedrooms

MORSTON
Morston Hall *The Street, Morston, Holt, Norfolk NR25 7AA (01263) 741041* £230 inc dinner, plus special breaks; 7 comfortable rms with country views. Attractive 17th-c flint-walled house in tidal village, with lovely quiet gardens, two small lounges, one with an antique fireplace, a conservatory, and hard-working friendly young owners; particularly fine modern english cooking (they also run cookery demonstrations and hold wine and food events), a thoughtful small wine list, and super breakfasts; croquet; cl Jan; dogs welcome away from public rooms; they are kind to families; partial disabled access; dogs welcome in bedrooms; £5

MUNDFORD
Crown *Crown St, Mundford, Thetford, Norfolk IP26 5HQ (01842) 878233* £65; 20 good rms. Friendly small village pub, originally a hunting inn and rebuilt in the 18th c, with an attractive choice of reasonably priced straightforward food, very welcoming staff, a happy atmosphere, and well kept real ales; dogs welcome; disabled access; dogs in some bedrooms if well behaved

NORTH WALSHAM
Beechwood *Cromer Rd, North Walsham, Norfolk NR28 0HD (01692) 403231* £130 inc dinner; 17 comfortable rms. Creeper-covered Georgian house once Agatha Christie's Norfolk hideaway, with a comfortable lounge and bar, charming owners and super staff, good, imaginative modern cooking in attractive dining room, nice breakfasts, and lovely garden; lots to do and see nearby; children over 10; dogs in bedrooms, £6, and in bar

OLD CATTON
Catton Old Hall *Lodge Lane, Old Catton, Norwich, Norfolk NR6 7HG (01603) 419379* £90; 7 comfortable rms. 17th-c former farmhouse with lots of original features such as oak timbers, flint walls, and inglenook fireplaces; cosy lounge, huge dresser in beamed no smoking dining room, hearty breakfasts (evening meals by prior arrangement), and attentive, welcoming owners; children over 12; dogs welcome if small, in some bedrooms

SWAFFHAM

Strattons *Ash Close, Swaffham, Norfolk PE37 7NH (01760) 723845* £**100**, plus special breaks; 8 interesting, pretty rms. No smoking and environment-friendly Palladian-style villa run by charming, warmly friendly owners with comfortable individually decorated drawing rooms, family photographs, paintings, lots of china cats (and several live ones), antiques, patchwork throws, fresh and dried flowers, and open fires; delicious highly imaginative food using local (and home-grown) organic produce, a carefully chosen wine list illustrated with Mrs Scott's own watercolours, and super breakfasts; big cupboard full of toys and games for children; garden with croquet; cl 24-26 Dec; dogs in bedrooms; £5.50

THORNHAM

Lifeboat *Ship Lane, Thornham, Hunstanton, Norfolk PE36 6LT (01485) 512236* £**78**, plus special breaks; 14 pretty rms, most with sea view. Rambling old white-painted stone pub, well placed by coastal flats, with lots of character in the main bar – open fires, antique oil lamps, low settles and pews around carved oak tables, big oak beams hung with traps and yokes, and masses of guns, swords and antique farm tools; several rooms lead off; enjoyable popular food in bar and elegant restaurant and well kept real ales; sunny conservatory with steps up to terrace with seats and playground; marvellous surrounding walks; children welcomed rather than tolerated; partial disabled access; dogs in bedrooms and bars

THORPE MARKET

Elderton Lodge *Cromer Rd, Thorpe Market, Norwich, Norfolk NR11 8TZ (01263) 833547* £**95**, plus special breaks; 11 rms. 18th-c shooting lodge for adjacent Gunton Hall, with lots of original features, fine panelling, a relaxing lounge bar with log fire, an airy conservatory where breakfast and lunch are served, and Langtry Restaurant with good food using fresh fish and game; six acres of mature grounds overlooking herds of deer; children over 6; partial disabled access; dogs in bedrooms and lounge; £5

TITCHWELL

Titchwell Manor Hotel *Main Rd, Titchwell, King's Lynn, Norfolk PE31 8BB (01485) 210221* £**90**, plus special breaks; 15 light, pretty rms. Comfortable hotel, handy for nearby RSPB reserve, and with lots of walks and footpaths nearby; roaring log fire, magazines and good naturalists' records of the wildlife, a cheerful bar, attractive no smoking brasserie restaurant (lots of seafood) with french windows onto lovely sheltered walled garden, good breakfasts, and particularly helpful licensees and staff; high tea for younger children; disabled access; dogs welcome in ground-floor bedrooms; £5

WARHAM

Three Horseshoes *The Street, Warham, Wells-next-the-Sea, Norfolk NR23 1NL (01328) 710547* £**52**; 5 rms, one with own bthrm. Basic but cheerful local with marvellously unspoilt traditional atmosphere in its three friendly gaslit rooms, simple furnishings, a log fire, very tasty generous bar food, decent wines, home-made lemonade, and very well kept real ales; bedrooms are in the Old Post Office adjoining the pub, with lots of beams and a residents' lounge dominated by an inglenook fireplace; cl 25-26 Dec; no children; dogs welcome

WINTERTON-ON-SEA

Fishermans Return *The Lane, Winterton-on-Sea, Great Yarmouth, Norfolk NR29 4BN (01493) 393305* £**70**; 3 rms reached by a tiny staircase. Traditional 300-year-old pub in quiet village, close to the beach, with warmly welcoming and helpful owners, a relaxed lounge bar with well kept real ales, open fire, good home-made food inc fresh fish (fine crabs in season), enjoyable breakfasts, and sheltered garden with children's play equipment; dogs welcome

Northamptonshire

Dog Friendly Pubs

CRICK
Red Lion *1 mile from M1 junction 18; A428*
You can't help but be impressed by the price of the generous helpings of good home-cooked lunchtime food at this pretty stone and thatched pub: sandwiches, and straightforward hearty main courses such as chicken and mushroom pie, plaice or vegetable pancake rolls. Prices go up a little in the evening when they do a wider range of dishes that might include wild mushroom lasagne, stuffed salmon fillet, roast duck and steaks; puddings such as lemon meringue pie, and a Sunday roast. Service is quick and friendly. The cosy low-ceilinged bar is relaxed and welcoming, with lots of comfortable seating, some rare old horsebrasses, pictures of the pub in the days before it was surrounded by industrial estates, and a tiny log stove in a big inglenook. The snug is no smoking. Four well kept beers on handpump include Greene King Old Speckled Hen, Hook Norton Best, Marstons Pedigree and Websters Yorkshire. There are a few picnic-sets under cocktail parasols on grass by the car park, and in summer you can eat on the terrace in the old coachyard, which is sheltered by a Perspex roof; lots of pretty hanging baskets.
Wellington ~ Lease Tom and Paul Marks ~ Real ale ~ Bar food (12-2, 6.30-9; not Sun evening) ~ (01788) 822342 ~ Children welcome lunchtimes only ~ Dogs welcome ~ Open 11-2.30, 6.15-11; 12-3, 7-10.30 Sun

FARTHINGSTONE
Kings Arms *Off A5 SE of Daventry; village signposted from Litchborough on former B4525 (now declassified)*
The handsome gargoyled stone exterior of this traditional little 18th-c country pub is nicely weathered, and very pretty in summer when the hanging baskets are at their best, and the tranquil terrace is charmingly decorated with flower and herb pots and plant-filled painted tractor tyres; the garden has a new pond. The village is picturesque, and there are good walks including the Knightley Way. Inside, there's plenty of character in the timelessly intimate flagstoned bar which has a huge log fire, comfortable homely sofas and armchairs near the entrance, whisky-water jugs hanging

from oak beams, and lots of pictures and decorative plates on the walls. A games room at the far end has darts, dominoes, cribbage, table skittles and board games. Hook Norton is well kept on handpump alongside a couple of guests such as Hop Back Crop Circle and Youngs, the short wine list is quite decent, and they have a few country wines; the outside gents' has an interesting newspaper-influenced décor. It's worth ringing ahead to check the limited opening and food serving times noted below as the licensees are sometimes away. Listed on a blackboard, dishes might include steak, ale and kidney filled yorkshire pudding, british cheese platter and scottish fish platter. They also retail a few carefully sourced food items, such as cheese, wine and olive oil.

Free house ~ Licensees Paul and Denise Egerton ~ Real ale ~ Bar food (Sat, Sun lunchtime only) ~ No credit cards ~ (01327) 361604 ~ Children welcome ~ Dogs welcome ~ Open 7-11; 12-3, 7(9 Sun)-11 Sat; closed weekday lunchtimes and Mon, Weds evenings

FOTHERINGHAY

Falcon *Village signposted off A605 on Peterborough side of Oundle*

Drinkers and diners experience an equally warm welcome at this comfortably civilised pub. The buzz of contented conversation fills the neatly kept little bar, which has cushioned slatback armchairs and bucket chairs, good winter log fires in a stone fireplace, and fresh flower arrangements. The no smoking conservatory restaurant is pretty, and if the weather's nice the attractively planted garden is particularly enjoyable. A very good range of drinks includes well kept Adnams and Greene King IPA on handpump, alongside a guest, usually from Nethergate or Potton, good wines with about 15 (including champagne) by the glass, organic cordials, and fresh orange juice. Locals gather in the much smaller tap bar, which has darts. The main draw though is the very well presented, inventive food from the seasonally changing bar menu. It's not cheap, but is worth the money, particularly the very good two-course bargain lunch menu (not Sunday): crispy duck spring rolls with spiced coleslaw, warm spicy salad of chick peas, garlic, roast red onions, peppers and spinach, calves liver steak with red wine shallot sauce and puddings such as puff pastry wrapped banana with toffee crunch ice-cream and hot chocolate sauce. The vast church behind is worth a visit, and the ruins of Fotheringhay Castle, where Mary Queen of Scots was executed, are not far away.

Free house ~ Licensees Ray Smikle and John Hoskins ~ Real ale ~ Bar food (12-2, 6.30-9.30) ~ Restaurant ~ (01832) 226254 ~ Children welcome ~ Dogs allowed in bar ~ Open 12-3, 6-11(6.30-10.30 Sun)

OUNDLE

Ship *West Street*

The constant comings and goings of local characters and buzz of happy chat fill the rooms of this easy-going community pub. Comfortably battered at the edges, it's a nice old building, made special by the friendly smiling service. The licensees have an interest in real ale so make an effort to source interesting and quickly rotated guest beers from brewers such as Abbeydale and Glentworth, which are then well kept alongside Bass and Oakham JHB, and a good range of malt whiskies. Enjoyable bar food in generous helpings is home-made where possible, and might include steak in ale pie, lemon chicken, stilton burger, and puddings. The heavily beamed lounge bar is made up of three rooms that lead off the central corridor, one of them no smoking at lunchtime. Up by the street there's a mix of leather and other seats, with sturdy tables and a log fire in a stone inglenook, and down one end a charming little panelled snug has button-back leather seats built in around it. The wood-floored public side has darts, dominoes, fruit machine and a jukebox. The friendly black and white pub cat you might see lounging around is called Midnight. The wooden tables and chairs out on the series of small sunny but sheltered terraces are lit at night.

Free house ~ Licensees Andrew and Robert Langridge ~ Real ale ~ Bar food (12-3, 7-9) ~ (01832) 273918 ~ Dogs welcome ~ Jazz last Sun in month ~ Open 11-11; 12-10.30 Sun ~ Bedrooms: £25(£30S)/£50S(£60B)

Dog Friendly Hotels, B&Bs and Farms

BADBY
Windmill *Main St, Badby, Daventry, Northamptonshire NN11 3AN (01327) 702363* £**72.50**, plus special breaks; 10 rms. Carefully modernised and warmly welcoming thatched stone inn with beams, flagstones and huge inglenook fireplace in front bar, a cosy comfortable lounge, a relaxed and civilised atmosphere, good generously served bar and restaurant food, and decent wines; fine views of the pretty village from car park; disabled access; dogs welcome

CRANFORD
Dairy Farm *12 St Andrews Lane, Cranford, Kettering, Northamptonshire NN14 4AQ (01536) 330273* £**50**; 4 comfortable rms. Charming 17th-c manor house of great character on an arable and sheep farm, with oak beams and inglenook fireplaces, good homely cooking using home-grown fruit and vegetables, kind, attentive owners, and garden with charming summer house and ancient dovecote; no smoking; cl Christmas; partial disabled access; dogs in annexe

DAVENTRY
Fawsley Hall *Fawsley, Daventry, Northamptonshire NN11 3BA (01327) 892000* £**190**; 43 fine rms. Lovely Tudor hotel with Georgian and Victorian additions set in quiet gardens designed by Capability Brown; smart, beautifully furnished antique-filled reception rooms with impressive décor, open fires, a Great Hall for afternoon tea, excellent food in the no smoking restaurant based in the original Tudor kitchens, and health and beauty treatment rooms; tennis, gym, putting green, and croquet; dogs welcome in bedrooms

OLD

Wold Farm *Harrington Rd, Old, Northamptonshire NN6 9RJ (01604) 781258* £60; 5 rms. No smoking 18th-c farmhouse in a quiet village, with spacious interesting rooms, antiques and fine china, hearty breakfasts in the beamed dining room, attentive welcoming owners, snooker table, and two pretty gardens; dogs welcome in bedrooms; £2

Northumbria

(County Durham, Northumberland and Tyneside)

Dog Friendly Pubs

BLANCHLAND
Lord Crewe Arms *B6306 S of Hexham*
Dating back to the 13th c, when the Premonstratensians built this remote village robustly enough to resist most border raiding parties, this fine inn is still separated from the rest of the world by several miles of moors, rabbits and sheep. Originally part of the monastery guest house, and then home to several distinguished families after the Dissolution in 1536, its tremendous age is evident everywhere. The narrow bar is housed in an unusual stone barrel-vaulted crypt, its curving walls being up to eight feet thick in some places. Plush stools are lined along the bar counter. Upstairs, the Derwent Room has low beams, old settles, and sepia photographs on its walls, and the Hilyard Room has a massive 13th-c fireplace once used as a hiding place by the Jacobite Tom Forster (part of the family who had owned the building before it was sold in 1704 to the formidable Lord Crewe, Bishop of Durham). Bar food includes filled rolls, wild mushrooms in creamy sauce, cumberland sausage with black pudding and mash, smoked salmon, prawn and tuna salad, and puddings; children's meals. Well kept Wylam Gold Tankard on handpump. The lovely walled garden was formerly the cloisters. *Free house ~ Licensees A Todd, Peter Gingell and Ian Press, Lindsey Sands ~ Real ale ~ Bar food ~ Restaurant ~ (01434) 675251 ~ Children welcome ~ Dogs allowed in bar and bedrooms ~ Open 11-11.30; 12-10.30 Sun ~ Bedrooms: £80B/£120B*

CARTERWAY HEADS
Manor House Inn *A68 just N of B6278, near Derwent Reservoir*
Superbly run by welcoming licensees, this bustling slate-roofed stone house continues to impress readers with its very good food, and they've now opened a deli, where you can buy local produce, as well as chutneys, puddings and ice-cream made in the kitchens. The delicious food is served in generous helpings, and might include locally smoked kippers or crayfish and mushroom crêpes, sausage, black pudding and mushrooms with bubble

and squeak; mouth-watering puddings and a local cheese platter; smiling service by the helpful young staff. There are good views from the partly no smoking restaurant. The locals' bar has an original boarded ceiling, pine tables, chairs and stools, old oak pews, and a mahogany counter. The comfortable lounge bar has a woodburning stove, and picture windows give fine views over moorland pastures; darts, dominoes, TV and piped music (only in the bar). They've around 70 malt whiskies to choose from, farm cider, and decent wines (with about eight by the glass), along with well kept Courage Directors, Theakstons Best, Charles Wells Bombardier and a guest from a local brewer such as Mordue on handpump. There are rustic tables out on a small side terrace and lawn; great views. Good breakfasts. *Free house ~ Licensees Moira and Chris Brown ~ Real ale ~ Bar food (12-9.30(9 Sun)) ~ Restaurant ~ (01207) 255268 ~ Children in eating area of bar and restaurant ~ Dogs allowed in bar ~ Open 11-11; 12-10.30 Sun; closed 25 Dec evening ~ Bedrooms: £38B/£60B*

NEWTON-BY-THE-SEA

Ship *Village signposted off B1339 N of Alnwick; Low Newton – paid parking 200 metres up road on right, just before village (none in village)*
Tucked into the top corner of a National Trust courtyard of low white-painted stone cottages, this charmingly simple refuge looks down over the sloping grassy square to the broad beach, and beyond to off-shore rocks packed with seabirds and sometimes seals. The plainly furnished bare-boards bar on the right has nautical charts on its dark pink walls, beams and hop bines. Another simple room on the left has some bright modern pictures on stripped stone walls, and a woodburning stove in its stone fireplace. It's very quiet here in winter (when opening times are complicated), when they have just one or two real ales including Black Sheep. In contrast, queues can quickly build up on hot summer days, when the beer range extends to two or three guests from local brewers such as Border, Mordue and Wylam; also decent wines, an espresso machine (colourful coffee cups, good hot chocolate), and good soft drinks. Made with fresh local ingredients, enjoyable lunchtime snacks could include local crab sandwiches, warm ciabattas with enterprising fillings, fishcakes and salad; while in the evening (when you must book), dishes might be venison rump steak, scallops, or local lobster (from June to October). Out in the corner of the square are some tables among pots of flowers, with picnic-sets over on the grass. *Free house ~ Licensee Christine Forsyth ~ Real ale ~ Bar food (please ring) ~ No credit cards ~ (01665) 576262 ~ Children welcome ~ Dogs welcome ~ Open all day in summer hols, otherwise please ring*

WELDON BRIDGE

Anglers Arms *B6344, just off A697; village signposted with Rothbury off A1 N of Morpeth*
The obliging landlord and his wife, and the friendly young staff go out of their way to make sure that visitors enjoy coming to this substantial hotel. Nicely lit and comfortable, the traditional turkey-carpeted bar is divided

into two parts: cream walls on the right, and oak panelling and some shiny black beams hung with copper pans on the left, with a grandfather clock and sofa by the coal fire, staffordshire cats and other antique ornaments on its mantelpiece, old fishing and other country prints, some in heavy gilt frames, a profusion of other fishing memorabilia, and some taxidermy. Some of the tables are lower than you'd expect for eating, but their chairs have short legs to match – different, and rather engaging. The no smoking side restaurant in a former railway dining car is more formal but light and airy, with crisp white linen and a pink carpet. Make sure you're hungry if you eat here – the enjoyable bar food comes in huge portions: dishes might include steak and ale pie or scampi, and mixed grill; puddings such as strawberry pavlova. Timothy Taylors Landlord is well kept on handpump alongside a couple of guests such as Black Sheep Bitter and Charles Wells Bombardier, also decent wines and an espresso machine; there may be almost imperceptible piped music. There are tables in the attractive garden with a good play area; they have rights to fishing on a mile of the River Coquet just across the road.
Free house ~ Licensee John Young ~ Real ale ~ Bar food ~ Restaurant ~ (01665) 570271 ~ Children welcome ~ Dogs allowed in bedrooms ~ Open 11-3, 6-11; 12-3, 6-10.30 Sun ~ Bedrooms: £35S/£55S

Dog Friendly Hotels, B&Bs and Farms

CHATTON
Old Manse *New Rd, Chatton, Alnwick, Northumberland NE66 5PU (01668) 215343* £64; 2 pretty rms. Down a sweeping drive this quietly set house has a relaxing lounge, super breakfasts and afternoon tea in elegant dining room (or on the terrace), and flower-filled back garden with summer house; free fishing (equipment available), lots of walks, nearby cycle hire, and riding; children over 12; dogs welcome in bedrooms

CHOLLERFORD
George *Chollerford, Hexham, Northumberland NE46 4EW (01434) 681611* £110, plus special breaks; 47 well equipped rms. Quiet hotel with fine gardens sloping down to the river, and the 17th-c bridge over North Tyne visible from the candlelit restaurant; kind service; swimming pool and leisure club; fishing, putting green, and mountain bike hire; limited disabled access; dogs welcome in two bedrooms only

CORNHILL-ON-TWEED
Tillmouth Park *Cornhill-on-Tweed, Northumberland TD12 4UU (01890) 882255* £140, plus special breaks; 14 spacious, pretty rms with period furniture. Solid stone-built country house in 15 acres of parkland, with comfortable relaxing lounges, open fires, a galleried hall, good food in bistro or restaurant, and a carefully chosen wine list; fishing, nearby golf, and shooting; lots to do nearby; cl 2 wks Feb; dogs welcome in bedrooms

CROOKHAM

Coach House *Crookham, Cornhill-on-Tweed, Northumberland TD12 4TD* *(01890) 820293* £**45**; 10 individual rms with fresh flowers and nice views, 8 with own bthrm. 17th-c farm buildings around a sunny courtyard, with helpful and friendly staff, an airy beamed lounge with comfortable sofas and big arched windows, good breakfasts with home-made preserves (which you can also take home), afternoon tea, and enjoyable dinners using local vegetables; lots to do nearby; good disabled access; dogs welcome in bedrooms

GATESHEAD

Eslington Villa *8 Station Rd, Low Fell, Gateshead, Tyne & Wear NE9 6DR* *(0191) 487 6017* £**84.50**, plus wknd breaks; 18 rms. Comfortable, extended Edwardian house in quiet residential area with some original features, a lounge with comfortably modern furniture and bay windows overlooking garden, good food in conservatory restaurant, and a friendly atmosphere; cl 4 days over Christmas; disabled access; dogs welcome in bedrooms

GRETA BRIDGE

Morritt Arms *Greta Bridge, Barnard Castle, County Durham DL12 9SE* *(01833) 627232* £**87.50**, plus special breaks; 23 rms. Smart, old-fashioned coaching inn where Dickens stayed in 1838 to research for *Nicholas Nickleby* – one of the interesting bars has a colourful Dickensian mural; comfortable lounges, fresh flowers, good open fires, and pleasant garden; coarse fishing; pets allowed; attractive garden with children's play area; disabled access; dogs in bedrooms, bar and lounge

HEADLAM

Headlam Hall *Headlam, Darlington, County Durham DL2 3HA (01325)* *730238* £**90**, plus special breaks; 34 pretty rms, in the main house and adjacent coach house. Peaceful Jacobean mansion in four acres of carefully kept gardens with a little trout lake, tennis court, and croquet lawn; elegant rooms, a fine carved oak fireplace in the main hall, stylish food in the four individually decorated rooms of the restaurant, and courteous staff; indoor swimming pool, snooker and sauna, and gym; cl 24-26 Dec; disabled access; dogs welcome in ground-floor coach house bedrooms

LONGFRAMLINGTON

Embleton Hall *Longframlington, Morpeth, Northumberland NE65 8DT* *(01665) 570249* £**95**; 13 comfortable, pretty and individually decorated rms. Charming hotel in lovely grounds surrounded by fine countryside, with a particularly friendly relaxed atmosphere and courteous staff; neat little bar, elegant lounge, log fires, excellent value bar meals, and very good food in the attractive dining room; disabled access; dogs welcome in bedrooms

LONGHORSLEY

Linden Hall *Longhorsley, Morpeth, Northumberland NE65 8XF (01670)*
516611 **£121**, plus special breaks; 50 individually decorated rms. Georgian
hotel in 450 acres of landscaped park with clay pigeon shooting, mountain
biking (bike hire available), 18-hole golf course, pitch and putt, croquet,
lots of leisure facilities inc a swimming pool, and health and beauty
treatments; pubby bar, elegant drawing room, and good food in attractive
restaurant; children in main restaurant early evening only; disabled access;
dogs welcome in two bedrooms only

NEWCASTLE UPON TYNE

Malmaison *Quayside, Newcastle upon Tyne, Tyne & Wear NE1 3DX (0191)*
245 5000 **£154.50**; 116 individually decorated and well equipped rms. In
a former Co-op warehouse and overlooking the river, this stylish hotel
(part of a small chain) is boldly decorated throughout, with contemporary
furniture and artwork, genuinely friendly staff, modern cooking in
fashionable brasserie, and decent breakfasts; disabled access; dogs welcome
in bedrooms; £10

ROMALDKIRK

Rose & Crown *Romaldkirk, Barnard Castle, County Durham DL12 9EB*
(01833) 650213 **£124**, plus special breaks; 12 rms – those in the main
house have lots of character. Smart and interesting old coaching inn by
green of delightful Teesdale village, with Jacobean oak settle, log fire, old
black and white photographs, and lots of brass in the beamed traditional
bar; cosy residents' lounge, very good imaginative food in bar and fine oak-
panelled restaurant, and well kept real ales and wines; cl Christmas; disabled
access; dogs welcome in bedrooms

STANNERSBURN

Pheasant *Stannersburn, Hexham, Northumberland NE48 1DD (01434)*
240382 **£70**, plus special breaks; 8 rms. Beautifully located unpretentious
17th-c stone inn close to Kielder Water and its quiet forests; traditional,
comfortable lounge, simple public bar, a happy mix of customers, good
food inc excellent fresh veg and enjoyable Sun lunch, well kept real ales, a
fine choice of malts, good welcoming service, and nice breakfasts; picnic-
sets in streamside garden; cl Mon/Tues during Nov-Mar; disabled access;
dogs welcome in bedrooms by arrangement

Nottinghamshire

Dog Friendly Pubs

CAUNTON
Caunton Beck *Main Street; village signposted off A616 Newark—Ollerton*
Almost new, but not new-looking this delightfully civilised dining pub was reconstructed using original timbers and reclaimed oak, around the skeleton of the old Hole Arms. Scrubbed pine tables, clever lighting, an open fire and country-kitchen chairs, low beams and rag-finished paintwork in a spacious interior make for a relaxed atmosphere. With lots of flowers and plants in summer, the terrace is a nice place to sit when the weather is fine. Its main focus is on the good well presented (though not cheap) food, which is served all day. As well as delicious sandwiches and a hearty english breakfast, the fairly elaborate monthly changing menu might include oatmeal crusted sardines with truffle, wilted rocket and parmesan, lemon and thyme chicken breast, and puddings such as orange pannacotta or chocolate brownie with maple syrup. They also do reasonably priced two- and three-course set menus (not Saturday evenings or lunchtime Sunday); no smoking restaurant. About half the wines on the very good wine list are available by the glass, and they've well kept Greene King Ruddles Best, Springhead, Marstons Pedigree and a guest such as Castle Rock on handpump; also espresso coffee. Service is pleasant and attentive; daily papers and magazines, no music.
Free house ~ Licensees Julie Allwood and Toby Hope ~ Real ale ~ Bar food (8am-10.30pm) ~ Restaurant ~ (01636) 636793 ~ Children in eating area of bar and restaurant ~ Dogs allowed in bar ~ Open 8am-12 midnight

HALAM
Waggon & Horses *Off A612 in Southwell centre, via Halam Road*
This heavily oak-beamed dining pub is well liked for its wide choice of enjoyable and often inventive food: lunchtime rolls or baked potatoes with unusual fillings; starters such as wild mushroom and fennel soup or fried squid, and main courses such as broad bean, cherry tomato and rocket risotto, and rib-eye steak topped with stilton. The bright and cheery open-plan area is well divided into smallish sections (an appealing black iron screen dividing off the no smoking part is made up of tiny african-style

figures of people and animals). Good sturdy high-back rush-seat dining chairs are set around a mix of solid mainly stripped tables, there are various wall seats, smaller chairs and the odd stout settle too, with lots of pictures ranging from kitten prints to Spy cricketer caricatures on walls painted cream, brick red and coffee; candles throughout give a pleasant night-time glow. Well kept Thwaites Original Bitter, Thoroughbred and Lancaster Bomber well kept on handpump; piped jazz. Out past a piano and grandfather clock in the lobby are a few roadside picnic-sets by the pretty window boxes.

Thwaites ~ Tenants Rebecca and William White ~ Real ale ~ Bar food (12-2.30, 6-9.30; not Sun evening) ~ Restaurant ~ (01636) 813109/816228 ~ Children welcome ~ Dogs welcome ~ Open 12-3, 5.30-11; 12-11 Sat; 12-10.30 Sun

LAXTON
Dovecote *Signposted off A6075 E of Ollerton*
You will need to book a table if you want to eat at this very welcoming red-brick free house, which manages to maintain a pubby atmosphere, despite the popularity of the food. The very friendly courteous service, buzzing atmosphere and honestly priced enjoyable food are what make it such an agreeable place – and it's usefully close to the A1. Served in big helpings, bar food includes steak and kidney pie, mushroom stroganoff, and sweet and sour battered chicken, with specials such as bass stuffed with prawns. The puddings are made by Aunty Mary, the landlord's aunt, who lives in the village. The central lounge has dark wheelback chairs and tables on wooden floors, and a coal-effect gas fire. This opens through a small bay (the former entrance) into a carpeted no smoking dining area. Around the other side, another little lounge leads through to a pool room with darts, fruit machine, pool, dominoes and piped music. They have well kept Marstons Pedigree and a couple of guests from brewers such as Charles Wells and Wychwood on handpump and around 10 wines by the glass. There are wooden tables and chairs on a small front terrace by a sloping garden, which has a disused white dovecote. As well as the two bedrooms, they have a site and facilities for six caravans. The pub stands next to three huge medieval open fields as Laxton is one of the few places in the country still farmed using the traditional open field system. Every year in the third week of June the grass is auctioned for haymaking, and anyone who lives in the parish is entitled to a bid – and a drink. You can find out more at the visitor centre behind the pub.

Free house ~ Licensees Stephen and Betty Shepherd ~ Real ale ~ Bar food (12-2, 6.30(7 Sun in winter)-9) ~ Restaurant ~ (01777) 871586 ~ Children in eating area of bar and restaurant ~ Dogs allowed in bar ~ Open 11.30-3, 6.30(6 Sat, 7 winter Sun)-11.30(10.30 Sun) ~ Bedrooms: £35B/£50B

Dog Friendly Hotels, B&Bs and Farms

LANGAR
Langar Hall *Church Lane, Langar, Nottingham, Nottinghamshire NG13 9HG (01949) 860559* £**130**, plus special breaks; 10 lovely, nicely old-fashioned rms, some in wing and courtyard as well. Fine country house in spacious grounds with family portraits in the hall and up the stairs, a friendly homely drawing room, library, small modern bar, pillared dining hall, antiques and fresh flowers, a relaxed informal atmosphere, lively, helpful owner and willing young staff, and very good food; dogs welcome in some bedrooms; £10

NOTTINGHAM
Harts *Standard Hill, Park Row, Nottingham, Nottinghamshire NG1 6FN (0115) 988 1900* £**142**; 32 well appointed quiet rms with fine views. Adjacent to the well-known restaurant of the same name, this is a smart and stylish purpose-built hotel in a traffic-free cul-de-sac on the site of the city's medieval castle; charming, friendly staff, lounge and snack bar, small exercise room, and private gardens; disabled access; dogs welcome in bedrooms; £5

NOTTINGHAM
Lace Market *29-31 High Pavement, Nottingham, Nottinghamshire NG1 1HE (0115) 852 3232* £**139**, plus special breaks; 42 modern, comfortable rms. Next to a lovely church, this Georgian town house has a relaxed atmosphere, friendly young staff, a convivial bar with daily papers, wood-strip floors and strong but subtle colours, good brasserie-style food in contemporary restaurant, and enjoyable breakfasts; dogs welcome in bedrooms; £20

SOUTHWELL
Old Forge *Burgage Lane, Southwell, Nottinghamshire NG25 0ER (01636) 812809* £**76**, plus special breaks; 4 rms. 200-year-old former blacksmith's house with welcoming owner, interesting furnishings, super breakfasts in conservatory overlooking the Minster, and pretty terrace; limited disabled access; dogs welcome in bedrooms; £2

Oxfordshire

Dog Friendly Pubs

FIFIELD
Merrymouth *A424 Burford—Stow*
Friendly and family run, this 13th-c country inn is popular for its good food. The simple but comfortably furnished L-shaped bar has nice bay-window seats, flagstones, horsebrasses and antique bottles hanging from low beams, some walls stripped back to the old masonry, and an open fire in winter. Except for five tables in the bar, the pub is no smoking; piped classical music. Served by efficient and attentive staff, the enjoyable bar food might include smoked mackerel pâté, creamy leek and prawn tart, cold home-baked ham, sausages with onion gravy, and rack of lamb; also daily specials such as pasta with smoked cheese and tomato sauce, and home-made puddings like raspberry marshmallow meringue. Well kept Adnams Broadside and Hook Norton Best on handpump, and decent wines. There are tables on a terrace and in the back garden (there may be a little noise from fast traffic on the road). The quaint bedrooms are well cared for. The Domesday Book mentions an inn on this site, and its name comes from the Murimuth family, who once owned the village.
Free house ~ Licensees Andrew and Timothy Flaherty ~ Real ale ~ Bar food ~ Restaurant ~ (01993) 831652 ~ Children welcome ~ Dogs welcome ~ Open 11-2.30, 6-10; 12-2.30, 7-10 Sun; closed Sun evening in winter ~ Bedrooms: £45S/£65B

HOOK NORTON
Gate Hangs High *Banbury Road; a mile N of village towards Sibford, at Banbury—Rollright crossroads*
The new courtyard garden is now open though there are still seats on the broad lawn behind this tucked-away country pub, with holly and apple trees, and fine views; the flower tubs and wall baskets are very colourful. The bedrooms in the converted barns are up and running, too; we'd be grateful for any feedback. The bar has joists in the long, low ceiling, a brick bar counter, stools and assorted chairs on the carpet, baby oil lamps on each table, a gleaming copper hood over the hearth in the inglenook fireplace, and hops over the bar counter. Well kept Hook Norton Best, Old Hooky

and Copper Ale on handpump, bottled beers, and decent wines; piped music and dominoes. Well liked bar food might include sandwiches, pork crackling with apple sauce, home-made soup, braised rabbit in cider and mustard, winter jugged hare or tuna steak with horseradish sauce, and home-made puddings such as banoffi pie; they have a good children's menu and do a two-course weekday set menu. You'll need to book for Saturday evening and Sunday lunch, in the slightly chintzy no smoking side dining extension.
Hook Norton ~ Tenant Stephen Coots-Williams ~ Real ale ~ Bar food (12.30-2.30, 6-10; all day summer Sun) ~ Restaurant ~ (01608) 737387 ~ Children in eating area of bar and restaurant ~ Dogs allowed in bar ~ Open 12-3(4 Sat), 6-11.30; 12-10.30 Sun; 12-5, 7-10.30 Sun in winter ~ Bedrooms: £40B/£60B

KELMSCOTT
Plough *NW of Faringdon, off A417 or A4095*
Not far from the Thames and the former summer home of William Morris, this is a rather pretty little inn. The small traditional beamed front bar has ancient flagstones and stripped stone walls, a good log fire, and the relaxed chatty feel of a real village pub with a good mix of customers. The pleasant dining area has attractively plain and solid furnishings, and bar food (often served in small and large helpings) such as roast ham and eggs, home-made lasagne, vegetable stir-fry or ploughman's, devilled kidneys and T-bone steak; evening choices may include home-made chicken and duck pâté with red onion jam, grilled tiger prawns, or roast duck breast with carrot and ginger purée; also puddings like baked apple pie. Well kept Hook Norton Best and maybe Nethergate Old Growler or Timothy Taylors Landlord on handpump, and Black Rat farm cider; piped music, pool, TV and darts. The garden is pretty, with seats among plantings of unusual flowers and aunt sally, and there are picnic-sets under cocktail parasols out in front. The Oxfordshire cycleway runs close by.
Free house ~ Licensee Martin Platt ~ Real ale ~ Bar food (12-2.30, 7-9; all day weekends) ~ Restaurant ~ (01367) 253543 ~ Children in eating area of bar and restaurant ~ Dogs allowed in bar ~ Live entertainment Sat evening ~ Open 11-11; 12-10.30 Sun; closed Mon ~ Bedrooms: £45S/£75B

LEWKNOR
Olde Leathern Bottel *Under a mile from M40 junction 6; just off B4009 towards Watlington*
This pleasant country pub is often used as a break from the M40 and so can get busy at lunchtimes. The two bar rooms have heavy beams in the low ceilings, rustic furnishings, open fires, and an understated décor of old beer taps and the like. The no smoking family room is separated only by standing timbers, so you won't feel segregated from the rest of the pub. Well liked bar food includes lunchtime filled baguettes, ham and eggs or all-day breakfast, and daily specials such as beef and Guinness pie or chicken and bacon caesar salad, with home-made puddings such as apple and mincemeat pie. Well kept Brakspears Bitter and Special on handpump, and eight wines by the glass. The attractive sizeable garden has plenty of picnic-sets under parasols, and a children's play area.

Brakspears ~ Tenant L S Gordon ~ Real ale ~ Bar food (12-2, 7-9.30; 12-2, 6-10 Fri/Sat) ~ (01844) 351482 ~ Children in restaurant and family room ~ Dogs welcome ~ Open 11-2.30(3 Sat), 6-11; 12-3, 7-10.30 Sun

MAIDENSGROVE

Five Horseshoes *W of village, which is signposted from B480 and B481; OS Sheet 175 map reference 711890*
This is a friendly country dining pub set on a lovely common high up in the Chiltern beechwoods and close to good local walks. The rambling main bar is furnished with mostly modern wheelback chairs around stripped wooden tables (though there are some attractive older seats and a big baluster-leg table), and there's a proper log fire in winter; the low ceiling in the main area is covered in banknotes from all over the world, mainly donated by customers. Enjoyable bar food under the new licensee includes baked filo parcel of goats cheese with red onion marmalade, rustic salad of smoked tuna, crab and papaya, chilli and garlic sausages with parsley mash and caramelised onion gravy, thai spiced vegetables with coriander rice, medallions of pork fillet cooked in a white stilton and apricot sauce, and rosemary roasted duck breast; there's also a barbecue menu with dishes such as minted lamb and mozzarella burger. The airy dining conservatory is no smoking. Well kept Brakspears Bitter, Special and a seasonal ale on handpump, and a good wine list. The three areas outside have a peaceful wooded outlook, and you often see red kites here.
Brakspears ~ Tenant Greg Fitzpatrick ~ Real ale ~ Bar food (not winter Sun evening) ~ Restaurant ~ (01491) 641282 ~ Children welcome ~ Dogs allowed in bar ~ Open 11-3, 6-11; 11-11 Sat; 12-10.30 Sun; 11-3, 6-11 Sat in winter; 12-6 Sun in winter

STANTON ST JOHN

Star *Pub signposted off B4027, in Middle Lane; village is signposted off A40 heading E of Oxford (heading W, you have to go to the Oxford ring road roundabout and take unclassified road signposted to Stanton St John, Forest Hill etc)*
This pleasant old pub has an attractive extension on a level with the car park. There are old-fashioned dining chairs, an interesting mix of dark oak and elm tables, rugs on flagstones, pairs of bookshelves on each side of an attractive inglenook fireplace (good blazing fires in winter), shelves of good pewter, terracotta-coloured walls with a portrait in oils, and a stuffed ermine; down a flight of stairs are little low-beamed rooms – one has ancient brick flooring tiles and the other quite close-set tables. Decent bar food includes sandwiches, chicken liver pâté, venison pie or moussaka, red thai chicken curry, and fillet of beef wellington, with puddings such as spotted dick. Well kept Wadworths IPA and 6X on handpump. The rather straightforward family room and conservatory are no smoking; piped music, darts, shove-ha'penny and dominoes. The walled garden has seats among the rockeries and children's play equipment.
Wadworths ~ Tenant Michael Urwin ~ Real ale ~ Bar food (not Sun evening) ~ No credit cards ~ (01865) 351277 ~ Children in family room ~ Dogs welcome ~ Open 11-2.30, 6.30-11; 12-2.30, 7-10.30 Sun

SWALCLIFFE
Stags Head *Bakers Lane, just off B4035*
Behind this charmingly picturesque thatched pub is a series of neatly terraced gardens with palm trees, a small fountain, several tables under a pergola, and a sensibly segregated play area. Inside, the low-beamed bar has a big woodburning stove at one end, a standard lamp beside it, and high-backed wooden pews and cushioned seats along the stone walls. Lots of little jugs hang from the ceiling, and the 'head' of a master of foxhounds rather than the fox. A lighter room has lots more tables, and a tiled fireplace, along with newspapers to read, plenty of books, and lists of various local events and activities; at night all the tables have candles. Half the pub is no smoking. Bar food includes duck and green peppercorn terrine with apricot dressing, chicken and bacon caesar salad, prawn stir-fry with egg noodles, mediterranean pork ribs, and specials like chicken, leek and spring onion risotto; children's menu as well. Well kept Black Sheep, Brakspears Bitter, and Wye Valley St George's Ale on handpump, and several wines by the glass; piped easy listening music, shove-ha'penny, cribbage, dominoes, and Tuesday evening bridge. A letting bedroom has its own kitchenette. They've two cats, a dog, a couple of chickens and two ducks. More reports please.
Free house ~ Licensees Ian and Julia Kingsford ~ Real ale ~ Bar food (12-2.15, 7-9.30; 12-4 Sun; not Sun evening, Mon, Tues lunchtime) ~ Restaurant ~ (01295) 780232 ~ Children welcome ~ Dogs welcome ~ Open 11-2.30(3 Sat), 6.30-11; 12-5 Sun; closed Sun evening, all day Mon, Tues lunchtime ~ Bedrooms: £35S/£60S

SWINBROOK
Swan *Back road a mile N of A40, 2 miles E of Burford*
This 17th-c country pub is in a lovely spot close to the River Windrush and its bridge, and there are old-fashioned benches outside by the fuchsia hedge. The tiny interior is cosy, peaceful and dimly lit, with simple antique furnishings and a woodburning stove in the flagstoned tap room and the back bar; darts, dominoes and cribbage. Well kept Archers Village Bitter, Greene King IPA and Old Speckled Hen, and Wadworths 6X on handpump, a choice of good coffees and herbal teas. Tasty bar food at lunchtime includes home-made soup, pasta with seafood or with sun-dried tomatoes and parmesan, home-made steak and kidney pie, and chicken filled with brie, wrapped in bacon and topped with pesto sauce; in the evening, there might be a starter for two people with smoked salmon, whitebait, breaded camembert, onion rings and garlic bread, and pork tenderloin with apricot, sage and cashew nut pâté; also puddings such as home-made apple crumble or chocolate fudge cake.
Free house ~ Licensee Bob Shepherd ~ Real ale ~ Bar food (not Sun evening) ~ (01993) 822165 ~ Well behaved children welcome away from bar ~ Dogs allowed in bar ~ Open 11.30-3, 6.30-11; 12-3, 7-10.30 Sun; closed 25 Dec

TADPOLE BRIDGE

Trout *Back road Bampton—Buckland, 4 miles NE of Faringdon*

Although drinkers do drop into this bustling place, most customers come to enjoy the particularly good, imaginative food. It's also a nice place to stay with some rooms overlooking the Thames (a new suite has its own terrace and overlooks both the garden and river). The L-shaped bar has plenty of seats and some rugs on flagstones, a modern wooden bar counter with terracotta wall behind, some stripped stone, and a large stuffed trout. Friendly and efficient staff serve well kept Brakspears Bitter, Youngs Bitter and a guest beer on handpump, and there are 12 wines by the glass, home-made sloe gin, cherry plum brandy and elderflower cordial; darts, dominoes, cribbage, backgammon and piped music. As well as filled baguettes, the attractively presented dishes might include bacon and game terrine, carpaccio of tuna with rocket and parmesan, scallops with veal sweetbreads, black pudding and apple jus (a delicious dish) or tomato and black olive risotto with roasted vegetables, roast local lamb with a puy lentil and bacon casserole, roast venison (from Blenheim), and daily specials such as almond-crusted red mullet fillet. Their well hung beef is normally charolais or aberdeen angus, and they do use a lot of good local produce – some from Mr Green's father's nearby farm. The restaurant is no smoking. The well kept garden is a lovely place to sit in summer, with small fruit trees, attractive hanging baskets, and flower troughs. They sell day tickets for fishing on a two-mile stretch.

Free house ~ Licensee Chris Green ~ Real ale ~ Bar food (not Sun evening) ~ Restaurant ~ (01367) 870382 ~ Children welcome ~ Dogs welcome ~ Open 11.30-3, 6-11; 12-3 Sun; closed Sun evening; evening 25 Dec, all day 26 Dec, 31 Dec and 1 Jan, 1st wk Feb ~ Bedrooms: /£80B

Dog Friendly Hotels, B&Bs and Farms

BURFORD

Lamb *Sheep St, Burford, Oxfordshire OX18 4LR (01993) 823155 £150*, plus special breaks; 15 rms. Very attractive 500-year-old Cotswold inn with lovely restful atmosphere, spacious beamed, flagstoned and elegantly furnished lounge, classic civilised public bar, bunches of flowers on good oak and elm tables, three winter log fires, antiques, modern british food in lovely restaurant, and pretty little walled garden; disabled access; dogs welcome in bedrooms, bar and lounges; £5

CHOLSEY

Well Cottage *Caps Lane, Cholsey, Wallingford, Oxfordshire OX10 9HQ (01491) 651959 £40*; 2 neatly kept, lemon-yellow rms in garden flat overlooking courtyard. Extended old workman's cottage with pretty rose-filled garden, open fire in homely sitting room, bird prints and paintings in dining room where breakfast is taken around one big table, and plenty of places nearby for evening meals; horse riding is available as the owners have four horses; disabled access; dogs must be well behaved; £15

CLIFTON
Duke of Cumberlands Head *Clifton, Banbury, Oxfordshire OX15 0PE (01869) 338534* £**85**; 6 rms in sympathetic extension. Pretty thatched 17th-c stone inn with a friendly atmosphere, very good food in bar and no smoking back restaurant, enjoyable breakfasts, log fire, well kept beers and wines, and helpful service; tables in garden; dogs welcome

KINGHAM
Mill House *Station Rd, Kingham, Chipping Norton, Oxfordshire OX7 6UH (01608) 658188* £**120**, plus special breaks; 23 good rms with country views. Carefully renovated 17th-c flour mill in seven acres with trout stream; comfortable spacious lounge, open log fire in lounge bar, original features such as two bread ovens, a cosy popular restaurant, and very good interesting food; disabled access; dogs welcome in bedrooms

KINGSTON BAGPUIZE
Fallowfields *Southmoor, Kingston Bagpuize, Abingdon, Oxfordshire OX13 5BH (01865) 820416* £**145**, plus special breaks; 10 rms. Delightful Gothic-style manor house with elegant, relaxing sitting rooms, open fires, imaginative food using home-grown produce in attractive conservatory dining room, courteous helpful service, and 12 acres of pretty gardens and paddocks; no smoking; lots to see nearby and plenty for children; cl 24-27 Dec; dogs in bedrooms; £5

MOULSFORD
Beetle & Wedge *Ferry Lane, Moulsford, Wallingford, Oxfordshire OX10 9JF (01491) 651381* £**185**, plus special breaks; 11 pretty rms, most with a lovely river view. Civilised riverside hotel where Jerome K Jerome wrote *Three Men in a Boat* and where H G Wells lived for a time (it was the Potwell in *The History of Mr Polly*); informal old beamed Boathouse Bar and lovely conservatory dining room (both with wonderful food – but must book), a carefully chosen wine list, open fires, fresh flowers, a riverside terrace and waterside lawn with moorings; nice walks; they are kind to families; disabled access; dogs welcome in bedrooms

OXFORD
Old Parsonage *1 Banbury Rd, Oxford OX2 6NN (01865) 310210* £**179**; 28 lovely rms. Handsome and civilised 17th-c parsonage, fairly central, with very courteous staff, good breakfasts and excellent light meals in cosy bar/restaurant; small lounge, open fires and fine paintings, and pretty little garden; they provide picnics; cl 25-27 Dec; dogs welcome in bedrooms

Randolph *Beaumont St, Oxford OX1 2LN (0870) 400 8200* £**170**, plus special breaks; 111 rms. Fine neo-gothick Victorian hotel facing the Ashmolean Museum; elegant comfortable day rooms, grand foyer, graceful restaurant with lovely plasterwork ceiling, and cellar wine bar; disabled access; dogs in bedrooms; £15

SHILLINGFORD
Shillingford Bridge Hotel *Shillingford Rd, Shillingford, Wallingford, Oxfordshire OX10 8LZ (01865) 858567* £**120**, plus special breaks; 40 rms. Riverside hotel with own river frontage, fishing and moorings, spacious comfortable bars and attractive airy restaurant (all with fine views), squash, outdoor heated swimming pool, and Sat dinner–dance; disabled access; dogs welcome away from restaurant; £7.50

SHIPTON-UNDER-WYCHWOOD
Shaven Crown *High St, Shipton-under-Wychwood, Chipping Norton, Oxfordshire OX7 6BA (01993) 830330* £**95**, plus special breaks; 8 comfortable rms. Densely beamed, ancient stone hospice built around striking medieval courtyard with seating by lily pool and roses; impressive medieval hall with a magnificent lofty ceiling, sweeping stairway and old stone walls, log fire in comfortable bar, intimate candlelit restaurant, well chosen wine list, good friendly service, warm relaxed atmosphere, and bowling green; partial disabled access; dogs welcome away from restaurant; £10

WOODSTOCK
Feathers *Market St, Woodstock, Oxfordshire OX20 1SX (01993) 812291* £**135**, plus special breaks; 20 individually decorated rms. Lovely old building with a fine relaxing drawing room and study, open fires, first-class friendly staff, a gentle atmosphere, daily changing imaginative food inc lovely puddings, and a sunny courtyard with attractive tables and chairs; dogs welcome in bedrooms and lounges

Shropshire

Dog Friendly Pubs

BRIDGES
Horseshoe *Near Ratlinghope, below the W flank of the Long Mynd*
In a picturesque streamside setting among deserted hills, this country pub (now with new licensees) is in good walking country, and handy for the Stiperstones. It's popular with walking groups, though you'll find locals here too. Warmed by a cosy fire, the down-to-earth yet comfortable bar has interesting windows, lots of pictures and toby jugs, and well kept Adnams Bitter, Bass and a changing guest such as Greene King Old Speckled Hen on handpump, and they've also farm cider. A small dining room leads off from here; winter darts and dominoes, and piped music. Tasty bar food such as local sausages, home-made steak and kidney pie, grilled trout and half a duck, with puddings such as apple pie. Tables are placed out by the little River Onny; the Long Mynd rises up behind. They have plans to turn the outbuildings into a restaurant, and maybe bedrooms. *Free house ~ Licensees Bob and Maureen Macauley ~ Real ale ~ Bar food (12-3, 6-9; 12-9 Sat/Sun) ~ (01588) 650260 ~ Children welcome ~ Dogs welcome ~ Open 11-11; 12-10.30 Sun; closed 25 Dec*

BURLTON
Burlton Inn *A528 Shrewsbury—Ellesmere, near junction with B4397*
The kind of place it's hard to tear yourself away from, this attractively restored old pub is well run by welcoming licensees. The food here is very good, and besides interesting specials such as mackerel with gooseberry and orange sauce, honey-glazed chicken breast stuffed with goats cheese, and duck stir-fry, an enticing choice of home-made bar food could include filled baguettes or baked potatoes, chicken, bacon and brie lasagne, and halibut with salmon gravadlax sauce; home-made puddings such as raspberry, pear and amaretto trifle. Readers recommend the Sunday roasts. There may be two set-time evening sittings in the restaurant. Everything seems meticulously arranged and well cared for, from the pretty flower displays in the brick fireplace or beside the neatly curtained windows, to the piles of *Country Living* and interior design magazines in the corner; there are a few sporting prints, spurs and brasses on the walls, open fires in

winter and dominoes and cribbage. French windows lead from the new garden dining room to the pleasant terrace, with its smart wooden furniture. There are eleven wines by the glass (in two sizes), and along with well kept Banks's, you'll find three continually changing guests from brewers such as Hop Back, St George's and Wye Valley. They now have disabled facilities. There are tables on a small lawn behind, with more on a strip of grass beyond the car park.

Free house ~ Licensee Gerald Bean ~ Real ale ~ Bar food (12-2, 6.30-9.45(7-9.30 Sun)) ~ Restaurant ~ (01939) 270284 ~ Well behaved children in eating area of bar and restaurant ~ Dogs welcome ~ Open 11-3, 6-11; 12-3, 7-10.30 Sun; closed bank hol Mon lunchtimes, 25-26 Dec and 1 Jan ~ Bedrooms: £50B/£80B

PICKLESCOTT
Bottle & Glass *Village signposted off A49 N of Church Stretton*

In a delightful spot below the north end of the Long Mynd, this nicely unspoilt 17th-c former farmhouse changed hands shortly before we went to press. The jovial old-school landlord is about to celebrate his 40th year in the trade, and his 30th as a licensee; he works hard to make sure everyone is happy, and on our visit effortlessly ran the bar while striking up conversations with various customers, many of whom were soon chatting to each other as if they were old friends. The nicest part of the pub is the small beamed and quarry-tiled candlelit bar, so it's good news that the lounge will be refurbished in a similar style; a third room will be opened up off the bar too, and each will have its own inglenook (logs in the huge one in the bar blaze away every day of the year). Very good home-made bar food (promptly served, in hearty helpings) might include stilton, pork and celery pâté, sausage and mash, steak, kidney and Guinness pie, fresh fish, and rack of lamb. Well kept Woods Parish and Shropshire Lad and a changing guest beer on handpump; unobtrusive piped music. After the changes are complete, around half the pub will be no smoking. Two cats and two dogs have moved with the landlords from Devon. There are a few picnic-sets in front.

Free house ~ Licensees Paul and Jo Stretton-Downes ~ Real ale ~ Bar food (12-2, 7-9; not Sun evening, or 25 Dec) ~ (01694) 751345 ~ Children in eating area of bar ~ Dogs allowed in bar ~ Open 12-2.30, 6-11

WISTANSTOW
Plough *Village signposted off A49 and A489 N of Craven Arms*

Woods beers are brewed next door to this pleasant pub, so the Woods Parish, Plough Special, Shropshire Lad and seasonal ales are very well kept on handpump (you can buy bottles of Woods beer to take away). A bonus is that the food is enjoyable too. Making good use of local suppliers, the seasonally changing menu might include local sausages with mash and onion gravy, steak and kidney suet pudding, and organic salmon with local asparagus; home-made puddings such as white chocolate rice pudding with blackcurrant sauce. On Sundays, the menu is limited to two roasts, a fish and a vegetarian option. Spotlessly kept, the pub is simply furnished with high rafters and cream walls, and a russet turkey carpet, oak or mahogany tables and chairs and welsh dressers to give the modernised bar a more homely feel. The games area has darts, pool, dominoes, fruit machine and piped music. Friendly staff serve Addlestone's and Weston's cider and about 15 wines by the glass, including a rosé. There are some tables under cocktail parasols outside.

Own brew ~ Real ale ~ Bar food (12-1.30, 6.30-8.30; not Mon, or Sun evening) ~ Restaurant ~ (01588) 673251 ~ Children in eating area of bar and family room ~ Dogs allowed in bar ~ Open 11.30-2.30, 6.30-11; 12-2.30, 7-10.30 Sun; closed Mon

Dog Friendly Hotels, B&Bs and Farms

BISHOP'S CASTLE
Castle Hotel *Market Sq, Bishop's Castle, Shropshire SY9 5BN* (01588) 638403 £70, plus special breaks; 6 spacious rms with fine views. On the site of the old castle keep, this enjoyable 17th/18th-c hotel has good fires, a relaxed and friendly atmosphere, lovely home-made food, well kept beers, and welcoming owners; crown bowling green at top of garden (available for residents); dogs by arrangement

CLUN
New House Farm *Clun, Craven Arms, Shropshire SY7 8NJ* (01588) 638314 £55; 2 rms. Remote 18th-c farmhouse near the Welsh border with plenty of surrounding hillside walks; no smoking homely rooms, packed lunches, good breakfasts, plenty of books, a country garden and peaceful farmland (which includes an Iron Age hill fort), and helpful friendly owner; cl end Nov–Easter; children over 10; dogs welcome in bedrooms by arrangement; £5; bring own bed, must be towelled down if wet

HOPTON WAFERS
Crown *Hopton Wafers, Kidderminster, Worcestershire DY14 0NB* (01299) 270372 £87.50, plus special breaks; 7 rms. Attractive creeper-covered stone inn in pleasant countryside, with interestingly furnished bar, inglenook fireplace, enjoyable food, decent house wines, beers and malt whiskies, friendly efficient service, and streamside garden; children over 12; dogs welcome in bedrooms by arrangement

KNOCKIN
Top Farmhouse *Knockin, Oswestry, Shropshire SY10 8HN* (01691) 682582 £50; 3 pretty rms. Most attractive Grade I listed black and white timbered house dating back to the 16th c, with friendly owners, lots of timbers and beams, a log fire in the restful comfortable drawing room, good

breakfasts in the large dining room, and an appealing garden; grand piano; children over 12; dogs in bedrooms

LONGVILLE
Longville Arms *Longville, Much Wenlock, Shropshire TF13 6DT (01694) 771206* £**55**; 5 comfortable rms in converted stables, with showers. Warmly friendly inn with two spacious bars, well kept real ales, a wide range of enjoyable food in the restaurant or lounge bar, superb breakfasts, and a large terrace overlooking the big children's play area; disabled access; dogs in bedrooms and in bar when food service has stopped

LUDLOW
Dinham Hall *Ludlow, Shropshire SY8 1EJ (01584) 876464* £**140**; 4 individually decorated rms, 2 in cottage. Late 18th-c manor house in quiet walled gardens opposite the ruins of Ludlow Castle, with restful lounges, open fires, and period furnishings, friendly, helpful staff, and creative french cooking in the elegant no smoking restaurant; dogs welcome in bedrooms; £7

LUDLOW
Wheatsheaf *Lower Broad St, Ludlow, Shropshire SY8 1PQ (01584) 872980* £**50**, plus special breaks; 5 comfortable oak-beamed rms with showers. Attractively furnished small 17th-c pub built into medieval town gate; traditional atmosphere, two log fires, lots of hops, timbers, and exposed stone walls, wide range of good food in bar and no smoking restaurant (super steaks), and real ales; dogs in bedrooms

NORTON
Hundred House *Bridgnorth Rd, Norton, Shifnal, Shropshire TF11 9EE (01952) 730353* £**99**, plus special breaks; 10 cottagey rms with swing and lavender-scented sheets. Carefully refurbished mainly Georgian inn with quite a sophisticated feel, neatly kept bar with old quarry-tiled floors, beamed ceilings, oak panelling and handsome fireplaces, elaborate evening meals using inn's own herbs, friendly service, good bar food, and excellent breakfasts; delightful garden; dogs in bedrooms if well behaved; £10

RHYDYCROESAU
Pen-y-Dyffryn Hall *Rhydycroesau, Oswestry, Shropshire SY10 7JD (01691) 653700* £**110**, plus special breaks; 12 rms with really helpful information packs about where to go. Handsome Georgian stone-built rectory in five acres with lovely views of the Shropshire and Welsh hills, and trout fishing, hill-walking and riding (shooting can be arranged); log fires in both comfortable lounges, good food using the best local ingredients, helpful staff, and a relaxed friendly atmosphere; children over 3; disabled access; dogs welcome away from restaurant

STREFFORD
Strefford Hall Farm *Strefford, Craven Arms, Shropshire SY7 8DE (01588) 672383* £**50**; 3 rms. No smoking Victorian stone-built farmhouse

surrounded by 360 acres of working farm; woodburner in sitting room, good breakfasts, and lots of walks; cl Christmas and New Year; disabled access; dogs welcome in bedrooms

WORFIELD
Old Vicarage *Hallon, Worfield, Bridgnorth, Shropshire WV15 5JZ (01746) 716497* £135, plus special breaks; 14 pretty rms. Restful and carefully restored Edwardian rectory in two acres; two airy conservatory-style lounges, very good interesting food in no smoking restaurant, a fine wine list, a cosseting atmosphere, and warmly friendly, helpful service; good disabled access; dogs welcome in bedrooms; £10

WREKIN
Buckatree Hall *Wrekin, Telford, Shropshire TF6 5AL (01952) 641821* £80; 62 rms, several with own balconies and many with lake views. Comfortable former hunting lodge dating from 1820, in large wooded estate at the foot of the Wrekin; extended and modernised with comfortable day rooms, enjoyable food in the Terrace Restaurant, and helpful attentive service; dogs welcome in bedrooms

WROCKWARDINE
Church Farm *Wrockwardine, Telford, Shropshire TF6 5DG (01952) 244917* £58, plus special breaks; 5 individual well equipped rms, most with own bthrm. Friendly Georgian farmhouse on very ancient site overlooking the attractive garden and church; a relaxed atmosphere, particularly good caring service, beams and log fire in lounge, and good daily changing food in traditionally furnished dining room; children over 10; dogs in certain bedrooms; £2

Somerset

Dog Friendly Pubs

ASHILL
Square & Compass *Windmill Hill; off A358 between Ilminster and Taunton; up Wood Road for 1 mile behind Stewley Cross service station; OS Sheet 193 map reference 310166*
Despite its nicely remote setting, you'll often find this unassuming country pub rather busy in the evenings with chatty locals – it's the sort of place that farmers turn up to on their tractors. There's an open fire and simple, comfortable furnishings in the bar, perhaps Beth the dog or the pub cats Daisy and Lilly, and well kept Exmoor Ale, St Austell HSD, and Windmill Hill Bitter on handpump. Generous helpings of enjoyable bar food includes daily specials such as cauliflower cheese topped with mushrooms or bacon, trio of local sausages with onion gravy, tagliatelle carbonara, and breast of duck with a port and cranberry sauce. Piped classical music at lunchtimes. There's a terrace outside and a garden with picnic-sets, views over the Blackdown Hills, and a children's play area. A new self-contained barn extension for weddings and parties has been opened in the grounds and will also act as a local arts centre.
Free house ~ Licensees Chris, Janet and Beth Slow ~ Real ale ~ Bar food (not Tues, Weds or Thurs lunchtimes) ~ (01823) 480467 ~ Children welcome ~ Dogs welcome ~ Open 12-2.30, 6.30-11; 12-2.30, 7-10.30 Sun; closed Tues, Weds and Thurs lunchtimes

BATCOMBE
Three Horseshoes *Village signposted off A359 Bruton—Frome*
As we went to press, the licensees were about to leave this honey stone pub, so we are keeping our fingers crossed that the new people will continue along the same vein. The chef is staying so there's no doubt that the good interesting food will remain quite a draw. As well as bar meals like filled ciabattas, ham and eggs and moules marinière with frites, there might be warm tart of local brie and avocado with blush tomato salsa, roast half duck with apricot and walnut stuffing, and grilled fillets of devon turbot; also puddings such as white and dark chocolate rum cappuccino mousse. The longish narrow main room has cream-painted beams and planks, local

pictures on the lightly ragged dark pink walls, built-in cushioned window seats and solid chairs around a nice mix of old tables, and a woodburning stove at one end with a big open fire at the other; there's a plain tiled room at the back on the left with more straightforward furniture. The no smoking, stripped stone dining room is pretty. Well kept Butcombe and a changing guest on handpump, 10 wines by the glass, and a dozen malt whiskies. The back terrace has picnic-sets, with more on the grass. The pub is on a quiet village lane by the church which has a very striking tower. Reports on the new regime please.

Free house ~ Licensees Charles and Claire Edmondson-Jones ~ Real ale ~ Bar food ~ Restaurant ~ (01749) 850359 ~ Children in restaurant ~ Dogs allowed in bar ~ Open 12-3, 6.30-11; 12-3, 7-10.30 Sun

BATH

Star *23 Vineyards; The Paragon (A4), junction with Guinea Lane*
An honest drinkers' pub and handy for the main shopping area, this old pub (with a new licensee) gives a strong sense of the past. It is set in a quiet steep street of undeniably handsome if well worn stone terraces, and the four (well, more like three and a half) small linked rooms are served from a single bar, separated by sombre panelling with glass inserts. They are furnished with traditional leatherette wall benches and the like – even one hard bench that the regulars call Death Row – and the lighting's dim, and not rudely interrupted by too much daylight. With no machines or music, chat's the thing here – or perhaps cribbage, dominoes, table skittles and shove-ha'penny. Particularly well kept Bass is tapped from the cask, and they have Abbey Bellringer, and guests such as Hop Back Summer Lightning, and Timothy Taylors Landlord on handpump, and quite a few malt whiskies. Filled rolls only (served throughout opening hours during the week), and Sunday lunchtime bar nibbles; friendly staff and customers. No children inside.

Punch ~ Lease Paul Waters ~ Real ale ~ Bar food (see text) ~ (01225) 425072 ~ Dogs welcome ~ Acoustic singers and folk Sun evenings ~ Open 12-2.30, 5.30-11; 12-11 Sat; 12-10.30 Sun

CHURCHILL

Crown *The Batch; in village, turn off A368 into Skinners Lane at Nelson Arms, then bear right*
Apart from the marvellous range of around 10 well kept real ales, an important part of this unspoilt little cottage's appeal to its enthusiastic supporters is its far from neat-and-clean style. The small and local stone-floored and cross-beamed room on the right has a wooden window seat, an unusually sturdy settle, and built-in wall benches; the left-hand room has a slate floor, and some steps past the big log fire in a big stone fireplace lead to more sitting space. Tapped from the cask, the real ales might include Bass, Bath SPA, Hop Back GFB and Chimera Red, Palmers Copper Ale, Gold, 200 and Tally Ho, and RCH Hewish and PG Steam. Straightforward lunchtime bar food includes good soup, sandwiches, filled baked potatoes, salads, daily specials like beef casserole, and puddings such

as well liked treacle pudding. Outside lavatories. They do get busy at weekends, especially in summer. There are garden tables at the front and a smallish back lawn, and hill views; the Mendip morris men come in summer. Good walks nearby.

Free house ~ Licensee Tim Rogers ~ Real ale ~ Bar food (12-2.30(3 weekends); not evenings) ~ No credit cards ~ (01934) 852995 ~ Children welcome ~ Dogs welcome ~ Occasional live band Sun ~ Open 12-11; 12-10.30 Sun

COMPTON MARTIN
Ring o' Bells *A368 Bath—Weston*
Even when this cheerful country pub is at its busiest, the landlord and his staff remain friendly and helpful. The cosy, traditional front part of the bar has rugs on the flagstones and inglenook seats right by the log fire, and up a step is a spacious carpeted back part with largely stripped stone walls and pine tables; the lounge is partly no smoking. Reasonably priced bar food includes stilton mushrooms, ham and eggs, lasagne, mushroom, broccoli and almond tagliatelle, a generous mixed grill, and puddings; best to get here early to be sure of a seat. Well kept Butcombe Bitter, Blond, and Gold, and guests like Bass and Robinsons Young Tom on handpump; darts in the public bar. The family room is no smoking, and has blackboards and chalks, a Brio track, and a rocking horse; they also have baby changing and nursing facilities, and the big garden has swings, a slide and a climbing frame. Blagdon Lake and Chew Valley Lake are not far away, and the pub is overlooked by the Mendip Hills.

Butcombe ~ Manager Roger Owen ~ Real ale ~ Bar food ~ Restaurant ~ (01761) 221284 ~ Children in family room ~ Dogs allowed in bar ~ Open 11.30-3, 6.30-11; 12-3, 7-10.30 Sun

CONGRESBURY
White Hart *Wrington Road, which is off A370 Bristol—Weston just E of village – keep on*
Although the names of the licensees are new, Paul and Rebecca worked for the previous tenants for quite a few years here. It's a pleasant companionable country pub, and the L-shaped carpeted main bar has a few heavy black beams in the bowed ceiling of its longer leg, country-kitchen chairs around good-sized tables, and a big stone inglenook fireplace at each end, with woodburning stoves and lots of copper pans. The short leg of the L is more cottagey, with wooden games and other bric-a-brac above yet another fireplace and on a delft shelf, lace and old-gold brocaded curtains, and brocaded wall seats. A roomy family Parlour Bar, open to the main bar, is similar in mood, though with lighter-coloured country-style furniture, some stripped stone and shiny black panelling, and big bright airy conservatory windows on one side; the restaurant is no smoking. Tasty bar food includes home-made soup, vegetarian dishes like cauliflower cheese or stilton, leek and walnut pie, home-made lasagne and steak pie, and puddings such as home-made fruit crumbles. Well kept Badger Best, Tanglefoot, and King & Barnes Sussex on handpump; perhaps faint music. There are picnic-sets under an arbour on the terrace behind, and the

garden has been landscaped; the hills you see are the Mendips.
Badger ~ Tenants Paul Merrick and Rebecca North ~ Real ale ~ Bar food ~ (01934) 833303 ~ Children in family room ~ Dogs welcome ~ Open 11.30-2.30, 6-11; 12-3, 7-10.30 Sun; closed 25 Dec

CROWCOMBE

Carew Arms *Village (and pub) signposted just off A358 Taunton—Minehead*
There's some emphasis on the food in this 17th-c beamed inn, and the smart, newly bare-boarded dining room has doors to one side leading to an outside terrace where you can eat in fine weather. The front bar has long benches and a couple of old long deal tables on its dark flagstones, a high-backed antique settle and a shiny old leather wing armchair by the woodburning stove in its huge brick inglenook fireplace, and a thoroughly non-PC collection of hunting trophies to remind you that this is the Quantocks. A back room behind the bar is a carpeted and gently updated version of the front one, and on the right is a library, and residents' lounge. Well kept Otter Bitter and Exmoor Ale and either Fox, Gold or Hart on handpump, eight wines by the glass, Lane's strong farm cider, and a dozen malt whiskies; dominoes, cribbage, darts, skittle alley, and piped music (only in the Garden Room). Bar food at lunchtime includes home-made vegetable samosas with minted yoghurt, potted brown shrimps, local sausages with red wine gravy, honey roasted pork and roast cod; evening dishes such as deep-fried goats cheese with red pepper marmalade, seared king scallops, chicken breast with creamed leeks and black pudding, and rump of lamb with rösti. Picnic-sets out on the back grass look over rolling wooded pasture, and the attractive village at the foot of the hills has a fine old church and church house.
Free house ~ Licensees Simon and Reg Ambrose ~ Real ale ~ Bar food ~ Restaurant ~ (01984) 618631 ~ Children welcome ~ Dogs allowed in bar ~ Live jazz Sun afternoon ~ Open 11-4, 6-11; 11-11 Sat; 12-10.30 Sun ~ Bedrooms: £25(£47B)/£50(£72B)

DOULTING

Waggon & Horses *Doulting Beacon, 2 miles N of Doulting itself; eastwards turn off A37 on Mendip ridge N of Shepton Mallet, just S of A367 junction; the pub is also signposted from A37 at the Beacon Hill crossroads and from A361 at the Doulting and Cranmore crossroads*
Particularly when the enthusiastic Mr Cardona is in, you can be sure of a genuine welcome to the wide mix of customers here. The rambling bar has studded red leatherette seats and other chairs, a homely mix of tables including antiques, and well kept Greene King IPA and a guest on handpump, a small, carefully chosen wine list, and cocktails. Two rooms are no smoking. Bar food includes spicy bean casserole or ham and eggs, salmon fishcakes with dill mayonnaise, ambitious daily specials, and puddings such as crème brûlée; good winter stews and game dishes. The big walled garden (with summer barbecues) is lovely: elderly tables and chairs stand on informal terracing, with picnic-sets out on the grass, and perennials and flowering shrubs intersperse themselves in a pretty and

pleasantly informal way. There's a wildlife pond, and a climber for children. Off to one side is a rough paddock with a horse and various fancy fowl, with pens further down holding many more in small breeding groups – there are some really quite splendid birds among them, and the cluckings and crowings make a splendidly contented background to a sunny summer lunch. They often sell the eggs, too. During the spring and autumn, there are some remarkable classical music and other musical events, and exhibitions of local artists' work that take place in the big raftered upper gallery to one side of the building.

InnSpired ~ Lease Francisco Cardona ~ Real ale ~ Bar food ~ Restaurant ~ (01749) 880302 ~ Children tolerated but must be well behaved and quiet ~ Dogs allowed in bar ~ Classical concerts and some jazz ~ Open 11.30-2.30, 6-11; 12-3, 7-11 Sun

EXFORD
Crown *The Green (B3224)*

Readers enjoy their visits to this comfortably upmarket Exmoor coaching inn. You can expect a friendly welcome from the licensees and their staff, the food and beer are good, and it's a nice place to stay, too. The two-room bar has a very relaxed feel, plenty of stuffed animal heads and hunting prints on the cream walls, some hunting-themed plates (this is the local hunt's traditional meeting place at New Year), and a good mix of chatty customers. There are a few tables fashioned from barrels, a big stone fireplace (with a nice display of flowers in summer), old photographs of the area, and smart cushioned benches; piped music and TV. Well kept Exmoor Ale and Gold and a guest such as Archers Best or Cotleigh Tawny on handpump; decent wine list (with some available by the half-carafe). To be sure of a table, it's best to book beforehand: sandwiches, soup, parma ham and avocado salad, leek and wild mushroom tagliatelle with blue cheese, braised lamb shank with herb mash; and daily specials such as salmon, green bean and new potato salad; good Sunday lunch. The rather smart dining room is no smoking. There's a delightful water garden behind – a lovely summer spot with a trout stream threading its way past gently sloping lawns, tall trees and plenty of tables. A smaller terraced garden at the side overlooks the village and the edge of the green. They have stabling for horses.

Free house ~ Licensee Hugo Jeune ~ Real ale ~ Bar food ~ Restaurant ~ (01643) 831554 ~ Children in eating area of bar ~ Dogs allowed in bar and bedrooms ~ Open 11-3, 6-11; 11-11 Sat; 12-11 Sun ~ Bedrooms: £65B/£95B

HUISH EPISCOPI
Rose & Crown *Off A372 E of Langport*

Known locally as 'Eli's' after the friendly landlady's father, this unspoilt thatched pub has been run by Mrs Pittard's family for well over 135 years, and Mrs Pittard was actually born in the pub (as was her mother). It's like a real step back in time, with the atmosphere and character as determinedly unpretentious and welcoming as ever. There's no bar as such – to get a drink (prices are very low), you just walk into the central flagstoned still room and choose from the casks of well kept Teignworthy Reel Ale or guests such as Butcombe Blond or Glastonbury Mystery Tor; also, several farm ciders (and local cider brandy). This servery is the only thoroughfare between the casual little front parlours with their unusual pointed-arch windows; genuinely friendly locals. Food is home-made, simple and cheap and uses local produce (and some home-grown fruit): generously filled sandwiches, cottage pie or stilton and broccoli tart, pork, apple and cider cobbler or steak in ale pie, and puddings such as sticky toffee pudding or chocolate torte; good helpful service. Shove-ha'penny, dominoes and cribbage, and a much more orthodox big back extension family room has pool, darts, fruit machine and jukebox; skittle alley and popular quiz nights. One room is no smoking at lunchtimes and early evening. There are tables in a garden outside, and a second enclosed garden with a children's play area. The welsh collie is called Bonny. Summer morris men, good nearby walks, and the site of the Battle of Langport (1645) is close by.

Free house ~ Licensee Mrs Eileen Pittard ~ Real ale ~ Bar food (12-2, 6-7.30; not Sun evening) ~ No credit cards ~ (01458) 250494 ~ Children welcome ~ Dogs welcome ~ Folk singers every 3rd Sat; irish night once a month in winter ~ Open 11.30-2.30, 5.30-11; 11.30-11 Fri and Sat; 12-10.30 Sun

LOVINGTON
Pilgrims Rest *B3153 Castle Cary—Keinton Mandeville*

There's no doubt that most visitors to this quietly placed and civilised country bar/bistro come to enjoy the very good food, but there are a few bar stools (and a frieze of hundreds of matchbooks) by a corner counter with nice wines by the glass and well kept Cottage Champflower on handpump, from the nearby brewery. There's a chatty, relaxed feel, and a cosy little maroon-walled inner area has sunny modern country and city prints, a couple of shelves of books and china, a cushioned pew, a couple of settees and an old leather easy chair by the big fireplace. With flagstones throughout, this runs into the compact eating area, with candles on tables, heavy black beams and joists, and some stripped stone; piped music. The landlord cooks using all fresh ingredients including local meat and cheeses and daily fresh fish: sandwiches on home-baked bread, asparagus and spring vegetable risotto, lemon sole with a dash of Noilly Prat, fillet steak in a light dijon sauce, and puddings such as crème brûlée. Perhaps better value are the fixed course meals; there is also a separate more formal carpeted no smoking dining room. The landlady's service is efficient and friendly, and there's a rack of daily papers. Picnic-sets and old-fashioned benches on the side grass, and the car park exit has its own traffic lights – on your way out line your car up carefully or you may wait for ever for them to change.

Free house ~ Licensees Sally and Jools Mitchison ~ Real ale ~ Bar food (see opening hours) ~ Restaurant ~ (01963) 240597 ~ Children welcome ~ Dogs allowed in bar ~ Open 12-3, 7-11; closed Sun evening, Mon, Tues lunchtimes; last 2 weeks Oct

MONKSILVER
Notley Arms *B3188*

New Zimbabwean licensees have taken over this bustling pub and Mr Deary welcomes fellow Springboks with biltong, ostrich fillet and bobotie. But there are plenty of locals and visitors too, which creates a friendly, unpretentious atmosphere. The beamed and L-shaped bar has small settles and kitchen chairs around the plain country wooden and candlelit tables, original paintings on the ochre-coloured walls, fresh flowers, and a couple of woodburning stoves; to be sure of a table you must arrive promptly as they don't take reservations. Generous helpings of reasonably priced food include country-style pâté, home-made tagliatelle with bacon, mushrooms and cream, aubergine tagine with dates and almonds with couscous, beef and Guinness pie or fresh cod fillet, locally reared sirloin steak, and puddings such as treacle tart with clotted cream; winter Sunday lunch. Well kept Exmoor Ale, Smiles Best, and Wadworths 6X on handpump, farm cider, and country wines; cribbage, dominoes and alley skittles; there's a bright no smoking little family room. Seats outside in the immaculate garden which runs down to a swift clear stream. This is a lovely village.
Unique (Enterprise) ~ Lease Russell and Jane Deary ~ Real ale ~ Bar food ~ (01984) 656217 ~ Children in family room if well behaved ~ Dogs welcome ~ Open 11.30-2.30, 6.30-11; 12-2.30, 7-10.30 Sun

PITNEY
Halfway House *Just off B3153 W of Somerton*

Although often packed out and perhaps a bit smoky, this old-fashioned pub has a really good friendly atmosphere, quite a mix of customers, and a fine range of up to 10 real ales. The three rooms all have roaring log fires and a homely feel underlined by a profusion of books, maps and newspapers. As well as six regular ales tapped from the cask such as Butcombe Bitter, Cotleigh Tawny, Hop Back Summer Lightning, and Teignworthy Reel Ale, there might be guests like Archers Golden, Hop Back Crop Circle, and RCH Pitchfork. They have 20 or so bottled beers from Belgium and other countries, Wilkins's farm cider, and quite a few malt whiskies; cribbage and dominoes. Good simple filling food includes sandwiches, filled baked potatoes, and a fine ploughman's with home-made pickle. In the evening they do about half a dozen home-made curries. There are tables outside.
Free house ~ Licensees Julian and Judy Lichfield ~ Real ale ~ Bar food (not Sun) ~ (01458) 252513 ~ Children in eating area of bar and restaurant ~ Dogs welcome ~ Open 11.30-3, 5.30-11; 12-3.30, 7-10.30 Sun; closed evening 25 Dec

ROWBERROW
Swan *Village signposted off A38 ¼ mile S of junction with A368*

After enjoying one of the surrounding walks, it's pleasant to sit with a drink by the pond in the attractive garden of this sizeable olde-worlde pub; tethering post for horses. Inside, there are low beams, some stripped stone, warm red décor, comic hunting and political prints, an ancient longcase clock, and huge log fires. Lunchtime sandwiches and filled baked potatoes,

as well as more substantial dishes such as ham and eggs, vegetable casserole, pesto chicken, beef in ale pie, and steaks. Well kept Bass, and Butcombe Bitter, Blond and Gold on handpump, eight wines by the glass, and Thatcher's cider. Note that they are very firm about keeping children out.
Butcombe ~ Managers Elaine and Robert Flaxman ~ Real ale ~ Bar food ~ (01934) 852371 ~ Dogs welcome ~ Open 12-3, 6-11; 12-3, 7-10.30 Sun; closed evenings 25 and 26 Dec and 1 Jan

SHEPTON MONTAGUE
Montague Inn *Village signposted just off A359 Bruton—Castle Cary*
The rooms in this popular little country pub are simply but tastefully furnished with stripped wooden tables, kitchen chairs and a log fire in the attractive inglenook fireplace, and there's a no smoking candlelit restaurant – which has french windows overlooking the gardens. Using fresh organic produce where possible, the interesting food might include home-made soup or chicken liver pâté, good antipasto, spinach, mushroom and brie lasagne, halibut steaks with salsa verde, and roast local lamb with port and redcurrant sauce; puddings as well; friendly service. If you do not pre-book a table, you may not get served. Well kept Greene King IPA and a guest tapped from the cask, a few wines by the glass, and local cider; shove-ha'penny. The pretty back garden and terrace have good views.
Free house ~ Licensees Julian and Linda Bear ~ Bar food (not Sun evening, Mon) ~ Restaurant ~ (01749) 813213 ~ Children in eating area of bar and restaurant ~ Dogs allowed in bedrooms ~ Open 11-2.30, 6-11; 12-2.30 Sun; closed Sun evening, Mon ~ Bedrooms: /£70S

STOKE ST GREGORY
Rose & Crown *Woodhill; follow North Curry signpost off A378 by junction with A358 – keep on to Stoke, bearing right in centre, passing church and follow lane for ½ mile*
Bustling and friendly, this popular country pub has been in the same family for 26 years. The cosy bar is decorated in a pleasant stable theme: dark wooden loose-box partitions for some of the interestingly angled nooks and alcoves, lots of brasses and bits on the low beams and joists, stripped stonework, a wonky floor, and appropriate pictures including a highland pony carrying a stag; many of the wildlife paintings on the walls are the work of the landlady, and there's an 18th-c glass-covered well in one corner. The two rooms of the dining room lead off here with lots of country prints and paintings of hunting scenes, animals and birds on the walls, more horsebrasses, jugs and mugs hanging from the ceiling joists, and candles in bottles on all tables. Generous helpings of enjoyable bar food (slightly more expensive in the evenings) include local home-cooked smoked ham and eggs, home-made steak and kidney pie, salmon fishcakes, scrumpy chicken, vegetable stroganoff, grilled skate wings, and puddings such as rhubarb crumble. Plentiful breakfasts, and Sunday roast; speedy, cheerful service, even when busy. The restaurants are no smoking. Well kept Exmoor Ale and Gold, and a guest such as Archers Village Bitter on handpump, and decent wines. Under cocktail parasols by an apple tree on

the sheltered front terrace are some picnic-sets; summer barbecues. The pub is in an interesting Somerset Levels village with willow beds still supplying the two basket works.

Free house ~ Licensees Stephen, Sally, Richard and Leonie Browning ~ Real ale ~ Bar food ~ Restaurant ~ (01823) 490296 ~ Children in restaurant ~ Dogs allowed in bar ~ Open 11.30-3, 6.30-11; 12-3, 7-10.30 Sun; closed evening 25 Dec ~ Bedrooms: £36.50(£46.50B)/£53(£73B)

WINSFORD
Royal Oak *In Exmoor National Park, village signposted from A396 about 10 miles S of Dunster*

There's usually a good mix of customers in this civilised and rather smart thatched inn which creates a pleasant, chatty atmosphere. The attractively furnished lounge bar has a cushioned big bay-window seat from which you can look across the road towards the village green and foot and packhorse bridges over the River Winn, tartan-cushioned bar stools by the panelled counter (above which hang horsebrasses and pewter tankards), armed and cushioned windsor chairs set around little wooden tables, and a gas-fired stove in the big stone hearth. Another similar bar offers more eating space with built-in wood-panelled seats creating booths, fresh flowers, and country prints; there are several pretty and comfortable lounges, and three no smoking rooms. Served by friendly staff, bar snacks might include lunchtime sandwiches and ploughman's, as well as home-made soup, lambs liver with onion gravy, aubergine and courgette lasagne glazed with goats cheese, and daily specials like smoked salmon and prawn tian with citrus dressing or pork steak with a rich cider and apple sauce; home-made puddings such as treacle tart. Well kept Brakspears Bitter and Butcombe Bitter on handpump; piped music.

Free house ~ Licensee Charles Steven ~ Real ale ~ Bar food ~ Restaurant ~ (01643) 851455 ~ Children in eating area of bar and restaurant ~ Dogs allowed in bar ~ Open 11-2.30, 6.30-11; 12-3, 7-11 Sun ~ Bedrooms: /£116B

WITHYPOOL
Royal Oak *Village signposted off B3233*

Even when this popular place is really busy (which it often is) the staff remain helpful and friendly. The beamed lounge bar has a fine raised log fireplace, comfortably cushioned wall seating and slat-backed chairs, and stags' heads, stuffed fish, several fox masks, sporting prints and paintings, and various copper and brass ornaments on its walls. The locals' bar (named after the barman Jake who has been here for over 26 years) has some old oak tables, and plenty of character. Good bar food includes nice lunchtime sandwiches, pasta with free range chicken breast, asparagus and cherry tomatoes in a cream and white wine sauce, wild mushroom risotto, and fillet of beef with sweet potato wedges; also daily specials such as savoy cabbage and bacon soup, home-cooked honey roast ham with free range fried eggs, and whole torbay sole. The restaurant is no smoking. Well kept Exmoor Ale and Gold on handpump, quite a few malt whiskies, and a decent wine list. There are wooden benches on the terrace, and just up the road, some grand views from Winsford Hill. The River Barle runs through the village itself, with pretty bridleways following it through a wooded combe further upstream. R D Blackmore stayed here while writing *Lorna Doone*.

Free house ~ Licensee Gail Sloggett ~ Real ale ~ Bar food (12-2, 6.30-9.30) ~ (01643) 831506 ~ Children in bottom bar and restaurant ~ Dogs allowed in bar and bedrooms ~ Open 11(12 Sun)-11 ~ Bedrooms: /£100B

Dog Friendly Hotels, B&Bs and Farms

BABINGTON

Babington House *Babington, Frome, Somerset BA11 3RW (01373) 812266* £**311**; 29 individually decorated, well equipped contemporary rms, 12 in coach house, 5 in stable block, 3 in lodge. Georgian mansion in lovely grounds with cricket and football pitches, indoor and outdoor swimming pools, walled garden, tennis courts and croquet; comfortable drawing room with evening Martini bar, library, Log Room, and bar, a particularly relaxed, informal atmosphere, helpful and welcoming young staff, enjoyable modern cooking, super breakfasts, and lots for children to do; cinema, videos and computers, various animals, gym, sauna and spa; dogs welcome in some bedrooms; £15

BARWICK

Little Barwick House *Barwick, Yeovil, Somerset BA22 9TD (01935) 423902* £**120**, plus special breaks; 6 attractive rms. Carefully run listed Georgian dower house in 3½ acres 2m S of Yeovil, and thought of as a restaurant-with-rooms; lovely relaxed atmosphere, log fire in cosy lounge, excellent food using local produce, a thoughtful wine list, super breakfasts, nice afternoon tea, and particularly good service; cl 2 wks Jan; dogs welcome in bedrooms; £5

BATH

Royal Crescent Hotel *16 Royal Crescent, Bath BA1 2LS (01225) 823333* £**210**, plus special breaks; 45 luxurious rms. Elegant Georgian hotel in glorious curved terrace, with comfortable antique-filled drawing rooms, open fires and lovely flowers; imaginative modern cooking in Pimpernel Restaurant (in summer you can eat in the delightful garden), and impeccable service; health spa, gym and croquet; they are kind to children; limited disabled access; dogs welcome; £25

BATHFORD

Eagle House *23 Church St, Bathford, Bath BA1 7RS (01225) 859946* £**74**, plus winter breaks; 8 rms, 2 in cottage with sitting room and kitchen. Friendly and relaxed B&B in Georgian house with homely furnishings and family mementoes, winter log fires, comfortable drawing room, nice continental breakfasts in no smoking breakfast room (full english is extra), and two-acre gardens with tennis, croquet, treehouse and swings; plenty to do nearby; cl 15 Dec-8 Jan; dogs welcome by arrangement; £3.50

BECKINGTON
Pickford House *Bath Rd, Beckington, Frome, Somerset BA11 6SJ (01373) 830329* £45; 5 rms, some with river view and most with own bthrm. Honey-coloured hilltop stone house, with open fire in sitting room, bar, delicious evening meals (by arrangement) and breakfasts, a relaxed friendly atmosphere, helpful courteous owners and friendly collie; big garden with swimming pool; you can take over the house with a group of friends for a gourmet weekend; partial disabled access; dogs welcome in some bedrooms, depending on size of dog

HATCH BEAUCHAMP
Farthings *Hatch Beauchamp, Taunton, Somerset TA3 6SG (01823) 480664* £105, plus special breaks; 10 spacious rms (inc a cottage suite) with thoughtful extras. Charming little Georgian house in three acres of gardens with helpful and hard-working long-serving owners, open fires in quiet lounge and convivial bar, and good varied food using fresh local produce; can arrange golf and other activities; children must be well behaved; dogs in Maple Cottage suite only, by arrangement

HOLFORD
Combe House *Holford, Bridgwater, Somerset TA5 1RZ (01278) 741382* £90, plus special breaks; 16 rms. Warmly friendly former tannery (still has waterwheel) in a pretty spot, with comfortable rooms, log fires, good home-made food, and a relaxed atmosphere; heated indoor swimming pool and tennis court; cl 1st 2 wks Jan; dogs welcome in some bedrooms; £3

HUNSTRETE
Hunstrete House *Hunstrete, Pensford, Bristol BS39 4NS (01761) 490490* £185, plus special breaks; 25 individually decorated rms. Classically handsome, mainly 18th-c country-house hotel on the edge of the Mendips, in 92 acres inc lovely Victorian walled garden and deer park; comfortable and elegantly furnished day rooms with antiques, paintings, log fires, fresh garden flowers, a tranquil atmosphere, excellent service, and very good food using home-grown produce when possible; croquet lawn, heated outdoor swimming pool, all-weather tennis court, and nearby riding; limited disabled access; dogs welcome in bedrooms; £10

LANGFORD BUDVILLE
Bindon Country House *Langford Budville, Wellington, Somerset TA21 0RU (01823) 400070* £115; 12 stylish bdrms. Tranquil 17th-c house designed as a bavarian hunting lodge and set in seven acres of formal and woodland gardens; comfortable, elegant drawing room, panelled bar, and intimate no smoking restaurant all decorated with Duke of Wellington memorabilia, enjoyable modern cooking, and a thoughtful wine list;

outdoor swimming pool, tennis, and croquet; dogs welcome in some bedrooms

LUXBOROUGH
Royal Oak *Luxborough, Watchet, Somerset TA23 0SH (01984) 640319* **£65**; 12 rms. Unspoilt and interesting old pub in idyllic spot, marvellous for exploring Exmoor; bar rooms with log fires in inglenook fireplaces, beams, flagstones, character furnishings and a thriving feel, four distinctive no smoking dining rooms, and good food and real ales; dogs welcome in bedrooms and bar area; £5

MILBORNE PORT
Old Vicarage *Sherborne Rd, Milborne Port, Sherborne, Dorset DT9 5AT (01963) 251117* **£70**, plus special breaks; 6 rms, some in annexe. Charming Victorian house with an interesting mix of furnishings from East and West, pleasant guest lounge and conservatory overlooking the gardens, good asian food, in no smoking dining room, cooked by Mr Ma at weekends, and enjoyable breakfasts; cl Jan; children over 5; partial disabled access; dogs in Coach House only; £5

NETHER STOWEY
Old Cider House *25 Castle St, Nether Stowey, Bridgwater, Somerset TA5 1LN (01278) 732228* **£60**, plus special breaks; 5 individually decorated rms. Carefully restored Edwardian house (previously used to produce cider) in secluded garden, with big comfortable lounge, log fire, delicious breakfasts and imaginative, candlelit evening meals using home-grown and local produce, and a small carefully chosen wine list; plenty of walks and dog friendly beaches nearby; dogs if well behaved are welcome; £3.50

NORTON ST PHILIP
George *High St, Norton St Philip, Bath BA3 6LH (01373) 834224* **£80**; 8 comfortable rms of real character. Carefully restored, exceptional building that has been offering hospitality to travellers for nearly 700 years; individual bars with trusses and timbering, fine old stone fireplaces, really heavy beams, 18th-c pictures, oak dressers and settles and so forth, a marvellous dining room, good food, real ales, decent wines, and organised, friendly service; a stroll over the meadow behind the pub (past the picnic-sets on the narrow grass pub garden) leads to an attractive churchyard around the medieval church whose bells struck Pepys (here on 12 June 1668) as 'mighty tuneable'; cl 25–26 Dec; dogs welcome in some bedrooms and other areas

SHEPTON MALLET
Charlton House and Mulberry Restaurant *Charlton Rd, Shepton Mallet, Somerset BA4 4PR (01749) 342008* **£165**, plus special breaks; 25 attractive and stylish rooms with nice extras, and large bthrms. Substantial Georgian hotel in landscaped grounds; bare-boarded rooms with oriental rugs, dark red walls with lots of old photographs and posters, and show-

casing the owners' Mulberry style of informal furnishings; smart dining room and three-bay conservatory, restored 18th-c orangery dining room, exceptionally good modern cooking, interesting wines, and helpful, efficient uniformed staff; seats on the back terrace overlooking a big lawn, and croquet; health spa; they are kind to children; disabled access; dogs welcome in one bedroom only

SOMERTON
Lynch Country House *4 Behind Berry, Somerton, Somerset TA11 7PD (01458)* 272316 £**49**; 8 prettily decorated rms, plus 3 extra in summer cottage. Carefully restored and homely Georgian house, with books in comfortable lounge, and good breakfasts (no evening meals) in airy room overlooking tranquil grounds and lake with black swans and exotic ducks; cl Christmas and New Year; disabled access; dogs welcome in bedrooms

STOGUMBER
Hall Farm *Station Rd, Stogumber, Taunton, Somerset TA4 3TQ (01984)* 656321 £**40**; 7 rms, most with own bthrm. Old-fashioned B&B – wonderfully unpretentious, with warmly friendly staff; cl Christmas and New Year; disabled access; dogs welcome in bedrooms if well behaved

STON EASTON
Ston Easton Park *Ston Easton, Bath BA3 4DF (01761)* 241631 £**150**; 22 really lovely rms. Majestic Palladian mansion of Bath stone with beautifully landscaped 18th-c gardens and 26 acres of parkland; elegant day rooms with antiques and flowers, an attractive no smoking restaurant with good food (much grown in the kitchen garden), fine afternoon teas, library and billiard room, and extremely helpful, friendly and unstuffy service; children over 7 in dining room; dogs in bedrooms at manager's discretion

TAUNTON
Castle *Castle Green, Taunton, Somerset TA1 1NF (01823)* 272671 £**170**, plus special breaks; 44 lovely rms. Appealingly modernised partly Norman castle, its front almost smothered in wisteria, with fine old oak furniture, tapestries and paintings in comfortably elegant lounges, really excellent modern english cooking, good breakfasts, a range of good value wines from a thoughtful list, and efficient friendly service; pretty garden; disabled access; dogs welcome in bedrooms; £10

WELLS
Infield House *36 Portway, Wells, Somerset BA5 2BN (01749)* 670989 £**52**; 3 comfortable rms (best view from back one). Carefully restored no smoking Victorian town house with period furnishings and family portraits, elegant lounge (with lots of local guidebooks), good breakfasts in dining room with Adam-style fireplace, evening meals by arrangement, and friendly personal service; children over 12; dogs welcome in bedrooms

WOOKEY HOLE

Glencot House *Glencot Lane, Wookey Hole, Wells, Somerset BA5 1BH* *(01749) 677160* £118; 13 rms, many with four-posters. In 18 acres of pretty gardens and parkland (with own cricket pitch), this Jacobean–style Victorian mansion has some fine panelling, carved ceilings, antiques and flowers in the public rooms and hallways, a friendly atmosphere, and good food in the restaurant; fishing, table tennis, snooker, and small indoor jet stream pool; two friendly dogs and pet pig, lots to do nearby; cl New Year; they are kind to children; dogs welcome in bedroom with access to terrace and garden

Staffordshire

Dog Friendly Pubs

BURTON UPON TRENT
Burton Bridge Inn *Bridge Street (A50)*
Readers enjoy the genuinely friendly atmosphere at this straightforward, bustling old brick local. It's the tap for Burton Bridge Brewery (out in the long old-fashioned yard at the back) which produces the Bitter, Festival, Golden Delicious, Gold Medal, Porter and Top Dog Stout that are well kept and served on handpump here. They also keep around 25 whiskies and over a dozen country wines. The simple little front area leads into an adjacent bar, separated from a no smoking oak-panelled lounge by the serving counter. The bar has wooden pews, plain walls hung with notices, awards and brewery memorabilia, and the lounge has oak beams, a flame-effect fire and old oak tables and chairs. Simple but hearty bar snacks include cobs, toasties, filled yorkshire pudding and ploughman's; the panelled upstairs dining room is only open at lunchtime. A blue-brick patio overlooks the brewery.
Own brew ~ Licensees Kevin and Jan McDonald ~ Real ale ~ Bar food (lunchtime only, not Sun) ~ No credit cards ~ (01283) 536596 ~ Children in eating area of bar ~ Dogs welcome ~ Open 11.30-2.15, 5-11; 12-2.15, 7-10.30 Sun; closed bank hol Mon lunchtime

WARSLOW
Greyhound *B5053 S of Buxton*
This very welcoming slate and stone-built pub is surrounded by pretty countryside and is handy for the Manifold Valley, Dovedale and Alton Towers. The side garden has picnic-sets under ash trees, with rustic seats out in front where window boxes blaze with colour in summer. Straightforward but cosily comfortable inside, the beamed bar has long cushioned antique oak settles (some quite elegant), houseplants in the windows, cheerful fires and a no smoking area. Reasonably priced home-made bar food includes lunchtime sandwiches, filled baked potatoes, sausage, egg and chips, as well as soup, thai-style fishcakes, vegetarian stuffed peppers, big battered cod or moroccan lamb, and puddings such as chocolate fudge cake; Wednesday night curries. They serve well kept Black

Sheep, Marstons Pedigree and a couple of changing guests such as Everards Perfick and Wadworths 6X on handpump, as well as 20 malt whiskies; TV, fruit machine, pool, darts, dominoes and piped music. Bedrooms are basic but good value, and a tasty breakfast is provided.

Free house ~ Licensees Jan and Andy Livesley ~ Real ale ~ Bar food (12-3, 6.30-9) ~ Restaurant ~ (01298) 84249 ~ Children in eating area of bar and family room ~ Dogs allowed in bar ~ Soft rock most Sats ~ Open 12-3, 6.30-11; 12-11(10.30 Sun) Sat; 12-3, 6.30-11(10.30 Sun) Sat, Sun in winter ~ Bedrooms: £17.50/£35

Dog Friendly Hotels, B&Bs and Farms

BETLEY
Adderley Green Farm *Heighley Castle Lane, Betley, Crewe, Cheshire CW3 9BA (01270) 820203* £**56**, plus special breaks; 3 rms. Georgian farmhouse on big dairy farm, with good breakfasts in homely dining room, and large garden; cl Christmas and New Year; children over 5; dogs in bedrooms by arrangement; £1

HOPWAS
Oak Tree Farm *Hints Rd, Hopwas, Tamworth, Staffordshire B78 3AA (01827) 56807* £**85**; 8 comfortable, spacious and pretty rms. Carefully restored no smoking farmhouse with elegant little lounge, fresh flowers, an attractive breakfast room, a friendly atmosphere, enjoyable breakfasts, gardens overlooking the River Tame, indoor swimming pool and steam room; cl Christmas–New Year; no children; dogs welcome in bedrooms

OAKAMOOR
Bank House *Farley Lane, Oakamoor, Stoke-on-Trent, Staffordshire ST10 3BD (01538) 702810* £**65**, plus special breaks; 3 lovely big rms. Carefully restored no smoking country home in neat gardens on the edge of the Peak National Park, with lovely views; log fire in comfortable drawing room, library, piano in the inner hall, and most enjoyable food (by prior arrangement using home-grown and local produce) – super home-made breads, brioches, pastries and jams and marmalade at marvellous breakfast; friendly dog and cats; lots to do nearby; cl Christmas; dogs welcome in bedrooms by prior arrangement

ROLLESTON ON DOVE
Brookhouse Hotel *Station Rd, Rolleston on Dove, Burton upon Trent, Staffordshire DE13 9AA (01283) 814188* £**115**, plus wknd breaks; 19 comfortable rms with Victorian brass or four-poster beds. Handsome ivy-covered William & Mary brick building in five acres of lovely gardens with comfortable antiques-filled rooms, and good food using seasonal local produce in elegant little dining room; children over 12; disabled access; dogs welcome in bedrooms

STOKE-ON-TRENT
Haydon House *Haydon St, Basford, Stoke-on-Trent, Staffordshire ST4 6JD* *(01782) 711311* £60; 23 rms, some in annexe. Family-run Victorian house with a relaxed, friendly atmosphere, attractive and comfortable cocktail lounge and conservatory, good food (popular locally) in no smoking restaurant, and an extensive wine list; dogs in bedrooms and public areas

TAMWORTH
Old Rectory *Churchside, Harlaston, Tamworth, Staffordshire B79 9HE* *(01827) 383583* £45; 4 attractive rms overlooking open countryside. Former Victorian rectory in large grounds in award-winning village; spacious sunny kitchen opening onto the garden with enjoyable breakfasts that include home-made preserves and local specialities; dogs welcome in bedrooms; £2.50

Suffolk

Dog Friendly Pubs

BUXHALL
Crown *Village signposted off B1115 W of Stowmarket; fork right by post office at Great Finborough, turn left at Buxhall village sign, then second right into Mill Road, then right at T-junction*
Given the quality of the imaginative food, it's not surprising that this welcoming 17th-c timber-framed country pub is so popular, and to be sure of a table, you must book. Skilfully cooked with fresh seasonal ingredients, monthly changing dishes might include fresh crab filo tart, duck and vegetable pancakes, grilled skate wing with brown shrimps, roasted pork loin and scottish lamb; home-made puddings such as rum truffle cake. They also do lunchtime bar snacks and sandwiches. Good service from the friendly landlord and pleasant staff. All the wines on their carefully chosen wine list are available by the glass, and they've also well kept Greene King IPA, Mauldons Bitter, Tindalls Best, and Woodfordes Wherry on handpump; smart coffees. The intimate little bar on the left has an open fire in a big inglenook, a couple of small round tables on a tiled floor, and low hop-hung beams. Standing timbers separate it from another area with pews and candles, and flowers in summer on big stripped oak or pine tables, and there's a further light and airy room which they call the Mill Bar. Plenty of seats and picnic-sets under parasols on the heated terrace, and they've a pretty garden, with nice views over gently rolling countryside.
Greene King ~ Lease Trevor Golton ~ Real ale ~ Bar food (not Sun evening) ~ Restaurant ~ (01449) 736521 ~ Well behaved children in restaurant ~ Dogs allowed in bar ~ Occasional live jazz ~ Open 12-3, 6.30-11; 12-3 Sun; closed Sun evening

EARL SOHAM
Victoria *A1120 Yoxford—Stowmarket*
It's no wonder the Earl Soham beers at this unpretentious little village pub are so well kept – the brewery is right across the road: on handpump, you might find Victoria Bitter, Albert Ale, Edward Ale and Empress of India Pale Ale, and they've local farm cider too. There's an appealingly easy-going local atmosphere in the bar, which is fairly basic and sparsely

furnished, with stripped panelling, kitchen chairs and pews, plank-topped trestle sewing-machine tables and other simple scrubbed pine country tables with candles, tiled or board floors, an interesting range of pictures of Queen Victoria and her reign, a piano, and open fires; cribbage and dominoes. Readers enjoy the home-made puddings, while other very reasonably priced bar food could include ploughman's, popular corned beef hash, vegetarian pasta dishes, beef casserole or winter Sunday roast; service is very friendly (but can be slow at times). There are seats on the raised back lawn, with more out in front. The pub is quite close to a wild fritillary meadow at Framlingham, and a working windmill at Saxtead.

Free house ~ Licensee Paul Hooper ~ Real ale ~ Bar food (till 10pm) ~ Restaurant ~ No credit cards ~ (01728) 685758 ~ Children in eating area of bar ~ Dogs welcome ~ Open 11.30-3, 6-11; 12-3, 7-10.30 Sun

GREAT GLEMHAM

Crown *Between A12 Wickham Market—Saxmundham and B1119 Saxmundham—Framlingham*

Nothing is too much trouble for the helpful staff or friendly licensees at this immaculately kept smart pub. It's worth booking for the popular bar food, which comes in generous helpings. Enjoyable dishes might include crispy whitebait, sausage, egg and chips, gammon and pineapple; with daily specials such as leek and goats cheese tart, lamb casserole, and fried rainbow trout; children's menu too. Past the sofas on rush matting in the big entrance hall, an open-plan beamed lounge has wooden pews and captains' chairs around stripped and waxed kitchen tables, local photographs and interesting paintings on cream walls, fresh flowers, and some brass ornaments; log fires in two big fireplaces. Well kept Greene King IPA and Old Speckled Hen are served from old brass handpumps; they've seven wines by the glass, and good coffee. A tidy, flower-fringed lawn, raised above the corner of the quiet village lane by a retaining wall, has some seats and tables under cocktail parasols; disabled access. The pub is in a particularly pretty village.

Free house ~ Licensees Barry and Susie Coote ~ Real ale ~ Bar food (not Mon) ~ (01728) 663693 ~ Children welcome ~ Dogs welcome ~ Open 11.30-3, 6.30-11; 12-3, 7-10.30 Sun; closed Mon

HUNDON

Plough *Brockley Green – nearly 2 miles SW of village, towards Kedington*

As it's set on top of one of the few hills around here, this remote pub has fine views over the Stour Valley. The neatly kept knocked-through bar has soft red brickwork, old oak beams and plenty of old standing timbers, cushions on low side settles, pine kitchen chairs and sturdy low tables, and plenty of horsebrasses. Outside, there are five acres of lovely landscaped gardens, and a pleasant terrace with an ornamental pool and good wooden furniture under a wisteria-covered pergola; croquet. Cheerful staff serve Greene King IPA, Woodfordes Wherry, and a guest such as Charles Wells Bombardier on handpump, and they've a carefully chosen wine list with a dozen by the glass, and 30 malt whiskies. Besides lunchtime sandwiches, tasty bar food might include soup, cajun chicken, steak pie or sun-dried tomato and goats cheese tart; on Friday evenings they have seafood specials such as monkfish thermidor poached in white wine. Part of the bar and all the restaurant are no smoking.

Free house ~ Licensees David and Marion Rowlinson ~ Real ale ~ Bar food ~ Restaurant ~ (01440) 786789 ~ Children in eating area of bar ~ Dogs welcome ~ Live jazz bank hol Mon lunchtime ~ Open 11-2.30, 6-11; 12-3, 7-10.30 Sun ~ Bedrooms: £45S(£50B)/£65S(£75B)

LONG MELFORD
Black Lion *Church Walk*

This comfortable hotel is somewhere you'd come for a civilised meal, rather than just a quick drink. One side of the oak serving counter is decorated in ochre, and, besides bar stools, has deeply cushioned sofas, leather wing armchairs and antique fireside settles, while the other, in shades of terracotta, has leather dining chairs around handsome tables set for the good bar food. The interesting changing menu could include crispy fried ham hash cakes, cauliflower cheese charlotte on roasted vegetables, steamed beef and suet pudding, and bass with Pernod sauce; also puddings such as chocolate brownie with honeycomb ice-cream. The restaurant is no smoking. Big windows with swagged-back curtains have a pleasant outlook over the green, and there are large portraits, of racehorses and of people. Service by neatly uniformed staff is friendly and efficient; the piped Radio Suffolk can be obtrusive. You'll find well kept (but not cheap) Adnams, and maybe Nethergate Suffolk County on handpump, and they've a fine range of wines by the glass, including champagne, 20 malt whiskies, and generous cafetière coffees; tortilla chips are set out in bowls. The Victorian walled garden is appealing.

Ravenwood Group ~ Manager Lahsen Ighaghai ~ Real ale ~ Bar food (12-2, 7-9.30(10 Fri/Sat)) ~ Restaurant ~ (01787) 312356 ~ Children welcome ~ Dogs welcome ~ Open 11-11; 12-10.30 Sun ~ Bedrooms: £85B/£109.50B

ORFORD
Jolly Sailor *Quay Street*

A good base for walkers, fishermen and bird-watchers, this unspoilt 17th-c brick pub is built mainly from wrecked ships' timbers. The several snugly traditional rooms have lots of exposed brickwork, and are served from counters and hatches in an old-fashioned central cubicle. There's an unusual spiral staircase in the corner of the flagstoned main bar – which also has 13 brass door knockers and other brassware, local photographs, two cushioned pews and a long antique stripped deal table, and an open woodburning stove in the big brick fireplace (with nice horsebrasses above it); a small room is popular with the dominoes and cribbage players. Adnams Bitter and Broadside are well kept on handpump. A short choice of straightforward food in generous helpings could include good battered local cod, skate, rock eel or flounder with chips, home-made steak pie or chilli con carne, and daily roasts; also a couple of evening specials; no sandwiches. There are lovely surrounding coastal walks and plenty of outside pursuits; several picnic-sets on grass at the back have views over the marshes. No children.

Adnams ~ Tenant Philip Attwood ~ Real ale ~ Bar food (12-2, 7.15-8.45; not Mon evening, nor Mon-Thurs evenings Nov-Easter) ~ No credit cards ~ (01394) 450243 ~ Dogs allowed in bar ~ Open 11.30-2.30, 7-11; 12-2.45, 7-10.30 Sun; closed evenings 25/26 Dec ~ Bedrooms: /£50S

STOKE-BY-NAYLAND
Crown *Park Street (B1068)*

Reopened towards the end of 2003 after complete refurbishment by a former landlord of the nearby Angel, in partnership with a director of Lay & Wheelers, the noted wine merchant, this has quickly proved a winner. It typifies the best sort of contemporary reinterpretation of what makes a good if rather upmarket pub. The careful interior design has a lot to do with this. There is plenty of room for either drinking or eating, most of it directly open to the three-sided bar servery, yet well divided, and with two or three more tucked-away areas too. The main area, with a big woodburning stove, has quite a lot of tables, in a variety of shapes, styles and sizes. Seating varies from deep armchairs and sofas to elegant dining chairs and comfortable high-backed woven rush seats – and there are plenty of bar stools. This all gives a good choice between conviviality and varying degrees of cosiness and privacy. With a subtle colour scheme of several gentle toning colours, cheerful wildlife and landscape paintings, quite a lot of attractive table lamps and carefully placed gentle spotlighting, low ceilings (some with a good deal of stripped old beams), and floors varying from old tiles through broad boards or dark new flagstones to beige carpet, the overall feel is of relaxation. There is a table of daily papers. The drink, food and service are all very good. They have Adnams Bitter and Explorer and Greene King IPA and Morlands Original on handpump, nicely served coffee (typically doing well over 100 cups a day), and take care with other drinks such as Pimms. The choice of wines is rewarding – an unusual feature is the glass-walled 'cellar' in one corner. They sell wines by the half-case to take away too, and suggest a different wine by the glass to go with each of their two dozen or so menu choices. The food is enterprising without being outlandishly unusual, taking care with ingredients (local free range chicken, pork, lamb, game and vegetables, crab from East Mersea, wild scotch salmon), and might include bouillabaisse with rouille, ham and mozzarella tart, baby vegetable risotto, charcuterie with home-baked bread, and specials such as sausage and mash, lemon sole or bass, and nice seasonal puddings like peach and blueberry tart with ice-cream. They are happy to do small helpings if you want. Service is good, prompt and thoughtful – and given a slightly continental touch by the wrap-around white aprons worn by all the friendly young staff. A sheltered back terrace has cushioned teak chairs and tables under big canvas parasols with heaters, looking out over a neat lawn to a landscaped shrubbery that includes a small romantic ruined-abbey folly. There are many more picnic-sets out on the front terrace. Disabled access is good, and the car park is big.

Free house ~ Licensee Richard Sunderland ~ Real ale ~ Bar food (12-2.30(3.30

Sun), 6-9.30(10 Fri, Sat; 9 Sun)) ~ Restaurant ~ (01206) 262001 ~ Children in restaurant ~ Dogs allowed in bar ~ Open 11-11; 12-10.30 Sun

Dog Friendly Hotels, B&Bs and Farms

ALDEBURGH
Wentworth *Wentworth Rd, Aldeburgh, Suffolk IP15 5BD (01728) 452312* £113; 35 rms, 7 in annexe which are more spacious. Comfortable and traditional hotel that has been in the same family for over 80 years and overlooks fishing huts and boats; plenty of comfortable seats, lounges with log fires, antiques and books, a convivial bar, cheerful long-standing staff, good enjoyable food in no smoking restaurant, nice breakfasts, and sunny terrace for light lunches; may cl 2 wks Christmas; partial disabled access; dogs welcome in bedrooms and lounges; £2

BILDESTON
Crown *High St, Bildeston, Ipswich, Suffolk IP7 7EB (01449) 740510* £99; 13 newly refurbished rms. Lovely timber-framed Tudor inn with a comfortable well furnished beamed lounge, open fires, good food in popular restaurant, welcoming courteous service, an attractive two-acre informal garden – and resident ghost; self-catering apartment; disabled access; dogs welcome; £10

BURY ST EDMUNDS
Angel *3 Angel Hill, Bury St Edmunds, Suffolk IP33 1LT (01284) 714000* £120, plus special breaks; 75 individually decorated rms. Thriving creeper-clad 15th-c country-town hotel with particularly friendly staff, comfortable lounge and relaxed bar, log fires and fresh flowers, and good food in elegant restaurant and downstairs medieval vaulted room (Mr Pickwick enjoyed a roast dinner here); disabled access; dogs welcome in bedrooms

CAMPSEY ASH
Old Rectory *Station Rd, Campsey Ash, Woodbridge, Suffolk IP13 0PU (01728) 746524* £85; 7 comfortable, pretty rms. Very relaxed and welcoming no smoking Georgian house by church, with charming owner and staff, log fire in comfortable and restful drawing room, quite a few Victorian prints, first-class food from a set menu in summer conservatory or two other dining rooms with more log fires, a good honesty bar, a sensational wine list with very modest mark-ups on its finest wines, and sizeable homely gardens; dogs in bedrooms

HADLEIGH
Edgehall *2 High St, Hadleigh, Ipswich, Suffolk IP7 5AP (01473) 822458* £65, plus special breaks; 8 pretty rms. Friendly family-run Tudor house with Georgian façade, comfortable carefully restored rooms, personal

service, traditional english cooking using home-grown produce in no smoking dining room, and attractive walled garden with croquet; self-catering also; dogs welcome away from dining areas; £5

HIGHAM
Old Vicarage *Higham Rd, Higham, Colchester, Essex CO7 6JY (01206) 337248* **£70**, plus special breaks; 3 rms, 2 with own bthrm. Charming Tudor house near quiet village with very friendly owners, pretty sitting room with fresh flowers, log fire and antiques, and enjoyable breakfasts in attractive breakfast room; play room with toys for children, grounds and fine gardens with river views (they have boats), tennis court, trampoline, and heated swimming pool; dogs welcome

HINTLESHAM
Hintlesham Hall *Hintlesham, Ipswich, Suffolk IP8 3NS (01473) 652334* **£155**, plus special breaks; 33 lovely rms. Magnificent mansion, mainly Georgian but dating from Elizabethan times, in 175 acres with big walled gardens, 18-hole golf course, outdoor heated swimming pool, croquet and tennis; restful and comfortable day rooms with books, antiques and open fires, fine modern cooking in several restaurants, a marvellous wine list, and exemplary service; snooker, sauna, steam room, gym and beauty salon; well behaved children over 10 in evening restaurant; disabled access; dogs welcome by prior arrangement, away from public areas

HORRINGER
Ickworth *Horringer, Bury St Edmunds, Suffolk IP29 5QE (01284) 735350* **£210**, plus special breaks; 27 rms, 11 in annexe. Lovely 18th-c house in marvellous parkland on a vast National Trust estate (formerly owned by the Marquess of Bristol), the east wing of which is a family-friendly hotel; elegant and traditional décor mixes with more contemporary touches, the atmosphere is relaxed and informal, and staff friendly and helpful; good, modern cooking in italian-style café, grand high tea for smaller children, crèches and clubs for children, games room with TV and computer games, wellies, bikes and adventure playground, riding, tennis, and swimming pool; spa and beauty treatments; disabled access; dogs welcome in bedrooms; £7.50

LAVENHAM
Angel *Market Pl, Lavenham, Sudbury, Suffolk CO10 9QZ (01787) 247388* **£75**, plus special breaks; 8 comfortable rms. No smoking, 15th-c inn with original cellar and pargeted ceiling in attractive residents' lounge, several Tudor features such as a rare shuttered shop window front, civilised atmosphere, good food in bar and restaurant, lots of decent wines, several malt whiskies, well kept real ales, thoughtful friendly service, and maybe live classical piano Fri pm; cl 25-26 Dec; disabled access; dogs welcome in one ground-floor room only; £10

LAVENHAM

Swan *High St, Lavenham, Sudbury, Suffolk CO10 9QA (01787) 247477*
£99; 51 smart rms. Handsome and comfortable Elizabethan hotel that incorporates several fine half-timbered buildings inc an Elizabethan house and the former wool hall; lots of cosy seating areas, interesting historic prints and alcoves with beams, timbers, armchairs and settees, good food in lavishly timbered no smoking restaurant with a minstrels' gallery (actually built only in 1965), afternoon teas, intriguing little bar, and friendly helpful staff; dogs in bedrooms; £5

LONG MELFORD

Bull *Hall St, Long Melford, Sudbury, Suffolk CO10 9JG (01787) 378494*
£120, plus special breaks; 25 rms, ancient or comfortably modern. An inn since 1580, this fine black and white hotel was originally a medieval manorial hall, and has handsome and interesting carved woodwork and timbering, and an old weavers' gallery overlooking the courtyard; a large log fire, old-fashioned and antique furnishings, enjoyable food, and friendly service; dogs (if small) in bedrooms; £5

ORFORD

Crown & Castle *Orford, Woodbridge, Suffolk IP12 2LJ (01394) 450205*
£120, plus special breaks; 18 well designed, stylish rms, 10 in garden with own terrace. Red brick and high gabled Victorian hotel by the Norman castle in this seaside village; a lovely relaxed informal atmosphere, cosy, deeply comfortable lounge, bar, exceptionally good modern british cooking with european and far eastern influences, super wine list with 20 by the glass (first-class children's menu), light lunches on terrace in summer, and excellent breakfasts; no smoking except in private dining room; dogs in garden rooms; £10; towels and treats supplied

ROUGHAM

Ravenwood Hall *Rougham, Bury St Edmunds, Suffolk IP30 9JA (01359) 270345* £105, plus special breaks; 14 comfortable rms with antiques, some rms in mews. Tranquil Tudor country house in seven acres of carefully tended gardens and woodland; log fire in comfortable lounge, cosy bar, good food in timbered restaurant with big inglenook fireplace (home-preserved fruits and veg, home-smoked meats and fish), a good wine list, and helpful service; croquet and heated swimming pool; they are kind to children and have themed occasions for them and lots of animals; disabled access; dogs welcome away from restaurant

SOUTHWOLD

Swan *Market Pl, Southwold, Suffolk IP18 6EG (01502) 722186* £140, plus winter breaks; 42 well appointed rms, some overlooking the market square. No smoking, 17th-c hotel with comfortable drawing room, a convivial bar, interesting enjoyable food in elegant no smoking dining room, fine wines, well kept real ales (the hotel backs onto Adnams Brewery), and polite helpful staff; children must be over 5 in evening dining room; dogs in bedrooms; £5

STOKE-BY-NAYLAND
Angel *Polstead St, Stoke-by-Nayland, Colchester, Essex CO6 4SA (01206)*
263245 £**75**; 6 comfortable rms. Civilised and elegant dining pub in Stour
Valley with Tudor beams in cosy bar, stripped brickwork and timbers, fine
furniture, huge log fire and woodburner, decent wines, and particularly
good, imaginative and reasonably priced bar food; cl 25–26 Dec and 1 Jan;
dogs in one bedroom

WESTLETON
Crown *The Street, Westleton, Saxmundham, Suffolk IP17 3AD (01728)*
648777 £**105**; 19 quiet, comfortable rms. Smart, extended country inn in
lovely setting with good nearby walks; comfortable bar, no smoking dining
conservatory, more formal restaurant, a wide range of enjoyable attractively
presented food (nice breakfasts, too), log fires, several well kept real ales,
decent wines, and a pretty garden with outside heaters; cl 25–26 Dec;
disabled access; dogs in some bedrooms; £4.50

WOODBRIDGE
Seckford Hall *Seckford Hall Rd, Great Bealings, Woodbridge, Suffolk IP13
6NU (01394) 385678* £**130**, plus special breaks; 32 comfortable rms.
Handsome red brick Tudor mansion in 34 acres of gardens and parkland
with carp-filled lake, putting, and leisure club with indoor heated pool,
beauty salon and gym in lovely tithe barn; fine linenfold panelling, huge
fireplaces, heavy beams, plush furnishings and antiques in comfortable day
rooms, good food (inc lovely teas with home-made cakes), and helpful
service; cl 25 Dec; dogs welcome in bedrooms; £7.50

WORLINGTON
Worlington Hall *Mildenhall Rd, Worlington, Bury St Edmunds, Suffolk
IP28 8RX (01638) 712237* £**80**; 9 comfortable rms with decanter of
sherry and fruit. 16th-c former manor house in five acres with a 9-hole
pitch and putt course, comfortable panelled lounge bar with log fire, good
food in relaxed candlelit bistro, and friendly staff; dogs in bedrooms and
lounge

Surrey

Dog Friendly Pubs

BETCHWORTH
Dolphin *Turn off A25 W of Reigate opposite B2032 at roundabout, and keep on into The Street; opposite the church*

This surprisingly unspoilt 16th-c village pub is usually busy with a good mix of locals, walkers and visitors and has a lovely welcoming atmosphere. The neat and homely front room has kitchen chairs and plain tables on the 400-year-old scrubbed flagstones, and the carpeted back saloon bar is black-panelled, with robust old-fashioned elm or oak tables. There are three warming fires, a nice chiming longcase clock, silenced fruit machine, darts, shove-ha'penny, cribbage and dominoes. As well as up to 18 wines by the glass, friendly staff serve well kept Youngs Bitter, Special, Waggle Dance and maybe a seasonal guest on handpump. It's best to arrive early, or book a table beforehand if you want to enjoy the generously served, good value bar food, which includes very popular breaded plaice and chips, beef or vegetable lasagne, and steaks, and daily specials such as dressed crab salad; puddings might be spotted dick. There are some seats in the small laurel-shaded front courtyard, and behind are picnic-sets on a terrace and lawn by the car park, opposite the church. Parking can be very difficult in summer. No children inside.

Youngs ~ Managers George and Rose Campbell ~ Real ale ~ Bar food (12-2.30, 7-10) ~ (01737) 842288 ~ Dogs allowed in bar ~ Open 11-3, 5.30-11; 11-11 Sat; 12-10.30 Sun

BLACKBROOK
Plough *On by-road E of A24, parallel to it, between Dorking and Newdigate, just N of the turn E to Leigh*

Children are catered for thoughtfully at this neatly kept pub, which has a better than average children's menu and a little swiss playhouse furnished with little tables and chairs in the secluded garden. Welcoming and enjoyable, the no smoking red saloon bar has fresh flowers on its tables and on the window sills of its large windows. Down some steps, the public bar has brass-topped treadle tables, old saws on the ceiling, and bottles and flat irons. Bar food includes nice bagels with inventive toppings, steak sandwich, and blackboard specials such as lentil, pea and ham soup, chicken and lime curry and roast rack of lamb. Well kept Badger Best, K&B Sussex and Tanglefoot, and a guest such as Gribble Fursty Ferret on handpump, 16 wines by the glass, and several ports; shove-ha'penny and cribbage. The countryside around here is particularly good for colourful spring and summer walks through the oak woods, and the pub's white frontage is covered in pretty hanging baskets and year round window boxes. There are tables and chairs outside on the terrace.

Badger ~ Tenants Chris and Robin Squire ~ Real ale ~ Bar food (not Mon evening) ~ (01306) 886603 ~ Children welcome ~ Dogs allowed in bar ~ Open 11-3, 6(7 Sun)-11.30

CHARLESHILL

Donkey *B3001 Milford—Farnham near Tilford; coming from Elstead, turn left as soon as you see pub sign*

Emphasis at this beamed cottagey pub is on the enjoyable (though not cheap) food. Friendly staff serve starters such as soup and thai-style fishcakes, and main courses such as hot and sour mushrooms on stir-fry vegetables, steak and Guinness pie, and bass fillet with king prawns. The bright saloon has lots of polished stirrups, lamps and watering cans on the walls, and prettily cushioned built-in wall benches, while the lounge has a fine high-backed settle, highly polished horsebrasses, and swords on the walls and beams; the dining conservatory is no smoking. All their wines are available by the glass, and you'll also find well kept Greene King IPA, Abbot and Old Speckled Hen on handpump; piped music. The garden is very attractive, with a terrace, plenty of seats, and a play area with a wendy house for children; the two friendly donkeys are called Pip and Dusty.

Greene King ~ Lease Lee and Helen Francis ~ Real ale ~ Bar food (12-2.30, 6-9) ~ Restaurant ~ (01252) 702124 ~ Children welcome ~ Dogs allowed in bar ~ Open 12-3, 6-11(11.30 Sat); 12-10.30 Sun; 12-3, 6-10.30 Sun in winter

COLDHARBOUR

Plough *Village signposted in the network of small roads around Leith Hill*

The charming licensee couple here clearly enjoy running this friendly old coaching inn. The two bars (each with a lovely open fire) have stripped light beams and timbering in the warm-coloured dark ochre walls, with quite unusual little chairs around the tables in the snug red-carpeted games room on the left (with darts), and little decorative plates on the walls; the one on the right leads through to the no smoking candlelit restaurant. From the pub's own Leith Hill Brewery, they serve Crooked Furrow and Tallywacker on handpump, along with three or four well kept real ales such as Ringwood Old Thumper, Shepherd Neame Master Brew and Ringwood Bold Forester; also Biddenden farm cider; piped music, darts, TV, shove-ha'penny, cribbage and dominoes. Enjoyable (though not cheap) bar food includes fried baby squid, roast beef or roasted vegetables in tomato sauce and melted goats cheese on fettucine pasta, confit of duck, and puddings such as mascarpone and lemon cheesecake. This is a peaceful setting in a hamlet high in the Surrey hills (good walks), and there are picnic-sets by tubs of flowers in front and in the terraced garden with its fish pond and waterlilies.

Own brew ~ Licensees Richard and Anna Abrehart ~ Real ale ~ Bar food (12-3, 6-9.30(9 Sun)) ~ Restaurant ~ (01306) 711793 ~ Children in eating area of bar and also in barn on Sun ~ Dogs allowed in bar ~ Open 11.30-11; 12-10.30 Sun ~ Bedrooms: £54S/£65S(£80B)

EASHING

Stag *Lower Eashing; Eashing signposted off A3 southbound, S of Hurtmore turn-off; or pub signposted off A283 just SE of exit roundabout at N end of A3 Milford bypass*

Also known as the Stag on the River, this attractive pub has a millstream running past the garden, making this a great place to be on a summer's day. Tucked down a narrow lane, the building itself has a Georgian brick façade, but dates back in part to the 15th c. Its opened up interior has a charming old-fashioned locals' bar on the right with red and black flooring tiles by the counter and well kept Courage Best, Fullers London Pride and Shepherd Neame Spitfire on handpump, about 14 wines by the glass and good coffee. A cosy gently lit room beyond has a low white plank ceiling, a big stag print and stag's head on the dark-wallpapered walls, some cookery books on shelves by the log fire, and sturdy cushioned chairs grouped around dark tables on the brick floor. An extensive blue-carpeted area rambles around on the left, with similar comfortable dark furniture, some smaller country prints and decorative plates on pink Anaglypta walls, and round towards the back a big woodburning stove in a capacious fireplace under a long mantelbeam. It's all rather smart yet cosily traditional, the thriving atmosphere helped along by attentive and chatty neatly dressed staff; there is a table of conservative daily papers, and they are kind to visiting dogs. Tasty lunchtime and early evening bar snacks include open ciabatta sandwiches, burgers and sausage and mash, while a big blackboard lists food such as moules marinière and venison steak; also puddings such as lemon cheesecake with berry fruits; no smoking restaurant. The riverside garden has picnic-sets and other tables under cocktail parasols among mature trees, and a terrace with some teak furniture, and more picnic-sets in a lantern-lit arbour.

Punch ~ Lease Marilyn Lackey ~ Real ale ~ Bar food (12-2.30(3 Sun), 6-9.30; not Sun, Mon evenings) ~ Restaurant ~ (01483) 421568 ~ Children in eating area of bar and restaurant ~ Dogs allowed in bar ~ Open 11-11; 12-10.30 Sun ~ Bedrooms: /£55S

ESHER

Marneys *Alma Road (one way only), Weston Green; heading N on A309 from A307 roundabout, after Lamb & Star pub turn left into Lime Tree Avenue (signposted to All Saints Parish Church), then left at T-junction into Chestnut Avenue*

Turning off the busy trunk road, it's a real surprise to find this cottagey little pub, in such a pleasant spot right on the edge of a well wooded common, beside an attractive church and close to a lively duck pond. There's not much room in the chatty low-beamed bar with its black and white plank panelling, shelves of hens and ducks and other ornaments, small blue-curtained windows, and perhaps horse racing on the corner TV. On the left, past a little cast-iron woodburning stove, a dining area (somewhat roomier but still small) has big pine tables, pews and pale country kitchen chairs. Well kept Bass, Courage Best and Flowers Original on handpump, just over a dozen wines by the glass (even pink champagne on our summer visit), enterprising soft drinks, norwegian schnapps and good coffee. The sensibly small choice of good interesting food has a scandinavian lean, and runs from baguettes to meatballs and red cabbage or good soused herring fillets; puddings such as almond and pear tart. They are happy to cater for small appetites. Service by friendly uniformed staff is quick and efficient; and they have daily papers. The pleasantly planted sheltered garden has black picnic-sets under purple canvas parasols, and the front terrace has dark blue cast-iron tables and chairs under matching parasols, with some more black tables too.

Free house ~ Licensee Henrik Platou ~ Real ale ~ Bar food (12-2.15; not evenings or Sun) ~ (020) 8398 4444 ~ Children welcome till 6pm ~ Dogs allowed in bar ~ Open 11-11; 12-10.30 Sun

LEIGH

Plough *3 miles S of A25 Dorking—Reigate, signposted from Betchworth (which itself is signposted off the main road); also signposted from South Park area of Reigate; on village green*

Helpful notices inside this tiled and weatherboarded cottage warn you not to bump your head on the very low beams in the cosy timbered dining lounge on the right, which is decorated with lots of local prints on white walls. On the left, a simpler more local pubby bar has a good bow-window seat, lots of different games including darts, shove-ha'penny, dominoes, table skittles, cribbage, Jenga, backgammon and shut-the-box; there's also piped music, an alcove fruit machine and occasional TV. Well kept real ales are Badger Best, Tanglefoot, Sussex, and a guest such as Gribble Fursty Ferret on handpump, and you can have a glass of anything on the decent wine list. The wide-ranging menu includes a big selection of sandwiches, baked potatoes, and blackboard specials such as creamy garlic mushrooms, steak pie, roasted vegetable mexican-style tortilla wrap, and puddings such as pavlova; you may need to book at the weekend. The pub is attractively placed by the village green, and picnic-sets under cocktail parasols in a pretty side garden (fairy-lit in the evening), and colourful hanging baskets make this especially pleasant in summer; nearby parking is limited.

Badger ~ Tenant Sarah Bloomfield ~ Real ale ~ Bar food (12-10(9.30 Sun)) ~ Restaurant ~ (01306) 611348 ~ Children in eating area of bar and restaurant ~ Dogs allowed in bar ~ Open 11-11; 12-10.30 Sun

MICKLEHAM

Running Horses *Old London Road (B2209)*

Picnic-sets on a terrace in front of this smartly substantial white-painted inn with its big sash windows, and lovely flowering tubs and hanging baskets take in a peaceful view of the old church with its strange stubby steeple, just across the quiet lane, and are a delightful place to pass a summer evening. Inside, the two calmly relaxing rooms of the bar are neatly kept and spaciously open plan with fresh flowers (in summer) in an inglenook at one end, lots of race tickets hanging from a beam, some really good racing cartoons, hunting pictures and Hogarth prints, dark carpets, cushioned wall settles and other dining chairs around straightforward pubby tables and bar stools. Adnams, Fullers London Pride, Shepherd Neame and Youngs are well kept on handpump alongside good, if pricey wines by the glass, from a serious list. As well as a tempting choice of bar food (not cheap) such as lunchtime chunky sandwiches, ciabatta toasties, smoked salmon and mussel linguine, steak, Guinness and mushroom pudding, there's also a more elaborate restaurant menu (which you can eat from in the bar), which might include carpaccio of peppered venison and fried bass with roast pear and almonds; also puddings such as sticky date and sultana pudding with butterscotch sauce. The restaurant area leads straight out of the bar and although it is set out quite formally with crisp white cloths and candles on each table, it shares the thriving atmosphere of the bar; piped music and professional staff.

Punch ~ Lease Steve and Josie Slayford ~ Real ale ~ Bar food (12-2.30, 7-9.30) ~ Restaurant ~ (01372) 372279 ~ Children in restaurant ~ Dogs welcome ~ Open 11.30-11; 12-10.30 Sun ~ Bedrooms: £94(£94S)(£105.75B)/ £105.75(£105.75S)(£141B)

REIGATE HEATH

Skimmington Castle *3 miles from M25 junction 8: through Reigate take A25 towards Dorking, then on edge of Reigate turn left past Black Horse into Flanchford Road; after ¼ mile turn left into Bonny's Road (unmade, very bumpy track); after crossing golf course, fork right up hill*

Readers are fond of this quaint old country pub. The bright main front bar leads off a small room with a central serving counter, with dark simple panelling and lots of keys hanging from the beams. There's a miscellany of chairs and tables, shiny brown plank panelling, well kept Adnams, Greene King Old Speckled Hen, Youngs Special and a guest such as Sharps Eden on handpump, with over a dozen wines by the glass, farm cider and even some organic spirits. The cosy back rooms are partly panelled too, with old-fashioned settles and windsor chairs; one has a big brick fireplace with its bread-oven still beside it – the chimney is said to have been used as a highwayman's look-out. Steps take you down to just three tables in a small but pleasant no smoking room at the back; shove-ha'penny, cribbage, dominoes, ring-the-bull, board games, and piped music. The bar food is good and popular, so you need to get here early for a table as they don't take bookings. Swiftly served dishes could include mushroom and spinach stroganoff, home-made fish or steak and kidney pie, lamb steak and rib-eye steak; irresistible puddings. In fine weather you can enjoy lovely views from the crazy-paved front terrace and tables on the grass by lilac bushes; more tables at the back overlook the meadows and the hillocks (though you may find the views blocked by trees in summer). The pub is remotely placed up a track, handy for the Greensand Way and there's a hitching rail outside for horses. No children.

Punch ~ Tenants Anthony Pugh and John Davidson ~ Real ale ~ Bar food (12-2.15(2.30 Sun), 7-9.30(9 Sun)) ~ (01737) 243100 ~ Dogs welcome ~ Folk jam session 2nd Tues in month ~ Open 11-3, 5.30(6 Sat)-11; 12-10.30 Sun

Dog Friendly Hotels, B&Bs and Farms

BAGSHOT
Pennyhill Park *College Ride, Bagshot, Surrey GU19 5ET (01276) 471774* £**260**, plus special breaks; 123 individually designed luxury rms and suites. Impressive Victorian country house in 120 acres of well kept gardens and parkland inc a 9-hole golf course, tennis courts, outdoor heated swimming pool, clay pigeon shooting, archery, fishing, and an international rugby pitch; friendly courteous staff, wood-panelled bar with resident pianist, comfortable two-level lounge and reading room, very good imaginative food in two restaurants, jazz Sun lunchtime, and terraces overlooking the golf course; disabled access; dogs in bedrooms and some other areas; £50

HASLEMERE
Deerfell *Blackdown, Haslemere, Surrey GU27 3LA (01428) 653409* £**50**; 3 comfortable rms, 1 with shared bthrm. Comfortable no smoking stone coach house with wonderful views and good nearby walks; generous meals in handsome dining room (ordered in advance), open fire in sitting room, pictures, antiques and old rugs, a sun room, good breakfasts, and friendly owners; cl mid-Dec-mid-Jan; children over 6; dogs by prior arrangement

HASLEMERE
Lythe Hill Hotel & Spa *Petworth Rd, Haslemere, Surrey GU27 3BQ (01428) 651251* £**184**, plus wknd breaks; 41 individually styled rms, a few in the original house. Lovely partly 15th-c building in 20 acres of parkland and bluebell woods (adjoining the NT hillside) with floodlit tennis court, croquet lawn, and jogging track; plush, comfortable and elegant lounges, a relaxed bar, two no smoking restaurants (one with french cooking, the other with traditional english), and good attentive service; spa with swimming pool, sauna, steam and beauty rooms and gym; disabled access; dogs in some bedrooms; £20

NUTFIELD
Nutfield Priory *Nutfield, Redhill, Surrey RH1 4EL (01737) 824400* £**175**, plus special breaks; 60 rms. Impressive Victorian gothick hotel in 40 acres of parkland with lovely elaborate carvings, stained-glass windows, gracious day rooms, a fine panelled library, cloistered restaurant, and even an organ in the galleried grand hall; extensive leisure club with indoor heated swimming pool; dogs welcome in bedrooms

Sussex

Dog Friendly Pubs

AMBERLEY
Black Horse *Off B2139*
After a walk along the South Downs Way, the garden of this very pretty pub is a restful place to enjoy a drink or lunch, and the views are lovely. The main bar has high-backed settles on flagstones, beams over the serving counter festooned with sheep bells and shepherds' tools (hung by the last shepherd on the Downs), and walls decorated with a mixture of prints and paintings. The lounge bar has many antiques and artefacts collected by the owners on their world travels; there are log fires in both bars and two in the no smoking restaurant. Well liked bar food includes home-made vegetable soup, home-made chicken liver pâté, sandwiches with salad and chips, lasagne or broccoli and pasta bake, and various curries or chicken with sauces. Well kept Charles Wells Bombardier and Greene King IPA on handpump, and several malt whiskies; piped music. The garden is a restful place.
Pubmaster ~ Tenant Gary Tubb ~ Real ale ~ Bar food (12-3, 6-9(10 Fri/Sat); all day Sun) ~ Restaurant ~ (01798) 831552 ~ Children in eating area of bar and restaurant (must be over 6) ~ Dogs welcome ~ Open 11-11; 12-10.30 Sun

CHILGROVE
White Horse *B2141 Petersfield—Chichester*
From outside, this former 18th-c coaching inn certainly looks the part, with its tiled roof and long white-painted façade covered with wisteria. Inside, it has a much more up-to-date feel, civilised and quietly upmarket – certainly more inn than pub, though service is so helpful and friendly that you do feel immediately welcome. The bar counter is made up from claret, burgundy and other mainly french wooden wine cases, and good wines by the glass, with an impressive range by the bottle, are a big plus here; they also have well kept Ballards on handpump. Dark brown deco leather armchairs and a sofa are grouped on dark boards here, and on either side are three or four well spaced good-sized sturdy tables with good pale spindleback side and elbow chairs on lighter newer boards; a feeling of freshness is accentuated by the big bow window, uncluttered cream walls

and ceiling, and clear lighting. There may be piped music, well reproduced. Besides a good range of sandwiches, spanish staff prepare enjoyable if not cheap light lunchtime dishes such as air-dried ham with melon or mediterranean fish soup, seared scallops, and sturdier dishes such as pork fillet with apple compote and port sauce. The bar has a woodburner on one side, and a log fire on the other. Past here, it opens into a similarly fresh-styled restaurant with comfortable modern seats and attractively laid tables. Outside, one neat lawn has white cast-iron tables and chairs under an old yew tree, and another has wooden benches, tables and picnic-sets under a tall flag mast; completely no smoking. This is a lovely downland valley with lots of fine walks nearby, and the road through is a good one, and fairly quiet. We have not yet heard from readers who have stayed in the eight bedrooms here, but would expect this to be a nice place to stay in. *Free house ~ Licensee Charles Burton ~ Real ale ~ Bar food (12-2, 6-10) ~ Restaurant ~ (01243) 535219 ~ Children welcome ~ Dogs welcome ~ Open 10-3, 6-10; closed Sun evening, Mon ~ Bedrooms: £47.50B/£95B*

EAST ASHLING
Horse & Groom *B2178 NW of Chichester*

Six bedrooms in a newly built wing have been added to this bustling and friendly country pub, and there's also a new conservatory restaurant extension overlooking the garden. With a good mix of customers, the front part is a proper bar with old pale flagstones and a woodburning stove in a big inglenook on the right, a carpeted area with an old wireless set, nice scrubbed trestle tables, and bar stools along the counter serving well kept Brewsters Hophead, Harveys Best, Hop Back Summer Lightning, and Youngs on handpump. They also have eight wines by the glass and Addlestones cider. A couple of tables share a small light flagstoned middle area with the big blackboard that lists changing dishes such as parsnip soufflé with cheddar cheese, steak in ale pie, and rack of lamb; also snacks such as sandwiches and filled baked potatoes, and home-cooked ham and eggs. The back part of the pub, entirely no smoking and angling right round behind the bar servery, has solid pale country-kitchen furniture on neat bare boards, and a fresh and airy décor, with a little bleached pine panelling and long white curtains. French windows lead out to a garden with picnic-sets under cocktail parasols. Always popular with local people in the know, the pub gets extremely busy on Goodwood race days. *Free house ~ Licensee Michael Martell ~ Real ale ~ Bar food (12-2.15, 6.30-9.15; not Sun evening) ~ Restaurant ~ (01243) 575339 ~ Children in eating area of bar and restaurant ~ Dogs allowed in bar and bedrooms ~ Open 12-3, 6-11; 12-6 Sun ~ Bedrooms: £40S/£60B*

EAST CHILTINGTON
Jolly Sportsman *2 miles N of B2116; Chapel Lane – follow sign to 13th-c church*

Even when this tucked-away and civilised Victorian dining pub is at its busiest, service remains friendly and helpful. The food is imaginative and extremely good, and includes a fixed-price menu, as well as cockle, tomato and saffron pasta, sicilian-style sardine fillets with couscous, fresh herb omelette, cornish hake fillet with fresh chanterelles, best end of local lamb, and puddings such as chocolate and griotte cherry loaf with coffee sauce. A couple of chairs by the fireplace are set aside for drinkers in the chatty little bar with stripped wood floors and a mix of furniture, but most people head for the smart but informal no smoking restaurant with contemporary light wood furniture, and modern landscapes on green-painted walls. Two well kept ales from breweries such as Brewsters, Dark Star or Mauldons are tapped from the cask, there's a remarkably good wine list with nine wines by the glass, farm cider, 68 malt whiskies, and quite a few natural fruit drinks. There are rustic tables and benches under gnarled trees in a pretty cottagey front garden with more on the terrace and the front bricked area, and the large back lawn with a children's play area looks out towards the South Downs; good walks nearby.

Free house ~ Licensee Bruce Wass ~ Real ale ~ Bar food (till 10 Fri and Sat) ~ Restaurant ~ (01273) 890400 ~ Children welcome ~ Dogs welcome ~ Open 12-2.30, 6-11; 12-4 Sun; closed Sun evening, all day Mon

EAST DEAN

Tiger *Pub (with village centre) signposted – not vividly – from A259 Eastbourne—Seaford*

This is a smashing old pub and a favourite with a great many customers. It's in an idyllic spot by a secluded sloping village green lined with similar low cottages, and the outside is brightened up with lovely flowering climbers and window boxes in summer. Inside, there are just nine tables in the two smallish rooms (candlelit at night) so space at peak times is very limited – particularly in winter when you can't stand outside or sit on the grass; they don't, in the best pub tradition, take bookings so you do have to arrive early for a table. There are low beams hung with pewter and china, polished rustic tables and distinctive antique settles, and old prints and so forth. Well kept Harveys Best with guests such as Adnams Best or Broadside, and Brakspears Bitter on handpump, and a good choice of wines with a dozen by the large glass; cribbage and dominoes. They get their fish fresh from Hastings, their lamb from the farm on the hill, all vegetables and eggs from another local farm, and meat from the local butcher. From a sensibly short but ever changing menu, the imaginative food at lunchtime might include a choice of 20 different ploughman's, home-made potato, leek and cheddar tart, fresh local crab salad or casserole of pork in cider; in the evening, there might be locally smoked breast of duck salad, rabbit stew with bacon and cream and fresh grilled fillets of bass. At lunchtimes on hot days and bank holidays they usually have only cold food. The South Downs Way is close by so it's naturally popular with walkers, and the lane leads on down to a fine stretch of coast culminating in Beachy Head. No children inside.

Free house ~ Licensee Nicholas Denyer ~ Real ale ~ Bar food ~ No credit cards ~ (01323) 423209 ~ Dogs welcome ~ Open 11-3, 6-11; 11-11 Sat; 12-10.30 Sun

EAST HOATHLY

Foresters Arms *Village signposted off A22 Hailsham—Uckfield (take south-easternmost of the two turn-offs); South Street*

The new young licensees have refreshed this village pub, giving it a bit of an emphasis on good reasonably priced food without losing its simplicity and relaxed local atmosphere. The bar has two small linked rooms, with just a handful of tables on its parquet floor (one in a bow window), simple pub seating including a sturdy winged settle, eau de nil wallpaper and dark woodwork; the one on the right has a small art nouveau fireplace under a big mirror, and its ceiling is papered with sheet music, from J S Bach to 'Yes! We Have No Bananas!' and french songs of a similar vintage. Back from here is a bigger room with a collection of musical instruments on one wall, a piano, and some sturdy cushioned oak settles; darts, cribbage, dominoes and shove-ha'penny. The food, all freshly cooked, might include fresh oysters, mushroom soup, sandwiches, filo-wrapped king prawns with a chilli dip, home-baked ham and egg or mussels steamed with cream (something of a speciality here), very popular beer-battered fish and mint-marinated local lamb chops; puddings too, and local cheeses with biscuits and fruit. With 24 hours' notice and for at least two people, they do a special paella – and more humbly, evening take-away fish and home-made chips or thai curry (not Sunday). On the left, a charming library-style no smoking carpeted dining room, not cut off from the rest of the pub, has just five candlelit tables. Under high beams, hop bines and copper pans, the mahogany bar counter has well kept Harveys Best on handpump, decent wines by the glass, and good coffee. There may be unobtrusive piped music. Service is informal, helpful and friendly, and there is good wheelchair access. A few picnic-sets with cocktail parasols stand out in front.

Harveys ~ Tenants Gary Skipsey and Lindsay Coates ~ Real ale ~ Bar food (12-2.30, 6.30-9.15) ~ Restaurant ~ (01825) 840208 ~ Children welcome if eating ~ Dogs welcome ~ Live music Thurs evening ~ Open 11-3, 5-11; 12-10.30 Sun

ELSTED

Three Horseshoes *Village signposted from B2141 Chichester—Petersfield; also reached easily from A272 about 2 miles W of Midhurst, turning left heading W*

In summer, the lovely garden here, with free-roaming bantams, plenty of tables, pretty flowers, and marvellous downland views, is quite a draw. But it's just as nice in winter as the snug little rooms have ancient beams and flooring, antique furnishings, lovely log fires, fresh flowers on the tables, attractive prints and photographs, candlelight, and a very congenial atmosphere. Popular, enjoyable bar food includes a generous ploughman's with a good choice of cheeses, chicken in dijon mustard or tomato and goats cheese tart, steak, kidney and Guinness pie (made by Joan for 23 years now), fresh seasonal crab and lobster, and delicious home-made puddings. The dining room is no smoking. Well kept changing ales racked on a stillage behind the bar counter might include Ballards Best, Cheriton Pots Ale, and Timothy Taylors Landlord, with guests like Fullers London Pride or Hop Back Summer Lightning; summer cider; dominoes.

Free house ~ Licensee Sue Beavis ~ Real ale ~ Bar food ~ (01730) 825746 ~
Well behaved children in eating areas ~ Dogs allowed in bar ~ Open 11-2.30, 6-
11; 12-3, 7-10.30 Sun

FITTLEWORTH
Swan *Lower Street*
Dating from 1382, this old coaching inn is popular with both those
popping in for a pint and a chat and with customers wanting an enjoyable
meal. The beamed main bar is comfortable and relaxed with windsor
armchairs and bar stools on the part stripped wood and part carpeted floor,
there are wooden truncheons over the big inglenook fireplace (which has
good winter log fires), and well kept Fullers London Pride, Greene King
Old Speckled Hen, and Wadworths 6X on handpump. There's an
attractive panelled room – part of the no smoking restaurant – that's
decorated with landscapes by Constable's brother George; piped music.
Well liked bar food includes lunchtime ploughman's, home-made soup,
home-made thai crab cakes with pineapple chutney, pie of the day or
sausages with onion gravy, sun-blush tomato risotto or calves liver on
parsnip mash; also home-made puddings like profiteroles or crème brûlée;
friendly, swift service. Perhaps the nicest place to sit in summer is at one of
the well spaced tables on the big back lawn, sheltered by flowering shrubs
and a hedge sprawling with honeysuckle; there are also benches by the
village lane in front of this pretty tile-hung inn. Good nearby walks in
beech woods.
Enterprise ~ Lease Robert Carey ~ Real ale ~ Bar food (not winter Sun evening) ~
Restaurant ~ (01798) 865429 ~ Children in eating area of bar and restaurant ~
Dogs allowed in bar ~ Open 11-3, 5(6 Sat)-11; 12-4, 7-10.30 Sun ~ Bedrooms:
£35B/£70B

FLETCHING
Griffin *Village signposted off A272 W of Uckfield*
This civilised and very well run old inn appeals to a wide mix of customers
– not always an easy thing to do. It's very popular locally with plenty of
chatty regulars enjoying the well kept real ales or the live jazz twice a week,
there are lots of customers who drive some distance to have an imaginative
meal (or residents staying overnight in the comfortable bedrooms), and
they allow well behaved children and dogs, too. The beamed and quaintly
panelled bar rooms therefore have a good bustling atmosphere, as well as
blazing log fires, old photographs and hunting prints, straightforward
furniture including some captains' chairs, and china on a delft shelf. There's
a small bare-boarded serving area off to one side, and a snug separate bar
with sofas and TV. As well as filled ciabattas, the extremely good food
might include a tuscan vegetable soup, grilled lemon-scented sardines with
fresh tomato sauce, sweet potato, oyster mushrooms and taleggio tart,
organic veal meatballs with tomato salsa on tagliatelle, and chargrilled
sirloin steak with home-made chips and béarnaise sauce; also puddings such
as chocolate brownie with chocolate sauce and crème fraîche. It does get
particularly busy on Sunday lunchtimes. Well kept Badger Tanglefoot,

Harveys Best, and King Horsham Best Bitter on handpump, and a fine wine list with a dozen (including champagne and sweet wine) by the glass, and fresh apple juice. The two acres of garden behind the pub look across fine rolling countryside towards Sheffield Park, and there are plenty of seats here and on a sheltered gravel terrace.

Free house ~ Licensees N Pullan and J Pullan ~ Real ale ~ Bar food (12-2.30, 7-9.30; not 25 Dec or evening 1 Jan) ~ Restaurant ~ (01825) 722890 ~ Children in eating area of bar and restaurant ~ Dogs allowed in bar ~ Jazz Fri evening and Sun lunchtime ~ Open 12-3, 6-11; 7pm opening Sun evening in winter; closed 25 Dec ~ Bedrooms: /£85B

ICKLESHAM
Queens Head *Just off A259 Rye—Hastings*

Bustling and friendly, this handsome pub is liked by a wide mix of customers; dogs, too, are welcome but must be kept on a lead. The open-plan areas work round a very big serving counter which stands under a vaulted beamed roof, the high beamed walls and ceiling of the easy-going bar are lined with shelves of bottles and covered with farming implements and animal traps, and there are well used pub tables and old pews on the brown patterned carpet. Other areas (two are no smoking and popular with diners) have big inglenook fireplaces, and the back room is now decorated with old bicycle and motorbike prints. Well kept Courage Directors, and Greene King IPA and Abbot, with guests like Grand Union Special, Whites 1066 Country Bitter, and Woodfordes Wherry on handpump; Biddenden cider, and quite a few wines by the glass. Reasonably priced, decent bar food includes sandwiches, home-made lentil and bacon soup, filled baked potatoes, home-made steak and kidney pudding, fresh fish dishes, and daily specials; prompt service from efficient staff. Shove-ha'penny, dominoes, cribbage, darts, and piped music. Picnic-sets look out over the vast, gently sloping plain of the Brede Valley from the little garden, and there's an outside children's play area, and boules. Good local walks.

Free house ~ Licensee Ian Mitchell ~ Real ale ~ Bar food (12-2.30, 6.15-9.30; all day Sat and Sun; not 25 or 26 Dec) ~ (01424) 814552 ~ Well behaved children in eating area of bar till 8.30pm ~ Dogs welcome ~ Live jazz/blues/folk Tues evening ~ Open 11-11; 12-10.30 Sun

LURGASHALL
Noahs Ark *Village signposted from A283 N of Petworth; OS Sheet 186 map reference 936272*

On the edge of a quiet village green, this charming 16th-c pub is run by friendly people. The two neatly furnished bars have warm log fires (one in a capacious inglenook), well kept Greene King IPA, Abbot and Old Speckled Hen on handpump, and several well polished trophies. The family room is decorated like the inside of an ark; darts. From a sensibly short menu, bar food includes ploughman's, hot wraps with fillings like crispy duck, spring onion, cucumber and hoi sin, salads, fresh cod in cider batter, chicken curry or steak and mushroom pie; also puddings such as dark chocolate brandy torte, and Sunday lunch. In summer, the flowering baskets are splendid, there's a back garden with seating, and picnic-sets on the grass in front are ideally placed for watching the local cricket team play. *Greene King ~ Tenant Bernard Joseph Wija ~ Real ale ~ Bar food (not Sun evening) ~ Restaurant ~ (01428) 707346 ~ Children in restaurant and family room ~ Dogs allowed in bar ~ Open 11-3, 6-11; 12-3, 7-10.30 Sun; closed Sun evening in winter*

PETWORTH
Welldiggers Arms *Low Heath; A283 towards Pulborough*
This interestingly combines good generous fresh food (not that cheap, but really good value for this part of the world) with the unassuming style and appearance of an ancient country pub as it might have been in the 1930s. The result is a thoroughly civilised atmosphere, chatty and relaxed. The smallish L-shaped bar has low beams, a few pictures (Churchill and gun dogs are prominent) on shiny ochre walls above a panelled dado, a couple of very long rustic settles with tables to match, and some other stripped tables; a second rather lower side room has a somewhat lighter décor. They have well kept Youngs on handpump, and decent wines. The changing food, all home-made, might include bacon and egg baps, crab tartlet, french onion soup, smoked salmon pâté, home-baked ham and egg, vegetarian wellington or a rich oxtail casserole, and puddings like bread and butter pudding; their speciality is seafood royale (for two, with lobster, king prawns, crab, oysters and so forth). Under the eye of the long-serving hands-on landlord, service is friendly and informal yet efficient; no music or machines. Outside, screened from the road by a thick high hedge, are plenty of tables and chairs on pleasant lawns and a terrace, looking back over rolling fields and woodland.
Free house ~ Licensee Ted Whitcomb ~ Real ale ~ Bar food ~ (01798) 342287 ~ Children welcome ~ Dogs welcome ~ Open 11-3, 6-11; closed Mon; closed Tues, Weds and Sun evenings

RUSHLAKE GREEN
Horse & Groom *Village signposted off B2096 Heathfield—Battle*
With a strong local following – though there are plenty of visitors, too – this attractively set pub has a good thriving atmosphere. On the right is the heavily beamed dining room with guns and hunting trophies on the walls, plenty of wheelback chairs around pubby tables, and a log fire. The little L-shaped bar has more low beams (watch your head) and is simply furnished with high bar stools and bar chairs, red plush cushioned wall seats and a few brocaded cushioned stools, and a brick fireplace with some brass items on the mantelpiece; horsebrasses, photographs of the pub and local scenes on the walls, and fresh flowers. A small room down a step has jockeys' colours and jockey photographs and watercolours of the pub. Listed on boards by the entrance to the bar, the large choice of popular bar food might include steak, kidney and Guinness suet pudding or toad in the hole with proper cumberland sausages and onion gravy, organic salmon, chicken breast coated in sesame seeds with stir-fried noodles, and puddings such as squidgy

chocolate meringue or orange brûlée cheesecake. Well kept Harveys Best and Shepherd Neame Master Brew and Spitfire on handpump, and several wines by the glass. The village green is just across the lane, and there are oak seats and tables (made by the landlord) in the cottagey garden with pretty country views.

Free house ~ Licensees Mike and Sue Chappel ~ Real ale ~ Bar food (12-2.30, 7-9.30(9 Sun)) ~ Restaurant ~ (01435) 830320 ~ Children welcome ~ Dogs welcome ~ Open 11.30-3, 5.30-11; 12-3, 7-10.30 Sun

RYE

Ypres Castle *Gun Garden; steps up from A259, or down past Ypres Tower*
Set at the base of the 13th-c Ypres Tower and museum and the even older St Mary's Parish Church, this friendly pub has lovely views from the windows and from the large, sheltered garden looking over the River Rother with its working fishing fleet, and on further to Romney Marsh and the sea. Inside, the bars are traditionally furnished with antique furniture and rugs and there's a big eclectic art collection, and a winter log fire surrounded by comfortable chairs. You can eat in the large no smoking room, the more informal bar area or the comfortable no smoking restaurant, and although bar food is served at lunchtime only, in the evening you can enjoy the restaurant food in the bar. From the lunchtime menu, there might be wild mushroom soup, filled baguettes, home-cooked ham and egg, caramelised onion and goats cheese quiche, and daily specials; in the evening there are main courses such as whole local plaice with fresh herbs, 10oz sirloin steak with brandy and peppercorn sauce, rack of local lamb or gloucester old spot pork steak with cider and apple sauce. Well kept Harveys Best and White 1066 Country Bitter with guests like Adnams Broadside, Fullers London Pride, and Charles Wells Bombardier on handpump, 10 wines by the glass, Weston's cider, and local fresh apple juice; shove-ha'penny, cribbage, dominoes, and piped music. During the September arts festival, several events are held here. Locals tend to call the pub 'Wipers' in true WW1 style.

Free house ~ Licensees Tom Cosgrove and Michael Gagg ~ Real ale ~ Bar food (12-2.30, 7-9; not Sun evening or winter Tues) ~ Restaurant ~ (01797) 223248 ~ Children allowed if eating but must be gone by 9pm ~ Dogs allowed in bar ~ Live music Fri evening ~ Open 11.30-3, 6-11; all day during school hols; 11.30-11 Sat; 12-4 Sun; closed Sun evening, winter Tues

SALEHURST

Salehurst Halt *Village signposted from Robertsbridge bypass on A21 Tunbridge Wells—Battle road*
Handy for the busy A21 and close to the church, this well liked little pub has a good bustling evening atmosphere; it tends to be quieter at lunchtime. The L-shaped bar has plain wooden tables and chairs on flagstones at one end, a cushioned window seat, beams, a little open brick fireplace, a time punch clock and olde-worlde pictures, and maybe fresh flowers; lots of hops on a big beam divide this from the beamed carpeted area with its mix of tables, wheelback and farmhouse chairs, and a half wall leads to a no

smoking dining area. Listed on boards, the bar food at lunchtime includes sandwiches, home-made burgers and beef and mushroom pie; with evening dishes such as sizzling tiger prawns in garlic and parsley butter, rump steak or roasted duck breast in a bitter orange and port sauce; puddings like banoffi pie. Well kept Harveys Best and a guest like Rother Valley Organic Bitter on handpump, and good wines. It can get very busy at weekends, so best to book in advance; piped music. The charming and pretty back garden is a suntrap in summer, and has terraces and picnic-sets for outside meals.

Free house ~ Licensees Claire and Hossein Refahi ~ Real ale ~ Bar food (12-2.30, 6.30-9.30; not Sun evening or Mon) ~ Restaurant ~ (01580) 880620 ~ Children welcome ~ Dogs allowed in bar ~ Open 12-3, 6.30-11(10.30 Sun); closed Mon exc bank hols

SINGLETON

Fox & Hounds *Just off A286 Midhurst—Chichester; heading S into the village, the main road bends sharp right – keep straight ahead instead; if you miss this turn, take the Charlton road, then first left*

Cosy and comfortable, this pretty 16th-c pub is run by friendly people. The partly panelled main bar has cream paintwork, a polished wooden floor, daily papers and books to borrow, and a good winter log fire. There's a second bar with red settles and another fire, a third flagstoned room on the left, and a further seating area off a side corridor; much of the pub is no smoking. Generous helpings of bar food at lunchtime includes home-made soup, cheese platter with pickles, pasta of the day, well liked shank of lamb in garlic and rosemary, and steaks; with more elaborate evening dishes such as seared marlin with a warm potato and basil salad or game pie using local game; puddings too, and Sunday roast. Well kept Fullers London Pride, Greene King IPA, and Ringwood Best on handpump, and decent wines by the glass; no music or machines. There are tables on an attractive small back terrace, and beyond that a big walled garden with colourful flowerbeds and fruit trees. The Weald & Downland Open-Air Museum is just down the road, and Goodwood Racecourse is not far away.

Enterprise ~ Lease Tony Simpson ~ Real ale ~ Bar food (all day summer weekends; not winter Sun evening) ~ (01243) 811251 ~ Children in family room ~ Dogs allowed in bar ~ Open 11.30-3, 6-11; 11.30-11 Sat; 12-10.30 Sun; 11.30-3, 6-11 Sat in winter

TROTTON

Keepers Arms *A272 Midhurst—Petersfield; pub tucked up above road, on S side*

The interesting décor here is worth a visit for that alone, and the walls throughout are decorated with some unusual pictures and artefacts that reflect Jenny's previous long years of travelling the world. The beamed L-shaped bar has timbered walls and some standing timbers, sofas by the big log fire, and ethnic rugs scattered on the oak floor. Elsewhere, there are a couple of unusual adult high chairs at an oak refectory table, two huge Georgian leather high-backed chairs around another table, an interesting medley of old or antique seats, and dining tables decorated with pretty candelabra, and bowls of fruit and chillis. There's also a north african-style room with a cushioned bench around all four walls, with a large central table, rare ethnic fabrics and weavings, and a big moroccan lamp hanging in the centre. The popular restaurant is no smoking. Interesting piped music ranges from Buddha bar-type music to classical. From a sensibly slimmed-down menu, bar food might include a lunchtime platter for two, hot chicken, bacon and mayonnaise panini, home-made pie of the day, and fresh seafood platter (Fridays only and must be ordered by Wednesday lunchtime); they also offer several dishes in starter and main course sizes: chargrilled chicken with thai vegetables and noodles; fresh crab with asparagus and hollandaise sauce. Well kept Ballards Best and Nyewood Gold, and Cheriton Pots on handpump, farm cider, and decent wines. Plenty of seats on the attractive, almost mediterranean-feeling front terrace. Dogs lunchtime only.

Free house ~ Licensee Jenny Oxley ~ Real ale ~ Bar food (not Sun evening, Mon) ~ Restaurant ~ (01730) 813724 ~ Children in restaurant ~ Dogs allowed in bar ~ Open 12-3, 6.30-10.30(11 Sat); 12-3 Sun; closed Sun evening, all Mon

WILMINGTON
Giants Rest *Just off A27*
Particularly well run, this comfortable Victorian pub has a really good bustling atmosphere and you can be sure of a warm welcome from the charming licensees. The long wood-floored bar and adjacent open areas, one with a log fire, are simply furnished with old pews and pine tables (each with their own bar game or wooden puzzle and much enjoyed by readers), and have well kept Harveys Best, Hop Back Summer Lightning, and Timothy Taylors Landlord on handpump; decent wines. Well liked and generously served, the bar food might include stilton and walnut pâté, garlic king prawns, beef in ale pie, savoury vegetable crumble, salmon fishcakes or home-cooked ham with bubble and squeak; also puddings like sticky date pudding or apple and blackberry pie. Sunday lunchtime is especially busy and there may not be much space for those just wanting a drink as most of the tables are booked by diners. There's a sizeable no smoking area, and smoking at tables is banned at weekends (it is allowed at the bar then); piped music. Plenty of seats in the front garden, and the pub is watched over by the impressive chalk-carved Long Man of Wilmington at the foot of the South Downs. Elizabeth David, the famous cookery writer, is buried in the churchyard at nearby Folkington; her headstone is beautifully carved and features mediterranean vegetables and a casserole.

Free house ~ Licensees Adrian and Rebecca Hillman ~ Real ale ~ Bar food ~ (01323) 870207 ~ Children in eating area of bar and restaurant ~ Dogs allowed in bar ~ Open 11-3, 6-11; 11-11 Sat; 12-10.30 Sun ~ Bedrooms: £40B/£45B

Dog Friendly Hotels, B&Bs and Farms

ALFRISTON
George *High St, Alfriston, Polegate, East Sussex BN26 5SY (01323) 870319*
£80, plus wknd breaks; 7 rms. 14th-c timbered inn opposite the intriguing
façade of the Red Lion, with massive low beams hung with hops, appropriately soft lighting, a log fire (or summer flower arrangement) in a huge
stone inglenook, lots of copper and brass, plenty of sturdy stripped tables,
and a thriving atmosphere; popular home-made food, a cosy candlelit
restaurant, nice breakfasts, well kept real ales, and a jovial landlord; seats out
in the charming flint-walled garden behind; cl 24–27 Dec; dogs in
bedrooms

BATTLE
Little Hemingfold Hotel *189 Hastings Rd, Battle, East Sussex TN33 0TT*
(01424) 774338 £92, plus special breaks; 12 rms, 6 on ground floor in
adjoining Coach House. Partly 17th-c, partly early Victorian farmhouse in
40 acres of woodland, with trout lake, tennis, gardens, and lots of walks;
comfortable sitting rooms, open fires, restful atmosphere and very good food
using home-grown produce at own candlelit table; children over 7; cl 2 Jan–
10 Feb; dogs welcome in bedrooms

BATTLE
Powder Mills *Powdermill Lane, Battle, East Sussex TN33 0SP (01424)*
775511 £120, plus special breaks; 40 rms, some in annexe. Attractive
18th-c creeper-clad manor house in 150 acres of park and woodland with
four lakes and outdoor swimming pool, and next to the 1066 battlefield;
country-house atmosphere, log fires and antiques in elegant day rooms,
attentive service, and good modern cooking in Orangery restaurant;
children over 10 in evening restaurant; disabled access; dogs welcome away
from restaurant

BRIGHTON
Grand *97-99 Kings Rd, Brighton, East Sussex BN1 2FW (01273) 224300*
£250, plus special breaks; 200 handsome rms, many with sea views.
Famous Victorian hotel with marble columns and floors and fine moulded
plasterwork in the luxurious and elegant day rooms; good service, very
good food and fine wines, popular afternoon tea in sunny conservatory, a
bustling nightclub, and health spa with indoor swimming pool; disabled
access; dogs welcome in bedrooms; £5

CHARLTON
Woodstock House *Charlton, Chichester, East Sussex PO18 0HU (01243)*
811666 £90, plus special breaks; 13 rms. 18th-c country house close to
Goodwood with a friendly, relaxed atmosphere, log fire in homely sitting
room, cocktail bar, imaginative food in attractive dining room (also open to

non-residents), and suntrap inner courtyard garden; lots to see nearby and plenty of downland walks; disabled access; dogs welcome if small, by arrangement

CHICHESTER

Suffolk House *East Row, Chichester, West Sussex PO19 1PD (01243) 778899* £**89**, plus winter breaks; 11 rms, some overlooking garden. Friendly Georgian house in centre and close to the cathedral, with homely comfortable lounge, little bar, traditional cooking in no smoking restaurant, good breakfasts, and small walled garden; disabled access; dogs by arrangement

CLIMPING

Bailiffscourt *Climping St, Climping, Littlehampton, East Sussex BN17 5RW (01903) 723511* £**195**, plus special breaks; 39 rms, many with four-poster beds, winter log fires and super views. Mock 13th-c manor built only 60 years ago but with tremendous character – fine old iron-studded doors, huge fireplaces, heavy beams and so forth – in 30 acres of coastal pastures and walled gardens: elegant furnishings, enjoyable modern english and french food, fine wines, a relaxed atmosphere, and spa with indoor swimming pool, outdoor swimming pool, tennis and croquet; children over 7 in restaurant; disabled access; dogs in bedrooms and lounges; £5

CUCKFIELD

Ockenden Manor *Ockenden Lane, Cuckfield, Haywards Heath, West Sussex RH17 5LD (01444) 416111* £**155**, plus special breaks; 22 individually decorated, pretty rms. Dating from 1520, this carefully extended manor house has antiques, fresh flowers and an open fire in the comfortable sitting room, good modern cooking in fine panelled restaurant, cosy bar, and super views of the South Downs from the neatly kept garden (in nine acres); dogs in 4 ground-floor bedrooms; £10

EAST HOATHLY

Old Whyly *Halland Rd, East Hoathly, Lewes, East Sussex BN8 6EL (01825) 840216* £**90**; 3 rms. Handsome 17th-c manor house in lovely garden with tennis court and swimming pool, fine antiques and paintings, delicious food, and super breakfasts with their own honey and eggs; plenty of walks nearby and very close to Glyndebourne (hampers can be provided); children must be well behaved; dogs welcome by arrangement

EASTBOURNE

Grand *King Edward's Parade, Eastbourne, East Sussex BN21 4EQ (01323) 412345* £**165**, plus special breaks; 152 rms, many with sea views. Gracious and very well run Victorian hotel, with spacious, comfortable lounges, lots of fine original features, lovely flower arrangements, imaginative food in elegant restaurants, and courteous helpful service; leisure club and outdoor pool and terraces; disabled access; dogs if small, by arrangement; £7

FAIRLIGHT

Fairlight Cottage *Warren Rd, Fairlight, Hastings, East Sussex TN35 4AG* *(01424) 812545* £**65**, plus winter breaks; 3 rms, one with four-poster. Comfortable and very friendly no smoking house in fine countryside with views over Rye Bay and plenty of rural and clifftop walks; big comfortable lounge (nice views), good breakfasts in elegant dining room or on new balcony; children over 10; dogs in bedrooms

FRANT

Old Parsonage *Church Lane, Frant, Tunbridge Wells, Kent TN3 9DX* *(01892) 750773* £**95**, plus special breaks; 4 very pretty rms, 2 with four-posters. Just two miles from Tunbridge Wells, this carefully restored imposing former Georgian rectory has antiques, watercolours and plants in elegant sitting rooms, a spacious Victorian conservatory, good food in candlelit dining room, and balustraded terrace overlooking quiet garden; several nearby walks; children over 7; dogs welcome in bedrooms

HASTINGS

Beauport Park *Battle Rd, Hastings, East Sussex TN38 8EA (01424) 851222* £**130**; 25 attractive rms. Georgian house set in 38 acres of gardens and woodland with outdoor heated swimming pool, tennis and putting green, and riding next door; log fire and a relaxed friendly atmosphere in the Georgian-style lounge, a large conservatory, good, enjoyable food, and restaurant and cocktail bar that overlook the formal italian and sunken gardens; dogs welcome in bedrooms and bar

LEWES

Shelleys *High St, Lewes, East Sussex BN7 1XS (01273) 472361* £**185**, plus special breaks; 19 pretty rms. Once owned by relatives of the poet, this stylish and spacious 17th-c town house is warm and friendly, with good food, nice breakfasts and bar lunches in elegant dining room, and seats in the quiet back garden; limited disabled access; dogs in bedrooms

NEWICK

Newick Park Hotel *Newick, Brighton, East Sussex BN8 4SB (01825) 723633* £**165**; 13 individually decorated, spacious rms inc 3 suites in a converted granary. Charming and carefully restored Georgian building in a huge estate of open country and woodland; organic walled kitchen garden, two lakes with fishing, pretty views, tennis, badminton, croquet, outdoor swimming pool, quad bikes, and tank driving; comfortable and spacious public rooms include a study, a sitting room, bar/morning room and elegant restaurant with enjoyable dinner-party food using home-grown produce and local game, and good breakfasts; dogs in one ground-floor room

PEASMARSH

Flackley Ash *London Rd, Peasmarsh, Rye, East Sussex TN31 6YH (01797) 230651* £**132**, plus special breaks; 45 individually decorated rms. Elegant red-brick Georgian house in five acres of neat gardens, with comfortable lounge and bar areas, good breakfasts in charming dining room with inglenook fireplace and conservatory extension, and indoor swimming pool, sauna and gym, croquet, and putting green; dogs in bedrooms; £7.50

RUSHLAKE GREEN
Stone House *Rushlake Green, Heathfield, East Sussex TN21 9QJ (01435) 830553* £125; 7 rms, some with four-posters. In a thousand acres of pretty countryside (with plenty of walks and country sports) and surrounded by an 18th-c walled garden, this lovely house was built at the end of the 15th c and extended in Georgian times; there are open log fires, antiques and family heirlooms in the drawing room, a quiet library, an antique full-sized table in the mahogany-panelled billiard room, wonderful food in the panelled dining room, fine breakfasts, and a cosseting atmosphere; cl Christmas; children over 9; dogs welcome in bedrooms

RYE
Jeakes House *Mermaid St, Rye, East Sussex TN31 7ET (01797) 222828* £94, plus special breaks; 11 rms (4 with four-posters) overlooking the rooftops of this medieval town or across the marsh to the sea, 10 with own bthrm. Fine 16th-c building, well run and friendly, with good breakfasts, lots of books, comfortable furnishings, swagged curtains, linen and lace, a warm fire, and lovely peaceful atmosphere; children over 11; dogs welcome in bedrooms and bar; £5

SHIPLEY
Goffsland Farm *Shipley Rd, Southwater, Horsham, West Sussex RH13 7BQ (01403) 730434* £44; 2 rms inc 1 family rm with own access. 17th-c Wealden farmhouse on 260-acre family farm with good breakfasts, and a friendly welcome; horse-riding and plenty of surrounding walks; children over 5; dogs welcome

TILLINGTON
Horse Guards *Tillington, Petworth, West Sussex GU28 9AF (01798) 342332* £70; 2 spacious clean rms and little self-catering cottage. Prettily set 18th-c dining pub in lovely village setting, with neatly kept and cosy beamed front bar, imaginative restaurant-style food, 10 wines by the glass, and real ales; dogs in bedrooms and in cottage

Warwickshire
(with Birmingham and West Midlands)

Dog Friendly Pubs

ALDERMINSTER
Bell *A3400 Oxford—Stratford*

The glow of lovingly polished wood warms the interior of this civilised dining pub. The neatly kept communicating rooms of the spacious bar have stripped slatback chairs around wooden tables on flagstones and wooden floors, little vases of flowers, small landscape prints and swan's-neck brass-and-globe lamps on cream walls and a solid-fuel stove in a stripped brick inglenook. It's run with enthusiastic verve by cheery licensees, and has a good menu which might include filled lunchtime baguettes (not Sun), starters such as spinach and parmesan soufflé or seafood cocktail, and main courses such as cashew, mushroom and apricot roast, steak and kidney pudding, and braised lamb shank; also home-made puddings such as fruit crumble or chocolate, brandy and almond torte. Do make it clear if you want to eat in the bar. The licensees put great effort into keeping the atmosphere flourishing by putting on lots of parties, food festivals, and classical and light music evenings. Well kept Greene King IPA and Abbot on handpump, alongside a good range of around a dozen wines and champagne by the glass, freshly squeezed juice, cocktails and various teas. Other than the bar, the pub is no smoking. They have high chairs, and children are particularly welcome. A conservatory and terrace overlook the garden and Stour Valley.

Free house ~ Licensees Keith and Vanessa Brewer ~ Real ale ~ Bar food ~ Restaurant ~ (01789) 450414 ~ Children welcome ~ Dogs allowed in bar and bedrooms ~ Open 12-2.30, 7-11(10.30 Sun); closed evening 24-27 Dec, 1 Jan ~ Bedrooms: £27(£45S)(£52B)/£48(£70S)(£70B)

ARMSCOTE
Fox & Goose *Off A3400 Stratford—Shipston-on-Stour*

This stylishly transformed blacksmith's forge – hovering comfortably somewhere between bistro and upmarket pub – is now entirely no smoking. Walls are painted a warm red in the small flagstoned bar and cream in the larger eating area, with bright crushed velvet cushions plumped up on wooden pews, a big gilt mirror over a log fire, polished floorboards and black and white etchings. In a quirky tableau above the dining room's woodburning stove, a stuffed fox stalks a big goose; piped jazz. Listed on a daily changing blackboard, the food puts together some imaginative and successful combinations of ingredients. There might be grilled garlic sardines, home-cured gravadlax on buckwheat blinis, home-made tagliatelle with goats cheese, roasted peppers, pesto and parsnip crisps, rib-eye steak, and home-made puddings. Service is charming and helpful. Well kept Ansells and a guest such as Adnams Broadside on handpump, mulled wine in winter, jugs of Pimms in summer, and well chosen wines including a choice of dessert wines. Bedrooms, which are named after characters in *Cluedo*, are mildly quirky, stylishly decorated and comfortable. Outside, the garden has an elegant vine-covered deck area overlooking a big lawn with tables, benches and fruit trees.

Free house ~ Licensee Rachel Hawkins ~ Real ale ~ Bar food (12-2.30, 7-9.30) ~ Restaurant ~ (01608) 682293 ~ Children in restaurant ~ Dogs allowed in bar ~ Open 12-3, 6-11(10.30 Sun) ~ Bedrooms: £45B/£90B

ASTON CANTLOW
Kings Head *Village signposted just off A3400 NW of Stratford*
This lovely old black and white timbered Tudor pub is a real picture in summer, with wisteria and colourful hanging baskets. There's particular praise from readers for the good often inventive food and the high standard of enthusiastic service from attentive young staff – it is popular, so you will need to book. The creative menu changes very regularly and meals are freshly prepared: maybe fried brie with raspberry vinaigrette, gorgonzola, spinach and mushroom cannelloni, or breast of duck with red cabbage and plum sauce; puddings such as warm chocolate brownie. The clean and comfortable village bar on the right is a nice mix of rustic surroundings with a civilised, gently upmarket atmosphere: flagstones, low beams, and old-fashioned settles around its massive inglenook log fireplace. The chatty quarry-tiled main room has attractive window seats and oak tables. Three well kept real ales on handpump include Greene King Abbot, M&B Brew XI and a guest such as Hook Norton Old Hooky, also decent wines; piped jazz. The garden is lovely, with a big chestnut tree. The pub is not far from Mary Arden's house in Wilmcote, and Shakespeare's parents are said to have married in the church next door.

Furlong Leisure ~ Manager David Brian ~ Real ale ~ Bar food (12-2.30, 7-10; 12-3, 7-9 Sun) ~ Restaurant ~ (01789) 488242 ~ Children welcome ~ Dogs allowed in bar ~ Open 11-3, 5.30-11; 11-11 Sat; 12-10.30 Sun

EDGE HILL
Castle *Off A422*
At its best by far on a sunny day when you can sit outside, and worth a look at the building itself, this beautifully positioned crenellated octagon tower is a folly that was built in 1749 by an 18th-c Gothic Revival enthusiast to mark the spot where Charles I raised his standard at the start of the Battle of Edge Hill. The big attractive garden (with aunt sally) has lovely glimpses down through the trees of the battlefield, and it's said that after closing time

you can hear ghostly sounds of battle – a phantom cavalry officer has even been seen galloping by in search of his severed hand. Inside, there are arched doorways, and the walls of the lounge bar, which has the same eight sides as the rest of the main tower, is decorated with maps, pictures and a collection of Civil War memorabilia. Straightforward bar food includes sandwiches, bean casserole, breaded cod, mixed grill, and puddings. Hook Norton Best, Old Hooky, one of their seasonal beers, and a guest such as Shepherd Neame Spitfire are well kept on handpump; also country wines, farm cider and around 30 malt whiskies. The public bar, with old farm tools for decoration, has darts, pool, cribbage, dominoes, fruit machine and piped music. Upton House is nearby on the A422, and Compton Wynyates, one of the most beautiful houses in this part of England, is not far beyond.

Hook Norton ~ Lease N J and G A Blann ~ Real ale ~ Bar food (12-2, 6-9) ~ (01295) 670255 ~ Children in eating area of bar ~ Dogs allowed in bar ~ Open 11.15-2.30, 6.15-11(11.30-11 wknds) ~ Bedrooms: /£70B

FARNBOROUGH
Inn at Farnborough *Off A423 N of Banbury*
The immaculately kept interior at this stylishly refurbished and civilised golden-stone house is a pleasant mix of the traditional and contemporary, with plenty of exposed stonework, and thoughtful lighting. The emphasis however is very much on the quite sophisticated changing blackboard menu. Very well prepared dishes, using local produce where possible, might include wild mushroom risotto with parmesan crisps and rocket salad, seared king scallops, baked goats cheese cheesecake with tomato and sweet pepper chutney, and roast rump of lamb with chorizo and moroccan spiced cassoulet. There's also a good value two- and three-course lunchtime and early evening menu (not Sat evening or Sun). Service is usually cheerfully attentive but can be slow. The beamed and flagstoned bar has neat blinds on its mullioned windows, a chrome hood in the old stone fireplace, plenty of fresh flowers on the modern counter, candles on wicker tables, and smartly upholstered chairs, window seats and stools. A stable door leads out to chic metal furnishings on a decked terrace. The dining room has nice wooden floors, a good mix of mismatched tables and chairs, and well chosen plants. Well kept Greene King Abbot and a couple of guest beers such as Highgate Davenports and Charles Wells Bombardier on handpump, and a good extensive wine list with about 17 by the glass. A machine dispenses Havana cigars; piped music. The landscaped garden is really delightful with a lovely sloping lawn, plenty of picnic-sets (one under a big old tree) and wandering hens. A string of white fairy-lights around the roof gives the exterior an elegant appearance at night.

Free house ~ Licensee Tony Robinson ~ Real ale ~ Bar food (12-3, 6-10.30) ~ Restaurant ~ (01295) 690615 ~ Children welcome ~ Dogs allowed in bar ~ Open 11-11

GREAT WOLFORD

Fox & Hounds *Village signposted on right on A3400 3 miles S of Shipston-on-Stour*

You do need to book a table if visiting this inviting 16th-c stone inn for a meal as they do reserve tables throughout the pub. The cosy low-beamed bar has a nice collection of chairs and old candlelit tables on spotless flagstones, antique hunting prints, and a roaring log fire in the inglenook fireplace with its fine old bread oven; piped music, darts (Sunday evening) and cribbage (Wednesday evening). An old-fashioned little tap room serves well kept Hook Norton and a couple of guests such as Bass and Timothy Taylors Landlord on handpump, and over 170 malt whiskies. Under new licensees, bar food might include cream of parsnip soup, roast figs with parma ham, spaghetti with cockles, clams, sun-dried tomatoes and garlic cream sauce, crispy duck leg with egg noodles, and puddings such as orange and almond cake with greek yoghurt; no smoking section. A terrace has green plastic furniture and a well.

Free house ~ Licensees Paul and Veronica Tomlinson ~ Real ale ~ Bar food (not Sun evening) ~ Restaurant ~ (01608) 674220 ~ Children in eating area of bar ~ Dogs welcome ~ Open 12-2.30(3 Sat, Sun), 6-11(10.30 Sun); closed Mon ~ Bedrooms: £45B/£70B

PRIORS MARSTON

Holly Bush *Village signposted from A361 S of Daventry (or take the old Welsh road from Southam); from village centre follow Shuckburgh signpost, then take first right turn by phone box*

This golden-stone 13th-c inn, once the village bakehouse, has recently been refurbished by a new owner. The main part is divided into small beamed rambling rooms by partly glazed timber dividers, keeping a good-sized bar as well as the main dining area, and there are flagstones, some bare boards, a good deal of stripped stone, and good sturdy tables in varying sizes. A log fire blazes in the big stone hearth at one end, and the central lounge area has a woodburning stove. Beside a second smaller and smarter no smoking dining area is a back snug with temptingly squashy leather sofas. Good bar food includes game pie or mushroom and spinach lasagne, roast salmon with mediterranean stuffing, rump steak, and puddings such as baked rhubarb and vanilla cheesecake; you can also eat from the impressive restaurant menu; friendly informal service from amiable staff. They have Fullers London Pride, Hook Norton Best and a guest such as Timothy Taylors Landlord well kept on handpump from the copper-topped bar counter, alongside a farm cider, and decent wines by the glass; there may be piped music. The sheltered garden behind has tables and chairs on the lawn, and this is an attractive village. We have not yet heard from readers who have stayed here, and look forward to reports.

Free house ~ Licensee Richard Saunders ~ Real ale ~ Bar food (12-2, 6.30-9.30; 12-2.30, 7-9 Sun) ~ Restaurant ~ (01327) 260934 ~ Children welcome in lounge area ~ Dogs welcome ~ Open 12-2, 5.30-11; 12-3, 6-11.30(7-10.30 Sun) Sat ~ Bedrooms: £40S/£45B

SHUSTOKE

Griffin *5 miles from M6 junction 4; A446 towards Tamworth, then right on to B4114 and go straight through Coleshill; pub is at Church End, a mile E of village*
Almost always bustling with a cheery crowd, the low-beamed L-shaped bar at this unpretentious country local has two stone fireplaces (one's a big inglenook) with warming log fires. Besides one nice old-fashioned settle the décor is fairly simple, from cushioned café seats (some quite closely packed) to sturdily elm-topped sewing trestles, lots of old jugs on the beams, beer mats on the ceiling and a fruit machine. The finest feature here is the interesting range of up to 10 real ales. From a servery under a very low heavy beam, Banks's Original and Marstons Pedigree are well kept alongside guests from small brewers such as Bathams, Everards, Exmoor, Hook Norton, Theakstons and Timothy Taylors; also country wines, farm cider, mulled wine and hot punch in winter. As well as a choice of 20 Warwickshire cheeses (you can buy them to take away), good value straightforward lunchtime bar food, served by friendly efficient staff, includes pie and chips, broccoli bake, and cod, chips and mushy peas; you may need to arrive early to get a table. There are old-fashioned seats and tables outside on the back grass, a play area and a large terrace.
Free house ~ Licensee Michael Pugh ~ Real ale ~ Bar food (12-2; not Sun or evenings) ~ No credit cards ~ (01675) 481205 ~ Children in conservatory ~ Dogs welcome ~ Open 12-2.30(2.45 Sun), 7-11(10.30 Sun)

WHARF

Wharf Inn *A423 Banbury—Southam, near Fenny Compton*
This open-plan pub, by Bridge 136 of the South Oxford Canal, very usefully serves food all day. They serve breakfast first thing, and later into the day the bar menu (which changes four times a year) might include mussels in creamy white wine sauce, vegetarian penne pasta and braised blade of beef with dumplings; friendly efficient service, and good freshly ground coffee. A smart tall-windowed dining area on the left has plain solid tables and high-backed chairs, a big oriental rug, cream walls, modern artwork, and end windows so close to the water that you feel right by it. A small central flagstoned bar has Adnams, Charles Wells Bombardier, Hook Norton Best and a guest on handpump. On the right is a pair of soft white leather settees by a feature coffee table, a modern woodburning stove, and some appealing mainly water-related pictures; a little snug beyond has a pile of children's books. Lighting throughout is good; disabled access and facilities; faint piped pop music. The slightly sloping waterside garden has picnic-sets and a playhouse on high stilts. They have moorings, and space for caravans.
Punch ~ Lease Kevin Partridge ~ Real ale ~ Bar food (8-9.30) ~ Restaurant ~ (01295) 770332 ~ Children welcome ~ Dogs allowed in bar ~ Open 8.30(10 in winter)-11(10.30 Sun)

Dog Friendly Hotels, B&Bs and Farms

BISHOP'S TACHBROOK
Mallory Court *Harbury Lane, Bishop's Tachbrook, Leamington Spa, Warwickshire CV33 9QB (01926) 330214* £**195**, plus special breaks; 29 comfortable rms. Fine ancient-looking house – actually built around 1910 – with elegant antiques and flower-filled day rooms, attentive staff, and excellent food using home-grown produce in oak-panelled restaurant; ten acres of lovely gardens with outdoor swimming pool, tennis, and croquet; children over 9; disabled access; dogs welcome in bedrooms by prior arrangement

BUBBENHALL
Bubbenhall House *Paget's Lane, Bubbenhall, Coventry, Warwickshire CV8 3BJ (02476) 302409* £**55**; 3 rms. Mainly Edwardian house in five acres of mature woodland with marvellous wildlife (including one of only two Dormouse Sanctuaries in the UK) and once the home of the Mini's designer; beams and a fine Jacobean staircase, TV lounge plus other comfortable ones, hearty breakfasts in elegant dining room, and a friendly, family atmosphere; tennis court; dogs by prior arrangement

HENLEY-IN-ARDEN
Ashleigh House *Whitley Hill, Henley-in-Arden, Solihull, West Midlands B95 5DL (01564) 792315* £**65**; 11 homely rms, some in former stable block. Edwardian house (mainly no smoking) in two acres of neatly kept grounds with original features, a comfortable residents' lounge and small bar, good breakfasts in spacious dining room (evening meal by arrangement), and conservatory overlooking the gardens; dogs welcome in bedrooms; £5

HOCKLEY HEATH
Nuthurst Grange *Nuthurst Grange Rd, Hockley Heath, Solihull, West Midlands B94 5NL (01564) 783972* £**165**, plus special breaks; 15 comfortable, spacious rms with lots of extras. Red-brick, creeper-clad Edwardian house in landscaped gardens, with light, airy and prettily decorated public rooms, lovely fresh flowers, enjoyable modern british cooking using home-grown produce, good breakfasts, and pleasant helpful staff; cl Christmas; disabled access; dogs welcome in bedrooms by prior arrangement

LOXLEY
Loxley Farm *Stratford Rd, Loxley, Warwick, Warwickshire CV35 9JN (01789) 840265* £**70**; 2 suites with their own sitting rooms in attractive barn conversion. Not far from Stratford, this tucked-away, thatched and half-timbered partly 14th-c house has low beams, wonky walls and floors, antiques and dried flowers, open fire, helpful friendly owners, and good Aga-cooked breakfasts; peaceful garden, and fine old village church; cl Christmas and New Year; dogs welcome in bedrooms

PILLERTON HERSEY

Dockers Barn Farm *Oxhill Bridle Rd, Pillerton Hersey, Warwick, Warwickshire CV35 0QB (01926) 640475* £**50**; 3 cosy, beamed rms. Quietly set and carefully converted 18th-c threshing barn surrounded by fields of sheep and ponies; friendly owners, flagstoned floors, beams, interesting collections, and family portraits, and 21 acres of wildlife-friendly garden and land; can use hot tub in garden; cl Christmas; children over 8; dogs welcome in Granary Suite only

SHERBOURNE

Old Rectory *Vicarage Lane, Sherbourne, Warwick, Warwickshire CV35 8AB (01926) 624562* £**85**; 7 rms with hand-carved four-posters and brass beds. Charming 17th-c country house with cosy sitting room, big log fire in inglenook fireplace, beams, flagstones and elm floors, honesty bar, and enjoyable breakfasts; cl Christmas and New Year; no children; dogs in Stable Block rooms only

STRATFORD-UPON-AVON

Melita *37 Shipston Rd, Stratford-upon-Avon, Warwickshire CV37 7LN (01789) 292432* £**72**, plus winter breaks; 12 well equipped, no smoking rms. Family-run Victorian hotel with carefully laid-out garden, comfortable lounge with open fire, extensive breakfasts; close to town centre and theatre; cl Christmas; disabled access; dogs welcome in bedrooms

Shakespeare *Chapel St, Stratford-upon-Avon, Warwickshire CV37 6ER (0870) 400 8182* £**130**, plus wknd breaks; 74 comfortable well equipped rms. Smart hotel based on handsome, lavishly modernised Tudor merchants' houses, with comfortable bar, good food, quick friendly service, and civilised tea or coffee in peaceful chintzy armchairs by blazing log fires; seats out in back courtyard; three mins' walk from theatre; disabled access; dogs welcome in bedrooms; £10

Wiltshire

Dog Friendly Pubs

AXFORD
Red Lion *Off A4 E of Marlborough; on back road Mildenhall—Ramsbury*
A wide choice of delicious food and friendly service make this pretty flint-and brick pub a reliable bet for an excellent meal. Besides lunchtime (not Sunday) filled rolls and baked potatoes, bar snacks (not Saturday evening or Sunday lunchtime) might include home-made turkey and ham pie or poached salmon; or you can choose more elaborate dishes from the à la carte menu such as spinach, dolcelatte and mascarpone tartlet, roast local partridge, and lots of interesting fish dishes; food is cooked freshly to order, so there may be a wait. The restaurant and bar eating area are no smoking. The beamed and pine-panelled bar has a big inglenook fireplace, and a pleasant mix of comfortable sofas, cask seats and other solid chairs on the parquet floor; the pictures by local artists are for sale. There are lovely views over a valley from good hardwood tables and chairs on the terrace outside the restaurant, and you get the same views from picture windows in the restaurant and lounge. Welcoming service from the attentive staff and landlord. Along with 18 sensibly priced wines by the glass, and around two dozen malt whiskies, you'll find well kept Hook Norton, Fullers London Pride and an occasional guest from a brewer such as Cottage on handpump. The sheltered garden has picnic-sets under parasols and swings.
Free house ~ Licensee Seamus Lecky ~ Real ale ~ Bar food ~ Restaurant ~ (01672) 520271 ~ Children welcome ~ Dogs allowed in bar ~ Open 12-3, 6.30-11; 12-3, 7-10.30 Sun; closed 25 Dec

BERWICK ST JAMES
Boot *B3083, between A36 and A303 NW of Salisbury*
The partly carpeted flagstoned bar of this flint and stone pub has a contented cosy atmosphere, a huge winter log fire in the inglenook fireplace at one end, sporting prints over a smaller brick fireplace at the other, and houseplants on its wide window sills. A charming small back no smoking dining room has a nice mix of dining chairs around four tables, and deep pink walls with an attractively mounted collection of celebrity boots. Wadworths IPA and 6X along with a changing guest such as Youngs

Best are well kept on handpump, and they have a few well chosen house wines, half a dozen malts and farm cider; piped jazz. The blackboard menu lists a good choice of reasonably priced food, made using lots of local produce (vegetables may even come from the garden), such as tasty baguettes, chilli con carne, red thai chicken curry or bass with ginger, spring onion and soy sauce; puddings too, and children's meals; service can be slow when it's busy. Very neatly kept, the sheltered side lawn has pretty flowerbeds, and some well spaced picnic-sets.

Wadworths ~ Tenant Kathie Duval ~ Real ale ~ Bar food (12-2.30, 6.30-9.30; not Mon) ~ Restaurant ~ (01722) 790243 ~ Children welcome ~ Dogs welcome ~ Open 12-3, 6-11; 12-3, 7-10.30 Sun; closed Mon lunchtime exc bank hols

BERWICK ST JOHN
Talbot *Village signposted from A30 E of Shaftesbury*
This attractive old pub is set in a peaceful and pretty village, with thatched old houses. The single long, heavily beamed bar is simply furnished with cushioned solid wall and window seats, spindleback chairs, a high-backed built-in settle at one end, and tables. The huge inglenook fireplace has a good iron fireback and bread ovens, and there are nicely shaped heavy black beams and cross-beams with bevelled corners; seats outside too. Reasonably priced bar food includes sausage and mash with onion gravy or cheese and mushroom omelette, home-made lasagne and grilled cajun chicken; also daily specials such as battered hake or pork with apple and cider. Bass, Ringwood Best, Wadworths 6X and a guest such as Shepherd Neame Spitfire are well kept on handpump, and they've farm cider; darts, cribbage.

Free house ~ Licensees Pete and Marilyn Hawkins ~ Real ale ~ Bar food ~ (01747) 828222 ~ Children in eating area of bar ~ Dogs welcome ~ Open 12-3, 6.30-11; 12-4 Sun; closed Sun evening, Mon exc bank hol lunchtime

DEVIZES
Bear *Market Place*
This old coaching inn has provided shelter to distinguished guests as diverse as King George III and Dr Johnson. These days you'll find a choice of 15 different wines by the glass, along with well kept Wadworths IPA, 6X and a seasonal guest on handpump, and they've a good choice of malt whiskies, and freshly squeezed juices. Cosier after a recent refurbishment, the big main carpeted bar has log fires, black winged wall settles and muted cloth-upholstered bucket armchairs around oak tripod tables; the classic bar counter has shiny black woodwork and small panes of glass. Separated from the main bar by some steps, a room named after the portrait painter Thomas Lawrence (his father ran the establishment in the 1770s) has dark oak-panelled walls, a parquet floor, a big open fireplace, shining copper pans, and plates around the walls; it's partly no smoking. As we went to press they had plans to change their menu, but bar food might include home-made soup, sandwiches, fish and chips, steak, and home-made puddings. There are buffet meals in the Lawrence Room, and you can eat these in the bar too. It's only a stone's throw from here to Wadworths

brewery, where you can buy beer in splendid old-fashioned half-gallon earthenware jars.

Wadworths ~ Tenant Andrew Maclachlan ~ Real ale ~ Bar food (11.30-2.30, 7-9.30) ~ Restaurant ~ (01380) 722444 ~ Children welcome ~ Dogs welcome ~ Open 11-11; 12-10.30 Sun; closed 25/26 Dec ~ Bedrooms: £50B/£75B

DONHEAD ST ANDREW

Forester *Village signposted off A30 E of Shaftesbury, just E of Ludwell; Lower Street*

This 14th-c thatched pub, in a charming village, changed ownership recently, but the resident manager who has built up its reputation over the last year or so is staying on in charge; there are no plans to alter the present very successful operation. The pub is well organised inside, with stripped tables in the welcoming and appealing bar, which usually has a few local regulars around the servery, and a log fire in its big inglenook fireplace. Here, a big blackboard lists the changing food. Very nicely cooked, this might include popular warm chicken salad, broad bean, asparagus, pea and parmesan risotto, smoked haddock or rib-eye steak, and delicious puddings such as poached apricots with shortbread. They have well kept Flowers Original, Ringwood Best and perhaps a guest beer such as Bass on handpump; the choice of wines by the glass is very good, and the atmosphere is warmly welcoming. The comfortable main dining room has more country-kitchen tables in varying sizes, nicely laid out with linen napkins, and attractive wrought-iron candlesticks – they sell these, if you like the design. A second smaller and cosier dining room is, like the first, no smoking. Service is pleasant and helpful, and there are no machines or piped music. Tables out on the good-sized recently reworked terrace have fine country views, and there are good walks nearby. The neighbouring cottage used to be the pub's coach house.

Free house ~ Licensee Darren Morris ~ Real ale ~ Bar food ~ Restaurant ~ (01747) 828038 ~ Children welcome ~ Dogs allowed in bar ~ Open 11-3, 6-11(10.30 Sun)

GREAT HINTON

Linnet *3½ miles E of Trowbridge, village signposted off A361 opposite Lamb at Semington*

Everything from bread and sausages to ice-cream is home-made at this attractive brick pub – very much somewhere to come to for an imaginative meal, rather than just a drink. The set lunch is excellent value, and to be sure of a table on the weekend, it's best to book a few weeks in advance. Well cooked by the dedicated chef/landlord, and served in the little bar or restaurant, the changing menu might include at lunchtimes filled focaccia or salads, smoked salmon and cod fishcakes and grilled rib-eye steak; evening dishes such as pork tenderloin filled with apple, red onion and truffles with honey and mustard sauce, and puddings such as lemon meringue cheesecake. The bar to the right of the door has a cream carpet and lots of photographs of the pub and the brewery, and there are bookshelves in a snug end part. The cosy restaurant is candlelit at night. As well as more than two dozen malt whiskies, and quite a few wines (with

eight by the glass), they serve well kept Wadworths 6X, and maybe a seasonal guest on handpump; piped music. In summer, the flowering tubs and window boxes with seats dotted among them are quite a sight.
Wadworths ~ Tenant Jonathan Furby ~ Real ale ~ Bar food (not Mon) ~ Restaurant ~ (01380) 870354 ~ Children welcome ~ Dogs allowed in bar ~ Open 11-2.30, 6-11; 12-3, 7-10.30 Sun; closed Mon

GRITTLETON
Neeld Arms *Off A350 NW of Chippenham; The Street*
The friendly licensees help generate a particularly convivial atmosphere at this 17th-c black-beamed pub. It's largely open-plan, with some stripped stone, a log fire in the big inglenook on the right and a smaller coal-effect fire on the left, flowers on tables, and a pleasant mix of seating from windsor chairs through scatter-cushioned window seats to some nice arts and crafts chairs and a traditional settle. The parquet-floored back dining area has yet another inglenook, with a big woodburning stove (even back here, you still feel thoroughly part of the action). From the substantial central bar counter, you can get well kept beers such as Bath Gem, Hook Norton, Hop Back Crop Circle and Wadworths 6X on handpump, with guests from brewers such as Hop Back and Wychwood; they've also a good choice of reasonably priced wines by the glass. Enjoyable food from changing blackboards might include lunchtime (not Sunday) ciabattas, fish, chips and mushy peas, and sausages or pie of the week; evening dishes such as salmon with parma ham or venison with redcurrant jus; puddings too. They do Sunday roast with local beef. It gets tremendously busy when the Badminton horse trials are on (and service can be slow). As we went to press, the terrace was gaining a pergola; look out for Soaky, the golden retriever who likes slops.
Free house ~ Licensees Charlie and Boo West ~ Real ale ~ Bar food ~ Restaurant ~ (01249) 782470 ~ Children welcome ~ Dogs welcome ~ Open 12-3, 5.30-11; 11.30-3.30, 5.30-11 Sat; 12-3.30, 6.30-11 Sun ~ Bedrooms: £40S(£40B)/£60S(£70B)

HINDON
Lamb *B3089 Wilton—Mere*
The best place to sit in this civilised solid hotel (handily open all day) is probably in the two slate-floored lower sections of the roomy long bar. There's a long polished table with wall benches and chairs, blacksmith's tools set behind a big inglenook fireplace, and at one end a window seat (overlooking the village church) with a big waxed circular table, spindleback chairs with tapestried cushions, a high-backed settle and brass jugs on the mantelpiece above the small fireplace; there are lots of tables and chairs up some steps in a third bigger area. Enjoyable (but not cheap) bar food might include ploughman's, steak and kidney pie, calves liver with apple and calvados mash or tuna loin with thai sauce, and puddings such as bread and butter pudding; Sunday roast too, and you can usually get cream teas throughout the afternoon. Pleasant staff serve four well kept Youngs beers on handpump (though this may change as the pub is due to be

bought by another pub group), and a good choice of wines by the glass; the range of whiskies includes all the malts from the Isle of Islay. There are picnic-sets across the road (which is a good alternative to the main routes west); parking is limited.

Youngs ~ Tenant Nick James ~ Real ale ~ Bar food ~ (01747) 820573 ~ Children welcome away from bar ~ Dogs welcome ~ Open 11-11; 12-10.30 Sun ~ Bedrooms: £55B/£80B

LOWER CHUTE

Hatchet *The Chutes well signposted via Appleshaw off A342, 2½ miles W of Andover*

A real stunner (you'll wish you'd brought your camera), this 16th-c thatched cottage is one of the county's most attractive pubs. They serve well kept Adnams, Otter and Timothy Taylors Landlord on handpump, along with a guest such as Ringwood Best, and there are 10 wines by the glass to choose from, and a range of country wines. With an unchanging, friendly local atmosphere, the very low-beamed bar has a mix of captains' chairs and cushioned wheelbacks around oak tables, and a splendid 17th-c fireback in the huge fireplace (which has a roaring log fire in winter); cribbage, dominoes, and piped music. Thursday night is curry night, when you can eat as much as you like. Other tasty bar food includes around half a dozen vegetarian dishes such as jambalaya, aubergine and two-cheese ravioli, plus lamb tagine, tiger prawns in filo pastry or smoked salmon salad; daily specials as well, and they do a good value Sunday roast. The restaurant is no smoking. There are seats out on a terrace by the front car park, or on the side grass, and there's a children's sandpit. They have only twin bedrooms.

Free house ~ Licensee Jeremy McKay ~ Real ale ~ Bar food (12-2.15, 6.30-9.30) ~ Restaurant ~ (01264) 730229 ~ Children in restaurant and family room ~ Dogs allowed in bar ~ Open 11.30-3, 6-11; 12-3.30, 7-10.30 Sun ~ Bedrooms: £55S/£60S

NEWTON TONY

Malet Arms *Village signposted off A338 Swindon—Salisbury*

Happy reports celebrate the food at this tiled flintstone pub, peacefully placed in a quiet village. The imaginative blackboard menu changes regularly, but might typically include beautifully presented smoked trout pâté, home-baked smoked ham, popular rump steak sandwich, tuna steak, and roast duck breast with spiced potato rösti; home-made puddings too. In winter they do Sunday roasts, and in summer you'll find tasty locally smoked food. Nice furnishings include a mix of different-sized tables with high winged wall settles, carved pews, chapel and carver chairs, and there are lots of pictures mainly from Imperial days. The main front windows are said to have come from the stern of a ship. There's a log and coal fire in a huge fireplace (as the paintwork between the black beams suggests, it can smoke a bit if the wind's strongly in the east). The welcoming landlord (who loves cricket) serves a couple of changing guests, usually from fairly local brewers, such as Ballard's and Triple fff, alongside well kept

Stonehenge Heelstone and Wadworths 6X on handpump. As well as decent wines and farm cider, they've 15 malt whiskies, and an espresso machine. The two pub jack russells are called Badger and Piper, and there's an african grey parrot called Steerpike. There are old-fashioned garden seats on the small front terrace, with some picnic-sets on the grass there, and more in a back garden which has a wendy house; there's also a little aviary. With a playing field opposite, and chickens and a horse paddock out behind, the pub looks over a chalk stream that you ford to drive to it – it's best to use an alternative route in winter, when it can be quite deep.

Free house ~ Licensee Noel Cardew ~ Real ale ~ Bar food (12-2.30, 6.30-10) ~ (01980) 629279 ~ Children in restaurant and family room ~ Dogs allowed in bar ~ Open 11-3, 6-11; 12-3, 7-10.30 Sun; closed 26 Dec, 1 Jan

NORTON

Vine Tree *4 miles from M4 junction 17; A429 towards Malmesbury, then left at Hullavington, Sherston signpost, then follow Norton signposts; in village turn right at Foxley signpost, which takes you into Honey Lane*

In an attractively converted 18th-c mill house, this civilised dining pub is a popular place for a well cooked meal. Three beautifully kept little rooms open together, with limited edition and sporting prints, a mock-up mounted pig's mask (used for a game that involves knocking coins off its nose and ears), lots of stripped pine, big church candles on the tables (the lighting's very gentle), and some old settles; look out for the friendly pub dog Clementine. There are picnic-sets in a two-acre garden which includes a pretty walled terrace and a good well fenced separate play area; two boules pitches. It's best to book if you want to eat here, especially at weekends. Besides baguettes made with home-baked bread (not Friday or Saturday evenings), a wide choice of imaginative (but not cheap) seasonally changing dishes might include foie gras and chicken liver terrine, woodland mushroom and feta risotto, marinated yellow fin tuna medallion with seaweed and chinese egg noodles, and roast pork wrapped in prosciutto; puddings such as white and dark chocolate torte, and a choice of three good Sunday roasts. One dining area is no smoking. Although the emphasis is on eating, there's a buoyant atmosphere, and drinkers do pop in; helpful attentive staff serve well kept Archers or Butcombe Bitter and, from an impressive list, around 16 wines are available by the glass. It's not the easiest place to find, so it feels more remote than its proximity to the motorway would suggest.

Free house ~ Licensees Charles Walker and Tiggi Wood ~ Real ale ~ Bar food (12-2(2.30 Sat), 7-9.30(9.45 Fri/Sat); 12-3, 7-9.30 Sun) ~ Restaurant ~ (01666) 837654 ~ Children welcome ~ Dogs welcome ~ Open 12-3, 6-11; 12-10.30 Sun

RAMSBURY

Bell *signposted off B4192 NW of Hungerford, or A4 W*

This spotlessly kept dining pub is nicely positioned in a smartly attractive village. Comfortably modernised, the airy bar has exposed beams, cream-washed walls, and two woodburning stoves; fresh flowers on polished tables add a welcome touch of colour. Victorian stained glass panels in one of the two sunny bay windows look out onto the quiet village street. There's a pleasantly relaxed chatty atmosphere, and the friendly landlord and his staff are welcoming. Good bar food might include sausages and mash, fish and chips, and beef stir-fry, or you can eat from the more elaborate à la carte menu in the bar, with dishes such as smoked duck salad or black pudding with scallops, lamb chump with potato purée, ratatouille and rosemary coulis; delicious puddings. Tables can be reserved in the restaurant. Wadworths IPA, 6X and an occasional guest beer are well kept on handpump. There are picnic-sets on the raised lawn; roads lead from this quiet village into the downland on all sides. The landlord has plans to add bedrooms during 2005.

Free house ~ Licensee Jeremy Wilkins ~ Real ale ~ Bar food (not Sun evening) ~ Restaurant ~ (01672) 520230 ~ Children welcome ~ Dogs allowed in bar ~ Open 12-3, 6-11; 12-3, 7-10.30 Sun

ROWDE
George & Dragon *A342 Devizes—Chippenham*
Fish-lovers can choose from a great selection of seafood, delivered fresh from Cornwall, at this attractive old dining pub. The seasonally changing menu (with the quality and price of an upmarket restaurant) might typically include grilled lemon sole or thai curry with hake, salmon and squid, and steamed bass; non-fishy choices such as guinea fowl and lentil soup, cheese soufflé, and fillet steak; puddings such as pecan tart with crème fraîche, and a selection of cheeses. No smoking dining room; if Ralph the ginger tom is around he may try and help you finish your meal. The bar is tastefully furnished, with plenty of dark wood, and a log fire with a fine collection of brass keys by it; the bare-floored dining room has quite plain tables and chairs, and is close enough to the bar to keep a pleasant chatty atmosphere. A couple of changing well kept real ales on handpump are from breweries such as Archers and Butcombe, and they've organic cider, and continental beers and lagers; shove-ha'penny, cribbage and dominoes. A pretty garden at the back has tables and chairs; the Kennet & Avon Canal is nearby.

Free house ~ Licensees Tim and Helen Withers ~ Real ale ~ Bar food (not Sun or Mon) ~ Restaurant ~ (01380) 723053 ~ Children in eating area of bar and restaurant ~ Dogs allowed in bar ~ Open 12-3, 7-11(10.30 Sun); closed Mon lunchtime, 25 Dec, 1 Jan

Dog Friendly Hotels, B&Bs and Farms

BRADFORD-ON-AVON
Woolley Grange *Woolley Green, Bradford-on-Avon, Wiltshire BA15 1TX (01225) 864705 £140*, plus winter breaks; 26 rms, with fruit and home-made biscuits. Civilised Jacobean manor house with a relaxed informal atmosphere, lovely flowers, log fires and antiques in comfortable and

beautifully decorated day rooms, and pretty conservatory; delicious food using local (or home-grown) produce, often organic, inc home-baked breads and muffins and home-made jams and marmalades for breakfast, marvellous staff, and swimming pool, tennis, badminton, and croquet; particularly well organised for families, with nannies and plenty of entertainment; disabled access; dogs welcome in bedrooms

CASTLE COMBE

Manor House *Castle Combe, Chippenham, Wiltshire SN14 7HR (01249)* 782206 £**180**, plus special breaks; 48 lovely rms, some in mews cottages just 50 yds from the house. 14th-c manor house in 360 acres of countryside inc an italian garden and parkland; gracious day rooms with panelling, antiques, log fires and fresh flowers, a warm friendly atmosphere, and very good innovative food; 18-hole golf course with full range of practice facilities, croquet, boules, and all-weather tennis court, and heated outdoor swimming pool; dogs in cottage rooms only; £15

CHICKSGROVE

Compasses *Lower Chicksgrove, Tisbury, Salisbury, Wiltshire SP3 6NB (01722)* 714318 £**75**, plus special breaks; 4 rms. Lovely thatched no smoking house in delightful hamlet with old bottles and jugs hanging from the beams, good freshly cooked food in newly refurbished dining room, well kept real ales, and peaceful farm courtyard, garden with new furniture, and play area; cl 25-26 Dec; disabled access; dogs welcome in bedrooms

COLLINGBOURNE KINGSTON

Manor Farm *Collingbourne Kingston, Marlborough, Wiltshire SN8 3SD (01264)* 850859 £**50**; 3 comfortable, very spacious rms with sofas and dining table, and country views. No smoking 17th-c farmhouse on working arable farm lived in by the same family since 1885; warmly welcoming owners, excellent hearty Aga-cooked breakfasts (you can collect your eggs from their free range chickens), packed lunches on request and several very good local pubs and restaurants; good walking, cycling and riding directly from the farm; their own private airstrip with aerial adventures on offer; dogs in bedrooms

CRUDWELL

Old Rectory Country House Hotel *Crudwell, Malmesbury, Wiltshire SN16 9EP (01666)* 577194 £**98**, plus special breaks; 12 big homely rms. Elegant, welcoming country-house hotel, formerly the rectory to the Saxon church next door; three acres of lovely landscaped Victorian gardens, an airy drawing room, interesting and enjoyable food in panelled no smoking restaurant, a relaxed atmosphere, and unpretentious service; dogs welcome in bedrooms

EASTON GREY

Whatley Manor *Easton Grey, Malmesbury, Wiltshire SN16 0RB (01666)* 822888 £**275**, plus special breaks; 23 sumptuous rms and 8 suites. Newly re-opened and very stylish Cotswold manor house in 12 acres of gardens, meadows and woodland; spacious and rather fine oak-panelled drawing room, pine-panelled lounge, log fires, italian furniture, silk rugs and limestone floors, a cosseting atmosphere, knowledgeable staff, classical french cooking with contemporary touches in two restaurants, and well stocked wine cellars; cinema and Spa Aquarias with thermal pools, gym, and hydrotherapy pool that extends outside with lovely valley views; children over 12; disabled access; dogs welcome in bedrooms; £15

HEYTESBURY

Angel *High St, Heytesbury, Warminster, Wiltshire BA12 0ED (01985) 840330* £75; 8 comfortable light rms. 16th-c coaching inn with armchairs, sofas, and a good fire in cosy homely lounge, a long chatty beamed bar, and good service from friendly staff; wide choice of consistently good food in charming back dining room that opens onto secluded garden; disabled access; dogs welcome in bedrooms, if small and well behaved

LACOCK

At the Sign of the Angel *Church St, Lacock, Chippenham, Wiltshire SN15 2LB (01249) 730230* £99, plus special breaks; 10 charmingly old rooms with antiques. This fine 15th-c house in a lovely NT village is full of character, with heavy oak furniture, beams and big fireplaces, a restful oak-panelled lounge, and good english cooking in three candlelit restaurants; cl Christmas period; dogs welcome in bedrooms

MALMESBURY

Old Bell *Abbey Row, Malmesbury, Wiltshire SN16 0BW (01666) 822344* £150, plus special breaks; 31 attractive rms. With some claim to being one of England's oldest hotels and standing in the shadow of the Norman abbey, this fine wisteria-clad building has traditionally furnished rooms with Edwardian pictures, an early 13th-c hooded stone fireplace, two good fires and plenty of comfortable sofas, magazines and newspapers; cheerful helpful service, very good food, and attractively old-fashioned garden; particularly well organised with facilities and entertainments for children; disabled access; dogs welcome in bedrooms; £7.50

PURTON

Pear Tree *Church End, Purton, Swindon, Wiltshire SN5 4ED (01793) 772100* £115, plus special breaks; 17 very comfortable, pretty rms. Impeccably run former vicarage with elegant comfortable day rooms, fresh flowers, fine conservatory restaurant with good modern english cooking using home-grown herbs, helpful caring staff, and 7½ acres inc a traditional Victorian garden; cl 26–30 Dec; disabled access; dogs in bedrooms

SALISBURY

Rose & Crown *Harnham Rd, Harnham, Salisbury, Wiltshire SP2 8JQ (01722) 399955* £130; 28 rms in the original building or smart modern extension. It's almost worth a visit just for the view – well nigh identical to that in the most famous Constable painting of Salisbury Cathedral; elegantly restored inn with friendly beamed and timbered bar, log fire, good bar and restaurant food, and charming Avonside garden; disabled access; dogs in bedrooms

TEFFONT EVIAS

Howards House *Teffont Evias, Salisbury, Wiltshire SP3 5RJ (01722) 716392* **£145**, plus special breaks; 9 rms. Partly 17th-c house in two acres of pretty gardens with ancient box hedges, croquet, and kitchen gardens; fresh flowers, beams and open fire in restful sitting room, delicious modern cooking in no smoking restaurant, fine breakfasts, and attentive, helpful staff; cl Christmas, last wk Feb, 1st wk Mar; dogs welcome away from restaurant; £7

WARMINSTER

Bishopstrow House *Bishopstrow, Warminster, Wiltshire BA12 9HH (01985) 212312* **£199**, plus special breaks; 32 sumptuous rms, some with jacuzzi. Charming ivy-clad Georgian house in 27 acres with heated indoor and outdoor swimming pools, indoor and outdoor tennis courts, fitness centre and beauty treatment rooms, and own fishing on River Wylye; very relaxed friendly atmosphere, log fires, lovely fresh flowers, antiques and fine paintings in boldly decorated day rooms, and really impressive food; disabled access; dogs in bedrooms; £10

Worcestershire

Dog Friendly Pubs

BERROW GREEN
Admiral Rodney *B4197, off A44 W of Worcester*
On Sundays they do a choice of three roasts at this civilised country inn. Attractively light and roomy throughout, the bare-boards entrance bar, with high beams and a sunny bow window, has big stripped kitchen tables and cushioned chairs, a traditional winged settle, and a woodburning stove in a fireplace that opens through to the comfortable no smoking lounge area. This has some carpet on its slate flagstones, dark red settees, a table of magazines and rack of broadsheet newspapers, quite a few board games, and prints of the Battle of the Saints, where Lord Rodney obliterated the french fleet in the Caribbean. A separate skittle alley has pool; also darts, Jenga, cribbage, dominoes, and perhaps piped music. It's popular with older crowds at lunchtime, and in the evening you'll find locals dropping in for a chatty drink. Besides a couple of tasty fresh cornish fish specials such as john dory fillets, enjoyable dishes include tortilla wraps, home-made pie, pizza or curry, along with restaurant dishes (which can also be eaten in the bar) such as pork fillet with apple, calvados and sage cream sauce; home-made puddings too. A rebuilt barn stepping down through three levels forms a charming end restaurant (mostly no smoking). Alongside well kept Wye Valley Bitter, they've three changing guests such as Cottage Hop n Drop, RCH East Street Cream and Woods Quaff, and you'll find a tempting choice of wines, and good bloody marys; cheerful service from the hands-on licensees. Out on a terrace and neat green, solid tables and chairs look over the Lower Teme valley (two of the three bedrooms share the views), and this is good walking territory. The friendly pub dog is called Penny.
Free house ~ Licensees Gillian and Kenneth Green ~ Real ale ~ Bar food (not Mon lunchtime exc bank hols) ~ Restaurant ~ (01886) 821375 ~ Children welcome ~ Dogs allowed in bar and bedrooms ~ Open 11-3, 5-11; 11-11 Sat; 12-10.30 Sun; closed Mon lunchtime exc bank hols ~ Bedrooms: £40S/£55B

BIRTSMORTON

Farmers Arms *Birts Street, off B4208 W*

Good value simple dishes at this pretty black and white timbered village pub might include sandwiches, well cooked macaroni cheese, fish and chips, chicken and vegetable curry, gammon and steak; also good puddings like spotted dick. Service is very welcoming, and there's a friendly bustling atmosphere. The neatly kept big room on the right, which has a no smoking area, rambles away under very low dark beams, with some standing timbers, and flowery-panelled cushioned settles as well as spindleback chairs; on the left an even lower-beamed room seems even cosier, and in both the white walls have black timbering; darts in a good tiled area, shove-ha'penny, cribbage, and dominoes. Sociable locals gather at the bar for Hook Norton Best and Old Hooky well kept on handpump, and there's also a changing guest from a brewer such as Wye Valley. You'll find seats out on the large lawn, and the pub is surrounded by plenty of walks. Please treat the opening hours we give below as approximate – they may vary according to how busy or quiet things are.

Free house ~ Licensees Jill and Julie Moore ~ Real ale ~ Bar food (12-2, 6.30-9.30) ~ No credit cards ~ (01684) 833308 ~ Children welcome ~ Dogs allowed in bar ~ Open 11-4, 6-11; 12-4, 7-10.30 Sun

HOLY CROSS

Bell & Cross *4 miles from M5 junction 4: A491 towards Stourbridge, then follow Clent signpost off on left*

The imaginative food is the big attraction at this comfortably civilised pub, although it's also popular with locals just out for an evening drink. Enticing dishes, from a changing menu, include lunchtime snacks (not Sunday) such as toasted muffin with potted chicken liver and port parfait, smoked haddock with scrambled egg, and grilled calves liver with bubble and squeak; a few daily specials such as roasted cornish brill with spinach and ricotta ravioli, and puddings might include sticky chocolate brownies and chantilly cream. The Sunday menu includes traditional roasts; they also do children's meals. With a classic unspoilt early 19th-c layout, the five small rooms and kitchen open off a central corridor with a black and white tiled floor: they give a choice of carpet, bare boards, lino or nice old quarry tiles, a variety of moods from snug and chatty to bright and airy, and an individual décor in each – theatrical engravings on red walls here, nice sporting prints on pale green walls there, racing and gundog pictures above the black panelled dado in another room. Two of the rooms have small serving bars, with well kept Banks's Bitter, Marstons Pedigree and maybe a guest such as Timothy Taylors Landlord on handpump. You'll find decent house wines, a variety of coffees, daily papers, coal fires in most rooms, perhaps regulars playing cards in one of the two front ones, and piped music. The pub cat is called Pumba. There's a terrace in the pleasant garden; fine views.

Enterprise ~ Tenants Roger and Jo Narbett ~ Real ale ~ Bar food (not 25 Dec, evening 26 Dec) ~ Restaurant ~ (01562) 730319 ~ Children in restaurant ~ Dogs allowed in bar ~ Open 12-3, 6-11; 12-4, 7-10.30 Sun; closed 25 Dec

KEMPSEY
Walter de Cantelupe *A38, handy for M5 junction 7 via A44 and A4440*
Readers highly recommend the tasty ploughman's at this welcoming and
unpretentious roadside inn and, to go with it, there's a good choice of
wines by the glass (they have regularly changing bin ends, and english
wines from a local vineyard). Boldly decorated in red and gold, the bar area
has an informal and well worn in mix of furniture, an old wind-up HMV
gramophone and a good big fireplace. The dining area has various plush or
yellow leather dining chairs, an old settle, a sonorous clock, and candles and
flowers on the tables. Cooked by the friendly landlord, using lots of local
produce, enjoyable well presented dishes might be glamorgan sausages with
mushroom gravy and mashed potato, chicken balti, and specials such as
beef and ale pie or cajun-spiced salmon; also puddings such as marmalade
bread and butter pudding, and you can buy jars of home-made chutney.
Well kept real ales on handpump such as Hobsons Best, Cannon Royall
Kings Shilling and Timothy Taylors Landlord; good service. The dining
area is no smoking; cribbage, dominoes and table skittles. There's a pretty
suntrap walled garden at the back; the sociable labrador is called Monti.
Free house ~ Licensee Martin Lloyd Morris ~ Real ale ~ Bar food (12-2(2.30
Sat), 6-9.30; 12-2.30, 7-8 Sun; not Mon exc bank hols) ~ Restaurant ~
(01905) 820572 ~ Children in restaurant ~ Dogs allowed in bar and bedrooms ~
Open 12-2(2.30 summer), 5.30-11; 11-2.30(3 summer), 6-11 Sat; 12-3.30(4
summer), 7-10.30 Sun; closed Mon exc bank hols, 25-26 Dec, 1 Jan ~ Bedrooms:
£38.50S(£49.50B)/£49.50S(£77B)

MALVERN
Nags Head *Bottom end of Bank Street, steep turn down off A449*
In a pleasant spot between the great mass of hill swelling up behind and the
plain stretching out below, this cheerfully bustling traditional tavern serves
up to 11 beers on handpump. Along with well kept Greene King IPA,
Marstons Pedigree and Woods Shropshire Lad, you'll find changing guest
beers from brewers such as Banks's, Bathams, Cottage, Holden's, Timothy
Taylors and Wye Valley. They also have a fine range of malt whiskies, and
decent wines by the glass; friendly young staff. A good variety of places to
sit rambles through a series of snug individually decorated rooms with one
or two steps between some, all sorts of chairs including some leather
armchairs, pews sometimes arranged as booths, a mix of tables with some
sturdy ones stained different colours, bare boards here, flagstones there,
carpet elsewhere, and plenty of interesting pictures and homely touches
such as house plants and shelves of well thumbed books; there's a coal fire
opposite the central servery. The pub attracts a good mix of customers
(with plenty of locals), and the mood is chatty and easy-going; broadsheet
newspapers and a good jukebox. Bar food might include goats cheese
ciabatta, soup, moroccan vegetable tagine and fish pie. In the evenings they
only serve meals in the extension barn dining room; they don't take
bookings, and it fills up quickly so get there early. Outside are picnic-sets
and rustic tables and benches on the front terrace and in a garden; there are
heaters, and umbrellas for wet weather.

Free house ~ Licensee Duncan Ironmonger ~ Real ale ~ Bar food (12-2, 6.30-8.30) ~ Restaurant ~ (01684) 574373 ~ Children welcome ~ Dogs welcome ~ Open 11-11; 12-10.30 Sun

Dog Friendly Hotels, B&Bs and Farms

AB LENCH
Manor Farm House *Ab Lench, Evesham, Worcestershire WR11 4UP* (01386) 462226 £80; 2 rms. Comfortable 250-year-old house in a rural spot with a lovely fenced-in half-acre garden; relaxing reception rooms, a study with TV, some interesting objects collected from around the world, enjoyable evening meals, nice breakfasts, and charming, friendly owners; children over 12; cl Dec-Jan; dogs welcome in bedrooms, if small

BROADWAY
Broadway Hotel *The Green, Broadway, Worcestershire WR12 7AA* (01386) 852401 £130; 20 well kept rms. Lovely 15th-c building, once a monastic guest house, with galleried and timbered lounge, cosy beamed bar, attractively presented food served by attentive staff in airy comfortable restaurant, and seats outside on terrace; dogs welcome in some bedrooms

Lygon Arms *High St, Broadway, Worcestershire WR12 7DU* (01386) 852255 £199, plus special breaks; 69 lovely period rms (some more modern, too). Handsome hotel where Oliver Cromwell and King Charles I once stayed; interesting beamed rooms, oak panelling, antiques, log fires, fine traditional food in the Great Hall with minstrels' gallery and heraldic frieze, excellent service, and charming garden; health spa; disabled access; dogs welcome in bedrooms; £25

EVESHAM
Evesham Hotel *Coopers Lane, off Waterside, Evesham, Worcestershire WR11 1DA* (01386) 765566 £124, plus special breaks; 40 spacious rms with games and jigsaws. Comfortably modernised and cheerful family-run hotel with a warmly friendly, relaxed and jokey atmosphere, popular restaurant with very good food (esp lunchtime buffet), huge wine and spirits list, and sitting room with games and toys; indoor swimming pool surrounded by table tennis and table football, and grounds with croquet, trampoline, swings and putting; particularly well organised for families (but they do not get overrun by children); cl 25-26 Dec; disabled access; dogs welcome in bedrooms only

HIMBLETON
Phepson Farm *Phepson, Droitwich, Worcestershire WR9 7JZ* (01905) 391205 £55, plus winter breaks; 6 rms, 4 in renovated farm buildings. Relaxed and friendly 17th-c farmhouse on small sheep farm with a fishing

lake; a comfortable guests' lounge, good breakfasts in separate dining room; self-catering also; cl Christmas and New Year; dogs by arrangement only

MALVERN
Cowleigh Park Farm *Cowleigh Park, Cradley, Malvern, Worcestershire WR13 5HJ (01684) 566750* £**62**; 3 rms. Carefully restored and furnished black and white timbered 17th-c farmhouse in own grounds, surrounded by lovely countryside, with good breakfasts and light suppers or full evening meals (prior booking); self-catering also; cl Christmas; children over 7; dogs welcome in bedrooms

MALVERN WELLS
Cottage in the Wood *Holywell Rd, Malvern, Worcestershire WR14 4LG (01684) 575859* £**99**, plus special breaks; 31 compact but pretty rms, some in separate nearby cottages. Family-run Georgian dower house with quite splendid views across the Severn Valley and marvellous walks from the grounds; antiques, log fires, comfortable seats and magazines in public rooms, and modern english cooking and an extensive wine list in attractive no smoking restaurant; dogs welcome in ground-floor bedrooms; £5

Yorkshire

Dog Friendly Pubs

APPLETON-LE-MOORS
Moors *Village N of A170 just under 1½ miles E of Kirkby Moorside*
Appropriately named, this unassuming little stone-built pub has tables in
the walled garden with quiet moors views, and there are moors walks
straight from here to Rosedale Abbey or Hartoft End. Inside, it is almost
totally no smoking, strikingly neat and fresh, and surprisingly bare of the
usual bric-a-brac. Sparse decorations include just a few copper pans and
earthenware mugs in a little alcove, a couple of plates, one or two pieces of
country ironwork, and a delft shelf with miniature whiskies; the whiteness
of walls and ceiling is underlined by the black beams and joists, and the
bristly grey carpet. Perfect for a cold winter evening, there's a nice built-in
high-backed stripped settle next to an old kitchen fireplace, and other
seating includes an unusual rustic seat for two cleverly made out of stripped
cartwheels; plenty of standing space. To the left of the bar, where you'll
probably find a few regulars, there's a games room with a pool table (the
one place you can smoke) and darts; dominoes. Well kept Black Sheep and
Theakstons Black Bull on handpump, and quite a few malt whiskies;
efficient service. The wide choice of food in the no smoking dining room
could include home-made chicken liver pâté, mushroom quiche, local
trout, and daily specials such as lamb casserole or guinea fowl in port; also
home-made puddings like bilberry flan. The bedrooms are in what used to
be a barn behind.
Free house ~ Licensee Janet Frank ~ Real ale ~ Bar food (not lunchtimes exc Sun
(will offer food to residents on Mon)) ~ Restaurant ~ No credit cards ~ (01751)
417435 ~ Children welcome ~ Dogs allowed in bar ~ Open 7-11; 12-3, 7-10.30
Sun; closed Mon ~ Bedrooms: £30S/£50B

ASENBY
Crab & Lobster *Village signposted off A168*
Handy for the A1, this interesting place has a rambling, L-shaped bar with
an interesting jumble of seats from antique high-backed and other settles
through settees and wing armchairs heaped with cushions, to tall and rather
theatrical corner seats; the tables are almost as much of a mix, and the walls

and available surfaces are quite a jungle of bric-a-brac, with standard and table lamps and candles keeping even the lighting pleasantly informal. There's also a no smoking dining pavilion with big tropical plants, nautical bits and pieces, and Edwardian sofas. Well liked bar food includes pressed terrine of potted beef, ham hock and foie gras with red onion and beetroot marmalade, moroccan spiced lamb shank, goan fish curry with coconut rice, and puddings like iced white chocolate and raspberry parfait. Well kept Courage Directors and John Smiths on handpump, and good wines by the glass from an interesting wine list; piped music. The gardens have bamboo and palm trees lining the paths, there's a gazebo at the end of the walkways, and seats on a mediterranean-style terrace. The opulent bedrooms (based on famous hotels around the world) are in the surrounding house which has three acres of mature gardens, and 180-metre golf hole with full practice facilities.

Free house ~ Licensee Mark Spenceley ~ Real ale ~ Bar food ~ Restaurant ~ (01845) 577286 ~ Children in eating area of bar and restaurant ~ Dogs welcome ~ Live entertainment Sun lunchtime ~ Open 11.30-2.30, 6.30-11; 12-3, 7-10.30 Sun ~ Bedrooms: /£150B

BRADFIELD

Strines Inn *From A57 heading E of junction with A6013 (Ladybower Reservoir) take first left turn (signposted with Bradfield) then bear left; with a map can also be reached more circuitously from Strines signpost on A616 at head of Underbank Reservoir, W of Stocksbridge*

After a visit to this isolated moorland inn – set in an area known as Little Switzerland – there are plenty of rambles all around to walk off a hearty good value meal; fine views from the picnic-sets, a safely fenced-in children's playground, and some rescued animals. The main bar has a welcoming atmosphere, black beams liberally decked with copper kettles and so forth, quite a menagerie of stuffed animals, homely red-plush-cushioned traditional wooden wall benches and small chairs, and a coal fire in the rather grand stone fireplace; there's a good mixture of customers. A room off on the right has another coal fire, hunting photographs and prints, and lots of brass and china, and on the left is another similarly furnished room; two rooms are no smoking. Under the new licensee, bar food includes home-made soup, hot panini bread with hot roast beef, mediterranean vegetable hot pot, filled giant yorkshire puddings or popular pie of the day, and daily specials such as cajun chicken or T-bone steak; also puddings like home-made apple pie. Well kept Adnams Broadside, Banks's Riding Bitter, and Marstons Pedigree on handpump, and several malt whiskies; piped music. The bedrooms have four-poster beds (one has an open log fire), and there's a self-catering cottage.

Free house ~ Licensee Bruce Howarth ~ Real ale ~ Bar food (12-2.30, 5.30-9 winter weekdays; all day in summer) ~ (0114) 285 1247 ~ Children welcome ~ Dogs welcome ~ Open 10.30-11; 10.30-10.30 Sun; 10.30-3, 5.30-11 weekdays and all day weekends in winter ~ Bedrooms: £45B/£67.50B

BREARTON

Malt Shovel *Village signposted off A61 N of Harrogate*

There's always a friendly welcome and a good relaxed atmosphere in this deservedly popular 16th-c village pub. As they don't take bookings, you do need to arrive early, but there is a waiting list system. Several heavily-beamed rooms radiate from the attractive linenfold oak bar counter with plush-cushioned seats and a mix of tables, an ancient oak partition wall, tankards and horsebrasses, an open fire, and paintings by local artists (for sale) and lively hunting prints on the walls; nearly half the pub is no smoking. Reliably good and reasonably priced bar food might include mussels steamed in white wine with garlic and cream, ploughman's, steak in ale or game pie, thai chicken curry, and bass with herb butter; puddings such as apple and bramble crumble. Well kept Black Sheep Bitter, Daleside Bitter, and Theakstons Best with a couple of guests such as Durham Magus or North Yorkshire Golden Ale on handpump, quite a few malt whiskies, and a small but interesting and reasonably priced wine list. Darts, shove-ha'penny, cribbage and dominoes. You can eat outside on the small terrace on all but the coldest of days as they have outdoor heaters; there are more tables on the grass. This is an attractive spot off the beaten track, yet handy for Harrogate and Knaresborough.

Free house ~ Licensee Leslie Mitchell ~ Real ale ~ Bar food (not Mon) ~ No credit cards ~ (01423) 862929 ~ Children welcome ~ Dogs welcome ~ Open 12-2.30, 6.45-11(10.30 Sun); closed Mon

CONSTABLE BURTON

Wyvill Arms *A684 E of Leyburn*

After an upstairs flood, much of this inn has been carefully redecorated and refurbished, and readers have been quick to voice their enthusiasm. The bar is still decorated with teak and brass, with mirrors along the back of the bar, ornate shelving, and a bar counter which came from a bank 30 years ago. There's a mix of seating, a finely worked plaster ceiling with the Wyvill family's coat of arms, and an elaborate stone fireplace. The second bar where food is served, has semi-circled, upholstered alcoves, a seventies jukebox with music for all ages, hunting prints and a mounted stag's head, and old oak tables; the reception area of this room includes a huge chesterfield which can seat up to eight people, another carved stone fireplace, and an old leaded church stained-glass window partition. Both rooms are hung with pictures of local scenes, and the restaurant is no smoking. Consistently good, enjoyable food served by friendly, helpful staff includes light lunches such as scrambled egg and smoked salmon, exotic mushroom lasagne, and rarebit and smoked haddock with roast cherry tomatoes; also super steak and onion pie, suckling pig, and monkfish wrapped in parma ham; delicious puddings like chocolate torte with an orange sorbet. The breakfasts and chips come in for special praise. Well kept Black Sheep, John Smiths Bitter, and Theakstons Best with a guest like Charles Wells Bombardier on handpump, and a thoughtful wine list; cribbage, dominoes, darts and piped music. The white bull terrier is called Tricky. There are several large wooden benches with large white parasols for outdoor dining. Constable Burton Gardens are opposite and worth a visit.

Free house ~ Licensee Nigel Stevens ~ Real ale ~ Bar food ~ Restaurant ~ (01677) 450581 ~ Children welcome ~ Dogs allowed in bar ~ Open 11-3, 6-11; 12-3, 7-10.30 Sun ~ Bedrooms: /£66B

CRAYKE
Durham Ox *Off B1363 at Brandsby, towards Easingwold; West Way*
As there is no shop in the village, the enterprising landlord here has started a little shop and fitted a small area by the door with shelves, a fridge, and scales and baskets for vegetables. The old-fashioned lounge bar has venerable tables and antique seats and settles on the flagstones, pictures and photographs on the dark red walls, interesting satirical carvings in its panelling (which are Victorian copies of medieval pew ends), polished copper and brass, and an enormous inglenook fireplace with winter log fires (flowers in summer). In the bottom bar is a framed illustrated account of the local history (some of it gruesome) dating back to the 12th c, and a large framed print of the original famous Durham Ox which weighed 171 stone. As well as daily specials, the tasty (if not cheap) bar food includes home-made soup, wild mushroom tortellini with roast peppers and salsa verde, grilled free range chicken breast, rib-eye steak or local lamb rump, and king prawn, pancetta and mango kebab; there's an early bird menu on Sundays through to Thursdays, and Friday evening fish and chips (best to book in advance). The restaurant is no smoking. Well kept Caledonian Deuchars IPA, John Smiths, Theakstons XB, and Charles Wells Bombardier on handpump, and 12 wines by the glass; piped music and dominoes. There are seats outside on a terrace and in the courtyard, and the comfortable bedrooms are in converted farm buildings. The tale is that this is the hill which the Grand Old Duke of York marched his men up; the view from the hill opposite is marvellous.

Free house ~ Licensee Michael Ibbotson ~ Real ale ~ Bar food (12-2.30, 6-9.30(8.30 Sun)) ~ Restaurant ~ (01347) 821506 ~ Children allowed but not in restaurant ~ Dogs allowed in bedrooms ~ Folk/easy listening live music Thurs evenings ~ Open 11-3, 6-11.30; 12-3, 7-10 Sun; closed 25 Dec ~ Bedrooms: £60B/£80B

EAST WITTON
Blue Lion *A6108 Leyburn—Ripon*
This busy dining pub, set on the edge of the green in a pretty village, places quite an emphasis on its popular food. The big squarish bar has high-backed antique settles and old windsor chairs on the turkey rugs and flagstones, ham-hooks in the high ceiling decorated with dried wheat, teazles and so forth, a delft shelf filled with appropriate bric-a-brac, several prints, sporting caricatures and other pictures on the walls, a log fire, and daily papers; the friendly labrador is called Archie. Restaurant-quality meals (with prices to match – some find them too steep for a Dales pub) might include hot roast beef sandwich with horseradish, lemon chicken, leek and sage risotto with gruyère cheese, creamed garlic mushrooms and tarragon

with home-made brioche, home-made tagliatelle carbonara or confit of duck leg with chorizo and choucroute, and chargrilled steak with red wine sauce. Well kept Black Sheep Bitter and Riggwelter, and Theakstons Best, and an impressive wine list with quite a few by the glass. Picnic-sets on the gravel outside look beyond the stone houses on the far side of the village green to Witton Fell, and there's a big, pretty back garden.

Free house ~ Licensee Paul Klein ~ Real ale ~ Bar food ~ (01969) 624273 ~ Children welcome ~ Dogs allowed in bar and bedrooms ~ Open 11-11; 12-10.30 Sun ~ Bedrooms: £53.50S/£69S(£79B)

FERRENSBY
General Tarleton *A655 N of Knaresborough*

Even when this rather smart and comfortable old coaching inn is very busy – which it usually is – service remains helpful and courteous. Although many customers do come to enjoy the good modern cooking, there are plenty of locals popping in for a drink and a chat. The beamed and carpeted bar has brick pillars dividing up the several different areas to create the occasional cosy alcove, some exposed stonework, and neatly framed pictures on the red walls; there's a mix of country-kitchen furniture and comfortable banquettes, a big open fire, and a door leading out to a pleasant tree-lined garden with smart green tables. From the menu, the interesting bar food includes thai spiced chicken, prawn and coconut soup, queenie scallops, terrine of duck with cumberland sauce, steak in ale pudding, and daily specials such as roast red-legged partridge, and spiced sea salt crusted halibut with roasted fennel; puddings like steamed treacle pudding with vanilla crème anglaise. Also a children's menu, and good breakfasts. Well kept Black Sheep Best and Timothy Taylors Landlord on handpump, over 20 good wines by the glass, and quite a few coffees. The courtyard eating area (and restaurant) are no smoking.

Free house ~ Licensee John Topham ~ Real ale ~ Bar food (12-2, 6-9.15) ~ Restaurant ~ (01423) 340284 ~ Children welcome ~ Dogs allowed in bedrooms ~ Open 12-3, 6-11(10.30 Sun) ~ Bedrooms: /£84.90B

LANGTHWAITE
Charles Bathurst *Arkengarthdale, a mile N towards Tan Hill; generally known as the CB Inn*

As well as refurbishing the kitchen in this well run inn, a new dining room has been built with wooden floors and views of Scar House, a shooting lodge owned by the Duke of Norfolk. The inn looks appropriately stolid from the outside, and is knocked through inside to make a long bar with light pine scrubbed tables, country chairs and benches on stripped floors, plenty of snug alcoves, and a roaring fire. The island bar counter has well kept Black Sheep Bitter and Riggwelter, John Smiths, and Theakstons Best on handpump, and a short but interesting list of wines; piped music, darts, pool, TV and dominoes. Using local ingredients and cooked by the licensee, the very popular food might include lunchtime filled baguettes, lamb kofta with spicy tomato salsa, mediterranean roast vegetables on couscous, loin of salmon with tagliatelle carbonara, slow roasted pork belly

with wilted spinach and wild mushrooms, and puddings such as sticky toffee pudding with caramel sauce. Best to book to be sure of a table; the dining room is partly no smoking. The bedrooms are pretty and comfortable, and there are fine views over Langthwaite village and Arkengarthdale.
Free house ~ Licensees Charles and Stacy Cody ~ Real ale ~ Bar food ~ (01748) 884567 ~ Children welcome ~ Dogs welcome ~ Open 11-11; 12-10.30 Sun; 3-11 Mon-Thurs in winter ~ Bedrooms: /£70B

LITTON
Queens Arms *From B6160 N of Grassington, after Kilnsey take second left fork; can also be reached off B6479 at Stainforth N of Settle, via Halton Gill*
This is a smashing little inn in a lovely setting with a friendly welcome, fine own-brewed ale, and proper home cooking. The main bar on the right has a good coal fire, stripped rough stone walls, a brown beam and plank ceiling, stools around cast-iron-framed tables on the stone and concrete floor, a seat built into the stone-mullioned window, and signed cricket bats. The left-hand room is an eating area with old photographs of the Dales around the walls. Well kept Litton Ale and Potts Beck Ale on handpump from their own micro-brewery; the family room is no smoking. Good, popular bar food includes filled baked potatoes, home-made rabbit pie or game pie, daily specials such as local blue cheese, onion, mushroom and black olive tart, roast lamb, halibut steak in seafood sauce, and a massive mixed grill; puddings like rhubarb crumble or syrup tart. Darts, dominoes, cribbage, and piped music. There are seats and a safe area for children in the two-level garden, and the views over the fells are stunning. Plenty of surrounding walks – a track behind the inn leads over Ackerley Moor to Buckden, and the quiet lane through the valley leads on to Pen-y-Ghent. Walkers enjoy staying here very much – and there is a walkers' room (price on request).
Free house ~ Licensees Tanya and Neil Thompson ~ Real ale ~ Bar food (12-2, 6.30-8; not Mon; no food Jan) ~ (01756) 770208 ~ Children in family room ~ Dogs allowed in bar ~ Open 12-3, 7-11; 11.30-3, 6.30-11(10.30 Sun) Sat; Sat opening 7pm in winter; closed Mon (exc bank hols) ~ Bedrooms: /£66S

MIDDLEHAM
White Swan *Market Place*
In a rather steep and pretty village, this pleasant coaching inn is set in the cobbled market place. It has a relaxed pubby atmosphere and is tastefully decorated in an understated way. The beamed and flagstoned entrance bar has a long dark pew built into the big window overlooking the sloping market square, and a mix of chairs around a handful of biggish tables. Well kept Black Sheep Best, Special and Riggwelter and John Smiths on handpump from the curved counter, 13 wines by the glass, and a couple of dozen malt whiskies, with friendly attentive service and a good inglenook log fire. A second beamed room on the right has a variety of tables and dining chairs, a red oriental rug on its black boards, and like the first is candlelit. There's a third broadly similar room behind and a no smoking

restaurant. Modestly priced bar food includes sandwiches, home-made soup, black pudding and bacon risotto, local sausages with grain mustard mash and gravy, battered fish and chips, steak in ale pie, and daily specials. *Free house ~ Licensees Andrew Holmes and Paul Klein ~ Real ale ~ Bar food (12-2.15, 6.30-9.15) ~ Restaurant ~ (01969) 622093 ~ Children welcome ~ Dogs welcome ~ Open 11-11; 12-10.30 Sun ~ Bedrooms: £47.50B/£59(£69B)*

MILL BANK
Millbank *Mill Bank Road, off A58 SW of Sowerby Bridge*

In deeply folded countryside close to the old mill towns of Calderdale, just off the main road through the Ryburn Valley, this is a notable country dining pub that draws people in from far around. Cottagey and traditionally Pennine from the outside, it has a calm, clean-cut minimalist modern décor with local touches such as chapel chairs and local photographs for sale. The interior is divided into the tap room, bar and no smoking restaurant, with well kept Adnams Broadside, Tetleys and Timothy Taylors Landlord on handpump, and 21 wines by the glass including champagne, port and pudding wines; it also has a specialised gin list. Discreet background music of a jazzy flavour. Outside is a terrace with a glass roof and fold-away windows that make the most of the glorious setting overlooking an old textile mill. Below this is a garden adorned with metal sculptures made from old farm equipment. Sandwiches are available along with the fixed-price menu, and dishes such as butternut squash soup, brandade of salted whiting with aubergine crisps and chorizo with saffron mayonnaise, venison and juniper sausages or braised shoulder of lamb, and bass fillet with mushroom and celeriac purée. Puddings are similarly innovative, and feature chocolate fondant cake with poached pear and vanilla ice-cream, in addition to a plate of selected vegetarian-suitable yorkshire cheeses. The fixed-price Sunday lunch menu is particularly good value. They're hoping to have accommodation during 2005. The former industrial hamlet of Mill Bank nearly disappeared under the bulldozers in the early 1970s, but was saved after a campaign by local residents and has now been wholeheartedly revived as a community. There is superb walking country nearby, with the Calderdale Way easily accessible from the pub.
Timothy Taylors ~ Licensee Joe McNally ~ Real ale ~ (01422) 825588 ~ Children in eating area of bar ~ Dogs allowed in bar ~ Open 12-3, 5.30-11; 12-10.30 Sun; closed Mon exc bank hols; closed 2 wks Oct, 1 wk Jan

OSMOTHERLEY
Golden Lion *The Green, West End; off A19 N of Thirsk*

There's no doubt that most customers come to this old stone-built dining pub to enjoy the particularly good, interesting food, and as it is so busy (especially at weekends) you must book to be sure of a table. The roomy beamed bar on the left, simply furnished with old pews and just a few decorations on its white walls, has a pleasantly lively atmosphere, candles on tables, well kept Hambleton Bitter, Timothy Taylors Landlord, and maybe Jennings Cumberland or John Smiths on handpump, a decent wine list and 40 malt whiskies; one side of the pub is no smoking. On the right, a similarly unpretentious eating area, brightened up with fresh flowers, has good value generous food which might include sandwiches, soups, creamy lemon risotto with caramelised onion, home-made spicy chilli chicken burger, spaghetti with fresh baby clams, home-made vegetable lasagne or chargrilled poussin, and puddings such as middle eastern orange cake with marmalade cream; several teas and coffees. There's also an airy no smoking dining room, mainly open at weekends. Benches out in front look across the village green to the market cross. As the inn is the start of the 44-mile Lyke Wakes Walk on the Cleveland Way, and quite handy for the Coast to Coast Walk, it is naturally popular with walkers.

Free house ~ Licensee Christie Connelly ~ Real ale ~ Bar food (12-3, 6-9.30) ~ Restaurant ~ (01609) 883526 ~ Children welcome ~ Dogs allowed in bar ~ Open 12-3.30, 6-11; 12-11 Sat; closed evening 25 Dec

WATH IN NIDDERDALE
Sportsmans Arms *Nidderdale road off B6265 in Pateley Bridge; village and pub signposted over hump bridge on right after a couple of miles*
You can be sure of a genuinely warm welcome from the courteous, friendly staff in this civilised restaurant-with-rooms – whether you are popping in for a quick drink, a more leisurely meal, or staying overnight in the very comfortable bedrooms. Using the best local produce – game from the moors, fish delivered daily from Whitby, and Nidderdale lamb, pork and beef – the carefully presented and prepared delicious food might include fresh soup, really excellent lunchtime sandwiches, their special salad with bacon, croûtons, olives, anchovies, and parmesan and pecorino cheeses on mixed leaves, locally smoked trout fillets, chicken breast with white wine, chive and mushroom sauce, and sirloin steak; puddings like sticky toffee pudding. The whole place is no smoking apart from the bar and the lounge. Well kept Black Sheep on handpump, a very sensible and extensive wine list, a good choice of malt whiskies, and several russian vodkas; open fires. Benches and tables outside. As well as their own fishing on the River Nidd, this is an ideal spot for walkers, hikers and ornithologists, and there are plenty of country houses, gardens and cities to explore.

Free house ~ Licensee Ray Carter ~ Real ale ~ Bar food ~ Restaurant ~ (01423) 711306 ~ Children welcome ~ Dogs allowed in bar ~ Open 12-2.30, 6.30-11; 12-3, 7-10.30 Sun; closed 25 Dec ~ Bedrooms: £50B/£90B

Dog Friendly Hotels, B&Bs and Farms

BAINBRIDGE
Rose & Crown *Bainbridge, Leyburn, North Yorkshire DL8 3EE (01969) 650225 £66*, plus special breaks; 12 comfortable rms. 15th-c coaching inn overlooking lovely green, with antique settles and other old furniture in beamed and panelled front bar, open log fires, cosy residents' lounge, big

wine list, and home-made traditional food in bar and restaurant; pets welcome by prior arrangement; disabled access; dogs in some bedrooms; £5

BLAKEY RIDGE
Lion *High Blakey, Kirkbymoorside, North Yorkshire YO62 7LQ (01751) 417320* £**60**, plus winter breaks; 10 good rms, most with own bthrm. The fourth-highest inn in England, this has spectacular moorland views, rambling beamed stripped stone bars, blazing fires, generous helpings of decent food served all day, good breakfasts, candlelit restaurant, quite a few real ales, and genuinely friendly licensees and staff; fine walking country; disabled access; dogs welcome in bedrooms

BOLTON ABBEY
Devonshire Arms *Bolton Abbey, Skipton, North Yorkshire BD23 6AJ (01756) 710441* £**220**, plus special breaks; 41 individually furnished rms with thoughtful extras. Close to the priory itself and in lovely countryside, this civilised former coaching inn owned by the Duke of Devonshire has been carefully furnished with fine antiques and paintings from Chatsworth; log fires, impeccable service, beautifully presented imaginative food, and super breakfasts; health centre; children over 12 in restaurant; disabled access; dogs in some bedrooms; not allowed near restaurants

BRADFORD
Victoria Hotel *Bridge St, Bradford, West Yorkshire BD1 1JX (01274) 728706* £**95**, plus special breaks; 60 well equipped rms with CD and video. Carefully renovated Victorian station hotel with many original features and lots of stylish character, bustling bar, popular and informal brasserie serving good modern food, and marvellous breakfasts, small private gym and sauna; disabled access; dogs welcome in bedrooms

BRAFFERTON
Laurel Manor Farm *Brafferton, North Yorkshire YO61 2NZ (01423) 360436* £**70**; 3 big beamed rms. Tall Georgian house with lovely views, surrounded by 28 acres of farmland: rare breeds, horses, fishing in the River Swale, 1,500 trees, carefully planted landscaped gardens, and croquet and tennis; open fire in comfortable sitting room, antiques and family photographs, aircraft models and pictures, good breakfasts and enjoyable candlelit family dinners using home-grown produce (by arrangement), and friendly, attentive owners; horses and other pets welcome in stable room; dogs welcome in bedrooms

CRAY
White Lion *Cray, Skipton, North Yorkshire BD23 5JB (01756) 760262* £**60**, plus special breaks; 8 comfortable rms all with showers. Welcoming little pub spectacularly isolated 335 metres (1,100 ft) up with super views, lots of walks, traditional feel with flagstones, beams and log fires, good bar food, and decent wines; residents only 25 Dec; partial disabled access; dogs in bedrooms and other areas; £3

HALIFAX

Holdsworth House *Holmfield, Halifax, West Yorkshire HX2 9TG (01422)* *240024* £120, plus wknd breaks; 40 traditional, individually decorated, quiet rms. Lovely, immaculately kept 17th-c house a few miles outside Halifax, with antiques, fresh flowers and fires in comfortable lounges, lots of sitting areas in the two bar rooms, friendly, particularly helpful staff, three carefully furnished dining rooms (one oak-panelled) with enjoyable food and very good wine list, and garden; disabled access; dogs welcome in bedrooms, bar, lounge and reception

HAROME

Pheasant *Mill St, Harome, Helmsley, North Yorkshire YO62 5JG (01439)* *771241* £100, plus special breaks; 12 rms. Family-run hotel with a relaxed homely lounge, and traditional bar with beams, inglenook fireplace and flagstones, good very popular food using their own eggs, vegetables and fruit, efficient service, and indoor heated swimming pool; cl Dec-Feb; children over 7; disabled access; dogs welcome in bedrooms by prior arrangement

HARROGATE

Alexa House *26 Ripon Rd, Harrogate, North Yorkshire HG1 2JJ (01423)* *501988* £70, plus winter breaks; 13 rms, some in former stable block. Attractive Georgian house with friendly staff, comfortable lounge, good home cooking in no smoking dining room, and marvellous breakfasts; good disabled access; dogs welcome in bedrooms

HAWNBY

Laskill Grange *Easterside, Helmsley, York, North Yorkshire YO62 5NB (01439) 798268* £66, plus special breaks; 6 rms, some in beamy converted outside building. Attractive and welcoming creeper-covered stone house on big sheep and cattle farm near Rievaulx Abbey; open fire, antiques and books in comfortable lounge, conservatory overlooking the garden, good food using home-grown produce, and own natural spring water; self-catering also; cl 25 Dec; partial disabled access; dogs in bedrooms if well behaved

HELMSLEY

Black Swan *Market Place, Helmsley, North Yorkshire YO62 5BJ (01439)* *770466* £150, plus special breaks; 45 well equipped and comfortable rms. Striking Georgian house and adjoining Tudor rectory with beamed and panelled hotel bar, attractive carved oak settles and windsor armchairs, cosy and comfortable lounges with lots of character, and a charming sheltered garden; dogs welcome in bedrooms and certain lounges; £10

KILBURN

Forresters Arms *Kilburn, York, North Yorkshire YO61 4AH (01347)* *868386* £62, plus special breaks; 10 clean, bright rms. Friendly old coaching inn opposite the pretty village gardens; sturdy but elegant furnishings made next door at Thompson mouse furniture workshop, big log fire in cosy lower bar, interesting Henry Dee bar in what was a stable with manger and stalls still visible, and enjoyable food in restaurant and beamed bar; cl 25 Dec; dogs welcome away from dining room

KNARESBOROUGH

Dower House *Bond End, Knaresborough, North Yorkshire HG5 9AL* (01423) 863302 £75, plus special breaks; 31 clean, comfortable rms. Creeper-clad 15th-c former dower house with attractively furnished public rooms of some character, good food in Terrace Restaurant, super breakfasts, helpful service, and leisure and health club; partial disabled access; dogs welcome in annexe bedrooms only

Newton House Hotel *5-7 York Place, Knaresborough, North Yorkshire HG5 0AD* (01423) 863539 £80, plus special breaks; 11 refurbished, very well equipped rms. Elegant family-run 18th-c house close to the river and market square, with a warm welcome for guests of all ages, comfortable sitting room with magazines, books, sweets and fresh fruit, and good, generous english breakfasts in no smoking dining room; no evening meals but plenty of places a short walk away; cl 1 wk Christmas; dogs in bedrooms and public sitting room/bar; bowls and blankets available

LEEDS

42 The Calls *Leeds, West Yorkshire LS2 7EW* (0113) 244 0099 £147.50, inc bottle of champagne, plus special breaks; 41 attractive rms using original features, with lots of extras, CD stereo with disc library, satellite TV and good views. Stylish modern hotel in converted riverside grain mill in peaceful spot overlooking the River Aire, with genuinely friendly staff, marvellous food in restaurant and next-door chic but informal Brasserie Forty-Four, and fine breakfasts; cl 4 days over Christmas; disabled access; dogs welcome in bedrooms

LEEDS

Malmaison *Sovereign Quay, Leeds, West Yorkshire LS1 1DQ* (0113) 398 1000 £154, plus wknd breaks; 100 spacious rms with CDs and air conditioning. Stylish hotel by the River Aire, with bold, modern furnishings, contemporary bar and brasserie, enjoyable food and decent breakfasts, and helpful friendly service; disabled access; dogs welcome in bedrooms; £10

LINTON

Wood Hall *Trip Lane, Linton, Wetherby, West Yorkshire LS22 4JA* (01937) 587271 £160, plus racing breaks; 44 spacious well furnished rms. Grand Georgian mansion in over a hundred acres of parkland by the River Wharfe; comfortable reception rooms, log fire, antiques and fresh flowers, and imaginative cooking in the no smoking restaurant; indoor swimming pool and health centre; disabled access; dogs welcome in courtyard bedrooms

LONG PRESTON
Maypole *Main St, Long Preston, Skipton, North Yorkshire BD23 4PH (01729) 840219* £**49.50**, plus winter breaks; 6 comfortable rms. Neatly kept 17th-c pub with generous helpings of enjoyable traditional food (and nice breakfasts) in spacious beamed dining room, open fire in lounge bar, real ales, and helpful service; dogs in bedrooms and bar

MALHAMDALE
Miresfield Farm *Malham, Skipton, North Yorkshire BD23 4DA (01729) 830414* £**56**; 10 rms. Spacious old farmhouse with good freshly prepared food in beamed dining room, pleasant conservatory and two lounges (one with open log fire), and lovely garden by stream and village green; partial disabled access; dogs welcome in bedrooms

MARKINGTON
Hob Green *Markington, Harrogate, North Yorkshire HG3 3PJ (01423) 770031* £**115**, plus winter breaks; 12 well equipped pretty rms. Lovely gardens and over 800 acres of rolling countryside surround this charming 18th-c stone hotel; comfortable and pretty lounge and garden room, log fires, antique furniture, fresh flowers, relaxed atmosphere, good interesting food, decent choice of wines, and friendly service; dogs welcome in bedrooms and main hall

MIDDLETON
Cottage Leas Country Hotel *Nova Lane, Middleton, Pickering, North Yorkshire YO18 8PN (01751) 472129* £**68**, plus special breaks; 12 comfortable rms. Delightful, peaceful 18th-c farmhouse with extensive gardens, comfortable informal rooms, beamed ceilings, open log fire in cosy lounge, a well stocked bar, and enjoyable creative food; partial disabled access; dogs in some bedrooms; £4.50

MONK FRYSTON
Monk Fryston Hall *Main St, Monk Fryston, Leeds, West Yorkshire LS25 5DU (01977) 682369* £**116**, plus special breaks; 29 comfortable rms. Benedictine manor house in 30 acres of secluded gardens with lake and woodland, an oak-panelled lounge and bar with log fires, antiques, paintings and fresh flowers, good honest food, and friendly helpful staff; disabled access; dogs welcome in bedrooms and public areas (not restaurant); £5

OTLEY
Chevin Country Park Hotel *Yorkgate, Otley, West Yorkshire LS21 3NU (01943) 467818* £**122**, plus special breaks; 49 rms, some in log lodges deep in the woods. Built of finnish logs with walks through 50 acres of birchwood (lots of wildlife), this comfortable, newly refurbished hotel has its own leisure club, good food in lakeside restaurant, and friendly service; tennis and fishing; disabled access; dogs welcome in bedrooms by prior arrangement only

PICKERING

White Swan *Market Place, Pickering, North Yorkshire YO18 7AA (01751) 472288* £**120**; 10 rms inc 2 suites. Former coaching inn and now a restaurant-with-rooms with a charming country atmosphere, panelling, and log fire in small and civilised front bar, another log fire in no smoking snug, an attractive no smoking dining room, and busy but comfortable family room; particularly good imaginative food using carefully sourced local produce; well kept real ales, and an impressive wine list; dogs in some bedrooms if well behaved

REETH

Arkleside *Reeth, Richmond, North Yorkshire DL11 6SG (01748) 884200* £**82**; 11 cosy no smoking rms including 2 suites. Former row of 17th-c lead miners' cottages with lovely Swaledale views, a friendly atmosphere, homely snug and bar, two comfortable lounges, super, imaginative food in candlelit restaurant, nice breakfasts, and helpful, polite service; children over 10; little garden, fishing on the River Swale, and plenty of good walks; dogs welcome away from public rooms

RICHMOND

Millgate House *Millgate, Richmond, North Yorkshire DL10 4JN (01748) 823571* £**80**; 3 rms, 2 overlooking the garden. Georgian town house with lots of interesting antiques and lovely plants, a peaceful drawing room, warm friendly owners offering meticulous attention to detail, and good breakfasts in charming dining room which also overlooks the garden; it is this award-winning small garden, with views over the River Swale and the Cleveland Hills beyond, that is so special, filled with wonderful roses, ferns, clematis and hostas – they have a booklet listing the plants; children over 10; dogs welcome in bedrooms

RIPLEY

Boars Head *Ripley, Harrogate, North Yorkshire HG3 3AY (01423) 771888* £**120**, plus special breaks; 25 charmingly decorated rms. In a delightful estate village, this fine old coaching inn has a relaxed, welcoming atmosphere, with comfortable sofas in attractively decorated lounges, long flagstoned bar, notable wines by the glass, fine food in bar and restful dining room, and unobtrusive service; games, videos and special menus for children; disabled access; dogs welcome in some bedrooms (inc bed, bonio and bowls) and some public areas; £10

RIPON

Ripon Spa *Park St, Ripon, North Yorkshire HG4 2BU (01765) 602172* £**105**, plus special breaks; 40 individually furnished rms, many overlooking the grounds. Neatly kept friendly and comfortable Edwardian hotel with seven acres of charming gardens, yet only a short walk from the centre; attractive public rooms, winter log fires, and good food in bar and restaurant; disabled access; dogs in bedrooms

RIPPONDEN
Thurst House Farm *Ripponden, Sowerby Bridge, West Yorkshire HX6 4NN* *(01422) 822820* £60; 3 comfortable rms with views. 17th-c former farmhouse in a quiet rural spot with a cosy interior, open fire in sitting room, plenty of books to read, super breakfasts with home-made bread and conserves and free range eggs, good traditional english evening meals using home-grown produce, and plenty to do nearby; children over 8; cl Christmas and New Year; dogs welcome in bedrooms by special arrangement

SEDBUSK
Stone House *Hawes, North Yorkshire DL8 3PT (01969) 667571* £90, plus special breaks; 23 rms, 5 with own conservatories. Small, warmly friendly Edwardian hotel in a stunning setting with magnificent views; country-house feel and appropriate furnishings, attractive oak-panelled drawing room, billiard room, log fires, and exemplary service offering good local information; pleasant extended dining room with excellent wholesome food (special needs catered for) inc super breakfasts, and reasonable choice of wines; wonderful walks; P. G. Wodehouse stayed here as a guest of the original owner who employed a butler called Jeeves – it was on him that Wodehouse based his famous character; cl Jan; good disabled access; dogs welcome away from dining room

SKIRLAUGH
Dowthorpe Hall *Skirlaugh, Hull, East Yorkshire HU11 5AE (01964)* *562235* £64; 3 rms. Reached down a long tree-lined drive, this fine Georgian house in its lovely garden is separate from the working farm; large comfortable and beautifully decorated drawing room, delicious meals using home-grown produce, nice breakfasts, and welcoming friendly owners; outdoor swimming pool and croquet; dogs welcome in bedrooms by prior arrangement

STUDLEY ROGER
Lawrence House *Studley Roger, Ripon, North Yorkshire HG4 3AY (01765)* *600947* £96; 2 spacious, lovely rms with peaceful views. Attractive Georgian house with two acres of lovely garden on the edge of Studley Royal and Fountains Abbey; fine antiques and pictures, log fires, good breakfasts, and delicious evening meals; cl Christmas and New Year; children by arrangement; dogs welcome by prior arrangement

THORNTON WATLASS
Buck *Thornton Watlass, Ripon, North Yorkshire HG4 4AH (01677) 422461* £70, plus fishing, racing and special breaks; 7 rms, most with own bthrm. Cheerful country pub overlooking cricket green in very attractive village, with interesting beamed rooms, open fire, jazz Sun lunchtimes, enjoyable food in no smoking dining room, and lots of nearby walks; cl pm 25 Dec; limited disabled access; dogs welcome in bedrooms

YORK

Dairy Guesthouse *3 Scarcroft Rd, York YO23 1ND (01904) 639367* £56;
5 attractive rms, most with own bthrm. Carefully restored and recently
refurbished no smoking Victorian house with lots of original features and
attention to detail, enjoyable breakfasts with vegetarian and vegan dishes,
warmly hospitable atmosphere, and charming little flower-filled courtyard;
cl Jan; disabled access; dogs welcome in bedrooms

Grange Hotel *1 Clifton, York YO30 6AA (01904) 644744* £155, plus
special breaks; 30 individually decorated rms with antiques and chintz.
Close to the Minster, this Regency town house has elegant public rooms,
an open fire, newspapers, good breakfasts, excellent restaurant food (there's
also a brasserie), and warmly friendly staff; car park; disabled access; dogs
welcome in bedrooms

London

Dog Friendly Pubs

Archery Tavern *Bathurst Street, W2, opposite the Royal Lancaster hotel*
A useful stop for visitors to this side of Hyde Park, this welcoming and nicely kept Victorian pub is next to a little mews housing some riding stables, so you can sometimes hear the sound of hooves clopping past the door. Taking its name from an archery range that occupied the site for a while in the early 19th c, it has several comfortably relaxing, pubby areas around the central servery. On the green patterned walls are a number of archery prints, as well as a history of the pub and the area, other old prints, dried hops, and quite a few plates running along a shelf. Well kept Badger Best, King & Barnes Sussex and Tanglefoot on handpump. A big back room has long tables, bare boards, and a fireplace; darts, TV, a big stack of board games, fruit machine, piped music (loudish at times). Bar food typically includes sandwiches, soup, and daily specials such as chicken, leek and stilton pie; they may do breakfasts on weekend mornings. There's lots more seating in front of the pub, under hanging baskets and elaborate floral displays, and some nicely old-fashioned lamps.
Badger ~ Manager Mac MacGlade ~ Real ale ~ Bar food (12-3, 6-9.30) ~ (020) 7402 4916 ~ Children welcome ~ Dogs welcome ~ Open 11-11; 12-10.30 Sun

Colton Arms *Greyhound Road, W14*
Kept exactly the same by its dedicated landlord for the last 40 years, and very much a family concern, this genuinely unspoilt little gem is like an old-fashioned country pub in town. The main U-shaped front bar has a log fire blazing in winter, highly polished brasses, a fox's mask, hunting crops and plates decorated with hunting scenes on the walls, and a remarkable collection of handsomely carved 17th-c oak furniture. That room is small enough, and the two back rooms are tiny; each has its own little serving counter, with a bell to ring for service. Well kept Caledonian Deuchars IPA, Fullers London Pride and Shepherd Neame Spitfire on handpump (when you pay, note the old-fashioned brass-bound till); the food is limited to sandwiches (weekday lunchtimes only). Pull the curtain aside for the door out to a charming back terrace with a neat rose arbour. The pub is next to the Queens Club tennis courts and gardens

Enterprise ~ Tenants N J and J A Nunn ~ Real ale ~ Bar food (12-2 weekdays only) ~ No credit cards ~ (020) 7385 6956 ~ Dogs welcome ~ Open 12-3, 5.30-11 Mon-Fri; 12-3.30, 7-11(10.30 Sun) Sat; Sun 1-4 winter

Dove *Upper Mall, W6*

Said to be where *Rule Britannia* was composed, this old-fashioned tavern is one of London's most famous riverside pubs, and if you're lucky enough to secure a spot on the delightful back terrace it's hard not to consider it one of the nicest. The main flagstoned area, down some steps, has a few highly prized teak tables and white metal and teak chairs looking over the low river wall to the Thames reach just above Hammersmith Bridge, and there's a tiny exclusive area up a spiral staircase. You'll often see rowing crews out on the water. By the entrance from the quiet alley, the front bar is cosy and traditional, with black panelling, and red leatherette cushioned built-in wall settles and stools around dimpled copper tables; it leads to a bigger, similarly furnished room, with old framed advertisements and photographs of the pub. They stock the full range of Fullers beers, with well kept ESB, London Pride and seasonal beers on handpump: no games machines or piped music. Bar food includes sandwiches, soup, thai fishcakes with sweet chilli sauce, grilled sausages and mash or steak and ale pie, fish and chips or calves liver with crispy bacon and red wine gravy, and daily specials. The pub isn't quite so crowded at lunchtimes as it is in the evenings. A plaque marks the level of the highest-ever tide in 1928.

Fullers ~ Manager Alison Juliff ~ Real ale ~ Bar food (12-2.30, 5-9 Mon-Sat; 12-4 Sun) ~ (020) 8748 9474 ~ Dogs welcome ~ Open 11-11; 12-10.30 Sun

Fox & Hounds *Latchmere Road, SW11*

The garden has been extensively refurbished at this big Victorian local, with plenty of new planting and the addition of big parasols and heaters for winter. Although there's an emphasis on the excellent mediterranean food it's still very much the kind of place where locals happily come to drink. Changing every day, the bar food might include spinach and nutmeg soup with yoghurt, a good antipasti, spaghetti with field mushrooms, chilli, thyme and parmesan, pan-fried cod fillet with spiced black beans, coriander and chorizo, and creamy Italian cheeses with pear and grilled bread. The pub can fill quickly, so you may have to move fast to grab a table. The spacious, straightforward bar has bare boards, mismatched tables and chairs, two narrow pillars supporting the dark red ceiling, photographs on the walls, and big windows overlooking the street (the view partially obscured by colourful window boxes). There are fresh flowers and daily papers on the bar, and a view of the kitchen behind. Two rooms lead off, one rather cosy with its two red leatherette sofas. Well kept Adnams Broadside, Fullers London Pride and Harveys Sussex on handpump; the carefully chosen wine list (which includes a dozen by the glass) is written out on a blackboard. The appealingly varied piped music fits in rather well.

Free house ~ Licensees Richard and George Manners ~ Real ale ~ Bar food (12-2.30, 7-10.30 (10 Sun); not Mon lunchtime) ~ (020) 7924 5483 ~ Children welcome in eating area till 7pm ~ Dogs welcome ~ Open 12-2.30 (not

Mon), 5-11 Mon-Thurs; 12-11 Fri, Sat; 12-10.30 Sun; closed Mon lunchtime; 24 Dec-1 Jan; Easter Sat/Sun

Prospect of Whitby *Wapping Wall, E1*
Claiming to be the oldest pub on the Thames (it dates back to 1543), this entertaining pub was for a long while better known as the Devil's Tavern, thanks to its popularity with smugglers and other ne'er-do-wells. The river views can hardly be bettered, so over the centuries it's been a favourite with some of the capital's best-known figures. Pepys and Dickens were both frequent callers, Turner came for weeks at a time to study the scene, and in the 17th c the notorious Hanging Judge Jeffreys was able to combine two of his interests by enjoying a drink at the back while looking down over the grisly goings-on in Execution Dock. With such a lively history it's no wonder they do rather play on it; the tourists who flock here lap up the colourful tales of Merrie Olde London, and only the most unromantic of visitors could fail to be carried along by the fun. The pub is an established favourite on the evening coach tours, but is usually quieter at lunchtimes. Plenty of bare beams, bare boards, panelling and flagstones in the L-shaped bar (where the long pewter counter is over 400 years old), and a river view towards Docklands from tables in the waterfront courtyard. Well kept Charles Wells Bombardier, Fullers London Pride and Greene King Old Speckled Hen on handpump, and quite a few malt whiskies. Bar meals are served all day, from a menu including sandwiches and filled baked potatoes, various burgers, and jamaican jerk spiced chicken. One room (with good river views) is no smoking; fruit machine, golf game.
Spirit Group ~ Manager Christopher Reeves ~ Real ale ~ Bar food (12-9.30) ~ Restaurant ~ (020) 7481 1095 ~ Children welcome ~ Dogs welcome ~ Open 11.30-11; 12-10.30 Sun

Spaniards Inn *Spaniards Lane, NW3*
Tales of hauntings and highwaymen continue to draw the crowds to this busy former toll house, which now has a more practical claim to fame: they recenty introduced the world's first automatic dog-wash, perfect for cleaning canines who've enjoyed themselves a little too enthusiastically on the Heath. Dating back to 1585, the low-ceilinged oak-panelled rooms of the attractive main bar are full of character, with open fires, genuinely antique winged settles, candle-shaped lamps in shades, and snug little alcoves. But for many visitors the highlight is perhaps the charming garden, nicely arranged in a series of areas separated by judicious planting of shrubs. A crazy-paved terrace with slatted wooden tables and chairs opens onto a flagstoned walk around a small lawn, with roses, a side arbour of wisteria and clematis, and an aviary. You may need to move fast to bag a table out here in summer. Served all day, bar food includes ciabattas, mushroom and leek risotto, and steak and kidney pudding; they do a paella on Saturdays and a choice of roasts on Sundays. The food bar is no smoking at lunchtimes; upstairs, the Georgian Turpin Room is no smoking all day. Well kept Adnams, Charles Wells Bombardier, Marstons Old Empire, Shepherd Neame Spitfire and a guest like Everards Tiger on handpump –

though in summer you might find the most popular drink is their big jug of Pimms; newspapers, fruit machine. The pub is believed to have been named after the Spanish ambassador to the court of James I, who had a private residence here. It's fairly handy for Kenwood. Parking can be difficult.

Mitchells & Butlers ~ Manager Matthew O'Keefe ~ Real ale ~ Bar food (11-10;12-9 Sun) ~ (020) 8731 6571 ~ Children welcome ~ Dogs welcome ~ Open 11-11(12 Sat during July/Aug Kenwood concerts); 12-10.30 Sun

White Cross *Water Lane*

On fine days the busy paved garden in front of this perfectly-set Thames-side pub can feel rather like a cosmopolitan seaside resort; plenty of tables overlook the water, and in summer there's an outside bar. Though it can get crowded, it's a delightful spot, with a certain wistful charm in winter as well. Inside, the two chatty main rooms have something of the air of the hotel this once was, with local prints and photographs, an old-fashioned wooden island servery, and a good mix of variously aged customers. Two of the three log fires have mirrors above them – unusually, the third is below a window. A bright and airy upstairs room has lots more tables, and a pretty cast-iron balcony opening off, with a splendid view down to the river. From a servery at the foot of the stairs, lunchtime bar food includes good sandwiches, salads, a variety of sausages, and plenty of daily changing specials, including a roast. Well kept Youngs Bitter, Special and seasonal beers on handpump, and a dozen or so carefully chosen wines by the glass; service is friendly and civilised, even when the pub is at its busiest. Fruit machine, dominoes. It pays to check the tide times if you're leaving your car by the river; one visitor discovered just how fast the water can rise when on returning to his vehicle he found it marooned in a rapidly swelling pool of water, and had to paddle out shoeless to retrieve it. It's not unknown for the water to reach right up the steps into the bar, completely covering anything that gets in the way. Boats leave from immediately outside for Kingston and Hampton Court.

Youngs ~ Managers Ian and Phyl Heggie ~ Real ale ~ Bar food (12-3) ~ (020) 8940 6844 ~ Dogs welcome ~ Open 11-11; 12-10.30 Sun; closed 25 Dec (exc 12-2)

Dog Friendly Hotels and B&Bs

22 Jermyn Street Hotel *22 Jermyn St SW1Y 6HP* (020) 7734 2353 £268.75; 5 rms and 13 suites – spacious with deeply comfortable seats and sofas, flowers, plants, and antiques. Stylish little hotel owned by the same family for over 80 years and much loved by customers; no public rooms but wonderful 24-hr service, helpful notes and suggestions from the friendly owners, in-room light meals, and a warm welcome for children (with their own fact sheet listing shops, restaurants, and sights geared towards them, free video library, old-fashioned and electronic games, and own bathrobes); disabled access; dogs if small, in bedrooms by prior arrangement

41 *41 Buckingham Palace Rd SW1W 0PS (020) 7300 0041* £**288**, 20 stylish black and white rms with working gas fires and state-of-the-art technology. Small, intimate hotel opposite the Royal Mews and close to shops and theatres; club lounge serving fine breakfasts and all-day snacks, friendly, helpful staff, and use of two health clubs; dogs welcome in bedrooms, if small (they do ask for a sizeable returnable deposit)

Chesterfield *35 Charles St W1X 8LX (020) 7491 2622* £**210**, plus special breaks; 110 well equipped, pretty rms. Charming hotel just off Berkeley Sq, with particularly courteous helpful staff, afternoon tea in panelled library, a relaxed club-style bar with resident pianist, and fine food in attractive restaurant or light and airy conservatory; dogs welcome in bedrooms

Conrad London *Chelsea Harbour SW10 0XG (020) 7823 3000* £**194**; 160 luxury suites. Spacious hotel tucked away in the quiet modern enclave of the Chelsea Harbour development and overlooking its small marina; enjoyable modern cooking in Aquasia restaurant and bar, friendly service, and health club; disabled access; dogs welcome (if small) at management discretion

Hazlitts *6 Frith St W1V 5TZ (020) 7434 1771* £**240**, plus special breaks; 23 rms with 18th- or 19th-c beds and free-standing Victorian baths with early brass shower mixer units. Behind a typically Soho façade of listed early Georgian houses, this is a well kept and comfortably laid-out little hotel that's very handy for the West End; good continental breakfasts served in your bedroom, snacks in the sitting room, lots of restaurants all around; kind, helpful service; dogs in bedrooms if small

Knightsbridge Hotel *10 Beaufort Gardens SW3 1PT (020) 7584 6300* £**240**; 44 well equipped and individually designed bdrms and suites. Stylish hotel in a quiet tree-lined street, with an african feel in the high-ceilinged drawing room, a library decorated in soft, relaxing colours (both with sandstone fireplaces), original modern art, and honesty bar; no meals (though light continental breakfast is included) but plenty of restaurants nearby; dogs welcome in bedrooms at manager's discretion

L'Hotel *28 Basil St SW3 1AS (020) 7589 6286* £**176.25**; 12 well equipped rms. Small family-owned french-style city hotel, near Harrods, and set above the neatly kept, well run Metro wine bar where continental breakfasts are served – as well as good modern french café food; friendly staff; disabled access; dogs by prior arrangement; £15

Malmaison *Charterhouse Sq EC1 6AH (020) 7012 3700* £**127**, plus special breaks; 97 stylish, modern, very well equipped rms. Large, elegant red-brick Victorian hotel converted from a nurses' residence for St

Bartholomew's hospital and set in the cobbled courtyard of leafy
Charterhouse Sq; imaginative modern cooking in brasserie (exceptionally
good steaks and popular Sunday brunch, too), chic bar set off the spacious
lobby, with comfortable sofas, and helpful, attentive service; dogs welcome
in bedrooms and given a bowl and blanket; £10

Rubens *39 Buckingham Palace Rd SW1W 0PS (020) 7834 6600* **£194**,
plus special breaks; 172 well equipped, individually furnished rms inc
luxurious suites in the Royal Wing. Opposite Buckingham Palace and near
Victoria Station, this attractive hotel has comfortable day rooms inc lounge
with views of the Royal Mews, open fire in bar, and library restaurant with
fine international food; dogs welcome in bedrooms by arrangement (they
may ask for a sizeable refundable deposit)

Scotland

Dog Friendly Pubs

ABOYNE
Boat *Charlestown Road (B968, just off A93)*
They serve well kept Bass along with a couple of real ales from brewers such as Caledonian and Houston at this welcoming country inn. The fresh battered haddock is very popular, and other reasonably priced bar food includes lunchtime sandwiches, mince and tatties, and lasagne; while in the evening there are also a few more elaborate choices such as pork and vegetable kebabs, chargrilled tuna steak, and puddings such as lemon syllabub. They use plenty of fresh local produce, and are happy to accommodate special requests. As you step inside, the first thing you'll notice is the model train, often chugging around just below the ceiling, making appropriate noises. There are also scottish pictures and brasses in the two areas downstairs, and a bar counter that runs down the narrower linking section, and games in the public-bar end. Spiral stairs take you up to a roomy additional dining area, which is no smoking. The atmosphere is relaxed and pubby, with an openable woodburning stove, and friendly service. Right by the River Dee, the pub used to serve the ferry that it's named for; there are tables outside, and they have a self-catering flat.
Free house ~ Licensee Wilson Forbes ~ Real ale ~ Bar food (12-2(2.30 Sat/Sun), 5.30-9(9.30 Fri/Sat)) ~ Restaurant ~ (01339) 886137 ~ Children welcome ~ Dogs allowed in bar and bedrooms ~ Open 11-2.30, 5-11(12 Fri/Sat); 11-11 Sun; closed 25/26 Dec and 1/2 Jan

GAIRLOCH
Old Inn *Just off A832/B8021*
It's not just the freshly cooked food or the great choice of beers that makes this 18th-c inn such a lovely place to visit – as one couple commented 'the staff could not have been more helpful and friendly, it seemed that they took a real pleasure in making our stay enjoyable'. Nicely placed at the bottom of Flowerdale Glen, the pub is tucked comfortably away from the modern waterside road, but only yards away from the little fishing harbour, and handy for pleasant beaches. Picnic-sets are prettily placed outside by the trees that line the stream as it flows past under the old stone bridge, and

on the opposite side are more trees with high crags above (look out for eagles). There are pleasant wooded walks up the glen, the ancestral home of Clan MacKenzie, to the Flowerdale waterfall. The well kept changing beers are a big draw, with anything from three to a dozen on offer: favourites include Adnams Broadside, Houston Peterswell, and Isle of Skye Red Cuillin and Blind Piper (the hotel's own blend of Isle of Skye ales rather in the way that Broadside was originally a blend of other Adnams ales, and named after a famed local 17th-c piper), with guests from brewers such as Atlas, Caledonian, Orkney. They have a lot of enjoyable fairly priced wines by the glass, a decent collection of malt whiskies, and you can get speciality coffees. The good food is popular, and fresh locally landed fish is a speciality, with home-made langoustine ravioli commonly on the board, and mussels, crabs, lobster, skate, haddock and hake often cropping up too. The regular bar menu includes wild venison sausages, seafood grill, and puddings such as clootie dumpling and custard; lunchtime open sandwiches as well. The landlady makes her own chutneys and preserves – and grows many of the herbs they use. It's nicely decorated with paintings and murals on exposed stone walls, and the cheerfully relaxed public bar has chatty locals; darts, TV, pool, fruit machine and jukebox. The restaurant is no smoking.

Free house ~ Licensees Alastair and Ute Pearson ~ Real ale ~ Bar food (12-2, 7-9; 12-9.30 in summer) ~ Restaurant ~ (01445) 712006 ~ Children welcome ~ Dogs allowed in bar and bedrooms ~ Scottish music most Thurs-Sat evenings ~ Open 11-1(12 Sat); 12.30-11.30 Sun ~ Bedrooms: £37.50B/£69B

INVERARAY
George *Main Street E*

The bustling flagstoned bar of this comfortably modernised inn (run by the same family since 1860) shows plenty of age in its exposed joists, old tiles and bared stone walls. You'll find antique settles, cushioned stone slabs along the walls, carved wooden benches, nicely grained wooden-topped cast-iron tables, lots of curling club and ships' badges, and a cosy log fire in winter. Swiftly served by friendly staff (you order at the table), generously served enjoyable bar food includes good scampi and chips, gammon and pineapple with cumberland sauce, and salmon grilled with lemon and parsley butter. They are building a new conservatory restaurant. Two well kept changing beers include one from Fyne along with a guest such as Caledonian Deuchars IPA on handpump, and they've over 100 malt whiskies; darts, dominoes, pool and TV, but no bar games in summer. Nicely placed in the centre of this little Georgian town, stretching along Loch Fyne in front of Inveraray Castle, the pub is well placed for the great Argyll woodland gardens, best for their rhododendrons in May and early June; there are good nearby walks – you may spot seals or even a basking shark or whale. Some of the individually decorated bedrooms (reached by a grand wooden staircase) have jacuzzis and four-poster beds.

Free house ~ Licensee Donald Clark ~ Real ale ~ Bar food (12-9.30) ~ Restaurant ~ (01499) 302111 ~ Children welcome ~ Dogs welcome ~ Open 11(12 Sun)-12 ~ Bedrooms: £35B/£60S(£120B)

ISLE OF WHITHORN
Steam Packet *Harbour Row*

There's usually quite a bustle of yachts and inshore fishing boats in the picturesque working harbour – and you can watch it all from the large picture windows of this friendly inn. Swiftly served by helpful staff, the food is good, with changing evening specials such as steamed roast vegetable tartlet with three-cheese sauce and roast duck breast with root vegetable mash. Other well cooked dishes might include glamorgan sausages, steamed mussels with tomato and pesto sauce, and puddings such as chocolate terrine with mixed fruits; they do children's meals too. The comfortable low-ceilinged bar is split into two: on the right, plush button-back banquettes and boat pictures, and on the left, green leatherette stools around cast-iron-framed tables on big stone tiles, and a woodburning stove in the bare stone wall. Bar food can be served in the lower-beamed dining room, which has excellent colour wildlife photographs, rugs on its wooden floor, and a solid-fuel stove, and there's also a small eating area off the lounge bar. The conservatory is no smoking. Theakstons XB is well kept on handpump, along with a guest such as Houston Killellan, and they've two dozen malt whiskies, and a good wine list, with half a dozen by the glass; pool and dominoes. There are white tables and chairs in the garden. Several of the bedrooms have good views. Boat trips leave from the harbour; you can walk up to the remains of St Ninian's Kirk, on a headland behind the village.
Free house ~ Licensee John Scoular ~ Real ale ~ Bar food (12-2, 6.30-9) ~ Restaurant ~ (01988) 500334 ~ Children welcome away from bar ~ Dogs allowed in bar and bedrooms ~ Open 11(12 Sun)-11(12 Sat); closed Mon-Thurs 2.30-6 in winter; closed 25 Dec ~ Bedrooms: £25B/£50B

KINGHOLM QUAY
Swan *B726 just S of Dumfries; or signposted off B725*

Visitors enjoy coming to this well run little pub, and the friendly staff are kind to families. The neat and comfortable public bar has well kept Theakstons Best on handpump, and good house wines; TV and quiet piped music. A short (but temptingly reasonably priced) selection of pubby food is served in the well ordered lounge or at busy times in the restaurant. Enjoyable dishes might include haggis with melted cheese, liver and bacon, steak pie or battered haddock; evening specials such as rack of ribs or seafood risotto, and puddings such as sticky toffee pudding. Half the food service area is no smoking. The small garden has tables and a play area. In a quiet spot overlooking the old fishing jetty on the River Nith, the pub is handy for the Caerlaverock nature reserve with its multitude of geese.
Free house ~ Licensees Billy Houliston, Tracy Rogan and Alan Austin ~ Real ale ~ Bar food (12-2, 5-9) ~ (01387) 253756 ~ Children welcome ~ Dogs allowed in bar ~ Open 11.30-2.30, 5-10(11 Fri); 11.30-11 Sun

KIPPEN
Cross Keys *Main Street; village signposted off A811 W of Stirling*

Tables in the garden of this unpretentious and cosily comfortable 18th-c inn have good views towards the Trossachs. Popular with locals, the lounge is straightforward but welcoming with a good log fire; there's a coal fire too in the attractive no smoking family dining room. The menu changes every day, and enjoyable dishes are made using lots of fresh local produce; you can get smaller helpings for children. Generously served by friendly staff, bar food might include smoked salmon and prawn marie rose parcel, home-made lasagne or lamb casserole, with puddings such as home-made sticky toffee pudding; they also do sandwiches. Belhaven 80/- and maybe Harviestoun Bitter & Twisted are well kept on handpump, and they've more than 30 malt whiskies; piped music, and dominoes and TV in the separate public bar. The brightly lit exterior is a cheering sight on a cold winter night.

Free house ~ Licensees Mr and Mrs Scott ~ Real ale ~ Bar food (12-2, 5.30-9; 12.30-9 Sun) ~ Restaurant ~ (01786) 870293 ~ Children welcome ~ Dogs allowed in bar and bedrooms ~ Open 12-2.30, 5.30-11; 12-12 Sat; 12.30-11 Sun; closed 25 Dec, 1 Jan ~ Bedrooms: /£60S(£50B)

PITLOCHRY
Moulin *Kirkmichael Road, Moulin; A924 NE of Pitlochry centre*
A real bonus at this imposing 17th-c white-painted inn are the real ales, which are brewed in the little stables across the street: Ale of Atholl, Braveheart, Moulin Light, and the stronger Old Remedial are superbly kept on handpump (they do group brewery tours by arrangement). They also have around 40 malt whiskies. Although it has been much extended over the years, the bar, in the oldest part of the building, still seems an entity in itself. Above the fireplace in the smaller room is an interesting painting of the village before the road was built (Moulin used to be a bustling market town, far busier than upstart Pitlochry), while the bigger carpeted area has a good few tables and cushioned banquettes in little booths divided by stained-glass country scenes, another big fireplace, some exposed stonework, fresh flowers, and local prints and golf clubs around the walls; bar billiards, shove-ha'penny, cribbage, dominoes and an old-fashioned fruit machine. The extensive bar menu includes mussels with garlic and cream, haggis, neeps and tatties, macaroni cheese, game casserole, and puddings such as sticky whisky fudge cake; from 12 till 6pm they also serve baked potatoes and sandwiches. In the evening, visitors enjoy eating in the restaurant. Surrounded by tubs of flowers, picnic-sets outside look across to the village kirk; there are rewarding walks nearby. The rooms are comfortable and breakfast is good; they offer good value three-night breaks out of season.

Own brew ~ Licensee Heather Reeves ~ Real ale ~ Bar food (12-9.30; not 25 Dec) ~ Restaurant ~ (01796) 472196 ~ Children in eating area of bar and restaurant ~ Dogs allowed in bar ~ Open 12-11(11.45 Sat) ~ Bedrooms: £50B/£65S(£75B)

PLOCKTON
Plockton Hotel *Village signposted from A87 near Kyle of Lochalsh*
The very friendly staff help make a visit to this bewitching little hotel

special; the food is very good too, and this is a charmingly relaxed place to stay (visitors rave about the breakfasts). Forming part of a long, low terrace of stone-built houses, the inn is set in a lovely National Trust for Scotland village. Tables in the front garden look out past the village's trademark palm trees and colourfully flowering shrub-lined shore, and across the sheltered anchorage to the rugged mountainous surrounds of Loch Carron; a stream runs down the hill into a pond in the landscaped back garden. With a buoyant bustling atmosphere, the welcoming comfortably furnished lounge bar has window seats looking out to the boats on the water, as well as antiqued dark red leather seating around neat Regency-style tables. The separate public bar has darts, pool, shove-ha'penny, dominoes, TV and piped music. The food is popular, so it is a good idea to book at busy times if you want a table. Well cooked, using lots of fresh local ingredients, dishes might include herring in oatmeal or skye mussels, highland venison casserole, home-made soup (with their own bread), haggis and whisky, and poached salmon; they also do children's meals, and from 9 till 10 you can get basket meals. The snug and Courtyard restaurant are no smoking. Well kept Caledonian Deuchars IPA and Isle of Skye Hebridean Gold on handpump, and bottled beers from the Isle of Skye brewery, along with a good collection of malt whiskies, and a short wine list. More than half of the no smoking bedrooms in the adjacent building have sea views – one even has a balcony and woodburning stove. A hotel nearby changed its name a few years ago to the Plockton Inn, so don't get the two confused.
Free house ~ Licensee Tom Pearson ~ Real ale ~ Bar food (12(12.30 Sun)-2.15, 6-9; basket meals till 10) ~ Restaurant ~ (01599) 544274 ~ Children in eating area of bar and restaurant ~ Dogs allowed in bar ~ Live music summer Weds evenings ~ Open 11-12(11.45 Sat); 12.30-11 Sun; closed 25 Dec ~ Bedrooms: £55S(£45B)/£90B

SKEABOST
Skeabost House Hotel *A850 NW of Portree, 1½ miles past junction with A856*

The new owner of this splendidly grand-looking hotel, developed from a Victorian hunting lodge, plans to hold regular concerts on the lawn, and on Saturday nights there's live music in the bar. She's also redecorated the high-ceilinged bar (which is now more for residents), added a new restaurant and extended some of the bedrooms; a fine panelled billiards room leads off the stately hall. The wholly separate public bar has darts, pool, TV, jukebox, and even its own car park. Isle of Skye Red Cuillin is well kept on handpump, and they've over 100 malt whiskies, including their own and some rare single-year bottlings. Enjoyable food (which you can eat in the bar) might include lamb hot pot, wild mushroom and asparagus risotto, oysters, steaks, and puddings such as banana cheesecake; they also do bar snacks on Saturday and three-course meals on Sunday. All the eating areas are no smoking. The hotel has 12 acres of secluded woodland and gardens, with glorious views over Loch Snizort; it's said to have some of the best salmon fishing on the island, and there's a golf course too. The price we show for bedrooms is for the cheapest room; prices can be much higher.

Free house ~ Licensee Helen Myers ~ Real ale ~ Bar food (10-11) ~ Restaurant ~ (01470) 532202 ~ Children in eating area of bar and family room ~ Dogs allowed in bar ~ Open 11-2, 5-11; 11-12.30 Sat; 12-11 Sun ~ Bedrooms: /£90S(£90B)

STEIN

Stein Inn *End of B886 N of Dunvegan in Waternish, off A850 Dunvegan—Portree; OS Sheet 23 map reference 263564*

With views over the sea to the Hebrides, tables outside this 18th-c inn are an ideal place to sit with a whisky (they've over 100 to choose from), and watch the sunset. Inside, the original public bar has great character, with its sturdy country furnishings, flagstone floor, beam and plank ceiling, partly panelled stripped-stone walls and peat fire, and there is a comfortable no smoking lounge and no smoking dining area. The games area has a pool table, and darts, dominoes and cribbage; there may be piped radio. The evening crowd of local regulars (where do they all appear from?) and the owners are welcoming; good service from the smartly uniformed staff. Isle of Skye Red Cuillin or (brewed by Isle of Skye for the pub) Reeling Deck is well kept on handpump, along with a couple of guests from brewers such as Cairngorm and Orkney. Using local fish and highland meat, the very short bar menu might include good ploughman's, breaded haddock, and 8oz sirloin steak, with specials such as home-made soup, and lemon chicken; puddings too. There's a lively children's inside play area, and showers for yachtsmen. The pub is tranquilly set in a small untouched village just above a quiet sea inlet. Some of the bedrooms have sea views; we are told that it's well worth pre-ordering the tasty smoked kippers if you stay here.

Free house ~ Licensees Angus and Teresa Mcghie ~ Real ale ~ Bar food (12-4, 6-9.30(9 Sun); not Mon exc bank and summer hols) ~ (01470) 592362 ~ Children in eating area of bar, family room and restaurant till 8.30pm ~ Dogs welcome ~ Open 11-12(12.30 Sat); 12.30-11 Sun; 4-12 wkdays, 12-12 Sat, 12.30-11 Sun in winter; closed 25 Dec, 1 Jan ~ Bedrooms: £24.50S/£64S

TAYVALLICH

Tayvallich Inn *B8025, off A816 1 mile S of Kilmartin; or take B841 turn-off from A816 2 miles N of Lochgilphead*

Great for sunny days, the terrace of this simply furnished bar/restaurant has lovely views over the yacht anchorage and water, and there's a garden too. Service is friendly, and people with children are made to feel welcome. One little room has local nautical charts on the cream walls, exposed ceiling joists, and pale pine upright chairs, benches and tables on its quarry-tiled floor; piped music. It leads into a no smoking dining conservatory, from where sliding glass doors open onto the terrace. With seafood freshly brought in by local fishermen from the bay of Loch Sween just across the lane, the short but enticing menu might include deep-fried whitebait, tagliatelle with porcini mushrooms, truffle oil and parmesan, home-made fish pie, scottish rib-eye steak, and local langoustines; puddings such as crème brûlée, and fresh milk shakes too. There are 20 malt whiskies including a full range of Islay malts, and Caledonian 80/- on handpump.

Free house ~ Licensee Roddy Anderson ~ Bar food (12-2, 6-10; 12-10 wknds, see below in winter) ~ Restaurant ~ (01546) 870282 ~ Children in eating area of bar and restaurant ~ Dogs allowed in bar ~ Live music two Sats a month ~ Open 11-12(1 Sat); 12-12 Sun; 5-11(12 Fri) Weds-Fri in winter; closed Mon-Tues, and lunchtime Weds-Fri in winter

WEEM
Ailean Chraggan *B846*
Visitors think very highly of this welcoming little family-run hotel, a lovely place to stay or come to for a meal. You can eat in either the comfortably carpeted modern lounge or the mainly no smoking dining room, and good changing dishes might include soup, sandwiches, half a dozen oysters, roast pheasant salad, tomato, chickpea and kidney bean curry, venison steak with red wine jus, and hot chocolate pudding; children's meals too. It's a good idea to book at busy times. They've a very good wine list, and there are around 100 malt whiskies; winter darts and dominoes. The atmosphere is friendly, and you're likely to find chatty locals in the bar. Two terraces outside give lovely views to the mountains beyond the Tay, sweeping up to Ben Lawers (the highest in this part of Scotland).
Free house ~ Licensee Alastair Gillespie ~ Bar food ~ Restaurant ~ (01887) 820346 ~ Children welcome ~ Dogs allowed in bar and bedrooms ~ Open 11(12.30 Sun)-11; closed 25-26 Dec, 1-2 Jan ~ Bedrooms: £45B/£90B

Dog Friendly Hotels, B&Bs and Farms

ACHILTIBUIE
Summer Isles Hotel *Achiltibuie, Ullapool, Ross-shire IV26 2YQ (01854) 622282* **£125**; 13 comfortable rms. Beautifully placed above the sea towards the end of a very long and lonely road; warm, friendly, well furnished hotel with delicious set menus using fresh ingredients (in which it's largely self-sufficient), a choice of superb puddings and excellent array of uncommon cheeses; pretty watercolours and flowers; cl mid-Oct-Easter; children over 8; dogs welcome in bedrooms (not to be left unattended)

APPLECROSS
Applecross Inn *Shore St, Applecross, Strathcarron, Ross-shire IV54 8LR (01520) 744262* **£70**; 7 rms, all with breathtaking sea views over Sound of Raasay, some with shared bthrms. Gloriously placed informal inn with tables out by shore, simple comfortable and friendly bar, log or peat fire in lounge, small restaurant with excellent fresh fish and seafood; cl 25 Dec and 5 Jan; dogs welcome

ARDEONAIG
Ardeonaig Hotel *Ardeonaig, Killin, Perthshire FK21 8SY (01567) 820400* **£75**, plus special breaks; 16 rms. Extended 17th-c farmhouse on south

shore of Loch Tay, with log fire in snug and lounge, library with fine views, bistro or formal dining using fresh local produce; salmon fishing rights on the loch – as well as fishing for trout and charr – a drying and rod room, and boats and outboards; shooting, stalking and pony trekking can be arranged, lots of surrounding walks; cl early Jan; dogs welcome in bedrooms; £10

ARDUAINE

Loch Melfort Hotel *Arduaine, Oban, Argyll PA34 4XG (01852) 200233* £118, plus special breaks; 26 rms, gorgeous sea views. Comfortable hotel popular in summer with passing yachtsmen (hotel's own moorings), nautical charts and marine glasses in airy modern bar, own lobster pots and nets so emphasis on seafood, pleasant foreshore walks, outstanding springtime woodland gardens; cl Jan; disabled access; dogs welcome in some bedrooms

AUCHENCAIRN

Balcary Bay *Auchencairn, Castle Douglas, Kirkcudbrightshire DG7 1QZ (01556) 640217* £114, plus special breaks; 20 rms with fine views. Once a smugglers' haunt, this charming and much liked hotel has wonderful views over the bay, neat grounds running down to the water, comfortable public rooms (one with log fire), a relaxed friendly atmosphere, good enjoyable food inc super breakfasts, and lots of walks; cl 1 Dec–mid-Feb; disabled access; dogs welcome in bedrooms

AUCHTERARDER

Gleneagles Hotel *Auchterarder, Perthshire PH3 1NF (01764) 662231* £330, plus special breaks; 270 individually decorated rms. Grand hotel in lovely surroundings with attractive gardens and outstanding leisure facilities: three championship golf courses inc the PGA Centenary Course, shooting, riding, fishing, health spa, tennis, squash, croquet and even falconry, lots of children's activities inc playroom with arts and crafts; comfortable, elegant high-ceilinged day rooms, a fine bar, exceptional service, pianists, enjoyable food using local produce (much is home-grown) in four restaurants, famous afternoon teas; disabled access; dogs welcome in bedrooms; £15

AVIEMORE

Lynwilg House *Aviemore, Inverness-shire PH22 1PZ (01479) 811685* £60; 3 rms. Attractive, quietly set 1930s-style house in four acres of landscaped gardens with open fire in spacious lounge, lovely breakfasts with their own free range eggs and home-baked bread, super dinners using home-grown produce, and charming owners; plenty to do nearby; cl Nov-Dec, Jan; children over 5; dogs in one bedroom

BALLATER

Auld Kirk *31 Braemar Rd, Ballater, Aberdeenshire AB35 5RQ (01339) 755762* £60, plus special breaks; 7 attractive rms, inc 2 family rms. 19th-c church converted to a hotel in 1990, still with bell tower, stained glass and exposed rafters; original pillared pine ceiling in refurbished restaurant, other public rooms with homely décor; cl 25-27 Dec; disabled access; dogs welcome in bedrooms

BALLATER
Balgonie Country House *Braemar Pl, Ballater, Aberdeenshire AB35 5NQ (01339) 755482* £**130**, plus special breaks; 9 pretty rms. Quietly set and spotless Edwardian house with fine views from four acres of mature gardens, particularly helpful friendly owners, fresh flowers, games and books in lounges, and most enjoyable food using the best local produce in charming dining room; cl 6 Jan-1 Mar; dogs in bedrooms by prior arrangement (not to be left unattended)

BIGGAR
Shieldhill Castle *Quothquan, Biggar, Lanarkshire ML12 6NA (01899) 220035* £**118**, plus special breaks; 16 large, well equipped rms. Fortified partly 12th-c manor with 16th-c additions and set in rolling hills and farmland; log fires in atmospheric wood-panelled rooms including comfortable lounge, fine food in carved high-ceilinged and large windowed restaurant, and friendly, helpful staff; fishing, stalking, and shooting nearby; disabled access; dogs welcome away from dining areas

BRIDGE OF CALLY
Bridge of Cally Hotel *Bridge of Cally, Blairgowrie, Perthshire PH10 7JJ (01250) 886231* £**80**, plus winter breaks; 18 rms. In an acre of grounds along the River Ardle, this former drovers' inn is a friendly family-run place with good value home-made food using seasonal game in popular restaurant and comfortable bar; dogs welcome

CALLANDER
Poppies *Leny Rd, Callander, Perthshire FK17 8AL (01877) 330329* £**56**, plus special breaks; 9 rms. Small private hotel with excellent food in popular and attractive candlelit dining room, comfortable lounge, helpful friendly owners, and seats in the garden; children over 12; cl Jan; dogs welcome in bedrooms

CLACHAN SEIL
Willowburn *Clachan Seil, Isle of Seil PA34 4TJ (01852) 300276* £**152** inc dinner; 7 rms facing the water. Simple little white hotel on the shore of Clachan Sound, with enthusiastic, welcoming owners, open fire and local guidebooks in straightforward lounge, bar with lovely views, imaginative food using local and home-grown produce and delicious breakfasts in airy dining room overlooking water; guests' dogs get a letter from the hotel's pets; lots of wildlife; dogs welcome away from eating areas

CROMARTY
Royal *Marine Terrace, Cromarty, Ross-shire IV11 8YN (01381) 600217* £**70**, plus special breaks; 10 newly refurbished rms. Traditional waterfront

hotel (you may see dolphins) with friendly owners and staff, attractive lounges, bars and sun lounge, garden and good home cooking with an emphasis on seafood; gets very busy in summer; dogs welcome in bedrooms

CULLEN

Seafield Hotel *Cullen, Buckie, Banffshire AB56 4SG (01542) 840791* £80; 19 attractively furnished, spacious rms. No smoking 19th-c former coaching inn with an easy-going, comfortable and friendly atmosphere, carefully reburbished residents' lounge and convivial bar, log fires, fresh flowers and antiques, good enjoyable food using plenty of local fresh fish (and of course the famous cullen skink soup) in informal restaurant, nice breakfasts, helpful staff, and fine sandy beach just 5 minutes away; lots to do nearby; dogs welcome in bedrooms; £5

DALCROSS

Easter Dalziel Farm *Dalcross, Inverness IV2 7JL (01667) 462213* £48; 3 rms with shared bthrm. Early Victorian farmhouse on 210 acres of family-run mixed farm (beef cattle and grain) with friendly helpful owners, log fire in lounge, good scottish breakfasts in big dining room and – when farm commitments allow – evening meal using own beef, lamb and veg; self-catering cottages, too; cl Christmas and New Year; dogs welcome by arrangement away from restaurant

DERVAIG

Druimard Country House *Dervaig, Tobermory, Isle of Mull PA75 6QW (01688) 400345* £135 inc dinner, plus special breaks; 7 rms. Peaceful Victorian country house with wonderful views across the glen and River Bellart, friendly helpful owners, comfortable lounge and conservatory, lots of pictures, books and magazines, good breakfasts, excellent food using the best local produce; the Mull Little Theatre is in the grounds; cl Nov-Mar; disabled access; dogs welcome in bedrooms, some with direct access to garden

DRUMBEG

Drumbeg *Drumbeg, Lairg, Highland IV27 4NW (01571) 833236* £54; 6 traditional and attractive rms. Isolated little highland hotel in a fine setting surrounded by hills and with views of Drumbeg Loch; comfortable lounge and small reading room, simply furnished restaurant with lovely water views, a woodburning stove, and delicious french and italian country cooking using local produce and cooked by the owners, and a carefully chosen small wine list; cl 2 wks early Dec, 2 wks Jan; dogs welcome in bedrooms

DRUMNADROCHIT

Polmaily House *Drumnadrochit, Inverness IV63 6XT (01456) 450343* £126, plus special breaks; 11 light, elegant rms. Very relaxing and comfortable hotel in 18 acres, with drawing room and library, open fire and excellent food in the no smoking restaurant (wonderful packed lunches too); a happy place for families with well equipped indoor play area with lots of supervised activities, baby sitting and listening, hundreds of children's videos, plenty of ponies and pets, evening children's club, indoor heated swimming pool, tennis, croquet, fishing, boating and riding; disabled access; dogs welcome in bedrooms; £5 (£10 if a big dog)

DULNAIN BRIDGE

Auchendean Lodge *Dulnain Bridge, Grantown-on-Spey, Murrayshire PH26 3LU (01479) 851347* **£160** inc dinner, plus special breaks; 5 comfortable rms. Edwardian hunting lodge with wonderful views over the Spey Valley to the Cairngorm mountians; Arts and Crafts-style architecture, two lounges with plenty of pictures and knick-knacks, a piano for guests' use, and warm log fire, enthusiastic owners, good, interesting meals using home-grown and local produce, super breakfasts with home-made marmalade and jams, and lovely garden; Bess the owner's dog loves taking other dog friends for walks in the nearby woods and moors; children over 12; cl Nov-Easter; dogs in bedrooms and one lounge; £5

DUNBLANE

Cromlix House *Cromlix, Dunblane, Perthshire FK15 9JT (01786) 822125* **£235**, plus special breaks; 14 rms inc 8 spacious suites. Walking, loch and river fishing or shooting on 2,000 acres around this rather gracious country house; relaxing day rooms with fine antiques and family portraits, an informal atmosphere, very good food using local produce in two dining rooms, and courteous service; cl Jan; dogs welcome in bedrooms

EAST HAUGH

East Haugh House *East Haugh, Pitlochry, Tayside PH16 5TE (01796) 473121* **£138** inc dinner, plus special breaks; 13 rms, 5 in converted bothy, some with four-posters and one with open fire. Turreted stone house with lots of character, delightful bar in cream and navy with a fishing theme, house-party atmosphere and particularly good food inc local seafood, game in season cooked by chef/proprietor, and home-grown vegetables in new restaurant; excellent shooting, stalking and salmon and trout fishing on surrounding local estates; cl 20-27 Dec; disabled access to one room; dogs welcome in ground-floor bedrooms with direct access outside; £5

EDINBURGH

Malmaison *1 Tower Pl, Leith, Edinburgh EH6 7DB (0131) 468 5000* **£153.70**, plus special breaks; 100 stylish rms with CD players and satellite TV. Converted baronial-style seamen's mission in the fashionable docks area of Leith with very good food in the downstairs french brasserie, cheerful café bar, gym, and friendly service; free parking; disabled access; dogs welcome in bedrooms if small; £10

Seven Danube Street *7 Danube St, Edinburgh EH4 1NN (0131) 332 2755* **£100**; 5 fine rms with plenty of extras. Quietly placed Georgian house with charming helpful owners, comfortable lounge, a relaxed homely atmosphere, marvellous breakfasts served at one big table, and small garden; no smoking; cl Christmas; dogs by arrangement

ERISKA
Isle of Eriska Hotel *Ledaig, Oban, Argyll PA37 1SD (01631) 720371* £250; 19 rms. In a wonderful position on small island linked by bridge to mainland, impressive baronial hotel with very relaxed country house atmosphere, log fires and pretty drawing room, excellent food, exemplary service, and comprehensive wine list; leisure complex with indoor swimming pool, sauna, gym and so forth, lovely surrounding walks, and 9-hole golf course, clay pigeon shooting and golf – and plenty of wildlife inc tame badgers who come nightly to the library door for their bread and milk; cl Jan; children over 5 in pool and evening restaurant (high tea provided); disabled access; dogs welcome in bedrooms

FINTRY
Culcreuch Castle *Fintry, Glasgow G63 0LW (01360) 860555* £116, plus special breaks; 14 individually decorated rms (inc 4 family rms) with lovely views. Central Scotland's oldest inhabited castle, nearly 700 years old, in beautiful 1,600-acre parkland and surrounding hills and moors, with log fires and antiques in the public rooms, good freshly prepared food in candlelit panelled dining room, and a friendly relaxed atmosphere, play area; 8 modern holiday lodges, too; disabled access; dogs in bedrooms and other areas by arrangement; £4

GARVE
Inchbae Lodge *Garve, Ross-shire IV23 2PH (01997) 455269* £50, plus special breaks; 16 rms, some in chalets (which have fine mountain views). Former hunting lodge in lovely highland setting with comfortable homely lounges, winter log fires, small bar (liked by locals), and good fixed-price evening meals using fresh local produce; lots of wildlife, marvellous walks; cl Christmas; disabled access; dogs in chalet rooms

GATEHOUSE OF FLEET
Cally Palace *Gatehouse of Fleet, Castle Douglas, Kirkcudbrightshire DG7 2DL (01557) 814341* £176 inc dinner, plus special breaks; 55 rms. 18th-c country mansion, a hotel since 1934, with marble fireplaces and ornate ceilings in the public rooms, relaxed cocktail bar, enjoyable food in elegant dining room (smart dress required), evening pianist and Sat evening dinner dance, helpful friendly staff, 18-hole golf course, croquet and tennis, indoor leisure complex with heated swimming pool, private fishing/ boating loch; cl Jan, cl wkdys in Feb; disabled access; dogs welcome in bedrooms

GIFFORD
Tweeddale Arms *Gifford, Haddington, East Lothian EH41 4QU (01620) 810240* £75, plus special breaks; 14 rms. Civilised late 17th-c inn in quiet

village, with comfortable sofas and chairs in tranquil lounge, gracious dining room, wide choice of good daily changing food, and charming service; disabled access; dogs welcome in some bedrooms; £10

GIGHA

Gigha Hotel *Isle of Gigha PA41 7AA (01583) 505254* **£120** inc dinner, plus special breaks; 13 rms, most with own bthrm. Traditional family-run hotel, small and attractive with lots of charm, bustling bar (popular with yachtsmen and locals), neatly kept comfortable residents' lounge, and local seafood in restaurant; self-contained cottages too; cl Christmas; dogs welcome in bedrooms

GLASGOW

Malmaison *278 West George St, Glasgow G2 4LL (0141) 572 1000* **£154.50**; 72 smartly quirky very comfortable rms. Stylishly converted church with greek façade, striking central wrought-iron staircase, a relaxed contemporary atmosphere, friendly staff, enjoyable french food in attractive brasserie/bar; gym; disabled access; dogs if small in bedrooms; £10

One Devonshire Gardens *Glasgow G12 0UX (0141) 339 2001* **£224**; 35 opulent rms. Elegant cosseting hotel a little way out from the centre, with luxurious Victorian furnishings, fresh flowers, exemplary staff, and fine modern cooking in the stylish restaurant; dogs welcome in bedrooms

GLENDEVON

Tormaukin *Glendevon, Dollar, Clackmannanshire FK14 7JY (01257) 781252* **£90**; 12 comfortable rms, some in converted stable block. Neatly kept 18th-c inn in good walking country, with loch and river fishing, lots of golf courses in reach, beamed dining room and softly lit bar, very good food using fresh local produce (soup and coffee all day), and fine breakfasts; also a self-catering chalet; cl 2nd wk Jan; disabled access; dogs welcome in some bedrooms

GLENELG

Glenelg Inn *Kirkton, Glenelg, Kyle, Ross-shire IV40 8JR (01599) 522273* **£178** inc dinner, plus special breaks; 7 individually decorated and comfortable rms, all with fine views. Overlooking Skye across its own beach, carefully renovated old stables with relaxed bar, comfortable sofas and blazing fires, friendly staff and locals, good food using local venison, local hill-bred lamb and lots of wonderfully fresh fish and seafood, and quite a few whiskies; the drive to the inn involves spectacular views from the steep road (and the pretty drive to Glen Beag broch is nice); disabled access; dogs welcome away from dining room

GLENROTHES

Balbirnie House *Markinch, Glenrothes, Fife KY7 6NE (01592) 610066* **£190**, plus special breaks; 30 rms. Fine Georgian country house in 400-acre park landscaped in Capability Brown style, with fresh flowers, open fires and antiques in gracious public rooms, extremely good inventive food, and a big wine list; disabled access; dogs welcome in bedrooms; £15

GULLANE
Greywalls *Duncar Rd, Gullane, East Lothian EH31 2EG (01620) 842144* £260, plus special breaks; 23 individually decorated rms. Overlooking Muirfield golf course, this beautiful family-run Lutyens house has antiques, open fires and flowers in its comfortable lounges and panelled library, very good food and fine wines in the restaurant, impeccable service, and lovely Gertrude Jekyll garden, all of a piece with the perfect design of the house; cl Nov-Mar; disabled access; dogs welcome in bedrooms

INNERLEITHEN
Traquair Arms *Innerleithen, Peebles-shire EH44 6PD (01896) 830229* £70, plus special breaks; 15 comfortable rms. Very friendly hotel with interesting choice of good food in attractive dining room, cosy lounge bar, friendly service, superb local Traquair ale, and nice breakfasts; cl 25-26 Dec, 1 Jan; disabled access; dogs welcome away from restaurant

INVERNESS
Bunchrew House *Bunchrew, Inverness IV3 8TA (01463) 234917* £140, plus special breaks; 14 individually decorated rms. Friendly 17th-c mansion west of town by Beauly Firth with fine views and landscaped gardens, log fire in the elegant panelled drawing room, and traditional cooking using local produce, local game and venison; cl Christmas; dogs welcome in bedrooms; £10

Dunain Park *Inverness IV3 8JN (01463) 230512* £158; 13 rms inc 6 suites with own lounge. 18th-c italianate mansion in six acres of well tended gardens and woodland, a short walk from the River Ness and Caledonian Canal; charming owners, traditional homely décor with family photographs and china ornaments, log fires and fresh flowers, wonderful food using home-grown produce and local game, fish and aberdeen angus meat, generous breakfasts, and 200 whiskies; small warm swimming pool, sauna, lots of walks and golf courses nearby; cl 5-21 Jan; disabled access; dogs welcome in bedrooms

ISLE ORNSAY
Eilean Iarmain *Isle Ornsay, Isle of Skye IV43 8QR (01471) 833332* £125, plus winter breaks; 16 individual rms inc 4 suites (those in main hotel best), all with fine views. Sparkling white hotel with gaelic-speaking staff and locals, big cheerfully busy bar, two pretty dining rooms with lovely sea views, and very good food; disabled access; well behaved dogs welcome

Kinloch Lodge *Isle Ornsay, Isle of Skye IV43 8QY (01471) 833214* £110, plus winter breaks; 14 rms. Surrounded by rugged mountain scenery at the head of Loch Na Dal, this charming white stone hotel has a relaxed atmosphere in its comfortable and attractive drawing rooms, antiques, portraits, flowers, log fires, and good imaginative food; cookery demonstrations; children by arrangement; cl 22-28 Dec; dogs welcome in bedrooms by arrangement

KELSO
Ednam House *Ednam, Kelso, Roxburghshire TD5 7HT (01573) 224168* £111; 32 rms (the original ones are the nicest) inc 2 suites. Large Georgian manor house by the River Tweed with three acres of gardens and owned by the same family since 1928; three distinctive lounges with antiques and plenty of comfortable seating, two bars (one with fishing theme), excellent food in large candlelit dining room (lovely informal atmosphere) that overlooks the river, and particularly good, friendly service; shooting and fishing by arrangement; genuine welcome for children; cl 2 wks over Christmas and New Year; dogs welcome away from restaurant

KILBERRY
Kilberry Inn *Kilberry, Tarbert, Argyll PA29 6YD (01880) 770223* £85, plus special breaks; 3 ground-floor rms. Homely and welcoming inn on west coast of Knapdale with fine sea views, old-fashioned character, very good traditional home cooking relying on fresh local ingredients; no smoking throughout; cl Nov– Mar; disabled access; dogs in bedrooms

KILCHRENAN
Taychreggan Hotel *Kilchrenan, Taynuilt, Argyll PA35 1HQ (01866) 833211* £127, plus special breaks; 19 rms. Civilised and extensively refurbished hotel with fine garden running down to Loch Awe, comfortable airy bar, attractively served lunchtime bar food, polite efficient staff, good freshly prepared food in no smoking dining room, careful wine list, dozens of malt whiskies, and pretty inner courtyard; cl 6 wks Jan/Feb; no children; dogs welcome in some bedrooms; £4

KILNINVER
Knipoch *Knipoch, Oban, Argyll PA34 4QT (01852) 316251* £146, plus winter breaks; 20 rms. Elegant very well kept Georgian hotel in lovely countryside overlooking Loch Feochan; fine family portraits, log fires, fresh flowers and polished furniture in comfortable lounges and bars, carefully chosen wines and malt whiskies, and marvellous food inc their own smoked salmon; dogs welcome in bedrooms

KINCLAVEN BY STANLEY
Ballathie House *Stanley, Perth PH1 4QN (01250) 883268* £178, plus special breaks; 42 pretty rms, some luxurious and some in newer building with river views from balconies. On a vast estate with fine salmon fishing on the River Tay (lodges and facilities for fishermen) and plenty of sporting opportunities, this turreted mansion has a comfortable and relaxed drawing room, separate lounge and bar, good enjoyable modern scottish cooking, croquet and putting; limited disabled access; dogs welcome in bedrooms

KINNESSWOOD
Lomond Country Inn *Main St, Kinnesswood, Kinross KY13 9HN (01592)*
840253 £70, plus special breaks; 10 comfortable rms, 8 in an extension.
Attractive little inn in village centre with views across Loch Leven (nice
sunsets), open fires, informal bustling bar, well kept real ales, and good
reasonably priced bar and restaurant food using local produce; disabled
access; dogs welcome in bedrooms

KIRKTON OF GLENISLA
Glenisla Hotel *Glenisla, Blairgowrie, Perthshire PH11 8PH (01575) 582223*
£50, plus special breaks; 14 individually decorated rms. Friendly 17th-c
mansion west of town by Beauly Firth with fine views and landscaped
gardens, log fire in the elegant panelled drawing room, and traditional
cooking using local produce, local game and venison; cl 22-26 Dec; dogs
welcome in bedrooms; £5

LOCKERBIE
Dryfesdale Hotel *Dryfebridge, Lockerbie, Dumfries-shire DG11 2SF (01576)*
202427 £95, plus wknd breaks; 16 rms, 7 on ground floor. Relaxed and
comfortable former manse in five acres, open fire in homely lounge, good
food in pleasant restaurant, garden and lovely surrounding countryside,
putting and croquet; cl Christmas; good disabled access; dogs welcome in
bedrooms; £4

MELROSE
Burts *Market Sq, Melrose, Roxburghshire TD6 9PN (01896) 822285* £98,
plus special breaks; 20 rms. Welcoming 18th-c family-run hotel close to
abbey ruins in delightfully quiet village; coal fire in bustling bar, residents'
lounge, consistently popular imaginative food, exceptional breakfasts; cl
24-26 Dec; dogs welcome in bedrooms and lounge only

MINNIGAFF
Creebridge House *Creebridge, Newton Stewart, Wigtownshire DG8 6NP*
(01671) 402121 £80, plus special breaks; 19 rms inc 2 with four-posters.
Attractive country-house hotel in three acres of gardens with relaxed
friendly atmosphere, open fire in comfortable drawing room, cheerful bar,
and big choice of delicious food inc fine local fish and seafood in garden
restaurant; dogs welcome in bedrooms

NENTHORN
Whitehill Farm *Nenthorn, Kelso, Roxburghshire TD5 7RZ (01573) 470203*
£48; 4 rms, 3 with shared bthrm. Comfortable farmhouse on mixed farm
with fine views, big garden, log fire in sitting room, and good home cooking;
no babies; cl Christmas and New Year; dogs welcome away from kitchen

ONICH
Allt-Nan-Ros *Onich, Fort William, Inverness-shire PH33 6RY (01855)*
821210 £110, plus special breaks; 20 rms, many with views over the

gardens to the water. Victorian shooting lodge with fine scottish food, friendly atmosphere, bright airy rooms, and magnificent views across Loch Linnhe and the gardens; cl Dec/Jan but open New Year; disabled access; dogs in bedrooms; £3

PEAT INN

Peat Inn, Cupar, Fife KY15 5LH (01344) 840206 **£165**, plus special breaks; 8 luxurious suites. Famous restaurant-with-rooms: beams and white plaster walls, log fires and comfortable sofas, friendly service, fine interesting food using the best local produce inc plenty of game and seafood, and an excellent wine list; cl evenings of Sun and Mon, 25 Dec, 1 Jan; disabled access; dogs welcome in bedrooms

PITLOCHRY

Killiecrankie House Hotel *Killiecrankie, Pitlochry, Perthshire PH16 5LG (01796) 473220* **£130**, plus special breaks; 10 spotless rms. Comfortable country hotel in spacious grounds with splendid mountain views, mahogany-panelled bar with stuffed animals and fine wildlife paintings, cosy sitting room with books and games, a relaxed atmosphere, friendly owners, and excellent well presented, locally sourced food and good wine list in elegant restaurant; cl Jan-early Feb; disabled access; dogs welcome in two bedrooms; £10

PORT APPIN

Airds Hotel *Port Appin, Appin, Argyll PA38 4DF (01631) 730236* **£320** inc dinner, plus special breaks; 12 lovely rms. Instantly relaxing 18th-c inn with lovely views of Loch Linnhe and the island of Lismore, blissfully comfortable day rooms, professional courteous staff, and charming owners; the food is exceptional (as is the wine list), there are lots of surrounding walks, with more on Lismore (small boat every hour), clay pigeon shooting and riding; cl 5-26 Jan; children over 8 for dinner; dogs welcome in bedrooms by prior arrangement; £10

PORTPATRICK

Knockinaam Lodge *Portpatrick, Stranraer, Wigtownshire DG9 9AD (01776) 810471* **£230** inc dinner; 10 individual rms. Lovely very neatly kept little hotel with comfortable pretty rooms, open fires, wonderful food, and friendly caring service; dramatic surroundings, with lots of fine cliff walks; children over 12 in evening restaurant (high tea at 6pm); dogs welcome in some bedrooms; £15

PORTREE

Rosedale *Quay Brae, Portree, Isle of Skye IV51 9DB (01478) 613131* **£70**, plus special breaks; 18 rms, many with harbour views. Built from three fishermen's cottages with lots of passages and stairs, this family-run waterfront hotel has two traditional lounges, small first-floor restaurant with freshly cooked popular food, lots of whiskies in the cocktail bar, helpful staff, marvellous views; cl Nov-Mar; dogs welcome in three bedrooms and in lounge

RAASAY
Isle of Raasay Hotel *Isle of Raasay, Kyle, Ross-shire IV40 8PB (01478) 660222* £59, plus special breaks; 12 rms. Victorian hotel with marvellous views over the Sound of Raasay to Skye, popular with walkers and bird-watchers, home-made food with an emphasis on fresh fish; no petrol on the island; disabled access; dogs welcome in bedrooms; £2

SCARISTA
Scarista House *Scarista, Harris, Isle of Harris HS3 3HX (01859) 550238* £150, plus special breaks; 5 rms, some in annexe. Marvellously wild countryside and empty beaches surround this isolated small hotel with its antiques-furnished rooms, open fires, warm friendly atmosphere, plenty of books and records (no radio or TV), an impressive wine list, and good food in candlelit dining room using organic home-grown vegetables and herbs, hand-made cheeses, their own eggs, home-made bread, cakes, biscuits, yoghurt and marmalade, and lots of fish and shellfish; excellent for wildlife, walks and fishing; disabled access; cl Christmas and occasionally in winter; dogs welcome in bedrooms

SCONE
Murrayshall House *Perth PH2 7PH (01738) 551171* £130, plus special breaks; 41 rms inc 14 suites, plus lodge which sleeps 6. Handsome mansion in 300-acre park, very popular with golfers (it has two of its own courses); comfortable elegant public rooms, warm friendly staff, relaxed atmosphere, imaginative food, and good wines; disabled access; dogs in bedrooms

SCOURIE
Scourie Hotel *Scourie, Lairg, Sutherland IV27 4SX (01971) 502396* £80; 20 rms with views to Scourie Bay. A haven for anglers, with 36 exclusive beats on 25,000-acre estate; snug bar and cocktail bar, two comfortable lounges and good food using plenty of local game and fish in smart no smoking dining room; cl Oct-Apr; dogs welcome in bedrooms and public rooms (not near food areas)

SHIEL BRIDGE
Kintail Lodge *Glenshiel, Kyle, Ross-shire IV40 8HL (01599) 511275* £65, plus special breaks; 12 good value big rms. Pleasantly informal and fairly simple former shooting lodge on Loch Duich, with magnificent views, four acres of walled gardens, newly refurbished residents' lounge bar and comfortable sitting room, good well prepared food inc local seafood in new conservatory restaurant, and fine collection of malt whiskies; cl Jan-mid-Feb; dogs welcome in bedrooms; £3.50

SHIELDAIG
Tigh an Eilean *Shieldaig, Strathcarron, Ross-shire IV54 8XN (01520) 755251* £120, plus special breaks; 11 rms. Attractive hotel in outstanding position with lovely view of pine-covered island and sea, kayaks, private fishing and sea fishing arranged, within easy reach of NTS Torridon Estate,

Beinn Eighe nature reserve and Applecross peninsula; new bar extension in pub part, pretty woodburner in one of two comfortable residents' lounges with well stocked honesty bar, library, modern dining room with delicious food inc home-baked bread; cl end Oct–Mar; dogs welcome in bedrooms

SPEAN BRIDGE

Letterfinlay Lodge *Letterfinlay, Spean Bridge, Inverness-shire PH34 4DZ* *(01397) 712622* £**80**, plus special breaks; 13 rms, most with own bthrm. Secluded and genteel family-run country house with picture window in extensive modern bar overlooking loch; elegantly panelled small cocktail bar, good popular food, friendly attentive service; grounds run down through rhododendrons to the jetty and Loch Lochy; fishing can be arranged; cl Nov–Easter; dogs welcome away from dining room; £2

SPITTAL OF GLENSHEE

Dalmunzie House *Glenshee, Blairgowrie, Perthshire PH10 7QG (01250)* *885224* £**120**, plus special breaks; 16 rms with own bthrm. Old-fashioned former Victorian shooting lodge, off A93, peacefully set in huge estate among spectacular mountains, plenty of walks within it, and own golf course; family-run atmosphere with enthusiastic young australian staff, enjoyable food using local produce, and tasty breakfasts; disabled access; dogs welcome in bedrooms

STRONTIAN

Kilcamb Lodge Hotel *Strontian, Acharacle, Argyll PH36 4HY (01967)* *402257* £**110**, plus winter breaks; 11 rms. Warm friendly little hotel in 28 acres by Loch Sunart, with log fires in two lounges, carefully cooked food using fresh ingredients from organic kitchen garden, fine choice of malt whiskies in small bar, and a relaxed atmosphere; beach, fishing boat, four moorings and jetty; dogs welcome in bedrooms; £3.50

SWINTON

Wheatsheaf *Main St, Swinton, Duns, Berwickshire TD11 3JJ (01890) 860257* £**95**; 7 rms with baths or showers. Warmly friendly inn with exceptionally good food, a pleasantly decorated and relaxed main lounge plus small pubby area, new reception lounge, and no smoking front conservatory; garden play area for children; cl 24–26 Dec; dogs welcome in bedrooms

TARBERT

Columba Hotel *East Pier Rd, Tarbert, Argyll PA29 6UF (01880) 820808* £**74**, plus special breaks; 10 rms. In a peaceful position on Loch Fyne with views of the surrounding hills, this family-run hotel has log fires in the friendly bar and lounge, an informal and relaxed atmosphere, very enjoyable food using fresh local produce, and quite a few malt whiskies; dogs welcome in bedrooms

Stonefield Castle *Stonefield, Tarbert, Argyll PA29 6YJ (01880) 820836* £**160** inc dinner, plus special breaks; 33 rms. With wonderful views and surrounding wooded grounds, this scottish baronial mansion has comfortable public rooms and decent restaurant food; snooker room; dogs welcome in bedrooms; £10

TOMINTOUL
Argyle House 7 *Main St, Tomintoul, Ballindalloch, Banffshire AB37 9EX (01807) 580766* £36; 5 rms, most with own bthrm. Small family-run guest house, originally a temperance hotel, and recently carefully renovated; library with books for guests to borrow, good breakfasts in dining room, and a genuine welcome from the friendly owners; lots to do nearby; dogs welcome in bedrooms

Wales

Dog Friendly Pubs

CAPEL CURIG
Bryn Tyrch *A5 W of village*
In the heart of Snowdonia, this remote but welcoming country inn is popular with walkers and climbers. Big picture windows run the length of one wall, with views across the road to picnic-sets on a floodlit patch of grass by a stream running down to a couple of lakes, and the Snowdon Horseshoe in the distance. Comfortably relaxed, the bar has several easy chairs round low tables, some by a coal fire with magazines and outdoor equipment catalogues piled to one side, and a pool table in the plainer hikers' bar. Wholesome food, with an emphasis on vegetarian and vegan dishes, is generously served to meet the healthy appetite of anyone participating in the local outdoor attractions – very much what this place is about. Bar menu includes yellow pepper, onion and tomato salad, courgette and feta filo pie, grilled trout, and puddings such as mocha meringue sundae. You can also pop in here for a cup of one of the many coffee blends or Twinings teas that are listed on a blackboard, and served with a piece of vegan cake. Well kept Bass, Flowers IPA and Whitbreads Castle Eden on handpump, and quite a few malt whiskies; shove-ha'penny and dominoes. There are tables on a steep little garden at the side. More reports on the refurbished bedrooms (some have views, £10 cleaning charge for dogs) please.
Free house ~ Licensee Rita Davis ~ Real ale ~ Bar food ~ Restaurant ~ (01690) 720223 ~ Children welcome ~ Dogs allowed in bedrooms ~ Open 12-11(10.30 Sun); closed Mon, Tues Nov-Feb (but open school and bank hols) ~ Bedrooms: £39(£45B)/£52(£59B)

CRICKHOWELL
Bear *Brecon Road; A40*
This charming old coaching inn is a delight from the moment you catch your first glimpse of its aged flower-bedecked white frontage, which seems to sit so comfortably in its corner of this nice old town. It's well run and spotlessly kept, with a calmly civilised atmosphere in the comfortably decorated, heavily beamed lounge, which has fresh flowers on tables, lots of

little plush-seated bentwood armchairs and handsome cushioned antique settles, and a window seat looking down on the market square. Up by the great roaring log fire, a big sofa and leather easy chairs are spread among rugs on the oak parquet floor. Well kept Bass, Brains Rev James, Hancocks HB and Greene King Old Speckled Hen on handpump, as well as malt whiskies, vintage and late-bottled ports, unusual wines (with about a dozen by the glass) and liqueurs (with some hops tucked in among the bottles) and local apple juice; the family bar is partly no smoking. Friendly helpful staff serve bar food which includes chicken liver parfait with cumberland sauce and toasted brioche, faggots with chips and peas, sausage and mash, braised hock of welsh lamb, and puddings such as dark chocolate and orange mousse; the more elaborate restaurant menu is pricier, and their Sunday lunch is very popular. You can eat in the garden in summer; disabled lavatories.

Free house ~ Licensee Judy Hindmarsh ~ Real ale ~ Bar food (12-2, 6-10) ~ Restaurant ~ (01873) 810408 ~ Children in eating area of bar and family room ~ Dogs welcome ~ Open 11-3, 6-11; 12-3, 7-11 Sun ~ Bedrooms: £57(£57S)(£77B)/£75(£75S)(£95B)

FELINFACH
Griffin *A470 NE of Brecon*

From the main road you can't miss this restauranty pub, with its bright orangey-red external paintwork. Inside, the back bar is quite pubby in an up-to-date way, with three leather sofas around a low table on pitted quarry tiles, by a high slate hearth with a log fire, and behind them mixed stripped seats around scrubbed kitchen tables on bare boards, and a bright blue and ochre colour scheme. An upright piano stands against one wall – the acoustics are pretty lively, with so much bare flooring and uncurtained windows. The two smallish no smoking front dining rooms, linking through to the back bar, are attractive: on the left, mixed dining chairs around mainly stripped tables on flagstones, and white-painted rough stone walls, with a cream-coloured Aga cooker in a big stripped-stone embrasure; on the right, similar furniture on bare boards, with big modern prints on terracotta walls. Table settings are classy, service is charming, and the good food (they are proud of never sourcing anything from further away than 15 miles) might include lunchtime dishes such as roast butternut soup, open sandwiches and braised leg of rabbit with haricot beans and chorizo stew. A pricier evening menu includes dishes such as wild mushroom tagliatelle and rump of lamb. They have a good choice of wines by the glass (in three sizes), and Tomos Watkin OSB and one of their seasonal beers on handpump. There may be piped Radio Wales in the bar. We have not yet heard from people who have stayed here, but would expect good news about their white bedrooms. Wheelchair access is good, and there are tables outside.

Free house ~ Licensee Charles Inken ~ Real ale ~ Bar food (lunchtime only) ~ Restaurant ~ (01874) 620111 ~ Children welcome ~ Dogs welcome ~ Open 12-3.30, 6-11; 12-11(10.30 Sun) Sat; closed Mon lunchtime ~ Bedrooms: £67.50B/£92.50B

HAY-ON-WYE
Kilverts *Bullring*

It's the enjoyably relaxed atmosphere that makes this friendly informal hotel such a pleasure for locals and visitors alike. Calm and understated, with no piped music or machines, the airy high-beamed bar has some stripped stone walls, *Vanity Fair* caricatures, a couple of standing timbers, candles on well spaced mixed old and new tables, and a pleasant variety of seating. You can watch the world go by from tables in a small front flagstoned courtyard (with outdoor heaters) or while away the hours by the fountain in a pretty terraced back garden. Enjoyable bar food from a sensibly balanced menu is served in generous helpings, and includes lunchtime filled baguettes or sandwiches, about a dozen pizzas, thai-style fishcakes, beef and ale pie, spinach and mushroom roulade, and 12oz rump steak; welcoming service; no smoking restaurant. They've an extensive wine list with about a dozen by the glass, as well as three real ales such as Brains Rev James, Hancocks HB and Wye Valley Butty Bach on handpump, farm cider, and good coffees; piped music. There's a £5.50 cleaning charge for dogs in the comfortable bedrooms.

Free house ~ Licensee Colin Thomson ~ Real ale ~ Bar food (12-2, 7-9.30) ~ Restaurant ~ (01497) 821042 ~ Children in eating area of bar and restaurant ~ Dogs welcome ~ Open 9-11(10.30 Sun); may close earlier in winter ~ Bedrooms: £50S/£70S(£80B)

MONKNASH
Plough & Harrow *Signposted Marcross, Broughton off B4265 St Brides Major—Llantwit Major – turn left at end of Water Street; OS Sheet 170 map reference 920706*

Dating back to the early 12th c, this evocative country pub was originally part of a monastic grange. It's solidly built with massively thick stone walls. The dimly lit unspoilt but welcoming main bar (which used to be the scriptures room and mortuary) seems hardly changed over the last 70 years. There's a log fire in a huge fireplace with a side bread oven large enough to feed a village, as well as a woodburning stove with polished copper hot water pipes. The heavily black-beamed ceiling has ancient ham hooks, an intriguing arched doorway to the back, and a comfortably informal mix of furnishings that includes three fine stripped pine settles on the broad flagstones. The room on the left has lots of Wick rugby club memorabilia (it's their club room); daily papers, darts, dominoes, cribbage and piped music. Around seven well kept real ales on handpump or tapped from the cask might include Shepherd Neame Spitfire, Tomos Watkin Crw Haf, Worthingtons and Wye Valley Hereford Pale along with a couple of frequently changing guest beers from thoughtfully sourced brewers such as Breconshire or Cottage. Bar food could include three-cheese ploughman's or spaghetti bolognese, cod and chips, and puddings such as rhubarb crumble. Staff are friendly, and it can get crowded at weekends, when it's popular with families. In a peaceful spot not far from the coast near Nash Point, it's an enjoyable walk from here down to the sea, where you can pick up a fine stretch of the coastal path. There are picnic-sets in the front garden, which has a boules pitch, and they hold barbecues out here in summer.

Free house ~ Licensee Lynne Moffat ~ Real ale ~ Bar food (12-2, 6-9) ~ Restaurant ~ (01656) 890209 ~ Children in eating area of bar ~ Dogs welcome ~ Live music Sun evening and some Sats ~ Open 11-11; 12-10.30 Sun

RAGLAN

Clytha Arms *Clytha, off Abergavenny road – former A40, now declassified*

Doing very well at the moment, this beautifully positioned old white house with its long verandahs and diamond paned windows is a great all-rounder. It stands in its own extensive well cared-for grounds – a mass of colour in spring – on the edge of Clytha Park. Inside is comfortable, light and airy with scrubbed wood floors, pine settles, big faux fur cushions on the window seats by big windows, a good mix of old country furniture and a warming coal fire. Don't miss the murals in the lavatories. Run by charming licensees, it's the sort of relaxed place where everyone feels welcome, from locals who've walked here for a pint in the spotlessly kept bar (solidly comfortable furnishings and a couple of good fires), to diners in the contemporary linen-clothed restaurant. The very reasonably priced bar menu is well balanced with soundly imaginative dishes: spaghetti with tomato and basil sauce, half a dozen oysters, charcuterie, wild boar sausages with potato pancakes, chicken breast with parmesan crust and pasta, or grilled queen scallops. The restaurant menu is pricier and more elaborate. An impressive choice of drinks includes Bass, Felinfoel Double Dragon and Hook Norton, three interesting changing guest beers (around 300 different ones a year) from brewers such as Brains, Caledonian and Fullers, an extensive wine list with about a dozen or so by the glass, Weston's farm cider and a changing guest cider – even home-made perry. The restaurant and lounge are no smoking; darts, shove-ha'penny, boules, table skittles, cribbage, dominoes, draughts and chess. The two friendly labradors are Beamish and Stowford and there's an english setter.

Free house ~ Licensees Andrew and Beverley Canning ~ Real ale ~ Bar food (12.30-2.15, 7-9.30; not Sun evening or Mon) ~ Restaurant ~ (01873) 840206 ~ Children welcome ~ Dogs allowed in bar ~ Open 12-3, 6-11; 12-11 Sat; 12-10.30 Sun; closed Mon lunchtime ~ Bedrooms: £50B/£70B

SHIRENEWTON

Carpenters Arms *Mynydd-bach; B4235 Chepstow—Usk, about ½ mile N*

New licensees weren't planning any big changes at this former country smithy – indeed we hope not, as its main appeal is its proper pubby atmosphere. The series of small interconnecting rooms have lots to look at, from chamber-pots and a blacksmith's bellows hanging from the planked ceiling of one lower room, which has an attractive Victorian tiled fireplace, to a collection of chromolithographs of antique royal occasions under another room's pitched ceiling (more chamber-pots here). Furnishings run the gamut too, from one very high-backed ancient settle to pews, kitchen chairs, a nice elm table, several sewing-machine trestle tables and so forth; it's popular with locals (especially for Sunday lunch); shove-ha'penny, cribbage, dominoes, table skittles, backgammon, bar billiards, and piped pop music. Beers now come from the Punch list so the range has changed a little: Bass, Flowers IPA, Fullers London Pride, Shepherd Neame Spitfire and Wadworths 6X on handpump. Bar food is likely to be straightforward. The pub is handy for Chepstow.

Punch ~ Tenants Sue and Terry Thomas ~ Real ale ~ Bar food (not Sun evening) ~ No credit cards ~ (01291) 641231 ~ Children in family room ~ Dogs welcome ~ Open 11-2.30, 6-11; 12-3, 7-11 Sun

TALYLLYN

Tynycornel *B4405, off A487 S of Dolgellau*
Idyllically peaceful, this comfortably civilised hotel is in a delightful position nestling peacefully below high mountains – Cadair Idris opposite (splendid walks) and Graig Goch behind – overlooking a charming lake. Though not at all pubby, it's relaxed and friendly, and in summer the attractively planted side courtyard is a pleasant place for afternoon tea. It's immaculately kept, with deep armchairs and enveloping sofas around low tables, a central log fire, and big picture windows looking out over the water, as well as big bird prints, local watercolours, and a good range of malt whiskies (the serving bar, with keg beer, is tucked away behind). Enjoyable lunchtime bar food might include good sandwiches, courgette and tomato soup, thai green vegetable curry, steamed salmon fillet or burgundy beef casserole in a yorkshire pudding. Also puddings such as tangy lemon tart; courteous service from the uniformed staff. There's a no smoking restaurant and conservatory. Guests have the use of a sauna and fishing facilities, and can hire boats on the lake.

Free house ~ Licensee Thomas Rowlands ~ Bar food (lunchtime only) ~ Restaurant ~ (01654) 782282 ~ Children welcome ~ Dogs allowed in bedrooms ~ Open 11-11; 12-10.30 Sun ~ Bedrooms: £50S/£100B

TINTERN

Cherry Tree *Pub signposted up narrow Raglan road off A446, beside Royal George; parking very limited*
A new bar at this white-painted late 16th-c stone cottage (delightfully approached across a little stone slab bridge over a tiny stream) has been built using reclaimed materials to blend with the traditional character of the original building – now with slate floors throughout. The new area has dark wood furniture, and leads into the original beamed and lime-washed bar, which has a plain serving counter in one area and a good open fire in another; cribbage, darts, cards, dominoes and piped music. Look out for Guinness the dog. Generous good value food, made using lots of fresh local ingredients, might include mushroom and ricotta tortellini, spicy meatballs with couscous, beef and ale pie, as well as quickly changing daily specials such as sizzling crevettes and their famous paella (for two). Tapped straight from the cask, Hancocks HB is well kept alongside changing guests from brewers such as Felinfoel, Timothy Taylors and Wye Valley. They also serve farm cider, just over a dozen wines by the glass and milk shakes. It's in a quiet and attractive spot, yet only half a mile or so from the honey-pot

centre of Tintern, and there are tables out in a charming garden, and on a green patio; disabled access is difficult.

Free house ~ Licensees Jill and Steve Pocock ~ Real ale ~ Bar food (12-3, 6-9; 12-9 wknds) ~ Restaurant ~ (01291) 689292 ~ Children in eating area of bar ~ Dogs allowed in bar ~ Open 12-11(10.30 Sun); 12-3, 5-11 winter ~ Bedrooms: /£50B

TRELLECK
Lion *B4293 6 miles S of Monmouth*

The landlord's father is hungarian and brings in some of the ingredients that are used in the interesting authentic hungarian specialities at this smallish stone-built pub. A blackboard hung with dried peppers above one fireplace lists a choice of these dishes, such as peppers filled with minced pork and rice with sweet tomato sauce, hungarian sausage and egg baked with sour cream and cheese, and fried pork steak with cream cheese. Other food includes baguettes, filled baked potatoes, home-made vegetarian hotpot, grilled salmon steak or chicken kiev. There's a step up to the no smoking dining area. The unpretentious open-plan bar has one or two black beams in its low ochre ceiling, a mix of furnishings including some comfortable brocaded wall seats and tub chairs, old red plush dining chairs, a hop-hung window seat, varying-sized tables, and log fires in two fireplaces opposite each other. There's a small fish tank in a wall recess, and another bigger one in the lobby by the lavatories; piped music. A colourful galaxy of pumpclips in the porch and on a wall show the splendid range of quickly changing guest beers from brewers such as Archers and Milton, which are well kept alongside Bath SPA and Wye Valley Butty Bach, and they've around 30 malt whiskies. There are some picnic-sets and an aviary out on the grass. The pub is opposite the church, and handy for the standing stones; bedrooms in a nearby cottage.

Free house ~ Licensees Tom and Debbie Zsigo ~ Real ale ~ Bar food (12-2, 7-9) ~ Restaurant ~ (01600) 860322 ~ Children welcome ~ Dogs allowed in bar ~ Open 12-3, 6(7 Mon)-11; 12-3, 6.30-11 Sat; 12-3 Sun; closed Sun evening ~ Bedrooms: /£65S

TY'N-Y-GROES
Groes *B5106 N of village*

The food at this attractive old hotel is good (if not cheap), and it's in a charming spot, making it a nice place to stay. Past the hot stove in the entrance area, the spotlessly kept homely series of rambling, low-beamed and thick-walled rooms are nicely decorated with antique settles and an old sofa, old clocks, portraits, hats and tins hanging from the walls, and fresh flowers. A fine antique fireback is built into one wall, perhaps originally from the formidable fireplace in the back bar, which houses a collection of stone cats as well as cheerful winter log fires; one area is no smoking. There's also an airy verdant no smoking conservatory. Ind Coope Burton and Tetleys are well kept on handpump, and they've a good few malt whiskies, kir, and a fruity Pimms in summer; light classical piped music at lunchtimes, and a live harpist a couple of times a month. Well presented dishes might include grilled mushrooms with stilton, garlic and lemon, chicken curry with saffron rice or home-made lasagne, and daily specials such as game casserole, local lamb steak and bass. As well as puddings such as pecan and syrup tart, they do delicious home-made ice-creams. Run by the same family for the last 19 years, and said to have been the first Welsh pub to be properly licensed – in 1573 – it enjoys magnificent views over the Vale of Conwy and the distant mountains. The neatly kept, well equipped bedrooms (some have terraces or balconies) also have views, and in summer it's a pleasure to sit outside in the pretty back garden with its flower-filled hayricks.

Free house ~ Licensee Dawn Humphreys ~ Real ale ~ Bar food (12-2.15, 6.30-9) ~ Restaurant ~ (01492) 650545 ~ Children in family room till 7pm; must be over 10 in restaurant ~ Dogs allowed in bedrooms ~ Open 12-3, 6.30(6 Sat)-11(10.30 Sun) ~ Bedrooms: £79B/£95B

USK

Nags Head *The Square*

Visitors are full of enthusiastic praise for this charming old coaching inn. Though doing well in all respects, it's the really friendly welcome (it's been in the same family for over 35 years) and the tasty food that really seem to hit the mark. Generously served well presented dishes (concentrating on local produce) could include home-made soup, home-made steak pie, vegetable pancakes, delicious rabbit pie, and interesting specials including seasonal game dishes (lovely on a cold winter evening). You can book tables, some of which may be candlelit at night. With a friendly chatty atmosphere, the beautifully kept traditional main bar has lots of well polished tables and chairs packed under its beams (some with farming tools), lanterns or horsebrasses and harness attached, and various sets of sporting prints and local pictures – look out for the original deeds to the pub. Tucked away at the front is an intimate little corner with some african masks, while on the other side of the room a passageway leads to the pub's own busy coffee bar (open between Easter and autumn). Built in the old entrance to the courtyard, it sells snacks, teas, cakes and ice-cream, and tables spill out from here on to the front pavement. A simpler room behind the bar has prints for sale, and perhaps a knot of sociable locals. They do 15 wines by the glass, along with well kept Brains SA, Buckleys Best and Rev James on handpump, 12 malt whiskies and a farm cider; quiet piped music. The church in Usk is well worth a look.

Free house ~ Licensees the Key family ~ Real ale ~ Bar food (11.30-1, 6-10) ~ Restaurant ~ (01291) 672820 ~ Children welcome ~ Dogs allowed in bar ~ Open 11-3(3.30 Sun), 5.30-11(10.30 Sun)

Dog Friendly Hotels, B&BS and Farms

ABERDOVEY

Penhelig Arms *Terrace Rd, Aberdovey, Gwynedd LL35 0LT (01654) 767215* **£78**, plus special breaks; 15 comfortable rms, 4 in annexe impressively furnished, with harbour views. In a fine spot overlooking the sea, with cosy bar, open fires, delicious food with emphasis on daily-delivered fresh local fish in no smoking restaurant, extensive (and fairly priced) wine list with 30 by the glass (champagne, too), splendid breakfasts, and charming friendly service; lovely views of Dovey estuary; cl 25–26 Dec; dogs welcome in bedrooms; £3

ABERSOCH

Porth Tocyn Hotel *Bwlch Tocyn, Pwllheli, Gwynedd LL53 7BU (01758) 713303* **£110**, plus special breaks; 17 attractive rms, most with sea views. On a headland overlooking Cardigan Bay, a lovely place to stay – with a refreshingly sensible and helpful approach to families (though not solely a family hotel) – and with a new conservatory; very friendly hard-working owners and staff, several cosy interconnecting sitting rooms with antiques and fresh flowers, most enjoyable traditional cooking in the restaurant (lots of options such as light lunches, high teas for children as they must be over 7 for dinner in the restaurant, and imaginative Sun lunches); lots of space in the pretty garden, heated swimming pool in summer, hard tennis court; cl mid-Nov to mid-Mar; disabled access; dogs welcome in bedrooms by prior arrangement

BEDDGELERT

Sygun Fawr Country House *Beddgelert, Caernarfon, Gwynedd LL55 4NE (01766) 890258* **£68**, plus special breaks; 12 rms. Spectacular scenery surrounds this secluded 17th-c hotel, with lots of surrounding walks; beams, stripped stone walls, inglenooks, and a restful atmosphere, a varied imaginative menu, antiques and an informal atmosphere in the restaurant and new dining conservatory, and 20 acres of mountainside and gardens; cl Jan; dogs in bedrooms and bar; £3

BETWS-Y-COED

Ty Gwyn *Betwys-y-coed, Gwynedd LL24 0SG (01690) 710383* **£64**, plus special breaks; 13 pretty rms, most with own bthrm. Welcoming and well run 17th-c coaching inn with interesting old prints, furniture and bric-a-brac, good food and friendly service; pleasant setting overlooking river and a very good base for the area; children free if sharing parents' room; cl Mon–Weds in Jan; disabled access; dogs welcome in bedrooms; £5

BROAD HAVEN

Druidstone Hotel *Broad Haven, Haverfordwest, Dyfed SA62 3NE (01437) 781221* **£130**; 11 rms and 5 cottages, some with sea view, shared bthrms. Alone on the coast above an effectively private beach with exhilarating cliff walks, this roomy and very friendly hotel, run by a very nice family, has something of a folk-club and Outward Bound feel at times; it's extremely winning if you take to its unique combination of good wholesome and often memorably inventive food, slightly fend-for-yourself approach amid elderly furniture, and glorious seaside surroundings; self-catering cottages, two with wheelchair access; dogs welcome away from restaurant

CAERNARFON
Seiont Manor *Llanrug, Caernarfon, Gwynedd LL55 2AQ (01286) 673366*
£180, plus special breaks; 28 luxurious rms. Fine hotel built from the original farmstead of a Georgian manor house, in 156 acres of mature parkland; open fires and comfortable sofas in lounge, restful atmosphere in library and drawing room, imaginative food in restaurant's four interconnecting areas, and leisure suite with swimming pool, gym and sauna; dogs welcome in bedrooms

CONWY
Sychnant Pass House *Sychnant Pass Rd, Conwy, Gwynedd LL32 8BJ (01492) 596868* **£80**; 10 rms. Victorian house in two acres among the foothills of the Snowdonia National Park; big comfortable sitting rooms, log fires, a relaxing, friendly atmosphere, and enjoyable food (the restaurant is open to non-residents, too); dogs welcome away from restaurant

CRICCIETH
Mynydd Ednyfed Country House *Caernarfon Rd, Criccieth, Gwynedd LL52 0PH (01766) 523269* **£75**; 8 individually decorated rms, some with four-posters. Beautifully set 400-year-old house in 8 acres of garden, orchard, paddock and woods with lovely views overlooking Tremadog Bay, and once home to Lloyd George's family; traditional lounge bar, enjoyable food using local produce in comfortable dining room and airy conservatory, and friendly staff; cl 22 Dec–4 Jan; dogs if small and well behaved in bedrooms only; £5

EGLWYSFACH
Ynyshir Hall *Eglwysfach, Machynlleth, Dyfed SY20 8TA (01654) 781209* **£125**, plus special breaks; 9 individually decorated, no smoking rms, two with four-posters. Carefully run Georgian manor house in 14 acres of landscaped gardens adjoining the Ynyshir coastal bird reserve, with particularly good service, antiques, log fires and paintings in the light and airy public rooms, extremely good food using home-grown vegetables, and delicious breakfasts; lots to do nearby; may cl 3 wks Jan; children over 9; disabled access to ground-floor rms; dogs welcome in two bedrooms; £3

FISHGUARD
Manor Town House *Main St, Fishguard, Dyfed SA65 9HG (01348) 873260* **£65**; 6 comfortable rms, most with sea views. Georgian house with fine views of harbour from sheltered garden, a guests' lounge with books, an attractive, well planned basement restaurant with delicious home-made food using fresh local produce, and enjoyable breakfasts (and pre-dinner drinks) out on the terrace overlooking the sea in good weather; cl Christmas, and Nov–Jan; dogs welcome in bedrooms by arrangement

GELLILYDAN
Tyddyn Du Farm *Gellilydan, Blaenau Ffestiniog, Gwynedd LL41 4RB (01766) 590281* **£70**, plus special breaks; 4 ground-floor, private stable

and long barn suites with Jacuzzi baths, fridges and microwaves, one with airbath. 400-year-old farmhouse on working farm in the heart of Snowdonia, with beams and exposed stonework, and big inglenook fireplaces in lounge; children can help bottle-feed the lambs, and look at goats, ducks, sheep and shetland ponies; fine walks, inc short one to their own roman site; partial disabled access; dogs welcome away from dining room

GILWERN
Wenallt Farm *Twyn-wenallt, Gilwern, Abergavenny, Gwent NP7 0HP (01873) 830694* £**56**; 7 rms. Friendly and relaxing 16th-c welsh longhouse on 40 acres of farmland in the Brecon Beacons National Park, with oak beams and inglenook fireplace in big drawing room, a TV room, good food in dining room, packed lunches on request, and lots to do nearby; cl Christmas; dogs welcome in bedrooms

LLANABER
Llwyndu Farmhouse *Llanaber, Barmouth, Gwynedd LL42 1RR (01341) 280144* £**78**, plus special breaks; 7 charming rms, most with own bthrm, some in a nicely converted 18th-c barn. Most attractive 16th-c farmhouse just above Cardigan Bay, with a warm welcome from friendly owners, big inglenook fireplaces, oak beams, mullioned windows, relaxing lounge, enjoyable breakfasts, and good imaginative food in candlelit dining room; cl 25-26 Dec; dogs welcome in bedrooms

LLANARMON D C
West Arms *Llanarmon Dyffryn Ceiriog, Llangollen, Clwyd LL20 7LD (01691) 600665* £**109**, plus special mid-week breaks; 15 rms. Charming and civilised 16th-c inn with heavy beams and timbers, log fires in inglenook fireplaces, lounge bar interestingly furnished with antique settles, sofas in the old-fashioned entrance hall, comfortable locals' lounge bar, good food, and friendly quiet atmosphere; the lawn runs down to the River Ceiriog (fishing for residents); disabled access; dogs welcome away from restaurant; £6

LLANDELOY
Lochmeyler Farm *Llandeloy, Haverfordwest, Dyfed SA62 6LL (01348) 837724* £**50**, plus special winter breaks; 15 pretty rms with videos (they have a video library). Attractive creeper-covered 16th-c farmhouse on 220-acre working dairy farm; two lounges (one no smoking), traditional farmhouse cooking in pleasant dining room, mature garden, and welsh cakes on arrival; can walk around the farm trails; cl Christmas and New Year; partial disabled access; dogs welcome in bedrooms

LLANDRILLO
Tyddyn Llan *Llandrillo, Corwen, Clwyd LL21 0ST (01490) 440264* £**130**; 13 pretty rms. Elegant and relaxed Georgian house with three acres of lovely gardens and surrounded by the Berwyn mountains; fresh flowers in

comfortable public rooms, enjoyable food using the best ingredients, and an impressive wine list; fine forest walks (guides available), and watersports, fishing and horse riding can be arranged; cl 19–29 Jan; disabled access; dogs welcome in bedrooms; £5

LLANDUDNO
St Tudno *15 North Parade, Llandudno, Gwynedd LL30 2LP (01492) 874411* **£105**, plus special breaks; 18 individually decorated rms, some with sea view. Opposite the pier, this well run, smart Victorian seaside hotel has genuinely helpful and friendly staff, Victorian-style décor in restful no smoking sitting room, a convivial bar lounge, relaxed coffee lounge for light lunches, and attractive, newly refurbished italian-style restaurant; small indoor pool; dogs in bedrooms only; £10

LLANFAIR D C
Eyarth Station *Llanfair Dyffryn Clwyd, Ruthin, Clwyd LL15 2EE (01824) 703643* **£54**, plus special breaks; 6 pretty rms. Carefully converted old railway station with quiet gardens and wonderful views, a friendly relaxed atmosphere, log fire in airy and comfortable beamed lounge, good breakfasts and enjoyable suppers in dining room (more lovely views), sun terrace and heated swimming pool, and lots of walks; cl Feb; disabled access; dogs welcome in bedrooms by arrangement; £4

LLANGAMMARCH WELLS
Lake *Llangammarch Wells, Powys LD4 4BS (01591) 620202* **£140**, plus special breaks; 19 charming, pretty rms with fruit and decanter of sherry. Particularly well run 1860s half-timbered hotel in 50 acres with plenty of wildlife, well stocked trout lake, clay pigeon shoots, tennis, riding or walking their two friendly labradors; deeply comfortable tranquil drawing room with antiques, paintings and log fire, wonderful afternoon teas (in summer under the chestnut tree overlooking the river), courteous service, fine wines and good modern british cooking in elegant candlelit dining room, and liberal breakfasts; children over 7 in evening dining room; disabled access; dogs welcome in some bedrooms; £6

LLANSANFFRAID GLAN CONWY
Old Rectory Country House *Llanrwst Rd, Glan Conwy, Colwyn Bay, Clwyd LL28 5LF (01492) 580611* **£169** inc dinner, plus special breaks; 6 deeply comfortable rms. Georgian house in pleasant gardens with fine views over Conwy estuary, Conwy Castle and Snowdonia; delightful public rooms with flowers, antiques and family photos, delicious food of the highest restaurant standards, and marvellous wines; good breakfasts, warmly friendly staff; cl 15 Dec–15 Jan; children under 9 months or over 5; dogs in coach house only

LLANWDDYN
Lake Vyrnwy Hotel *Llanwddyn, Oswestry, Powys SY10 0LY (01691) 870692* **£120**, plus special breaks; 35 rms, the ones overlooking the lake

are the nicest – and quietest. Large impressive Tudor-style mansion overlooking lake in 40 square miles of forestry, with lots of sporting activities (esp fishing); conservatory looking over the water, log fires and sporting prints in the comfortable and elegant public rooms, relaxed atmosphere, bar, and good food using their own lamb and game from the estate, and home-made preserves, chutneys, mustards and vinegars; enjoyable teas too; dogs welcome in bedrooms; £10

LLANWRTYD WELLS
Carlton House *Dolycoed Rd, Llanwrtyd Wells, Powys LD5 4RA (01591)* *610248* **£65**, plus special breaks; 6 well equipped rms. Warmly friendly owners run this comfortable Edwardian restaurant-with-rooms, and there's a relaxing little sitting room with plants and antiques, an attractive dining room with original panelling and log fire, exceptionally good modern british cooking using top-quality local produce (delicious puddings and home-made canapés and petits fours), super breakfasts with home-made bread and marmalade, and a thoughtful wine list; cl 10-29 Dec; dogs welcome in bedrooms

LLECHRYD
Castell Malgwyn *Llechryd, Cardigan, Dyfed SA43 2QA (01239) 682382* **£75**; 19 attractive rms. Handsome, creeper-covered 18th-c house with 40 acres of woodland, a mile of river frontage (fishing, falconry and shooting), and lots of walks; homely comfortable lounge, convivial bar lounge, enjoyable food and nice breakfasts, friendly staff, and plenty of regular guests; dogs welcome in bedrooms; £10

MONMOUTH
Riverside Hotel *Cinderhill St, Monmouth, Gwent NP25 5EY (01600)* *715577* **£61.85**, plus special breaks; 17 rms. Comfortable, warmly welcoming bustling hotel overlooking River Monnow and the 13th-c fortified gatehouse, with good value bar meals, enjoyable food in newly refurbished restaurant, a bustling lounge bar, and conservatory; disabled access; dogs welcome in bedrooms and bar

MONTGOMERY
Dragon *Market Sq, Montgomery, Powys SY15 6PA (01686) 668359* **£79.50**, plus special breaks; 20 rms. Attractive black and white timbered small hotel with a pleasant grey-stone tiled hall, comfortable residents' lounge, beamed bar, restaurant using local produce; indoor swimming pool, sauna; dogs welcome in bedrooms

NANTGWYNANT
Pen-y-Gwryd *Nantgwynant, Caernarfon, Gwynedd LL55 4NT (01286)* *870211* **£68**, plus special breaks; 16 rms, some with own bthrm. In two acres, this cheery hotel is by the Llanberis Pass in Snowdonia National Park; warm log fire in simply furnished panelled residents' lounge, rugged slate-floored bar that doubles as mountain rescue post; lots of climbing

mementoes and equipment, friendly, chatty games room (lots of walkers, climbers and fishermen), hearty enjoyable food, big breakfasts, and packed lunches; sauna in the trees and outdoor swimming pool, table tennis; private chapel; cl Nov-Dec and mid-week Jan-Feb; disabled access; dogs welcome in bedrooms, bar and lounge; £2

OXWICH

Oxwich Bay Hotel *Oxwich, Swansea, West Glamorgan SA3 1LS (01792) 390329* **£72**, plus special breaks; 13 rms. Comfortable hotel on edge of beach in a lovely area, with dedicated friendly staff, food served all day, restaurant/lounge bar with panoramic views, summer outdoor dining area, and a welcome for families; cl 24-25 Dec; dogs welcome in bedrooms; £5

PRESTEIGNE

Radnorshire Arms *High St, Presteigne, Powys LD8 2BE (01544) 267406* **£72.50**, plus special breaks; 19 rms. Rambling handsomely timbered 17th-c hotel with old-fashioned charm and an unchanging atmosphere, elegantly moulded beams and fine dark panelling in the lounge bar, latticed windows, enjoyable food (inc morning coffee and afternoon tea), separate no smoking restaurant, well kept real ales, and politely attentive service; dogs welcome in bedrooms

PWLLHELI

Plas Bodegroes *Efailnewydd, Pwllheli, Gwynedd LL53 5TH (01758) 612363* **£60**; 11 rms. Lovely Georgian manor house, aptly described as a restaurant-with-rooms, in tree-filled grounds and fronted by a 200-year-old beech avenue; comfortably restful rooms, enjoyable modern cooking using superb fresh local produce and very good wine list in no smoking restaurant, very nice breakfasts, and genuinely friendly, helpful staff; cl Dec-Feb; dogs welcome in bedrooms

RHAYADER

Beili Neuadd *Rhayader, Powys LD6 5NS (01597) 810211* **£52**; 3 rms with log fires, and newly converted stone barn with 3 bunkhouse rms. Charming partly 16th-c stone-built farmhouse in quiet countryside (they have their own trout pools and woodland), with beams, polished oak floorboards, and nice breakfasts in new garden room; self-catering also; cl Christmas; children over 8; dogs by arrangement

ST BRIDES WENTLOOG

West Usk Lighthouse *St Brides Wentloog, Newport, Gwent NP10 8SF (01633) 810126* **£95**; 3 rms. Unusual ex-lighthouse – squat rather than tall – that was on an island in the Bristol Channel (the land has since been reclaimed); modern stylish furnishings, lots of framed record sleeves (Mr Sheahan used to work for a record company), informal atmosphere, good big breakfasts, and a Rolls-Royce drive to good local restaurant; flotation tank, aromatherapy, reflexology, and other complementary therapies, roof garden with palm trees, vines and a barbecue, and lots of nearby walks; dogs welcome in bedrooms by arrangement; £5

ST DAVID'S
Warpool Court *St David's, Haverfordwest, Dyfed SA62 6BN (01437) 720300* £140, plus special breaks; 25 rms. Originally built as St David's cathedral school in the 1860s and bordering NT land, this popular hotel has lovely views over St Bride's Bay; Ada Williams's collection of lovely hand-painted tiles can be seen in the public rooms, food in the elegant restaurant is imaginative (good for vegetarians too), and staff are helpful; quiet gardens, heated summer swimming pool, tennis, exercise room, table tennis, pool and croquet; cl Jan; dogs welcome in bedrooms; £6

TAL-Y-BONT
Lodge *Tal-y-Bont, Conwy, Gwynedd LL32 8YX (01492) 660766* £70, plus special breaks; 14 rms. Friendly little modern hotel in over three acres on the edge of Snowdonia, with open fire, books and magazines in comfortable lounge, generous helpings of popular food using lots of home-grown produce in no smoking restaurant, and good service; lots of walks; well behaved pets welcome; good disabled access; dogs welcome in bedrooms; £3

TINTERN PARVA
Parva Farmhouse Hotel *Tintern, Chepstow, Gwent NP16 6SQ (01291) 689411* £76, plus special breaks; 9 comfortable rms. Friendly stone farmhouse built in 17th c, with leather chesterfields, woodburner and honesty bar in large beamed lounge, books (no TV downstairs), and very good food and wine (inc wine using locally grown grapes) in cosy restaurant; 50 yds from River Wye and lovely surrounding countryside; partial disabled access; dogs welcome in bedrooms (must not be left unattended); £3.50

Channel Islands

Dog Friendly Pubs

ROZEL
Rozel Bay Hotel
Tucked away at the edge of a sleepy little fishing village, this friendly inn is just out of sight of the sea. The bar counter (Bass, Charles Wells Bombardier and Courage Directors under light blanket pressure) and tables in the traditional-feeling and cosy little dark-beamed back bar are stripped to their original light wood finish, and there are dark plush wall seats and stools, an open granite fireplace, and old prints and local pictures on the cream walls. Leading off is a carpeted area with flowers on big solid square tables. Piped music, and TV, darts, pool, cribbage and dominoes in the games room. The good value short pubby menu includes big helpings of food such as fish and chips, bangers and mash, beef and ale pie and puddings. The upstairs restaurant now concentrates on fresh fish in a relaxed rustic french atmosphere, with up to 10 fish dishes a day and good value specials. The pub has an attractive steeply terraced, partly covered, hillside garden.
Randalls ~ Lease Ian King ~ Real ale ~ Bar food (12-2(3 Sun), 6-8.30) ~ Restaurant (not Sun evening) ~ (01534) 863438 ~ Children welcome ~ Dogs allowed in bar ~ Open 11-11

ST BRELADE
Old Portelet Inn *Portelet Bay*
This popular 17th-c farmhouse is often busy, particularly with families and visitors to the island. It's well placed at the head of a long flight of granite steps, giving views across Portelet (Jersey's most southerly bay) as you go down to a sheltered cove. Children will be happily occupied in either the supervised indoor play area (entrance 60p) or another one outside, watching the kiddies' entertainment they sometimes put on during the summer, or with board games in the wooden-floored loft bar. The picnic-sets on the partly covered flower-bower terrace by a wishing well are a good place to relax, and there are more seats in the sizeable landscaped garden with lots of scented stocks and other flowers. Generous helpings of bar food, served by neatly dressed friendly staff, includes sandwiches, filled

baked potatoes, chilli nachos, moules marinière, steak and mushroom pie, and puddings such as chocolate fudge cake. The low-beamed downstairs bar has a stone bar counter (well kept Bass and Courage Directors kept under light blanket pressure and reasonably priced house wine), a huge open fire, gas lamps, old pictures, etched glass panels from France and a nice mixture of old wooden chairs on bare oak boards and quarry tiles. It opens into the big timber-ceilinged no smoking family dining area, with standing timbers and plenty of highchairs; TV, cribbage, dominoes, and very audible piped music; disabled and baby-changing facilities.

Randalls ~ Manager Stephen Jones ~ Real ale ~ Bar food (12-9) ~ (01534) 741899 ~ Children welcome ~ Dogs allowed in bar ~ Live music 2 or 3 nights a week in summer, 1 in winter ~ Open 9-11

Old Smugglers *Ouaisne Bay*

The welcoming bar at this straightforward pub has thick walls, black beams, log fires, and cosy black built-in settles, also well kept Bass and two guests from brewers such as Greene King and Ringwood on handpump; sensibly placed darts as well as cribbage. Bar food includes soup, vegetarian spring roll with sweet chilli dip, burgers, battered cod, duck breast with orange and brandy sauce, and steaks. A room in the restaurant (the only area with piped music) is no smoking. The building is a conversion of a row of old fishermen's cottages, and is picturesquely set on a lane just above the beach with interesting views over one of the island's many defence towers from a weatherproof porch.

Free house ~ Licensee Nigel Godfrey ~ Real ale ~ Bar food (12-2, 6-9; not Sun evening Nov-Mar) ~ Restaurant ~ (01534) 741510 ~ Children welcome ~ Dogs allowed in bar ~ Open 11-11.30

ST JOHN
Les Fontaines *Le Grand Mourier, Route du Nord*

In a pretty spot on the north coast and a nice place for a pint after a walk (well kept Bass and Charles Wells Bombardier), this former farmhouse is a popular local haunt. The best part is the public bar where you're likely to hear the true Jersey patois – look out for a worn, unmarked door at the side of the building, or as you go down the main entry lobby towards the bigger main bar, go through the tiny narrow door on your right. In here you'll find very heavy beams in the low dark ochre ceiling, massively thick irregular red granite walls, cushioned settles on the quarry-tiled floor and antique prints. The big granite-columned fireplace with a log fire warming its unusual inglenook seats may date back to the 14th c, and (a rarity these days) has kept its old smoking chains and side oven. The carpeted main bar is a marked contrast, with plenty of wheelback chairs around neat dark tables, and a spiral staircase leading up to a wooden gallery under the high pine-raftered plank ceiling; one large area is no smoking; piped music. A bonus for families is Pirate Pete's, a supervised play area for children (entry 50p for half an hour), though children are also welcome in the other rooms. Bar food includes ploughman's, sweet and sour chicken, cumberland sausage, and specials such as baked lamb shank, grilled local plaice, and lobster or crab salad. Seats on a terrace outside have good views, although lorries from the nearby quarry can mar the atmosphere.

Randalls ~ Manager Hazel O'Gorman ~ Real ale ~ Bar food (12-2.15(2.45 Sun), 6-9(8.30 Sun) ~ (01534) 862707 ~ Children in eating area of bar and restaurant ~ Dogs allowed in bar ~ Open 11-11

ST OUEN'S BAY
La Pulente *Start of Five Mile Road*

It's the impressive location that makes this civilised pub special. There are sweeping views across the endless extent of Jersey's longest beach from the terrace, lounge (no smoking) and conservatory. The carpeted eating area upstairs has ragged walls and scrubbed wood tables, and leads off on to the terrace; piped music. Cheerful and busy, the public bar has a surfing theme, with photographs and prints on the walls, well kept Bass and Courage Directors on handpump, and a jukebox, darts, pool, fruit machine and TV. Very enjoyable bar food, served by friendly staff, includes sandwiches, baked potatoes, fried chicken breast with asparagus and leek tart, and daily specials such as spaghetti with feta and mushrooms, and bass fillet with scallops.

Randalls ~ Manager Julia Wallace ~ Real ale ~ Bar food (12-2.15, 6-9; not Sun evening) ~ Restaurant ~ (01534) 744487 ~ Children welcome in lounge area ~ Dogs allowed in bar ~ Open 11-11

Answers to Dog Quiz

1. 6.8 million
2. Greyfriars Bobby
3. 42
4. Bullseye
5. Saint Bernard
6. Scraps
7. 19 mph
8. Petra
9. Nipper
10. Sirius
11. Nana
12. Depends on where you live – from £0 through a £50 fixed penalty (common in towns) to a maximum of £1,000
13. Susie
14. Seth
15. Timmy
16. Laika
17. Toby
18. Labrador, dachshund, cocker spaniel, cairn terrier, shetland sheepdog, basset hound, cavalier king charles spaniel, beagle
19. Toto
20. Shadow
21. Montmorency
22. Mutley
23. Finding the stolen Jules Rimet World Cup trophy just before England won it in 1966
24. Tyke
25. Dennis the Menace
26. Pal
27. Basenji – though it can howl, growl and even yodel
28. Perdita
29. P G Wodehouse
30. Scooby snacks
31. Dr Who
32. On top of his kennel
33. The PDSA's Dickin Medal
34. One million
35. All of them except lily pollen which can be fatal to cats
36. Sadie

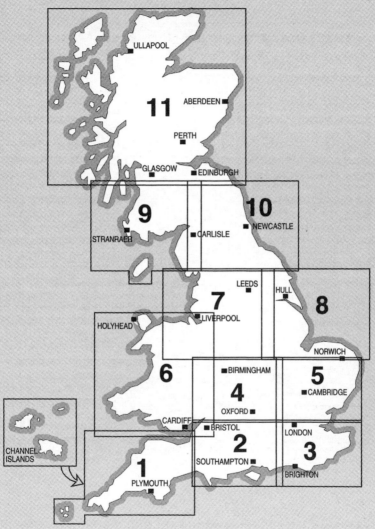

Key to map areas

Reference to sectional maps

﹏﹏ Motorway	● **Totnes**	Dog friendly pub
﹏﹏ Major road	◉ **Lynton**	Dog friendly accommodation
− − − County boundary	■ **BODMIN**	Place name to assist location

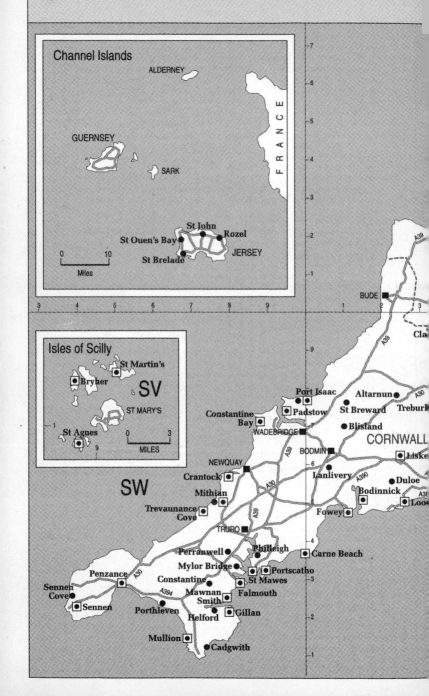

1

Channel Islands

ALDERNEY

F R A N C E

GUERNSEY

SARK

St John
St Ouen's Bay ● ● Rozel
St Brelade ● JERSEY

0   10
Miles

Isles of Scilly

St Martin's
● Bryher

SV

ST MARY'S

St Agnes ●

0   3
MILES

BUDE ■

A39

A39

Cla

Port Isaac ●   Altarnun ●
● Padstow   St Breward ●   Trebur
Constantine
Bay ●   ● Blisland   A30
WADEBRIDGE ■

CORNWALL

BODMIN ■   ● Liske

NEWQUAY ■   Lanlivery ●   A390   ● Duloe
Crantock ●   Bodinnick ●
Mithian ●   A38
Trevaunance ●   Fowey ●   Loo
Cove   A39

TRURO ■

SW   Perranwell ●   Philleigh ●   ● Carne Beach

Mylor Bridge ●   ● Portscatho
Penzance ■   Constantine ●   St Mawes ●
Sennen   A30   Mawnan   Falmouth
Cove ●   A394   Smith ●   Gillan ●
● Sennen   Porthleven ●   Helford ●
Mullion ●   ● Cadgwith

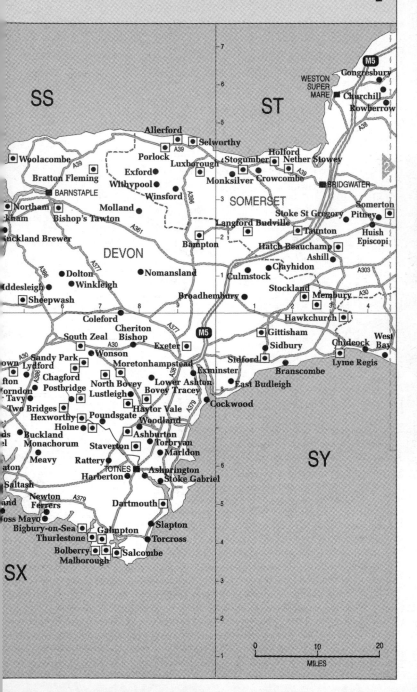

1

SS

ST

WESTON
SUPER
MARE

M5

Congresbury

Churchill

Kowberrow

A38

Allerford

A39

Selworthy

Porlock

Luxborough

Holford

Stogumber

Nether Stowey

Exford

Withypool

Monksilver

Crowcombe

A39

Winsford

A396

BRIDGWATER

Woolacombe

A39

Bratton Fleming

BARNSTAPLE

Molland

Northam

kham

Bishop's Tawton

uckland Brewer

A361

Langford Budville

Bampton

ddesleigh

Sheepwash

Dolton

Winkleigh

Nomansland

Culmstock

Coleford

Cheriton
Bishop

South Zeal

Wonson

Exeter

A30

M5

own

Sandy Park

Lydford

Chagford

Postbridge

orndon
Tavy

Two Bridges

Hexworthy

Holne

Buckland
Monachorum

Meavy

aton

Saltash

Newton
Ferrers

oss Mayo

Bigbury-on-Sea

Thurlestone

Bolberry

Malborough

Salcombe

SX

Moretonhampstead

North Bovey

Lustleigh

Bovey Tracey

Lower Ashton

Haytor Vale

Poundsgate

Woodland

Ashburton

Staverton

Torbryan

Marldon

Rattery

TOTNES

Harberton

Ashprington

Stoke Gabriel

Dartmouth

Galmpton

Slapton

Torcross

SOMERSET

Stoke St Gregory

Somerton

Pitney

Taunton

Huish
Episcopi

Hatch Beauchamp

Ashill

Clayhidon

Stockland

Membury

A303

A30

Hawkchurch

Gittisham

Sidbury

Chideock

West
Bay

Sidford

Branscombe

Lyme Regis

Exminster

East Budleigh

Cockwood

A379

DEVON

A377

A386

A30

A386

A38

A377

Broadhembury

SY

0   10   20
MILES

7

6

5

3

2

1

7

6   8   9   1   2   3   4

1

6

5

8

4

3

2

1

A38

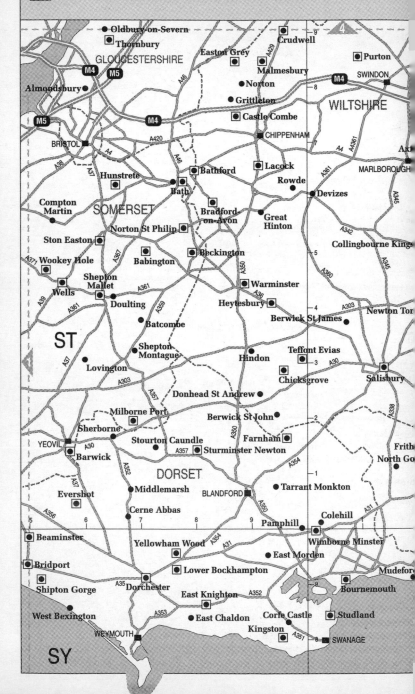

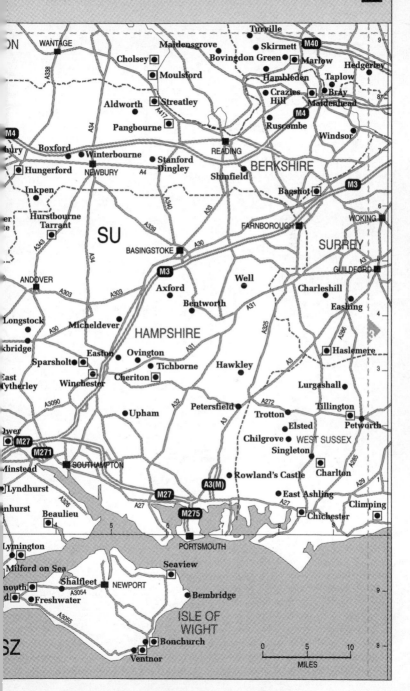

2

Turville
Skirmett
Maidensgrove
WANTAGE
Bovingdon Green
Marlow
M40
Hedgerley
Cholsey
Hambleden
Taplow
Moulsford
Crazies
Bray
Hill
Maidenhead
Aldworth
Streatley
Pangbourne
Ruscombe
Windsor
M4
Boxford
Winterbourne
READING
Hungerford
Stanford
BERKSHIRE
NEWBURY
Dingley
Inkpen
Shinfield
Bagshot
M3
Hurstbourne
Tarrant
WOKING
SU
FARNBOROUGH
BASINGSTOKE
SURREY
M3
GUILDFORD
ANDOVER
Well
Charleshill
Axford
Eashing
Bentworth
Longstock
Micheldever
HAMPSHIRE
Haslemere
xbridge
Easton
Ovington
East
Sparsholt
Tichborne
Hawkley
ytherley
Cheriton
Winchester
Lurgashall
Tillington
Upham
Petersfield
Petworth
Trotton
Elsted
Chilgrove
WEST SUSSEX
M27
Singleton
Minstead
M271
SOUTHAMPTON
Charlton
Lyndhurst
A3(M)
Rowland's Castle
nhurst
Beaulieu
East Ashling
Climping
M275
Chichester
Lymington
PORTSMOUTH
Milford on Sea
Seaview
nouth
Shalfleet
NEWPORT
d
Freshwater
Bembridge
ISLE OF
WIGHT
SZ
Bonchurch
0   5   10
Ventnor
MILES

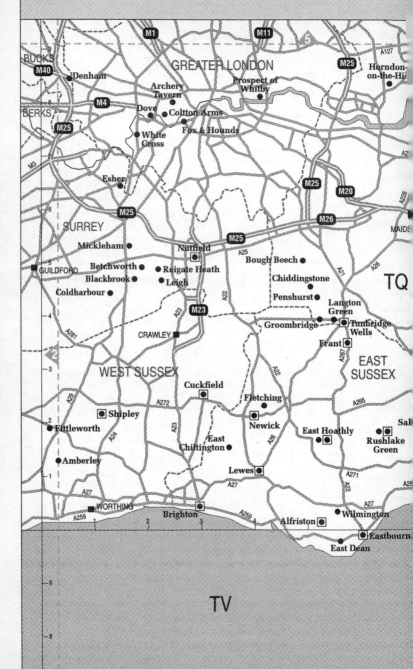

3

BUCKS
M40
M1
M11
GREATER LONDON
M25
Horndon-on-the-Hill
A127
Denham
Archery Tavern
Prospect of Whitby
M4
BERKS
M25
Dove
Coltton Arms
Fox & Hounds
White Cross
A2
M3
M25
Esher
M25
M20
A228
M26
SURREY
M25
MAIDS
A21
A26
Mickleham
Nutfield
A25
Bough Beech
TQ
GUILDFORD
Betchworth
Reigate Heath
Chiddingstone
Blackbrook
Leigh
Penshurst
Coldharbour
Langton Green
A281
A22
M23
Groombridge
Tunbridge Wells
A23
Frant
EAST SUSSEX
CRAWLEY
A267
WEST SUSSEX
Cuckfield
A272
Fletching
A265
A29
Shipley
A23
Newick
A21
Fittleworth
A24
East Chiltington
East Hoathly
Sal
Rushlake Green
Amberley
A26
Lewes
A271
A2
A27
WORTHING
Brighton
Alfriston
Wilmington
A259
A259
Eastbourn
East Dean
TV

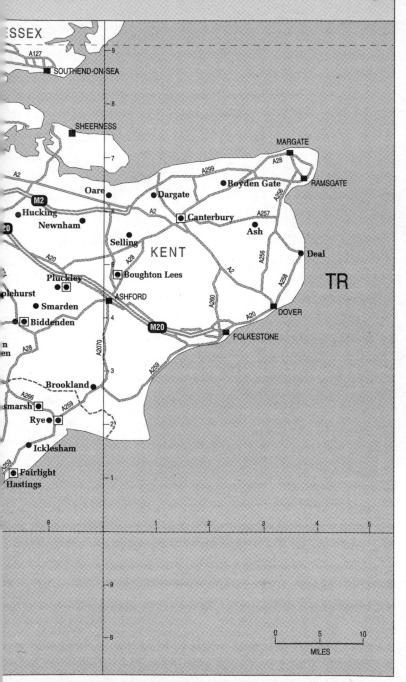

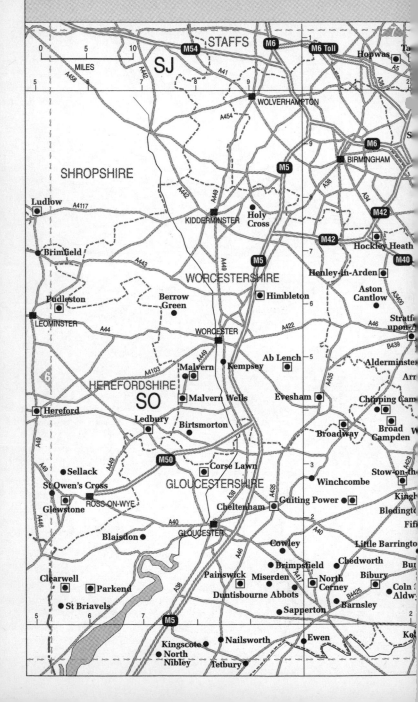

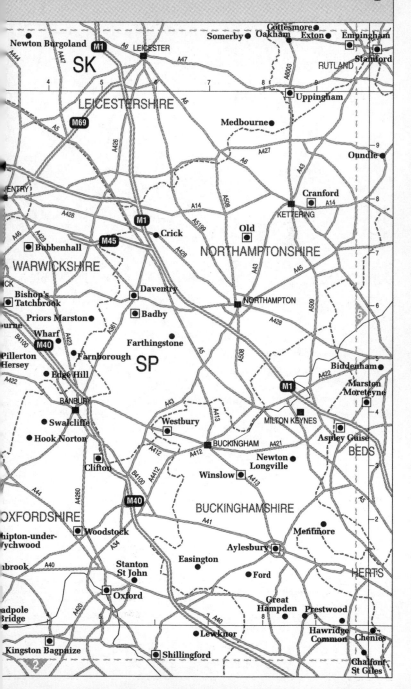

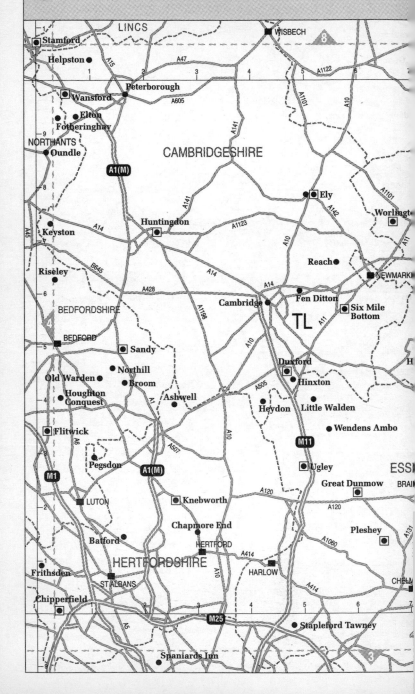

5

LINCS

Stamford

Helpston

WISBECH

A15

A47

A1122

Peterborough

A605

Wansford

A141

A101

A10

Elton

Fotheringhay

NORTHANTS

CAMBRIDGESHIRE

Oundle

A1(M)

Ely

A1101

Worlingt

A142

Huntingdon

A1123

A10

Keyston

A14

Reach

NEWMARK

Riseley

B645

A428

A14

A14

Fen Ditton

A17

BEDFORDSHIRE

A1198

Cambridge

TL

Six Mile
Bottom

BEDFORD

Sandy

Duxford

H

Old Warden

Northill

Broom

A10

A505

Hinxton

Houghton
Conquest

Ashwell

Heydon

Little Walden

Flitwick

A6

A507

Wendens Ambo

M11

M1

Pegsdon

A1(M)

Ugley

ESS

Great Dunmow

BRAI

LUTON

Knebworth

A120

A120

Chapmore End

Pleshey

A1060

A13

Batford

HERTFORD

A414

Frithsden

HERTFORDSHIRE

A10

HARLOW

CHELM

ST ALBANS

A414

Chipperfield

A5

M25

Stapleford Tawney

Spaniards Inn

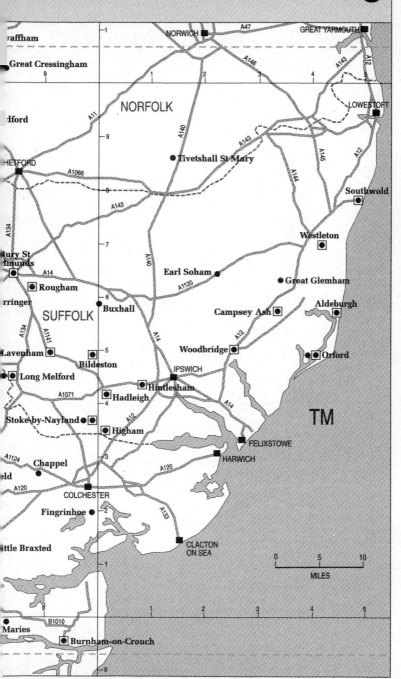

5

waffham

Great Cressingham
9

NORFOLK

NORWICH

A47

GREAT YARMOUTH

A146

A143

A12

1

2

3

4

A11

A140

A143

LOWESTOFT

lford

9

HETFORD

A1066

Tivetshall St Mary

A143

8

A145

A12

Southwold

A143

A134

7

A140

Westleton

Bury St Edmunds

A14

Rougham

Earl Soham

A1120

Great Glemham

Aldeburgh

rringer

6

Buxhall

SUFFOLK

A144

Campsey Ash

A134

A1141

Lavenham

5

Bildeston

A14

Woodbridge

A12

Orford

IPSWICH

Long Melford

A1071

Hintlesham

4

Hadleigh

A14

Stoke-by-Nayland

A12

Higham

TM

A1124

Chappel

3

A120

FELIXSTOWE

eld

A120

A133

HARWICH

COLCHESTER

Fingrinhoe

2

A133

ttle Braxted

CLACTON ON SEA

0   5   10

MILES

1

9

B1010

1   2   3   4   5

Maries

Burnham-on-Crouch

9

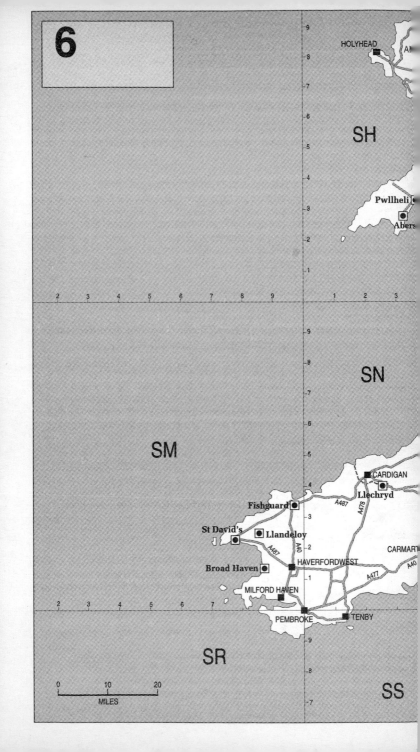

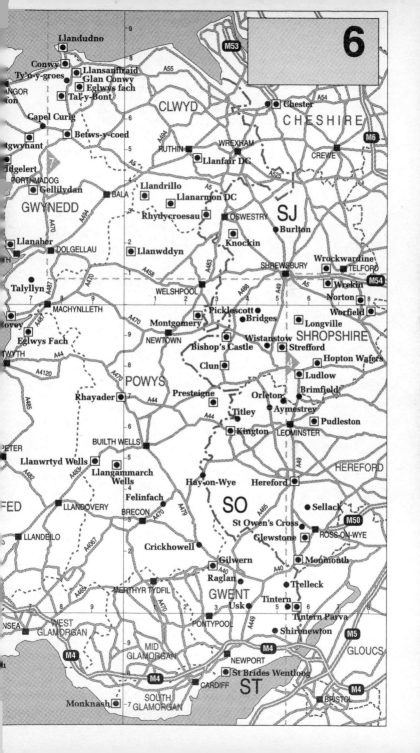

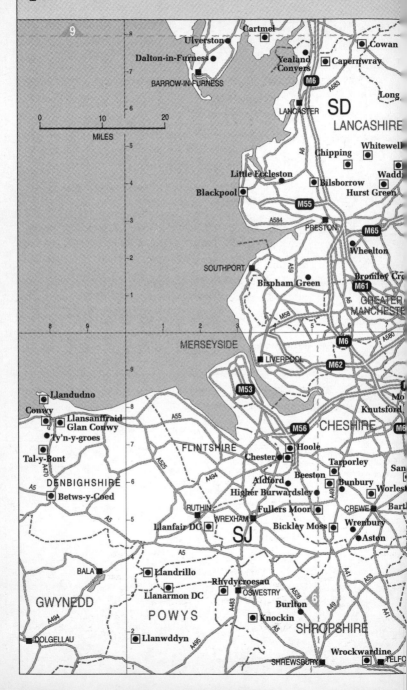

7

Cartmel
Ulverston • Cowan
Dalton-in-Furness • Yealand • Capernwray
Conyers
BARROW-IN-FURNESS M6 A683 Long

LANCASTER SD
LANCASHIRE

Whitewell
Chipping
A6
Little Eccleston Wadd
Bilsborrow Hurst Green
Blackpool

M55
A584 PRESTON
M65
Wheelton
SOUTHPORT A59 Bromley Cr
Bispham Green M61
A6 GREATER
MANCHESTER
M58
MERSEYSIDE M6 A580

LIVERPOOL M62

M53 Mo
Llandudno Knutsford
Conwy Llansanffraid M56 CHESHIRE M6
Glan Conwy A55
Ty'n-y-groes FLINTSHIRE Hoole
Tal-y-Bont Chester Tarporley San
A70 A525 A494 Beeston
A5 DENBIGHSHIRE Aldford Bunbury Worles
Betws-y-Coed Higher Burwardsley CREWE Bart
RUTHIN Fullers Moor
Llanfair DC WREXHAM Bickley Moss Wrenbury
SJ Aston
A5
Llandrillo
BALA Rhydycroesau
Llanarmon DC OSWESTRY A528 A53
GWYNEDD POWYS Burlton A49 A41
Knockin
A494 A5 SHROPSHIRE
DOLGELLAU A495 Wrockwardine
Llanwddyn SHREWSBURY TELFO

MILES
0 10 20

9

8
7
6
5
4
3
2
1

8 9 1 2 3

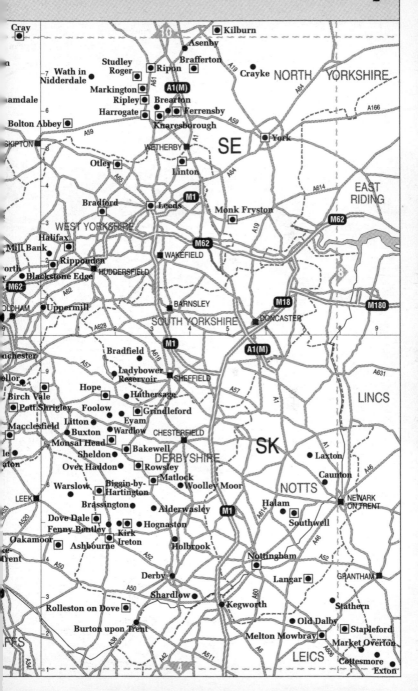

7

Cray

Kilburn
Asenby
Brafferton
Studley
Roger Ripon Crayke NORTH YORKSHIRE
Wath in
Nidderdale
Markington A1(M)
Ripley Brearton
Harrogate Ferrensby
Knaresborough
Bolton Abbey
York
WETHERBY SE
Otley
Linton
EAST RIDING
Bradford Leeds M1
Monk Fryston
WEST YORKSHIRE M62
Halifax
Mill Bank M62
Ripponden WAKEFIELD
Blackstone Edge HUDDERSFIELD
M62 M18 M180
Uppermill BARNSLEY
OLDHAM SOUTH YORKSHIRE DONCASTER
M1 A1(M)
Bradfield
Manchester LINCS
Ladybower
Reservoir SHEFFIELD
Birch Vale Hope Hathersage
Pott Shrigley Foolow Grindleford
Macclesfield Litton Eyam
Buxton Wardlow CHESTERFIELD
Monsal Head Bakewell SK
Sheldon Laxton
Over Haddon Rowsley Caunton
Matlock NOTTS
Warslow Biggin-by- Woolley Moor
Hartington
LEEK Brassington Alderwasley M1 Halam
Dove Dale Southwell
Fenny Bentley Kirk Hognaston
Oakamoor Ireton
Ashbourne Holbrook
Trent Nottingham
Derby Langar GRANTHAM
Shardlow
Rolleston on Dove Kegworth Stathern
Old Dalby
Burton upon Trent Stapleford
Melton Mowbray Market Overton
Cottesmore
LEICS Exton
FES

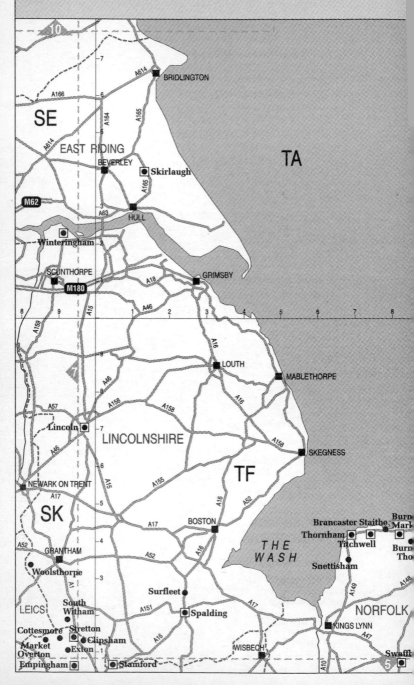

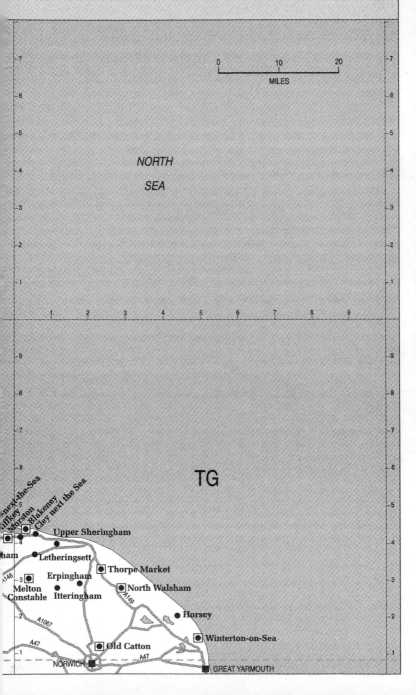

8

0   10   20
MILES

NORTH

SEA

TG

next-the-Sea
iffley
Morston
Blakeney
Cley next the Sea
Upper Sheringham
ham
Letheringsett
A148
Thorpe Market
Erpingham
Melton
Constable   North Walsham
Itteringham
A149
A1067
Horsey
A47
Winterton-on-Sea
Old Catton
NORWICH   A47   GREAT YARMOUTH

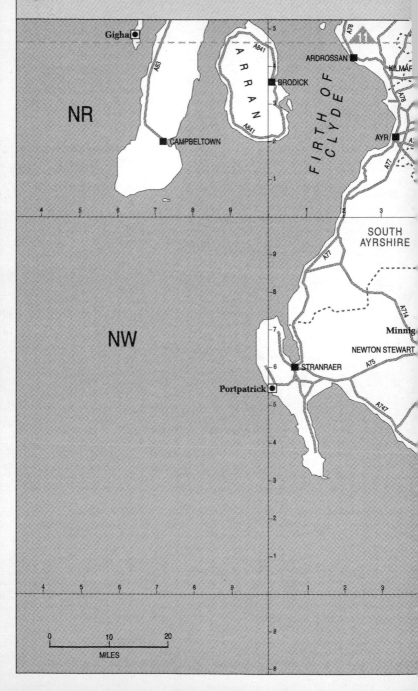

Gigha

A83

ARRAN

A841

BRODICK

NR

CAMPBELTOWN

A841

FIRTH OF CLYDE

ARDROSSAN

KILMAR

A78

A78

AYR

A77

A7

SOUTH
AYRSHIRE

A77

A714

Minnig

NEWTON STEWART

A75

NW

STRANRAER

A76

Portpatrick

A747

0   10   20
MILES

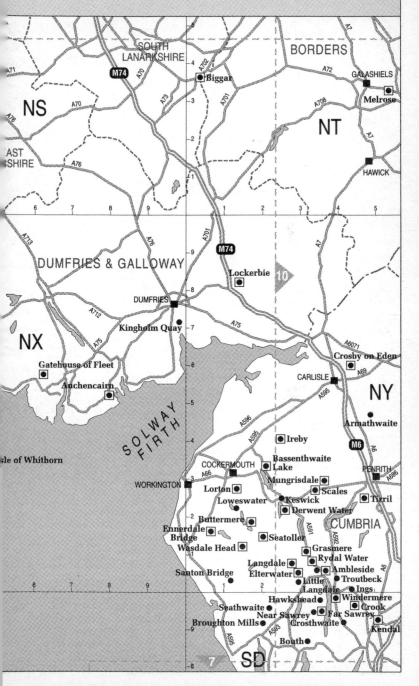

9

NS

EAST
SHIRE

A71

A76

A70

A76

A713

A712

A75

NX

Isle of Whithorn

SOUTH
LANARKSHIRE

M74

A70

A73

A701

Biggar

A72

BORDERS

GALASHIELS

Melrose

A708

NT

A7

HAWICK

DUMFRIES & GALLOWAY

A76

A701

M74

Lockerbie

A7

10

DUMFRIES

Kingholm Quay

Gatehouse of Fleet

Auchencairn

SOLWAY
FIRTH

A75

A6071

Crosby on Eden

A69

CARLISLE

A595

NY

Armathwaite

M6

A6

A596

Ireby

Bassenthwaite
Lake

A595

COCKERMOUTH

A66

WORKINGTON

Lorton

Loweswater

Mungrisdale

Scales

Keswick

Derwent Water

PENRITH

A592

Tirril

CUMBRIA

Buttermere

Ennerdale
Bridge

Seatoller

A591

Wasdale Head

Grasmere

Rydal Water

Langdale

Elterwater

Ambleside

Troutbeck

Santon Bridge

Little
Langdale

Ings

Windermere

Hawkshead

Crook

Seathwaite

Near Sawrey

Far Sawrey

Kendal

Broughton Mills

Crosthwaite

A593

Bouth

SD

7

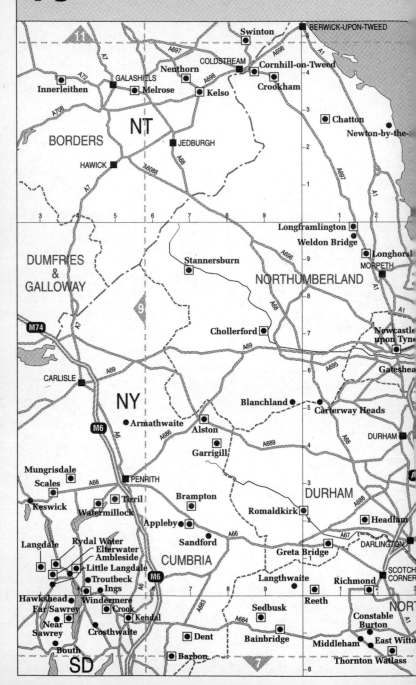

Swinton
BERWICK-UPON-TWEED
Nenthorn
COLDSTREAM
Cornhill-on-Tweed
GALASHIELS
Crookham
Innerleithen
Melrose
Kelso
Chatton
Newton-by-the-
NT
BORDERS
JEDBURGH
HAWICK
Longframlington
Weldon Bridge
DUMFRIES
&
GALLOWAY
Stannersburn
Longhorsl
MORPETH
NORTHUMBERLAND
M74
Chollerford
Newcastle
upon Tyne
CARLISLE
Gateshea
NY
Blanchland
Carterway Heads
Armathwaite
Alston
DURHAM
Mungrisdale
Garrigill
Scales
PENRITH
DURHAM
Keswick
Tirril
Brampton
Watermillock
Romaldkirk
Headlam
Langdale
Appleby
DARLINGTON
Rydal Water
Sandford
Elterwater
Greta Bridge
SCOTCH
Ambleside
CUMBRIA
CORNER
Little Langdale
Troubeck
Langthwaite
Richmond
Hawkshead
Ings
Reeth
NOR
Far Sawrey
Windermere
Crook
Sedbusk
Constable
Near
Kendal
Burton
Sawrey
Crosthwaite
Dent
Bainbridge
East Witto
Bouth
Middleham
SD
Barbon
Thornton Watlass

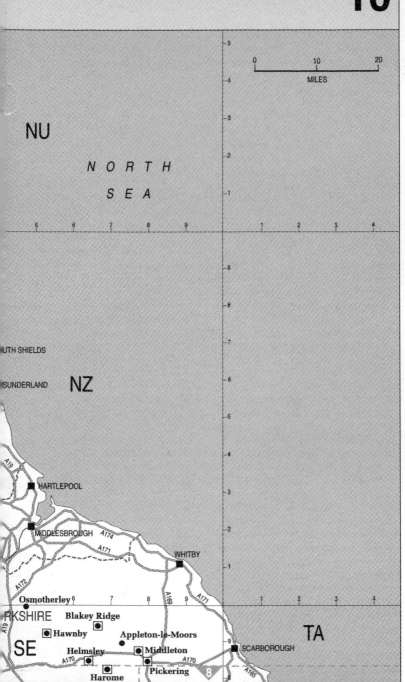

NU

N O R T H

S E A

0   10   20
MILES

5   6   7   8   9   1   2   3   4

9

8

7

UTH SHIELDS

SUNDERLAND   NZ

6

5

4

A19

3

■ HARTLEPOOL

2

■ MIDDLESBROUGH   *A174*

A171

■ WHITBY   1

A172

Osmotherley 6   7   8   A169   9   A171

RKSHIRE   Blakey Ridge   1   2   3   4

● Hawnby   Appleton-le-Moors   TA

SE   Helmsley   ● Middleton   9   ■ SCARBOROUGH

A170   A170

Harome   Pickering   A185

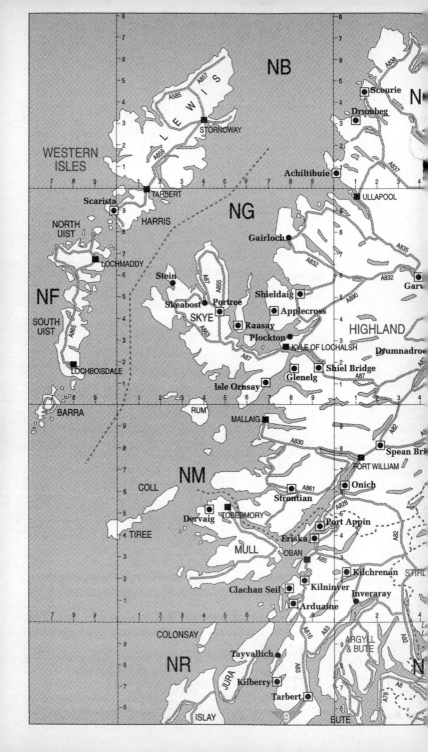

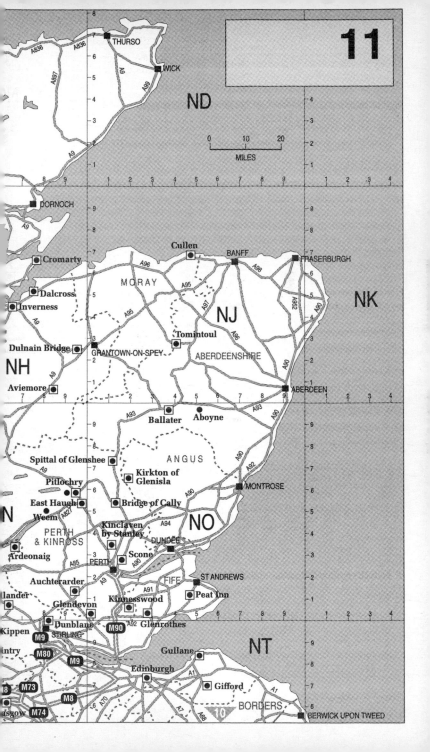